RESTORING THE BIBLICAL CHRIST

RESTORING THE BIBLICAL CHRIST

Is Jesus God?

Jason Kerrigan

Restoring the Biblical Christ

Copyright © 2025 Jason Wayne Kerrigan

Unless otherwise noted, Bible quotations are from the KJV. I often added bold text, etc. to Bible quotations, but I did not change any English wording, unless specifically noted.

I desire for the message of these books to spread as far and as inexpensively as possible.

I hope to get the information from my books on at least one website, organized with links and maybe search capabilities to aid the reader. I also hope to get the information of my books into a free app form (so people can easily access this information freely). I authorize such projects. I only require that, unless being translated, the wording is unchanged. In cases of translation, please be diligent to make the meanings as close to the English meaning as possible. I also authorize audio book versions/translations of my books to be produced. If some new or other form of media is desired to convey the book's information faithfully and righteously, I also authorize that. Regardless of who produces what, my permission remains open for everyone.

Regarding physical reproductions of my books in English: Anyone who wants to republish my books can do so, provided that the books are published in their entirety without any changes to the wording. Reproductions of my books can be sold publicly, and any profits can be kept by the seller or used however they see fit. Regardless of who reproduces or sells the books, I reserve the copyright and continue to extend my reproduction permission to all freely. This copyright page must be included in any physical reproductions of my books. Any intentional changes to the wording, including this copyright page (other than a changed/added ISBN number), voids my permission for that reproduction.

Regarding physical reproductions/translations of my books into languages other than English: My books can be translated into other languages freely, as long as there is a genuine effort to accurately convey the meaning of the text being translated. Any intentional alteration to word or phrase meanings, or any new meanings brought in which do not convey what I intended in the book voids my permission. The books, if translated accordingly, may be sold or given away as the translator sees fit and the profits from those particular sales are at their discretion. I also permit that up to 700 words may be added on a new page and that this single additional page can be included in the book immediately after this copyright page. Any information the translator wants to include on that single page is allowable. That page will not be a required inclusion within any subsequent translations (even if those translations are in the same language).

PDF files for my books can be found at:

https://tinyurl.com/y536c5a7

Any portions of my books can be reproduced for private use. For those who want to quote my books in products meant to be sold, follow standard fair-use copyright law liberally.

I can currently be reached at the following email:

restoringthebiblicalchrist@gmail.com

Table of Contents

1. **Monotheism vs. Polytheism** 1
   Jesus Nearly Declared a Roman God 1
   Justin Arguing with Jews about "Another God" 2
   The Ebionites 4
   Artemon Asserts Jesus "a Mere Man" 6
   Theodotus and Artemon 7
   Proof of Artemon's Claim 11
   The Synods at Antioch 12
   The Apostolic Weight of Antioch 15
   The Doctrine of Antioch 16

2. **How Error Became Prominent** 19
   Rome Adopts Christianity 19
   Alexandria's Doctrinal Schism 20
   The Council of Nicaea 24
   Christianity Rejects the Nicene Doctrine 29
   The Doctrine of Arius 29
   Theodosius Enforces the Nicene Doctrine 33

3. **One True God** 35
   Christ Reveals God 35
   The Image is Called by the Name of the Archetype 36
   1 John 5:20 – There is Only One True God 43
   John 14:9 – Did Jesus Claim to be the Father? 47
   Did Some Men See the Father Himself? 49
   Satan is not the God of this World 51
   1 Corinthians 8:4-6 – Not Many Real Gods 54

4. **Begotten of God** 55
   Same Nature = Same God? 55
   Philo on Being a Son of God 56

"Born of" Should be Translated as "Begotten" 59
Begotten Explained 61
How was Jesus the "Only-Begotten"? 64
When was Jesus Begotten? 66
Jesus from the Seed of David 66
"I will be to Him a Father" 68
Not by Water Only, but by Blood 71
Jesus' Blood was not Divine in Nature 73
Acts 20:28 is not Speaking of God's Blood 74
Matthew 1:23 – Emmanuel, God with Us 78

5. **From Heaven** **85**
Interesting Quotes from Philo 85
The Common Biblical Unitarian Explanation 86
Other Men in the Bible Came from Heaven 87
John 3:31 – "Cometh from Heaven" 88
John 3:13-21 – Who is Speaking? 91
John 3:13 – The Son of Man from Heaven 94
John 6:33 & 38 – "Cometh Down from Heaven" 95
John 6:62 – "Ascend up Where He was Before" 97
God Sent Jesus into the World 99

6. **Philippians Chapter Two** **101**
Philippians 2:6 – Who Being in the Form of God 101
Philippians 2:6 – Equal to God 107
Took on Him the Form of a Servant 108
The Likeness of Men / As a Man 109
Philippians 2:9-11 – The Name Above Every Name 111
Why Isaiah 45:23 is Quoted in Philippians 2:10-11 114

7. **Conscious Preexistence?** **117**
Matthew 23:37 – "O Jerusalem" 117
John 17:5 – "Before the World" 118
1 Peter 1:11 – The Spirit of Christ in the Prophets? 120
First-Person Narrative Messianic Prophecies 122
1 Peter 3:18-20 – Preached in the Days of Noah 123
Micah 5:2 – "From Everlasting"? 129
Hebrews 7:3 – Christ and Melchisedec 131
Hebrews 13:8 – "Yesterday" = Eternity Past? 134

8. **John 8:58 – Before Abraham** 135
   No Connection to Exodus 3:14 135
   How Others Have Translated John 8:58 138
   The Day of Christ 140
   Abraham "Saw" the Day of Christ 141
   Γενέσθαι – Past or Future 143
   Before Abraham What? 145
   Ἐγώ Εἰμι – Possibilities and Conclusion 147

9. **Resurrection** 159
   The Shroud of Turin 159
   Christ Begotten Completely at the Resurrection 161
   Philo on Being Begotten of God 163
   Romans 1:4 – Appointed Son of God by Resurrection 164
   John 10:17-18 – Jesus Laid Down His Life Daily 167
   God Raised Others from the Dead through Christ 172
   The Scriptures Call Jesus a Prophet 173
   John 2:19 – Jesus Raised Himself from the Dead? 176
   God Raised Christ from the Dead 180
   Did the Resurrection Prove Christ was Divine? 181

10. **Created Christ & New Creation** 183
    Revelation 3:14 – Beginning of the Creation 183
    Colossians 1:15 – Firstborn of All Creation 186
    All "Other" Things Created Through Christ? 188
    Colossians 1:16 – Why Past Tense Verbs? 191
    Proverbs 8:22 – "The LORD Created Me" 195

11. **Our Lord** 199
    The Word "Lord" Does Not Mean "God" 199
    1 Corinthians 8:6 – Christ is Our One Lord 202
    Is God Called "Our" Lord in this Present Time? 206
    Can't Serve Two Masters / "Masters" on Earth 213
    1 Timothy 6:15 – Describing the Father, Not Jesus 215
    King of Kings and Lord of Lords 217
    Daniel 7:14 – Men will Serve God 220
    Why God will Judge Mankind through Christ 221
    Jesus' Everlasting Kingdom / Returned to God 224

12. Hebrews Chapter One 227

Hebrews 1:2 – Through Christ? 227
Hebrews 1:3 – Image of His Confidence 230
Hebrews 1:8 – Thy Throne, O God? 234
Psalm 45:6 – The Hebrew Nouns are Ambiguous................... 239
Psalm 45 – The Context Does Not Support "O God" 240
"Thy Throne is God" – An Odd Translation?............................ 244
The Manuscripts Support "Thy Throne is God" 246
What about the Context in Hebrews Chapter One?.................. 247
Hebrews 1:10-12 – Not Addressed to the Son 250
Why is Psalm 102:24-27 Quoted?... 254

13. John 1 – The Word.. 257

What Does "the Word" Mean?... 258
The Word – It or He?.. 259
John 1:1b – The Word was "with" God?................................... 261
John 1:1c – The Word was God 266
John 1:1a – In the Beginning... 267
John 1:3 – "By Means of" the Word 268
John 1:4 – Life in the Word.. 270
John 1:6-7 – John Prepares the Way for God 271
John 1:12 – His Name 272
John 1:14 – The Word was Made Flesh 274

14. John 1:18... 279

Only-Begotten or One-Of-A-Kind? 279
Only Begotten Son or Only Begotten God? 280
Μονογενής Υἱός – The Manuscript Evidence 282
The Ante-Nicene Fathers... 283
Μονογενής Θεός – The Phrase Never Used............................ 285
The Internal Evidence 286
The Testimony of Clement of Alexandria 287
Valentinian Influence in 2nd Century Alexandria 288
Valentinus Introduced Corrupted Texts 291
How Trustworthy is Papyrus 66? 293
The Valentinian Motive.. 295

15. Fifth Chapter of John 301
John 5:23 – Honor the Son Even as the Father 301
Jesus Refused to be Called "Good Master" 304
God Alone is "Good" / Christ the "Good" Shepherd 305
John 5:18 – Equal with God? 306
John 5:19 – Actions of Christ all Actions of God? 309

16. Tenth Chapter of John 311
John 10:30 – "I and the Father are One [Essence?]" 311
Understanding "I and the Father are One" 314
Paul of Samosata – How God and Jesus are One 317
John 10:27-29 – The Security of the Sheep 318
John 10:34-35 – Jesus' Defense / "Ye are Gods" 323

17. John 12:37-41 329
Not One, but Two Texts Being Quoted 329
How Were They Blinded? 330
The Glory Pertained to the Miracles 333
The Common Explanation Fails 334

18. Christ and Worship 337
The Worship that is Given to Jesus 337
Why the Angel Would Not Let John Worship Him 340
Why Peter Would Not Let Cornelius Worship Him 341
Matthew 4:10 / Luke 4:8 – Worship [Only?] God 342

APPENDIXES

A. Common Inquiries: The Old Testament 347

B. Common Inquiries: The New Testament 353

C. Revelation 3:14 Ἀρχή contd 367

D. Firstborn in the Old Testament 375

E. Holy Spirit 383

F. Angel of the LORD 401

G. Infancy Narratives Spurious? 405
Contradictory Infancy Narratives 405
The Genealogies Pertain to Joseph 409

Julius Africanus	411
Jesus, Son of Man	419
Symmachus, the Expert Witness	423
Jerome and "The Authentic Gospel of Matthew"	426
Trypho's Gospel, Justin's Memoirs	428
Origin of the Matthew Infancy	440
Basilides' Claim to Matthias/Matthew	448
Luke, Without an Infancy Narrative	451
The First Infancy Narrative Added to Luke	453
"Isn't Luke that Ebionite Adoptionist?"	456
The Adoptionists Lose	461
Aristides of Athens	464
Concluding Remarks	466

H. Paul of Samosata on Jesus' Birth 469

I. Epistles of Ignatius Spurious? 473

J. Trinity in 1 Clement? 485

K. Theophilus "of Antioch" 489

REFERENCE NOTES 505

SCRIPTURE INDEX 541

"Jesus of Nazareth, a man approved of God among you by miracles and wonders and signs, which God did by him in the midst of you."

—The Apostle Peter
(Acts 2:22)

Chapter One

Monotheism vs. Polytheism

We find a record in the Book of Acts where polytheists, seeing a miracle done by Paul, instantly began to call him a god.

> "And when the people saw what Paul had done, they lifted up their voices, saying in the speech of Lycaonia, The gods are come down to us in the likeness of men." (Acts 14:11)

Paul was no god, however. Neither was his companion, Barnabas. Yet, the pagans instantly drew the conclusion that they were gods when they beheld the miracle. Not only that, but they identified them as the gods that they *already* worshipped and were familiar with.

> "Barnabas they called Zeus, and Paul, because he was the chief speaker, they called Hermes. And the priest of Zeus, whose temple was in front of the city, brought oxen and garlands to the gates and wanted to offer sacrifice with the people." (Acts 14:12-13 RSV)

This tendency of men to interpret the supernatural by their own societal traditions nearly resulted in Paul and Barnabas being identified as Roman gods (see also Acts 28:6). If this was the polytheists' reaction to a single miracle performed by Paul, what did they say about the resurrected Jesus?

Jesus Nearly Declared a Roman God

According to Tertullian (writing around 200 AD), Jesus himself was nearly identified as one of the Roman gods by Emperor Tiberius (who was only Emperor till 37 AD).[1] Eusebius, a Christian historian writing in the 4th century, relays the account as follows:

> And when the wonderful resurrection and ascension of our Saviour were already noised abroad, in accordance with an ancient custom which prevailed among the rulers of the provinces, of reporting to the emperor the novel occurrences which took place in them, in order that nothing might escape him, Pontius Pilate informed Tiberius of the reports which were noised abroad through all Palestine concerning the resurrection of our Saviour Jesus from the dead. He gave an account also of other wonders which he had learned of him, and how, after his death, having risen from the dead, he was now believed by many to be a God. They say that Tiberius referred the matter to the Senate, but that they rejected it, ostensibly because they had not first examined into the matter (for an ancient law prevailed that no one should be made a God by the Romans except by a vote and decree of the Senate).[2]

It was easy to see, from the very outset, that the pagans hearing about Jesus were going to interpret his identity through their own polytheistic ideologies.

> "[The Greek philosophers] said, 'He [Paul] seems to be a proclaimer of foreign gods,' because he preached to them Jesus and the resurrection." (Acts 17:18 NKJV)

The further Christianity became distanced from its monotheistic Jewish roots, the more polytheistic it leaned.

Justin Arguing with Jews about "Another God"

We see a striking example of the contrast between Jewish and Roman beliefs about Christ in Justin Martyr's *Dialogue with Trypho* (written 160 AD). Here, a Roman philosopher tries to convince a Jew, Trypho, that Jesus was "another God" who was subordinate to the Maker of all things.

> Then I [Justin Martyr] replied, "I shall attempt to persuade you, since you have understood the Scriptures, [of the truth] of what I say, that **there is, and that there is said to be, another God** and Lord subject to the Maker of all things; who is also called an

Angel, because He announces to men whatsoever the Maker of all things—above whom there is no other God—wishes to announce to them." ... And Trypho said, "Certainly; but you have not proved from this that there is **another God** besides Him who appeared to Abraham, and who also appeared to the other patriarchs and prophets." ... Then I replied, "Reverting to the Scriptures, I shall endeavour to persuade you, that He who is said to have appeared to Abraham, and to Jacob, and to Moses, and who is called God, is **distinct from Him who made all things**,—**numerically**, I mean, not [distinct] in will. For I affirm that He has never at any time done anything which He who made the world—above whom there is no other God—has not wished Him both to do and to engage Himself with."[3]

In this writing, we actually see a Roman philosopher, Justin, trying to persuade a Jew, Trypho, that there is "another God," whom he identifies as Jesus. *"Another God"!?!?* Perhaps what is even more noteworthy than that is the admission by Justin Martyr that there were Christians living in 160 AD who believed Jesus was a normal man, not even born of a virgin.

> "Now assuredly, Trypho," I continued, "[the proof] that this man is the Christ of God does not fail, **though I be unable to prove that He existed formerly as Son of the Maker of all things, being God, and was born a man by the Virgin**. But since I have certainly proved that this man is the Christ of God, whoever He be, even if I do not prove that He pre-existed, and submitted to be born a man of like passions with us, having a body, according to the Father's will; in this last matter alone is it just to say that I have erred, and not to deny that He is the Christ, though it should appear that He was **born man of men**, and [nothing more] is proved [than this], that He has become Christ by election. For **there are some**, my friends," I said, "of our race, who **admit that He is Christ, while holding Him to be man of men**."[4]

According to Justin, there were Christians in 160 AD who believed in Christ while asserting that he was "born man of men" *in contrast* to Justin's belief that Christ existed formerly, as God, and was born through a virgin. Trypho, the Jew with whom Justin spoke, replied thus:

> And Trypho said, "Those who affirm him to have been **a man**, and to have been anointed by election, and then to have become Christ, appear to me to speak more plausibly than you who hold those opinions which you express. **For** we all expect that Christ will be **a man** [born] **of men**."[5]

Elsewhere, while speaking to polytheists, Justin says Jesus can rightly be called "the Son of God" even if he was not born of a virgin. Then he says those polytheists should accept a virgin birth claim since they *already* believed Perseus, "the son of Zeus," was born of a virgin as well.

> "Moreover, the Son of God called Jesus, even if only a man by ordinary generation, yet, on account of His wisdom, is worthy to be called the Son of God; for all writers call God the Father of men and gods. … And if we even affirm that He was born of a virgin, accept this in common with what you accept of Perseus."[6]

The Ebionites

As Justin showed in 160 AD, there were very ancient Christians who believed Jesus was a normal human being. This, according to Trypho the Jew, was the expectation of the Jewish people. It is obvious that Trypho himself was not a Christian, but what about those early Jews who *were* Christians? What happened to *them?* What did *those* Jewish Christians believe? Who were *they?* According to the records we have, those early Jewish Christians were known as *the Ebionites*. One early Christian writer named Origen, writing 248 AD, had this to say of them:

> Ebion signifies "poor" among the Jews, and those Jews who have received Jesus as Christ are called by the name of Ebionites.[7]

According to Origen: **1.** *Ebion* (a Hebrew word) signifies *poor.* **2.** This term was used *among* the Jews. **3.** This term was applied to *Jewish Christians*. So, we have a *Hebrew* term that was applied *by* Jews *to* Jews who received Christ. Do you see the implications of this? Since Christianity *began* with the Jews, it makes sense to look for Jewish roots amongst early

Christian sects when attempting to trace doctrine back to the earliest Christian communities. *All* of the apostles, mind you, were Jews.

> "The name Ebionites was probably used in Jerusalem as a designation of the Christians there."
> —*Arthur Cushman McGiffert, Ph. D.*[8]

Why were the early Jewish Christians called *poor?* Well, *poor* was how Jesus himself described his Jewish disciples. Luke 6:20 says Jesus "lifted up his eyes on **his disciples**, and said, **Blessed be ye poor**: for yours is the kingdom of God." Now, obviously, the term *poor* is inherently more generalized, but very early on in the Christian movement, at least in Jerusalem, *the poor* (*i.e., Ebionites*) was "the church's self-designation."[9]

Later on, in the 3rd century, we find the term *Ebionite* being used to describe *two* sects of Christians continuing to live as traditional Jews.

> "There are some who accept Jesus, and who boast on that account of being Christians, and yet would regulate their lives, like the Jewish multitude, in accordance with the Jewish law,—and these are the twofold sect of Ebionites, who either acknowledge with us that Jesus was born of a virgin, or deny this, and maintain that He was begotten like other human being."
> —*Origen, 248 AD*[10]

In the latter half of the 4th century, Epiphanius confusedly referred to the *original* group of Ebionites as *Nazarenes*, naming an *offshoot* of that group *Ebionites*.[11] Notwithstanding, when the Christian movement began, no such distinction between Ebionites and Nazarenes (Acts 24:5) existed.

> "The word 'Nazarenes' was, in fact, in the beginning a general name given to the Christians of Palestine by the Jews (cf. Acts xxiv. 5), and as such synonymous with 'Ebionites.'"
> —*Arthur Cushman McGiffert, Ph. D.*[12]

According to Epiphanius, the Nazarenes, formerly known as Ebionites, could be traced back to the Jewish community fleeing Jerusalem prior to its destruction in 70 AD, having been warned by Christ.

> **All the disciples** had settled in Pella after their remove from Jerusalem—Christ having told them to abandon Jerusalem and withdraw from it because of the siege it was about to undergo. And they settled in Peraea for this reason and, as I said, lived their lives there. It was from this that the Nazoraean sect had its origin.[13]

The Ebionites have origins that trace back to the community of disciples fleeing Jerusalem prior to 70 AD. It behooves us, therefore, to consider what this community of early Christians believed about Jesus. So, what *did* they believe? Around 324 AD, Eusebius described them as follows:

> Ebionites ... considered [Jesus] **a plain and common man** and justified only by his advances in virtue and that **he was born of the virgin Mary by natural generation**. With them the observance of the law was altogether necessary,[14] as if they could not be saved only by faith in Christ and a corresponding life. **Others**, however, besides these, but of the same name [Ebionites], avoided the absurdity of the opinions maintained by the former, **not** denying that the Lord was born of the Virgin by the Holy Ghost, and yet **in like manner not acknowledging his preexistence**.[15]

The Ebionites were not considered heretics until after the mid-2nd century,[16] even though they were known to believe Jesus was a normal man who did not preexist his birth and, generally,[17] that he was not born of a virgin (Appendix G shows that the virgin birth theme was not part of the original Gospels). *What more need be said?* The Ebionites can be traced back to the earliest followers of Jesus Christ. Despite some recorded variations in their beliefs, *none* of the Ebionites ever believed Jesus was God himself or that he consciously preexisted his humanity.

Artemon Asserts Jesus "a Mere Man"

As we saw with the Ebionites, the earliest Jewish Christian belief maintained that Jesus was a normal man who did not consciously preexist his humanity. One notable early Christian holding this same view was a man named Artemon. This Artemon lived in the capital of Rome, teaching there at the end of the 2nd century. He made a very interesting claim that what he taught was in fact the same doctrine handed down by the apostles of Christ. Eusebius of Caesarea (a 4th century Christian historian) recites a certain anonymous record concerning Artemon.

> "They [the Artemonites] assert," said he, "that all those primitive men and the apostles themselves, both received and taught these things as they are now taught by them, and that the truth of the gospel was preserved until the times of Victor ... but that from [Victor's] successor Zephyrinus, the truth was mutilated."[18]

Eusebius is quoting an unidentified individual (Hippolytus? Caius? Calistus?) who was opposed to Artemon. The same individual attempted to refute Artemon's claim that his doctrine was maintained during the time of Victor (who was the bishop of Rome from 189-199 AD), writing thus:

> How then could it happen ... that those until the times of Victor, preached the gospel after this manner? And how are they so devoid of shame to utter these falsehoods against Victor, well knowing that Victor excommunicated that currier Theodotus, the leader and father of this God-denying apostasy, as **the first one that asserted Christ was a mere man**? For had Victor entertained the sentiments which their impious doctrine promulgates, how could he have expelled Theodotus, the **inventor** of this heresy?[19]

In such a way, it was asserted that Artemon's claims were not true. If Victor (an *earlier* bishop of Rome) excommunicated Theodotus, who "was the first one that asserted Christ was a mere man," then how could Artemon say that the truth was maintained *until* the time of Victor and subsequently mutilated under Victor's successor, Zephyrinus? Let's briefly respond to the erroneous accusations against Artemon.

Theodotus and Artemon

To begin with, Theodotus was *not* the "first one" to assert that Christ was a mere man (as Artemon's accuser stated). Justin Martyr showed that there were Christians in his day (160 AD) who believed this. This was decades before Victor was even bishop of Rome (189-199 AD). Furthermore, the

Ebionites also claimed Jesus was a normal man long before any of these occurrences.

> "The Artemonites were certainly correct in maintaining that the adoptionism which they held was, at least in essential principles, an ancient thing, and their opponents were wrong in denying it."
>
> —*Arthur Cushman McGiffert, Ph. D.*[20]

Notwithstanding, when Artemon's accuser says Theodotus was excommunicated for "inventing" a "God-denying" heresy, he is somewhat correct. However, the accuser misrepresents the facts when he *confines* Theodotus' excommunication to an assertion that "Christ was a mere man." Epiphanius, writing 375 AD, conveys the whole matter, which he learned "from written works,"[21] as follows:

> Theodotus of Byzantium ... at the outset of persecution—I cannot say which one—he with some others was arrested by the governor of the city and was subjected to examination for Christ's sake ... Theodotus, however, fell into transgression by denying Christ ... But as a supposed lame excuse for himself he **invented the following new doctrine** that said, "I didn't deny God, I denied a man." ... Thereafter he, and the Theodotians whose founder he was, **taught this doctrine of his** and said that Christ was a mere man **begotten of a man's seed**. ... Theodotus says next that he has not committed sin by denying Christ. "For," says he, "Christ himself has said, 'All manner of blasphemy shall be forgiven men,' and, 'Whosoever speaketh a word against the Son of Man, it shall be forgiven him.'[22]

Theodotus' new doctrine centered around *an excuse to deny Christ during persecution*. Regardless of what Theodotus *based* his conclusion on, his *conclusion itself* (that denying Christ under persecution is excuseable) was the novel heresy and explains why Victor excommunicated him. Theodotus apparently invented this heresy between 189-199 AD (during the time of Victor) to excuse his own former denial of Christ while he himself was under persecution. *This* was the "new doctrine." If we dismiss the *denying-Christ-under-persecution* aspect of Theodotus' Christology, we find that he taught "Christ was a mere man begotten of a man's seed."

Thus, since Artemon's Christology was said to be like that of Theodotus, Artemon likely *also* asserted that "Christ was a mere man begotten of a man's seed." As we have already seen, that doctrine of Artemon was not something "invented" by Theodotus, and neither of them were the first to bring such a doctrine forth. Artemon said that "all those primitive men and the apostles themselves both received and taught these things as they are now taught by them." We have previously discussed how this doctrine *at least* traced back to the Ebionites.

Other than the aforementioned sources, our information regarding Theodotus is largely confined to the writings of Hippolytus (170-235 AD). As you will see, Hippolytus presents a different account regarding Theodotus than what we found in the writings of Epiphanius. According to Hippolytus, writing sometime after 222 AD, Theodotus apparently taught *contradicting* doctrines about Christ.

Hippolytus writes thus:

> But Theodotus of Byzantium introduced a heresy of the following description, alleging that all things were created by the true God; whereas that Christ, he states, in a manner similar to that advocated by the Gnostics already mentioned, made His appearance according to some mode of this description. And Theodotus affirms that **Christ is a man of a kindred nature with all men**, but that He surpasses them in this respect, that, according to the counsel of God, **He had been born of a virgin**, and the Holy Ghost had overshadowed His mother. This heretic, however, maintained that **Jesus had not assumed flesh in the womb of the Virgin, but that afterwards Christ descended upon Jesus at His baptism in form of a dove**. And from this circumstance, the followers of Theodotus affirm that at first miraculous powers did not acquire operating energy in the Saviour Himself. **Theodotus, however, determines to deny the divinity of Christ**. Now, opinions of this description were advanced by Theodotus.[23]

Notice how he asserts that Theodotus taught Christ was "born of a virgin," which seems to blatantly *contradict* Epiphanius' written sources. Furthermore, in Hippolytus, the statement that "Jesus had not assumed flesh in the womb of the virgin" smacks of *Gnosticism* and *contradicts* the other statement that he makes—"Christ is a man of kindred nature with all men." Hippolytus appears to be attributing *contradictory* opinions to the *same* man. Furthermore, the statement, "Theodotus affirms that Christ ... had been born of a virgin," does not match the subsequent statement that "afterwards Christ descended upon Jesus at His baptism" (this might reflect a common strawman argument used to discredit adoptionist Christology[24]). It seems here that Hippolytus' [corrupted?] text has confounded at least two *different* views and is arguing with itself about what Theodotus taught. This conflation of views related to Theodotus is carried through when Hippolytus describes the "followers of Theodotus" as well.

> "[Theodotus taught that Jesus] at his baptism in Jordan received Christ, who came from above and descended (upon him) in form of a dove. ... But (among the followers of Theodotus) some are disposed (to think) that never was this man made God, (even) at the descent of the Spirit; whereas others (maintain that he was made God) after the resurrection from the dead."
>
> —*Hippolytus of Rome*[25]

Clearly there is a great deal of variation in what Hippolytus attributed to both Theodotus and to his adherents. Yet, despite the chaos, even Hippolytus' record hints at Theodotus' rejection of a virgin birth as well, because he traces Theodotus' Christology to Cerinthus and the Ebionites.

> But a certain **Cerinthus** ... asserted that the world was not made by the primal Deity... And he supposed that Jesus was **not generated from a virgin**, but that he was born son of Joseph and Mary, just in a manner similar with the rest of men ... But there was a certain **Theodotus** ... he acknowledges that all things were created by God. Forcibly appropriating, however, (his notions of) Christ from the school of the Gnostics, and **Cerinthus** and **Ebion**... [26]

Cerinthus and the Ebionites *both* asserted that Christ was not born of a virgin. The Gnostics, to whom Hippolytus *also* traces Theodotus' doctrine, believed something entirely different. Why does Hippolytus attribute contradictory doctrines to both Theodotus *and* to his adherents? Perhaps Hippolytus is laying more at Theodotus' doorstep than is merited.

Bypassing the confusion in Hippolytus' record, we are left with the records of Eusebius and Epiphanius, who do not trace anything Gnostic to Theodotus himself. Thus, accepting these two agreeing witnesses over the witness of Hippolytus (which doesn't even agree with itself), we can conclude, in agreement with scholars like Bart D. Ehrman,[27] that both Theodotus and Artemon taught "Christ was a mere man begotten of a man's seed." Accordingly, Artemon claimed that "all those primitive men and the apostles themselves, both received and taught these things" as well "and that the truth of the gospel was preserved until the times of Victor" but "from his successor Zephyrinus, the truth was mutilated."

Proof of Artemon's Claim

There is evidence to support Artemon's claim that Christological doctrines at Rome were indeed altered under Bishop Zephyrinus. *A Dictionary of Early Christian Biography* describes Zephyrinus' time as bishop as follows:

> [Zephyrinus'] reign was marked by serious disturbance at Rome owing to doctrinal controversies and consequent schism.[28]

"Doctrinal controversies and consequent schism" *did* occur during Bishop Zephyrinus' reign (199-217 AD). This was due, in part, to the influence of a man named Callistus, who "induced [Zephyrinus] for his own purposes, the declare generally for, but sometimes against, the Patripassians [Modalists asserting the Father himself was crucified]."[29] Artemon claimed that the true Christian doctrine was mutilated under Zephyrinus. Since history does show a fluctuating doctrine under Zephyrinus, Artemon's assertions are already vindicated in part.

Although we are not told much about what Artemon himself taught (outside the correlations to Theodotus' doctrine), there was another prominent individual who is known to have believed the same as Artemon. This man, known as Paul of Samosata (having been born in Samosata, Syria), was the bishop of Antioch from 260-272 AD. Epiphanius, writing in the 4th century, says, "[Paul] revived the sect of Artemon."[30] And Eusebius, also writing in the 4th century, equates the doctrine of Paul to that of Artemon in these words, "The heresy of Artemon, which Paul of Samosata again attempted to revive among us."[31] Eusebius' labeling of Paul's doctrine as "heresy" is due to Eusebius' view of what "orthodoxy" was during the time of his own 4th century writings, which encompassed the Nicene Crisis. We will discuss the Council of Nicaea (325 AD) later, but first we are going to look at a time *prior* to that, in which Paul of Samosata lived.

The Synods at Antioch

Christians often suffered persecution from Rome's government before Gallienus became the emperor of Rome in 253 AD. Yet, upon being made emperor, Gallienus issued his edict of toleration in favor of the Christians and a time of peace toward Christianity ensued. This timeframe, during which the Christians had favor with Rome, is known as the "Little Peace of the Church." One of the letters issued by Emperor Gallienus during this time still survives to this day. It was addressed to bishops in general, but *specifically named* the bishop of Rome and the bishop of Alexandria.[32] The bishop of Alexandria at that time was *Dionysius of Alexandria*. This Dionysius would incite others against Paul of Samosata, the bishop of Antioch, for his beliefs and lead the charge for his deposition.

The acceptance of Christians into Roman society during the *Little Peace of the Church* likely spurred on the desire for one homogenous presentation to Roman society of just what the Christian doctrine actually was. However, there was no homogenous presentation at that time. The church was scattered. Up to this point, different communities often held different and contradictory beliefs about Christ. In an attempt to subjugate the Christology of others, Dionysius, the bishop of Alexandria organized the Synods of Antioch (held 264-269 AD). During the Synods of Antioch, those doctrines being taught in Antioch were compared to prominent Alexandrian and Roman interpretations. One of the chief matters of dispute between the bishops of Alexandria and Rome and the bishop of Antioch was the nature of Christ's pre-human existence. The doctrine being taught in Antioch was that Christ's "pre-existence was simply in the divine foreknowledge."[33] Since Christ's pre-human existence was confined to the mind of God, Paul of Samosata, the bishop of Antioch, defined Christ's pre-existence as being the *same-nature* (ὁμοούσιος) with God. To Paul, this meant that Jesus did not exist *outside* of God as a conscious being, but remained in the essence of God, being *in the mind of God himself.*

Eusebius of Caesarea, writing several decades later as an opponent of Paul of Samosata, describes the first gatherings at Antioch in these words:

> All, therefore, having frequently convened at different times, discussed various subjects and questions at every meeting. The adherents of the Samosatians attempted to conceal and cover over their unorthodoxy, while at the same time those on the other side used every effort to unmask and bring to light the heresy and blasphemy of the man against Christ.[34]

The first meetings did not result in Paul's "excommunication." Even so, Paul was eventually pronounced a heretic in 269 AD after being examined by Malchion, "the head of the sophist's Greek school of sciences at Antioch."[35] Following Paul's debate with the Greek sophist, a letter condemning Paul was written by the hand of that same Malchion[36] (as one representing the sentiments of several bishops in attendance). The letter of Malchion, wherein the bishop of Antioch was pronounced a heretic, was, like Gallienus' edict, also specifically addressed to the bishop of Rome and the bishop of Alexandria. Nevertheless, despite the attempts of those bishops to remove the bishop of Antioch, Queen Zenobia, the Jewess who ruled over Syria (and Antioch) during that time, would not allow it. However, when Zenobia was conquered in 272 AD by Emperor Gallienus' successor, Emperor Aurelian, the bishops of Alexandria and Rome (the two largest cities in the Roman Empire) entreated the new emperor of Rome to pronounce a judgment against Paul on their behalf.

A Dictionary of Early Christian Biography records their appeal to Aurelian in these words:

> The Catholic prelates represented to him what they termed Paul's "audacity." Aurelian relegated the decision to the bp. of Rome and the Italian prelates, decreeing that the residence should belong to the one they recognized by letters of communion.[37]

Thus, by Roman decree, Paul was removed from his bishopric in 272 AD.

According to the historical records, Paul of Samosata's doctrine was the same as that of Artemon. The letter sent from Malchion affirmed this. According to Eusebius, Malchion's letter contained the following words [note that Artemas here is the same person as Artemon]:

> [Paul] parades with the execrable heresy of Artemas (for why should we not mention his father) ... We have been compelled, therefore, to excommunicate this man who sets himself up in opposition to God, and is unwilling to yield, and to appoint another bishop in his place over the catholic church ... But the other [*i.e.,* Paul] may write to Artemas if he pleases, and those that think with Artemas may have communion with him.[38]

Apparently, Artemon was still living (still in Rome?) and in communion with others of like faith. Since Artemon was still living at that time, being very aged by then, and since he was apparently known to many, including all those [allegedly?] involved in sending and receiving the letter, it is unlikely that the men seeking to condemn Paul would have been able to identify Paul's doctrine with that of Artemon unless it was, in fact, identifiable. I also see in Malchion's letter evidence that Paul was not formerly acquainted with Artemon, because his potential communion with Artemon is proposed as something new. Hence, we have two ancient and separate theological branches (Artemon in Rome and Paul in Antioch) who were proclaiming the same thing, despite not being in fellowship while doing so. This gives credence to the notion that they were both drawing from a preexisting and thus more ancient train of thought.

Even though the letter from Malchion said Paul of Samosata could write to Artemon for communion, Paul was hardly desperate for acceptance from the distant Artemon. Despite the opposition to Paul from the Alexandrian and Roman bishops, Paul was still in fellowship with many Christians in the East. The letter written by Malchion criticizes how Paul was still supported by "those bishops and presbyters of the neighboring districts and cities" and "the inhabitants of Antioch" and "the presbyters and deacons about him."[39]

The Apostolic Weight of Antioch

We know from history that Simon Peter (the apostle Peter) was once the bishop of Antioch and that Antioch was the headquarters of Paul of Tarsus (the apostle Paul) during his missionary journeys. Hence, the fact that Artemon *claimed* his doctrine was handed down by the apostles, coupled with the fact that this doctrine was so prominent in Antioch, gives credence to Artemon's assertion that the doctrine taught by him was indeed passed down from the apostles of Christ. I believe it was precisely because of the weight of testimony that Antioch held in relation to the original Christian doctrine that someone afterward felt the need to forge documents under Ignatius' name (a former bishop of Antioch). Let the reader note that Ignatius of Antioch reportedly died at Rome in 117 AD, yet Artemon's accuser (Hippolytus?), while writing in Rome during the early 3rd century and referencing men who declared Jesus to be God beforehand, made no mention of any works of Ignatius, writing thus:

> For who knows not the works of Irenaeus and Melito, and the rest, in which Christ is announced as God and man?[40]

If the epistles attributed to Ignatius, which *repeatedly* identify Jesus as God himself, were known at that time, Ignatius' writings would have been at the *forefront*, because Ignatius was *more ancient* than *both* Irenaeus and Melito and was also bishop of a city, Antioch, that had a *greater connection* to the apostles' doctrine than the districts of those other men, Lyons and Sardis. *Ignatius was reportedly a disciple of the apostle John himself! Why, then, weren't **any** references made to his epistles in **any** of the early Christian debates?* This *same* Ignatius allegedly wrote an epistle to the Christians at Rome, declaring things clearly at odds with Artemon, *so why didn't Artemon's opponent bring up Ignatius' epistle in Rome shortly thereafter?* This *same* Ignatius was *the bishop of Antioch **before*** Paul of Samosata became *the bishop of Antioch, so why didn't Paul's opponents make mention of Ignatius' letters as proof that Paul deviated from his predecessors?* (Note: This line of reasoning is also applicable to and evidence of my assertion in Appendix K, that *To Autolycus* was not actually written by Theophilus of Antioch). It is also noteworthy that none of Ignatius' epistles were ever quoted during the Nicene Crisis, either.

Scholars widely confess that eight out of the fifteen epistles allegedly written by Ignatius are total forgeries. The remaining seven epistles are also confessed by scholars to have been severely corrupted. Some scholars (see Appendix I) even argue that *all* the epistles attributed to Ignatius are total forgeries.

The Doctrine of Antioch

Having established the premise, that we may discover the doctrine of the apostles by examining the doctrine of Antioch, let's look at what Paul of Samosata, bishop of Antioch from 260-272 AD, asserted regarding Jesus.

Eusebius only records the following concerning his doctrine.

- The bishop of Antioch "taught that he [Jesus] was in nature but a common man."[41]
- Malchion wrote, "He does not wish to confess with us that the Son of God descended from heaven."[42]

Notice that there is no mention here of any Gnostic beliefs. All we see is that Paul said Jesus was, in regard to his nature, a common man and that he did not descend from heaven (we will discuss these things as we proceed).

A Dictionary of Early Christian Biography relays the doctrine of Paul of Samosata in the following:

> Paul held the pure humanity of Christ, "He was not before Mary, but received from her the origin of His being" (Athan. *de Synod*. p. 919, c. iii. s. 10). His pre-existence was simply in the divine foreknowledge. ... He was convicted, according to Eusebius, of asserting that Christ was mere man deemed specially worthy of divine grace (Eus. H. E. vii. 27). He taught also that as the Logos is not a Person, so also the Holy Spirit is impersonal, a divine virtue belonging to the Father and distinct from Him only in conception.[43]

Malchion wrote that Paul "does not wish to confess with us that the Son of God descended from heaven."[44] According to Paul, Jesus "existed in predestination before the ages, but was manifested in actual being from Nazareth."[45]

> "For they [the Samosatians] believe that the Word is like the word in a human heart, and the sort of wisdom everyone has in his human soul if God has given him understanding. They therefore say that God, together with his Word, is one person. ... They say, 'Jesus was a man, and yet God's Word inspired him from on high.'"
>
> —*Epiphanius*[46]

Unlike Paul of Somasata, the bishops of Alexandria and Rome believed that Jesus was a conscious being *prior* to his birth. In order to differentiate Jesus' pre-human existence from the mind/plan of God, those bishops correspondingly rejected Paul of Samosata's *same-nature* (ὁμοούσιος) terminology. Hence, in the latter half of the 3rd century, the bishops of the Roman Empire's two largest cities were claiming that Jesus existed in a different essence than God prior to his humanity, as a conscious being who descended from heaven and became a man.

Contrary to the opinions of some, we *never* find Paul of Samosata affirming a virgin birth (see Appendix H). However, we *do* see his doctrine associated with Artemon, who was in turn associated with the doctrine of Theodotus. Therefore, since Theodotus taught "Christ was a mere man begotten of a man's seed," it is likely that Paul of Samosata held that same belief. We may even see some correlation between Paul and the Ebionites, because Epiphanius described the Ebionites as "Jews in every way and nothing else."[47] Compare that to how he also said Paul's adherents "do not have circumcision or keep the Sabbath, but hold Jewish views on everything else."[48] Was it really a *bad* thing to "hold Jewish views"? As we said before, *all* of the apostles were Jews. And remember that Epiphanius himself traced the Ebionites back to Pella, where he said "all the disciples had settled ... after their remove from Jerusalem."

Some might assume that the only "Jewish views" abandoned by Western Christianity were pre-Christian observances of Mosaic law, but that is not the case. For example, around the middle of the 2nd century there was a well-known conflict between the Roman bishop and a prominent Eastern bishop regarding the annual rememberence of Jesus' death and resurrection (commonly referred to now as *Easter*). The Eastern bishop, Polycarp, Bishop of Smyrna, traveled to Rome, where the bishop of Rome attempted to persuade him to abandon his Eastern tradition. Irenaeus, writing around 180 AD, recounts the event as follows.

> For neither could Anicetus [the bishop of Rome] persuade Polycarp [the bishop of Smyrna] to forego the observance [in his own way], inasmuch as these things had been **always [so] observed by John the disciple of our Lord, and by other apostles with whom he had been conversant.**[49]

So, Polycarp, who was a bishop in the East, received his date of remembrance from John and other apostles. Yet, this apostolic tradition was afterward rejected at the Council of Nicaea (which we will discuss in the next chapter). In accordance with the Council of Nicaea's decision to prefer the Roman date, the emperor of Rome issued the following injunction.

> "That we may have nothing in common with the usage of the parricides and murderers of our Lord; and as that order is most convenient which is observed by all the churches of the West, as well as those of the southern and northern parts of the world, and also by some in the East … that the custom which prevails with one consent in the city of Rome, and throughout all Italy [etc.] … and to have no fellowship with the perjury of the Jews … that the most holy feast of Easter should be celebrated on one and the same day."
>
> —*Constantine, Emperor of Rome*[50]

As time progressed, the Christian concepts which could be traced back to the Jewish apostles became increasingly overshadowed by a desire to hold up novel Roman ideas as orthodoxy.

Chapter Two

How Error Became Prominent

In chapter one we looked at a period in early church history known as the *Little Peace of the Church*. That peace was termed *little* because it would not last. Persecution from Rome would soon begin again under the reign of Emperor Diocletian (284-305 AD). This persecution, primarily enforced in the East (there were many slaughtered at Alexandria), would wreak havoc amongst Christian communities and cast the former Alexandrian and Roman bishops' pursuit of homogeneity into a time of disorganization and reset. Yet, like the peace, the persecution would be short lived as well. Soon, an emperor would arise who would change everything.

Rome Adopts Christianity

Christianity as a whole was already widespread throughout the Roman Empire when Constantine became Emperor in 306 AD. Yet, rather than violently opposing the constant spread of the Christian movement, as some of the previous emperors of Rome had done, Constantine decided to embrace it and assimilate Christianity into Roman society. In 313 AD, Emperor Constantine, who recently "converted" to Christianity, suddenly began issuing state support for the Christian churches and clergymen.

Constantine's actions were in stark contrast to the conduct of the previous Roman Emperor, Diocletian, who persecuted the Christians severely during his own reign. Those Christians who refused to sacrifice to the Roman gods under the reign of Diocletian were imprisoned, tortured, and killed. Now, under Constantine, Christian clergy were getting government benefits, exemption from taxes, and extremely high social status. Consequently, throngs of people began seeking to attain the elaborate positions in the churches, so much so that Roman officials wrote to Constantine complaining that they could not find enough men to fill the governmental positions within their cities—the men qualified for those political careers were now opting for priestly ones instead. In response, Constantine issued an order prohibiting men to enter into the priesthood who were eligible for civic duties.

Prior to the establishment of the Roman papacy, the highest position that one could have in societal Christianity was that of a bishop. There was only one bishop per city, and he was to oversee the Christian activities therein. The larger the city, the more political power the bishop tended to have and the more widespread his doctrinal influences tended to become. Within the larger cities there were also a number of presbyters (often called *priests* or *pastors*) who presided over individual churches within the jurisdiction of their local bishop. In this construct, presbyters were considered inferior to the bishop in authority.

Alexandria's Doctrinal Schism

Boasting a population upwards of one million and second in importance only to the capital city of Rome itself, Alexandria was a massive Egyptian metropolis located along the coast of the Mediterranean Sea within the western half of the Roman Empire. Due to the greatness of the city, the metropolitan bishop presiding over Alexandria was in a very powerful position, even having uninhibited access to the Egyptian grain supply, which he could have distributed among the massive Alexandrian populace as he saw fit (a quirk that was eventually used to retain the favor of Alexandria's populace against outside influences). It is difficult to overstate the magnitude of power that was once wielded by the bishop of Alexandria within Christendom and, under Constantine, within the politics of Rome itself.

In the beginning of the 4th century a man named Achillas served only a single year as the bishop of Alexandria before appointing his successor. One of the candidates for the position was a presbyter (pastor) named Arius, who was at that time about 56 years old.

> Arius was the parish priest, as he may be described, of the church of Baukalis, the oldest and most important of the churches of

> Alexandria ... He had been a possible successor at the last vacancy of the "Evangelical Throne."[51]

Arius was considered for the position of Alexandria's next bishop. Yet, in 312 AD, Bishop Achillas named Alexander as his successor instead.

Shortly after becoming bishop, Alexander was standing by a window at his beach house waiting for some guests to arrive. There he saw a group of boys playing on the shore, pretending to baptize one another in the sea.

> He therefore sent for the children and had them brought into his presence. In the investigation that followed it was discovered that one of the boys, who was no other than the future Primate of Alexandria [Athanasius], had acted the part of the bishop, and in that character had actually baptized several of his companions in the course of their play. Alexander, who seems to have been unaccountably puzzled over the answers he received to his inquiries, determined to recognize the make-believe baptisms as genuine; and decided that Athanasius and his playfellows should go into training in order to fit themselves for a clerical career.[52]

Athanasius, the boy who was pretending to be a bishop on the beach, was born sometime around 296-298 AD, so he was 14-16 years of age at this time (312 AD). Not long thereafter, Alexander invited Athanasius to be his secretary and to share in his meals. Thus, Athanasius had a growing relationship and influence upon the Alexandrian bishop. While still a teenager (or, at the most, 20 years old), Athanasius composed two works, *Against the Pagans* and *The Incarnation.* It was in these works that Athanasius declared his view that the Son of God had no beginning, but was instead from all eternity coexistent with the Father. Alexander began to favor Athanasius' doctrine and, having knowledge that Arius was teaching otherwise at the "oldest and most important" church in Alexandria, called the presbyter in to discuss the matter. Arius declared his beliefs to Alexander and afterwards went back to his duties as a local pastor. Yet, the issue was not settled in Alexander's mind and he decided to hold a meeting of the Alexandrian clergy in order to discuss the subject further. Prior to the meeting, Alexander sent for a statement of faith from those regional clergymen who believed as Arius did. Accordingly, a letter was sent from them declaring that the Father existed before the Son.

The letter contained the following words:

> To our blessed pope and bishop, Alexander. The presbyters and deacons in union with the Lord bid you greetings. Our belief **which comes from our forefathers and which we have learned from you as well**, blessed pope, is as follows: ... God, who is the cause of all, is **the only one without beginning**. The Son, on the other hand, who was begotten of the Father (though not in time) and who **was created** and established before the ages, **did not exist prior to his begetting** ... And therefore [God] is also before Christ, **as we have learned from you when you have preached in the congregation**.[53]

Two Egyptian bishops, Theonas of Marmarica and Secundus of Ptolemais, Arius, five other presbyters, and six deacons signed the document declaring that Alexander previously taught the beliefs which they now held to. Yet, apparently desirous of reconsidering the accurateness of his own previous beliefs, Alexander proceeded to call the aforementioned meeting of the Alexandrian clergy. Arius was present. This meeting is where the conflict between Arius and Alexander explodes.

A Dictionary of Early Christian Biography accredits Sozomen (a 5th century Trinitarian historian whose works covered Christian events from 323–439 AD) as having effectively sorted through the myths surrounding the Council of Nicaea in order to relay the facts:

> Like Socrates, Sozomen is habitually trustworthy, and a conscientious and serious writer. In his account of the council of Nicaea, which may be taken as a favourable specimen of his work as a whole, he seems to have drawn from the best sources, to have proceeded with care, and to have made a sufficiently good choice among the apocryphal traditions and innumerable legends which in the 5th cent. obscured the reports of this great council.[54]

The reason why I have referred to Sozomen's reliability as a historian is because Sozomen recorded how Alexander himself, the bishop of Alexandria, vacillated back and forth between doctrinal positions during this controversial meeting at Alexandria.

A Dictionary of Early Christian Biography states the following:

> According to Sozomen, **Alexander seemed to waver between the Arian and anti-Arian positions**. Ultimately he asserted in strong terms the coequality of the Son; whereupon Arius criticized his language as savouring of the Sabellian error which had "confounded the persons."⁵⁵

Amazing! Sozomen records the monumental shift of the Alexandrian bishop's own theology. And because Arius would not follow suit, the Alexandrian bishop flexed his political muscle and began persecuting Arius and the rest of the clergy present who sided with him.

Sozomen writes:

> During the debate, Alexander seemed to incline first to one party and then to the other; finally, however, he declared himself in favor of those who affirmed that the Son was consubstantial and coeternal with the Father, and he commanded Arius to receive this doctrine, and to reject his former opinions. Arius, however, would not be persuaded to compliance, and many of the bishops and clergy considered his statement of doctrine to be correct. Alexander, therefore, ejected him and the clergy who concurred with him in sentiment from the church. Those of the parish of Alexandria, who had embraced his opinions, were the presbyters Aithalas, Achillas, Carpones, Sarmates, and Arius, and the deacons Euzoius, Macarius, Julius, Menas, and Helladius. Many of the people, likewise, sided with them: some, because they imagined their doctrines to be of God; others, as frequently happens in similar cases, because they believed them to have been ill-treated and unjustly excommunicated.⁵⁶

Arius subsequently wrote a letter to Eusebius, bishop of Nicomedia, which contained the following words:

> We are vehemently opposed and persecuted, and every engine is set in motion against us by the bishop ... Eusebius, your brother, bishop of Caesarea, and Theodotus and Paulinus, Athanasius [bishop of Anagastus], Gregorius and Aetius, and **all the bishops of the East**, affirm, that God, who is without a beginning, **existed before the Son**. ... We are persecuted, because we have said that **the Son has a beginning**. But God is without a beginning. On this account we are persecuted, and because we said that he is of things not existing. Thus we have said, because he is not a part of God, nor of any subject matter. On this account we are persecuted.[57]

And in a letter from that same Eusebius, bishop of Nicomedia, to Paulinus, bishop of Tyre, Eusebius says:

> We have **never heard** that there are two unbegotten beings, nor that one has been divided into two, nor have we learned or believed that it has ever undergone any change of a corporeal nature; but we affirm that the unbegotten is one and one also that which exists in truth by Him, yet was not made out of His substance.[58]

Nevertheless, although it was previously unheard of, this doctrine of Athanasius, now being promoted by the super-bishop of Alexandria, began causing major disturbances within Constantine's empire.

The Council of Nicaea

Constantine assembled a council of bishops at Nicaea in 325 AD to settle this divisive dispute. Eusebius of Caesarea read a statement of faith aloud at the council, which contained the following words (except for the portion I have underlined, which was likely added at a later date[59]):

> We believe in one God, the Father Almighty, Maker of all things visible and invisible; and in one Lord Jesus Christ, the Word of God, God of God, light of light, life of life, the only begotten Son,

the first born of every creature, begotten of the Father before all ages, by whom also all things were made; who for our salvation was made flesh and conversed among men; who suffered, and rose again the third day, and ascended to the Father, and will come again with glory to judge the living and the dead. We also believe in one Holy Spirit; <u>believing every one of these to be and subsist, the Father truly the Father, and the Son truly the Son, and the Holy Spirit truly the Holy Spirit; as also our Lord, when he sent his disciples to preach, said, "Go teach all nations, baptizing them in the name of the Father and of the Son, and of the Holy Spirit."</u> We solemnly affirm that we thus hold and thus think, and have so held formerly, and will hold even unto the death, and will always continue in this faith, anathematizing every impious heresy. We testify before Almighty God and our Lord Jesus Christ, that we have believed this sincerely, and from the heart, from the time that we were capable of knowing ourselves, and now also truly think and speak, being prepared to show by sufficient proofs, and to convince your minds, that we have so believed in times past, and have preached accordingly.[60]

Theodoret (393-457 AD) describes Constantine's reaction upon hearing the statement of faith in the following:

Having made this representation of our faith, there was no pretense for contradiction. But our pious emperor himself was the first to declare, that it was extremely well conceived, and that it expressed his own sentiments, exhorting all to assent to, and sign it, that they might unite in its doctrines, **with the addition only of the single word** *consubstantial* [ὁμοούσιος – homoousios]; which he explained by asserting that he did not use the term with reference to corporeal affections, and that the Son did not subsist from the Father, either by division or abscission, since it was impossible that an immaterial, intellectual and incorporeal nature could admit of any bodily affection; but that it must be understood in a divine and mysterious manner.[61]

Now, when combining the statement of faith read by Eusebius with the homoousios term used by Paul of Samosata, it appears that Constantine was *affirming* the view of Paul of Samosata (even if only to appease the Eastern half of his empire). Had the final statement of faith *only* added the word *homoousios*, the Nicene Creed would have been in agreement with Paul—the prehuman existence of Christ thus being confined to the mind of God—and there would have been nothing in the final text contrary to Arius, either. Yet, that was *not* the only change that was made to the statement of faith. At the behest of Constantine, the homoousios term was indeed included, but they *also* made several *other* changes as well.

Theodoret records the reaction of the presiding bishops to the homoousios terminology and their corresponding alterations to the statement of belief as follows (notice the subtle changes):

> It was thus that our most wise and religious emperor argued on this subject. But the bishops, **taking occasion from the word consubstantial [ὁμοούσιος], committed to writing the following form**: We believe in one God, the Father Almighty, Maker of all things visible and invisible. And in one Lord Jesus Christ, the Son of God, the only begotten of the Father, that is, of the essence of the Father; God of God, Light of Light, **true God of true God**; begotten, **not made**, consubstantial [ὁμοούσιος] with the Father, by whom all things were made, both in heaven and on earth; who for us men, and for our salvation, descended, was incarnate, and was made man, and suffered, and rose again the third day: he ascended into heaven, and shall come to judge the living and the dead: and in the Holy Spirit. **But** the holy catholic and apostolic Church of God **anathematizes** those who affirm that there was **a time when the Son was not**, or that he **was not before he was begotten**, or that he was **made of things not existing**: or who say, that the Son of God was of any other substance or essence, or created, or liable to change or conversion.[62]

The new creed was now *targeting* Arius' beliefs. Arius *did* say the Son was not before he was begotten. Arius *also* said the Son was made of things not existing. His letter to Eusebius of Nicomedia, which we read previously, asserts both of these views.

> **All the bishops of the East**, affirm, that God, who is without a beginning, existed before the Son. ... We are persecuted, **because we have said that the Son has a beginning**. But God is without a beginning. On this account we are persecuted, **and because we said that he is of things not existing**. Thus we have said, because he is not a part of God, nor of any subject matter. On this account we are persecuted.[63]

When Arius says Christ was not a *part* of God, he is *denying* that the Son's *origin* was the result of God's nature being *separated* from him to produce a second person. In his letter to Eusebius of Nicomedia, Arius writes:

> "But if the terms 'from Him,' and 'from the womb,' and 'I came forth from the Father, and I am come, be understood by some to mean as if a part of Him, one in essence or as an issue, then the Father is according to them compounded and divisible and alterable and material, and, as far as their belief goes, has the circumstances of a body, Who is the Incorporeal God."[64]

Arius was about 70 years old during his "trial" at Nicaea. During the council's procession the bishop of Myra (Nicolaus of Myra), struck a blow to the seventy-year old presbyter's head. This gives us an adequate picture of the dominating attitude towards Arius during the trial. *What was going on here?* Arius was not even allowed the dignity of presenting his defense properly. His written presentation was torn to pieces. Who were these abusers of old men?

> Sabinus, bishop of Haraclea in Thrace ... derided the fathers of Nicea as ordinary and ignorant men.[65]

Arius was an Alexandrian *presbyter* challenging the decision of the Alexandrian *bishop*. Could it be that this was *the* issue that determined the result of the Nicene Council? It was certainly the issue that brought the Council of Nicaea about. As such, this Alexandrian bishop vs. Alexandrian presbyter theme plausibly remained prominent. Remember, those assembled at the council were themselves bishops, now highly esteemed in Roman society as such. How would an announcement that Rome favored a presbyter over a bishop bring their own episcopate into dispute?

Although there were some bishops in attendance that sided with Arius, the limited record we have shows that those bishops were also being treated harshly as well. For example, Eusebius of Nicomedia, to whom Arius appealed, also had a written statement of faith prepared which, upon his reading, "excited so much indignation that it was rent in pieces and Eusebius was overwhelmed with confusion."[66] After this, we find Eusebius and others who sided with Arius being pressed to affirm propositions that they did not feel comfortable with.

> The prelates again asked the Arians, who seemed to be few in number, if they allowed that the Son was not a creature but the alone power, wisdom, and image of the Father and in no respect whatever different from him, and that he was true God. It was observed that Eusebius and his adherents made signs to one another that all these particulars might agree to men, for men too, said they, were called the image and glory of God. ... And as to their denominating the Son true God, that occasioned them no embarrassment, for he was so truly, because he was made so.[67]

The domineering fiasco playing out at this aggressive council was having an effect. Eventually, the majority of assembled bishops agreed to the creed's wording (though they had differing concepts in mind regarding its terminology). Constantine opined that the council's majority was divinely inspired and exhorted all in attendance to sign the document. Arius refused. Constantine exiled him, along with two Egyptian bishops—Theonas of Marmarica and Secundus of Ptolemais—for refusing to sign the Nicene Creed. Three other bishops (Eusebius of Nicomedia, Theognis of Nicaea, and Maris of Chalcedon) who *did* sign the creed *afterwards* recanted for having done so. They wrote a letter to Constantine, which said:

> We committed an impious act, O Prince, by subscribing to a blasphemy from fear of you.[68]

Yet, having initially secured an appearance of unity at the council, Constantine hoped that Christendom would now unite under the Nicene doctrine. He thus had the results published throughout his empire, so that all might adhere to it.

Christianity Rejects the Nicene Doctrine

The vast majority of Christians rejected the Nicene Creed. There was such an objection to it that Constantine reversed his position two years later (327 AD) and Arius was recalled from exile after a subsequent trial at the Council of Nicomedia. Bishop Alexander died in 328 AD, and Athanasius (the boy who was pretending to baptize on the beach) replaced him as the new bishop of Alexandria (not yet being 30 years of age). Several councils condemned Athanasius thereafter and Arius' views were pronounced as orthodox.

We see proof of Arius' claim that the bishops of the East did agree with him, because another synod was held in Antioch in 341 AD, where ninety-seven bishops produced a written statement which read as follows:

> We have not been followers of Arius—how could bishops, such as we, follow a Presbyter?—nor did we receive any other faith besides that which has been handed down from the beginning. But, after taking on ourselves to examine and to verify his faith, we admitted him rather than followed him.[69]

The bishops affirmed that they had not followed Arius, but rather examined him by the tenets of faith handed down to them from the beginning. In finding his beliefs to be orthodox, they received him accordingly. *Astonishing!* Arius was the one who was orthodox.[70] Yet, he is erroneously considered by many today to be *the* archetypal heretic.

The Doctrine of Arius

Arius has been misunderstood as if he believed Jesus pre-existed as a conscious being prior to his humanity. Though some of Arius' non-Trinitarian contemporaries (subsequently miscategorized as "Arians") *did* believe this about Jesus, that was *not* the case with Arius himself. Within his letter to Eusebius of Nicomedia, Arius described himself as a "fellow-disciple of Lucian."[71] This places Arius within the theological school of *Lucian of Antioch*, who was himself a pupil of Paul of Samosata. Arius' belief, therefore, is easily traced back to Paul of Samosata.[72]

The New Encyclopedia Britannica says the following regarding Lucian:

> Later critics, including Alexander of Alexandria, during the Council of Nicaea in 325, associated Lucian's school with the condemned theological revisions of Arius and his attack on the absolute divinity of Christ. Lucian, in 269, had also been implicated with the denounced teachings of the Atiochian bishop Paul of Samosata.[73]

Paul of Samosata believed that Jesus preexisted in the mind of God, but not as a conscious being. Likewise, a careful examination of Arius' beliefs will show that, while asserting that Christ did exist before his birth, he held the same persuasion as Paul of Samosata. In fact, those siding with Arius were said to think "like the Samosatene"[74] (*i.e.,* like Paul of Samosata) by Athanasius, who also said they were "openly reviving the statements of the Samosatene."[75]

> "The Son is not unbegotten, nor in any manner a part of the unbegotten, or of any matter subject to him; but **in will and design he existed before all times and ages**."
>
> *—Arius*[76]

Arius lived in Alexandria. I see some similarities in his statements about existing in the mind of God that with what I find in Philo of Alexandria's writings. Philo of Alexandria (50 BC–20 AD) was a Levite theologian who wrote about creation existing in the mind of God before anything external to God was made. According to Philo, God created all things in an archetypal form *within his own reasoning* before he created the visible version of creation, which was *patterned after* that preconceived archetype of creation existing only in the mind of God. Even though Arius would have largely opposed the allegorical methodology of Philo,[77] I do see some common ideas existing between Philo, Arius, and early Christian thought in general. For example, *2 Clement*, written 95-140 AD, says:

> So, then, brethren, if we do the will of our Father God, we shall be members of the first church, the spiritual,—that which was created before sun and moon ... (for the Scripture, saith, "God created man male and female;" the male is Christ, the female the church,) and that the Books and the Apostles teach that the church is not of the

present, but from the beginning. For it was spiritual, as was also our Jesus, and was made manifest at the end of the days in order to save you.[78]

And *The Shephard of Hermas,* written around 150 AD, says something similar.

> "[The elderly woman is] the Church," he replied. I said to him, "Why, then, is she elderly?" "Because," he said, "she was created before all things [πάντων πρώτη ἐκτίσθη]; therefore she is elderly, and for her sake [διὰ ταύτην] the world was formed.[79]

How could the Church have been created before all things? And how could 2 Clement say it had the same kind of former existence as Jesus?

Regarding creation existing first in the mind of God, Philo writes thus:

> When [God] had determined to create this visible world, [he] previously formed that one which is **perceptible only by the intellect** ... But **that world which consists of ideas**, it were impious in any degree to attempt to describe or even to imagine: but how **it was created**, we shall know if we take for our guide a certain image of the things which exist among us. When any city is founded through the exceeding ambition of some king or leader who lays claim to absolute authority, and is at the same time a man of brilliant imagination, eager to display his good fortune, then it happens at times that some man coming up who, from his education, is skillful in architecture, and he, seeing the advantageous character and beauty of the situation, first of all sketches out **in his own mind** nearly all the parts of the city ... Then, having received in his own mind, as on a waxen tablet, the form of each building, he carries in his heart the image of a city, perceptible as yet only by the intellect, the images of which he stirs up in memory which is innate in him, and, still further, engraving them in his mind like a good workman, keeping his eyes fixed on his model, he begins to raise the city of stones and wood, making the corporeal substances to resemble each of the incorporeal ideas. Now we must form a somewhat similar opinion of God, who, having determined to found a mighty

> state, first of all conceived its form in his mind, according to which form **he made a world perceptible only by the intellect**, and then completed one visible to the external senses, using the first one as a model. As therefore the city, when previously shadowed out in the mind of the man of architectural skill had no external place, but was stamped solely in the mind of the workman, so in the same manner neither can the world which existed in ideas have had any other local position except **the divine reason** (τὸν θεῖον λόγον) **which made them**.[80]

In Philo's theology, there was a perfect version of creation existing only in the mind of God which came before any of the things created external to God. Although Philo asserted that God's archetypal design of creation was "before everything and … was conceived before everything,"[81] this conceptual construct was confined to the divine reasoning itself. Like Philo, Arius described Christ as "begotten apart from time by the Father … being begotten apart from time before all things."[82] Since the archetypal model of creation was something conceived in God, yet not created external to God, Philo described it as "neither being uncreate as God, nor yet created as you, but being in the midst of these two extremities."[83] Likewise, Arius described Christ's pre-human state as "perfect creature of God, but not as one of the creatures; offspring, but not as one of things begotten."[84] The Son was not created like something that is created, but rather as something conceived internal to God. This accords with the doctrine of Paul of Samosata.

Jesus' pre-human existence, being only in the mind of God, was described by Arius as "non-existing," which Alexander relays in the following:

> Arius, Achilles, Aithales, Carpones, the other Arius, Sarmates, who were formerly priests; Euzoius, Lucius, Julius, Menas, Helladius, and Gaius, formerly deacons; and with them Secundus and Theonas, who were once called bishops. And the words invented by them, and spoken contrary to the mind of Scripture, are as follows:—"God was not always the Father; but there was a time when God was not the Father. The Word of God was not always, but was made 'from things that are not;' for He who is God **fashioned the**

non-existing from the non-existing; wherefore there was a time when He was not."[85]

Arius and those with him asserted that Christ only came into actual existence when he became a man. Alexander, who even associates Arius' doctrine with the Ebionites,[86] clearly affirms this in the following quote.

> It is on this account, beloved brethren, that without delay I have stirred myself up to inform you of the unbelief of certain persons who say that "There was a time when the Son of God was not;" and "He who previously had no existence subsequently came into existence; and **when at some time He came into existence He became such as every other man is**."[87]

After the Synod of Antioch declared that Arius was orthodox in 341 AD, another council was held at Rimini in 359 AD, where over four hundred bishops (more bishops than were at Nicaea) signed a creed renouncing the Nicene doctrine.

> In any case, the council [of Rimini] was a sudden defeat of [Nicene] orthodoxy, and St. Jerome could say: "The whole world groaned in astonishment to find itself Arian."[88]

Theodosius Enforces the Nicene Doctrine

The Nicene doctrine was on its way to extinction. If it were not for the Nicene oriented background of Theodosius,[89] who became the emperor of Rome in 379 AD, the Nicene sect may have been obliterated altogether.

A Dictionary of Early Christian Biography shows how, after taking the throne, Theodosius began a persecution against the "Arians" while promoting the "Athanasians" back into authoritative positions throughout the Roman Empire:

> His [Theodosius'] accession was the turning-point which secured the triumph of Trinitarian orthodoxy over the Arianism dominant in the East for at least the previous 40 years. **Theodosius turned**

what seemed in many places an obscure and conquered sect into a triumphant church, whose orthodoxy, on this point at least, never afterwards wavered.[90]

Once again it was the political system of Rome, not the independent and free discourse of men, that pushed forward the Nicene doctrine. Emperor Theodosius issued an edict in 380 AD announcing the persecution of anyone who did not accept the Nicene doctrine. The new Roman emperor's edict (the Edict of Thessalonica) contained the following enactment:

> According to the apostolic teaching and the doctrine of the Gospel, let us believe in the one deity of the Father, Son, and Holy Spirit, in equal majesty and in a holy Trinity. We authorize the followers of this law to assume the title Catholic Christians; but as for the others, since in our judgment they are foolish madmen, we decree that they shall be branded with the ignominious name of heretics, and shall not presume to give their conventicles the name of churches. They will suffer in the first place the chastisement of divine condemnation, and second, the punishment that our authority, in accordance with the will of heaven, shall decide to inflict.[91]

This time the emperor's decision stuck. And, by various means, the doctrine enforced by Emperor Theodosius has persisted from then until now. It is not difficult to trace the Christological breadcrumbs back to Rome. The Vatican (historic center of Nicene Trinitarianism) is still located inside the city of Rome to this day. Prior to the 16th century Protestant Reformation, the Roman Catholic church had the largest theological sway in Christendom at large. And, for the most part,[92] the Protestant split (protesting against certain practices of the Catholic church) hardly went so far as to divest itself of Roman traditions handed down through Catholicism. In fact, even in our modern day, Christian societies not only retain matters of doctrine from Rome, but also certain holidays as well. Although an exhaustive inquiry into the retained influence of Rome on today's Christianity is beyond the scope of this book, suffice it to say that Easter bunnies and Christmas trees have nothing to do with Jesus. They are instead vestigial relics from the pagan culture of Rome, historically assimilated into Christianity, passed on through Catholicism, retained through the Protestant split, and socially preserved in our modern day.

Chapter Three

One True God

Christ Reveals God

The Bible very clearly states that Christ is the image of God (2 Corinthians 4:4). The meaning of this is simple to understand—God is one and Christ is the image, reflection, or representation of that one God. Rather than expressing himself, Christ revealed the person of God.

Jesus shows how he reveals the actions of God, saying:

> "Verily, verily, I say unto you, The Son can do nothing of himself, but what he seeth the Father do: for what things soever he doeth, these also doeth the Son likewise." (John 5:19)

Christ did those things that he saw the Father do, and in this way, God was revealed through him.

And pay close attention to the following words of Christ:

> "My doctrine is not mine, but his that sent me. If any man will do his will, he shall know of the doctrine, whether it be of God, or whether I speak of myself." (John 7:16-17)

Notice in this last passage how Jesus said:

> "My doctrine is **not mine, but his** that sent me." (John 7:16)

And then:

> "If any man will do his will, he shall know of the doctrine, **whether** it be of God, **or whether** I speak of myself." (John 7:17)

Christ proclaimed that he spoke of God *rather* than of himself. His statement would be very misleading if he were trying to identify himself as God.

And again, Jesus says:

> "I can of mine own self do nothing: as I hear, I judge: and my judgment is just; because I seek not mine own will, but the will of the Father which hath sent me." (John 5:30)

Jesus did not seek his own will, but the will of the Father. Hence, we see that there are two wills. Christ was always subjecting his own will to God so that God would be revealed in him.

This is why Jesus said:

> "Whosoever shall receive me, receiveth **not me**, but him that sent me." (Mark 9:37)

And again:

> "Jesus cried and said, He that believeth on me, believeth **not on me**, but on him that sent me." (John 12:44)

The fact that Jesus said men believing on him were **not believing on him**, but on the Father, is rarely (if ever) acknowledged in our modern day. Yet, his statement is very fundamental. Christ was not expressing the things that were of *himself*, but rather the things that were of *God*. Therefore, by receiving Christ, you weren't receiving Christ (who was subjecting his will to God), but you were instead receiving God (who was being revealed through Christ's subjection).

The Image is Called by the Name of the Archetype

Arius, and those agreeing with him, acknowledged that Jesus is called *God*. Yet, they simultaneously confessed that Jesus was a normal man. How do these things fit together? The answer to this becomes evident when we look at how, throughout the Bible, a representative or image of someone is called by the name of the one whose attributes are being revealed through them.

Here is an example of a man being addressed by the name of someone whose attributes were being manifested through him:

> "[Jesus] turned and said unto Peter, Get thee behind me Satan."
> (Matthew 16:23)

Does this mean that Peter *was* Satan because Jesus *called* him Satan? It plainly says:

> "He turned and said **unto Peter**, Get thee behind me **Satan**."
> (Matthew 16:23)

It is clear to whom Jesus was speaking. Jesus refers to Peter as "Satan" in this passage. Yet, does this mean that Peter was *literally* Satan? Of course not.

And notice also how Jesus referred to Judas as a "devil," saying:

> "Have I not chosen you twelve, and one of you **is a devil**?"
> (John 6:70)

Judas was not *literally* a devil, but the devil *was* working through him, and therefore he was called by the name of the archetype whose attributes were being manifested.

It may even be that it was not Satan himself who was working through Peter and Judas, because Satan's *demons* are also called "Satan" as well. This is obviously true, because once when the Pharisees were accusing Jesus of casting out *demons* by the prince of the demons, Jesus responded to them by saying:

> "**If Satan casts out Satan**, he is divided against himself; how then will his kingdom stand? ... But if it is by the Spirit of God that I **cast out demons**, then the kingdom of God has come upon you."
> (Matthew 12:26, 28 RSV)

Satan's demons are called *Satan* because the attributes of Satan are manifested in them. Similarly, the angels of God are sometimes called God as well:

After seeing an angel of God, Manoah says:

> "We have seen God." (Judges 13:22)

The context shows that Manoah only saw "an angel of the LORD." (Judges 13:21.) However, since the angel was acting as God's personal representative *to* Manoah, he was therefore called God *by* Manoah.

> "Moreover, [angels] are more than once called gods; because in their ministry, as in a mirror, they give us an imperfect representation of divinity."
> —*John Calvin*[93]

This principle regarding the image being called by the name of its archetype may also be applied when a man serves as a sort of prototype for another man. This is why Jesus called John the Baptist "Elias," saying:

> "For all the prophets and the law prophesied until **John**. And if ye will receive it, **this is Elias**, which was for to come."
> (Matthew 11:13-14)

Since Jesus refers to John the Baptist by the name *Elias*, does this mean that John the Baptist *was* Elias? No. Some of the Levites asked John, "Art thou Elias?" And John answered, "I am not." (John 1:21.)

Albert Barnes comments on why John the Baptist was called Elias, saying:

> The prophet Malachi predicted that Elijah should be sent before the coming of the Messiah, to prepare the way for him (Malachi 4:5,6). By this was evidently meant, not that he should appear in person, but that one should appear with a striking resemblance to him; or, as Luke (Luke 1:17) expresses it, "in the spirit and power of Elijah."[94]

According to Barnes, John was referred to *as* Elias because he came "in the spirit[95] and power *of* Elias." (Luke 1:17.) Although Elias' *personal* attributes were not revealed in John, certain *ministerial* attributes identified with Elias were (which made John somewhat of an Elias replica).

Let's look at another example. The Pharisees accused Jesus of casting out demons *by Beelzebub,* saying:

> "This fellow doth not cast out devils, but **by Beelzebub** the prince of the devils." (Matthew 12:24)

Yet, Jesus equates this with *being called Beelzebub* when he, describing how his followers would be persecuted as he was, says:

> "If they have **called the master of the house Beelzebub**, how much more shall they call them of his household?" (Matthew 10:25)

Doing works *by* Beelzebub is equated to being *called* Beelzebub.

Again, Jesus himself is referred to as *David* in Ezekiel 34:23, as every commentary on the Bible will admit, yet this is not because Jesus was *himself* David, but rather because of certain commonalities he had with David, the righteous King of Israel. Additionally, Jesus is called "the Son of David" in the New Testament (Matthew 1:1, etc.). So, biblically, Jesus is called *both* David *and* the Son of David, yet *no one* asserts that Jesus is literally David himself. However, when Jesus is called God and the Son of God, many *do* affirm that this necessarily means Jesus is God himself.

So far, by the preceding examples, we have seen how individuals in the Bible were often called by the name of the archetype whose attributes were being expressed through them:

- Jesus called Peter Satan, though Peter is not Satan himself.

- Jesus called Judas a devil, though Judas was not literally a devil.

- Satan's demons were called Satan, though they are not Satan himself.

- An angel of the LORD was called God, though God is not an angel.

- John the Baptist was called Elias, but he was not Elias himself.

- Jesus equated acting in the power of Beelzebub to being called Beelzebub, yet that doesn't mean Beelzebub himself.

- Jesus is called David, but he was not David in a literal sense.

In light of all these examples, it is evident that, biblically, individuals were often called by the name of the one whom they represented or expressed. Furthermore, the Bible not only proves this principle, but also proves that this principle should be applied *in regard to Jesus being God*.

Exodus 7:1 reads thus:

> "And the LORD said unto Moses, See, **I have made thee a god** to pharaoh: and Aaron thy brother shall be thy prophet."

Here, in the Hebrew language, the word translated as "a god" is *elohim*, which may also be, and usually is, translated as "God."

The Bible says:

> "Hear O Israel, The LORD our **God** (*Elohim*) is one LORD."
> (Deuteronomy 6:4)

Therefore, a correct translation of Exodus 7:1 could very well be:

> "I have made thee **God** unto Pharaoh."

That is *not* to say that Moses was himself God, but rather that God's judgments (etc.) were being revealed *through* Moses, and thus he was God's expression to Pharaoh. Someone might say that Exodus 7:1 means that Pharaoh, who already believed in many gods, thought that Moses was also a literal god too, but that is incorrect. Pharaoh understood that Moses was God's representative (Exodus 5:1-3, 8:25-29, etc.). Furthermore, God already spoke of this principle to Moses in a previous passage, saying:

> "And he (Aaron) shall be thy spokesman unto the people: and he shall be ... to thee instead of a mouth, and thou shalt be to him (Aaron) **instead of God**." (Exodus 4:16)

Here, the phrase "instead of God" is also translated from the word *elohim*, which doesn't mean *instead of God*, but simply *God*. This obviously does not mean that Moses was a *replacement* for God to Aaron, but rather that Moses was the one through whom God revealed himself *unto* Aaron. In this way, Moses was (not in any literal sense) made God to Aaron.

God said that he made Moses God to Pharaoh and Aaron. With that being said, pay close attention to the content of Deuteronomy 18:17-19.

> "And the LORD said unto [Moses], They have well spoken that which they have spoken. I will raise them up a prophet from among their brethren, **like unto thee**, and will put my words in his mouth; and he shall speak unto them all that I shall command him. And it shall come to pass, that whosoever will not harken unto my words which he shall speak in my name, I will require it of him."
> (Deuteronomy 18:17-19)

This prophecy was fulfilled in Jesus, as the Scriptures say:

> "And he (God) shall send Jesus Christ, which before was preached unto you ... For Moses truly said unto the fathers, A prophet shall the Lord your God **raise up unto you** of your brethren, **like unto me**; him shall ye hear in all things whatsoever he shall say unto you. And it shall come to pass, that every soul, which will not hear that prophet, shall be destroyed from among the people. ... Unto you first God, having **raised up his Son Jesus**, sent him to bless you, in turning away every one of you from his iniquities."
> (Acts 3:20, 22-23, 26)

The Bible says that Moses was made "God" to Pharaoh and to Aaron. This principle was thus validated in regard to Moses. The prophecy that one would come who was "like unto Moses" was fulfilled in Christ. It is inconsistent to say that Moses was called God in one way, but Jesus, who was *like unto* Moses, is called God in an entirely different manner. The most consistent interpretation is that Christ would be called God in the same way as Moses was, since he was "like unto" Moses. Moses spoke the revealed words of God unto men and therefore he was called God. The coming prophet (Christ) was to do the same, as the Scripture said:

> "I will raise them up a prophet from among their brethren, **like unto thee**, and will put my **words in his mouth**; and he shall **speak unto them all that I shall command him**."
> (Deuteronomy 18:18)

And Jesus says this of himself:

> "For I have not spoken of myself; but the Father which sent me, he **gave me a commandment, what I should say, and what I should speak**." (John 12:49)

Both Moses and Christ are called God because the *only true God,* the Father, was revealed through them.

> "[Arius said] that 'the Word is not the very God;' 'though He is called God, yet He is not very God,' but 'by participation of grace, He, as others, is God only in name."
> —*Athanasius*[96]

Do not misunderstand my words, I am not implying that those in whom God is revealed will be deified (made literal gods). In fact, I do not say that we should even *call* men God at this present time. Although Jesus and Moses were called God in the Bible, using some of the grammatical peculiarities of the past in our modern day would only cause misunderstanding.

Examples:

- Even though the King James Bible translators wrote that people *worshipped* men who were in high positions (Luke 14:10, Revelation 3:9, etc.), we no longer apply the word *worship* in that manner in our modern day. We now only use the word *worship* in reference to the homage that is due to God alone (worship will be discussed in depth in chapter eighteen).

- Within the biblical Hebrew language, references to a *singular* noun are sometimes written in the *plural* form (majestic plural) in order to express the greatness of that noun (Genesis 42:30, Job 40:15, etc.), but such a practice is not common to us now.

Languages change. When the Bible was written, different grammatical quirks were used than we use now. It is evident that one such quirk was the application of an archetype's title to others. Hence, we should not reject that principle where biblical studies are concerned, even though we don't speak in that way now.

1 John 5:20 – There is Only One True God

The Bible specifically describes the Father as the "true God" in three instances:

- "These words spake Jesus, and lifted up his eyes to heaven, and said, **Father** ... this is life eternal, that they might know thee **the only true God**, and Jesus Christ, whom thou hast sent." (John 17:1, 3)

- "Ye turned to God from idols to serve the living and **true God**; And to wait for **his** Son from heaven, whom **he** raised from the dead, even Jesus." (1 Thessalonians 1:9-10)

- "And we know that the Son of God is come, and hath given us an understanding, that we may know **him that is true**, and we are in **him** that is true, even in **his** Son Jesus Christ. **This is the true God**, and eternal life." (1 John 5:20)

There has been some deal of controversy over whether this last passage, 1 John 5:20, designates Christ as the true God rather than the Father. I will address this issue in a moment, but first let's briefly consider what it means to say "true God." In the following passage, consider how there are two tabernacles. One tabernacle was the original archetype, designated as the "true" tabernacle, and the other was a copy of that true one, patterned after its design.

> "[Jesus is a] minister of the sanctuary, and of **the true tabernacle**, which the Lord pitched, and not man ... For if he were on earth, he should not be a priest, seeing that there are priests that offer gifts according to the law: Who serve unto **the example and shadow of heavenly things**, as Moses was admonished of God when he was about to make **the tabernacle**: for, See, saith he, that thou **make all things according to the pattern shewed to thee** in the mount." (Hebrews 8:1-5)

The tabernacle Moses built was an image of the true tabernacle, yet it served as a representation of the true to men on earth. Thus men, incapable of beholding heavenly things, might, by seeing the image of the heavenly, understand what those heavenly things were. Likewise, there is one true God, and Christ is his image. We cannot behold the true God, but we see him through seeing his revealed image, namely Christ. The image is not the true. The image is patterned after the true. So, when we read "true God" we should understand that this not only distinguishes him from false gods, but it also distinguishes him from his image.

Now, let's look at 1 John 5:20, which reads:

> "And we know that the Son of God is come, and hath given us an understanding, that we may know him that is true, and we are in him that is true, even in his Son Jesus Christ. **This is the true God**, and eternal life." (1 John 5:20)

Does this refer to Christ as the true God? No. Consider the following passage:

> "These words spake Jesus, and lifted up his eyes to heaven, and said, **Father** ... this is life eternal, that they might know **thee the only true God**, and Jesus Christ, whom thou hast sent." (John 17:1, 3)

The only true God, according to Jesus, is the Father. Why then would anyone go contrary to such a plain statement and allege that Christ is designated as the true God in 1 John 5:20? Primarily because "This is the true God" is written immediately after the words "Jesus Christ."

> "And we know that the Son of God is come, and hath given us an understanding, that we may know him that is true, and we are in him that is true, even in his Son **Jesus Christ. This is the true God**, and eternal life." (1 John 5:20)

Since the words "Jesus Christ" are nearest to the words "This is the true God" some have perceived that Christ was being called the true God in this text. Admittedly, this is a grammatical possibility. The Greek commentators will explain, however, that the closest antecedent isn't the deciding factor here.

Westcott comments thus:

> As far as the grammatical construction of the sentence is concerned the pronoun (οὗτος) may either refer to 'Him that is true' or to 'Jesus Christ.' **The most natural reference however is to the subject not locally nearest but dominant in the mind of the apostle** (compare 1 John 2:22, 2 John 7, Acts 4:11, 7:19). This is obviously 'He that is true' further described by the addition of 'His Son.' Thus the pronoun gathers up the revelation indicated in the words which precede ... This Being—this One who is true, who is revealed through and in His Son, with whom we are united by His Son—is the true God.[97]

The context clearly identifies the Father as the "true" one before stating, "this is the true God."

> "And we know that the Son of God is come, and hath given us an understanding, that we may know **him that is true**, and we are in **him that is true**, even in **his** Son Jesus Christ. **This** is the **true God**, and eternal life." (1 John 5:20)

God, the Father, is thus already identified as the "true" one two times in 1 John 5:20 before we find, "This is the true God." That alone is strong evidence that "the true God" refers back to the Father.

It is noteworthy that some manuscripts, like the 5th century Codex Alexandrinus, actually read as follows:

> "And we know that the Son of God is come, and hath given us an understanding, that we may know **the true God**, and we are in him that is true, even in his Son Jesus Christ. This is the true God, and eternal life." (1 John 5:20)

This specifically states that the true God is the Father of Jesus. Notwithstanding, I agree with Bruce Metzger, who argues that this is probably not the original reading, stating that "copyists added θεόν [God]" to "clarify the reference of the adjective."[98] Even so, the antiquity of this variant only adds support for the correct interpretation of the text, namely, that the true God is the Father.

Another reason why some think "the true God" refers to Christ is because of what is written *after* "the true God."

> "This is the true God, **and eternal life**." (1 John 5:20)

Since Jesus is elsewhere identified as "the life" (John 11:25, 14:6), some have argued that the eternal life in 1 John 5:20 is also referring to Jesus, thus presenting him in total as "The true God and eternal life." However, the eternal life in 1 John 5:20 is not referring to a person, but rather to *knowing God.*

> "And we know that the Son of God is come, and hath given us an understanding, **that we may know him that is true ... this is** the true God, and **eternal life**." (1 John 5:20)

This coincides with Jesus' statement:

> "**Father** ... this is life eternal, **that they might know thee the only true God**." (John 17:3)

The "eternal life" in both of these passages is *to know God*. While this is stated more explicitly in John 17:3, the contents of 1 John 5:20 are too theologically symmetric to John 17:3 to dismiss the corresponding theme—*the Father is the true God and knowing him is eternal life*. After speaking of knowing the true God in the first part of 1 John 5:20, the author then points back to that:

> "...we may **know him** that is true ... **This** is the true God and [knowing him] is eternal life."

I believe, therefore, that the pronoun οὗτος (the word translated as "this" when it says, "this is the true God and eternal life") not only refers back to God, but also to how knowing God is effectual unto eternal life.[99]

> "The Father and the Son, God and Jesus Christ, are always so definitely distinguished throughout the whole Epistle, that it would be strange if, at the close of it, and moreover, just after both subjects have been similarly distinguished immediately before, Christ—without further explanation, too—should be described as ὁ ἀληθινὸς Θεὸς."
>
> —J. E. Huther[100]

John 14:9 – Did Jesus Claim to be the Father?

A common passage of Scripture pointed out by Modalists (who say that Jesus is the Father himself) is John 14:8-9. In this passage, Philip says to Jesus:

> "Lord show us the Father, and it sufficeth us." (John 14:8)

Jesus replies to Philip's request, saying:

> "Have I been so long time with you, and hast thou not known **me**, Philip? he that hath seen me hath seen the Father?" (John 14:9)

The Modalists say that Christ was claiming to be the Father himself in this passage. I admit that it could be taken as such in isolation. However, let's look at Christ's statement in its proper context.

Immediately before Philip asked Jesus to show him the Father, Jesus said:

> "If ye had known me, ye should have known the Father **also**: and from henceforth ye know him, and have seen him." (John 14:7)

Notice how Jesus says, "If ye had known me, ye should have known the Father **also**." The word *also* represents two, not one.

Also notice here how Jesus informs his disciples that they have *already* seen the Father.

> "If ye had known me, ye should have known the Father also: and from henceforth ye know him, and **have seen him**." (John 14:7)

Philip did not comprehend the manner in which he had already seen the Father, which consequently led him to ask Jesus to show the Father to him. Yet, the Father was *already* being shown to Philip, because the Father was being revealed *through Jesus all along* (for which cause Jesus is called the image of God).

Suppose I was to show you an image (a photograph) of Abraham Lincoln, informing you that once you have seen that image you have seen Abraham Lincoln as well. Now suppose that after you stare at that image for ten minutes you were to say to me, "Will you show me Abraham Lincoln now?" I could say, "Has *the image* been in your face all along, and yet have you not seen *it* (the image)? Don't you know that when you have seen the image you have seen Abraham Lincoln as well? How can you say, 'Show me Abraham Lincoln'?"

Jesus is the image of God (2 Corinthians 4:4). He already told Philip that those who saw him had seen the Father, so when Philip afterwards requested that Jesus show him the Father, Jesus responded by saying:

> "Have I been so long time with you, and yet hast thou not known **me**, Philip? **he that hath seen me hath seen the Father; and how sayest thou then, Shew us the Father**?" (John 14:7-9)

Since the Father was *constantly* being revealed through Christ, for Philip to ask Christ to show him the Father demonstrated either disregard or unbelief concerning the fact that the Father was already being *revealed* through Christ all along. Christ is the image of God, so when Philip or anyone else saw Christ, they also saw God.

EXAMPLE	**JOHN 14:7-9**
The photograph is an image of Abraham Lincoln	Christ is the Image of the Father
When you have seen the image you have seen Abraham Lincoln	When you have seen Christ you have seen the Father (v.7, 9)
After seeing the image, someone says, "Show me Abraham Lincoln"	After seeing Christ, Philip says, "Show us the Father" (v.8)
Reply: "Has the image been in your face all along, and yet have you not seen it? When you have seen the image you have seen Abraham Lincoln as well? How can you say, 'Show me Abraham'?"	Jesus' reply: "Have I been so long time with you, and yet hast thou not known me, Philip? he that hath seen me hath seen the Father; and how sayest thou then, Shew us the Father?" (v.9)

Did Some Men See the Father Himself?

The Bible clearly teaches that no man has ever seen God:

> "No man hath seen God at any time." (1 John 4:12)

No man can see God because God is invisible:

> "The King eternal, immortal, invisible, the only wise God."
> (1 Timothy 1:17)

However, there are instances where *angels representing God* appeared to men and occasioned such statements as, "We have seen God." (Judges 13:22.) Even so, there are also instances where God was seen *sitting on his throne* and I don't believe those were visions of angels (and, on his throne, God is distinct from Christ as well. See Daniel 7:13, Revelation 5:7). Regarding seeing God on his throne, Daniel says his "garment was white as snow, and the hair of his head like the pure wool." (Daniel 7:9.) Now, this *is* akin to what we read of the angel sent to John (Revelation 1:1), who is described thus, "His head and his hairs were white like wool, as white as snow; and his eyes were as a flame of fire." (Revelation 1:14.) Here in Revelation 1:14 we see that an *angel* (if we take him as the angel of Revelation 1:1), is described as having an extremely white head with eyes that are like fire. Compare that to how Daniel also describes an angel later in his writings, "His face [was] as the appearance of lightning, and his eyes as lamps of fire." (Daniel 10:6.) John and Daniel give similar descriptions, but one says *his head was as white as snow* with fiery eyes and the other says *his face was like lightning* with fiery eyes. So, by comparison, it seems to me that the extremely white head may *also* be bright light, which would appear like lightning closer up. Those things were said of angels, but they could also account for how the Ancient of Days is described as having extremely white hair (Daniel 7:9).

Now, what I am proposing about God here, which may apply in a lesser sense to the angels, is this, "God is light." (1 John 1:5.) Just as light is invisible until it is separated into colors (like when it passes through a prism or when we see a rainbow), so also the invisible God has at times let "himself" be seen, not in his invisible essence, but *perhaps* in *a by-product* of his invisible essence. Thus, when men "saw God on his throne," it was always *like bright light* and *like the colors of a rainbow*.

- "Upon the likeness of **the throne** was the likeness as the appearance of a man above upon it. ... as the appearance of **the bow that is in the cloud in the day of rain**, so was the appearance of the brightness round about." (Ezekiel 1:26-28)

- "He that sat was to look upon like a jasper and a sardine stone: and there was **a rainbow** round about **the throne**, in sight like unto an emerald." (Revelation 4:3)

See the rainbow terminology? Now, when you see a rainbow, the colors closest to heaven are reddish (like a jasper and a sardine stone) and then, extending beyond that, you see green (like the color of an emerald), and then you see blue (like a sapphire), which is also the final color that extends out from God's throne into the distance (Exodus 24:10, Revelation 4:6). So, it seems to me that God is invisible, like light, but he can present himself to the sight of men just as light is visible when separated into colors. Notwithstanding, even if light becomes visible when, for example, it shines on a prism, the visible white light striking that prism and the visible colors extending from that white light *do not originate* where those things are seen. Rather, the light is all around, expansive, and the visible only slightly portrays the invisible. So also, God is not contained in the visible expression when men see him. Rather, he "fills heaven and earth" (Jeremiah 23:24) and is always "dwelling in the light which no man can approach unto; whom no man hath seen, nor can see." (1 Timothy 6:16.)

Philo (a Jewish writer we will discuss shortly) comments on appearances of God as follows:

> To those souls which are still in the body he must appear in the resemblance of the angels, though without changing his nature (for he is unchangeable), but merely implanting in those who behold him an idea of his having another form, so that they fancy that it is his image, not an imitation of him, but the very archetypal appearance itself.[101]

Satan is not the God of this World

It is so often said these days that Satan is "the god of this world." People make this claim based on an incorrect interpretation of 2 Corinthians 4:4, which says:

> "In whom the god of this world hath blinded the minds of them that believe not, lest the light of the glorious gospel of Christ, who is the image of God, should shine unto them." (2 Corinthians 4:4 KJV)

Satan is *not* referred to here as "the god of this world." The word "god" in this verse is translated from the phrase ὁ Θεὸς, which means *the God*. The fact that our English versions do not capitalize the *g* when it says, "the *god* of this world," is irrelevant, because the Greek text *never* capitalizes the first letter of a word unless that word is a name, written as the first word in a quotation, or written at the beginning of a new paragraph. The Greek word θεος is a title, but it is not a name, hence it is not even capitalized when used to identify the Father himself. In light of this fact, it is the *content* and *context* of 2 Corinthians 4:4 (not the capitalization) which must determine whether a false god (god) is being spoken of rather than the true God (God).

Although 2 Corinthians 4:4 says that the God of this world "blinded the minds of them which believe not, lest the light of the glorious gospel of Christ should shine unto them," this does not mean that it is automatically Satan who did that blinding. Rather, it is *God* who gave blinded eyes to the unbelievers:

> "According as it is written, God (ὁ Θεὸς) hath given them the spirit of slumber, eyes that they should not see, and ears that they should not hear; unto this day." (Romans 11:8)

This passage clearly shows that it was God, the *only* God, who blinded their minds by giving them "the spirit of slumber, eyes that they should not see, and ears that they should not hear." Yet, God did not blind their minds so that they wouldn't have a *chance* to believe, but rather because they had *already refused* to believe.

> "Whom the God (ὁ Θεὸς) of this world hath blinded the minds **of them which believe not**" (2 Corinthians 4:4)

And elsewhere the Scriptures also say:

> "They received not the love of the truth, that they might be saved. And for this cause God (ὁ Θεὸς) shall send them strong delusion, that they should believe a lie: That they all might be damned who believed not the truth, but had pleasure in unrighteousness."
> (2 Thessalonians 2:10-12)

It is because men already refuse to believe the truth that they are blinded.

> "And even as they did not like to retain God in their knowledge, God (ὁ Θεὸς) gave them over to a reprobate mind." (Romans 1:28)

Irenaeus, writing 180 AD, commented on 2 Corinthians 4:4 as follows:

> For one and the same God [that blesses others] inflicts blindness upon those who do not believe, but who set Him at naught; just as the sun, which is a creature of His, [acts with regard] to those who, by reason of any weakness of the eyes cannot behold his light; but to those who believe in Him and follow Him, He grants a fuller and greater illumination of mind. In accordance with this word, therefore, does the apostle say, in the Second [Epistle] to the Corinthians: "In whom the God of this world hath blinded the minds of them that believe not, lest the light of the glorious Gospel of Christ should shine [unto them]." And again, in that to the Romans: "And as they did not think fit to have God in their knowledge, God gave them up to a reprobate mind, to do those things that are not convenient." Speaking of antichrist, too, he says clearly in the Second to the Thessalonians: "And for this cause God shall send them the working of error, that they should believe a lie; that they all might be judged who believed not the truth, but consented to iniquity."[102]

I take τοῦ αἰῶνος τούτου ("of this world") here as *of this age*, "specifically (Jewish) a Messianic period" (Strong's #G165). Taking "this age" as *the Messianic age* has solid contextual support. Notice how the flow of thought leading up to 2 Corinthians 4:4 specifically contrasts the two Messianic and Mosaic ages. Notice also how the phrase, "blinded the minds," (4:4,) is a follow up to, "their minds were blinded." (3:14.)

> "Who also hath made us able ministers of καινῆς διαθήκης (**a new** covenant) ... But their minds were **blinded**: for until this day remaineth the same vail untaken away in the reading of the **old** testament ... Therefore seeing we have **this** ministry ... In whom ὁ θεὸς τοῦ αἰῶνος τούτου (the God of **this** age) hath **blinded** the minds of them which believe not." (2 Corinthians 3:6, 14, 4:1, 4)

1 Corinthians 8:4-6 – Not Many Real Gods

One of the most commonly misapplied texts used to assert the existence of multiple gods is 1 Corinthians 8:5, which reads:

> "For though there be that are called gods, whether in heaven or in earth, (as there be gods many, and lords many)" (1 Corinthians 8:5)

When Paul says that there are many gods he is not saying many *real* gods. The surrounding context indicates that Paul was speaking of *false* gods:

> "We know that an **idol** is nothing in the world, and that **there is none other God but one**. For though there be that are **called** gods, whether in heaven or in earth, (as there be gods many, and lords many,) **But to us there is but one God, the Father**."
> (1 Corinthians 8:4-6)

Paul is without a doubt *contrasting* the "many" gods of the pagan religions with the "one" God of the Christian faith.

> "For great is the **LORD**, and greatly to be praised: he is also to be feared above all gods. For all the gods of the people are idols: but the LORD made the heavens." (1 Chronicles 16:25-26)

Although some texts refer to "gods" in a way that is not identifying them with *false* Gods, there remains "none other God but one." (1 Corinthians 8:4.) The instances describing "gods" in an affirmative manner are all found in the Old Testament (except for John 10:34-35, which we will discuss in chapter sixteen). The Old Testament was written in the Hebrew language, wherein the word for "gods" can also be translated as "God." Hence, they were likely called "God" in the same way that Moses was in Exodus 7:1.

Chapter Four

Begotten of God

Was Christ begotten of God by coming out of the Father's own divine essence? Was it a natural process in which the Father reproduced a consubstantial offspring? Is there a difference between the nature of Christ's sonship and our sonship?

Same Nature = Same God?

I once read a book entitled *Mere Christianity,* written by C.S. Lewis, wherein he made the following assertion:

> A man begets human babies ... What God begets is God, just as what man begets is man.[103]

Do you see the species terminology? When man begets man, this does not refer to a reproduction of the *same* man, but it rather introduces a *different* man who is *a member of the same species* of man. Man does not beget himself. Therefore, if we were to draw a parallel between "man begetting man" and "God begetting God," as C.S. Lewis does, this would mean that God does not beget the *same* God, but a *different* God who is *a member of the same species* of God. God is an individual, not a species. Therefore, Lewis' analogy is misleading. Since God is an individual, then the Son, who is not the same individual as the Father, cannot, in any absolute sense, be the same God as the Father himself.

In 213 AD, Tertullian said:

> A father must necessarily have a son in order to be a father. So, likewise, a son must have a father to be a son. However it is one thing to *have,* and another thing to *be.* For example, in order

> to *be* a husband I must *have* a wife. However, I can never myself be my own wife. In like manner, in order to *be* a father, I must *have* a son, for I never can be a son to myself.[104]

The Father and the Son cannot be the same individual, and therefore (since God *is* an individual) the Son cannot be the same God as the Father. When God is spoken of as a species consisting of multiple persons, this effectively robs God of his own individuality and reduces him from one conscious person down to a substantial classification ... a *what* rather than a *who*. Such a conclusion would be admitted on our part if Scripture demanded it, but it does not, as this book demonstrates. In summary, even if the Son *were* begotten from the essence of the Father, this still would not make Jesus God himself.

Philo on Being a Son of God

Philo of Alexandria (50 BC to 20 AD) talks about how men are born of God, but it does not pertain to a reproduction of substance. Rather, he presents "born of God" as denoting a person who is *in a fixed state of attentiveness on God* instead of on natural things.

> Some men are born of the earth, and some are born of heaven, and some are born of God (θεοῦ γεγόνασιν): those are born of the earth, who are hunters after the pleasures of the body, devoting themselves to the enjoyment and fruition of them, and being eager to provide themselves with all things that tend to each of them. Those again are born of heaven who are men of skill and science and devoted to learning; for the heavenly portion of us is our mind, and the mind of every one of those persons who are born of heaven studies the encyclical branches of education and every other art of every description, sharpening, and exercising, and practising itself, and rendering itself acute in all those matters which are the objects of intellect. Lastly, those who are born of God (θεοῦ [γεγόνασιν]) are priests and prophets, who have not thought fit to mix themselves up in the constitutions of this world, and to become cosmopolites, but who having raised themselves above all the objects of the mere outward senses, have departed and fixed their views

on that world which is perceptible only by the intellect, and have settled there, being inscribed in the state of incorruptible incorporeal ideas.[105]

Philo described Abraham as initially being fixated on the natural heavens, but afterward switching his focus to God, which Philo equates to Abraham being born of God.

> Accordingly, Abraham, as long as he was abiding in the land of the Chaldaeans, that is to say, in opinion, before he received his new name, and while he was still called Abram, was a man born of heaven, investigating the sublime nature of things on high, and all that took place in these regions, and the causes of them, and studying everything of that kind in the true spirit of philosophy; on which account he received an appellation corresponding to the pursuits to which he devoted himself: for the name Abram, being interpreted, signifies the sublime father, and is a name very fitting for the paternal mind, which in every direction contemplates sublime and heavenly things: for the mind is the father of our composite being, reaching as high as the sky and even farther. But when he became improved, and was about to have his name changed, he then became a man born of God (γίνεται ἄνθρωπος θεοῦ), according to the oracle which was delivered to him, "I am thy God, take care that thou art approved before me, and be thou Blameless."[106]

Philo describes those focused on God as "born of God." However, to Philo, there was a clear difference between being focused on God and actually obtaining knowledge *from* God. In his view, being a son of God himself—having knowledge of God without mixture—was plausible, but seemingly out of reach. Yet, being a son *of reasoning*—having knowledge of God *through contemplation*—was something that we *could* achieve.

> But they who have real knowledge, are properly addressed as the sons of the one God, as Moses also entitles them, where he says, "Ye are the sons of the Lord God." And again, "God who begot Thee;" and in another place, "Is not he thy father?" Accordingly, it is natural for those who have this disposition of soul to look upon nothing as beautiful except what is good, which is the citadel

> erected by those who are experienced in this kind of warfare as a defense against the end of pleasure, and as a means of defeating and destroying it. And even if there be not as yet any one who is worthy to be called a son of God, nevertheless let him labour earnestly to be adorned according to his first-born word (τὸν πρωτόγονον αὐτοῦ λόγον), the eldest of his angels, as the great archangel of many names; for he is called, the authority (ἀρχὴ), and the name of God, and the Word (λόγος), and man according to God's image, and he who sees Israel. For which reason I was induced a little while ago to praise the principles of those who said, "We are all one man's Sons." For even if we are not yet suitable to be called the sons of God, still we may deserve to be called the children of his eternal image, of his most sacred word; for the image of God is his most ancient word (λόγος ὁ πρεσβύτατος).[107]

The varied terminology Philo uses may make it seem like he was referring to a conscious being as the Logos, but he was not. He was instead, in his normal usage of allegorical interpretation, referring to things that all *represented the rational mind*.[108] For example: Notice in the above excerpt that Philo describes the reasoning (λόγος) as "man according to God's image." Now see how Philo also describes this "man according to God's image" as "the species of the soul" called "mind and reason."

> God is the archetypal pattern of rational nature, and that man is the imitation of him, and the image formed after his model; not meaning by man that animal of a double nature, but the most excellent species of the soul which is called mind and reason (νοῦς καὶ λόγος).[109]

Notice how λόγος was translated as *reason* in the above quotation. In Philo's writings, man's reasoning faculty is patterned after God's reasoning faculty, and both are called *reason* (λόγος). To Philo, since man was not hearing from God himself, he had to rely on his ability to *contemplate* God. Thus, men *could* be a pupil of that reasoning ability—the λόγος which was inherent to God and reproduced in man as a sort of ambassador—but Philo did not consider himself nor his hearers as pupils of God himself. In regard to that absolute knowledge from God, Philo says, "For even if we are not yet suitable to be called the sons of God," as if that knowledge was beyond his ability. Yet, direct knowledge from God without mixture *was* made known to Christ. And this explains Jesus' profound proclamation that "no man knoweth … who the Father is, but the Son, and he to whom the Son will reveal him." (Luke 10:22.) Therefore, in the terminology of Philo, Jesus would have been claiming to have access to pure, non-speculative information from God.

"Born of" Should be Translated as "Begotten"

I have heard many people, from varying viewpoints, say that *only* Christ is *begotten* of God. And thus, according to them, Christ is the Son of God in such a way that does not apply to God's other "non-begotten" sons. However, there are actually *many* biblical passages where men other than Christ are unquestionably presented as *begotten* of God:

In Deuteronomy 32:18, as it reads in the Septuagint, Moses speaks unto the children of Israel, saying:

> "Thou hast forsaken God that **begot** thee, and forgotten God who feeds thee." (Deuteronomy 32:18 LXX)

The Hebrew Masoretic text says something slightly different:

> "Of the Rock that **begat** thee thou art unmindful, and hast forsaken God that formed thee." (Deuteronomy 32:18 KJV)

Instead of saying "God" begot the Israelites the Hebrew text says that "the Rock" begot them. However, since God is declared to be "the Rock" in the same chapter (Deuteronomy 32:3-4), the thought remains the same. According to the Bible, God begot the Israelites.

We also see God declaring this fact himself in the Septuagint text of Isaiah 1:2, saying:

> "I have **begotten** and reared up children, but they have rebelled against me." (Isaiah 1:2 LXX)

There are also New Testament examples of men being begotten of God as well. When translated correctly, as in the *American Standard Version,* 1 John 5:1 says:

> "Whosoever believeth that Jesus is the Christ is **begotten** of God: and whosoever loveth him that begat loveth him also that is begotten of him." (1 John 5:1 ASV)

This scripture clearly shows that those who believe that [the real[110]] Jesus is the Christ are *begotten* of God. The fact that Christians are begotten of God is very evident in many other New Testament passages as well, but (due to inconsistent translations) the Greek word γεννάω (gennao), which means *begotten,* has often been translated as "born" whenever it is applied to Christians, but "begotten" whenever it is applied to Christ.

- In reference to God begetting Christ, γεννάω is translated as "begotten" in Acts 13:33, Hebrews 1:5, 5:5, and possibly 1 John 5:18.

- In reference to God begetting Christians, γεννάω is translated as "born" in 1 John 2:29, 3:9, 4:7, 5:1, 5:4, 5:18.

The same Greek word that describes Christ as "begotten" of God is also used to describe Christians as "born" of God. So, when some of the English versions say that Christians are "born of God," this is the same as being "begotten of God."

Example: The KJV renders 1 John 2:29 as, "Ye know that every one that doeth righteousness is **born** of him." Yet, other English translations justifiably translate it as, "Ye know that every one that doeth righteousness is **begotten** of him." (ASV, YLT, Darby)

Adam Clarke commented on the correct translation of γεννάω in 1 John 2:29, saying:

> The words "born of him" (ἐξ αὐτοῦ γεγέννηται), should be translated "hath been begotten of him," which is the literal signification of the word, from γεννάω, *(gennao) I beget.*[111]

This is true. Yet, does this mean that those who are "begotten" of God *become* the God who begot them? Of course not. So, let's be consistent in our studies and not allege that Christ is God himself because *he* is begotten of God. Being begotten of God in no way suggests that the one who is begotten becomes the begetter.

Begotten Explained

In biblical terms, being begotten of someone does not necessarily denote the reproduction of matter. Notice how Paul says that he begot the church in Corinth:

> "For though ye have ten thousand instructors in Christ, yet have ye not many fathers: for in Christ Jesus I have **begotten** you through the gospel." (1 Corinthians 4:15)

Paul begot the Christians at Corinth, but he was not saying that the church at Corinth came out of his essence.

And again, this is not what Paul meant when he said:

> "I beseech thee for my **son** Onesimus, whom I have **begotten** in my bonds." (Philemon 10)

Does this mean that Onesimus came out of Paul's essence? No. According to its biblical usage, the word *begotten* may also be used to signify the reproduction of *character*. The same Greek word, γεννάω, that describes how both Christ and Christians are begotten of God is also used in those passages that describe how Paul begot sons as well (Philemon 10, 1 Corinthians 4:15). So then, according to the Scriptures, the word *begotten* does not necessarily refer to producing children out of one's substance. Paul was not referring to a physical and natural begetting process, but rather to a process by which others became "imitators" of him in relation to character (as he imitated Christ. 1 Corinthians 11:1).

This is why he says:

> "For though ye have ten thousand instructors in Christ, yet have ye not many **fathers**: for in Christ Jesus I have **begotten** you through the gospel. Wherefore I beseech you, **be ye followers of me**." (1 Corinthians 4:15-16)

Paul also says elsewhere:

> "Whatever you have learned or received or heard from me, or seen in me—put into practice." (Philippians 4:9 NIV)

The one begotten does what the father who begot him does, and thus, in a *characteristic* sense, the begetter is reproduced in the one who is begotten. This is what the Bible means when it speaks of *God* begetting children. According to the Bible, those who are begotten of God do as God does and those who are begotten of the devil do as the devil does:

> "If ye know that he is righteous, ye know that every one also that doeth righteousness is begotten of him. ... My little children, let no man lead you astray: he that doeth righteousness is righteous, even as he is righteous: he that doeth sin is of the devil; for the devil sinneth from the beginning. To this end was the Son of God manifested, that he might destroy the works of the devil. Whosoever is begotten of God doeth no sin, because his seed abideth in him: and he cannot sin, because he is begotten of God. In this the children of God are manifest, and the children of the devil: whosoever doeth not righteousness is not of God, neither he that loveth not his brother." (1 John 2:29, 3:7-10 ASV)

God's character is reproduced in the children of God. Satan's character is reproduced in the children of Satan. Therefore, when we think of God begetting children, we should often think in terms relative to *character* and *actions*. God does not undergo some sort of natural reproductive process by which his substance is divided into distinct persons. Rather, the *character* and *actions* of God are manifested within the children of God through the indwelling operation of God's Spirit. By God's Spirit abiding *in* them, God's character is revealed *through* them, and they are thereby begotten *of* him.

Let's look at another biblical example that shows how a father can beget sons regardless of substantial processes. The Bible shows that the physical offspring of Abraham are not his only children, because, in another sense, those who *do the works* of Abraham are his children as well (Romans 4:12-18, Galatians 3:7). Likewise, some who *are* his physical offspring are not his children in regard to their *character* and *actions*.

Jesus spoke to some of the physical descendants of Abraham and said:

> "I know that ye are Abraham's seed." (John 8:37)

And again, he says to them:

> "**Your father Abraham** rejoiced to see my day" (John 8:56)

Christ clearly acknowledged that those men with whom he spoke were Abraham's children in regard to their genealogical descent. However, Christ shows that those men were *not* children of Abraham in regard to their character, saying:

> "**If ye were Abraham's children, ye would do the works of Abraham**. But now ye seek to kill me, a man that hath told you the truth that I have heard of God: this did not Abraham. **Ye do the deeds of your father ... the devil**." (John 8:39-41, 44)

Christ shows that there is a wholly different way to be Abraham's children that clearly doesn't involve a reproduction of substance. The Jews to whom Christ spoke were Abraham's *physical* descendants. Yet, in regard to their *character,* they were not Abraham's children, but were instead declared to be children of the devil.

So, there are two ways in which a person may be a child of Abraham:

1. According to physical reproduction

2. According to reproduction of character

It is this latter connotation that Paul refers to when he speaks of *begetting* the Christians at Corinth. This is also the reasoning behind those passages that speak of *Christ's* children (Isaiah 49:20-21, Isaiah 53:10). Nevertheless, the *source* of all godly fatherhood is God and, in that regard, *he alone* is to be referred to as our Father (Matthew 23:9). It is solely God, the Father, who is *the source* of the godly character passed down to all.

> "For both he that sanctifieth (Christ) and they who are sanctified (those in Christ) are all of one (God): for which cause he (Christ) is not ashamed to call them brethren." (Hebrews 2:11[112])

None of these things point to a reproduction of substance. In biblical terms, being a son of someone does not necessarily refer to coming out of their substance. Paul calls Elymas a "child of the devil," (Acts 13:10,) but Elymas was not produced of Satan's substance. Likewise, Jesus was not talking about coming out of God's substance when he said, "Love your enemies ... do good to them ... pray for them ... **that ye may be the children of your Father which is in heaven**." (Matthew 5:44-45.)

> "Let us take it, as an example, that the apostle Paul has as his physical father some Jew, probably an unbeliever; but that he also has a **father** in God, **on whose character he modelled his life**. Well, then, if someone is going to trace his physical descent, which father would he be likely to mention? ... He who is reborn in God, however, has other forebears recorded, his forebears in God, although they are not his actual ancestors at all, but only "as was supposed" because of their **similarity of character**."
>
> —*Eusebius of Caesarea, 339 AD*[113]

How was Jesus the "Only-Begotten"?

The Greek word translated as "begotten" in the Bible is γεννάω (gennaō), but the Greek word used when the Bible says "only-begotten" is different. Instead of using γεννάω, *only-begotten* is translated from μονογενής (monogenēs), which is itself formed from the two words μόνος (monos), which means *only*, and γίνομαι (ginomai). This latter word, γίνομαι, does not *inherently* mean *to be born*, but rather *to come into existence, to be*.

Although γίνομαι *by itself* is not the *usual* verb for "born," μονογενής, being a *composite* of μόνος + γίνομαι, is always used to indicate a parent's only child (Judges 11:34 LXX, Luke 7:12, 9:42, etc.). Thus, it is rendered *only-begotten*. Since Jesus is "the only-begotten Son of God," (John 3:18,) this means Jesus was designated, in some sense, the *only existing child of God*. So, was this because he was *the only human born of a virgin?* According to the infancy narratives (see Appendix G), Jesus *became* the Son of God *because of the virgin birth.*

Luke 1:35 reads as follows:

> "And the angel answered and said unto her, The Holy Ghost shall come upon thee, and the power of the Highest shall overshadow thee: **therefore** also that holy thing which shall be born of thee shall be called the Son of God." (Luke 1:35)

Gabriel (the angel speaking to Mary) informs Mary that Christ will be called the Son of God *because of* the manner in which she would become pregnant. Since the *reason* for Christ being called the Son of God, according to Luke 1:35, was the virgin birth, Christ was *not* viewed as the Son of God prior to that causal event. Like Luke, the Book of Matthew also declares a virgin birth while making no mention of any prehumen existence or sonship, beginning simply with these words:

> "The book of the generation of Jesus Christ, the son of David, the son of Abraham." (Matthew 1:1)

The word translated here as *generation* is γένεσις (genesis), which means *beginning* or *origin* (*lit.* "The book of the beginning of Jesus Christ"). If we accept the virgin birth narratives found in Luke and Matthew (See Appendix G), Jesus being the *only* virgin-born man could easily supply the meaning of *only-begotten Son*. However, *the Book of Luke and of Matthew **never** refer to Jesus as the only-begotten Son*. This term is *only* applied to Christ within the books of John and 1 John. Furthermore, the author of those same books *also* declares that *others* are *begotten of God* if they do the works of God (see the previous heading *Begotten Explained*). Therefore, being consistent with the specific author's usage, it would seem that Christ was called the only-begotten Son *because he was the only one* *doing the deeds of God and abstaining from sin* (1 John 3:9). I intend to explore another angle for why Jesus is called God's only-begotten Son in the revision of my book *Explaining the Cross: Why did Jesus have to die?*

When was Jesus Begotten?

As we saw under the subheading *Begotten Explained*, a father can beget children, biblically speaking, when actions originating in him are replicated afterward by someone else. For example, when Genesis 4:21 says, "Jubal was the father of all such as handle the harp and organ," this means that he was the first to do such things and everyone playing the harp and organ afterward was performing actions that originated with him. In the case of Christ being begotten of God, he began to do those miraculous works originating in God after his baptism. This is when God anointed him "with the Holy Spirit and with power," after which Jesus "went about doing good,[114] and healing all that were oppressed of the devil." (Acts 10:38 cf. Luke 4:18.) After this event, Jesus said his words (John 12:49-50) and miraculous actions (John 5:19-20) were from God.

In his book titled *The Orthodox Corruption of Scripture,* Bart D. Ehrman *masterfully* argues that the original statement of God in Luke 3:22 was not, "Thou art my beloved Son; *with thee I am well pleased*," (RSV,) but rather, "Thou art my Son, *this day have I begotten thee*."[115] However, *A Textual Commentary on the Greek New Testament* says this latter reading "appears to be secondary, derived from Ps. 2.7."[116] I explain my theory for why "This day have I begotten thee" *may* have been a later addition by Ariston of Pella in Appendix G. Despite disagreements regarding events at Jesus' *baptism*, scholars *agree* that "Thou art my Son, this day have I begotten thee" was authentically applied to Jesus' *resurrection* (Acts 13:33). That correlation is discussed in chapter nine herein.

Jesus from the Seed of David

There is a consistent testimony in Scripture that the Jewish Messiah would be a physical descendant of David. Accordingly, the New Testament authors emphasized that point as something of great importance.

> "Concerning his Son Jesus Christ our Lord, which was made of the seed of David according to the flesh." (Romans 1:3)

God assured David that, from his loins, he would bring the promised Messiah.

> "God had sworn with an oath to [David], that of the fruit of his loins, according to the flesh, he would raise up Christ to sit on his throne." (Acts 2:30)

Even in sections of the Bible that assert a virgin birth, Jesus is *still* referred to as a descendant of David (which was explained historically as *Jesus took his flesh from Mary, who was herself a descendant of David*).

> "And the angel said to her, 'Do not be afraid, Mary, for you have found favor with God. And behold, you will conceive in your womb and bear a son, and you shall call his name Jesus. He will be great, and will be called the Son of the Most High; and the Lord God will give to him the throne of **his father David**.'" (Luke 1:30-32 RSV)

As I see it, the virgin birth concept was likely a very early *addition* to the Luke text which inadvertently negates the entire purpose of listing Joseph's genealogy in Luke 3 (see Appendix G). Regardless, Jesus' Davidic lineage according to the flesh, among those who believed he was born of a virgin and among those who did not, has been attested to from the earliest days of Christianity.

> "Remember that Jesus Christ of the seed of David was raised from the dead according to my gospel." (2 Timothy 2:8)

Through his Davidic descent, Jesus was also a descendant of David's relatives, most notably of Abraham (Galatians 3:16). The apostle Paul, an Israelite of the Tribe of Benjamin, made the following comment:

> "For I could wish that myself were accursed from Christ for my brethren, my kinsmen according to the flesh: Who are Israelites … Whose are the fathers, and of whom as concerning the flesh Christ came." (Romans 9:3-5)

"I will be to Him a Father"

Despite the fact that David was Jesus' natural ancestor (2 Timothy 2:8), in some aspects Jesus was not the son of David, but the Son of God.

> "And Jesus answered and said, while he taught in the temple, How say the scribes that Christ is the Son of David? For David himself said by the Holy Ghost, The LORD said to my Lord, Sit thou on my right hand, till I make thine enemies thy footstool."
>
> (Mark 12:35-36)

God promised David that he would be a father to David's coming Seed. The words of God are recorded as follows:

> "And when thy days be fulfilled, and thou shalt sleep with thy fathers, I will set up **thy seed** after thee, which **shall proceed out of thy bowels**, and I will establish his kingdom. He shall build an house for my name, and I will stablish the throne of his kingdom for ever. **I will be his father**, and **he shall be my son**."
>
> (2 Samuel 7:12-14)

This was fulfilled in a *representative* sense in Solomon (1 Chronicles 28:6), although he himself was not the one whose throne would be established "forever." As is common, Old Testament examples serve as allegories (Galatians 4:24) for New Testament fulfilments (Deuteronomy 18:15 w/ Acts 3:22-26, Genesis 22:14 w/ Galatians 3:16, Psalm 110:4 w/ Hebrews 7:3, Psalm 40:6-7 w/ 1 Corinthians 5:7, Hebrews 8:1-5, 10:1-4).

> "For unto which of the angels said he at any time ... I will be to him a Father, and he shall be to me a Son?" (Hebrews 1:5)

In regard to his flesh, Jesus was the Son of David, but there was another manner in which Jesus was also the Son of God. We previously discussed an example which showed how the physical descendants of Abraham were simultaneously said to be Abraham's children (John 8:37, 56) as well as children of the devil (John 8:44). This shows that a person can be the physical descendant of a man whilst also being the child of a spiritual being. Those same Jews who Jesus referred to as children of the devil

(John 8:44) claimed that both Abraham (John 8:53) and God (John 8:41) was their father.

> "Then said they to him, We be not born of fornication; we have one Father, even God." (John 8:41)

The Jews claimed that God was their father. What did they mean? It could be a claim that God was the one who *educated* them. One Jewish Midrash says, "He that educateth the child is called a father, not he that begets it."[117] When God took Israel as a nation for himself in the days of Moses, he began to say things like, "I am a father to Israel." (Jeremiah 31:9.)

> "When Israel was a child, then I loved him, and called my son out of Egypt." (Hosea 11:1)

God was a father to Israel in regard to his dealings with them. He redeemed them from Egypt, gave them their culture, educated them, provided for them, and brought them up from their onset to be his people.

Moses speaks to Israel of how God was a father to them, saying:

> "Do ye thus requite the LORD, O foolish people and unwise? is not he thy father that hath bought thee? hath he not made thee, and established thee? … For the LORD'S portion is his people; Jacob is the lot of his inheritance. He found him in a desert land, and in the waste howling wilderness; he led him about, he instructed him, he kept him as the apple of his eye. As an eagle stirreth up her nest, fluttereth over her young, spreadeth abroad her wings, taketh them, beareth them on her wings: So the LORD alone did lead him, and there was no strange god with him." (Deuteronomy 32:6, 9-12)

So, it was in regard to bringing them forth as a nation and bringing them up in his ways that he is called their father.

> "Wilt thou not from this time cry unto me, My father, thou art the guide of my youth?" (Jeremiah 3:4)

Likewise, Jesus was brought up by God. As with Israel, this may not have *begun* at his *human* birth, but that *might*[118] be indicated in Psalm 22.

> "My God, my God, why hast thou forsaken me? ... But thou art he that took me out of the womb: thou didst make me hope when I was upon my mother's breasts. I was cast upon thee from the womb: thou art my God from my mother's belly." (Psalm 22:1, 9-10)

It is wrong for a father to beget children and not train them. So, if Jesus *were* produced by God through a virgin—Appendix G shows this is not the case—God would have apparently been *responsible* to *be* a father to the virgin born child, training him up in the right way from his youth.

> "And when he was twelve years old, they went up to Jerusalem after the custom of the feast. And when they had fulfilled the days, as they returned, the child Jesus tarried behind in Jerusalem; and Joseph and his mother knew not of it. ... And it came to pass, that after three days they found him in the temple, sitting in the midst of the doctors, both hearing them, and asking them questions. And all that heard him were astonished at his understanding and answers. And when they saw him, they were amazed: and his mother said unto him, Son, why hast thou thus dealt with us? behold, thy father and I have sought thee sorrowing. And he said unto them, How is it that ye sought me? wist ye not that I must be about my Father's business? ... And Jesus increased in wisdom and stature, and in favour with God and man." (Luke 2:42-43, 46-49, 52)

Although God would seemingly be obligated to train up a virgin born child, he is, according to Scripture, a father to orphans as well.

> "A father of the fatherless, and a judge of the widows, is God in his holy habitation." (Psalm 68:5)

See Appendix G for how Jesus was sometimes considered the Son of Joseph, though Joseph was deceased. Regardless of human parentage, God *did* raise up Jesus by *being* a father to him through constant interaction. Since Jesus "was not rebellious" to that interaction, he correspondingly advanced in the purposes of God.

> "The Lord GOD hath given me the tongue of the learned, that I should know how to speak a word in season to him that is weary:

he wakeneth morning by morning, he wakeneth mine ear to hear as the learned. The Lord GOD hath opened mine ear, and I was not rebellious, neither turned away back. I gave my back to the smiters, and my cheeks to them that plucked off the hair: I hid not my face from shame and spitting." (Isaiah 50:4-6)

Thus, since God was a father to Jesus, the Son of God exemplified the resulting attributes one would expect and was thereby differentiated from the former prophets.

> "In many and various ways God spoke of old to our fathers by the prophets; but in these last days he has spoken to us by a Son."
> (Hebrews 1:1-2 RSV)

Not by Water Only, but by Blood

The Bible teaches that being born of blood is related to bloodline (John 1:13) and being born of water is related to a woman's labor (her water breaking) (John 3:4-6). The same author who recorded the meanings of being born of blood and of water said that Jesus came, not by water only (as one who merely was born through a woman), but also by blood (as being of a bloodline) (1 John 5:6). I am going to reproduce my comment from *The Salvation Bible Commentary* on 1 John 4:2-3 here, where I discuss these things.

1 John 4:2-3

Kerrigan

2. Jesus Christ is come – Perfect active participle verb, expressing an action *completed in the past*—"having come" (YLT). At the time this was written, Jesus already came in the flesh.

1 John 5:6 gives us more detail as to how he came, reading thus:

"This is he that came by water and blood, even Jesus Christ; not by water only, but by water and blood."[119]

When it says *by water*, this is in reference to the natural birth of a woman (when her water breaks). Comp. John 3:4-6. When it says *by blood*, this is in reference to genealogical descent, by which Jesus partook of the Abrahamic/Davidic bloodline. Comp. John 1:13. For Christ's genealogical connection to Abraham and David, see Gal. 3:16, Isa. 11:1, Luke 1:31-32, Rom. 1:3, Acts 2:30 w/ Psalm 132:11, 2 Tim. 2:8.

In the flesh – The same flesh that we have.

"Forasmuch then as the children are partakers of flesh and blood, he also himself likewise took part of the same." (Heb. 2:14)

3. And every spirit that confesseth not that Jesus Christ is come in the flesh is not of God: and this is that spirit of antichrist – This pertains to the Gnostic doctrine that Jesus was a transcendent being who merely came *through* Mary, but had no real flesh from her. This Antichrist doctrine ties into the *multiverse, parallel dimensions* concept being propagated in our modern day. According to the Antichrist doctrine, Jesus, in a parallel dimension where the future has already occurred, was born a real flesh and blood human in fulfillment of Rev. 12:1-5, but, they assert, he also died in that future dimension. Never accept a narrative regarding billionaires and a royal actress as the authentic fulfilment of Revelation 12. (To understand Revelation 12, comp. Rev. 12:1-2 w/ Gen. 37:9 and Gal. 4:22-26; Rev. 12:5 with Gal. 4:19). After "death," this pseudo-Jesus transcends his dimension and comes out of the abyss ("transcendence beyond time and space") in the final years of our own dimension—teaching men here how to transcend as he, allegedly, did before them. This Antichrist, according to them, will once again transcend time and space when the real Christ returns (at least they think he will transcend, but he is actually going into the lake of fire). After his alleged transcendence at the end, which will never occur, the same being comes out in the past, not as a man who has flesh, but as the Jesus of history, whom they define as a transcendent being not connected to this material world—including the flesh. In short, they will assert that the Antichrist is truly Jesus, who, by a transcendence beyond time and space, travels back in time to do those things we read about in the Bible. So, to them, the historic Jesus is a transcendent human who has come through a parallel dimension and entered our world, appearing as a man, but having no real flesh—not really hungering or thirsting, not really having blood, not really dying on the cross, not really rising from the dead. This is not a new deception, but an old one. It is the Antichrist doctrine. Not only do they say Yahweh, blessed be his name, is an evil deity, but they oppose him on every front. They say that Jesus was of another deity who wasn't Yahweh. They allege that Yahweh and the Father are different, rejecting any biblical texts that contradict their delusion, being ignorant as to what the Scriptures actually teach.

Jesus' Blood was not Divine in Nature

Some theologians have asserted that the *composition* of Christ's blood was divine. According to them, it was that divine composition which made Christ's blood acceptable to the Father. Is this a scriptural doctrine? No, it isn't. Jesus was a genuine man and he had the same kind of blood as all other men have.

The Bible says:

> "Forasmuch then as the children are partakers of flesh and **blood**, he (Christ) also himself likewise took part of the **same**."
> (Hebrews 2:14)

The Bible does not say *anywhere* that Christ was able to atone for man's sin because of the composition of his blood. Yet, I have heard many mainstream theologians assert this very thing, attempting to support such a claim by using the following reasoning:

> "Science proves that the blood type of a child comes from its father, not its mother, and therefore Jesus had God's blood because he was the Son of God, born of a virgin."

The reasoning behind this argument is unsound. How can we compare such scientific facts—which are only relative to the natural fertilization process between a man and a woman—with how Christ was allegedly conceived, of a *virgin*? It may be a scientific fact that a child's blood type is determined by his or her father, but that is in regard to the ***natural*** intercourse between a woman and a man that results in the *natural* conception of a child. God did not have natural relations with Mary, and so the natural passing on of blood isn't even a relevant factor. In fact, God does not even *have* blood, so how could "God's blood" have been *passed on* to Christ? Why do some people suppose that a natural conception bears identical and parallel facts to an alleged conception that was *not* natural? The two are not the same and would not share a comparable process.

Was it too hard for God to take *only* the blood and flesh from the womb of Mary and form Christ's body? No. John the Baptist said:

> "I say unto you, That God is able **of these stones** to raise up children unto Abraham." (Luke 3:8)

Or is it necessary for God to pass on a father's blood whenever a child is born? It is not at all necessary. **Adam had blood, but he had no natural father** (yet he was called "the son of God" in Luke 3:38). God formed Adam out of the dust, so why couldn't God form Jesus out of flesh and blood from his mother's body? If we do not automatically assume that Adam had "God's blood" then why assert this regarding Christ?

Why then would Christ have been born of a virgin? If the application of the Isaiah 7:14 prophecy were accurate (applied to Christ in Matthew 1:23), the virgin birth was simply "a sign" that God was with his people.

> "Therefore the Lord himself shall give you a **sign**; Behold, a virgin shall conceive, and bear a son, and shall call his name Immanuel."
> (Isaiah 7:14)

Note: We will discuss the Isaiah 7:14 prophecy in detail by the end of this present chapter.

In summary, although I believe the virgin birth narratives were later additions to the original Gospels (See Appendix G), even a virgin birth would not mean that Jesus had "God's blood."

Acts 20:28 is not Speaking of God's Blood

Depending on what version of the Bible you read, you might find a statement in Acts 20:28 that says God purchased the church "with his own blood."

> "Take heed therefore unto yourselves, and to all the flock, over the which the Holy Ghost hath made you overseers, to feed the church of **God**, which he hath purchased with **his own blood**."
> (Acts 20:28 KJV)

Some versions say, "His own blood," (KJV,) while others say, "The blood of his own," (Darby,) or, "The blood of his own Son." (RSV.) So why is there such a difference in the readings? Well, the difference doesn't start with the English versions. There are different readings in the Greek manuscripts from which the English versions are derived. Some versions represent Greek texts that read τοῦ (the) ἰδίου (his own) αἵματος (blood), while others represent Greek texts that read τοῦ (the) αἵματος (blood) τοῦ (of) ἰδίου (his own). The first reading states that God purchased the church "with his own blood," but the latter says he purchased the church "with the blood of his own." It is the second reading, "The blood of his own," that is found in the earliest manuscripts.[120] The original reading of the Greek in Acts 20:28 didn't read, "His own blood," but rather, "The blood of his own." Some English versions of the Bible were translated from less reliable Greek manuscripts, because that's all they had. As manuscripts were discovered, collected, and as the field of textual criticism expanded, the more ancient reading began to be preferred. Hence, we find readings of Acts 20:28 like that of *The Holy Scriptures: A New Translation from the Original Languages* by J. N. Darby:

> "Take heed therefore to yourselves, and to all the flock, wherein the Holy Spirit has set you as overseers, to shepherd the assembly of God, which he has purchased with **the blood of his own**."
> (Acts 20:28 Darby)

John Darby made the following comments regarding the accuracy of his Acts 20:28 translation:

> I am fully satisfied that this is the right translation of ver.28. To make it a question of the divinity of Christ (which I hold to be of the foundation of Christianity) is absurd. It has been questioned whether "of his own" can be used thus absolutely in the singular. But we have it in John 15:19, and in the neuter singular for material things, Acts 4.32. The torturing of the passage by copyists arose, I believe, from not seeing the real sense of it; a touching expression of the love of God.[121]

Some translations of Acts 20:28 include the word "Son" after "his own" in order to clarify that the text refers to "the blood of *his own Son*." The

Revised Standard Version includes the understood noun *Son* within its translation of Acts 20:28, which reads:

> "Take heed to yourselves and to all the flock, in which the Holy Spirit has made you overseers, to care for the church of God which he obtained with the blood of his own Son." (Acts 20:28 RSV)

Although the word "Son" is not stated within the Greek text of Acts 20:28, the fact of the matter is that the word ἰδίου (his own) can refer to an *understood noun* even when that noun is not stated within the text. Confirmation of this fact, as Darby pointed out, can be seen in how the word ἰδίου is used (in the accusative case – ἴδιον) in John 15:19, which says:

> "If ye were of the world, the world would love **its own** (τὸ ἴδιον)." (John 15:19)

John 15:19 is speaking of a category of people who belong to the world even though it doesn't say, "The world would love its own *people*." (c.f. John 1:11.) Likewise, Acts 20:28 is speaking of *a person* who belongs to God even though it doesn't say, "God purchased the church with the blood of his own *Son.*" Some translations may even read, "His own blood," in the text body, but you can still find the more ancient reading, "Blood of his own," in the apparatus. The NIV, for example, reads, "His own blood," in the main body of the text, but you can often find a footnote on the same page that says, "Or *with the blood of his own Son.*" The *NIV Study Bible* has a more extensive collection of notes than the standard NIV Bible, and the note on Acts 20:28 therein reads thus:

> *his own blood:* Lit. "the blood of his own one," a term of endearment (such as "his own dear one," referring to his own Son).[122]

The consistent testimony of the ancient manuscripts and the consistent message of the Bible in general is not that God has blood, but that God purchased the church with the blood of his own, "the **blood** of Jesus Christ **his Son**." (1 John 1:7)

There has been another issue of controversy as to what the original reading of Acts 20:28 was, but it is not in regard to "his own blood" vs. "the blood of his own." Instead, it is whether the original text read, "The church of *God* which he purchased with the blood of his own," or, "The church of *the Lord* which he purchased with the blood of his own." Bruce Metzger says that the manuscript evidence is "singularly balanced between 'church of God' and 'church of the Lord.'"[123] Likewise, Henry Alford says "the manuscript authority ... is weighty on both sides."[124] Truly it is. There are significant ancient manuscripts that attest to both of these readings. Notwithstanding, the scholars are now widely agreed that the original text contained "the church of God" reading rather than "the church of the Lord." Unfortunately, however, many of the commentaries that are still in circulation only address this issue, arguing in favor of the "church of God reading," but then stop short of even addressing the difference between "his own blood" and "the blood of his own."[125] Alford, for example, goes to great lengths arguing strongly for the "church of God" reading. Yet, despite his Greek text having τοῦ (the) αἵματος (blood) τοῦ (of) ἰδίου (his own) as the preferred reading and τοῦ (the) ἰδίου (his own) αἵματος (blood) in the apparatus as the less likely of the two, he doesn't even mention the significance of this in his comments. Instead, he seems to take for granted that the text means "his own blood" regardless of the wording. That, however, is not the case. In **all** of the places where the word ἰδίου is used it **always** (without exception) appears **before** the noun that it modifies.[126] Since the original reading is τοῦ (the) αἵματος (blood) τοῦ (of) **ἰδίου** (his own), placing ἰδίου **after** αἵματος, to be consistent, the noun being referred to as "his own" is **not** "the blood." The fact that the text reads "the blood of his own" is truly pivotal to a correct understanding of this passage.

I recommend reading Bruce Metzger's entries for Acts 20:28 in *A Textual Commentary on the Greek New Testament* for a fuller treatment of the text, but I will only cite a small portion of his comments here:

> It may well be, as Lake and Cadbury point out, that after the special meaning of ὁ ἰδίου (discussed in the previous comment) had dropped out of Christian usage, τοῦ ἰδίου of this passage was misunderstood as a qualification of αἵματος ("his own blood"). "This misunderstanding led to two changes in the text: τοῦ αἵματος τοῦ ἰδίου was changed to τοῦ ἰδίου αἵματος (influenced by Heb. ix 12?), which is neater but perverts the sense, and θεοῦ was changed

to κυρίου by the Western revisers, who doubtless shrank from the implied phrase 'the blood of God.'"[127]

Matthew 1:23 – Emmanuel, God with Us

In Matthew 1:23 we find a prophecy from Isaiah 7:14 being applied to the account of Christ's birth.

> "And she shall bring forth a son, and thou shalt call his name JESUS: for he shall save his people from their sins. Now all this was done, that it might be fulfilled which was spoken of the Lord by the prophet, saying, Behold, a virgin shall be with child, and shall bring forth a son, and they shall call his name Emmanuel, which being interpreted is, God with us." (Matthew 1:21-23 KJV)

The prophecy applied here is from Isaiah 7:14, where, in the *King James Version*, we read:

> "Therefore the Lord himself shall give you a sign; Behold, a virgin shall conceive, and bear a son, and shall call his name Immanuel." (Isaiah 7:14 KJV)

The *King James Version* says a "virgin" was going to bear a son. However, the Hebrew word *almah* which is translated as "virgin" in the KJV doesn't actually mean *virgin*. It might, however, *imply* that meaning inasmuch as it denotes a *young woman who has reached marriageable age*. Still, if the Hebrew text were emphasizing virginity, it could have used the Hebrew word *betulah* (virgin) instead of *almah* (young maiden), since *betulah* actually does mean *virgin*. Notwithstanding, the Septuagint, which predates the birth of Christ, translates *almah* in Isaiah 7:14 as παρθένος (*parthenos*), which, in the Greek language, does mean *virgin*. Or, at least, it *came* to mean that.

> "[Parthenos] originally also meant 'young woman,' but later it came to mean what we mean by 'virgin.'" —*Bart D. Ehrman*[128]

When the Septuagint was originally produced (around 250 BC), παρθένος did not mean *virgin*. We can find evidence for this in the Septuagint itself, because it calls Dina, Jacob's daughter, a παρθένος *after* she was no longer a virgin. *The Septuagint with Apocrypha*, translated by Sir Lancelot C.L. Brenton, reads as follows (I have added the parenthesis to relay the Greek text being translated):

> "And Sychem the son of Emmor the Evite, the ruler of the land, saw her; and he took her, and lay with her, and humbled her. And he was attached to the soul of Dina the daughter of Jacob, and he loved **the damsel** (τὴν παρθένον), and he spoke kindly to **the damsel** (τῆς παρθένου)." (Genesis 34:2-3 LXX)

Here, we find παρθένος (in the accusative and genitive cases) used twice of Dina *after* Shechem already had intercourse with her. Hence, in the Septuagint, παρθένος did *not* mean *virgin*. Compare also the redundance of Genesis 24:16, "a virgin (παρθένος), neither had any man known her."

As time went on, after παρθένος became identified with *virginity*, some men *retranslated* the Tanakh into Greek, rendering Isaiah 7:14's *almah* as ἡ νεᾶνις (the young woman) to avoid the anachronistic confusion. However, the prophecy of Isaiah 7:14 was already being associated with a virginal birth of Christ around that same time (first half of the 2nd century). Hence, early Christians like Justin Martyr and Irenaeus correspondingly accused those new translations of *altering* the *meaning* of Isaiah 7:14 in order to deny the virgin birth.[129] Regardless, there are no textual variants in Genesis 34 regarding Dina. She is called a παρθένος within every Greek translation even after losing her virginity. Hence, even if we retain παρθένος when Isaiah 7:14 says a young woman would conceive and bear a son, this does not necessitate conception while remaining a virgin.

Even if we allowed the term *virgin* in Isaiah 7:14, this *still* would not mean a woman became pregnant *while remaining* a virgin. It is not difficult to understand how a young woman, who *was* a virgin *when the prophecy was given*, could be prophesied to bear a son *as a result of* her *future* marriage and intercourse. In fact, this seems to be the implication.

> "In place of what the evangelist Matthew says: 'She shall have in her womb,' it was written in the prophet: 'She shall receive in her womb.'"
> —*Jerome, Commentary on Matthew 1:23*[130]

Some readings of the Septuagint say the παρθένος "*shall **have** in her womb,*" but others say she "*shall **receive** in her womb.*" It is the latter reading that was affirmed by Jerome. And this kind of terminology was used when a woman *received seed* from a man and became pregnant.[131]

> "The promise itself [refers to] the mother, who at the time when the prophecy was uttered was still a virgin."
> —*Heinrich Meyer*[132]

Both the Hebrew and the Greek indicate that a *particular* young woman is in view. The fact that the article is used in the prophecy when Isaiah says "**the** virgin shall conceive" (Isaiah 7:14) coincides with "**the** prophetess" (Isaiah 8:3) who conceived and gave birth immediately after that prophecy was given.

> "Therefore the Lord himself will give you a sign. Behold, a young woman shall conceive and bear a son ... And I went to the prophetess, and she conceived and bore a son." (Isaiah 7:14, 8:3 RSV)

Most commentaries I see take the words *the prophetess* in Isaiah 8:3 as designating *the wife of Isaiah*. I think this view is probably correct. The consensus seems to be that the prophet Isaiah takes a virgin/maiden to be his bride after speaking to Ahaz and she then becomes pregnant. Even though she would no longer be a virgin *after* Isaiah took her to wife, she could easily have been *known as such when the prophecy was first announced.*

The correct interpretation of this text could be as simple as:

1. Isaiah was betrothed to a specific woman who was coming of age.
2. Isaiah refers to her as what she is known to be when the prophecy was given, namely, the virgin/maiden.

3. Isaiah says that this particular virgin/maiden betrothed to him, once he took her to wife, would have a son.

4. Before that son was old enough to know right from wrong, the threat would be over.

I believe this is correct. Hence, I conclude that the young woman betrothed to Isaiah was probably a virgin when the prophecy was given, but was not a virgin when she conceived.

Contextually, the birth of this child was to be a sign of assurance to Judah that God was with them to defend them against their enemies. Here is the contextual threat which occasioned the prophecy:

> "And it came to pass in the days of Ahaz the son of Jotham, the son of Uzziah, king of Judah, that Rezin the king of Syria, and Pekah the son of Remaliah, king of Israel, went up toward Jerusalem to war against it." (Isaiah 7:1 KJV)

Isaiah then goes to Ahaz, King of Judah, to deliver a message from God assuring him of God's protection.

> "And Jehovah spake again unto Ahaz, saying, **Ask thee a sign of Jehovah thy God**; ask it either in the depth, or in the height above. But Ahaz said, I will not ask, neither will I tempt Jehovah. And he said, Hear ye now, O house of David: Is it a small thing for you to weary men, that ye will weary my God also? Therefore **the Lord himself will give you a sign**: behold, a virgin shall conceive, and bear a son, and shall call his name Immanuel. Butter and honey shall he eat, when he knoweth to refuse the evil, and choose the good. **For before the child shall know to refuse the evil, and choose the good, the land whose two kings thou abhorrest shall be forsaken**." (Isaiah 7:10-16 ASV)

This entire scenario related to God's protection for Judah against invading armies. Before the prophesied child was old enough to know the difference between right and wrong, the threat from the kings of Damascus and Samaria would be over. The sign of this child being born, however, was not presented as very exceptional. Instead, the option to choose a *different* sign than this was initially given to King Ahaz. God said to Ahaz, "Ask thee a sign of the LORD thy God; ask it either in the depth, or in the height above." When Ahaz refused to ask, the Lord himself opted for the sign of a child's birth. Before that prophesied child was old enough to know right from wrong, the two enemy kings' campaign would have ceased, and the boy would already be eating those finer foods now prevented by the ongoing siege.

This prophecy was fulfilled shortly thereafter, in the days of Isaiah.

> "And I went unto the prophetess; and **she conceived, and bare a son**. Then said the LORD to me, Call his name Mahershalalhashbaz. For **before the child shall have knowledge to cry, My father, and my mother, the riches of Damascus and the spoil of Samaria shall be taken away** before the king of Assyria."
> (Isaiah 8:3-4 KJV)

The fact that this prophecy was fulfilled during the days of Isaiah is typically agreed upon by most scholars, but is also believed by some to have a second fulfillment in the birth of Jesus. This is the most prevalent view within the Christian commentaries I have read. Yet, if it *were* a prophecy with a double fulfillment, *why do so many assert that the first child called Emmanuel was **not** God while simultaneously asserting that Jesus **is** shown to be God **because** he is called by that exact same name?*

> "The name *Emmanuel* may be understood as an assertion, *God is with us;* and then it is not necessarily a divine name. It was therefore given also to a boy who was born in the time of Isaiah."
>
> —*Johann Bengel*[133]

The fact that the child's literal name was Mahershalalhash (meaning, *swift to the prey*) would not negate him being called Emmanuel any more than the literal name Jesus would negate Jesus being called Emmanuel.

God was with Judah at that time to defend them against their enemies. This is the reason why the name is given to the child. The comfort given to Judah by the fulfillment of this prophecy is declared in the immediate context.

> "...**O Immanuel**. Associate yourselves, O ye people, and ye shall be broken in pieces; and give ear, all ye of far countries: gird yourselves, and ye shall be broken in pieces; gird yourselves, and ye shall be broken in pieces. Take counsel together, and it shall come to nought; speak the word, and it shall not stand: **for God is with us**." (Isaiah 8:8-10 KJV)

The armies that came against them would not prevail because of the fact that God was with Judah at that time. It had nothing to do with a woman birthing the Messiah hundreds of years later. Nor did it entail that the woman would be a virgin when she became pregnant. Hence, the prophecy of Isaiah 7:14 is entirely misinterpreted and misapplied in Matthew 1:23. See Appendix G, where it is shown that the virgin birth narrative, including Matthew 1:23, was *added* to the Gospel of Matthew sometime after it was written.

Before we move on to the next subject, we should address the notable objection of some early Christians here, who said that such a normal conception between a husband and wife "is a daily occurrence" and "the pregnancy and giving birth of a young female cannot possibly be anything of a sign."[134] Their objection is answered by the context in which the prophecy was given. Judah was facing the possibility of a devastating war, so the prophet taking a new wife and having a son by her was an indication of continued safety. Contrast this with what God said to Jeremiah:

> "Thou shalt **not take thee a wife, neither shalt thou have sons or daughters in this place**. For thus saith the LORD concerning the sons and concerning the daughters that are born in this place, and concerning their mothers that bare them, and concerning their fathers that begat them in this land; **They shall die of grievous deaths**." (Jeremiah 16:2-4)

God was going to destroy Jerusalem in Jeremiah's day, so God told Jeremiah not to take a wife or have children in light of that coming destruction. Thus, when Isaiah did the opposite, taking a wife and having a son by her, this was confirmation of protection and a secure future.[135] Furthermore, the child, once born, would represent a visible time marker. The people of

Judah could watch his growth, knowing that, "before the child shall have knowledge to cry, My father, and my mother," their crisis would end.

Chapter Five

From Heaven

I formerly believed that Jesus was a conscious heavenly being prior to his humanity. While basing this belief upon several passages found within the Gospel of John, it often troubled me that there was no indication of preexistent consciousness or "coming down from heaven" within any of the Synoptic Gospels (Matthew, Mark, Luke) or in Acts. In this chapter we will discuss how the Gospel of John, when properly understood, is not presenting a doctrine at variance with the other Gospels. First, however, I want to point out a couple of intriguing quotes from Philo.

Interesting Quotes from Philo

Philo (an Alexandrian Jew that lived during the time of Christ) spoke about how a man can *ascend to heaven* in regard to his soul's inquiries.

> For how could a mortal nature at the same time remain where it was and also emigrate? or how could it see what was here and what was on the other side? or how could it sail round the white sea, and at the same time traverse the whole earth to its furthest boundaries, and inspect the customs and laws of the nations on all the affairs and bodies which are in existence? On separating them from the things of the earth, … how could it **fly through the air from earth to heaven**, and investigate the natures which exist in heaven … And now, having gone not only to the very boundaries of earth and sea, but also to those of air and heaven, it has not stopped even there, thinking that the world itself is but a brief limit for its continued and unremitting course. And it is eager to advance further; and, if it can possibly do so, to comprehend the incomprehensible nature of God, even if only as to its existence.[136]

Philo talked about how a man in the service of God, being focused on him, draws close to God, but afterwards he, being occupied in the things of man, "descends from heaven," though he never left his body or consciously existed prior to his body.

> But every wise man is within friendship, even if he be dwelling at a distance, not merely in a different country, but in another climate and region of the world. But, according to Moses, a friend is so near to one as to differ in no respect from one's own soul, for he says, "the friend who is like thy Soul."[137] And again he says, "The priest shall not be a man by himself, when he goeth into the holy of holies, until he cometh out;"[138] speaking not with reference to the motions of the body, but to those of the soul; for the mind, while it is offering holy sacrifices to God in all purity, is not a human but a divine mind; but when it is serving any human object, it then **descends from heaven** (καταβὰς ἀπ' οὐρανοῦ) and becomes changed, or rather it falls to the earth and goes out, even though the mind may still remain within.[139]

Philo describes man's contemplative ability as something whereby man travels beyond his bodily confines and even into heaven. Yet, when man afterward begins focusing on earthly matters, he is described as "descending from heaven." Although I don't use Philo's comments on descending from heaven to interpret the Book of John, I do think they are worth consideration inasmuch as Philo was a 1st century Jew living during the times of Christ. Perhaps we simply view Jesus' *descending from heaven* statements differently than a 1st century Jewish theologian would have.

The Common Biblical Unitarian Explanation

There are several passages in the Book of John that say Jesus comes from heaven (John 3:13, 3:31, 6:32, 38, 62, 8:23, etc.). In order to understand what the Bible means when it says *Jesus* came from heaven, Biblical Unitarians make a comparison to *other* things in the Bible that are said to come down from heaven (Mark 8:11, 11:30, John 3:27, James 1:17, etc.). For example, Jesus spoke of the John's baptismal ministry as being "from heaven:"

> "The baptism of John, was it **from heaven**, or of men?"
> (Mark 11:30)

No one imagines John's baptism floating down from the sky to earth just because it is said to be "from heaven." We understand, rather, that being "from heaven" means his baptism was ordained by God in heaven and was divinely inspired. How much more, then, could we say that Christ was from heaven without asserting any floating down from heaven ideas? This certainly helps us to understand how Jesus could be from heaven, yet I would like to add some additional thoughts on the subject.

Other Men in the Bible Came from Heaven

It is noteworthy that men *other than Jesus* went into heaven, came from thence, and ministered subsequent to that experience. For example, Paul says:

> "I knew a man in Christ above fourteen years ago, (whether in the body, I cannot tell; or whether out of the body, I cannot tell: God knoweth;) such an one caught up to the third heaven."
> (2 Corinthians 12:2)

John also says he went to heaven:

> "After this I looked, and, behold, a door was opened in heaven: and the first voice which I heard was as it were of a trumpet talking with me; which said, Come up hither, and I will shew thee things which must be hereafter. And immediately I was in the spirit: and, behold, a throne was set in heaven, and one sat on the throne."
> (Revelation 4:1-2)

Both Paul and John went to heaven and then afterward shared some aspects of what they saw. It is plausible that Jesus experienced something similar, but perhaps in greater magnitude. Contrariwise, it is unlikely that Paul and John would have experienced greater heavenly revelations than Jesus. Indeed, we could *infer* an experience similar to theirs by the mere fact that Jesus *says* he came from heaven. If Jesus in fact had such an experience prior to his public ministry on earth, this could account for the texts where Jesus says he came from heaven. I will not assert this as a definitive explanation, however, because it is unproveable.

John 3:31 – "Cometh from Heaven"

In John 3:31, John the Baptist says:

> "He that **cometh from above** is above all: he that is of the earth is earthly, and speaketh of the earth: he that **cometh from heaven** is above all." (John 3:31)

We have previously discussed Jesus' declarations that those who believed on and received him did *not* believe on and receive *him*, but believed on and received *God*.

- "He that believeth on me, believeth not on me, but on him that sent me." (John 12:44)

- "Whosoever shall receive me, receiveth not me, but him that sent me." (Mark 9:37)

Jesus also said that those who saw him saw the Father who sent him.

- "He that hath seen me hath seen the Father." (John 14:10)

- "He that seeth me seeth him that sent me." (John 12:45)

Essentially, what we have in Jesus' statements is a supplanting of his own identity with that of God's identity. Yet, this is not to say that Jesus had no identity of his own, but that what he presented to men did not originate from himself, but from God. Jesus obediently conveyed the expressions of God to men rather than expressions that originated from himself.

> "For I have not spoken of myself; but the Father which sent me, he gave me a commandment, what I should say, and what I should speak. And I know that his commandment is life everlasting: whatsoever I speak therefore, even as the Father said unto me, so I speak." (John 12:49-50)

When thinking about "who" Jesus was and is, we have to think in terms of his *persona*, which, by his obedience, is God.

Webster's Dictionary defines the word *persona* as follows:

> *Persona* … the personality that a person (such as an actor or politician) projects in public : IMAGE

Jesus' *persona* was *the revelation of God.* Jesus spoke the words of the Father (John 17:8), which words were given to him by means of the Holy Spirit.

> "For he whom God hath sent speaketh the words of God: **for** God giveth not the Spirit by measure unto him." (John 3:34)

In the above text, Jesus speaking the words of God is directly attributed to God giving the Spirit to him "without limit." (NLT.) As such, his persona, the revelation of God, is thus attributed to the Holy Spirit, which in every one of the four Gospels is shown to have descended from heaven.

- "And Jesus, when he was baptized, went up straightway out of the water: and, lo, **the heavens were opened** unto him, and he saw **the Spirit of God descending** like a dove, and lighting upon him:" (Matthew 3:16)

- "And straightway coming up out of the water, he **saw the heavens opened**, and **the Spirit** like a dove **descending** upon him:" (Mark 1:10)

- "And **the Holy Ghost descended** in a bodily shape like a dove upon him, and a voice came from heaven, which said, Thou art my beloved Son; in thee I am well pleased." (Luke 3:22)

- "And John bare record, saying, I saw **the Spirit descending from heaven** like a dove, and it abode upon him." (John 1:32)

The persona of Jesus is owed to the descent of the Spirit from heaven, therefore Jesus, in regard to his persona, descended from heaven at that time. In short, whenever we see texts that refer to Jesus coming from heaven, I believe this should be taken in reference to "who" he is (the origin of his persona) not "what" he is (a man). This could explain why Jesus says the Jews *did know* where he was from on the one hand, but then *also* says they *did not know* where he was from. Clearly, he has two different categories of origin in mind.

- "Ye both know me, and ye know whence I am." (John 7:28)

- "I know whence I came, and whither I go; but ye cannot tell whence I come, and whither I go." (John 8:14)

Notice the phrases Jesus used in John 8:14, "Ye cannot tell whence I come, and whither I go." Now compare that carefully to what Jesus says in John 3:8, "[Thou] canst not tell whence **it** [τὸ πνεῦμα – *the Spirit* or *the wind*] cometh, and whither it goeth: **so is every one that is born of the Spirit**." There is a striking similarity between "whence I come, and whither I go" and "whence it cometh, and whither it goeth: so is every one that is born of the Spirit." The origin of both, according to Jesus, is not discernable to men. Most theologians interpret "born of the Spirit" as the experience of people who, *during their human lives*, become filled with the Holy Spirit. Yet, they do not conclude from this that such individuals, now born of the Spirit from heaven, must have therefore preexisted their own humanity.

When men saw Jesus, they saw the Father, because that persona descended from heaven and was now supplanting Jesus' own personal traits through his obedient submission. In such a way, Jesus came "out from" (John 17:8) and "forth from" the Father" (John 16:27-28)—Jesus relates these phrases to *speaking the words God gave him* (John 17:8).

Notice how the following passage pulls all of the aforementioned factors together.

> "**He that cometh from above** is above all: he that is of the earth is earthly, and speaketh of the earth: **he that cometh from heaven** is above all. And **what he hath seen** [comp. John 8:38] **and heard, that he testifieth**; and no man receiveth his testimony. He that hath received his testimony hath set to his seal that God is true.

For he whom God hath sent **speaketh the words of God**: for **God giveth not the Spirit by measure unto him**." (John 3:31-34)

1. Christ is from heaven, in reference to his persona inasmuch as **2.** He speaks the words of God, which is due to **3.** God giving the Spirit to him without measure.

John 3:13-21 – Who is Speaking?

John 3:13 speaks of Jesus having descended from heaven. Yet, contrary to popular opinion, those words were not necessarily spoken *by* Jesus.

> "No one has ascended into heaven but he who descended from heaven, the Son of man." (John 3:13 RSV)

Even though most of our contemporary English Bible publishers print John 3:16-21 in red letters (thereby implying that the words are Christ's), these are possibly the words of the Gospel's author (incorrectly assumed to be John[140]). In his commentary on the third chapter of John, Marvin Vincent, author of *Vincent's New Testament Word* Studies, shows why he does not believe that all of the "red letter" words in the third chapter of John are Christ's, writing thus:

> The interview with Nicodemus closes with ver. 15; and the succeeding words are John's. This appears from the following facts:
>
> **1.** The past tenses *loved* and *gave,* in ver. 16, better suit the later point of view from which John writes, after the atoning death of Christ was an accomplished historic fact, than the drift of the present discourse of Jesus before the full revelation of that work.
>
> **2.** It is in John's manner to throw in explanatory comments of his own (1:16-18; 12:37-41), and to do so abruptly.
>
> **3.** Ver. 19 is in the same line of thought with 1:9-11 in the Prologue; and the tone of that verse is historic, carrying the sense of past rejection, as *loved* darkness; *were* evil.

> **4.** The phrase *believe on the name* is not used elsewhere by our Lord, but by John (1:12; 2:23; 1 John 5:13).
>
> **5.** The phrase *only-begotten son* is not elsewhere used by Jesus of himself, but in every case by the Evangelist (1:14, 18; 1 John 4:9).
>
> **6.** The phrase *to do truth* (ver. 21) occurs elsewhere only in 1 John 1:6[141]

The reasons Vincent gives for believing that John 3:16-21 contains the narrative words of the Gospel's author, rather than the words of Christ, are solid. However, Christ's interview with Nicodemus actually may have ended in John 3:**12** (rather than Vincent's proposal of John 3:**15**). This means that the author's own narrative would begin from John 3:13 onward. The fact of the matter is that, grammatically speaking, everything in John 3:13-15 can be attributed to the author's narrative. In John 3:13 the phrase "*has gone up* into heaven" is in the perfect tense (indicating *a completed past event*). The author, who penned John 3:13 long after Christ's bodily ascension, was almost certainly *referring to the post-resurrection bodily ascension of Christ into heaven*. The evidence points us to conclude as much, since *every* other instance where the Bible speaks of Christ *ascending into heaven* is *always* referring to his *post-resurrection bodily ascension into heaven* (Psalm 68:18, John 6:62[?], 20:17, Acts 2:34, Ephesians 4:8-10, Hebrews 9:24, 1 Peter 3:22).

Notice what Jesus says while speaking *prior* to his post-resurrection ascension.

> "Touch me not; for **I am not yet ascended to my Father**: but go to my brethren, and say unto them, I ascend unto my Father, and your Father; and to my God, and your God." (John 20:17)

An early Christian belief that John 3:13 is referring *back* to Christ's post-resurrection ascension also accounts for the appearance of the phrase "who is in heaven" found in the *King James Version*—"And no man hath ascended up to heaven, but he that came down from heaven, even the Son of man **which is in heaven**." This phrase is present in quotations of John 3:13 as early as 160 AD.[142] Some even think it was the original reading.[143]

In John 3:14 the phrase, "must the Son of man *be lifted up*," uses an aorist infinitive verb, which, alone, does not indicate a past, present, or future event. If John 3:14 truly contains the narrative words of the author (and it almost certainly does) then it should be understood of the *past* crucifixion. The Greek verb δεῖ (dei), which is used when John 3:14 says "*must* the Son of man be lifted up," is a present indicative verb. It is not unusual for the author of John to use the present tense in reference to a past event. This is demonstrated by his usage of the same present indicative verb (δεῖ) in John 20:9, which says:

> "The first day of the week cometh Mary Magdalene early, when it was yet dark, unto the sepulchre, and seeth the stone taken away from the sepulchre. Then she runneth, and cometh to Simon Peter, and to the other disciple, whom Jesus loved, and saith unto them, They have taken away the Lord out of the sepulchre, and we know not where they have laid him. ... For as yet they knew not the Scripture, that he **must** (δεῖ) rise again from the dead."
> (John 20:1-2, 9)

This is describing events that occurred *after* Christ's resurrection, therefore John 20:9 contains the author's *present tense* narrative account regarding a *past* event.

The *NIV Study Bible* notes that:

> John ... sometimes used the present tense when speaking of the past.[144]

This is why the NIV translates the present tense verb used in John 20:9 in the past tense, saying:

> "They still did not understand from the scripture that Jesus **had to** (δεῖ) rise from the dead." (John 20:9 NIV)

Just as the author of John used the present tense verb δεῖ while referring to a past event in John 20:9 (the resurrection of Christ), so also he used the same present tense verb δεῖ while referring to a past event in John 3:14 (Christ's crucifixion). The usage of the present tense in reference to a past event is not peculiar to John. This was actually quite common within the Greek language.

Although the phrase "Son of man" is used elsewhere in the Gospel of John *only when quoting Christ* (eight times), this does not mean that the phrase could not have been used in the author's own narrative in John 3:13-14 as well. In comparison, Christ refers to himself as the Son of man *thirteen* times in the Gospel of Mark. Yet, although Mark himself only employs the phrase *twice*[145] in his own narrative, no one disputes the fact that those words are genuinely his.

In light of these things, it is almost certain that John 3:13-15 contains the narrative words of the Gospel's author rather than those of Jesus. Hence, Jesus was not speaking to Nicodemus of having *already* ascended into heaven. Rather, the narrator was writing *after* all of these things transpired, speaking of Jesus' post-resurrection ascension into heaven instead.

John 3:13 – The Son of Man from Heaven

John 3:13 refers to the Son of man descending from heaven, saying:

> "No man hath ascended up to heaven, but **he that came down from heaven, even the Son of man**." (John 3:13)

We previously saw that John 3:13 might pertain to Christ's *present* abode in heaven *after* his post-resurrection bodily ascension. Yet, when the text says, "He that came down from heaven," we understand that *this* action (coming down from heaven) *preceded* his ascension into heaven, because "came down" is translated from an aorist participle verb (καταβάς), which demonstrates and action that *precedes* the action of the main verb (ἀναβέβηκεν – *hath ascended up*). Hence, Jesus, in some way, came down from heaven *prior to his ascension* into heaven.

As we discussed earlier in this chapter under the heading *John 3:31 – "Cometh from Heaven,"* Jesus' coming from heaven is related to that heavenly *persona* he exhibited after receiving the Holy Spirit from heaven. Notice the specific terminology that Jesus uses right before it is said that he came from heaven.

> "Verily, verily, I say unto thee, We speak that we do know, and **testify that we** [comp. John 1:15, 3:26] **have seen**; and ye **receive not our witness**. If I have told you earthly things, and ye believe not, how shall ye believe, if I tell you **of heavenly things**? And no man hath ascended up to heaven, but he that came down from heaven…" (John 3:11-13)

He speaks of testifying of what he has seen and says his witness is not received. This precise terminology is repeated in John 3:31-34.

> "He that **cometh from above** is above all: he that is of the earth is earthly, and speaketh of the earth: he that cometh from heaven is above all. And **what he hath seen** and heard, that **he testifieth; and no man receiveth his testimony**. He that hath received **his testimony** hath set to his seal that God is true. **For** he whom God hath sent speaketh the words of God: **for God giveth not the Spirit by measure unto him**." (John 3:31-34)

Jesus testifying to what he has seen, correlated to no man receiving his testimony, is *directly related to how he speaks the words of God because God has given the Spirit to him without measure*. The heavy contextual emphasis on this principle leads me to believe that we should take Jesus' *coming down from heaven* in John 3:13 as reference to his heavenly persona.

John 6:33 & 38 – "Cometh Down from Heaven"

In John 6:33 & 38, Jesus speaks of himself as being the bread that comes down from heaven.

- "For the bread of God is he which **cometh down** (καταβαίνων – present active participle) from heaven, and giveth life unto the world." (John 6:33)

- "For **I came down** (καταβέβηκα – perfect active indicative) from heaven, not to do mine own will, but the will of him that sent me." (John 6:38)

The explanations given at the beginning of this chapter may fit here as well. Notwithstanding, I propose that John 6:33-38 *may* have Christ's *future* return from heaven in view. I say this due to the following factors:

1. Although Jesus was already the bread from heaven before his death, the bread they are exhorted to eat is Christ's flesh, which he says he "will give" for the life of the world (John 6:51). This was involving a *future event*, when Jesus died on the cross.

2. The eternal life that the bread from heaven brings would therefore not be given until *after* Christ's death, so the context must pertain to life subsequent to that death. The present active participle verb καταβαίνων ("is coming down from heaven") in John 6:32 would thus be taken as a futuristic present verb. Daniel B. Wallace describes the futuristic present tense as follows, "The present tense may be used to describe a future event, though it typically adds the connotation of immediacy and certainty. Most instances involve verbs whose *lexical* meaning involves anticipation (such as ἔρχομαι, **-βαίνω**, πορεύομαι, etc.). This usage is relatively common."[146]

3. The precise timing when eternal life would be experienced is stated to be "in the last day." (John 6:39-40.) When Christ would "raise him up" who believed on him. Jesus said, "Marvel not at this: for the hour is coming, in the which all that are in the graves shall hear his voice, And shall come forth; they that have done good, unto the resurrection of life." (John 5:28-29.)

4. This consummation of eternal life occurs when Christ returns from heaven. "For the Lord himself **shall descend from heaven** with a shout, with the voice of the archangel, and with the trump of God: and **the dead in Christ shall rise** first." (1 Thessalonians 4:16.)

5. Since the life given by partaking of the bread is subsequent to Christ's death and since the resurrection at the last day is contextually in view, which scripturally occurs when the Lord "descends from heaven," I propose that that future coming down from heaven is possibly in view when, contextually speaking of the last day, Jesus says, "For **I came down from heaven ... to do ... the will of him that sent me**. And **this** is the Father's will which hath sent me, that of all which he hath given me I should lose nothing, but **should raise it up again at the last day**." (John 6:38-39.) He is seemingly talking about coming down from heaven to raise up all that is given to him at the last day.

6. The perfect active indicative verb καταβέβηκα ("I came down") would therefore have to be taken as looking back from that future event, subsequent to Christ's death—looking back from the time when all those who are Christ's have come to him in the New Jerusalem *after* Christ "came down" from heaven and raised them up at the last day. This futuristic usage of a perfect tense verb would be categorized as a Proleptic (Futuristic) Present. In Daniel B. Wallace's *Greek Grammar Beyond the Basics*, he says, "The perfect can be used to refer to a state resulting from an antecedent action that is future from the time of speaking."[147] He then lists a few examples of the perfect tense being used in reference to the future, including one from Romans 13:8, where the perfect active indicative verb πεπλήρωκεν is translated "hath fulfilled." Rendering John 6:38 along these same lines, it would read, "I will have come down from heaven." This clarifies how Jesus could have been speaking of his future descent from heaven, which occurs prior to the saints being gathered unto him when they are raised up at that last day.

John 6:62– "Ascend up Where He was Before"

Regarding John 6:62, the explanations given at the beginning of this chapter may fit here. However, I believe Jesus was possibly talking about how his disciples (whom he now addressed) would see proof of his claim to eternal life when he himself ascended *from the grave* back to where he was before he died (*i.e.*, walking the earth). He is contextually focused on being *made alive*, not on going up into heaven.

> "But Jesus, knowing in himself that his disciples murmured at it, said to them, 'Do you take offense at this? Then what if you were to see the Son of man ascending where he was before? It is the spirit that **gives life**…'" (John 6:61-63 RSV)

Although "ascend" is not typically used to denote "resurrection," we do see it used as such in the Septuagint (the Greek translation of the Old Testament).

> "For if a man **go down** (καταβῇ) to the grave, he shall not **come up again** (ἀναβῇ)." (Job 7:9 LXX)

Here, in Job 7:9, the same root word ἀναβαίνω is used that we find in Jesus' statement in John 6:62. In Job 7:9, it is obviously referring to coming back up to where a man was before he "went down" into the grave. Thus, we do have a scriptural precedent for taking ἀναβαίνω (ascend up) as referring to the resurrection. As with Job 7:9, where a man "goes down" to the grave, Jesus' condition while dead was clearly referred to as "descended."

- "Or, Who shall descend into the deep? (that is, to bring up Christ again from the dead.)" (Romans 10:7) (Note: The Hebrew MSS and the LXX read, "Who shall go beyond the sea," in Deuteronomy 30:13, that verse Paul is here referencing. The *Cambridge Greek Testament for Schools and Colleges* says, "St Paul takes the sea, as surely Moses took it, to be the antithesis of "heaven" the "great *deep*;" and thus the idea is of exploring depth rather than breadth. The *Jerusalem Targum* on Deuteronomy has a remarkable paraphrase: "Neither is the law beyond the great sea, that thou shouldest say, O that we had one like Jonah the prophet, to descend into the depths of the sea, and bring it to us!" (Etheridge's Translation.) To Moses, sky and sea were suggestive of heights and depths of supernatural mystery.")

- "Now that he ascended, what is it but that he also descended first into the lower parts of the earth?" (Ephesians 4:9) (Note: Paul is here referring to Psalm 68:18-22.)

- "He seeing this before spake of the resurrection of Christ, that his soul was not left in hell, neither his flesh did see corruption." (Acts 2:31)

Such terminology is common throughout the Bible.

- "I will go down into the grave." (Genesis 37:35)

- "Let not his hoar head go down to the grave in peace." (1 Kings 2:6)

- "Let death seize upon them, and let them go down quick into hell." (Psalm 55:15)

- "But those that seek my soul, to destroy it, shall go into the lower parts of the earth." (Psalm 63:9)

- "For the grave cannot praise thee, death can not celebrate thee: they that go down into the pit cannot hope for thy truth." (Isaiah 38:18)

- "Yet have they borne their shame with them that go down to the pit: he is put in the midst of them that be slain." (Ezekiel 32:25)

It makes perfect sense, therefore, to take Jesus' resurrection as "ascending" back to where he was before he "descended" into the grave. Some may reply that Jesus' ascension is necessarily connected to his claim to be the bread of life that first descended, but I think, rather, that his ascension back from the grave was referenced as proof that he could also raise up those believing on him in the last day (John 6:44).

God Sent Jesus into the World

There are several texts that speak of God sending Jesus into the world (John 3:17, 10:36, 1 John 4:9, etc.). These passages do not mean that Jesus began *outside* of Earth and was afterward sent *to* Earth. Rather, when the

Bible speaks of being *sent into the world* it means *sent out into society*. This is why Jesus, while praying to God, could say that his disciples were sent into the world just as he was.

> "As thou hast sent me into the world, even so have I also sent them into the world." (John 17:18)

Some things said of Christ which would *seem* to be exceptional are also said regarding his disciples. For example, although Jesus says, "I am not of this world," (John 8:23,) he *also* said, "The world hath hated [the disciples], because **they are not of the world, even as I am not of the world**." (John 17:14.) Jesus was not of this world *in the same way* that the disciples were not of this world. Likewise, Jesus was sent into the world in the *same way* that his disciples were sent into the world.

Jesus sent his disciples into the world on a ministerial mission.

> "Then he called his twelve disciples together, and gave them power and authority over all devils, and to cure diseases. And he **sent** them to preach the kingdom of God, and to heal the sick."
> (Luke 9:1-2)

The disciples' mission into society, to heal sickness and to preach the kingdom of God, was the same mission God sent Jesus on as well.

> "[Jesus said] The Spirit of the Lord is upon me, because he hath anointed me to preach the gospel to the poor; he hath **sent me** to heal the brokenhearted, to preach deliverance to the captives, and recovering of sight to the blind, to set at liberty them that are bruised, To preach the acceptable year of the Lord." (Luke 4:18-19)

Chapter Six

Philippians Chapter Two

Philippians chapter two has some very famous passages that relate to the person of Christ. We will be focusing our attention primarily on Philippians 2:6-11, where we find statements regarding Christ being in the form of God, being equal to God, having the name above every name, etc.

Philippians 2:6 – Who Being in the Form of God

Philippians 2:6 reads like this in the *King James Version:*

> "Who, being in the form of God, thought it not robbery to be equal with God:" (Philippians 2:6 KJV)

The NIV incorrectly translates the text as "very nature."

> "Who, being in **very nature** God, did not consider equality with God something to be used to his own advantage"
> (Philippians 2:6 NIV)

The NIV translation is unjustifiable. The Greek text of Philippians 2:6 says nothing about "nature." The word that the NIV incorrectly renders "nature" is the Greek word μορφή (morphe).

In his commentary on Philippians 2, John Lightfoot admits that μορφή (morphe) does not mean *nature* or *essence,* saying:

> μορφή is not the same as φύσις (nature) or οὐσία (essence).[148]

The literal definition of (μορφή) is given by Lighfoot later on in his commentary, where he writes:

> Μορφή, like σχῆμα, originally refers to the organs of sense. ... μορφή corresponds to 'form.' It comprises all of those sensible qualities, which striking the eye lead to the conviction that we see such and such a thing. The conviction indeed may be false, for the form may be a phantom; but to the senses at all events the representation of the object conceived is complete.[149]

This is a good description of the literal meaning of μορφή. Notwithstanding, Lightfoot extends his definition for μορφή beyond this when he says:

> Though μορφή is not the same as φύσις (nature) or οὐσία (essence), yet the possession of the μορφή involves participation in the οὐσία also.[150]

His two definitions contradict one another, because in the one instance he says that the underlying essence is included in the form, but elsewhere that the form may not represent an underlying essence at all. How can the following definition given by Lightfoot be reconciled to his former statement that "μορφή involves participation in the οὐσία also"?

> [Μορφή] comprises all of those sensible qualities, which striking the eye lead to the conviction that we see such and such a thing. The conviction indeed may be false, for the form may be a phantom.[151]

This latter definition does not include essence, but indeed may exclude it, since what is perceived may not really be there at all. It is this definition that is vindicated in Scripture.

Other than the two times μορφή is used in Philippians 2, the only other place in the New Testament where μορφή appears is Mark 16:12, which the NIV translates as:

> "Afterward Jesus appeared in a different **form** (μορφή) to two of them while they were walking in the country." (Mark 16:12 NIV)

Notice how the NIV translates μορφή accurately in Mark 16:12, but shows inconsistency in its translation of the same word in Philippians 2. The usage of the word μορφή in Mark 16:12 (where "Jesus appeared in a different μορφή") proves that μορφή does not imply *essence,* because:

1. The same event where Jesus appeared to the two men in a different μορφή is recorded in Luke 24:15-31, which specifically attributes the different form of Jesus to how the two men's "eyes were holden that they should not know him." (24:16.) It isn't the essence of Christ that causes the two disciples to see Jesus in a different form, it is their own handicapped perception.

2. Jesus' different form in Mark 16:12 can't be interpreted as "his resurrected form/essence instead of his former mortal form/essence." When the text says he "appeared in a different form," the form is shown to be different, not from his mortal condition, but his other post-resurrection appearances. The context reads, "Now **when Jesus was risen** early the first day of the week, **he appeared first** to Mary Magdalene, out of whom he had cast seven devils. And she went and told them that had been with him, as they mourned and wept. And they, when they had heard that he was alive, and had been seen of her, believed not. **After that he appeared in another form** unto two of them, as they walked, and went into the country. And they went and told it unto the residue: neither believed they them. **Afterward he appeared** unto the eleven as they sat at meat." (Mark 16:9-14.)

After his resurrection, Jesus appeared first to Mary, then in a different form to the two men walking, and afterwards to the eleven remaining apostles (Judas Iscariot was no longer with them). This clearly differentiates his "different form" (NIV) from the form he appeared in elsewhere after his resurrection. If we allowed *essence* or *nature* as the definition for μορφή, this would mean that Jesus appeared in at least two different essences after his resurrection. This, however, cannot be inferred inasmuch as the difference in his μορφή was attributed specifically to the perceptive ability of the men to whom he appeared. The word μορφή means *form* and pertains to the perception of the beholder, not to the nature of that which is beheld. So, what does the Bible mean when it says Jesus was "in the form of God"? It must denote that he was a visible presentation of God to those who beheld him.

Philippians 2:6 is typically regarded by commentators as describing Christ's existence prior to becoming human. Hence, Joseph Thayer writes:

> Phil. ii. 6 ... is to be explained as follows : *who, although* (formerly when he was λόγος ἄσάρκος) *he bore the form* (in which he appeared to the inhabitants of heaven) *of God.*[152]

He refers to a time before the Word was human (λόγος ἄσάρκος means *word without flesh*) and says that Christ bore the form of God when he was formerly beheld by heavenly beings. This is an example of how Philippians 2:6 is taken as describing Christ's existence before becoming a man. I disagree with Thayer that this passage pertains to Christ's prehuman state. I believe that when it says Jesus "subsisted (ὑπάρχω huparchō) in the form of God," this pertains to his life on earth where he lived as the image of God. Jesus often said things like, "He that hath seen me hath seen the Father." (John 14:9.) It makes sense to take "subsisting in the form of God" to mean *his state was such as God was constantly revealed through him to others.*

Christ is "the image of the *invisible* God," (Colossians 1:15,) so we cannot take "form of God" in its natural sense as *a visible* form of the God who is *invisible* (though some have concluded by "form of God" that God also must have actual hands and feet like a man[153]). The form of God beheld in Christ must then pertain to the confines in which that which is invisible may be beheld—not by natural eyes, but by "the eyes of your understanding." (Ephesians 1:18.) When Jesus said that the ones who saw him saw the Father, he never implied similarity in physical features. Instead, he always qualified seeing the Father as *seeing the immaterial qualities of God revealed through him.*

Jesus explains the manner in which seeing him included seeing the Father:

> "If ye had known me, ye should have known my Father also: and from henceforth ye know him, and have seen him. Philip saith unto him, Lord, **shew us the Father**, and it sufficeth us. Jesus saith unto him, Have I been so long time with you, and yet hast thou not known me, Philip? he that hath seen me hath seen the Father; and how sayest thou then, Shew us the Father? Believest thou not that

I am in the Father, and the Father in me? **the words that I speak unto you I speak not of myself**: but the Father that dwelleth in me, he doeth the works. Believe me that I am in the Father, and the Father in me: or else **believe me for the very works' sake**."

(John 14:7-11)

Seeing the Father in Christ was not accomplished by a glimpse of the natural eye, but by an interaction over time, during which the immaterial attributes of God were manifested and contemplated. Beholding Christ as the image of God, therefore, was accomplished through perception.

If seeing Jesus with the natural eye meant that men beheld the form of God, how then could Christ say to those who were presently looking at him, "Ye have neither heard [the Father's] voice at any time, **nor seen his shape** (εἶδος)"? (John 5:39)

Jesus said:

> "...the works which the Father has granted me to accomplish, these very works which I am doing, bear me witness that the Father has sent me. And the Father who sent me has himself borne witness to me. His voice you have never heard, **his form you have never seen**; and you do not have his word abiding in you, for you do not believe him whom he has sent." (John 5:36-38 RSV)

This was spoken to men who did not believe in him. They were blind to who he really was, namely the image of God. Notice that he says they did not hear the Father's voice. Hearing the voice of the Father doesn't mean hearing with the natural ear, but it too pertains to perception. Consider the following words of Christ that show hearing pertains to perception:

> "Why do ye not understand my speech? even because ye cannot hear my word. ... He that is of God heareth God's words: ye therefore hear them not, because ye are not of God." (John 8:43, 47 KJV)

They heard him, naturally speaking, but his words did not have entry into their hearts to the extent of perceiving the reality of them. Thus he said, "Ye cannot hear my word." The words went to all, but the perception of those words is what Christ has in view. It was on this wise, while speaking to men who did not believe, that Jesus said, "You have never heard his voice nor seen his shape."

> "His voice you have never heard, his form (εἶδος) you have never seen; and you do not have his word abiding in you, **for** you do not believe him whom he has sent." (John 5:37-38 RSV)

They did not see the "form" (εἶδος) of the Father because they did not believe, not because they did not see Jesus with their natural eyes.

Now, εἶδος (eidos), which we just saw translated as "form" in John 5:37, and μορφή, which is translated as "form" in Philippians 2:6, have a very similar meaning. Indeed, *Thayer's Lexicon* defines them both with nearly the exact same words:

- μορφή – the form by which a person or thing strikes the vision; the external appearance[154]

- εἶδος – that which strikes the eye; which is exposed to view[155]

Since the beholding of God's εἶδος referred to the immaterial attributes revealed through Christ, perceived only by those who believed, it is no stretch to take μορφή in the same sense. The εἶδος and the μορφή of God were exhibited in Christ, but only those who believed perceived that reality. In the case of Philippians 2:6, Christ constantly "subsisted[156] in the form of God," that is, *the ever-present underlying reality of Christ was that he expressed God's attributes to men.* This was not always beheld by all who saw him, but he himself knew that this was his status. Nevertheless, he did not use his status as the image of God to promote a self-centered lifestyle. He was a true example of someone being humble despite their high status. This is precisely what Paul intended to convey to his readers, presenting Christ as the example they should follow.

> "Let nothing be done through strife or vainglory; but in lowliness of mind let each esteem other better than themselves. Look not every man on his own things, but every man also on the things of others. Let this mind be in you, which was also in Christ Jesus: Who, being

in the form of God, thought it not robbery to be equal with God: But made himself of no reputation, and took upon him the form of a servant" (Philippians 2:3-7)

Philippians 2:6 – Equal to God

There isn't a consensus as to how the second clause of Philippians 2:6 should be translated. Some render it, "Thought it not robbery to be equal to God," showing that Christ, in himself, thought equality with God was rightfully self-applicable. Others render the text as, "Did not consider his equality with God as something to be clung to," showing that he was willing to set aside the nobility of his status in order to serve. I believe either translation is grammatically possible, but, due to the context, the latter is probably the correct one. Regardless of which translation of Philippians 2:6 is preferred, the equality that Christ has with God is not in question. In the first version, Jesus considers equality with God as applicable to himself. In the second version, that equality with God is assumed as reality. Jesus was equal to God, and even if Philippians 2:6 did not affirm this, we still have John 5:18.

> "[Jesus] said also that God was his Father, making himself equal with God." (John 5:18 KJV)

Throughout this book we have seen that being the Son of God meant that Jesus acted in accordance with the attributes of God. This provides the meaning for being equal to God in John 5:18 (see chapter fifteen herein, subheading *John 5:18 – Equal with God*). Likewise, Philippians 2:6 says that Jesus subsisted in the form of God, not because of how men beheld him with the natural eye, but because they saw the immaterial attributes of God revealed through him. In every instance, this equality with God is attributed to acting in sync with God.

The equality with God is qualified by Paul in Philippians 2:6 as *equality in the sense that Christ was in the form of God.* Notice how he connects "being equal to God" to "being in the form of God."

> "**Who, being** in the form of God, **thought** it not robbery to be equal with God:" (Philippians 2:6 KJV)

Christ's equality with God is predicated upon him being in the form of God. The manner of equality with God in Philippians 2:6 is therefore defined within the verse itself. Being in the form of God, he thus considered himself equal to God. Christ never asserted that he was equal to God in every respect. On the contrary, he clearly says, "My Father is greater than I." (John 14:28.) Yet, inasmuch as the Father was revealed through him, he was, in that regard, equal to God, or, as John 10:30 says, "one" with the Father.

Took on Him the Form of a Servant

Philippians 2:7-8 is commonly thought to describe how Christ, as a pre-incarnate being, consciously emptied himself of his heavenly glory and became a human. This, however, is not what the text says. This passage is describing how Jesus, during his humanity, humbled himself to function as a servant despite his glorious position as the image of God.

> "Who, being in the form of God, thought it not robbery to be equal with God: But made himself of no reputation, and took upon him the form of a servant, and was made in the likeness of men: And being found in fashion as a man, he humbled himself, and became obedient unto death, even the death of the cross." (Philippians 2:6-8)

When Philippians 2:7 says, "He took upon him the form of a servant," this is the second instance where μορφή appears in Philippians 2. The meaning here is, Jesus appeared to others as a servant *in his mannerisms* (rather than acting arrogantly as the image of God).

Jesus spoke of how he carried himself as a servant of others, saying:

> "And he said unto them, The kings of the Gentiles exercise lordship over them; and they that exercise authority upon them are called benefactors. But ye shall not be so: but he that is greatest among you, let him be as the younger; and he that is chief, as he

that doth serve. For whether is greater, he that sitteth at meat, or he that serveth? is not he that sitteth at meat? but I am among you as he that serveth." (Luke 22:25-27)

In this passage, Jesus says he conducted himself around his disciples as a servant would. This, however, does not mean that he "was" their servant. On the contrary, he was their Lord. On one occasion, Jesus washed the feet of his disciples—this was an act identifiable with a servant. Yet, he acknowledges his *actual* position over them even while taking on the *appearance* of their servant.

> "So after he had washed their feet, and had taken his garments, and was set down again, he said unto them, Know ye what I have done to you? Ye call me Master and Lord: and ye say well; for so I am. If I then, your Lord and Master, have washed your feet; ye also ought to wash one another's feet. For I have given you an example, that ye should do as I have done to you." (John 13:12-15)

Christ was not their servant by "very nature," but only in appearance, inasmuch as he "took upon him the form (μορφή) of a servant."

The Likeness of Men / As a Man

Philippians 2:7(b) says that Christ "was made in the likeness of men." This does not mean that he transitioned from being non-human to being human. The Greek word for "likeness" is ὁμοίωμα (homoiōma), which denotes a similarity, but not an actuality.[157] Some have taken the fact that Christ was made in the likeness of men so far as to assert that Philippians 2:7 is affirming *Docetism,* which was an early Gnostic doctrine that claimed Jesus only "seemed" to be a man, but was not.[158] This doctrine, if truly held by Paul, would put him at odds with other New Testament authors.[159] However, Paul is not asserting Docetism, because he isn't talking about Jesus "appearing like a real man even though he was not." We need only to look at a section of Paul's first letter to the Corinthians to learn what Paul had in mind in Philippians 2.

1 Corinthians 9:18-22 is a key text when trying to understand Philippians 2:7-8. Paul describes his own ministry in similar terms that he used to describe Christ's.

Philippians 2:6-8	1 Corinthians 9:18-22
Who, being in the form of God, thought it not robbery to be equal with God: But made himself of no reputation, and took upon him the form of a servant	For though I be free from all men, yet have I made myself servant unto all (9:19)
and was **made** (γίνομαι) in the likeness of men	I am **made** (γίνομαι) all things to all men (9:22)
And being found in fashion **as** (ὡς) a man	And unto the Jews I became **as** (ὡς) a Jew (9:20)

The bottom entry of the right-hand chart is from 1 Corinthians 9:20, where Paul writes:

> "And unto the Jews I became as a Jew, that I might gain the Jews."
> (1 Corinthians 9:20 KJV)

Paul was "by nature" a Jew, as he states in his Epistle to the Galatians:

> "**We who are Jews by nature** (φύσει), and not sinners of the Gentiles …" (Galatians 2:15 KJV)

Yet, he says in 1 Corinthians 9:20 that he became "as a Jew." Clearly, being "as a Jew" does not exclude one from being an actual Jew (cf. Philemon 9). Contextually, Paul is speaking of taking on mannerisms common to the Jewish people. Paul was made *in the likeness* of a Jew in regard to mannerisms, although he *was* a Jew in regard to his nature. The same concept is being conveyed in Philippians 2:7-8 in regard to Christ.

> "**But made himself of no reputation, and took upon him the form of a servant** (that is, he, by adopting the mannerisms of a servant, appeared as such), **and was made in the likeness of men** (he was not made similar to multiple men, as if he looked like a *composite* of many men, but this instead means that he made himself equal in presentation to typical men): **And being found in fashion** (σχῆμα schāma - outward appearance[160]) **as a man** (like Paul, who, being an actual Jew, took on Jewish cultural mannerisms and thus appeared outwardly as the typical Jew. Christ was an actual man, but, despite his uncommon status, presented himself socially in such a way that was typical to the common man), **he humbled himself** (refusing to draw on his glory for selfish gain, especially during his trials before Herod and Pilate), **and became obedient unto death, even the death of the cross**."
>
> (Philippians 2:6-8)

Philippians 2:9-11 – The Name Above Every Name

Philippians 2:9 says that God has given Jesus the name that is above every name.

> "Wherefore God also hath highly exalted him, and given him the name which is above **every** name." (Philippians 2:9 KJV)

Does having a name above "every" name mean that Jesus must be the same individual as God? If not, does that mean that Christ's name, being above every name, is above God's name as well? Absolutely not. The word "all" is not used within the Bible in an exclusively absolute sense, as if to automatically eliminate any possible exception whatsoever.

Hebrews 2:8 says:

> "[God] hast put **all things** in subjection under his (Christ's) feet.

For in that he (God) put all in subjection under him, he left nothing that is not put under him." (Hebrews 2:8)

However, 1 Corinthians 15:27 shows that there *is* an exception to "all things" under Christ, saying:

"When he saith **all** (πᾶς) things are put under him (Jesus), it is manifest (δῆλος) that he (God) is excepted, which did put all things under him." (1 Corinthians 15:27)

Now, why is it that the previous passage (Hebrews 2:8) did not let us know that God is excepted from all things put under Christ? Could it be that such a thing is considered *obvious,* and thus goes unspoken? Now then, if it is obvious that the one who put "**all** (πᾶς)" things under Jesus is excepted from those things under him, shouldn't it be equally just as obvious that the name of the one who *gave* Jesus a name above "every (πᾶς)" name would be excepted as well? The words "all" and "every" are not used in the Bible in such a way that automatically excludes any possibility of exception.

Having said that, I don't think the above explanation of *a name above every name* except *God's name* is necessarily the correct interpretation of the passage in Philippians 2. It is interesting that Philippians 2:9 has the article before "name," (τὸ ὄνομα,) so as to emphasize "*the* name." Could it be that the Father, in a sense, gave Jesus his own name? That sounds awkward if we think of a name as *a proper title,* but the Bible doesn't always use *name* in that regard. Sometimes the Bible uses the word *name* to denote *attributes that pertain to the one so named.* We see this clearly in Exodus 34:14, which says:

"The LORD, whose name is Jealous, is a jealous God."
(Exodus 34:14)

His "name is" jealous, because "he is" jealous, not because that is his literal name. The word name, in Bible terms, often signifies *attributes.* Could it be that Jesus was given the name of the Father in the sense that the attributes of the Father were revealed through him? Indeed, Philippians 2:8-9 says that the name was given to Jesus because of his obedience unto death, so it appears that the name was not given until after the resurrection. Jesus does say, after his resurrection, that he has a "new name."

> "I will write upon him the name of my God ... and I will write upon him **my new name**." (Revelation 3:12)

Could the new name given to Jesus be the name of God? Could Jesus being given the name of God mean that he was given the attributes of God? While it is true that Jesus already manifested the attributes of God prior to his resurrection, those attributes were manifested to a greater extent after God raised him from the dead. (See chapter nine under the subheadings *Romans 1:4 – Declared Son of God by Resurrection* and also *Christ Begotten Completely at the Resurrection.*)

During Christ's prayer in John 17, he actually said that the Father gave him his own name.

> "Holy Father, keep them in your name, the name which you have given me, that they may be one even as we are." (John 17:11 NASB)

Some versions read, "Your name, **those** (οὕς) you gave me," which would have Jesus praying that the Father keep through his own name the disciples that were given to him, but that is not the original reading.[161] The true reading is, "Your name, **which** (ᾧ) you gave me." This means that the Father gave his name to Jesus.

It makes sense to interpret *given the name above every name* as *given the attributes of the God who is greater than all.* Jesus is not reigning by his own power, but by the power of the Father revealed in him.

This is why God says he is the one subduing all things under Christ:

> "Sit on my right hand **until I make** thine enemies thy footstool." (Hebrews 1:13)

And yet Christ is also said to be subduing all things himself, yet by a certain working of power, namely, God's power.

> "... according to the working whereby he (Jesus) is able even to subdue all things unto himself." (Philippians 3:20)

It is God who is subduing all things under Christ, but Christ, by the power of God, is subduing all things in sync therewith. Hence, Christ is reigning by the power of God.

Jesus was given the *name, i.e., attributes* of God after his resurrection to such an extent that all things are being brought under his dominion as he functions in the power of God. I believe the careful student can discover also that this is the meaning of Christ sitting at the right-hand of the power of God (Luke 22:69). Once we understand that "sitting at the right hand of God" refers to *reigning with God in the might of God,* the meaning of Hebrews 1:8-13 becomes clearer. We are somewhat digressing from the meaning of Philippians 2:9-11, however, so let's sum up the point and see how it applies to our text.

The Father gave his name to Jesus who now rules by the attributes of God. Let's look again at Philippians 2:9-11 and incorporate this into our interpretation.

> **"Therefore God has highly exalted him and bestowed on him the name which is above every name** (Jesus now rules in the strength of God's attributes, and no one is greater than God)**, that at the name of Jesus** (who now embodies the attributes of God) **every knee should bow, in heaven and on earth and under the earth, and every tongue confess that Jesus Christ is Lord, to the glory of God the Father** (who is glorified in the dominion of Christ which reflects the power of the Father's own attributes)."
> (Philippians 2:9-11)

Why Isaiah 45:23 is Quoted in Philippians 2:10-11

Isaiah 45:23 is applied in Philippians 2:10-11. Paul, the author of Philippians, cites Isaiah 45:23 in Romans 14:11, so we will look there for his accepted reading of the text.

"For it is written, As I live, saith the Lord, every knee shall bow to me, and every tongue shall confess **to God**." (Romans 14:11)

Compare that with Paul's words in Philippians 2:10-11.

"That **at** the name of Jesus every knee should bow, of things in heaven, and things in earth, and things under the earth; And that every tongue should confess **that** Jesus Christ is Lord, to the glory of God the Father." (Philippians 2:10-11 KJV)

Notice that Philippians 2:11 does not say that every tongue will confess "to" Christ. It is God that the confession is made to here.

Romans 14:11	**Philippians 2:10-11**
"For it is written, As I live, saith the Lord, every knee shall bow to me, and every tongue shall **confess to** God."	"At the name of Jesus every knee should bow ... and every tongue should **confess that** Jesus Christ is Lord, to the glory of God the Father."

This speaks of the judgment day, as the context of Romans 14 shows:

"For we shall all stand before the judgment seat of Christ. For it is written, As I live, saith the Lord, every knee shall bow to me, and every tongue shall confess to God. So, then every one of us shall give account of himself to God." (Romans 14:10-12)

The judgment seat is Christ's, but the account will also be given to God, who will judge the world through the agency of Christ.

"Because he hath appointed a day, in the which he will judge the world in righteousness by (ἐν) that man whom he hath ordained; whereof he hath given assurance unto all men, in that he hath raised him from the dead." (Acts 17:31 KJV)

Chapter Seven

Conscious Preexistence?

Matthew 23:37 – "O Jerusalem"

There is an instance in Matthew 23:37 where Jesus weeps over Jerusalem and says these words:

> "O Jerusalem, Jerusalem, thou that killest the prophets, and stonest them which are sent unto thee, how often would I have gathered thy children together, even as a hen gathereth her chickens under her wings, and ye would not!" (Matthew 23:37)

Although this does not say anything about Jesus having a conscious preexistence, I used to refer to this text as possibly indicating that he had. Jesus seems to speak of a *prolonged* interaction with Jerusalem in which he wanted to gather the city under his sheltering care. This sounds like something that would be easily said by God (compare 2 Esdras 1:30), but not so easily said by Jesus as a man. I now believe that this passage was Jesus speaking the words of God in the first person. The evidence for this is that, right before he says these things, he also says:

> "Wherefore, behold, **I send** unto you prophets, and wise men, and scribes: and some of them ye shall kill and crucify…"
>
> (Matthew 23:34)

Here, he says, "**I** send" without any indicators that he is speaking the words of God, just as he went on to say of Jerusalem, "How often would **I** have gathered thy children," as he continued his discourse. Yet, when we compare the parallel passage from Luke, he attributes these words to *the wisdom of God.*

"Therefore also **said the wisdom of God, I will send** them prophets and apostles, and some of them they shall slay ..." (Luke 11:49)

This text, though worded slightly different, is a parallel passage to Matthew 23:34. In Matthew, Jesus says "I send," but in Luke it is the wisdom of God that says, "I send." In both instances Jesus is speaking, but in Luke we see that the words are attributed to God. So, I believe that the lament over Jerusalem, being contained in the same discourse, is also attributed to God (I will cover how Christ speaks the words of God more in chapter nine, subheading *John 2:19 – Jesus did not Raise Himself from the Dead*).

Compare the following examples where *speaking by the wisdom given* can sometimes be equated to *the Holy Spirit speaking* and *the Spirit of the Father speaking*.

- "Settle it therefore in your hearts, not to meditate before what ye shall answer: For I will give you **a mouth and wisdom**, which all your adversaries shall not be able to gainsay nor resist." (Luke 21:14-15)

- "But when they arrest you and deliver you up, do not worry beforehand, or premeditate what you will speak. But whatever is given you in that hour, speak that; for it is not you who speak, but **the Holy Spirit**." (Mark 13:11 NKJV)

- "But when they deliver you up, take no thought how or what ye shall speak: for it shall be given you in that same hour what ye shall speak. For it is not ye that speak, but **the Spirit of your Father** which speaketh in you." (Matthew 10:19-20)

John 17:5 – "Before the World"

While praying to the only true God (John 17:3), Jesus speaks of glory he had with him prior to the world. Here, I would like to relay the entry on this passage from the Racovian Cetechism (a 17th century non-Trinitarian publication), which reads:

> That a person may have had something, and consequently may have had glory, with the Father before the world was, without its being to be therefore concluded that he then actually existed, or that he possessed the same nature as the Father, is evident from 2 Tim. i. 9, where the apostle says of believers, that grace was given to them before the world began. Besides, it is here stated that Christ prayed for this glory : which is wholly incompatible with a divine nature. But the meaning of this passage is, that Christ beseeches God to give him in actual possession, with himself, the glory which he had with him, in his purposes and decrees, before the world was. For it is often said that a person has something with any one, when it is promised, or is destined for him : on this account believers are frequently said by this evangelist to have eternal life. Hence it happens that Christ does not say absolutely that he had the glory, but that he had it WITH THE FATHER ; as if he had said, that he now prayed to have actually conferred upon him that glory which had been laid up for him with the Father of old, and before the creation of the world.[162]

Although John 17:5 *could* be taken as a reference to Jesus' glory in the preexistent plan of God (compare 1 Corinthians 2:7), I think it *may* not mean that. The Greek verb translated as "was" when John 17:5 says, "before the world *was*," is a *present infinitive verb*. That same verb (εἶναι) is sometimes used in reference to *future occurrences postulated in the present* (Luke 20:27 of the *future* resurrection; 1 Corinthians 7:32 "to be" without concern in the *future* instead of getting married, etc.). Furthermore, "glory *which I had,*" (KJV,) could also be translated, "glory *I have been having*" (εἶχον *imperfect indicative*, which everywhere else in the New Testament means *had up to the present time*. Luke 19:20, 3 John 13). Jesus says he gave the glory God gave to him to his disciples as well (John 17:22). It is therefore logical that Jesus is speaking of glory he was experiencing *in this world* (John 2:11, 11:14) which he expected to *carry over after his resurrection* (John 13:31-32), much like the saints in *this world* now experience *"the powers of the world to come."* (Hebrews 6:5.)

> "And now, O Father, glorify thou me with thine own self with the glory which εἶχον **[I have been having up until now]** with thee before **the world** εἶναι **[to be]**." (John 17:5)

Hebrews 2:5 says that God put "the world to come" in subjection to Christ. This present world will pass away (Hebrews 1:10-11). Since Jesus' "kingdom is not of this world," (John 18:36,) he is plausibly speaking of the world to come. However, the fact that Jesus speaks of *this* world in John 17:6 may seem to push "the world" in verse 5 into the same "this world" category of verse 6, but Jesus elsewhere spoke of this world and the world to come in close proximity without confounding the two (Matthew 12:32).

1 Peter 1:11 – The Spirit of Christ in the Prophets?

In 1 Peter, we find the following words:

> "Of which salvation the prophets have enquired and searched diligently, who prophesied of the grace that should come unto you: Searching what, or what manner of time the Spirit of Christ which was in them did signify, when it testified beforehand the sufferings of Christ, and the glory that should follow." (1 Peter 1:10-11)

Here, the English translations suggest that "the Spirit of Christ" was in the prophets of old. However, the text should not be translated as:

> "What or what manner of time the Spirit of Christ which was in them did signify …"

But it should instead be translated in this way:

> "What or what manner of time of Christ the Spirit which was in them did signify …"

The prophets were inquiring into the coming of Christ and into things involving him. The context demonstrates this conclusively. However, some have felt that the Spirit must have been the Spirit of Christ because of the Greek word order.

The Greek text reads as follows:

ἐραυνῶντες   εἰς   τίνα   ἢ   ποῖον   καιρὸν   ἐδήλου
searching   into   what   or   what sort   of time   was signifying

τὸ   ἐν   αὐτοῖς   πνεῦμα   Χριστοῦ
the   in   them   Spirit   of Christ   (1 Peter 1:11)

The placement of the possessive form of Χριστός (Christ), appearing at the end and just after the word πνεῦμα (Spirit), makes it seem like the Spirit is of Christ. However, compare that to the Greek structure we find just a few verses later in 1 Peter 1:19, which reads:

ἀλλὰ   τιμίῳ   αἵματι   ὡς   ἀμνοῦ   ἀμώμου   καὶ
but   by precious   blood   as   of a lamb without blemish   and

ἀσπίλου   Χριστοῦ
without spot   of Christ   (1 Peter 1:19)

If we translate 1 Peter 1:19 in the same way that 1 Peter 1:11 is usually translated, it would read, "Without spot of Christ." Yet, we know this is not what is meant. In 1 Peter 1:19, despite Χριστοῦ appearing "in unusual position," (Robertson,) where "ἀσπίλου ["spot"] is in antecedent apposition to Χριστοῦ," (Meyer,) the "difficult" construction "owing to the term 'Christ's' being thrown to the end," (Schaff,) does not *demand* that we read the text as, "Spot of Christ." Every English translation of 1 Peter 1:19 testifies to this assertion. It is within the bounds of consistency, therefore, to assert that the same author, using a similar syntactical arrangement a few sentences prior, did not mean "Spirit of Christ" in 1 Peter 1:11. Just as it is correct to take Χριστοῦ as modifying the word "blood," in 1 Peter 1:19—"By the precious blood of Christ ... without spot"—so also it is correct to take Χριστοῦ as modifying "what, or what manner of time" in 1 Peter 1:11—"What or what manner of time of Christ the Spirit which was in them did signify."

The Companion Bible, by E.W. Bullinger, presents a slightly different rendering than I propose.

> These words "of Christ" should come after "signify."[163]

Bullinger's translation would thus be:

> "What or what manner of time the Spirit which was in them did signify of Christ …"

As I see it, the similar structure of 1 Peter 1:19 better supports the word order I have proposed, but the *meaning* of Bullinger's rendering is the same—The Spirit was testifying about things pertaining to Christ. This is incontrovertibly *the point* being conveyed in 1 Peter 1:11, whereas the notion that Christ's own Spirit is in view is contextually foreign.

First-Person Narrative Messianic Prophecies

There are several prophecies in the Old Testament that present the words of Christ in the first-person narrative. For example, Psalm 22:1 says:

> "My God, my God, why hast thou forsaken me?" (Psalm 22:1)

We know that these words were spoken by Christ while on the cross (Mark 15:34). How is it that we find first-person narrative words spoken by Christ in prophecies? How is it that prophecies speak of things yet to occur in the past tense? Some will say that Jesus transcended time and spoke these things through prophets of old, as one who had experienced these things in an alternate timeline. This whole transcendence-beyond-time doctrine will tie into the Antichrist agenda soon to be revealed (they will say that Christ dies in the end times, transcended time and came out in the past as a transcendent human through a virgin). Such conclusions are not necessitated by first-person Messianic prophecies, however.

Consider how Isaiah speaks a prophecy about Israel rejecting Christ as a historic event.

> "He is despised and rejected of men; a man of sorrows, and acquainted with grief: and **we hid** as it were our faces from him; he was despised, and **we esteemed him not**." (Isaiah 53:3)

Although Isaiah did not hide his face from Christ, he speaks first-person narrative words while representing the future deeds of Israel. Likewise, David did not experience the things prophesied in Psalm 22, etc., but he spoke as representing the future experience of Christ.

> "For David speaketh **concerning him**, I foresaw the Lord always before my face, for he is on my right hand, that I should not be moved: Therefore did my heart rejoice, and my tongue was glad; moreover also my flesh shall rest in hope: Because thou wilt not leave my soul in hell, neither wilt thou suffer thine Holy One to see corruption. Thou hast made known to me the ways of life; thou shalt make me full of joy with thy countenance. Men and brethren, let me freely speak unto you of the patriarch David, that he is both dead and buried, and his sepulchre is with us unto this day. Therefore **being a prophet**, and knowing that God had sworn with an oath to him, that of the fruit of his loins, according to the flesh, he would raise up Christ to sit on his throne; He **seeing this before spake of the resurrection of Christ**, that his soul was not left in hell, neither his flesh did see corruption." (Acts 2:25-31)

Just as Isaiah saw the future rejection of Christ and spoke as one representing Israel, so also David saw the future resurrection of Christ, his descendant, and spoke as one representing Christ. In both instances, events are spoken of in the past tense, but that occurs in the Hebrew language while conveying certainty as to future outcomes. This was very common in prophetic utterances, but also used in general when a future event was viewed as certain (Genesis 45:9-10 *lit.* "Thou *hast dwelt* in the land of Goshen"; Exodus 17:4 *lit.* "They *have stoned* me," etc.).

1 Peter 3:18-20 – Preached in the Days of Noah

In 1 Peter 3:18-20, we find the following words:

> "For Christ also hath once suffered for sins, the just for the unjust, that he might bring us to God, being put to death in the flesh, but quickened by the Spirit: By which also he went and preached unto the spirits in prison; Which sometime were disobedient, when once

the longsuffering of God waited in the days of Noah, while the ark was a preparing, wherein few, that is, eight souls were saved by water." (1 Peter 3:18-20)

Confusion has arisen because of the portion that says, "Quickened by the Spirit: By which also he went and preached unto the spirits in prison." How did Jesus go preach unto the spirits in prison by the Spirit? There are several scholars who believe that the original text read as follows:

- "He was made alive in the Spirit. In it Enoch went and preached even to those spirits..." (Goodspeed)

- "He came to life in the Spirit. (It was in the Spirit that Enoch also went and preached to the imprisoned spirits..." (Moffatt)

The reading that includes the word "Enoch" is preferred by some scholars since the narrative matches the details of Enoch very precisely. However, there aren't any extant manuscripts of 1 Peter that contain the name Enoch, so the inclusion of the name by some scholars is based upon a conjecture that the original Greek uncial manuscript(s) were copied incorrectly. There were no spaces between words in those manuscripts and all of the letters were written as capital letters. Hence, it is supposed that the Greek for, "And Enoch," which would look like ENWXKAI, was mistakenly transcribed by a copyist as saying, "In which also," which would look like ENWKAI. There is no manuscript to prove that this occurred, however. So, despite its plausibility (which is not unreasonable), it remains unproven.

A.T. Robertson, author of *Robertson's Word Pictures in the New Testament*, gives an overview of scholars who have preferred the Enoch reading:

> In which also (ἐν ᾧ καί). That is, in spirit (relative referring to πνεύματι). But, a number of modern scholars have followed Griesbach's conjecture that the original text was either Νῶε καὶ (Noah also), or Ἐνὼχ καὶ (Enoch also), or ἐν ᾧ καὶ Ἐνώχ (in which Enoch also) which an early scribe misunderstood or omitted Ἐνώχ καὶ in copying (ὁμοιοτέλευτον). It is allowed in Stier and Theile's

Polyglott. It is advocated by J. Cramer in 1891, by J. Rendel Harris in *The Expositor* (1901), and *Sidelights on N.T. Research* (p. 208), by Nestle in 1902, by Moffatt's New Translation of the New Testament. Windisch rejects it as inconsistent with the context. There is no manuscript for the conjecture, though it would relieve the difficulty greatly.[164]

In the Book of Enoch (cited in Jude 14-15), Enoch goes during the days of Noah to preach to the Watchers (the angels) who took the daughters of men to themselves and began corrupting humanity. Those angels, which are called *spirits* (Hebrews 1:7), were cast into prison to await their coming judgment. So then, during the days before the flood, Enoch went and preached to the spirits which are now imprisoned. This historic event was a prominent theme in the mind of the early Christians.

Jude refers to the imprisoned angels in his epistle:

> "And the angels which kept not their first estate, but left their own habitation, he hath reserved in everlasting chains under darkness unto the judgment of the great day." (Jude 6)

When Jude refers to those angel's punishment, he is using it as *an example* of how God will punish apostate men as well in a similar fashion.

> "And the angels which kept not their first estate, but left their own habitation, he hath reserved in everlasting chains under darkness unto the judgment of the great day. Even as Sodom and Gomorrha, and the cities about them in like manner, giving themselves over to fornication, and going after strange flesh, are set forth for an example, suffering the vengeance of eternal fire. Likewise also these filthy dreamers defile the flesh … to whom is reserved the blackness of darkness for ever." (Jude 1:6-8, 13)

Peter also mentions the imprisoned angels, to whom Enoch preached, and, like Jude, he corresponds their judgment with the future judgment of ungodly men.

> "For if God spared not the angels that sinned, but cast them down to hell, and delivered them into chains of darkness, to be reserved unto judgment; And spared not the old world, but saved Noah the eighth person, a preacher of righteousness, bringing in the flood upon the world of the ungodly; ... The Lord knoweth how to deliver the godly out of temptations, and to reserve the unjust unto the day of judgment to be punished." (2 Peter 2:4-5, 9)

Peter brought forth the example of the angels being imprisoned before the flood in 2 Peter 2 to exemplify ungodly men being reserved for judgment.

The fact that Jude and Peter refer to the angels being imprisoned before the flood gives us clear precedent for taking 1 Peter 3 in the same fashion. In 1 Peter 3, Peter is clearly talking about spirits (angels) who were in disobedience during the days of Noah.

> "In which he went and preached to the spirits in prison, who formerly did not obey, when God's patience waited in the days of Noah, during the building of the ark." (1 Peter 3:19-20 RSV)

The spirits who were preached to and imprisoned are distinctly identified as *those who were disobeying in the days of Noah*. Therefore, Peter is *not* talking about preaching to dead saints, etc. I have no doubt that Peter is referencing the events recorded in the Book of Enoch. And, since Enoch was the one who preached to those specific spirits now imprisoned, I have no doubts that Peter identifies Enoch as the preacher of 1 Peter 3:19-20.

Having said all of that, we must understand *why* Peter is referring to the fallen angels, the preaching of Enoch, the flood of Noah and those saved during that judgment. When we understand *the reason* behind the reference, it becomes clear that, whether we incorporate the word "Enoch" or not, the same point is being made.

Let's consider the factors:

1. Biblically, the circumstances that preceded the flood in Noah's day are going to be similar to the circumstances preceding the judgment by fire that is about to come upon the earth (Luke 17:26). Peter refers

to the historic destruction of the ungodly by water as being replicated somewhat in this next judgment by fire (2 Peter 3:5-7).

2. As we saw in the examples from 2 Peter and Jude, the reference to the angels being imprisoned until judgment was brought up as a *representation* of how ungodly men in this age would eventually be judged as well. The same is true in 1 Peter 3-4. Peter is talking about Christians being persecuted (1 Peter 3:14-16) and how those who persecute them will be judged *in the end* (1 Peter 4:4-5). The persecutors were not being punished yet, but like with the imprisoned angels, their sentence was being announced beforehand.

3. Peter brings up the salvation of Noah, being saved by the flood from the corruption overflowing the earth, as an example of how we are saved as well in baptism.

> "By which also he went and preached unto the spirits in prison; Which sometime were disobedient, when once the longsuffering of God waited in the days of Noah, while the ark was a preparing, wherein few, that is, eight souls were saved by water. The **like figure** whereunto even baptism doth also now save us."
>
> (1 Peter 3:18-20)

So then, let's consider the parallels. **1.** Peter says the way Noah was saved by water is likened unto how we are saved in baptism. **2.** Peter says the angels who were the cause of Noah's troubles are reserved till judgment, making a parallel to how those men persecuting Christians will be judged as well. **3.** Peter refers to how Enoch, though he was translated by the Spirit into an invisible dimension, pronounced judgement against those angels while Noah was awaiting his salvation, *which is paralleled to how Jesus is now pronouncing judgment against the persecutors of Christians, though he too has been translated by the Spirit into the heavens.*

Peter is comparing Jesus' current state to the state of Enoch, who, like Jesus, was already announcing coming judgment within a realm unseen by men before that punishment took place.

Philo comments thus on Enoch's translation:

> What is the meaning of the expression, "He was not found because God translated him?" (Genesis 5:24.) In the first place, the end of virtuous and holy men is not death but a translation and migration, and an approach to some other place of abode. In the second place, in this instance something marvelous did take place; for he was supposed to be carried off in such a way as to be invisible, for then he was not found: and a proof of this is, that he was sought for as being invisible, not only as having been carried away from their sight, since translation into another place is nothing else than a placing of a person in another situation; but it is here suggested, that he was translated from a visible place, perceptible by the outward senses, into an incorporeal idea, appreciable only to the intellect. This mercy also was bestowed on the great prophet, for his sepulchre also was known to no one.[165]

Enoch was translated into an invisible dimension and was pronouncing judgment before the flood, so also Jesus is now in heaven, unseen by men, and is pronouncing judgment before the coming fire.

In the Bible, when Jesus is paralleled to an event in history, he is sometimes referred to *as if he were there*, though he was *only represented there in a type*.

> "And [the Israelites in the wilderness] did all drink the same spiritual drink: for they drank of a spiritual rock that followed them: and the rock was Christ." (1 Corinthians 10:4 ASV)

This example is not stating that Jesus was *literally* the rock from whence they drank the water. Likewise, even if we take 1 Peter 3:19 as "Jesus went and preached in the Spirit," we understand that Jesus is equated to the historic event in which Enoch alone preached thus whilst demonstrating a type of the ascended Christ. The fact that Enoch was placed in judgment over the angels is likely also the reason why Peter goes on to say:

> "The resurrection of Jesus Christ: Who is **gone into heaven**, and is on the right hand of God; **angels** and authorities and powers being made subject unto him." (1 Peter 3:21-22)

Micah 5:2 – "From Everlasting"?

One of the primary "proof texts" cited by those who say that Christ has existed from eternity past is Micah 5:2, which the *King James Version* renders as:

> "But thou, Bethlehem Ephratah, though thou be little among the thousands of Judah, yet out of thee shall he come forth unto me that is to be ruler in Israel; whose goings forth have been from of old, **from everlasting**." (Micah 5:2 KJV)

This is indeed a messianic prophecy, but when the KJV says that the Messiah's goings forth is from "everlasting" it misrepresents the original Hebrew thought conveyed. Neither the Hebrew Old Testament text, nor the Greek Septuagint literally refer to eternity past.[166]

The words "from everlasting" in the KJV rendering of Micah 5:2 are translated from two Hebrew words םוי (yom) and םלוע (olam). These words do not denote eternity past. In fact, they are used elsewhere within passages that *cannot* be understood as describing eternity past.

Deuteronomy 32:7 says:

> "Remember **the days** (םוי) **of old** (םלוע), consider the years of many generations: ask thy father, and he will shew thee; thy elders, and they will tell thee." (Deuteronomy 32:7)

Israel was told to remember former events that, while very ancient, were not from everlasting, as the context shows:

> "Remember **the days** (םוי) **of old** (םלוע), consider the years of many generations: ask thy father, and he will shew thee; thy elders, and they will tell thee. **When** the most High divided to the nations their inheritance, when he separated the sons of Adam, he set the bounds of the people according to the number of the children of Israel." (Deuteronomy 32:7-8)

Another passage demonstrating how the Hebrew words םוי (yom) and םלוע (olam) are used, is Micah 7:14, which says:

> "Feed thy people with thy rod, the flock of thine heritage, which dwell solitarily in the wood, in the midst of Carmel: let them feed in Bashan and Gilead, as **in the days** (םוי) **of old** (םלוע)."
> (Micah 7:14)

Again, these words do not denote "eternity" but rather "ancient days." The Hebrew text of Micah 5:2 says Christ's goings forth are from ancient days, not from eternity past.

The same reasoning that pertains to the Hebrew text of Micah 5:2 also pertains to the Greek Septuagint text of Micah 5:2 as well, which reads:

> "...his goings forth are from the beginning, even from **the days** (ἡμερῶν) **of old** (αἰῶνος)." (Micah 5:2 LXX)

The exact same Greek phrase from Micah 5:2 (LXX), ἡμερῶν αἰῶνος, is also used in Deuteronomy 32:7:

> "Remember **the days** (ἡμερῶν) **of old** (αἰῶνος), consider the years for past ages: ask thy father, and he shall relate to thee, thine elders, and they shall tell thee." (Deuteronomy 32:7 LXX)

The Septuagint refers to ancient "days" (ἡμερῶν) rather than eternity past. Hence, the Septuagint text, like the Hebrew text, does not promote the "eternity" past translation of Micah 5:2.

- "...from of old, from **ancient times**." (Micah 5:2 NIV)
- "...from of old, from **ancient days**." (Micah 5:2 RSV)
- "...are of old, From **the days of antiquity**." (Micah 5:2 YLT)

This text does not say anything about "eternity past," and is simply referring to the prophesied Messiah's centuries-old descent, in reference to his genealogy, which was traced back to David and even to Abraham.

"Hath not the scripture said, That Christ cometh of the seed of David, and out of the town of Bethlehem, where David was?" (John 7:42)

Hebrews 7:3 – Christ and Melchisedec

There has been quite a bit of confusion regarding the comparison between Christ and Melchisedec that is found in Hebrews 7:3.

> "[Melchisedec, who was] without father, without mother, without descent, having neither beginning of days, nor end of life; but made like unto the Son of God; abideth a priest continually."
> (Hebrews 7:3)

If someone does not understand the context in which this scripture is presented, they may assume that Melchisedec did not have a father, mother, genealogy, beginning of days, or end of life. However, that is not what the writer is saying. Instead, the point being conveyed is that there is *nothing recorded* about Melchisedec's genealogy *in the Scriptures*, and there is *no record* of his beginning or ending. The writer was alluding to the fact that none of those things are recorded about Melchisedec, not that they didn't pertain to him in general.

Albert Barnes comments on this passage accurately, saying:

> **Without father**. The phrase *without father* (ἀπάτωρ) means, literally, one who has no father ... the apostle says that there was no such genealogical table in regard to Melchizedek. There was no record made of the name either of his father, his mother, or any of his posterity. ... The meaning of the word rendered "without father" here is, therefore, *one the name of whose father is not recorded in the Hebrew genealogies*. **Without mother**. The name of whose mother is unknown, or is not recorded in the Hebrew genealogical tables. Philo calls Sarah ἀμήτορα (without mother) probably because her mother is not mentioned in the sacred records. The Syriac[167] has given the correct view of the meaning of the apostle. In that version it is, "Of whom neither the father nor mother are recorded in the genealogies." **Without descent**,

> [margin], *pedigree*. The Greek word ἀγενεαλόγητος means *without genealogy; whose descent is unknown*. He is merely mentioned himself, and nothing is said of his family or of his posterity. **Having neither beginning of days, nor end of life**. The obvious meaning of the phrase is, that, *in the records of Moses*, neither the beginning nor the close of his life is mentioned. It is not said when he was born, or when he died; nor is it said that he was born, or that he died. ... There was no account of the commencement or close of his office as a priest, but, *so far as the record goes*, it is just as it would have been if his priesthood had neither beginning nor end.[168]

Albert Barnes gives a good exposition of these statements in regard to their application to Melchisedec. However, although Hebrews 7:3 is making a parallel between Melchisedec and Christ, all of these statements made about Melchisedec are not (and cannot be) applied to Christ. Unlike Melchisedec, Jesus has a mother in the Scriptures. Furthermore, Jesus has a genealogy that is recorded in Luke 3:23-38, but the writer of Hebrews describes Melchisedec as "without genealogy." Therefore, it cannot be that Christ is like Melchisedec in *all* of the aspects mentioned in Hebrews 7:3. Instead, the writer is specifying one particular point that is made immediately prior to his comparison, saying that Melchisedec was like the Son of God in that particular sense.

> "He is without father or mother or genealogy, and has neither beginning of days **nor end of life, but resembling the Son of God he continues a priest for ever**." (Hebrews 7:3 RSV)

Melchisedec (as far as the record shows) did not cease to be a priest, but instead "abideth a priest forever." Historically, his priesthood is presented as *something that did not end*. Likewise, since Christ has risen from the dead and now lives forever, his priesthood (not only on the basis of record, but also in reality) shall not end either.

The context clearly shows that it is the duration of their priesthood that is being compared:

> "Jesus has gone as a forerunner on our behalf, having become a high priest **for ever** after the order of Melchiz'edek. ... [Melchiz'edek] is without father or mother or genealogy, and has neither beginning of days **nor end of life, but resembling the Son of God he continues a priest for ever**. See how great [Melchiz'edek] is! Abraham the patriarch gave him a tithe of the spoils. ... This man who has not their [Levitical] genealogy received tithes from Abraham ... Here tithes are received by mortal men; there, by one of whom it is testified [due to no record of his death] that he lives. ... **In the likeness of Melchiz'edek, [Jesus] has become a priest**, not according to a legal requirement concerning bodily descent but **by the power of an indestructible life**. For it is witnessed of him, "Thou art a priest **for ever**, after the order of Melchiz'edek." ... Those who formerly became priests took their office without an oath, but this one was addressed with an oath, "The Lord has sworn and will not change his mind, 'Thou art a priest for ever.'" This makes Jesus the surety of a better covenant. The former priests were many in number, because **they were prevented by death from continuing in office; but he holds his priesthood permanently, because he continues for ever**." (Hebrews 6:20, 7:3, 4, 6, 8,15-17, 21-24 RSV)

The author of Hebrews was specifically comparing Christ to Melchisedec in regard to the perpetuity of their priesthood. He was not comparing Christ to Melchisedec in regard to having no father, no mother, no genealogy, **and no beginning of days**.

> "There is no record of his father or mother or any of his ancestors–no beginning or end to his life. He remains a priest forever, resembling the Son of God." (Hebrews 7:3 NLT)

Hebrews 13:8 – "Yesterday" = Eternity Past?

Some have asserted that an eternal past is implied within the text of Hebrews 13:8, which says:

> "Jesus Christ the same **yesterday**, and today, and forever."
> (Hebrews 13:8)

They argue that the word "yesterday" in this passage clearly signified eternity past. The Greek word that is translated as "yesterday" in Hebrews 13:8 is ἐχθές (echthes), which literally means *yesterday*. This exact same word is also used in John 4:52, which says:

> "Then inquired he of them the hour when he began to amend. And they said unto him, **yesterday** (ἐχθές) at the seventh hour the fever left him." (John 4:52)

Now, if ἐχθές means *eternity past* then the man who was healed in this passage never had a fever in the first place, and thus it never left him at all! Yet, this would be absurd. It is also absurd to say that "yesterday" implies eternity past when it is used of Jesus in Hebrews 13:8. Even if there *is* some extended meaning for the word "yesterday" in Hebrews 13:8 (which I believe there is), in no way, by any reasonable standard, does that necessitate that the extension be stretched to ***infinity!?!?***

Chapter Eight
John 8:58 – Before Abraham

No Connection to Exodus 3:14

The King James Version records Jesus' words in John 8:58 as:

"Before Abraham was, I am." (John 8:58 KJV)

The Greek text of Jesus' statement is as follows:

πρὶν   Ἀβραὰμ   γενέσθαι   ἐγὼ   εἰμί
before Abraham   shall have   I   am   (John 8:58)
                  come to be

This is commonly mistaken as connected to the phrase, "I am that I am," in Exodus 3:14. The Greek Septuagint text of Exodus 3:14 reads:

ἐγώ   εἰμι   ὁ   ὤν
I   am   the one   who is   (Exodus 3:14 LXX)

Notice that God does *not* say, "I am the ἐγώ (*egō* - I) εἰμι (*eimi* - am)," but *instead*, "I am ὁ (*ho* - the one) ὤν (*ōn* - who is)." Then, in the same verse, God does *not* tell Moses to present him as, "Ἐγώ εἰμι," but *rather* goes on to say:

"Say unto Israel ὁ (the one) ὤν (who is) has sent me."
(Exodus 3:14 LXX)

So, God was not saying, "I am that I am," but, "I am the One who is." God refers to himself with these same words in Revelation 1:8 (comp. Revelation 1:4):

> "Ἐγώ (I) εἰμι (am) ... ὁ (the one) ὤν (who is)." (Revelation 1:8)

The phrase Jesus used was *not* the same phrase God used of himself. Jesus never said, "Ἐγώ (I) εἰμι (am) ὁ (the one) ὤν (who is)." Instead, he said, "Before Abraham was, ἐγώ (I) εἰμι (am)." (John 8:58.) Simply saying, "Ἐγώ (I) εἰμι (am)," cannot rightfully be taken as a claim to be God. While still in the discussion with God, Moses himself said, "Ἐγώ (I) εἰμι (am) weak and slow tongued." (Exodus 4:10 LXX.)

> "Then Abner looked behind him, and said, Art thou Asahel? And he answered, **Ἐγώ εἰμι**." (2 Samuel 2:20 LXX)

Furthermore, the phrase, "Ἐγώ (I) εἰμι (am)," is spoken by men other than Jesus in the New Testament. In fact, just a few verses after John 8:58, a man whom Jesus healed used the exact same phrase.

> "Some said, This is he: others said, He is like him: but he said, **Ἐγώ εἰμι**." (John 9:9)

In the English translations, the translators add the word "he" after "I am" to make the man say, "I am *he*," but "he" is not present in the original Greek text (which is why the word *he* is italicized in the KJV).

> "Some said, This is he: others *said*, He is like him: *but* he said, I am *he*." (John 9:9 KJV with italics retained)

The KJV uses italicization to indicate that a word was *added* which was not in the original manuscripts. In John 9:9, the word "he" is added after "I am" to clarify the man's claim concerning himself ("I am *he, the man that was healed*"). Sometimes additional words are necessary during translation to clarify the meaning of texts and *every* English translation implements this necessary practice.

Notice how the following translations *add* words to translate the blind man's statement, "Ἐγώ εἰμι":

- "Yes, I am the same one!" (NLT)
- "I am the man." (NIV)
- "I am the one." (NASB)
- "I am the man." (RSV)

Translating ἐγώ εἰμι as "I am," in John 9:9 would be confusing to the English reader, so the English versions add words to clarify the meaning of the text.

Let's look at another verse in the Bible where English versions have translated ἐγώ εἰμι as something other than just "I am" for clarity.

> "And as they did eat, he said, Verily I say unto you, that one of you shall betray me. And they were exceeding sorrowful, and began every one of them to say unto him, Lord, ἐγώ εἰμι?"
>
> (Matthew 26:21-22)

The disciples were asking if they were going to be the one who betrayed Jesus, but their response literally translates to "Lord, I am?" We *understand* that this means, "I am [going to be the one to betray you]?" Thus, the translators make adjustments to convey that meaning.

- "Lord, is it I?" (KJV)
- "Am I the one, Lord?" (NLT)
- "Surely you don't mean me, Lord?" (NIV)
- "Surely not I, Lord?" (NASB)
- "Is it I, Lord?" (RSV)

No one tries to translate these texts as "I AM, Lord?" to imply the disciples were asking Jesus if they were "the Great I AM" of Exodus 3:14. Yet, when it comes to Jesus' ἐγώ εἰμι (I am) statements, some English versions put the ultra-literal translation, "I am," in all caps to insinuate a connection to "the I AM of Exodus 3:14."

> "Then the high priest asked him, 'Are you the Messiah, the Son of the Blessed One?' Jesus said, 'I AM.'" (Mark 14:62 NLT)

Jesus simply says, "Ἐγώ εἰμι," as a response to the question "Are you the Messiah?" He is *obviously* saying, "Yes, I am that one," not, "I AM the one who spoke to Moses out of the burning bush!" The "Jesus is claiming to be God" bias demonstrated in many of the English versions is quite astounding.

How Others Have Translated John 8:58

While I honor Daniel B. Wallace for his scholarly work, I want to bring attention to how even notable Greek scholars of our present day still employ a great deal of bias in their considerations of John 8:58. In Wallace's book, *Greek Grammar Beyond the Basics*, he demonstrates such bias while commenting on the *New World Translation* (the translation used by the *Jehovah's Witnesses*).

Wallace writes thus:

> The translators of the *New World Translation* understand the implications of ἐγώ εἰμι here, for in the footnote to this text in the *NWT*, they reveal their motive for seeing this as a historical present: "It is not the same as ὁ ὤν (*ho ohn'*, meaning 'The Being' or "The I AM') at Exodus 3:14, LXX." In effect, this is a negative admission that if ἐγώ εἰμι is *not* a historical present, then Jesus is here claiming to be the one who spoke to Moses at the burning bush, the I AM, the eternally existing One, Yahweh (cf. Exod. 3:14 in the LXX, ἐγώ εἰμι ὁ ὤν).[169]

This excerpt is a stain on Wallace's work. While I do not agree with the *New World Translation's* rendering of John 8:58, the translators are absolutely correct that ἐγώ εἰμι is not the same as ὁ ὤν in Exodus 3:14 (a *fact* that English readers *should* be made aware of and which modern-day theologians ceaselessly fail to acknowledge to the laity). Furthermore, the *New World Translation's* reading, "Before Abraham came into existence, I have been," is absolutely a grammatical possibility. Although I would not classify "I have been" as a historical present, there are translations, even some from Trinitarian academics, that do seem to take ἐγώ εἰμι as a historical present (Catholics rendering the text, "I was before

Abraham,"[170] and a Lutheran's translation, "I was in existence before Abraham was ever born."[171]) Such translations don't stem from a desire to disprove the Trinitarian belief, but are strictly the result of grammatical considerations. John 8:58 *can* be translated from the "historical present" viewpoint.

> "I existed before Abraham was born!" (*Goodspeed, An American Translation, 1935*)

In addition to the historical present ("I was"), some translators have taken ἐγώ εἰμι as a present perfect progressive (also called a *present perfect continuous*), which is how I would classify the *New World Translation's* rendering ("I have been").[172] This use of present tense verbs in relation to past events conveys *continued, unbroken existence from the past into the present*. *Greek Grammar*, by Herbert Weir Smyth, talks about this use of present tense verbs in the following excerpt:

> **1885. Present of Past and Present Combined.**—The present, when accompanied by a definite or indefinite expression of past time, is used to express an action begun in the past and continued in the present. The 'progressive perfect' is often used in translation. Thus, πάλαι θαυμάζω *I have been long* (and am still) *wondering* P. Cr. 43b. Cp. *iamdudum loquor*. So with πάρος, ποτέ. This use appears also in the other moods.[173]

Consider the following example of the present perfect progressive tense, where a present tense verb (ἐστε – *este*, "ye are") is used in relation to a past event.

> "And ye also shall bear witness, because **ἐστε** (literally, "ye are") with me from the beginning." (John 15:27)

If someone wanted to "prove" that the disciples were transcendent beyond time (as so many want to say of God and of Jesus), they could render the present indicative verb ἐστε as "ye are."

> "And ye also shall bear witness, because **ye are** with me from the beginning." (John 15:27, translating ἐστε as "ye are")

No one translates the text that way, because no one is trying to prove the disciples are transcendent beyond time. Instead, translators unanimously convey the meaning that was intended in this text.

> "And ye also shall bear witness, because **ye have been** with me from the beginning." (John 15:27)

Let's look at another example of the present perfect progressive tense. In John 14:9, Jesus uses εἰμί (the same present tense verb in John 8:58).

> "Jesus saith unto him, **εἰμί** (literally, "I am") so long time with you, and yet hast thou not known me, Philip?" (John 14:9)

All would agree that this is an example of the present perfect progressive tense, which is why we always find εἰμί translated in John 14:9 as showing *continued, unbroken existence from the past into the present* ("Have I been," KJV). Although I do not take εἰμί in John 8:58 as a present perfect progressive tense verb, it *can* be taken as such from a grammatical standpoint. We will discuss other possible translations of John 8:58, but I wanted to first lay some groundwork for showing **1.** Sometimes words are added to ἐγώ εἰμι during translation and **2.** The phrase ἐγώ εἰμι can be translated as a present perfect progressive (also called a *present perfect continuous*). Now, let's look at the *context* surrounding Jesus' statement before we continue our discussion of possible translations for John 8:58.

The Day of Christ

One thing that I never see emphasized when people comment on John 8:58 is Jesus' reference to "his day" in John 8:56.

> "Your father Abraham rejoiced to see **my day**." (John 8:56)

"The Day of Christ" (Luke 17:24, 1 Corinthians 1:8, 5:5, 2 Corinthians 1:14, Philippians 1:6, 10, 2:16, 2 Thessalonians 2:2[174]) is when Jesus returns, the trumpet sounds, and the "dead" in Christ rise to meet him in the air (1 Thessalonians 4:16). The Bible unanimously presents the "Day of Christ" as that future day when Jesus returns to gather his people.

"For as the lightning, that lighteneth out of the one part under heaven, shineth unto the other part under heaven; so shall also the Son of man be in **his day**." (Luke 17:24 comp. Matthew 24:27 ff.)

This is the day Jesus referred to when he said, "Abraham rejoiced to see my day." (John 8:56.) Abraham will receive his promised inheritance on the Day of Christ. *That* is the day Abraham looked forward to. The Jews misunderstood Jesus as if he were promising eternal life in this present world. Thus, they compared his claim to the fact that Abraham and the prophets were all already dead.

"Then said the Jews unto him, Now we know that thou hast a devil. Abraham is dead, and the prophets; and thou sayest, If a man keep my saying, he shall never taste of death. Art thou greater than our father Abraham, which is dead? and the prophets are dead: whom makest thou thyself?" (John 8:52-53)

Jesus' teaching was that men would not die anymore *after the resurrection*, as we see in the following:

"But they which shall be accounted worthy to obtain **that world**, and **the resurrection from the dead**, neither marry, nor are given in marriage: **Neither can they die any more**." (Luke 20:35-36)

This is what he was talking about in John 8 as well.

"Verily, verily, I say unto you, If a man keep my saying, **he shall never see death**." (John 8:51)

Jesus was talking about eternal life after the resurrection, which occurs on the Day of Christ.

Abraham "Saw" the Day of Christ

Even though the Bible always talks about the Day of Christ as a future event, some may object that Jesus had a day during the lifetime of Abraham in mind, because he says:

> "Your father Abraham rejoiced to see my day: and he **saw** it, and **was** glad." (John 8:56)

Even many of the Trinitarian commentaries will say that Abraham "saw" the Day of Christ *ahead of time*, though it had *not yet occurred*.

> "He saw it – See Hebrews 11:13; 'These all died in faith, not having received (obtained the fulfillment of) the promises, but having seen them afar off, and were persuaded of them,' etc."
>
> —*Albert Barnes*[175]

This is how I understand the text as well. However, I want to clarify that when Jesus says Abraham "saw" his day, the Greek verb he uses, εἴδω, is often used to denote *perception,* specifically *perception of a future prophetic event*.

- "These all died in faith, not having received the promises, but having **seen** (aorist participle of εἴδω = saw them before their deaths) them afar off, and were persuaded of them, and embraced them, and confessed that they were strangers and pilgrims on the earth." (Hebrews 11:13)

- "The woman saith unto him, I **know** (perfect indicative of εἴδω) that Messias cometh, which is called Christ: when he is come, he will tell us all things." (John 4:25)

- "Martha saith unto him, I **know** (perfect indicative of εἴδω) that he shall rise again in the resurrection at the last day." (John 11:24)

- "These things said Esaias, when he **saw** (aorist indicative of εἴδω) his glory, and spake of him." (John 12:41)

So, when Jesus says, "Abraham rejoiced to see my day: and he saw it, and was glad," (John 8:56,) this could definitely be taken as *Abraham perceived the future Day of Christ and was glad.*

Γενέσθαι – *Past or Future*

The aorist infinitive verb normally translated as "was" ("Before Abraham **was**, I am") is γενέσθαι (*genesthai*).

πρὶν	Ἀβραὰμ	**γενέσθαι**	ἐγὼ	εἰμί	
before	Abraham	was	I	am	(John 8:58)

It is possible to translate John 8:58 as depicting a *past* state of Abraham ("Before Abraham *was*"). However, that same Greek verb translated "was," is also used within the New Testament to depict a *future* "coming to be."

Here are some examples where γενέσθαι is used within the New Testament while a future occurance is in view.

- "Whosoever will **be** (γενέσθαι) great among you" (Matthew 20:26)

- "I will make you to **become** (γενέσθαι) fishers of men." (Mark 1:17)

- "And whosoever of you **will be** (γενέσθαι) the chiefest, shall be servant of all." (Mark 10:44)

- "Then Agrippa said unto Paul, Almost thou persuadest me **to be** (γενέσθαι) a Christian." (Acts 26:28)

- "Who against hope believed in hope, that he **might become** (γενέσθαι) the father of many nations" (Romans 4:18)

Did you see how γενέσθαι is used in reference to the future? Again, γενέσθαι can grammatically refer to *either* the past or the future. Even so, the *majority* of instances where γενέσθαι appears in the New Testament do refer to the *future*. What is even more significant than that is how γενέσθαι is used within the Book of John itself.

Here is a list of every instance in the Book of John (KJV) where γενέσθαι appears. Notice how every instance outside of John 8:58 is referring to an anticipated (*i.e.,* future) occurrence.

- "But as many as received him, to them gave he power **to become** (γενέσθαι) the sons of God." (John 1:12)

- "Nicodemus answered and said unto him, How can these things **be** (γενέσθαι)?" (John 3:9)

- "Wilt thou **be made** (γενέσθαι) whole?" (John 5:6)

- "Jesus said unto them, Verily, verily, I say unto you, Before Abraham **was** (γενέσθαι), I am." (John 8:58)

- "Will ye also **be** (γενέσθαι) his disciples?" (John 9:27)

- "Now I tell you before it **come** (γενέσθαι), that, when it is come to pass, ye may believe that I am he." (John 13:19)

- "And now I have told you before **it come to pass** (γενέσθαι), that, when it is come to pass, ye might believe." (John 14:29)

Outside of John 8:58, **the Book of John *only* uses γενέσθαι *when anticipated (i.e., future) events are in view*.**[176] Is John 8:58 truly the sole exception? Obviously, any translation of John 8:58 that conveys an anticipated event would be more harmonious with the author's style of writing. John 8:58 and John 14:29 even share the same syntactic combination of πρὶν (before) and γενέσθαι (come to be), where "before it comes to be" is the meaning of the latter.[177]

- εἴρηκα   ὑμῖν   **πρὶν**   **γενέσθαι**
  I have told   you   before   it comes to be   (John 14:29)

- **πρὶν**   Ἀβραὰμ   **γενέσθαι**   ἐγὼ   εἰμί
  Before   Abraham   comes to be   I   am   (John 8:58)

Before Abraham What?

Often when γενέσθαι is used, the sentence goes on to state the *object* of the verb γενέσθαι (e.g., Jesus didn't say, "I will make you to become," but, "I will make you to become *fishers of men*."). We don't have a stated object in John 8:58. It only says, "Before Abraham γενέσθαι." That is why Abraham simply *coming to be* is accepted as the intended meaning.

> "Nicodemus answered and said unto him, How can these things **be** (γενέσθαι)?" (John 3:9)

The verb γίνομαι (the root word of γενέσθαι) has broad applications, being used of things coming to be (or coming on the scene), whether in their origination, or corresponding to some kind of development. Unlike ἐγώ εἰμι, where the object can be implied, I don't see examples of implied objects in the New Testament where γίνομαι is concerned. From my research, without a *stated* object, γίνομαι simply means the subject noun *happens* or *comes to be*. This leaves us with at least four *possible* meanings for, "Before Abraham γενέσθαι."

1. "Before Abraham has come to be [in existence in the past]" – This would progress from the Jews' reference to the past in John 8:57, "Thou art not yet fifty years old, and hast thou seen Abraham?" This is the view we find in most English translations of the Bible.

2. "Before Abraham comes to be [at the resurrection]" – This agrees with Jesus' contextual reference to the Day of Christ, which *everywhere else* denotes the coming of Christ when the saints will be resurrected and rewarded. It also matches Jesus' contextual discussion of eternal life, which will come into effect at the resurrection and include Abraham. Furthermore, this view retains γενέσθαι as depicting an *anticipated* event, agreeing with how γενέσθαι is used *everywhere else* within the Book of John. For examples where γίνομαι is associated with the resurrection, see Luke 20:33, "Therefore in the resurrection whose wife of them γίνεται (is she)?"; 1 Corinthians 15:20, "But now is Christ risen from the dead, and ἐγένετο (become) the firstfruits of them that slept." For γενέσθαι without a stated object, compare Acts 10:40, which literally reads, "This one God raised up on the third day and gave him openly to be." (τοῦτον ὁ θεὸς ἤγειρεν τῇ τρίτῃ ἡμέρᾳ καὶ ἔδωκεν αὐτὸν ἐμφανῆ γενέσθαι.) In Acts 10:40 αὐτὸν ("him," *i.e.,* the resurrected Christ) precedes γενέσθαι, as Ἀβραὰμ (Abraham) does in John 8:58. I take γενέσθαι in Acts 10:40 as "to be" (*i.e.,* to be alive). Compare Acts 1:3. If some argue that it means "openly appear" after his resurrection, as most translators seem to take it, the same could be said regarding Abraham in John 8:58. Compare Luke 13:28.

Unlike the previous view, this has the Jews *misinterpreting* Jesus' words within their John 8:57 response. Yet, this is demonstrably what occurred.

> "They pervert the question. Christ had said, 'Abraham saw my day:' on the contrary, they ask him, 'Hast thou seen Abraham?'"
>
> —*John Lightfoot*[178]

The Jews *often* misunderstood Jesus' words. Whatever emphasis we place on the understanding of the Jews in relation to their attempted stoning of Jesus in John 8:59, we should not think that John 8:58 suddenly produced their desire to kill Jesus. Prior to John 8:59, Jesus twice said that those men were *already* going about to kill him (John 8:37, 40). They were actively trying to build a justification for capital punishment within an "are you greater than Abraham" framework (John 8:53). They found Jesus' statement in John 8:58 opportunistic inasmuch as he finally, in some respect, asserted priority to Abraham.

3. "Before Abraham comes to be [Abraham, the Father of many nations]" – The name Abraham literally means *the father of many nations*. We will discuss this possibility a little more as we proceed.

4. "Before Abraham has come to be [in his current state of bodily decay]" – This refers to the state that Abraham has transitioned into and remained in during the time of Jesus' speaking. Taken as Abraham's current state, John 8:58 would mean *before Abraham himself came to be in that state* **not** *before the state Abraham came to be in.* Hence, the historic time near Abraham's death would be in view. I see this perspective as invalid and I will not discuss it as we proceed.

Ἐγώ Εἰμι – *Possibilities and Conclusion*

Now, we will look at possible ways to translate ἐγώ εἰμι in keeping with the aforementioned potential meanings of the Abrahamic clause of John 8:58. I will go through seven possibilities. The correct interpretation, as I see it, is the seventh. Some of the proposals will incorporate *implied* predicates. Implied predicates are quite normal when ἐγώ εἰμι is concerned and this is acknowledged by Trinitarian scholars as well.

A.T. Robertson comments on the possibility of implied predicates in his entry for John 8:24.

> *That I am he* (*hoti egō eimi*). Indirect discourse, but with no word in the predicate after the copula *eimi.* Jesus can mean either "that I am from above" (verse 23), "that I am the one sent from the Father or the Messiah" (7:18, 28), "that I am the Light of the World" (8:12), "that I am the Deliverer from the bondage of sin" (8:28, 8:31f., 36), "that I am" without supplying a predicate in the absolute sense as the Jews (Deut. 32:39) used the language of Jehovah (cf. Isa. 43:10 where the very words occur *hina pisteusēte — hoti egō eimi*).[179]

Robertson was a Trinitarian and a Greek Scholar, so there is no room for anyone to imply bias in his acknowledgment that ἐγώ εἰμι could have an implied predicate in John 8:24. Although I have doubts that a predicate *is* implied in John 8:58, many have interpreted the passage with an implied predicate and I want to acknowledge the validity of their efforts.

Without further ado, here are the seven proposals for how John 8:58 *could* be understood. I would not espouse all of these as quality interpretations. I am only acknowledging them as grammatical possibilities.

1. "Before Abraham has come to be [in existence in the past], I have been." – Although I do not believe this is what Jesus intended, this is how many have understood the text. Typically, this would denote Christ existing since before Abraham came to exist (which is how the *Jehovah's Witness'* see the text). Taking the text as Jesus consciously preexisting [as a spiritual being] before Abraham came to be is supported by the Jew's preceding statement, "Thou art not yet fifty years old, and hast thou seen Abraham?" (John 8:57.) A claim to be existing since before Abraham, who died, while claiming to have the truth that brings eternal life (John 8:51) would be taken as a claim to be greater than Abraham (John 8:53) and infuriate the Jews enough to explain the attempted stoning in John 8:59. This view is not preferable inasmuch as it presents John 8:58 with a sole exception to how γενέσθαι is used everywhere else within the Book of John. It also departs from Jesus' contextual theme of the resurrection. Additionally, I don't see this first explanation as preferable since there is no mention of Jesus consciously preexisting in Matthew, Mark, Luke, Acts, etc. which would have undoubtedly been acknowledged by the authors if that had been their view. Therefore, taking John 8:58 as denoting conscious preexistence is not favorable when we assume New Testament harmonization. Notwithstanding, this was apparently how some early Christians understood the text. Irenaeus writes, "And as he was from Abraham, so did he also exist before Abraham."[180] Arius viewed Christ as existing before Abraham as well, being the first of God's conceptualized creation. In that sense, some have taken ἐγώ εἰμι here as, "I have been existing *in the plan of God* before Abraham," or, "*I was predetermined, promised by God*" (Grotius).[181] This would possibly harmonize with the rest of the New Testament, but seems to be an improbable theme when the contextual flow of John 8 is considered.

2. "Before Abraham comes to be [at the resurrection on the Day of Christ], I am [he who will raise him]." – This view fits well with Jesus' contextual discussion of eternal life (John 8:51) and matches the reference to his day, when he returns to resurrect those in him, which Abraham looked forward to. This view also harmonizes with the rest of the Book of John by retaining γενέσθαι as an anticipated event. The inference is *Jesus is claiming to be the necessary precursor present before Abraham is resurrected*. We see something similar to this in his discussion with Martha about Lazarus a few chapters later in John 11.

> "Jesus saith unto her, Thy brother shall rise again. Martha saith unto him, I know that he shall rise again **in the resurrection at the last day**. Jesus said unto her, Ἐγώ εἰμι ἡ ἀνάστασις (**I am** the resurrection), and the life: he that believeth in me, though he were dead, yet shall he live." (John 11:23-25.)

Here, Jesus says ἐγώ εἰμι with a supplied predicate, namely, *the resurrection and the life*. By saying, "I am the resurrection," Jesus claims to be the embodiment of the hope of resurrection. Grammatically speaking, something similar could have been implied in Jesus ἐγώ εἰμι statement in John 8:58. And notice how Jesus went on to tell Martha, "And whosoever liveth and believeth in me **shall never die**." (John 11:26.) Compare that with John 8:51, "Verily, verily, I say unto you, If a man keep my saying, he **shall never see death**." It is easy to see that Jesus had the same idea in mind within both passages. In one discourse, where the resurrection at the last day is mentioned, he claimed, "I am the resurrection," while in the other discourse, where the Day of Christ is mentioned, he says, "I am," without a supplied predicate. It does not seem a stretch to infer that a similar concept could have been conveyed in both instances. If it was implied that Abraham would only rise again because of Christ, this would have infuriated the Jews hearing him who already asked if Jesus was claiming to be greater than Abraham (John 8:53). This could account for their desire to stone Jesus in John 8:59. I see this view as leaning somewhat heavily on supplied inference and therefore do not think it is preferable.

3. "Before Abraham comes to be [at the resurrection on my day], I am [the Christ]." – This view is similar to the previous view, but is more refined inasmuch as it has Jesus claiming to be the Christ. We know that ἐγώ εἰμι in Luke 21:8 means, "I am [Christ]," because of the corresponding statement in Matthew 24:5, where Jesus doesn't only say, "Ἐγώ εἰμι," but, "Ἐγώ εἰμι ὁ Χριστός (I am the Christ)." This is why the English translators *add* the word "Christ" in their rendering of Luke 21:8. It is perfectly acceptable from a grammatical standpoint to do the same in John 8:58. The Jews were expecting the Christ to come before the future resurrection of Abraham occurred. There was so much emphasis on the coming of the Messiah at that time that an "I am he" statement could have easily been intended and received as "I am the Christ."

"Art thou **he that should come**, or do we look for another?"
(Matthew 11:3)

Jesus' statement could simply be interpreted as, "Before Abraham comes to be [at the resurrection], I am [he who was to come]." This would, compared to John 8:24, be a more explicit claim to be the Christ, because it refers to a culturally recognized Messianic event sequence. The Messiah was to come first and restore the kingdom to Israel (Acts 1:6). Abraham and the saints would correspondingly be resurrected and experience that kingdom as well (Luke 13:28). Claiming to be the Christ was, by some, considered a capital offense (Mark 14:61-64, Luke 4:18-29) and would explain the Jews' attempt to stone Jesus in John 8:59. This explanation of John 8:58 retains the use of γενέσθαι as an anticipated event. I find this particular explanation to be simple and highly plausible. Compare John 11:25-27.

4. "Before Abraham comes to be [at the resurrection on the Day of Christ], I am [to be resurrected]" – This *reuses* the verb γενέσθαι after ἐγώ εἰμι. "Before Abraham shall have come to be, I am to be." Since γενέσθαι is an infinitive verb, it does not specify 3rd person (*he* comes to be) or 1st person (*I* come to be), but can be used for either. Thus, γενέσθαι could be applicable to both Abraham and Christ in John 8:58. In 1 Corinthians 15:45, we see an example of a single Greek verb, the same verb used in John 8:58 (but with γίνομαι as an aorist indicative), being applied in two clauses, but only *stated* in the first clause. Since that single verb is implied in the second clause, but not stated therein, the KJV supplies the verb within the second clause using italics.

> "And so it is written, The first man Adam was made a living soul; the last Adam *was made* a quickening spirit." (1 Corinthians 15:45 with KJV italics retained)

The KJV uses italics to show that it added words not existing in the manuscripts from which it was translated. Following that same model for John 8:58, we would have, "Before Abraham comes to be, I am *to be*." Although we don't see the ἐγώ εἰμι + verb construction in the New Testament, it does exist in the Septuagint (the Greek translation of the Old Testament). There, we see examples like ἐγώ εἰμι πορεύομαι (I am going) (1(3^{182}) Kings 2:2). See also Judges 6:18, 2 Samuel 13:28, 24:17, 2 Kings 4:13, 10:9, 22:20 for more examples of the ἐγώ εἰμι + verb construction. Although the examples in the LXX have *indicative* verbs after ἐγώ εἰμι, infinitive verbs can and do sometimes follow indicative verbs ("[Noun] **is** (indicative) **to [verb]** (infinitive)"), so there is no problem reading an understood γενέσθαι after εἰμι in *that* regard. The particular verb γενέσθαι in John 8:58 is even more in line with the use of ἐγώ εἰμι as a copula in the New Testament than those [few] examples in the LXX. Nevertheless, despite having examples of the ἐγώ εἰμι + verb structure in the LXX, which helps sustain this proposal as a possibility, John 8:58 would be the *only* instance in the entire New Testament which followed that format (and that is *assuming* the verb is to be understood after ἐγώ εἰμι). To be fair, the sentence structure in John 8:58 is different than the other New Testament instances where ἐγώ εἰμι is used, so a comparison may not be as decisive as one might think. As to why the Jews would feel compelled to stone Jesus in John 8:59, those who came to be before others were viewed as having a greater position (1 Timothy 2:12-13), so Jesus specifically claiming to be the "firstborn from the dead" (Colossians 1:18) in contrast to Abraham would have been offensive to them. Despite this proposal potentially being able to squeeze through grammatical loopholes, I just see it as very unlikely from a syntactical point of view. I have presented the best case I know how for this proposal here and I think others would be hard pressed to find better examples from Scripture to validate its consideration. I searched, with a mind to argue *for* this proposal, and found the evidence lacking.

5. "Before Abraham comes to be [the father of many nations], I am [that seed to be multiplied]." – The name "Abraham" means "the father of many nations." The Racovian Catechism, a 17th century confession of faith, takes the position that Jesus spoke concerning Abraham becoming *the father of many nations*. "It is apparent," they said, "that Christ might have with propriety admonished the Jews to believe that he was the light of the world before Abraham should become the father of many nations, and thus the divine grace be transferred from them to other nations."[183] This view harmonizes with the rest of the Book of John by retaining γενέσθαι as an anticipated event, namely, Abraham becoming the father of the Gentiles as a result of Christ's coming.

> "Against hope [Abraham] believed in hope, that he γενέσθαι ("might become") the father of many nations." (Romans 4:18)

See also Galatians 3:7-8. After Christ's death and resurrection, the light was given to *the Gentiles* (literally, *the nations*) (Acts 26:23). The Racovian Catechism spoke of the divine grace being "transferred," which is not scriptural terminology, but we do see, "For if the casting away of them [the Jews] be the reconciling of the world." (Romans 11:15.) The greatest weakness I see here is that we must *infer* that the *meaning* of Abraham's name was intended. Having said that, Abram's name being changed to Abraham truly was a monumental event in Scripture with a clear emphasis on the *meaning* of his name.

> "As for me, behold, my covenant is with thee, and thou shalt be a father of many nations. Neither shall thy name any more be called Abram, but thy name shall be Abraham; for a father of many nations have I made thee." (Genesis 17:4-5)

The Racovian Catechism's emphasis on the *meaning* of *Abraham*, along with its *imminent fulfilment* during Christ's earthly ministry is scripturally grounded. Even so, I doubt this view, as such, is what Jesus had in mind.

6. "Before Abraham has come to be [in existence in the past], I am [in a state of perpetual existence]." – This view departs from the anticipatory use of γενέσθαι everywhere else within the Book of John by asserting that γενέσθαι is historical. As such, this view is similar to the first proposition we discussed, "Before Abraham has come to be [in existence in the past], I have been." Like that proposition, this view finds contextual support within the Jew's preceding statement, "Thou art not yet fifty years old, and hast thou seen Abraham?" (John 8:57.) This interpretation is different from that first proposition, however, inasmuch as it does not focus on Jesus' existence *from* the past to the present, but instead sees Jesus as possessing a transcendent existence outside of time. Since this is arguably not how ἐγώ εἰμι is used anywhere else in Scripture, and definitely not anywhere else by Jesus, such novelty regarding ἐγώ εἰμι makes this proposition doubtful. The transcendent interpretation of ἐγώ εἰμι is typically held by Trinitarians who have learned that Jesus' words in John 8:58 were not a claim to be "the I AM" of Exodus 3:14. Many still refuse to let the common misconception go, however, and try to *infer* a connection to Exodus 3:14. Although none of the *early* Christians saw a connection to Exodus 3:14, we do see Chrysostom, within his *Homilies on St. John* (386-397 AD), correlating Jesus' statement in John 8:58 with a transcendent existence of God, associating ἐγώ εἰμι therewith.

> But wherefore said He not, "Before Abraham was, I was," instead of "ἐγώ εἰμι"? As the Father uses this expression, "ἐγώ εἰμι," so also does Christ; for it signifies continuous Being, irrespective of all time.[184]

Thus, we see a correlation made as early as 386 AD with the ἐγώ εἰμι sayings of God, in which ἐγώ εἰμι is apparently thought to entail transcendence. Of course, I do not agree with Chrysostom, who was apparently averse to the "present perfect progressive" we discussed earlier. Those ἐγώ εἰμι sayings of God that he alleged were similar to John 8:58 are found in the Book of Isaiah (Isaiah 41:4, 43:10, 46:4 LXX). A particular correlation is often made by Trinitarian scholars between God's ἐγώ εἰμι statement in Isaiah 43:10 and Jesus' ἐγώ εἰμι statement in John 13:19.

Spoken by God:

> "... **that** (ἵνα) ye may know and **[ye may] believe** (πιστεύσητε) and understand that **I am** (ἐγώ εἰμι)" (Isaiah 43:10 LXX)

Spoken by Christ:

> "... **that** (ἵνα), when it is come to pass, **ye may believe** (πιστεύσητε) that **I am** (ἐγώ εἰμι)." (John 13:19)

When we focus on the similarities between these two verses, it may seem at first that Jesus was *quoting* Isaiah 43:10. However, when we look closer, we see that the two have different wording and are not the same. Regardless, even if they *were* worded the same, similarity between two clauses preceding personal identification does not demand a correspondence between those identities.

- "**And** (καὶ) **they shall know** (γνώσονται) **that** (ὅτι) I am the LORD (ἐγώ εἰμι κύριος)" (Ezekiel 33:29 LXX)

- "... **and** (καὶ) **they shall know** (γνώσονται) **that** (ὅτι) a prophet was in their midst (προφήτης ἦν ἐν μέσῳ αὐτῶν)." (Ezekiel 33:33 LXX)

"I am (ἐγώ εἰμι)" is not a title. Rather, as we noted before when the healed blind man in John 9:9 said, "I am (ἐγώ εἰμι)," the phrase is often used to mean, "I am [he, that one implied within the present context]." God can say fulfilled prophecies affirm who he is in Isaiah 43:10 and Jesus can say fulfilled prophecies affirm who he is as well in John 13:19 (John 7:40, 9:17, 17:8, Acts 3:22). This does not mean they are claiming to be the same individual.

7. "Before Abraham comes to be [at the resurrection on my day], I am [in a state of perpetual existence]." – This proposal is stronger than the previous interpretation inasmuch as it retains γενέσθαι as relating to an anticipated event (the resurrection of Abraham). This view, like the previous one, requires ἐγώ εἰμι to denote a perpetual existence. However, in this view Jesus would have meant perpetual existence *into the future*, not an existence that transcended time before Abraham. I will show that this was sometimes the case in other instances where ἐγώ εἰμι was used without a predicate. Furthermore, by comparing it to some of Christ's other ἐγώ εἰμι statements, I will endeavor to demonstrate that this could indeed be what Christ intended in this particular instance.

Any of us could say we are existing before Abraham is resurrected. It would probably sound unusual, however, for us to say, "Before Abraham comes to be, we are." When we say things *are*, without any predicate, it sounds like we are expressing perpetuity. For example, if we say, "The weather is nice," we think of something *temporary*. If we drop the article and the predicate and simply say, "Weather is," we think more along the lines of *perpetual existence*. A similar principle exists in the Greek language. This is especially true in *some* cases where ἐγώ εἰμι is used. For example, we find instances within the Septuagint where cities claiming "I am" (ἐγώ εἰμι) are proven wrong when they afterward come to ruin.

> "This is the rejoicing city that dwelt carelessly, that said in her heart, **I am (ἐγώ εἰμι)**, and there is none beside me: how is she become a desolation, a place for beasts to lie down in! every one that passeth by her shall hiss, and wag his hand." (Zephaniah 2:15)

John Calvin commented on this text as follows:

> By these words the Prophet means, that Nineveh was so blinded by its splendor that it now defied every change of fortune. ... Thus

then the Prophet shows in few words what was the cause of the ruin of Nineveh: it thought that its condition on the earth was fixed and perpetual.[185]

Nineveh dwelt carelessly because it thought its continued existence was assured into the future. This expectation of perpetual existence was expressed by the words "ἐγώ εἰμι." In contrast to that boast of perpetual existence, it came to ruin. This is a clear example of how ἐγώ εἰμι, without a predicate, can be a claim to perpetual existence. See the same boast by Babylon in Isaiah 47:7-10. Note that these cities did *not* believe they *were without a beginning* or that they *existed outside of time*. Ἐγώ εἰμι did not mean any of those things in regard to those cities, it only conveyed perpetual existence *into the future*.

The Septuagint reading of Isaiah 46:3-4 has ἐγώ εἰμι spoken twice by God in such a way that seems to convey perpetual existence across long periods of time.

> "Hear me, O house of Jacob, and all the remnant of Israel, who are borne by me from the womb, and taught by me from infancy, even to old age: **I am (ἐγώ εἰμι)**; and until ye shall have grown old, **I am (ἐγώ εἰμι)**: I bear you, I have made, and I will relieve, I will take up and save you." (Isaiah 46:3-4 LXX)

God is constantly in existence from their youth until they have grown old. I believe this is a good example of ἐγώ εἰμι denoting a state of perpetual existence into the future as well.

Now, having demonstrated that ἐγώ εἰμι can denote perpetual existence, compare Jesus' statements with that concept.

> "Then said Jesus unto them, When ye have lifted up the Son of man, then shall ye know that ἐγώ εἰμι" (John 8:28)

When Jesus spoke of being *lifting up*, this meant *lifted up on the cross*.

> "[Jesus said] And I, if I be **lifted up from the earth**, will draw all men unto me. **This he said, signifying what death he should die**." (John 12:32-33)

The Jews responded to Jesus talking about his death by contrasting their expectation that the Messiah would continue on forever.

> "The people answered him, We have heard out of the law that Christ abideth for ever: and how sayest thou, The Son of man must be lifted up?" (John 12:34)

They were confused by how he could be the Christ if he was to be crucified, because they "heard out of the law that Christ abideth for ever." I believe Jesus was confirming that he would abide forever when he said, "When ye have lifted up the Son of man, then shall ye know that ἐγώ εἰμι." (John 8:28.) That means, once they tried to end Jesus' life, they would learn that his existence would continue on perpetually (*i.e.,* Jesus would continue on forever as a result of his resurrection, despite his crucifixion).

Taking ἐγώ εἰμι to denote perpetual existence results in John 8:58 being interpreted, "Before Abraham comes to be [at the resurrection], I am [in an unbroken state of perpetual existence into the future]." This would have infuriated the Jews who perceived his claim to eternal life as a claim to be greater than Abraham.

> "[Jesus said] Verily, verily, I say unto you, If a man keep my saying, he shall **never see death**. Then said the Jews unto him, Now we know that thou hast a devil. **Abraham is dead**, and the prophets; and thou sayest, If a man keep my saying, he shall never taste of death. **Art thou greater than our father Abraham, which is dead?** and the prophets are dead: whom makest thou thyself?"
> (John 8:51-53)

It is evident that a claim to live forever would have been viewed as a confirmation to their inquiry, "Art thou greater than our father Abraham, which is dead?" This explains why they would have attempted to stone Jesus in John 8:59.

Someone might object to my conclusion here by pointing out that Jesus was going to die after making his statement in John 8:58. How could he claim to continue on forever at that time if he was about to be killed? Sometimes ἐγώ εἰμι would be used to denote a state that was "about to be." Jesus used ἐγώ εἰμι in this way in John 7:34-36, 12:26, 14:3, 17:24, but, unlike John 8:58, each of these instances say **ὅπου εἰμὶ ἐγὼ** ("**where I am**"). Notwithstanding, those instances do have εἰμι used of a future state. Smyth's *Greek Grammar* says, "Εἰμὶ is regularly future (*I shall go*) in the indicative present."[186] Εἰμὶ does not *always* mean "I shall go" when future situations are concerned, however, because Jesus says, "And now **I am** (εἰμὶ) no more in the world," when he was *about to leave* the world. Still, we don't have ἐγώ εἰμι used of an imminent state without ὅπου, but only εἰμὶ alone. If there are examples *outside* of the New Testament where ἐγώ εἰμι, without ὅπου, means "I am *about to be* existing," I do not know of them. There are examples where *other* present tense verbs are used to denote something is *about to be* in the near future. Compare Luke 13:32, which literally reads:

> "… I do cures to day and to morrow, and the third day **I am** perfected." (Luke 13:32)

The verb (τελειοῦμαι) translated in the KJV as "I shall be perfected" is a present tense verb, as εἰμὶ is. If we understand Jesus as referring to the eternal state he was *about* to be in, we may take εἰμὶ in a similar way to τελειοῦμαι in Luke 13:32, etc. Thus, we might conclude that Jesus was *about to be* in a perpetual state of existence. However, restricting our conclusions to examples where εἰμὶ itself is used, Jesus was most likely speaking of his existence *continuing unabated from the time of his speaking* in John 8:58. In other words, it would not be, "*I am about to be at my resurrection and continue existing perpetually* before Abraham comes to be," but, "*I am existing and will exist perpetually* before Abraham comes to be at his resurrection."

Someone might object that such a statement was impossible, since Jesus was about to die shortly after speaking these words? How could Jesus be the Christ who "abideth forever" (John 12:34) if he was soon to be crucified and buried? This is not problematic, because the Bible presents Jesus existence as continuing, despite his death.

> "Ye men of Israel, hear these words; Jesus of Nazareth, a man approved of God among you by miracles and wonders and signs, which God did by him in the midst of you, as ye yourselves also

> know: Him, being delivered by the determinate counsel and foreknowledge of God, ye have taken, and by wicked hands have **crucified and slain**: Whom God hath raised up, having loosed the pains of death: because **it was not possible** that he should be holden of it. **For** David speaketh concerning him, I foresaw the Lord always before my face, for he is on my right hand, that I should not be moved: Therefore did my heart rejoice, and my tongue was glad; moreover also my flesh shall rest in hope: Because thou wilt not leave my soul in hell, **neither wilt thou suffer thine Holy One to see corruption**. ... He seeing this before spake of **the resurrection of Christ**, that his soul was not left in hell, **neither his flesh did see corruption**. This Jesus hath God raised up, whereof we all are witnesses." (Acts 2:22-27, 31-32)

Peter equates Jesus to his flesh, so *Jesus* did not cease to be, because *his flesh* did not cease to be.

> "Thou wilt not leave my soul in hell, neither wilt thou suffer **thine Holy One** to see corruption. ... His soul was not left in hell, neither **his flesh** did see corruption." (Acts 2:27, 31)

Jesus no more ceased to be than Lazarus, who was dead for four days before his resurrection; or the young girl whom Jesus raised from the dead, of whom he said, "The damsel is not dead, but sleepeth." (Mark 5:39.) Similarly, David spoke of Christ, saying, "My flesh shall rest in hope." (Acts 2:26.) And if anyone contest that Christ ceased to be, it should not be any who espouse the perpetual existence of Christ with that unbiblical epithet, "the Great I AM," for then they contradict their own views.

In summary, I conclude that this last proposal, or possibly proposal three, is the correct view. Either are to be preferred above the Trinitarian view, because they both **1.** Retain the anticipatory use of γενέσθαι found everywhere else within the Book of John, **2.** Retain the thematic flow of resurrection on the Day of Christ, **3.** Account for why Abraham saw that resurrection day and was glad, **4.** Emphasize Jesus' own words above the Jews' misunderstanding, **5.** Do not require a novel use of ἐγώ εἰμι within Jesus' sayings, **6.** Are not contrary to the earliest Christian beliefs.

Chapter Nine

Resurrection

The Shroud of Turin

We have ample witness to the resurrection in the various books and letters that were compiled to make up the New Testament. Not only this, but Old Testament prophecy, written before Jesus was born, attests to his resurrection as well. Additionally, I am convinced that we have *scientific* proof of the resurrection, inasmuch as there is a mountain of evidence that the Shroud of Turin is authentic. The Shroud of Turin is a very ancient linen burial cloth that has a photographic negative image of a crucified man infused into its fibers. The man in the image has pierced hands, pierced feet, a wound in his side, lash marks that match perfectly with the Roman flagrum, puncture wounds from something placed on his head (the "crown of thorns"), etc. What is more, even with all of today's technology, the image on the Shroud, with its three-dimensional aspects, still cannot be duplicated. I am convinced that this is the actual burial cloth that wrapped Jesus' body at the time of his miraculous resurrection. The evidence in favor of its authenticity is quite frankly undeniable. Unfortunately, many who only take a cursory glance at the information often find the invalid results of radiocarbon testing performed in 1988 and, failing to understand the entirety of the matter, turn and walk away. If you are unfamiliar with the Shroud of Turin and the radiocarbon tests done, I suggest watching *Unwrapping the Shroud,* a Discovery Channel documentary, as a brief introduction to the subject. As the video shows, the test sample taken from the edge of the Shroud contained dyed cotton fibers from a repair done to the cloth (probably around 1532 in Chambery, France). The far less ancient cotton fibers that were interwoven with the older, original linen fibers of the Shroud caused inaccurate radiocarbon test results. This is not a wishful theory, but a scientific fact.

Consider the following extract from *Studies on the Radiocarbon Sample from the Shroud of Turin,* published in the peer-reviewed scientific journal *Thermochimica Acta:*

> Preliminary estimates of the kinetics constants for the loss of vanillin from lignin indicate a much older age for the cloth than the radiocarbon analyses. The radiocarbon sampling area is uniquely coated with a yellow-brown plant gum containing dye lakes. Prolysis-mass-spectrometry results from the sample area coupled with microscopic and microchemical observations prove that the radiocarbon sample was not part of the original cloth of the Shroud of Turin. The radiocarbon date was thus not valid for determining the true age of the shroud.[187]

Science "proves" that the radiocarbon test was "not valid for determining the true age of the Shroud." Furthermore, other factors "indicate a much older age for the cloth than the radiocarbon analyses." So, what then is the correct date range? Consider the following excerpt from *The Shroud of Turin: First Century After Christ!*

> "Four independent analyses (FT-IR, Raman, multiparametric mechanical, and numismatic) all make it possible to maintain with relative certainty that the Shroud is contemporaneous with the time of Jesus Christ."
>
> —*Giulio Fanti and Pierandrea Malfi*[188]

It is beyond the scope of this book to delve into this subject extensively, but an honest investigation of evidence for the Shroud of Turin will speak for itself. This amazing artifact preserves for us an independent testimony of the death, burial, and miraculous resurrection of Jesus Christ.

- "And Joseph took the body, and **wrapped it in a clean linen shroud**, and laid it in his own new tomb, which he had hewn in the rock; and he rolled a great stone to the door of the tomb, and departed." (Matthew 27:59-60 RSV)

- "Now the Lord, when he had given **the linen cloth** unto the servant of the priest, went unto James and appeared to him." (The Gospel According to the Hebrews[189])

Christ Begotten Completely at the Resurrection

The Bible speaks of Jesus as being "born" from the dead (Colossians 1:18, Revelation 1:5). While proclaiming the Gospel at a synagogue in Antioch, Paul spoke the following words regarding Christ's resurrection:

> "But God raised him from the dead: And he was seen many days of them which came up with him from Galilee to Jerusalem, who are his witnesses unto the people. And we declare unto you glad tidings, how that the promise which was made unto the fathers, God hath fulfilled the same unto us their children, in that **he hath raised up Jesus again; as it is also written in the second psalm, Thou art my Son, this day have I begotten thee**. And as concerning that he raised him up from the dead, now no more to return to corruption, he said on this wise, I will give you the sure mercies of David. Wherefore he saith also in another psalm, Thou shalt not suffer thine Holy One to see corruption." (Acts 13:30-35)

Paul equated Jesus' resurrection with his being begotten of God when he said:

> "God hath ... raised up Jesus again, as it is also written in the second Psalm, 'Thou art my Son, this day have I begotten thee.'"
> (Acts 13:33)

Furthermore, this event, according to Paul, was a fulfilment of the promise made to the fathers.

> "**The promise** which was made unto the fathers, God hath fulfilled the same unto us their children, **in that** he hath raised up Jesus again; **as it is also written** in the second psalm, Thou art my Son, this day have I begotten thee." (Acts 13:32-33)

God promised that he would send the Messiah as an *everlasting* king over Israel (2 Samuel 7:12-14, Isaiah 9:7). *That* is the promise that Israel was waiting for. Yet, in order for God's promise to be fulfilled, Jesus could not *cease to be* at his crucifixion. Jesus had to live forever.

> "The people answered [Jesus, saying], **We have heard out of the law that Christ abideth for ever**: and how sayest thou, The Son of man must be lifted up (*i.e.,* crucified)?" (John 12:33-34)

God's promise was not negated when Christ died, but it was rather fulfilled through Christ's resurrection, by which resurrection Christ even now continues to reign.

God *also* promised an *everlasting priest* who would redeem Israel from their sins. This promise was fulfilled by Christ's resurrection as well.

> "For he (God) testifieth, Thou (Christ) art a priest **for ever** after the order of Melchisedec. ... By so much was Jesus made a surety of a better testament. And [the Levites] truly were many priests, because they were not suffered to continue by reason of death: But this man, because **he continueth ever**, hath an unchangeable priesthood. Wherefore he is able also to save them to the uttermost that come unto God by him, seeing **he ever liveth** to make intercession for them." (Hebrews 7:17, 22-25)

For Christ to be a priest forever, he had to rise from the dead. The author of Hebrews refers to the resurrection as a fulfillment of Psalm 2, just as Paul did in Acts 13:32-33.

> "So also Christ glorified not himself to be made an high priest; but he that said unto him, Thou art my Son, **today have I begotten thee**. As he saith also in another place, Thou art a priest **for ever** after the order of Melchisedec." (Hebrews 5:5-6)

The writer clearly shows that the quotation, "Thou art my Son, today have I begotten thee," is intricately joined to the fact that Christ would live forever. This is because "this day have I begotten thee" truly is a reference to the resurrection of Christ into immortality.

Philo on Being Begotten of God

Philo talks about how men are not begotten of God in regard to their earthly nature.

> "And God created man, taking a lump of clay from the earth, and breathed into his face the breath of life: and man became a living soul." The races of men are twofold; for one is the heavenly man, and the other the earthly man. Now the heavenly man, as being born in the image of God, has no participation in any corruptible or earthlike essence. But the earthly man is made of loose material, which he calls a lump of clay. On which account he says, not that the heavenly man was made, but that he was fashioned according to the image of God; but the earthly man he calls a thing made, and not begotten (γέννημα) by the maker.[190]

Philo contrasts the "earthly man" with the "heavenly man," asserting that the latter is "begotten" by God. Philo uses much allegory in his writings, and I am not asserting that his works are on par with Scripture, but it is interesting that we find similar terminology to that of Philo's heavenly man and earthly man within the writings of Paul (though not used by Paul in allegorical fashion).

Paul speaks of the earthy man as our present bodies, but the heavenly man as our bodies to come at the resurrection.

> "But now hath Christ been raised from the dead, the firstfruits of them that are asleep. For since by man came death, by man came also the resurrection of the dead. For as in Adam all die, so also in Christ shall all be made alive. But each in his own order: Christ the firstfruits; then they that are Christ's, at his coming. ... But some one will say, How are the dead raised? and with what manner of body do they come? ... The first man is of the earth, earthy: the second man is of heaven. As is the earthy, such are they also that are earthy: and as is the heavenly, such are they also that are heavenly. And as we have borne the image of the earthy, we shall also bear the image of the heavenly."
>
> (1 Corinthians 15:20-23, 35, 44-49 ASV)

So, in the *terminology* of Philo—applied somewhat differently than by other Jews of his day—the heavenly man is "begotten of God," but the earthly man is not.

> "[We] which have the first-fruits of the Spirit, even we ourselves groan within ourselves, **waiting for the adoption**, to wit, **the redemption of our body**." (Romans 8:23)

In one sense we are "now" Sons of God, yet in another sense we are still "waiting for the adoption" that will occur at the resurrection (*i.e.,* "the redemption of our body").

> "For our conversation is in heaven; from whence also we look for the Saviour, the Lord Jesus Christ: Who shall change our vile body, that it may be fashioned like unto his glorious body, according to the working whereby he is able even to subdue all things unto himself." (Philippians 3:20-21)

Romans 1:4 – Appointed Son of God by Resurrection

When describing our resurrected state, Paul says:

> "So also is the resurrection of the dead. It [the body] is sown in corruption; it is raised in incorruption: It is sown in dishonour; it is raised in glory: it is sown in weakness; it is raised **in** (ἐν) **power** (δυνάμει): It is sown a natural body; it is raised a spiritual body."
> (1 Corinthians 15:42-44)

The same Greek phrase, ἐν δυνάμει (*en dunamei*), that is translated here as "in power" is also translated "in power" when *Christ's* resurrection is described.

> "[Christ] who through the Spirit of holiness was appointed the Son of God **in power** [ἐν δυνάμει] by his resurrection from the dead: Jesus Christ our Lord." (Romans 1:4 NIV, brackets and bold mine)

Paul is here contrasting the weakness of Jesus' pre-resurrection body with the empowered condition of the post-resurrection body.

> "For though he was crucified through weakness, yet **he liveth by the power of God** (ζῇ ἐκ δυνάμεως θεοῦ)." (2 Corinthians 13:4)

This phrase "by the power of God" uses the Greek preposition ἐκ (ek), which, according to the *Strong's Concordance*, is "a primary preposition denoting *origin* (the point *whence* action or motion proceeds)."[191] After Jesus died, the life he now has *came from* the miraculous power of God.

Jesus was *appointed* to this life from God subsequent death because he lived in holiness prior to death, according to a spirit of holiness.

> "[Christ] who **through the Spirit of holiness** [κατὰ πνεῦμα ἁγιωσύνης] was appointed the Son of God in power by his resurrection from the dead: Jesus Christ our Lord." (Romans 1:4 NIV, brackets and bold mine)

When Paul says Christ was appointed the Son of God according to *a*[192] *spirit of holiness* (πνεῦμα ἁγιωσύνης), this is *different* than when the Bible says *Holy Spirit* (πνεῦμα ἅγιον) elsewhere. The phrase we find in Romans 1:4 is a *genitive of quality*, "and contains the specific character of the πνεῦμα."[193] So, a spirit—think of *spirit* here as *mindset*—that has the character of holiness was the basis for Jesus being appointed Son of God at his resurrection. That is, because his spirit was governed by holiness, Jesus was declared the Son of God in power at the resurrection. The antithesis of *spirit of holiness* (spirit governed by holiness), is found in Romans 8:3, where we find Jesus had "the likeness of sinful flesh." Here the phrase "sinful flesh" (σαρκὸς ἁμαρτίας) is also a *genitive of quality*, denoting *flesh that is governed by sin*. Jesus had the same flesh as we do (Hebrews 2:14), but though his flesh was *like* the flesh governed by sin, Jesus' flesh, being the same nature as ours, was not governed by sin, but was kept under subjection by his spirit. This is precisely what we must do as well. And there is a *parallel* made in Romans between Christ and us in this regard.

- "Concerning his Son Jesus Christ our Lord, which was made of the seed of David **according to the flesh** (κατὰ σάρκα); And declared to be the Son of God with power, **according to the spirit of holiness** (κατὰ πνεῦμα ἁγιωσύνης), by the resurrection from the dead." (Romans 1:3-4)

- "For they that are **after the flesh** (κατὰ σάρκα) do mind the things of the flesh; but they that are **after the Spirit** (κατὰ πνεῦμα) the things of the Spirit. ... Therefore, brethren, we are debtors, not to the flesh, to live **after the flesh** (κατὰ σάρκα). For if ye live **after the flesh** (κατὰ σάρκα), ye shall die: but if ye **through the Spirit** (πνεύματι) do mortify the deeds of the body, ye shall live. For as many as are **led by the Spirit of God**, they are the sons of God." (Romans 8:5, 12-14)

The 4th century Latin Vulgate wording of Romans 1:4 is interesting.

> "Who was **predestinated** (*praedestinatus*) the Son of God in power, according to the spirit of sanctification, **from** (*ex*) the resurrection of our Lord Jesus Christ from the dead."
> (Romans 1:4 Vulgate)

This reading says Jesus was "predestinated the Son of God in power ... from the resurrection." This is also how we find the text quoted by Irenaeus in the 2nd century.[194] This agrees with the conclusions we have made thus far in this chapter.

Alexander of Alexandria relates the views of Arius and those with him as follows (notice the excellent "therefore" point from Hebrews 1:9):

> "We are also able," say these accursed wretches, "to become like Him, the sons of God; for it is written,—I have nourished and brought up children." When the continuation of this text is brought before them, which is, "and they have rebelled against Me," and it is objected that these words are inconsistent with the Saviour's nature, which is immutable, they throw aside all reverence, and affirm that God foreknew and foresaw that His Son would not rebel against Him, and that He therefore chose Him in preference to all

others. They likewise assert that He was not chosen because He had by nature any thing superior to the other sons of God; for no man, say they, is son of God by nature, nor has any peculiar relation to Him. He was chosen, they allege, because, though mutable by nature, His painstaking character suffered no deterioration. ... To establish this insane doctrine they insult the Scriptures, and bring forward what is said in the Psalms of Christ, "Thou hast loved righteousness and hated iniquity, **therefore** thy God hath anointed thee with the oil of gladness above thy fellows."[195]

John 10:17-18 – Jesus Laid Down His Life Daily

Many say that Christ was speaking of an ability to raise himself from the dead in John 10:17-18, where he says:

> "I lay my life down for the sheep ... Therefore doth my Father love me, because I lay down my life, that I might take it again. No man taketh it from me, but I lay it down of myself. I have power to lay it down, and I have power to take it up again. This commandment have I received of my Father." (John 10:15, 17-18)

When Christ said these things, he was not referring *exclusively* to his death and resurrection, instead he was referring to the laying aside of his own personal interests in general. The Bible compares the way that Christ laid down his life for us with the way that we should lay down our lives for the brethren, saying:

> "He laid down his life for us: and we ought to lay down our lives for the brethren." (1 John 3:16)

Do you see how this passage *parallels* the way in which Christ laid down his life for us with the way that we ought to lay down our lives for one another? When Jesus spoke of laying down *his* life, he said:

> "No man taketh it from me, but I **lay it down** (θεῖναι) of myself." (John 10:18)

The exact same Greek word that is translated as "lay down" in Christ's statement, θεῖναι (*theinai*), is also used when 1 John 3:16 says we ought to lay down our own lives, saying:

> "We ought to **lay down** (θεῖναι) our lives for the brethren."
> (1 John 3:16)

It is obvious that this isn't speaking exclusively of *dying* for the brethren when we look at the context.

> "By this we know love,[196] because he laid down his life for us. And we also ought to lay down our lives for the brethren. But whoever has this world's goods, and sees his brother in need, and shuts up his heart from him, how does the love of God abide in him?"
> (1 John 3:16-17 NKJV)

The *losing of* or *laying down of* one's life is not an exclusive reference to death, but it is instead spoken of in regard to laying aside one's own personal self-interests in general. In that sense, Christ laid down his own life on a daily basis.

Contextually, Christ's statement about laying down his life coincided with his analogy of a shepherd laying down his life for his sheep whenever a wolf attacks. Since that is obviously a life and death situation, some might think that Christ was referring specifically to physical death, as when a shepherd gets killed by a wolf when attempting to defend his sheep. Indeed, Jesus *does* contextually speak of laying down his life when the wolf attacks, saying:

> "I am the good shepherd: the good shepherd giveth his life for the sheep. But he that is an hireling, and not the shepherd, whose own the sheep are not, seeth the wolf coming, and leaveth the sheep, and fleeth: and the wolf catcheth them, and scattereth the sheep."
> (John 10:11-12)

Howbeit, it is just this text, when understood correctly, that will show that Christ was *not* speaking exclusively of dying for the sheep. A shepherd does not go to the wolf with the intention of dying. In fact, if the wolf kills the shepherd, that could leave the sheep without any remaining protection at all. While a shepherd laying down his life for his sheep does include the *possibility* that the wolf would kill him, it does not demand that outcome.

In *Barnes' Notes on the New Testament,* Albert Barnes comments on the manner in which the shepherd gives his life for the sheep, saying:

> **Giveth his life** – A shepherd that regarded his flock would hazard his own life to defend them. When the wolf comes, he would still remain to protect them. To *give his life,* here, means the same as not to fly, or to forsake his flock; to be willing to expose his life, if necessary, to defend them.[197]

The *climax* of Christ laying down his own life was indeed the cross, but that does not negate the fact that Christ also set aside his life for us *prior* to that event. Even before the cross Christ was already laying down his life for his sheep, denying his own self-interests in order to save others.

Jesus was *not* speaking of a *future* event in John 10:14-18 when he referred to laying down his own life. He didn't speak in the *future tense,* so as to say:

> "I **will lay** down my life."

Instead, he always spoke in the *present tense,* saying:

- "I **lay** (τίθημι – present active indicative) down my life for the sheep." (John 10:15)

- "Therefore doth the Father love me, because I **lay** (τίθημι – present active indicative) down my life." (John 10:17)

- No man taketh it from me but I **lay** (τίθημι – present active indicative) it down of myself." (John 10:18)

Christ was laying down his own life all along. Furthermore, when he said that no one takes his life (John 10:18), he *couldn't* have been referring exclusively to his crucifixion, because when he was crucified someone *did take* his life.

> "He was led like a sheep to the slaughter; and like a lamb dumb before his shearer, so opened he not his mouth: In his humiliation his judgment was taken away: and who shall declare his generation? For **his life is taken** from the earth." (Acts 8:32-33)

When Jesus spoke of laying down his life, he was referring to his own freewill choice to abandon his life in this world in order to seek and to save that which was lost. The self-denying life that Christ now lived was not forced upon him by default, but it was instead something that he *chose* to accept. If he wanted to then he could have taken this life up again. This is why he said:

> "I lay it down on my own initiative. I have freedom to lay it down, and I have freedom to take it up again." (John 10:18[198])

The word I translate here as "freedom" (or "power" in the KJV) is the Greek word ἐξουσία (*exousia*), which is given the following definition in the *Strong's Concordance*:

> **ἐξουσία** - (in the sense of *ability*); *privilege, i.e.* (subj.) *force, capacity, competency, freedom,* or (obj.) *mastery* (concr. *magistrate, superhuman, potentate, token of control*), **delegated influence**.[199]

The definition for the word ἐξουσία simply refers to *ability* (in one respect or another). The emphasis of John 10:18 is focused upon Christ's *freewill ability to choose* to lay down his life or to take it again. This is obvious because of how Jesus begins his statement, saying:

> "I lay it down on my own initiative..." (John 10:18 NASB)

Christ was not speaking of the *ability to raise himself from the dead,* but he was instead referring to his own *ability to choose* whether or not he would lay down his life as a whole. Jesus had to choose to obey God, even as we do. The choice that he made to lay down his life was actually a choice to obey God,[200] because God *commanded* Jesus to lay down his life, which is why he says:

> "No one has taken it away from me, but I lay it down on **my own initiative**. I have freedom to lay it down, and I have freedom to take it up again. This **commandment** I received from my Father."
> (John 10:18)

In fact, Christ's relationship with God was *dependent* upon his obedience to God. Jesus himself showed this, saying:

> "**If** you obey my commands, you will remain in my love, **just as** I have obeyed my Father's commands and remain in his love."
> (John 15:10 NIV)

The Father continued to love Christ *because of* Christ's obedience to the Father's commandments. This principle also applies to how Christ obeyed God by laying down his life, which is why Jesus says:

> "For this reason the Father loves me, because I lay down my life ... This commandment I received from my Father."
> (John 10:17-18 NASB)

Jesus also showed how his obedience to God was the reason why the Father did not *leave* him, saying:

> "And he that has sent me is with me; he has not left me alone, **because** I do always the things that are pleasing to him."
> (John 8:29 Darby)

Jesus even showed that he had to obey the commandment of God in order to partake of life everlasting as well, saying:

> "For I have not spoken of myself; but the Father which sent me, **he gave me a commandment**, what I should say, and what I should speak. And I know that **his commandment is life everlasting**: whatsoever I speak **therefore**, even as the Father said unto me, so I speak." (John 12:49-50)

God commanded Christ to lay down his life for the sheep. Jesus refused to take up his life in this present world so that he would be able to take up the eternal life that was to come.

Jesus told his disciples:

> "He that findeth his life shall lose it: and he that loseth his life for my sake shall find it." (Matthew 10:39)

And again, he says:

> "He that loveth his life shall lose it; and he that hateth his life in this world shall keep it unto life eternal." (John 12:25)

This is the equivalent of Jesus' words:

> "I lay down my life, that I might take it again." (John 10:17)

When he says, "I lay down my life, **that** I might take it again," he is referring to the laying down of his life in this world so that he could take it up again in the eternal life.

God Raised Others from the Dead through Christ

It was God who raised Christ from the dead, but God also gave Christ the authority to raise others from the dead as well.

> "[Jesus] called Lazarus out of his grave, and raised him from the dead." (John 12:17)

Christ gave that same ability (which God gave to him) to his disciples, sending them out with the following commission:

> "Heal the sick, cleanse the lepers, **raise the dead**, cast out devils: freely ye have received, freely give." (Matthew 10:8)

Although the disciples could raise the dead (which shows that miracles don't make a person God), we should not assume that they had this ability independent of Christ. Neither should we suppose that Christ had that same ability independent of God.

God *gave* Christ the ability to raise men from the dead:

> "For as the Father raiseth up the dead, and quickeneth them; even so the Son quickeneth whom he will. ... For as the Father hath life in himself; so hath he **given** to the Son to have life in himself."
>
> (John 5:21, 26)

It was the power of God working *through* Christ that gave him the authority to do such things.

Peter shows that God was the source of Christ's miracles, saying:

> "Ye men of Israel, hear these words; Jesus of Nazareth, a man approved of God among you by miracles and wonders and signs, which **God did by him** in the midst of you, as ye yourselves also know." (Acts 2:22)

This scripture, as well as several others, show us that it was God's power working through Christ which gave him the authority to do miraculous deeds. Therefore, since God is the *source* of Christ's miracles, whenever we see certain passages of Scripture that refer to *Christ* raising men from the dead, we should understand that this was accomplished by God's power working *through* Christ.

The Scriptures Call Jesus a Prophet

There are primarily two passages of Scripture that allegedly say Jesus would raise himself from the dead. We already discussed one of these passages under the subheading *John 10:17-18 – Jesus Laid Down His Life Daily.* The second passage is John 2:19, which says:

> "Jesus answered and said unto them, Destroy this temple, and in three days I will raise it up." (John 2:19)

God was actually speaking *through* Christ in this passage, declaring that *he* would resurrect the temple of Christ's body after it was destroyed (*i.e.*, crucified).[201] Yet, the context shows *Jesus* speaking these words, so how could God have spoken this? We will discuss this passage more as we proceed, but we must first acknowledge a certain scriptural truth, namely, that *Christ was a prophet.* This factor is critical in correctly understanding this particular resurrection text. How do we know that Jesus was a prophet? Do the Scriptures specifically refer to Christ as a prophet? Yes indeed.

Jesus' own disciples said:

> "**Jesus of Nazareth was a prophet** mighty in deed and word before God and all the people." (Luke 24:19)

God also refers to Christ as a prophet while speaking to Moses in Deuteronomy 18:17-19, which says:

> "And the LORD said unto me (Moses), They have well spoken that which they have spoken. I will raise them up a **Prophet** from among their brethren, **like unto thee**, and will put my words in his mouth; and he shall speak unto them all that I shall command him (*c.f.* John 12:49). And it shall come to pass, that whosoever will not hearken unto my words which he shall speak in my name, I will require it of him." (Deuteronomy 18:17-19)

Peter shows that this coming prophet was Jesus, saying:

> "And he (God) shall send Jesus Christ, which before was preached unto you ... For Moses truly said unto the fathers, A **prophet** shall the Lord your God **raise up unto you** of your brethren, like unto me; him shall ye hear in all things whatsoever he shall say unto you. And it shall come to pass, that every soul, which will not hear that **prophet**, shall be destroyed from among the people. ... Unto you first God, **having raised up his Son Jesus**, sent him to bless you, in turning away every one of you from his iniquities."
> (Acts 3:20, 22-23, 26)

Hence, Jesus is the fulfillment of God's promise to send a prophet like Moses.

- Jesus did not correct the woman at the well when she said to him:

    "I perceive that thou art a prophet." (John 4:19)

- The crowds called Jesus a prophet (Matthew 21:11, Luke 7:16).

There can be no doubt that Christ was truly referred to as a prophet by those who knew him. In fact, Jesus even refers to himself as a prophet:

- When Jesus "**was come into his own country**" (Matthew 13:54) the people did not receive him; "And they were offended in him. But Jesus said unto them, A **prophet** is not without honour, save **in his own country**." (Matthew 13:57)

- When Jesus was on his way to Jerusalem to be crucified, some Pharisees tried to get him to flee by saying that Herod would kill him, but Jesus said, "I must walk today, and tomorrow, and the day following: for it cannot be that a **prophet** perish out of Jerusalem." (Luke 13:31-33)

Jesus Christ, even according to his own proclamations, was truly a prophet. So then, what *is* a prophet? A prophet is, although not exclusively, someone who speaks God's words. Christ fits this description perfectly, because it is clearly stated in the Scriptures that Christ "speaketh the words of God." (John 3:34.) With that being said, when God's words would come to the prophets in the Old Testament, they would speak the words of God in the *first-person narrative.* There are hundreds of examples of this throughout Isaiah, Jeremiah, Ezekiel, etc. God spoke through the prophets of old in the first-person narrative and God *also* spoke through Christ in the same way:

> "God who at sundry times and in divers manners spake in time past unto the fathers by the prophets, Hath in these last days spoken unto us by his Son." (Hebrews 1:1-2)

If God spoke through Christ in the same way that he spoke through the Old Testament prophets,[202] why is it that every time God has spoken through Christ some assume that Christ must have spoken those things concerning himself?

John 2:19 – Jesus Raised Himself from the Dead?

It was God's words that Christ spoke when he said:

> "Destroy this temple, and in three days I will raise it up." (John 2:19)

In this passage, *God* is speaking *through Christ* concerning the raising of the temple of Christ's body.

Someone might object to this conclusion since the introduction to God's declaration says:

> "**Jesus answered and said unto them**, Destroy this temple, and in three days I will raise it up." (John 2:19)

Indeed, Christ *did* speak these words. However, the question is *not* whether or not Christ *spoke* the words, but the question is *rather* whether the words that Christ spoke were God's words or his own. The author of the Gospel of John only states that Jesus *said* these words, and that does *not* eliminate the possibility that they were the prophetic words of God. In fact, it is normal for the author of John to record the words of God as the sayings of the prophet through whom God spoke.

Compare the styles of Paul and the author of the Gospel of John in the following examples.

Paul shows that *God* spoke *through Isaiah* when he says:

> "Well **spake the Holy Ghost by Esaias** the prophet unto our fathers, Saying, Go unto this people, and say, Hearing ye shall hear, and shall not understand; and seeing ye shall see, and not perceive: For the heart of this people is waxed gross, and their ears are dull of hearing, and their eyes have they closed; lest they should see with their eyes, and hear with their ears, and understand with their heart, and should be converted, and **I** [God] **should heal them**."
> (Acts 28:25-27)

And yet the author of John records these words from Isaiah 6:9-10 as having been spoken ***by Isaiah***:

> "Therefore they could not believe, because that **Esaias said** again, He hath blinded their eyes, and hardened their heart; that they should not see with their eyes, nor understand with their heart, and be converted, and **I** [God] **should heal them**." (John 12:39-40)

Just as Isaiah said, "**I** should heal them," though he was evidently speaking the words of God, so also Jesus said, "I will raise it up," while speaking the words of God as well.

The fact that God spoke through Christ in John 2:19 is also implied *grammatically,* because the *active* voice of the verb used in John 2:19 does not match the *passive* voice of the verb used in John 2:22.

- John 2:19 says, "...in three days **I will raise** (ἐγερῶ) it."

    Here, the Greek verb ἐγερῶ (egeirō) is in the *active voice,* which shows that the speaker is *performing* the resurrection.

- John 2:22 says, "...therefore **he was raised** (ἠγέρθη) from the dead." (ASV)

    Here, the verb is in the *passive voice,* ἠγέρθη (egerthe). The passive voice shows Jesus *receiving* the resurrection.

The author of John could have easily written, "Therefore **he raised himself** from the dead," using an active verb with a reflexive pronoun to show that Christ was both the initiator and recipient of the action (as he does two verses later in John 2:24, etc.). However, that was not the point he was trying to convey (and that point is not conveyed anywhere else in the Bible either). God performed the action (hence the active voice is used in John 2:19) and Christ received the action (hence the passive voice is used in John 2:22).

Further proof that Christ was speaking God's words in John 2:19 is also found in John 2:22, which says:

> "When therefore he was raised from the dead, his disciples remembered that he spake this; and **they believed the scripture**, and the word which Jesus had said." (John 2:22 ASV)

What scripture was it that the disciples believed regarding Christ's resurrection? Does the scripture that the disciples believed speak of Jesus resurrecting himself? Or does it speak of God resurrecting Jesus instead?

Albert Barnes accurately shows which scripture it was that the disciples believed in his commentary on this verse, saying:

> **They believed the scripture** – The Old Testament, which predicted his resurrection. **Reference here must be made to Psalm 16:10**, comp. Acts 2:27-32, Acts 13:35-37; Psalm 2:7, comp. Acts 13:33. They understood those scriptures in a sense different from what they did before.[203]

Albert Barnes correctly states that the scripture believed by the disciples was Psalm 16:10, which says:

> "For thou wilt not leave my soul in hell; neither wilt thou suffer thine Holy One to see corruption." (Psalm 16:10)

This is *precisely* the passage that the disciples refer to immediately after Christ's resurrection, saying:

> "For David speaketh concerning him [Jesus], I foresaw the Lord always before my face, for he is on my right hand, that I should not be moved: Therefore did my heart rejoice, and my tongue was glad; moreover also my flesh shall rest in hope: Because thou wilt not leave my soul in hell, neither wilt thou suffer thine Holy One to see corruption. Thou hast made known to me the ways of life; thou shalt make me full of joy with thy countenance."
> (Acts 2:25-28 KJV)

Now, someone may think that the disciples were quoting David's words as if they applied to David himself, but they were not. David spoke Christ's words prophetically in the first-person narrative. The disciples showed that these words were prophetic concerning Christ's resurrection.

> "Men and brethren, let me freely speak unto you of the patriarch David, that he is both dead and buried, and his sepulcher is with us unto this day. Therefore being a prophet, and knowing that God had sworn with an oath to him, that of the fruit of his loins, according to the flesh, he would raise up Christ to sit on his throne; He seeing this before **spake of the resurrection of Christ**, that **his** soul was not left in hell, neither **his** flesh did see corruption. **This Jesus hath God raised up**, whereof we all are witnesses."
> (Acts 2:29-31)

Thus, it was Christ who said:

> "My flesh shall rest in hope: Because thou wilt not leave my soul in hell, neither wilt thou suffer thine Holy One to see corruption."
> (Psalm 16:10, Acts 2:26-27)

The fact that *this* is the passage of Scripture that the disciples believed (and thus quoted) after Christ's resurrection is very important, because it clearly demonstrates that Christ was *dependent upon God* for his resurrection.

Look again at what Christ says:

> "My flesh shall rest in hope: **Because thou** [God] wilt not leave my soul in hell, **neither wilt thou** [God] suffer thine Holy One to see corruption." (Psalm 16:10, Acts 2:26-27)

By these words it is manifestly evident that Christ was dependent upon God to resurrect his body. Would Christ really have said such things if he could raise *himself* from the dead? No. Instead, it was *God* who spoke *through* Christ in John 2:19, saying, "I will raise it up." And after Christ was raised, John 2:22 says that the disciples remembered those words and believed a scripture (Psalm 16:10) which showed God raising a dependent Christ from the grave.

Christ was entirely dependent upon God to raise him from the dead, as the Scriptures say:

> "[Jesus] offered up prayers and supplications with strong crying and tears unto him that was able to save him from death, and was heard in that he feared." (Hebrews 5:7)

God Raised Christ from the Dead

The fact that God raised Christ from the dead is a fundamental truth that is attested to throughout the Bible. Notice how the writers of the New Testament often rehearse the fact that Christ was resurrected by God.

- "The Prince of life, whom God hath raised from the dead; whereof we are witnesses." (Acts 3:15)

- "Jesus Christ of Nazareth, whom ye crucified, whom God raised from the dead." (Acts 4:10)

- "Him God raised up the third day, and shewed him openly." (Acts 10:40)

- "But God raised him from the dead." (Acts 13:30)

- "He that raised up Christ from the dead shall also quicken your mortal bodies." (Romans 8:11)

- "That if thou shalt confess with thy mouth the Lord Jesus, and shalt believe in thine heart that God hath raised him from the dead, thou shalt be saved." (Romans 10:9)

- "We have testified of God that he raised up Christ." (1 Corinthians 15:15)

- "Knowing that he which raised up the Lord Jesus shall raise up us also by Jesus." (2 Corinthians 4:14)

- "God, who hath raised him from the dead …" (Colossians 2:12)

- "Ye turned to God from idols to serve the living and true God; And to wait for his Son from heaven, whom he raised from the dead, even Jesus." (1 Thessalonians 1:9-10)

- "Who by him do believe in God, that raised him up from the dead, and gave him glory; that your faith and hope might be in God." (1 Peter 1:21)

And the Scriptures even specifically say that it was "the Father" who raised Christ from the dead.

- "Jesus Christ, and God the Father, who raised him from the dead."
(Galatians 1:1)

The Son of God was resurrected by God, the Father. This is the testimony of Scripture.

Did the Resurrection Prove Christ was Divine?

There is an erroneous argument circulating these days that says Christ's resurrection, in and of itself, proved that Jesus was God himself. Yet, how is that in any way a valid argument? I really do not see any grounds for making such a claim. We too shall be raised from the dead, but that does not make us divine.

The difference in Christ's resurrection and our own is in regard to *timing,* not divinity.

> "But now is Christ risen from the dead, and become the **firstfruits** of them that slept. For since by man came death, by man came also the resurrection of the dead... But every man in his own **order**: **Christ the firstfruits; afterwards they that are Christ's** at his coming." (1 Corinthians 15:20-21, 23 KJV)

Our resurrection will not prove that we are divine and Christ's resurrection did not prove that he was divine either.

Chapter Ten
Created Christ & New Creation

As believers, we are looking forward to "new heavens and a new earth, wherein dwelleth righteousness." (2 Peter 3:13.) This is the new and coming creation of God that the saints will inhabit for all eternity. God said, "I create new heavens and a new earth." (Isaiah 65:17.) Correspondingly, the inhabitants of New Earth will be new creations as well. In this chapter, we will discuss passages that say Christ is the beginning of God's creation as well as texts that speak of this new creation as a whole being made through Christ.

Revelation 3:14 – Beginning of the Creation

Christ clearly describes himself as the beginning of the creation of God in Revelation 3:14, saying:

> "And unto the angel of the church of the Laodiceans write; These things saith the Amen, the faithful and true witness, **the beginning of the creation of God**." (Revelation 3:14)

The meaning of this passage is obvious—Christ is the beginning, the first part, of the creation of God.

When Christ says that he is the "beginning of the creation of God" in Revelation 3:14, the word translated as "beginning" is the Greek word ἀρχή (*arche*, pronounced ar-khay'). When standing on its own, without any constricting factors, ἀρχή simply means *beginning*. Since there is nothing to constrict the meaning of ἀρχή in Revelation 3:14, Christ literally declares himself to be the "the *beginning* of the creation of God."

Henry A. Alford, a 19th century New Testament scholar, acknowledges the uninhibited significance of the word ἀρχή in Revelation 3:14, saying:

> The mere word ἀρχή would admit the meaning that Christ is the first created being.[204]

The word ἀρχή is used in a partitive genitive construction in Revelation 3:14. The partitive genitive phrase, "beginning of the creation of God," leaves no doubt that Christ is truly the first part of God's creation. Throughout the entirety of the New Testament, *wherever* the word ἀρχή is followed by a genitive phrase ("beginning of the _____"), that which is called the ἀρχή is *always* included as *part, the first part*, of the category that follows *without exception* (See Appendix C). If consistency means anything, as it should, this is very strong evidence that Jesus is included in God's creation.

Here are a few of the many examples demonstrating how the word ἀρχή, when presented in a partitive genitive phrase, is included as part of the specified group or category:

- "A land which the LORD thy God careth for: the eyes of the LORD thy God are always upon it, from the **beginning (ἀρχή) of the year** even unto the end of the year." (Deuteronomy 11:12 LXX.) The beginning of the year is the first part of the year.

- "So Gideon, and the hundred men that were with him, came unto the outside of the camp in the **beginning (ἀρχή) of the middle watch**; and they had but newly set the watch: and they blew the trumpets, and brake the pitchers that were in their hands." (Judges 7:19 LXX.) The beginning of the watch is the first part of the watch.

- "The **beginning (ἀρχή) of the gospel** of Jesus Christ, the Son of God." (Mark 1:1.) The beginning of the gospel (written by Mark) is the first part of the gospel (it is the first sentence).

- "This **beginning (ἀρχή) of miracles** did Jesus in Cana of Galilee, and manifested forth his glory; and his disciples believed on him." (John

2:11.) <u>The beginning of miracles (changing the water into wine) was the first public miracle recorded in the Gospel of John and is included among the category of miracles.</u>

- "And saying, Where is the promise of his coming? for since the fathers fell asleep, all things continue as they were from the **beginning** (ἀρχή) **of the creation**." (2 Peter 3:4.) <u>The beginning of creation is included among creation and is therefore a part of creation as well.</u>

- "These things saith the Amen, the faithful and true witness, **the beginning** (ἀρχή) **of the creation of God**." (Revelation 3:14.) <u>The beginning of creation is included among creation and is therefore a part of creation as well (hence the speaker, Christ, was created).</u>

Although the meaning of ἀρχή is universally accepted in those other texts, some, due to their theological positions, have rejected the meaning of ἀρχή in Revelation 3:14. Many will not allow Christ to say that he is the "beginning of the creation of God," asserting that ἀρχή should be translated as something other than "beginning" in this passage. While there are rare occasions when the word ἀρχή (being restricted by the context) does carry a meaning other than *beginning*, it *never* does so *anywhere* in the New Testament when it is used in the partitive genitive construction (as in Revelation 3:14). Hence, when Christ is said to be the "ἀρχή of the creation of God" this is very strong evidence that the biblical Christ is also a part, the first part, of God's creation.

Albert Barnes made the following concession in regard to Christ's statement in Revelation 3:14:

> If it were demonstrated from other sources that Christ was, in fact, a created being, and the first that God had made, it cannot be denied that this language would appropriately express that fact.[205]

Albert Barnes shows that Revelation 3:14 "undeniably" contains grammatical language that may "appropriately" express the fact that Christ was the first of God's creation. And indeed it does. The fact that Christ is the beginning of God's creation is the obvious and literal meaning of this text.

Colossians 1:15 – Firstborn of All Creation

In Colossians 1:15 we see a clear affirmation of the created origin of Christ. The best translation of this text into English reads as follows:

> "He is the image of the invisible God, **the firstborn of all creation**." (Colossians 1:15 NASB, ASV, Darby)

The phrase translated here as "the firstborn of all creation" literally reads like this in the Greek:

> πρωτότοκος πάσης κτίσεως
>   firstborn   of all   creation (Colossians 1:15)

This little three-word phrase is both simple and conclusive. Christ is the firstborn of all creation. This phrase "firstborn of all creation" is a partitive genitive construction, which grammatically shows that the subject is part of and included in the category of things mentioned.

Some theologians have completely fabricated an alternative, non-literal[206] definition of the word πρωτότοκος (prōtotokos) in an attempt to avoid the literal conclusion demanded in this text. In support of their claim that πρωτότοκος doesn't mean *firstborn*, they say that the Bible sometimes uses the word *firstborn* in such a way that actually *requires* a non-literal definition. And therefore (by claiming that there are other non-literal examples of *firstborn* within the Bible) they assert that *firstborn* does not necessarily have to be understood literally in Colossians 1:15 either. Out of the *one hundred and sixteen* times that the word "firstborn" appears in the Bible (KJV), there are typically only *five* proposed examples from the Old Testament, and only one example from the New Testament, where *firstborn* is said to be non-literal. The five Old Testament passages proposed as containing a non-literal usage of *firstborn* are Exodus 4:22, Job 18:13, Psalm 89:27, Isaiah 14:30, and Jeremiah 31:9 (See Appendix D for a detailed discussion proving that *firstborn* actually retains its meaning in all of these OT texts). The only *New* Testament text proposed by Trinitarians as contextually requiring a non-literal definition of *firstborn* is Colossians 1:18, which says:

> "And [Christ] is the head of the body, the church: who is the beginning, the **firstborn from the dead**; that in all things he might have the preeminence." (Colossians 1:18 KJV)

It has been argued that Paul couldn't have used the word *firstborn* literally in Colossians 1:18, because he says Jesus was "the firstborn from the dead." Jesus was not literally the first person who was raised from the dead in the Bible, so how can "firstborn from the dead" apply to him in a literal way? It is true that many people (like Lazarus) were *raised* from the dead, but no one, other than Christ, has been *born* from the dead. The former is temporary, when a person is raised back to life from the dead in their same mortal body only to die again. The latter is the *final* resurrection from the dead, when a person's body is changed and they become immortal. Being "born" from the dead (which is what Colossians 1:18 actually says) implies more than merely being revived (c.f. Luke 20:36).

Whenever Paul speaks of the resurrection from the dead (as in Colossians 1:15) he is almost always referring to the final resurrection rather than the temporal one. Notice what he says:

> "So also is **the resurrection of the dead**. It (the body) is sown in corruption; it is raised in incorruption: It is sown in dishonour; it is raised in glory: it is sown in weakness; it is raised in power: It is sown a natural body; it is raised a spiritual body. Behold, I shew you a mystery; We shall not all sleep, but we shall all be changed, In a moment, in the twinkling of an eye, at the last trump: for the trumpet shall sound, and **the dead shall be raised incorruptible**, and we shall be changed. For this corruptible must put on incorruption, and this mortal must **put on immortality**."
> (1 Corinthians 15:42-44, 51-53)

Paul says that at "the resurrection of the dead" (in reference to the final resurrection) we will put on immortality. When we acknowledge the *kind* of resurrection being described by Paul (when a person's body puts on immortality), we see that Christ is the first one who was resurrected from the dead in such a way:

> "But now is Christ risen from the dead, and become the firstfruits of them that slept. For since by man came death, by man came also the resurrection of the dead. For as in Adam all die, even so in Christ shall all be made alive. But every man in his own *order*: Christ the **firstfruits; afterward** they that are Christ's at his coming." (1 Corinthians 15:20-23)

And again, Paul says:

> "Having therefore obtained help of God, I continue unto this day, witnessing both to small and great, saying none other things than those which the prophets and Moses did say should come: That Christ should suffer, and that he should be the **first** that should rise from the dead, and should shew light unto the people, and to the Gentiles." (Acts 26:22-23)

Christ was the first who was raised from the dead in immortality. So then, since Paul is referring to the final resurrection, not a temporal one, even if we read the text as "first-raised from the dead" rather than "firstborn from the dead," Jesus is still, literally, first. Christ is literally the firstborn from the dead and thus *firstborn* is used literally in Colossians 1:18.

In light of Paul's literal usage of the word *firstborn* in Colossians 1:**18**, where he says "firstborn from the dead," we should ask why Paul would have used the exact same term in a non-literal sense *three verses earlier* in Colossians 1:**15**, where he says "firstborn of all creation." He would not ... He did not. When Paul says that Christ is "the firstborn of all creation" that is *exactly* what he means. **Just as Christ could not be called "firstborn from the dead" if he had not been dead, so also Christ could not be called "the firstborn of all creation" if he had not been created.**[207]

All "Other" Things Created Through Christ?

The Bible says "all things" were created through Christ in Colossians 1:16. Trinitarians argue that this refers to the creation that exists now, but I will argue that it pertains to the new creation yet to come. Either way, the following issue still arises: If Christ was truly created first and everything else is subsequently created through him, why doesn't the Bible say "all *other* things are created through him"? Isn't Christ necessarily *excluded* from things created when it says "all" things are created through him?

I suppose that by the same reasoning one could also say that Eve was not alive, because the Bible says:

> "Adam called his wife's name Eve; because she was the mother of **all** living." (Genesis 3:20)

Based upon this passage, someone could say:

> "Eve could not have been alive because she is the mother of *all* living. The text doesn't say she is the mother of all *other* living, so she is clearly excluded from the total category of living things."

What nonsense that would be! And it is also nonsense to say that Christ is not created simply because the Bible says "*all* things were created through him." (Colossians 1:16 ASV.) This is *especially* nonsense since Christ affirms himself to be the beginning of God's creation in Revelation 3:14.

The fact of the matter is that the Bible often uses the word "all" in such a way that *does* allow exceptions to the specified category. Eve was not the mother of either herself or Adam, and yet the Bible says that she is the "mother of *all* living." Thus, "mother of all living" manifestly has at least two exceptions. In the same way, Christ was not created through himself, and yet the Bible says that "all" things were created through him. He himself was created (Colossians 1:15, Revelation 3:14) and thus he is manifestly excepted from "all" things that were created through him.

The word "all" is *not* used within the Bible in an exclusively absolute sense, as if to automatically eliminate any possible exception whatsoever.

Hebrews 2:8 says:

> "[God] hast put **all things** in subjection under his (Christ's) feet. For in that he (God) put **all** in subjection under him, he left **nothing** that is not put under him." (Hebrews 2:8)

If somebody were to read Hebrews 2:8 without acknowledging Scripture as a whole then they might argue against the existence of any exception to those things that are put under Christ. However, 1 Corinthians 15:27 shows that there *is* an exception to "all things" under Christ, saying:

> "When he saith **all** things are put under him (Jesus), it is manifest that he (God) is **excepted**, which did put all things under him."
> (1 Corinthians 15:27)

Now, why is it that the previous passage (Hebrews 2:8) did not let us know that God is excepted from all things put under Christ? Could it be that such a thing is considered *obvious,* and thus goes unspoken? By the same standard, is it not also equally as obvious that Christ is necessarily excepted from those things that are created *through* him? Indeed. To say that Christ was created through himself would have been self-contradictory, therefore further clarification was entirely unnecessary. Christ was created first according to the Scriptures (Revelation 3:14) and all *other* things are subsequently created through him.

The Bible is full of examples where evident exceptions go unspoken. We read "all" and realize that "all other" is intended. Notwithstanding, when it comes to Christ and creation many theologians have criticized any Bible version that presents the understood word "other" within its translation, showing that "all [other] things" were made through Christ. It is true that the Greek text of Colossians 1:16 does not contain a word that can be translated as "other." Yet, we must be consistent. When it comes to less theologically charged verses, the more popular Bible translations often add the understood word "other" in passages like Luke 13:2, which literally says:

> "And Jesus answering said unto them, Suppose ye that these Galilaeans were sinners above **all** the Galilaeans, because they suffered such things?" (Luke 13:2 KJV)

Luke 13:2 says "*all* Galileans" in the Greek, not "all *other* Galileans." Notwithstanding, the translators of the NIV, NLT, NKJV, NASB and RSV all include the word "other" within this passage in order to show that "all *other Galileans*" are in view. Ever hear of any objections to the addition of the word "other" in *this* passage? I doubt it.

Colossians 1:16 – Why Past Tense Verbs?

When the Bible speaks of all things created in and through Christ in Colossians 1:16, it uses verbs that are normally taken in the "past tense."

> "For in him all things **were created** (ἐκτίσθη aorist indicative verb) ... All things **were created** (ἔκτισται perfect indicative verb) through him ..." (Colossians 1:16 RSV)

To the English reader, this looks like it must denote something historic. However, there are some instances where these kinds of Greek verbs may be taken as referring to future events as well. For example, aorist indicative verbs, which usually refer to a past event, are also *sometimes* used to show that a *future event* is *certainly going to occur.*

Daniel B. Wallace comments on the aorist indicative being used to describe a future event in his book *Greek Grammar Beyond the Basics*.

> The aorist indicative can be used to describe an event that is not yet past as though it were already completed. ... An author sometimes uses the aorist for the future to stress the certainty of the event. It involves a "rhetorical transfer" of a future event as though it were past.[208]

In light of this usage of aorist indicative verbs, some may think that *certainty of its occurrence* was intended in Colossians 1:16, which could have occasioned Paul's usage of an aorist indicative verb in reference to a future event. Since God *promised* to "make all things new," (Revelation 21:5,) Hypothetically, Paul could have emphasized the certainty of that new creation using an aorist indicative verb. On the other hand, some of the early Christians likely thought of a *planned* creation formerly existing in the mind of God (See chapter two herein, subheading *The Doctrine of Arius*). To them, Colossians 1:16 may have simply been viewed as *these things were constructed thus in the mind of God before anything outside of God was ever formed*. Notwithstanding these two postulations, there is a third option that better matches Paul's writing style.

Sometimes author's spoke of the future creation as having already taken place because they were *speaking as one viewing the existence of that future state*. This is expressed in Revelation 21, where John is seeing the future state of creation in "the vision" (Revelation 9:17) he had.

> "And I saw a new heaven and a new earth: for the first heaven and the first earth **were passed away** (παρῆλθεν – aorist indicative); and there was no more sea.[209]" (Revelation 21:1)

John obviously was not saying the present heaven and earth already passed away at that time, but he spoke in that manner, using the same kind of Greek verb Paul used in Colossians 1:16, because he was *speaking as one viewing the future state of things*. Now, there is absolutely a difference here, because John was having a vision of the future, but why couldn't Paul speak in that same way while beholding the future *contemplatively?* Like the Historic Present, where past events are spoken of with present tense verbs as if the narrator is present in the past, there also exists the Aorist for Future, where the narrator speaks as one witnessing the future while looking back on the past.

Smyth's *Greek Grammar* describes the Aorist for Future as follows:

> **Aorist for Future**. — The aorist may be substituted for the future when a future even is vividly represented as having actually occurred.[210]

An example of this aorist for future is in 2 Thessalonians 1:10, where Paul, as if speaking from the time of Christ's return, is looking back on the past.

> "When he comes to be glorified in his holy ones, and to be admired among all those who **have believed** (πιστεύσασιν – aorist participle) (because our testimony to you **was believed** (ἐπιστεύθη –

aorist indicative)) **in that day** (ἐν τῇ ἡμέρᾳ ἐκείνῃ)."

(2 Thessalonians 1:10 HNV[211])

Paul is speaking *retrospectively* here *as one looking back from the day when Christ returns*. Thus, Heinrich Meyer says, "In order to preserve the statement of *time* in ἐν τῇ ἡμέρᾳ ἐκείνῃ, one feels himself constrained to consider the *aorist* ἐπιστεύθη as placed for the *future*."[212]

Paul's method of speaking in his entry in 2 Thessalonians 1:10 is affirmed in Charles Ellicott's Bible commentary as well.

> **Because our testimony** – Introduced to show why the writers had said specially "in all them that believed" (the past tense is employed because it looks back from the Judgment Day to the moment when the gospel was offered and the divergence between believers and unbelievers began); the reason was, because among "all them that believed" the Thessalonians would be found included.
>
> **In that day** – Added at the end to make the readers look once more (as it were) upon the wonderful sight on which the writer's prophetic eyes were raptly fixed.[213]

Paul speaks as one "looking back from that day on the past" (Alford[214]), as one who is present during the future return of Christ. We see a similar instance of Paul looking back from a future state of things in Romans 8:29-30.

> "For whom he did foreknow, he also did predestinate to be conformed to the image of his Son, that he might be the firstborn among many brethren. Moreover whom he did predestinate, them he also called: and whom he called, them he also justified: and whom he justified, them he also **glorified** (ἐδόξασεν – aorist indicative)." (Romans 8:29-30)

This glorification of those who suffer with Christ will take place in the future, at the resurrection, during the new creation (Romans 8:17-23). Yet, *Paul uses an aorist indicative verb, describing that glorification as* *something that took place **in the past***. Like Romans 8:29-30, Paul is fast forwarding to the final state of things and speaking of its inception as *historic*, even though that final state was *yet to come*. I don't want to prolong this study by going through Romans 8:17-25 to explain something that is extremely obvious, namely that Paul is talking about the hope of the new creation to come. However, I do want to focus on Romans 8:29-30 in particular, where his discourse on the new creation leads up to. Here, we see something very similar to what we find in Colossians 1:15-16.

- "His Son, that he might be **the firstborn among many brethren** ... them he also **glorified**." (Romans 8:29-30)

- "He is the image of the invisible God, **the first-born of all creation**: for in him all things **were created**." (Colossians 1:15-16 RSV)

Now, since Paul spoke of a future event in Romans 8:29-30 using an aorist indicative verb, is it really any surprise that he also does so in his strikingly similar statement found in Colossians 1:15-16? When he describes Christ as "the firstborn of many brethren" in Romans 8:29, this is referring to Jesus' resurrected state (as the context shows, Romans 8:11, 13, 17-25). Paul has *the same thing in mind contextually* in Colossians 1:15-18, where he describes Christ as "the beginning, the firstborn from the dead." (Colossians 1:18.) To refer to someone as "firstborn among others" assumes that others are born in the same way. Paul speaks of those who are going to be born from the dead *in the future* as if they *were glorified already* in Romans 8:30. Paul likewise speaks of the *future* new creation as if it *was already created* in Colossians 1:16.

Paul is simply using the same writing style in Colossians 1:15-16 that we see him employ in Romans 8:29-30. In Romans 8:30, he speaks as looking back to the resurrection of the saints. In Colossians 1:16, he speaks as one looking back at the origin of the new creation. This is also evident by the way he begins Colossians 1:16 with ὅτι ("for").

> "... the first-born of all creation; **for** in him all things were created." (Colossians 1:15-16 RSV)

That particular creation he is firstborn of (the new creation) is what is created in him. He had to be created first,[215] referring to his resurrected state, and the rest of creation afterward is to be created in him (conformed to his attributes).

Paul is referring to the new creation in Colossians 1:16. The contextual focus is clearly on the hope we have of things to come, of which Christ was born first.

> "May you be strengthened with all power, according to his glorious might, for all endurance and patience with joy, giving thanks to the Father, who has qualified us to share in **the inheritance of the saints** in light. He has delivered us from the dominion of darkness and **transferred us to the kingdom of his beloved Son** (compare 2 Peter 1:11), in whom we have redemption, the forgiveness of sins. He is the image of the invisible God, the **first**-born of all creation; **for** in him all things were created, in heaven and on earth, visible and invisible, whether thrones or dominions or principalities or authorities—all things were created through him and for him. He is **before** all things, and in him all things hold together. He is the head of the body, the church; he is **the beginning**, the **first**-born **from the dead**, that in everything he might be pre-eminent.[216]" (Colossians 1:13-18 RSV)

Proverbs 8:22 – "The LORD Created Me"

Paul speaks of Christ as "the wisdom of God" in the New Testament, saying:

> "But unto them which are called, both Jews and Greeks, **Christ** the power of God, and **the wisdom of God**." (1 Corinthians 1:24)

Christ is called *wisdom* because he is *the revelation of the principle wisdom of God*. Christ is the wisdom of God *unto us* because he is *the intermediary in whom we receive God's wisdom*.

> "But of him are ye in Christ Jesus, who was made unto us wisdom from God, and righteousness and sanctification, and redemption:"
> (1 Corinthians 1:30 ASV)

This does not mean that Christ is God's own inherent wisdom in an absolute sense, but it rather means that the wisdom of God is revealed unto us *through* Christ. He is that wisdom personified to us.

Alexander, the bishop of Alexandria who began the persecution against Arius, describes Arius' belief regarding Christ being called *wisdom* in the following excerpt:

> [Arius teaches that] he is neither like the Father in regard to his essence, nor is he by nature either the Father's true Word, or true Wisdom. He is one of the things made and produced, but he is called Word and Wisdom inexactly, since he himself came into being by God's own Word and by the Wisdom of God, whereby God made not only all things, but him also.[217]

The fact that Christ is called the wisdom of God is pertinent to our present discussion, because there is a passage in the Old Testament where someone, who specifically identifies themself as Wisdom, says that God created them:

> "I, **wisdom**, dwell in prudence, and I find knowledge and discretion. ... **I have** counsel and sound **wisdom**, I have insight, I have strength. ... **The LORD created me** at the beginning of his work, the first of his acts of old. Ages ago I was set up, at the first, before the beginning of the earth. When there were no depths I was brought forth, when there were no springs abounding with water. Before the mountains had been shaped, before the hills, I was brought forth; before he had made the earth with its fields, or the first of the dust of the world. When he established the heavens, I was there, when he drew a circle on the face of the deep, when he made firm the skies above, when he established the fountains of the deep, when he assigned to the sea its limit, so that the waters might not transgress his command, when he marked out the foundations of the earth, then I was beside him, like a master workman;

and I was daily his delight, rejoicing before him always, rejoicing in his inhabited world and delighting in the sons of men."
(Proverbs 8:12, 14, 22-31 RSV)

Many of the early Christians thought at least *some* of this text applied to Christ. However, the fact is, Wisdom in Proverbs 8 is presented as *a female*. This cannot simply be explained away by grammatical gender either, because we are to call her our "sister."

"Say unto wisdom, Thou art my sister; and call understanding thy kinswoman." (Proverbs 7:4)

Many these days argue that the Wisdom in Proverbs 8 is simply a personification of an impersonal concept. This seems very likely, because *Folly* is *also* personified in the surrounding context as well.

"Folly is an unruly woman; she is simple and knows nothing."
(Proverbs 9:13 NIV)

Wisdom is depicted as a woman calling to those passing by in Proverbs 8:1-4. Folly is presented as a woman calling to those passing by in Proverbs 9:13-16. *Between these two personifications of impersonal concepts*, we have the passage where Christ is thought to be identified as the Wisdom who is speaking. Such an interpretation is contrary to the context, quite frankly, and I believe the language is simply personifying wisdom as a person, when it is not. Personifying things that are not conscious individuals is somewhat common in the Old Testament (compare, for example, Lamentations 1, where Jerusalem is personified as a woman).

Arius apparently correlated *some* of Proverbs 8 to Jesus (as did men like Athanasius,[218] though Epiphanius rejects the entire premise[219]). Even so, Arius likely understood it as *Christ was created before all things in the mind of God prior to having any conscious existence*.

"Because of the Arian handling of the doctrine of divine foreknowledge, it is sometimes extremely difficult to know whether they are referring to the earthly, the preexistent, or the postresurrection Son. As we have suggested above, the Arians could read

> back onto the preexistent one titles and status that he would receive as a recognition from God on the basis of his virtuous earthly life and death. This they did with the most important title for the redeemer, 'the Son.' Arius uses this appellation throughout fragments of the *Thalia* which have been preserved. Yet we have seen that Christ receives his adoption on the basis of his earthly ministry according to the Arian scheme. How are we to understand the use of the term *son* applied to the preexistent one? For example, Arius wrote in the *Thalia*:
>
>> The Unbegun (ἄναρχος) made (ἔθηκε) the son as beginning of the creatures (τῶν γενητῶν) [cf. Prov. 8:22a]. And having made this one he advanced (ἔθηκε) [him] for a son (εἰς υἱὸν) to himself.
>
> The text seems to refer to a precosmic son, but elsewhere the Arians have repeatedly stated that Jesus' sonship came by adoption on the basis of his virtuous life."
>
> —*Early Arianism—A View of Salvation*,
> *Robert C. Gregg and Dennis E. Groh*[220]

Whichever *portions* of Proverbs 7-9 *were* thought to apply to Christ, it is *obvious* that *the entirety* of what is said about Wisdom there cannot be applied thus, because Wisdom is described as *a woman*. It is obvious that this text was used by the Gnostics to support their *Sophia* (*i.e., Wisdom*) conceptions (they spoke of Sophia as of a conscious goddess). Early Gnostic assertions that *both* Sophia *and* Christ were described in Proverbs 7-9 undoubtedly led to such heretical ideas as, "Christ united to Sophia [and both] descended into [Jesus] and thus Jesus Christ was produced."[221] Their view that Wisdom was a female deity probably led them to see "her" whenever wisdom was described elsewhere in the Bible and, snowballing from there, they began to say *truth* was a woman goddess as well, and so on and so forth. We will discuss such Gnostic ideas in chapter 14.

Chapter Eleven

Our Lord

The Bible clearly teaches that Jesus is Lord. What exactly does this mean? Does this mean that Jesus is God? Or does the title *Lord* simply denote a position of authority? The declaration that Christ is Lord is certainly a fundamental Christian doctrine. In this chapter we will discuss what the Bible says on this subject.

The Word "Lord" Does Not Mean "God"

The Greek word that is translated as "Lord" in the New Testament is κύριος (kurios). Even though the word κύριος does not mean *God,* many people commonly interpret it as if it does. And thus, when Christ is called κύριος (Lord) some have understood this to be proof that Christ is God himself. However, title of *Lord* (κύριος) is also applied in the Bible to many people *other* than God and Christ.

Example: "Sarah obeyed Abraham, calling him **lord**[222] (κύριος)."
(1 Peter 3:6)

Was Sarah calling Abraham *God?* Absolutely not. So, we have a clear example here of someone other than God or Jesus being called *lord.* The word κύριος (lord) simply denotes *someone who is in ruling authority.* Sarah referred to Abraham as *her* lord (κύριος) because he was in authority over her, so also now we also refer to Christ as *our* Lord (κύριος) because he is in authority over us.

The Bible says:

> "The head of every man is Christ; and the head of the woman is the man; and the head of Christ is God." (1 Corinthians 11:3)

Christ *is* our Lord because God has placed him in a position of authority over us. We *call* Christ our "Lord" to acknowledge that fact.

There are also many other examples within the New Testament where men other than Jesus and Abraham are referred to as κύριος (Lord) as well. Yet, due to inconsistencies in translation processes this is sometimes not very evident in many of our English versions of the Bible.

Here are some places (KJV) where the word κύριος, translated as something other than *lord,* is applied to men other than Christ:

- **sir** – Matthew 13:27, 21:30, 27:63, John 12:21, Revelation 7:14

- **sirs** – Acts 16:30

- **masters** – Matthew 6:24, Luke 16:13, Acts 16:16, 16:19, Ephesians 6:5, 6:9, Colossians 3:22, 4:1

- **masters'** – Matthew 15:27

- **owners** – Luke 19:33

A consistent translation of the word κύριος as *lord* would show that *many* people, who were neither God nor Jesus, were called *lord.* No one argues that these others being called κύριος makes them God. However, whenever κύριος is applied to Christ there are many who take this as proof of divinity. For instance, in the study notes for Romans 10:9, the *NIV Study Bible* says:

> **Jesus is Lord**. The earliest Christian confession of faith, probably used at baptisms. In view of the fact that "Lord" (Greek *kyrios*[223]) is used over 6,000 times in the Septuagint (the Greek translation of the OT) to translate the name of Israel's God (Yahweh), it is clear that Paul, when using this word of Jesus, is ascribing deity to him.[224]

To say that Paul is clearly ascribing deity to Christ simply because he refers to Christ as "Lord" (κύριος) is based only upon circular reasoning.

One could also say:

> In view of the fact that "Lord" (Greek *kyrios*) is used over 6,000 times in the Septuagint (the Greek translation of the OT) to translate the name of Israel's God (Yahweh), it is clear that **Sarah**, when using this word of **Abraham**, is ascribing deity to him.

If someone *began* with the premise that Abraham was God then they could say that Sarah was acknowledging that fact when she referred to Abraham as κύριος as well. I do not doubt that you see the error of such reasoning.

While it is true that the Hebrew name *Yahweh* is translated into the Greek language as κύριος that does not mean that every time the word κύριος appears it automatically refers to Yahweh. Sometimes the word κύριος refers to God and other times it simply refers to someone who is in a position of authority. If we were to understand the word κύριος as an automatic reference to Yahweh, we would also have to understand the following scriptures as references to Yahweh as well:

- "The woman saith unto him, **Yahweh** (κύριος), I perceive that thou art a prophet." (John 4:19)

- "Jesus saith unto her, Woman, why weepest thou? Whom seekest thou? She, **supposing him to be the gardener**, saith unto him, **Yahweh** (κύριος), if thou have borne him hence, tell me where thou hast laid him, and I will take him away." (John 20:15)

- "The same came therefore to Philip, which was of Bethsaida of Galilee, and desired him, saying, **Yahweh** (κύριος), we would see Jesus." (John 12:21)

- "**Yahwehs** (plural form of κύριος), give unto your servants that which is just and equal; knowing that ye also have a **Yahweh** (κύριος) in heaven." (Colossians 4:1)

- "For though there be that are called gods, whether in heaven or in earth, (as there be gods many, and **Yahwehs** [plural form of κύριος] many)." (1 Corinthians 8:5)

- "The Lamb shall overcome them: for he is **Yahweh** (κύριος) of Yahwehs (plural possessive form of κύριος), and King of kings."
(Revelation 17:14)

As you can see, automatically taking κύριος to mean Yahweh every time that it appears would result in an utterly ridiculous understanding of the Bible. So then, let's determine by the context whether κύριος is referring to God or not.

1 Corinthians 8:6 – Christ is Our One Lord

This may be the proper place to discuss 1 Corinthians 8:6, which says:

> "But to us there is but one God, the Father, of whom are all things, and we in him; and one Lord Jesus Christ, by[225] whom are all things, and we by him." (1 Corinthians 8:6)

This is a very clear statement from Paul in which he acknowledges that Christians have only one God, the Father.

The Bible *never* says:

> "To us there is but one God, the Father, Son, and Holy Spirit."

Nor does it ever say:

> "To us there is but one God, Jesus Christ."

Instead, it identifies the Father as our one God, saying:

> "But to us there is but one God, the Father." (1 Corinthians 8:6)

This is in agreement with Christ's statement made in John 17:3, where, while praying, he says:

> "Father ... this is life eternal, that they might know thee the only true God." (John 17:1, 3)

Nevertheless, in order to defend the Nicene tradition, some theologians have attempted to reason away 1 Corinthians 8:6 by using the following argumentation:

> "The text says that the Father is our one God and it also says that Jesus is our one Lord. Though the Father is called our one God, and Jesus is called our one Lord, it is not saying that Jesus is not God just as it is not saying that God is not Lord. If the Father being called the *one God* over all Christians excludes Jesus from being our God, then, to be consistent, Jesus being called our *one Lord* must exclude the Father from being our Lord as well. Yet, this is not true, because, after all, there are many places throughout the Scriptures where the Father is called Lord and the Son is called God."

The catalyst for this argument is simply ignorance as to how the word κύριος is used. The fact of the matter is that God and Christ are called κύριος for different reasons. Abraham was Sarah's κύριος because he was in authority over her. *Lord* in that instance refers to authority. Jesus is called *Lord* in reference to his authority as well, inasmuch as God has given Jesus authority over his entire kingdom.

> "For he (God) hath put all things under his (Jesus') feet."
> (1 Corinthians 15:27)

It is because God has given the ruling authority over the kingdom to Christ that the Scriptures say:

> "God hath **made** that same Jesus, whom ye have crucified, both **Lord** (κύριος) and Christ."[226] (Acts 2:36)

This verse says that God made Jesus Lord. This is not saying God made Jesus *Yahweh*. Although one might argue this by comparing Exodus 7:1 (see p. 40), the context pertains to *a position* (Acts 2:34-35). God made Jesus *ruler* over the kingdom. So also when Paul says, "But to us there is but *one Lord* Jesus Christ," (1 Corinthians 8:6) he was referring to how Christ is the *one ruler* whom God has placed over us. God has made Christ to be the one ruler over the people of the kingdom of God. What then, does God not rule as well? Yes, he does, but only in an indirect sense, and that is because Jesus rules according to God's will. It is not that God is sometimes governing us and Jesus is governing us at other times. No. God does not go *around* Jesus to oversee us. We only know the will of God *through* Christ, not by direct interaction.

> "Neither knoweth any man the Father, save the Son, and he to whomsoever the Son will reveal him." (Matthew 11:27)

No man can know the Father except Christ reveals him, so also no man can know the *will* of the Father unless Christ reveals that will as well. We have one Lord, Jesus Christ, who reveals the will of God to us. It is by serving him that we serve God.

By way of an analogy, suppose that we had a job where there was only one supervisor with whom we ever interacted. Suppose also that this one supervisor of ours was ruling over the company for the owner of the company who had given him that position. Now suppose that the owner, having entrusted the entire business to the supervisor, never sought to command the employees at the business during the time of the supervisor's rule, but rather always permitted that supervisor to command the employees as he willed. And yet, suppose that the supervisor, who had the authority to rule as he willed, did not seek his own will while ruling the company, but instead ruled only according to the will of the owner. In this scenario, would we be able to say that we had *two* supervisors, or rather that we had only *one?* We would have only one supervisor no doubt. If the owner never ordered us, but rather gave that authority over to the supervisor alone, how could it be said that we had two supervisors? Even though the supervisor ruled according to the will of the owner, we would still have only one supervisor. This example expresses principles that are parallel to the manner in which Christ is Lord over God's kingdom.

The Bible says:

> "For **the Father judgeth no man**, but hath committed **all** judgment unto the Son." (John 5:22)

But after this, Jesus also said:

> "**I judge no man**" (John 8:15), but, "**as I hear, I judge**: and my judgment is just; because **I seek not mine own will, but the will of the Father**." (John 5:30)

God has committed "all" judgment over to Christ, but Christ judges only as he hears from God. This is also why the Bible says:

> "[Jesus,] **through the Holy Ghost had given commandments** unto the apostles." (Acts 1:2)

We have only one Master and Lord, Jesus Christ (Jude 4), but since Jesus rules according to the will of God, we are serving God as well when we obey him. So then, Jesus was given the place of rulership over the kingdom, but he does not rule that kingdom *independent of* God, but rather *according to* God. Hence, we still serve God as well even though we have only one Lord, Jesus Christ. This is why a Christian professes to be both "a servant of God **and** of the Lord Jesus Christ." (James 1:1.)

In reference to our previous owner/supervisor scenario, suppose that after the supervisor completed a certain project, he was to give the position of supervisor back over to the owner. At that time the owner would become the supervisor over the entire business again (and over the previous supervisor as well). This scenario contains similar principles to those Paul spoke of in 1 Corinthians 15:24-28, saying:

> "Then cometh **the end, when he** (Jesus) **shall have delivered the kingdom unto God**, even the Father; when he shall have put down all rule, and all authority and power. For **he** (Jesus) **must reign, till** he hath put all enemies under his feet. The last enemy that shall be destroyed is death. For he (God) hath put all things under his (Jesus') feet. But when he saith all things are put under him (Jesus), it is manifest that he (God) is excepted, which did put all things under him (Jesus). And when all things have been subdued unto him (Jesus), **then shall the Son himself also be subject unto him that put all things under him**." (1 Corinthians 15:24-28)

This shows that Jesus is the one reigning over the kingdom "**till**" the end (when he will deliver the kingdom's rulership to God). God has given the kingdom over to Jesus so that Jesus can rule (be Lord) over it until that time. God did not give the rulership of the kingdom to Jesus and somebody else. Jesus is the *one* Lord over the kingdom that God gave him.

Is God Called "Our" Lord in this Present Time?

We have already discussed how the Hebrew name for God, Yahweh, is often represented as κύριος in the Greek. There are many places within the New Testament where the title κύριος (Lord) is applied to God in that respect. So, *as a name,* God is often called κύριος. However, in reference to this present time, during which Christ is reigning over God's kingdom, God is never referred to *positionally* as "**our** Lord." That is a position he has given to Christ alone.

> "**The LORD** (ὁ κύριος) said **to my Lord** (τῷ κυρίῳ[227] μου), Sit thou on my right hand, till I make thine enemies thy footstool."
> (Mark 12:36)

Someone might argue against this by saying, "During the time that Jesus is described as our one Lord, the Bible still calls God '**our** Lord' as well, so then both God and Christ are our Lord at this time." This objection is not necessarily valid, however. In reference to the time frame during which Christ is reigning, God is *never* definitively referred to as "our Lord." Let's briefly look at the three places in the New Testament that allegedly refer to God as "our Lord" during this era.

Revelation 11:15 says:

> "And the seventh angel sounded; and there were great voices in heaven, saying, The kingdoms of this world are become the kingdoms of **our Lord**, and of his Christ; and he shall reign forever and ever." (Revelation 11:15)

It is true that this particular scripture calls God "our Lord," but this is referring to *the end,* when Christ delivers the kingdom up to his Father. How do we know this? Here is a brief explanation: Revelation 11:15 is describing the future events that will occur when the seventh trumpet is blown (Revelation 8:2, 8:6-9:14, 10:7, 11:15). The seventh trumpet is the *last* trumpet to be blown according to the Bible. Concerning this last trumpet, 1 Corinthians 15:51-54 says:

> "We shall not all sleep, but we shall be changed, In a moment, in the twinkling of an eye, **at the last trump**: for **the trumpet** shall sound, and the dead shall be raised incorruptible, and we shall be changed. ... **then** (at the last trump) **shall be brought to pass the saying that is written, 'Death is swallowed up in victory.'"**
> (1 Corinthians 15:51-52, 54)

Death is swallowed up in victory at the last trumpet. It is *after* death is swallowed up in victory that Christ delivers the kingdom to his Father:

> "Then cometh the end, when **he shall have delivered up the kingdom to God**, even the Father; **when** he shall have put down all rule and all authority and power. For **he must reign, till** he hath put **all** enemies under his feet. The **last** enemy that shall be destroyed is **death**." (1 Corinthians 15:24-26)

So, the following occurs once the seventh/last trumpet sounds:

1. Jesus has reigned *until* death was swallowed up in victory.

2. Jesus delivers the kingdom to God.

3. God is called "our Lord" at that time.

The context of Revelation 11:15 shows that God is called "our Lord" **after the seventh trumpet is blown**, and so this does not apply until *after* Christ gives the kingdom's rulership back to God.

> "And the **seventh angel sounded**; and there followed great voices in heaven, and they said, The kingdom of the world **is become** the kingdom of **our Lord**, and of his Christ: and he shall reign for ever and ever." (Revelation 11:15 ASV)

And thus, when God is called "our Lord" in Revelation 11:15 it is referring to that *future* event when Christ delivers the kingdom over to God, rather than this present time. Until the last trumpet, we have only one Lord according to the Scriptures and that is Jesus Christ.

Revelation 4:11 is also sometimes pointed to as a passage that refers to God as "our Lord." Yet, many English versions of the Bible do not even *hint* that God is called "our Lord" therein:

- "Thou art worthy, **O Lord**, to receive glory and honour and power." (Revelation 4:11 KJV)

- "Worthy art Thou, **O Lord**, to receive the glory, and the honour, and the power." (Revelation 4:11 YLT)

These translations represent the Greek reading found in the Textus Receptus.

Ἄξιος εἶ Κύριε
Worthy are you Lord   (Revelation 4:11a, Textus Receptus)

However, the more authoritative Greek text varies from the Textus Receptus, reading thus:

Ἄξιος εἶ ὁ κύριος καὶ ὁ θεὸς ἡμῶν
Worthy are you the Lord and the God of us
(Revelation 4:11a NA27)

Grammatically, the word ἡμῶν (hemōn) can either modify the *one* noun that immediately precedes it ("Lord and **our** God") or *both* of the preceding nouns in the text ("**our** Lord and God"). It is because of this that some English translations have rendered Revelation 4:11 in such a way that does refer to God as "our Lord."

"You are worthy, **our Lord and God**, to receive glory and honor and power." (Revelation 4:11 NIV)

Nevertheless, the Greek text that is used when translating Revelation 4:11 as "our Lord and God" can also be translated as "O Lord our God." This fact is demonstrated in *The New Living Translation:*

> "You are worthy, **O Lord our God**, to receive glory and honor and power." (Revelation 4:11 NLT)

Henry Alford was a notable Greek scholar and it is this latter translation, "O Lord and our," that we find in *Alford's Greek Testament.*[228] Thus, we have good testimony that "O Lord and our God" is a valid translation. Since the Greek text can either be translated as "our Lord and God" or "O Lord our God," whether God is actually called "our Lord" in Revelation 4:11 seems to be a matter of opinion. I admit, however, that I favor the translation, "You are worthy, our Lord and God." To me, this relays the Greek more accurately.

Let's assume that Revelation 4:11 *does* refer to God as "our Lord." This still does not show God being called "our Lord" during this present age. Contextually, the phrase in question was spoken in the confines of John's heavenly vision. Events that occur in visions are not always synchronized with real time (see Daniel 7:13-14, where Daniel sees God give the kingdom to Christ hundreds of years before that occurred). In John's vision, God is sitting on the throne (Revelation 4:2-11) with a sealed scroll (Revelation 5:1). An angel calls for anyone who is worthy to open the scroll, but *initially no one could be found* (Revelation 5:2-4).

> "And I saw a strong angel proclaiming with a loud voice, Who is worthy to open the book, and to loose the seals thereof? And no man in heaven, nor in earth, neither under the earth, was able to open the book, neither to look thereon. And I wept much, because no man was found worthy to open and to read the book, neither to look thereon." (Revelation 5:2-4 KJV)

Afterwards a declaration is made, "Behold, [Jesus] hath prevailed to open the book." (Revelation 5:5.) The scene portrayed in Revelation 5:4-12 shows Christ's redemptive work as just now taking place. In John's vision, the phrase ὁ κύριος καὶ ὁ θεὸς ἡμῶν is spoken beforehand. Hence, even if God is referred to as "our Lord" in Revelation 4:11, this is stated, as far as the vision is concerned, before the redemptive work of Christ was accomplished and thus, by extension, before Jesus received his kingdom. To some extent, therefore, whether God is actually called "our Lord" in Revelation 4:11 is irrelevant to our present discussion.

Someone might also think that God is being called "our Lord" in **2 Peter 3:15**, which says:

> "And account that the longsuffering of **our Lord** is salvation; even as our beloved brother Paul also according to the wisdom given unto him hath written unto you." (2 Peter 3:15)

A.T. Robertson says, "The Lord here is Christ."[229] Henry Alford agrees.[230] However, there is no consensus on the matter among scholars, as J.E. Huther states:

> "It is open to question whether ὁ κύριος ἡμῶν means God, or Christ."[231]

The fact that the phrase "our Lord" is used seems, in itself, to show that Christ is the referent. In addition to 2 Peter 3:15, Christ is specifically referred to as "our Lord" *six times* in 2 Peter alone.

- "Grace and peace be multiplied unto you through the knowledge of God, and of **Jesus our Lord**." (2 Peter 1:2)

- "For if these things be in you, and abound, they make you that ye shall neither be barren nor unfruitful in the knowledge of **our Lord Jesus Christ**." (2 Peter 1:8)

- "For so an entrance shall be ministered unto you abundantly into the everlasting kingdom of **our Lord** and Saviour **Jesus Christ**." (2 Peter 1:11)

- "Knowing that shortly I must put off this my tabernacle, even as **our Lord Jesus Christ** hath shewed me." (2 Peter 1:14)

- "For we have not followed cunningly devised fables, when we made known unto you the power and coming of **our Lord Jesus Christ**." (2 Peter 1:16)

- "But grow in grace, and in the knowledge of **our Lord** and Saviour **Jesus Christ**." (2 Peter 3:18)

Within the New Testament, Christ is specifically called "our Lord" *over seventy-five times.* On the other hand, since God has made Christ to be the one Lord over us, God is not presently referred to definitively as "our Lord" even once. Is this merely a coincidence? I think not. Hence, if the context can point to either God or Jesus as the referent of "our Lord," the weight is massively in favor of the latter.

Peter writes, "The μακροθυμία (long-suffering) of our Lord is salvation," and he then immediately adds, "even as our beloved brother Paul also according to the wisdom given unto him hath written unto you." (2 Peter 3:15) There is only one Pauline epistle written ***to a group*** of people in which "the μακροθυμία (long-suffering)" unto salvation is specifically mentioned. It speaks of the long-suffering *of God.*

> "Or despisest thou the riches of his goodness and forbearance and μακροθυμία (long-suffering); not knowing that the goodness of God leadeth thee to repentance?" (Romans 2:4)

Initially, this might look like it *must* be what Peter referred to since it deals with long-suffering unto salvation and was written by Paul. However, that is not the case, because Peter also says:

> "...even as our beloved brother Paul also according to the wisdom given unto him hath written unto you. As **in all his epistles, speaking in them of these things**..." (2 Peter 3:15-16)

Peter has in view Paul's encompassing themes, not particular wording. Although the μακροθυμία (long-suffering) of God is specified in Romans 2:4, Paul also acknowledges the μακροθυμία (long-suffering) of Jesus towards men unto salvation as well in his first epistle to Timothy.

> "This is a faithful saying, and worthy of all acceptation, that Christ Jesus came into the world to save sinners; of whom I am chief. Howbeit for this cause I obtained mercy, that in me first **Jesus Christ might shew forth all μακροθυμία (long-suffering)**, for a pattern to them which should hereafter believe on him to life everlasting." (1 Timothy 1:15-16)

Both the long-suffering of God and of Christ are presented in Paul's epistles, and not just where it is stated, but where it is implied thematically. The entire Christian theme is one of long-suffering towards men who were in sin with the intent that they would ultimately be reconciled to God. I do not want to go too far off on a long drawn out study here, but I will say in passing that the long-suffering of God and Jesus move in tandem. During Jesus' earthly ministry, after speaking of how men would ultimately perish unless they repent, Jesus spoke a parable of a caretaker over another man's vineyard. In this parable, the caretaker requests that a certain fruitless tree be given a few more years to bear fruit before it is destroyed.

> "...except ye repent, ye shall all likewise perish. He spake also this parable; A certain man had a fig tree planted in his vineyard; and he came and sought fruit thereon, and found none. Then said he unto the dresser of his vineyard, Behold, these three years I come seeking fruit on this fig tree, and find none: cut it down; why cumbereth it the ground? And he answering said unto him, Lord, let it alone this year also, till I shall dig about it, and dung it: And if it bear fruit, well: and if not, then after that thou shalt cut it down."
> (Luke 13:5-9)

The owner was patient for three years, but it still did not bear fruit. Yet, when he afterwards desired that the tree be removed, the gardener requested an additional three years. Both the owner of the vineyard and the gardener allowed the tree more time in hopes that it would bear fruit. This parable, spoken in the context of men having opportunity to repent, illustrates God's patience with men on behalf of Christ and how the long-suffering of God and the long-suffering of Christ go hand in hand. Peter could have potentially been referring to either God or Jesus when he said, "Account that the long-suffering of our Lord is salvation." (2 Peter 3:15.)

I believe that other clues in the context point to Jesus as the referent in 2 Peter 3:15. In the prior verse, 2 Peter 3:14, Peter writes:

> "Wherefore beloved, since ye look for such things, be diligent that ye may **be found of him** in peace, **without spot**, and blameless."
> (2 Peter 3:14)

Be found by whom? Who is it that is coming? It is Christ no doubt. Peter already referred to Christ's return in the same chapter (2 Peter 3:4, 8-9). He is now encouraging diligence to be found without "spot" upon his return. The Bible says Christ gave himself for the church "that he might **present it to himself** a glorious church, **not having spot**, or wrinkle, or any such thing." (Ephesians 5:27.) Hence, I believe that 2 Peter 3:14 has Christ in view, adding support for the same in 2 Peter 3:15. I recommend the comments by Henry Alford for a more extensive study on 2 Peter 3:15.

- "Jesus came and spake unto them, saying, All power is given unto me in heaven and in earth." (Matthew 28:18)
- "For the Father judgeth no man, but hath committed all judgment unto the Son." (John 5:22)
- "The Father loveth the Son, and hath given all things into his hand." (John 3:35)
- "God hath made that same Jesus, whom ye have crucified, both Lord and Christ." (Acts 2:36)
- "And call no man your father upon the earth: for one is your Father, which is in heaven. Neither be ye called masters: for one is your Master, even Christ." (Matthew 23:9-10)
- "There is one Lord, one faith, one baptism, one God and Father of all." (Ephesians 4:4-6)
- "To us there is but one God, the Father ... and one Lord Jesus Christ." (1 Corinthians 8:6)

Can't Serve Two Masters / "Masters" on Earth

If we have only one Lord, Jesus Christ, then how is it that the Bible speaks of also having "masters" (plural) here on earth as well?

Jesus said the following:

"No servant can serve two masters (κυρίοις – plural of κύριος)." (Luke 16:13)

And yet the Bible says elsewhere:

> "Servants be obedient to them that are your masters (κυρίοις – plural of κύριος)." (Ephesians 6:5)

When Paul says servants should obey their "masters" (plural) he uses the same Greek word that Jesus used when he said that no man could serve two "masters." The word translated as "masters" in both instances is the plural form of the word κύριος, which means *lord.* So how is it that Paul says those men who served Christ had other lords as well? How could a servant have another lord here on earth and still say that they had only *one* Lord, Jesus Christ? Were they being disobedient to the faith because they had a lord other than Jesus? Actually, the Bible *commands* servants to obey their earthly masters, so someone cannot truly be a servant of Christ without doing just that. A person **is** serving Christ *by* serving their earthly master.

This principle is shown to be true when Paul says:

> "**Servants, be obedient to them that are your masters according to the flesh**, with fear and trembling, in singleness of your heart, **as unto Christ**; Not with eye-service, as men-pleasers; but **as the servants of Christ, doing the will of God** from the heart; With good will doing service, **as to the Lord, and not to men**."
> (Ephesians 6:5-7)

So then, while the servant was serving the earthly master, he was simultaneously serving Christ. If the earthly master should command the servant to do something that Christ would not allow, at that time the servant would refuse to do the will of the earthly master and continue to do the will of that one master whom he had been serving all along. In this way, while having two masters, the servant has only one. He is serving the earthly master in his obedience to the heavenly master.

It is for this cause that Paul says:

> "For he that is called in the Lord, being a servant, is the Lord's freeman." (1 Corinthians 7:22)

The servant is freed from the earthly master and has become the servant of Christ. It is now in service to Christ that the servant continues to serve his old earthly master. Therefore, even those who have masters on earth may continue to have only one actual master, Jesus Christ.

1 Timothy 6:15 – Describing the Father, Not Jesus

Before we begin our discussion on the title *King of kings and Lord of lords,* we must first address a common misconception regarding who it is that is called "King of kings and Lord of lords" in 1 Timothy 6:15. Some have thought that 1 Timothy 6:15 is describing Christ since the preceding verse (1 Timothy 6:14) speaks of Christ's return.

1 Timothy 6:14-16 reads as follows in the *RSV:*

> "(14) I charge you to keep the commandment unstained and free from reproach until the appearing of our Lord Jesus Christ; (15) and this will be made manifest at the proper time by the blessed and only Sovereign, the King of kings and Lord of lords, (16) who alone has immortality and dwells in unapproachable light, whom no man has ever seen or can see. To him be honor and eternal dominion. Amen."

Although Christ is the subject of the last clause in verse 14, there is a transition made at the beginning of verse 15 that switches the focus to God, so that the entirety of the description in verses 15-16 is spoken of the Father.

> "The whole description applies to the Father, not to the Son."
> —*Henry Alford, on 1 Timothy 6:15-16*[232]

The blessed and only Potentate is the one setting the time of Christ's appearing. And since the blessed and only Potentate is the Father, 1 Timothy 6:14-15 lines up with the rest of Scripture, which says:

> "But **of that day and that hour** [when Christ shall return] knoweth no man, no, not the angels which are in heaven, **neither the Son, but the Father**." (Mark 13:32)

And again, Jesus says:

> "It is not for you to know **the times** or the seasons, **which the Father hath put in his own power**." (Acts 1:7)

The Father is the one who is setting the time of Christ's return. This is exactly what Paul is speaking of in 1 Timothy 6:15, saying:

> "The appearing of our Lord Jesus Christ: **Which in his own times** the blessed and only Potentate shall show."
> (1 Timothy 6:14-15)

Therefore, the blessed and only Potentate whom Paul identifies as the "King of kings and the Lord of lords" is the Father. After identifying God as the "King of kings and the Lord of lords," Paul goes on to describe the Father using language that is not applicable to the Son at all, saying:

> "The King of kings, and Lord of lords; Who only hath immortality, dwelling in the light which no man can approach unto; **whom no man hath seen**, nor can see." (1 Timothy 6:15-16)

Now, who will say that no man has ever seen Jesus? Of course men saw Jesus. Paul, the author of this text, even says that *he* saw Jesus (1 Corinthians 15:8). Therefore, he *couldn't* have been speaking of Jesus when he said:

> "... whom no man hath seen, nor can see." (1 Timothy 6:16)

The Bible clearly teaches that it is God, not Jesus, who has never been seen by man:

> "No man hath seen **God** at any time." (1 John 4:12)

Thus, it is obviously God who is being described in 1 Timothy 6:15-16. And since it is God who is described in that passage, it is also God, not Christ, who is called "King of kings and Lord of lords" therein.

> "The King of kings, and Lord of lords; Who only hath immortality, dwelling in the light which no man can approach unto; whom no man hath seen, nor can see." (1 Timothy 6:15-16)

King of Kings and Lord of Lords

Jesus is called "King of kings and Lord of lords" in Revelation 19:16 and God is also called "The King of kings, and Lord of lords" in 1 Timothy 6:15 (KJV). However, the Greek phrase that is used in the book of Revelation when Christ is called "King of kings and Lord of lords" is *not* the same Greek phrase that is used in 1 Timothy 6:15 when God is called "King of kings and Lord of lords." (KJV.)

The Greek phrase applied to Christ is:

Βασιλεὺς βασιλέων καὶ κύριος κυρίων
King of kings and Lord of lords (Revelation 19:16)[233]
        [noun]   **[noun]**

The Greek phrase that is applied to God is:

ὁ βασιλεὺς τῶν βασιλευόντων καὶ κύριος
The King of them being kings and Lord
                      [verb]

τῶν κυριευόντων
of them being lords (1 Timothy 6:15)
    [verb]

The English versions obscure it, but God's title expresses more of *the ruler over being ruler*. God has made Jesus Lord (Acts 2:36), but God is still the one who arranges the positions of authority within the kingdom that Jesus is Lord over.

A woman once came to Jesus and asked him to assign positions of authority to her two sons, saying:

> "Grant that these my two sons may sit, the one on thy right hand, and the other on the left, in thy kingdom." (Matthew 20:21)

Notice Jesus' response to her request:

> "To sit on my right hand, and on my left, is not mine to give, but it shall be given to them for whom it is prepared of my Father."
> (Matthew 20:23)

It is God who assigns positions of authority. God designs the governments and Christ is the ruler over those governments that God designs. And just as God assigns the positions of authority to others, so also he assigned the position of authority to Christ as well (Isaiah 55:4). God *gave* the kingdoms of the earth over to Jesus, as the Scriptures say:

> "I saw in the night visions, and, behold, one like the Son of man came with the clouds of heaven, and came to the Ancient of days, and they brought him near before him. And there was **given him** dominion, and glory, and a kingdom, that all people, nations, and languages, should serve him: his dominion is an everlasting dominion, which shall not pass away, and his kingdom that which shall not be destroyed." (Daniel 7:13-14)

This passage of Scripture shows that the kingdom that Christ is over was given to him by God. It is God, "the King of things pertaining to kings and the Lord of things pertaining to lords," who has appointed Christ Jesus to be "the King of kings and Lord of lords" (Revelation 17:14 & 19:16).

When Christ is called *King of kings and Lord of lords,* what does that mean? Albert Barnes writes:

> The phrase "king of kings," is a Hebraism, to denote a supreme monarch.[234]

The title "king of kings" does not simply mean that one king has two or more kings under him. Instead, this title is used to signify dominion over *all* of the kings of the earth.

Prior to making Christ the king of kings in the *New* Testament, God previously made someone else to be king of kings in the in the *Old* Testament. The prophet Daniel acknowledged Nebuchadnezzar as "king of kings," saying:

> "Thou, O king, art a **king of kings**: for the God of heaven hath given thee a kingdom, power, and strength, and glory."
> (Daniel 2:37, c.f. Ezra 7:12)

The Greek phrase that is used when Nebuchadnezzar is called "king of kings" in the Septuagint is the same Greek phrase that is used when Christ is called "king of kings" in the New Testament.[235] Nebuchadnezzar was made ruler over "all" men (Daniel 2:38, Jeremiah 27:6-8), and thus he was the supreme monarch over all of the kings of the world.

Notice how the prophet Daniel acknowledges that God *gave* Nebuchadnezzar that position of authority, saying:

> "Thou, O king, art a king of kings: for the God of heaven hath given thee a kingdom, power, and strength, and glory. And wheresoever the children of men dwell, the beasts of the field and the fowls of the heaven hath he given into thine hand, and hath made thee ruler over them all." (Daniel 2:37-38)

Nebuchadnezzar was only "king of kings" because God assigned that position to him.

> "The Most High ruleth in the kingdoms of men, and giveth it to whomsoever he will." (Daniel 4:17)

God gives the kingdoms of the earth to whomever he wants. However, Nebuchadnezzar failed to recognize that fact. Daniel warned Nebuchadnezzar of the consequences for not acknowledging that it was God who gave the kingdom to him, saying:

> "This is the interpretation, O king, and this is the decree of the Most High, which is come upon my lord the king: That they shall drive thee from men ... **till thou know that the Most High ruleth in the kingdom of men, and giveth it to whomsoever he will.**"
> (Daniel 4:24-25)

When Nebuchadnezzar said that he obtained the kingdom by his own strength, God took it from him (Daniel 4:31). Afterwards, when Nebuchadnezzar acknowledged that God gives it to whomever he wants, God gave the kingdom back to him (Daniel 4:36). Therefore, even though God gave the kingdoms of the earth to Nebuchadnezzar, he still decided when to remove him from his position and when to give it back.

> "He removeth kings, and setteth up kings." (Daniel 2:21)

The Bible says:

> "Let every soul be subject unto the higher powers. For there is no power but of God: **the powers that be are ordained of God.**"
> (Romans 13:1)

So also, the Bible says:

> "[Christ] was **ordained by God** to be the Judge of the quick and dead." (Acts 10:42)

God is over the positions of kings and rulers. When the time comes, he will depose all of the unrighteous kings and rulers on earth, establishing the king who we wait for, even Jesus Christ.

Daniel 7:14 – Men will Serve God

Since the Septuagint uses the word λατρεύω (a kind of service done to *God*) in Daniel 7:14, some say the verse contains proof that Jesus ("the Son of man") is God himself. That is an erroneous claim. Daniel 7:14 shows that, within the kingdom of Jesus Christ, men will serve the Father.

> "I saw in the night visions, and, behold, one like the Son of man came with the clouds of heaven, and came to **the Ancient of days**, and they brought him near before him. And there was given him dominion, and glory, and a kingdom, that all people, nations, and languages, should **serve him**." (Daniel 7:13-14)

When ancient kings (e.g., Nebuchadnezzar) were in power, their subjects were forced to serve the gods of those kings.

> "Nebuchadnezzar spake and said unto them, Is it true, O Shadrach, Meshach, and Abednego, do not ye **serve my gods**, nor worship the golden image which I have set up?" (Daniel 3:14)

Daniel 7:14 is about men serving *God* under the dominion of Jesus Christ. This is clear from the interpretation of Daniel's vision a few verses later.

> "I came near unto one of them that stood by, and asked him the truth of all this. So he told me, and made me know the interpretation of the things. ... **the Ancient of days** came, and judgment was given to the saints of the most High; and the time came that the saints possessed the kingdom. ... And the kingdom and dominion, and the greatness of the kingdom under the whole heaven, shall be given to the people of the saints of **the most High**, **whose** kingdom is an everlasting kingdom, and all dominions shall **serve** and obey **him**." (Daniel 7:16, 22, 27)

Why God will Judge Mankind through Christ

The Bible speaks of God judging the world in righteousness through a man, saying:

> "Therefore having overlooked the times of ignorance, God is now declaring to men that all people everywhere should repent, **because** he has fixed a day in which **he will judge the world in righteousness through a man** whom he has appointed, having furnished proof to all men by raising him from the dead."
> (Acts 17:30-31 NASB)

Jesus said the following:

> "The Father judgeth no man, but hath committed all judgment to the Son ... and hath given him authority to execute judgment also, **because** he is the Son of man." (John 5:22, 27)

Jesus is able to judge us "because he is the Son of man." In the Greek text of the above passage there is no direct article before "son of man." Hence, it can literally be translated as "a son of man" (Mark 3:28 and Ephesians 3:5 speak of men in general as "sons of men"). But why did God give Jesus the authority to judge because he is a son of man?

Around 304 AD, Lactantius wrote the following:

> If anyone gives men commandments for living and molds the characters of others he is obligated himself to practice the things that he teaches. Otherwise, [the student] will answer his teacher in this way: "I am not able to do the things you command, for they are impossible. ... Or, if you are so entirely convinced that it is possible to resist nature, you yourself practice the things you teach, so I can know that they are possible." But how can one practice what he teaches, unless he is like the teacher? For if the teacher is subject to no passion, a man may answer the teacher in this manner: "It is my wish not to sin. However, I am overpowered. For I am clothed with frail and weak flesh." Now, what will that teacher of righteousness say in reply to these things? How will he refute and convict a man who alleges the frailty of the flesh as an excuse for his faults—unless he himself will also be clothed with flesh—so that he can show that even the flesh is capable of virtue? You see, therefore, how much more perfect is a teacher who is mortal, for he is able to guide the one who is mortal. Therefore, let men learn and understand why the Most High God—when he sent his Ambassador and Messenger to instruct mortals with the commandments of his righteousness—willed for him to be clothed with mortal flesh.[236]

If God himself were to judge us directly someone might reply to God on judgment day, "But God, you don't know what it is like to be tempted like

I was. It was impossible for me to resist sin." Yet, since Jesus was made like us in all things (Hebrews 2:17), it is not possible for someone to reply to *him* in such a way.

Another reason why God has made Jesus Lord is because he already relegated a certain level of dominion over the earth to men.

> "The heaven, even the heavens, are the LORD'S: but **the earth hath he given to the children of men**." (Psalm 115:16)

God has given provincial dominion over the earth to man and will ultimately establish his kingdom on earth through a man, namely Jesus.

> "For not unto angels did he subject the world to come, whereof we speak. But one hath somewhere testified, saying, What is man, that thou art mindful of him? Or the son of man, that thou visitest him? Thou madest him a little lower than the angels; Thou crownedst him with glory and honor, And didst set him over the works of thy hands: Thou didst put all things in subjection under his feet. For in that he subjected all things unto him, he left nothing that is not subject to him. But now we see not yet all things subjected to him. But we behold him who hath been made a little lower than the angels, even Jesus, because of the suffering of death crowned with glory and honor, that by the grace of God he should taste of death for every man." (Hebrews 2:5-9 ASV)

I wrote this in the back of my Bible:

> Dominion on earth belongs to man (Ps. 115:16). Jesus' dominion is not compatible with the current sinful dominion. Perhaps a reason why Christ left and is not here or returned yet is because the dominion of sinful men must first reach its end. ... By God forbearing, he gives opportunity for men to repent, but the mark of the beast will set the damnation of men already, so coming afterward will, in most people, only consummate what was already appointed when they received the mark [of the beast]. A great and final division is thus made prior to the destruction of the [present] earth. There have been many judgments that destroyed nations, but

for the world to be judged thus, there must first be a one world government that encapsulates all and thus includes all in condemnation.

A great division is coming. There will be an attempt to bring everyone under the one-world Antichrist system. Once that outcome is set, God will again destroy this present age as he did when the old world of Noah became corrupt (Genesis 6:5-18, 2 Peter 3:3-13). As he reestablished humanity through one man at that time, he will do so again. This time, however, it will be through Jesus. And when Jesus returns, the new world will be inhabited, through means of the eternal resurrection, by those who throughout the ages have walked in the truth.

Jesus' Everlasting Kingdom / Returned to God

After the day of judgment, when God will judge the world through Jesus Christ, Jesus will give the kingdom's rulership back to God. Until then, God has given the rulership over to Jesus. Yet, the Bible also teaches that Christ will rule the kingdom *forever*.

> "Of the increase of his government and peace there shall be no end, upon the throne of David, and upon his kingdom, to order it, and to establish it with judgment and with justice from henceforth even for ever." (Isaiah 9:7)

And yet Paul says Jesus will give the kingdom back to God.

> "For he must reign till he hath put all enemies under his feet ... And when all things have been subdued unto him, then shall the Son himself also be subject unto him that put all things under him."
> (1 Corinthians 15:24-28)

How can Christ give the kingdom over to God and yet be said to reign forever? The fact of the matter is that there will be several rulers in God's kingdom. The saints, by means of the Messiah, "shall take the kingdom, and possess the kingdom for ever" *along with* Christ (Daniel 7:18). The resurrected saints will "reign with Christ." (Revelation 20:5.) After Jesus delivers the kingdom over to God, I believe that God will be the supreme monarch over the entire kingdom, and that Christ will also rule over the entire kingdom under God. However, in reference to how the saints will rule over the kingdom(s), I believe that we will each only be allotted certain areas within the kingdom of God and of Christ. This seems evident when we look at the following parable that Jesus spoke in Luke 19.

> "[Jesus] spake a parable, because he was nigh unto Jerusalem, and because they thought that the kingdom of God should immediately appear. He said therefore, A certain nobleman went into a far country to receive for himself a kingdom and to return. And he called his ten servants, and delivered to them ten pounds, and said unto them, Occupy till I come ... And it came to pass, that when he was returned, having received the kingdom, then he commanded those servants to be called unto him, to whom he had given the money, that he might know how much every man had gained by trading. Then came the first, saying, Lord, thy pound hath gained ten pounds. And he said unto him, Well, thou good servant: because thou hast been faithful in a very little, have thou authority over ten cities. And the second came, saying, Lord, thy pound hath gained five pounds. And he said likewise to him, Be thou also over five cities." (Luke 19:11-13, 15-18, c.f. Luke 22:28-30)

This parable depicts a ruler over an entire kingdom making his subjects rulers over various cities within that kingdom. Likewise, God will rule over all, and Christ will rule over all under God, and the saints will rule over parts of their kingdom under both God and Christ (though some may rule over the entire kingdom with God and Christ as well). In this way, God, Christ, and the saints will reign forever according to the Scriptures.

Chapter Twelve

Hebrews Chapter One

Anyone who has studied contemporary Christology has probably encountered a large emphasis on the first chapter of Hebrews. Several passages from that chapter have been misunderstood. We will presently examine some of those passages foremost relevant to the discussion at hand.

Hebrews 1:2 – Through Christ?

Hebrews 1:2 has been thought to show that all things were made *through* Christ (as an *agent* of God's creation). The meaning of this text largely hinges on how the Greek word διά (*dia*), when followed by a genitive noun or pronoun, can be understood.

Hebrews 1:2 presents διά followed by a genitive pronoun:

> "[Jesus] whom he [God] hath appointed heir of all things, **δι'** (same word as διά) **οὗ** (*hou*, genitive pronoun that means *whose*) also he made the worlds."

Since διά + a genitive often denotes an act was performed "through" that noun, Hebrews 1:2 is often taken to mean that God made the worlds *through* Christ. By this, men think that Christ must have been present and consciously involved in the origin of this creation. The Racovian Catechism argued that Hebrews 1:2 referred to the *new creation to come* being made through Christ, but I take a slightly different view on the text. I will discuss my beliefs, but first we will consider the footnote on Hebrews 1:2 within the Racovian Catechism (added sometime after its original publication). The footnote reads as follows:

> Grotius remarks that in his opinion this passage may without harshness be rendered, *propter quem mundum fecit,* "on whose account he made the world." And he shows in his commentary on this place, and on Heb. 1:10, that it was understood and believed among the Jews that the world had been created with a view to the Messiah. This interpretation would be more accordant with the bearing of the apostle's observations, and better harmonize with the preceding context:—that the Son of God was for this reason appointed heir of all things, that God had for, or with a view to, him, made the ages, or the world. For the Greek preposition διά with a genitive case may be rendered FOR, or "WITH A VIEW TO," as appears from a passage of Gregory Nazianzen, which, among others, is usually quoted as an example in the Lexicons. Δι' ἡμῶν την ανθρωπότητα Θεὸς υπέση. B. WISSOWATIUS.[237]

Hugo Grotius, whom the entry refers to, did make a case for taking Hebrews 1:2 as God making the world "with a view to" Christ (*i.e.,* God made all things with Christ in mind). Grotius refers the reader to Romans 6:4 in his *Annotations on the New Testament*. The reason why he believed Romans 6:4 was so important was because it presents διά with a genitive noun in such a way that διά seems to denote *on behalf of*.

> "Christ was raised from the dead **διὰ** the **glory (genitive noun)** of the Father." (Romans 6:4)

Was Christ raised from the dead *through* the glory of the Father or *on behalf of* the glory of the Father? If he was raised from the dead on behalf of the glory of the Father, then why couldn't we take Hebrews 1:2 to mean that God made the worlds (literally, *the ages*) *with Christ in view*?

A Greek-English Lexicon of the New Testament and Other Early Christian Literature comments on διά + a genitive noun as follows:

> At times διά w. gen. seems to have causal mng. (Radamacher² 142; POxy. 29, 2 [I AD] ἔδωκα αὐτῷ διὰ σοῦ=because of you; Achilles Tat. 3, 4, 5 διὰ τούτων=for this reason) διὰ τῆς σαρκός *because of the resistance of the flesh* Ro 8:3.—2 Cor 9:13; 1 J 2:12. —On the

use of διά w. gen. in Ro s. Schlaeger, La critique radicale de l'épître aux Rom.: Congr. d'Hist. du Christ. II 111f.[238]

Thus, we have one of the most renowned Greek-English lexicons affirming that διά + a genitive can be rendered "because of," or "for this reason."

Let's look at a couple of other examples of how English translations have rendered διά + a genitive while translating the New Testament.

Example 1. The NIV translates διά as "in view of" in Romans 12:1 when διά is followed by a genitive.

> "Therefore, I urge you, brothers and sisters, **in view of God's mercy** (διὰ τῶν οἰκτιρμῶν τοῦ θεοῦ), to offer your bodies as a living sacrifice, holy and pleasing to God—this is your true and proper worship." (Romans 12:1 NIV, parenthesis and bold added by me)

Trinitarian scholars have commented on the meaning of διά in this text as "contains the motive," (Meyer,) "presenting a motive," (Schaff,) "διά equivalent to *by an allusion to*," (Thayer,) "presenting the motive" (Vincent).

Example 2. The KJV translates διά as "for the sake" in Romans 15:30 when διά is followed by a genitive.

> "Now I beseech you, brethren, **for the Lord Jesus Christ's sake** (διὰ τοῦ κυρίου ἡμῶν Ἰησοῦ Χριστοῦ), and for the love of the Spirit, that ye strive together with me in your prayers to God for me." (Romans 15:30 KJV, parenthesis and bold added by me)

Trinitarian scholars have commented on the meaning of διά in this text as "It means probably out of love and regard to him," (Clarke,) "by means of a moving reference to," (Meyer,) "presenting a motive" (Schaff).

Applying all that we have seen, Grotius' assertion that Hebrews 1:2 can grammatically be translated, "… on whose account he made the world," seems to find vindication. As such, the text would mean *Christ is the heir of all things, on behalf of whom God made the world*. I used to believe this was the meaning of the text, but now I see things differently.

The meaning of Hebrews 1:2, as I now see it, relates to eternal matters, namely, how *God established the prophesied eternal matters through Christ*. The phrase in Hebrews 1:2 translated "made the worlds" is ἐποίησεν τοὺς αἰῶνας. The first word, ἐποίησεν, doesn't necessarily mean "he made," but simply carries the meaning "he did." Compare Hebrews 7:27, "This **he did** (ἐποίησεν) once." Contrast γεγονέναι ("were made") in Hebrews 11:3. Furthermore, τοὺς αἰῶνας does not literally mean "the worlds," but "the ages." This can definitely refer to *the future ages to come*, as we see in Hebrews 13:8, "Jesus Christ the same yesterday, and to day, **and for ever** (καὶ εἰς τοὺς αἰῶνας)." I propose the reading, "through whom he established the ages."

Hebrews 1:3 – Image of His Confidence

Many English translations render the Greek incorrectly in Hebrews 1:3, asserting that the "nature" or "substance" of God is in view.

> "Who being the effulgence of his glory, and the very image of his **substance**, and upholding all things by the word of his power, when he had made purification of sins, sat down on the right hand of the Majesty on high;" (Hebrews 1:3 ASV)

The word translated as "substance" in this passage is translated from the Greek word ὑπόστασις (hupostasis). Much debate has taken place over the years as to how this word should be translated here. However, one thing typically agreed upon is what the author of Hebrews intended by his use of the word in Hebrews 3:14.

> "For we are made partakers of Christ, if we hold the beginning of our **confidence** (ὑπόστασις) stedfast unto the end." (Hebrews 3:14)

The author means "confidence" here. This is how most English versions translate the word. There are only three instances within Hebrews where the author uses ὑπόστασις. In addition to Hebrews 1:3 and Hebrews

3:14, we find ὑπόστασις in Hebrews 11:1, where, like Hebrews 3:14, the word is again translated as "confidence."

- "Faith is the **confidence** (ὑπόστασις) that what we hope for will actually happen; it gives us assurance about things we cannot see."
(Hebrews 11:1 NLT)

- "Now faith is **confidence** (ὑπόστασις) in what we hope for and assurance about what we do not see." (Hebrews 11:1 NIV)

Since two out of the three instances where we find ὑπόστασις in Hebrews are already accepted as meaning "confidence," I submit that we take ὑπόστασις to mean "confidence" in Hebrews 1:3 as well.

I believe the true meaning of Hebrews 1:3 has usually been missed. Rather than ὑπόστασις being descriptive of Christ bearing God's image, which I do hold to be an indispensable truth, the meaning instead has reference to Christ's resurrection and how he, in his resurrected state, is the exact expression of his confidence. That is, *before he died, he had confidence in matters pertaining to his life after death and that is precisely what he now embodies as the resurrected Messiah.* The ὑπόστασις in Hebrews 1:3 does not refer to God's substance, but to Christ's confidence. The structure of the Greek text attests to this, reading as follows:

ὃς	ὢν	ἀπαύγασμα	τῆς	δόξης	καὶ	χαρακτὴρ	τῆς
who	being	off-shining	of the	glory	and	exact impress	of the

ὑποστάσεως	**αὐτοῦ**,	φέρων	τε	τὰ	πάντα	τῷ
confidence	**his**	bearing	and	things	all	in the

ῥήματι	τῆς	δυνάμεως	**αὐτοῦ**		
utterance	of the	power	**his**	(Hebrews 1:3)	

When Hebrews 1:3 says αὐτοῦ (*his*) twice, the first is usually taken by commentators as referring to God (God's substance), but the second is taken as referring to the Son (the Son's power). However, *both of these instances* are actually *referring to the Son*.

Henry Alford commented thus on Hebrews 1:3:

> ...the strict parallelism of the clauses would seem to require that αὐτοῦ here should designate the same person, as it does before, after τῆς ὑποστάσεως.[239]

The structure of Hebrews 1:3 favors the same referent for αὐτοῦ in both instances. Christ is in view throughout the passage and neither αὐτοῦ refers to God. Instead, the Son's confidence and power are in view.

Hebrews 1:3 pertains to the resurrected state of Christ. When it says he is the ἀπαύγασμα τῆς δόξης (the reflected radiance of the glory) this is equal to how the word δόξα (glory) is used elsewhere of the resurrection.

> "Christ was raised from the dead διά (*through* or *on behalf of*) τῆς (the) δόξης (glory) τοῦ (of the) πατρός (Father)." (Romans 6:4)

Christ was raised from the dead through (or *on behalf of*) the glory of God. Christ, after his resurrection, is the radiant reflection of that glory.

When Hebrews 1:3 says that Christ φέρων τε τά πάντα τῷ ῥήματι τῆς δυνάμεως (bears unto its end[240] all things in the utterance of his power) this is to say that he, in his resurrected state, is carrying out the extent of those things spoken beforehand in regard to the Messiah's power. The word for *power* here, δύναμις, may specify the resurrected condition of Christ's body since **1.** The author of Hebrews goes on to prove throughout his epistle that the Messiah had to be raised immortal to fulfill the prophecies. Compare Hebrews 7:16, "after the **power** (δύναμιν) of an endless life." **2.** We find δύναμις used elsewhere in the New Testament regarding the resurrected state. Notice how the following passage uses the same words[241] found in Hebrews 1:3 to describe the resurrection body.

> "So is it with the resurrection of the dead. What is sown is perishable, what is raised is imperishable. It is sown in dishonor, it is raised **in glory** (ἐν δόξῃ). It is sown in weakness, it is raised **in power** (ἐν δυνάμει)." (1 Corinthians 15:42-43 RSV)

Hebrews 1:3 ends by saying:

> "... when he had by himself purged our sins, sat down on the right hand of the Majesty on high." (Hebrews 1:3 KJV)

This is a continuation of the former thought, that Christ is carrying out the extent of what has been spoken regarding the Messiah. The author of Hebrews goes to great lengths to prove that Christ is **1.** the fulfillment of the prophesied High Priest who cannot die **2.** sitting at the right hand of God while all things are being subdued under him.

In regard to Jesus purging sins, this is not speaking of Christ's death on the cross specifically, but of what occurred *afterwards* in his ministry as High Priest. Of course, his death on the cross is a prerequisite to fulfilling his duty as our High Priest, but he did not complete the purging of our sins here on earth, but only after his resurrection and ascension into heaven.

> "So Christ has now become the High Priest over all the good things that have come. He has entered that greater, more perfect Tabernacle in heaven, which was not made by human hands and is not part of this created world. With his own blood—not the blood of goats and calves—he entered the Most Holy Place once for all time and secured our redemption forever." (Hebrews 9:11-12 NLT)

The purging of sins, as is prefigured in Old Testament High Priest symbolism, is not consummated at the time of the sacrifice, but at the time when that sacrifice is presented in the innermost sanctuary of the Tabernacle.

> "Behind the second curtain stood a tent called the Holy of Holies ... into the second only the high priest goes, and he but once a year, and not without taking blood which he offers for himself and for the errors of the people." (Hebrews 9:3,7 RSV)

Considering all that has been said on Hebrews 1:3, observe how nicely the context flows when understood of his resurrection.

> "Who being the reflected radiance of God's glory, who raised him from the dead, and the exact replication of his confidence regarding his life after death, and carrying out the extent of all the things spoken in the prophets regarding his miraculous immortal condition, after he had entered into the Most Holy Place and presented himself for our redemption, he sat down on the right hand of the

Majesty on high; having become so much better than the angels as he hath inherited a more excellent name than they. For unto which of the angels said he at any time, Thou art my Son, This day have I begotten thee?" (Hebrews 1:3-5, a dynamic rendering by me)

This last statement, "Thou art my Son, This day have I begotten thee," is shown by Paul in Acts 13:33 to be a resurrection text (see chapter nine herein, subheading *Christ Begotten Completely at the Resurrection*). A careful reading will show that when the author cites this resurrection prophecy, he is tying it into the preceding context and adding weight to his former assertion. This resurrection prophecy appears in Hebrews 1:5 because the resurrection was already in view in Hebrews 1:3.

> "So also Christ glorified not himself to be made an high priest; but he that said unto him, Thou art my Son, to day have I begotten thee. As he saith also in another place, Thou art a priest for ever after the order of Melchisedec. Who in the days of his flesh, when he had offered up prayers and supplications with strong crying and tears unto him that was able to save him from death, and was heard in that he feared; Though he were a Son, yet learned he obedience by the things which he suffered; And being made perfect, he became the author of eternal salvation unto all them that obey him; Called of God an high priest after the order of Melchisedec. ... Who is made, not after the law of a carnal commandment, but after the **power** (δύναμιν[242]) of an endless life." (Hebrews 5:5-10, 7:16)

Hebrews 1:8 – Thy Throne, O God?

Hebrews 1:8 depicts the Father addressing the Son as God in many of our English versions of the Bible:

- "But unto the Son he saith, Thy throne, O God..." (Hebrews 1:8, *King James Version,* 1611)

- "Your throne, O God, will last forever..." (Hebrews 1:8, *New International Version,* 1973)

Do these versions represent the correct translation of Hebrews 1:8? Compare those translations with the translations of Hebrews 1:8 listed below:

- "God is thy throne for ever and ever..." (Hebrews 1:8, *Daniel Mace New Testament*,1729)

- "God is thy throne for ever and ever..." (Hebrews 1:8, *Moffatt*, 1922)

Why do these versions of the Bible present, "God is thy throne," as a possible translation of Hebrews 1:8? Is this truly an acceptable translation of the Greek text? The truth of the matter is that, "Thy throne, **O God**," *and,* "Thy throne **is God**," are *both* grammatically possible translations of Hebrews 1:8. But how can both of these translations *accurately* express the grammar of a common Greek text when the thoughts they express are so different from one another? In order to grasp how this is possible we first need to attain a basic understanding of Greek noun usage.

In the English language a noun appears the same regardless of the role that it plays in a sentence (possessive nouns are an exception).

Example:

> "The man pushed the man toward the man and said, 'Hurry, man, the man's leg is broken.'"

In this sentence the noun *man* appears in the nominative, accusative, dative, genitive, and vocative positions. Yet, since the various ways that an English noun is *used* does not change the way that the English noun is *written,* then the word *man* continued to be written the exact same way ("man") regardless of the role that it played within the sentence. However, in the *Greek* language, the way that nouns are written *varies* from case to case. If we were to substitute the English word *man* with the Greek word for *man* (ἄνθρωπος), our example sentence would read as follows:

> "The ἄνθρωπος pushed the ανθρωπον towards the ανθρωπω and said, 'Hurry, ανθρωπε, the ανθρωπου leg is broken.'"

Did you notice how the noun's ending changed in accordance with how it was used in the sentence? The way that a Greek noun is *used* determines the way that the Greek noun is *written.*

Unlike Modern English, which really only has *two* cases, the common case (man) and the possessive or genitive case (man's), Koine Greek utilizes *five* different noun cases to show how a noun is used.

Those five cases are:

> **Nominative** – the subject noun of a sentence. "The **ἄνθρωπος** (man) pushed the ἄνθρωπος (man) towards the ἀνθρώπῳ (man) and said, 'Hurry, ἄνθρωπε (man), the ἀνθρώπου (man's) leg is broken.'"
>
> **Accusative** – the object noun of a sentence. "The ανθρωπος (man) pushed the **ἄνθρωπον** (man) towards the ἀνθρώπῳ (man) and said, 'Hurry, ἄνθρωπε (man), the ἀνθρώπου (man's) leg is broken.'"
>
> **Dative** – a noun that is the indirect object or recipient. "The ἄνθρωπος (man) pushed the ἄνθρωπον (man) towards the <u>ἀνθρώπῳ</u> (man) and said, 'Hurry, ἄνθρωπε (man), the ἀνθρώπου (man's) leg is broken.'"
>
> **Genitive** – a possessive noun. "The ἄνθρωπος (man) pushed the ἄνθρωπον (man) towards the ἀνθρώπῳ (man) and said, 'Hurry, ἄνθρωπε (man), the <u>ἀνθρώπου</u> (man's) leg is broken.'"
>
> **Vocative** – a noun being spoken to. "The ἄνθρωπος (man) pushed the ἄνθρωπον (man) towards the ἀνθρώπῳ (man) and said, 'Hurry, <u>**ἄνθρωπε**</u> (man), the ἀνθρώπου (man's) leg is broken.'"

The five cases for the word *God* appear as follows:

> **Nominative** - θεὸς
>
> **Accusative** - θεόν
>
> **Dative** - θεῷ
>
> **Genitive** - θεοῦ
>
> **Vocative** - θεέ

When God is being spoken *to* the Greek word for *God* usually appears in the *vocative* case, θεέ.

Matthew 27:46 demonstrates how the vocative noun θεέ is used within Greek grammar, saying:

> "My **God** (θεέ), My **God** (θεέ), why hast thou forsaken me?"
> (Matthew 27:46)

The Greek word for *God* appears in the vocative case (θεέ) in Matthew 27:46 because God *is being spoken to.* However, the Greek word for *God* in Hebrews 1:8 is **not** in the *vocative* case (which would show that God was being spoken to), but it is instead in the *nominative* case (which shows that God is the *subject* of the sentence).

> "But unto the Son he saith, Thy throne [is] **God** (θεὸς) forever and ever." (Hebrews 1:8)

The nominative θεὸς shows that "God" is the subject noun of the sentence.

Consider the following examples:

- "**God** (θεὸς) is a Spirit." (John 4:24)
- "**God** (θεὸς) is no respecter of persons." (Acts 10:34)
- "**God** (θεὸς) is a consuming fire." (Hebrews 12:29)
- "**God** (θεὸς) is well pleased." (Hebrews 13:16)
- "**God** (θεὸς) is thy throne." (Hebrews 1:8 Moffatt)

All of these passages demonstrate the proper use of the nominative noun θεὸς. Like the word θεὸς, the Greek word for "throne" in Hebrews 1:8 is *also* in the nominative case:

> ὁ   θρόνος   σου   ὁ   θεός
> the   throne   thy [is] the   God

Since both "God" and "throne" are in the nominative and are not connected by the word "and," these two subject nouns are being *paralleled* with one another. This *parallel* drawn between "God" and "throne" allows for the understood[243] linking verb "is" to be implemented whenever Hebrews 1:8 is translated into English ("God *is* thy throne," or, "Thy throne *is* God").

In light of all that has just been said, how is it grammatically possible for a *nominative* noun to be translated as if it were a *vocative* noun ("Thy throne, O **God** (ὁ θεὸς), is forever")? If Hebrews 1:8 truly intended to show that Christ was being addressed by the title "God" then wouldn't the writer have utilized the vocative case of the word "God" rather than the nominative case? Not necessarily.

The fact of the matter is that the nominative case can be understood as the vocative *if the text originated in/is quoted from a Semitic source*. Since the Old Testament is a Semitic source, whenever its contents are translated into the Greek, as it is whenever the New Testament writers *quote* Old Testament scriptures, the resulting Greek text often uses the nominative case as the vocative. A clear example of this can be found in Hebrews 10:7, which reads as follows:

> "Then said I, Lo, I come (in the volume of the book it is written of me,) to do thy will, O **God** (ὁ θεός)." (Hebrews 10:7)

This passage is translated from a Semitic source (Psalm 40:7-8), therefore the writer was able to use the nominative noun θεός in the place of a vocative noun. It is this categorical exception that grammatically allows the nominative noun θεός in Hebrews 1:8 (quoted from Psalm 45:6) to be understood as a vocative noun.

Since both translations ("Thy throne, O God," and, "Thy throne is God") are grammatically possible in Hebrews 1:8, we must turn to sources *outside* of the clause itself in order to discover which of these two translations was intended by the writer.

Psalm 45:6 – The Hebrew Nouns are Ambiguous

The passage quoted in Hebrews 1:8 is from Psalm 45:6. However, we cannot come to any conclusions regarding Hebrews 1:8 by looking to the Hebrew noun cases in Psalm 45:6, because Hebrew grammar does not contain a vocative case at all (the nominative is used as the vocative instead). This is why Greek *quotations* of Old Testament Hebrew do not contain vocative nouns either, even when the vocative case is obviously intended within the Hebrew text being quoted (as in Hebrews 10:7).

An obvious example of how Semitic nouns, even when used as vocative nouns, are translated as nominative nouns in the Greek can be seen by comparing the following two passages:

- "At the ninth hour Jesus cried out with a loud voice, "Eloi, Eloi, lama sabachthani?" which is **translated** (*from a Semitic language into Greek*), "My **God** (θεός - nominative), my **God** (θεός - nominative), why have you forsaken me?" (Mark 15:34 NASB)

- "And about the ninth hour Jesus cried with a loud voice, saying, Eli, Eli, lama sabachthani? **that is to say** (*the meaning, not the translation*), My **God** (θεέ - vocative), my **God** (θεέ - vocative), why hast thou forsaken me?" (Matthew 27:46)

Since the New Testament, assuming primacy, is generally not a translation of Hebrew or Aramaic into Greek, we see the Greek vocative noun being applied freely whenever someone is being addressed. Yet, when the New Testament *is* translating a Semitic source, the Greek text literally relays the ambiguity of the source being quoted. The fact that Hebrew grammar does not contain vocative nouns spills over into the Greek translation of the Hebrew and thus the ambiguity of the Greek text in Hebrews 1:8 is actually expressive of the ambiguity which already existed within the Hebrew text of Psalm 45:6.

Since the Septuagint is wholly a Greek translation from a Semitic source (Hebrew/Aramaic Old Testament), we frequently find the nominative being used as a vocative therein. Because of this, we cannot base our conclusions regarding Psalm 45:6 (which is quoted in Hebrews 1:8) upon the noun cases used in the Septuagint text either, because, being a Greek translation from a Semitic source, it simply reproduces the ambiguity found in its Hebrew counterpart.

Marvin Vincent, who prefers the vocative translation in Hebrews 1:8, concedes that the Hebrew text of Psalm 45:6 is ambiguous, saying:

> I retain the vocative, although **the translation of the Hebrew is doubtful**. The following renderings have been proposed: "thy throne (which is a throne) of God": "thy throne is (a throne) of God": "God is thy throne."[244]

In summary, whether or not Hebrews 1:8 is to be understood as vocative or nominative cannot be discovered by looking at the noun cases in Psalm 45:6.

Psalm 45 – The Context Does Not Support "O God"

Although the observance of noun cases does not help us determine the proper translation of Hebrews 1:8, some have advanced the notion that the *context* of Psalm 45 *does* support the translation "Thy throne, O God." However, as we shall see, the context of Psalm 45 actually strongly supports the translation "Thy throne is God" instead.

Note: In the following section we will be discussing the content of Psalm 45. Since the author of Hebrews utilizes the readings found in the Septuagint rather than the readings we find in the extant Hebrew Old Testament,[245] we too, in agreement with the author of Hebrews, will use the Septuagint reading of Psalm 45 as our primary text (which actually appears as Psalm 44 in the LXX).[246]

Psalm 45(44):2-4 – Some people may think that this passage *excludes* Christ from the category of mankind:

> "Thou [Christ] are **more beautiful than the sons of men**: grace has been shed forth on thy lips: therefore God has blessed thee forever. Gird thy sword upon thy thigh, O Mighty One, **in thy**

> **comeliness and in thy beauty**; and bend thy bow, and prosper, and reign." (Psalm 44:2-4 LXX)

The fact that this passage says that Christ is "more beautiful than the sons of men" does not *exclude* him from being a "son of man" himself (Christ is the Son of Abraham and of David). We can see the true meaning of this text by comparing it to the words of Isaiah 53:2-3, which says:

> "He (Christ) has **no form nor comeliness**; and we saw him, but **he had no form nor beauty**. But his form was ignoble, and **inferior to that of the children of men**." (Isaiah 53:2-3 LXX)

Isaiah 53:2-3 and Psalm 45(44):2 refer to Christ's pre-resurrection and post-resurrection appearance. Christ's pre-resurrection appearance was "inferior to that of the children of men," (Isaiah 53:3) but his post-resurrection appearance is "more beautiful than the sons of men" (Psalm 44:2 LXX). Both statements refer to Christ's persona. His appearance is being contrasted with the *normal* and *expected* appearance of those in the category of sons/children of men.

Another example of this type of "above/below the norm" contrast is found in Proverbs 30:2, which says:

> "Surely I am more brutish than any man, and have not the understanding of a man." (Proverbs 30:2 KJV)

The speaker is not excluding himself from the category that he is contrasted with ("man"). Likewise, Christ is not being excluded from the category that he is contrasted with in Psalm 45(44):2.

Psalm 45(44):5-6 – Some have attempted to formulate an argument in favor of the translation, "Thy throne, *O God*," based on the Hebrew parallelism located in Psalm 45(44):5-6.

In his book *Reasoning from the Scriptures with the Jehovah's Witnesses,*[247] Ron Rhodes says:

> Hebrews 1:8, as noted earlier, is actually a quotation from Psalm 45:6. It is important to note that in Psalm 45:5 *and* 6 we find a

clear example of Hebrew parallelism. This means the literary structure of one verse is seen to be identical to that of another. Theologian Millard Erickson notes that "God is your throne" is a "most unlikely interpretation, because the preceding verse in the Septuagint translation of the psalm which is being quoted begins, 'Thy weapons, O Mighty One, are sharpened,' and the nature of Hebrew parallelism is such as to require the reading, 'Thy throne, O God.'" In other words, verse five says, *"Thy weapons, O Mighty One"* (emphasis added). And because this verse has a literary structure that is parallel to verse 6, the only translation that does justice to verse 6 is, "Thy throne, *O God.*"[248]

Refuting this argument is not difficult. First of all, Psalm 45(44):5 does *not* read "Thy weapons, O Mighty One, are sharpened." The sentence structure in Psalm 45(44):5 actually appears as follows:

τὰ   βέλη   σου   ἠκονημένα   δυνατέ
the weapons thy [are] sharpened   Mighty One (Psalm 44:5 LXX)

Sir Lancelot C.L. Brenton shows the proper translation of this passage within *The Septuagint with Apocrypha,*[249] rendering it thus:

"Thy weapons are sharpened, Mighty One" (Psalm 44:5 LXX)

Why then does the aforementioned citation *misrepresent* the Septuagint text by asserting that it reads, "Thy weapons, O Mighty One, are sharpened"? Such a translation is clearly contrary to the word order present in Psalm 45(44):5. Therefore, the basis of his argument in favor of "Thy Throne, O God" is erroneously founded upon a misrepresentation of the Hebrew parallelism in the text. With that being said, let's look at the Hebrew parallelism in Psalm 45(44): 5-6 as it *truly* appears in the Septuagint:

(v.5) τὰ   βέλη   σου   ἠκονημένα
      the   weapons thy [are] sharpened   (Psalm 44:5 LXX)

(v.6) ὁ   θρόνος   σου   ὁ   θεός
      the throne   thy [is] the   God   (Psalm 44:6 LXX)

Here we see the true word order as it appears in the Septuagint. An accurate comparison of the Greek sentence structures in Psalm 45(44):5 & 45(44):6 shows that the Hebrew parallelism existing between these two passages gives strong support for the translation, "Thy throne *is God*," rather than, "Thy throne, *O God*." If we translate the sentence structure of Psalm 45(44):5 to match, "Thy throne, O God," then it would have to read, "Thy weapons, O Sharpened." This is unacceptable.

And what is more, the second line of Psalm 45(44):6 is also similar to the first line of Psalm 45(44):6 as well, producing a uniform structure both before and after Psalm 45(44):6a.

"Thy weapons | **are** | sharpened" (Psalm 44:5 LXX)

"Thy throne | **is** | God." (Psalm 45:6a)

"The scepter of thy kingdom | **is** | a scepter of righteousness."
(Psalm 44:6b LXX)

And to cap it all off, the extant *Hebrew* Old Testament (from which our English Old Testament is translated) *also* supports the Hebrew parallelism in favor of "Thy throne is God." Observe the Hebrew parallelism drawn between Psalm 45:5 (KJV, translated from the Hebrew text) with Psalm 45:6 (when translated "Thy throne is God"):

"Thine arrows | **are** | sharp in the heart of the king's enemies." (Psalm 45:5)

"Thy throne | **is** | God for ever and ever." (Psalm 45:6)

Both the Hebrew text and the Greek Septuagint support the parallelism in favor of "Thy throne is God." On the other hand, the alleged parallelism in favor of "Thy throne, O God," is not found in either. I believe that these facts provide compelling evidence in favor of the translation "Thy throne is God."

"Thy Throne is God" – An Odd Translation?

Many commentators have argued against the translation "Thy throne is God" using the following reasoning:

> To claim that Hebrews 1:8 should read, "God is thy throne forever," and that this shows that God is the source of Christ's authority is a completely odd way to make a point. In the Scriptures a "throne" is not the source of one's authority, but the place from which one rules. Thus, heaven is called "the throne of God" in Matthew 5:34. Surely God does not derive his authority from heaven!

In response to this, I would like to quote Dr. B.F. Westcott, co-editor of the *Westcott–Hort Greek New Testament*. Westcott commented on the translation "Thy throne is God" as follows:

> It is not necessary to discuss here in detail the construction of the original words of the Psalm. The LXX admits of two renderings: ὁ θεός can be taken as a vocative in both cases (*Thy throne, O God,... therefore, O God, thy God...*) or it can be taken as the subject (or the predicate) in the first case (*God is thy throne*, or *Thy throne is God...*), and in opposition to ὁ θρόνος σου in the second case (*Therefore God, even thy God...*). The only important variation noted in the other Greek versions is that of Aquila, who gave the vocative θεέ in the first clause (Hieron, *Ep.* lxv. *ad Princ.* § 13) and, as it appears, also in the second (Field, *Hexapla ad loc*). It is scarcely possible that אֱלֹהִים (elohim) in the original can be addressed to the king. The presumption therefore is against the belief that ὁ θεός is a vocative in the LXX. Thus on the whole it seems best to adopt in the first clause the rendering: *God is Thy throne* (or, *Thy throne is God*), that is "Thy kingdom is founded upon God, the immovable Rock"; and to take ὁ θεός as in apposition in the second clause.
>
> The phrase, "God is thy throne," is not indeed found elsewhere, but it is in no way more strange than Ps.lxxi. 3 *[Lord] be thou to me a rock of habitation ... Thou art my rock and fortress.* Is.xxvi. 4 (R.V.) *In the LORD JEHOVAH is an everlasting rock.* Ps.xc. 1

> *Lord, thou hast been our dwelling place.* Ps.xci. 1 *He that dwelleth in the secret place of the Most high ...* v. 2 *I will say of the Lord, He is my refuge and my fortress,* v. 9 *Thou hast made ... the Most High thy habitation.* Deut.xxxiii. 27 *The eternal God is thy dwelling-place.* Comp. Is. xxii. 23. For the general thought compare Zech. xii. 8.[250]

Adding to the list of Dr. Westcott, I would like to point out a few other texts similar to "Thy throne is God."

Psalm 16:5 says:

> "The LORD is the portion of mine inheritance and of my cup: thou maintainest my lot." (Psalm 16:5)

Here we see that God is referred to *as* the psalmist's "portion of inheritance." The psalmist went on to explain the meaning of this when he said, "Thou maintainest my lot." A "lot" is an inheritance, hence we see the psalmist referring to the one who *maintains* his inheritance *as* his inheritance. In the same way, the LORD who *maintains* Christ's throne *is* his throne.

Isaiah 12:2 says:

> "The LORD JEHOVAH is my strength and my song." (Isaiah 12:2)

The LORD who is the *cause* of the song *is* the song—God is the *cause* of Christ's throne, so God *is* his throne.

Psalm 71:3 says:

> "[LORD] thou hast given commandment to save me; for thou art my rock and my fortress." (Psalm 71:3)

The LORD who exercised authority to save him *is* the fortress in which he is saved—God exercises authority to establish Christ's throne, therefore God *is* his throne.

Psalm 118:14 says:

> "[The LORD] is become my salvation." (Psalm 118:14)

The LORD who *caused* him to be saved *is* his salvation—The LORD who *caused* Christ to rule *is* Christ's throne.

Like the examples we just listed, a throne can be descriptive of what *qualifies* one as a ruler rather than the *place* from which a person rules. It is God who qualifies the authority of Christ, and that is why the Bible says, "Thy throne is God."

The Manuscripts Support "Thy Throne is God"

Continuing the entry from Westcott, after the previous citation where he established the validity of the reading "Thy throne is God," he then says:

> This interpretation is required if we adopt the reading αὐτοῦ for σου.[251]

What he means is, there are certain extant manuscripts containing Hebrews 1:8 that say:

> "But unto the Son he saith, Thy throne ὁ θεός is for ever and ever: a sceptre of righteousness is the sceptre of **his** (αὐτοῦ) kingdom."

If the text to reads "his" while speaking to the Son, it is obvious that another, namely God, is being referred to in the third person. This reading **does not allow for** the interpretation, "*Unto the Son he says, Thy throne, O God ... his kingdom,*" but instead **requires**, "*Unto the Son he says, Thy throne is God ... his kingdom.*"

Bruce Metzger affirms this in *A Textual Commentary on the Greek New Testament*:

> Thus, if one reads αὐτοῦ the words ὁ θεός must be taken, not as the vocative (an interpretation that is preferred by most exegetes), but as the subject (or predicate nominative).[252]

The manuscripts that contain αὐτοῦ instead of σου are 𝔓46, which dates to around 200 AD, the 4th century Codex Sinaiticus, and the 4th century Codex Vaticanus. Although αὐτοῦ is probably not the original reading,[253] these manuscripts are strong witnesses that the early church did not accept "Thy throne, O God" as the correct interpretation of Hebrews 1:8. The manuscripts which have σου rather than αὐτοῦ allow for *both* interpretations (*Thy throne, O God* **and** *Thy throne is God*), however this very authoritative group of manuscripts from early Christianity **only** allows for the interpretation "Thy throne is God." Hence, we have very weighty evidence here that the early Christians interpreted Hebrews 1:8 as "Thy throne is God."

What about the Context in Hebrews Chapter One?

It has already been shown how the one who *establishes* Christ's throne can be referred to *as* his throne. But does the context surrounding Hebrews 1:8 support such an interpretation, showing that God is the one who *established* Christ's throne? *Definitely*.

One of the most common arguments made against the interpretation "Thy throne is God" is the allegation that it is contrary to **the context** of Hebrews chapter one. The reasoning behind this objection is as follows:

> If the translation, "God is thy throne," is correct then all that this verse means is that the Son's authority is derived from God; This in no way makes Jesus unique or greater than the angels, since this could be said of any of God's obedient angels. But the context is speaking of Christ's superiority over the angels. Therefore if the point of verse 8 was simply to demonstrate that Jesus' authority is derived from God then Jesus' superiority is not demonstrated in the least. After all, the angels *also* derived their authority from God.

This claim that Christ's superiority over the angels is not demonstrated within the translation "Thy throne is God" is erroneous. In reality, God as the source of Christ's **kingdom** *does* establish his greatness over the angels. Angels are not depicted as having a kingdom. Christ is depicted as a son ruling over the kingdom of his father. The Bible never says that an angel's throne (which shows a position of *rulership*) is God. So, for Christ to be said to reign (which "throne" signifies) indeed places him in a higher position than the angels. Christ is the Lord over God's kingdom. The angels are inferior to Christ because they are his servants. In fact, this is the **whole reason** why Psalm 104(103):4 is quoted in Hebrews 1:7, which says:

> "In speaking of the angels he says, He makes his **angels** winds, his **servants** flames of fire." (Hebrews 1:7 NIV)

Other than the fact that angels are identified as *servants*, this passage bears no relativity to the surrounding context whatsoever.

After identifying the angels as "servants" in Hebrews 1:7, the writer then immediately *contrasts* their subservient status with Christ's position as the Son ruling over the Father's kingdom, writing thus:

> "In speaking of the angels he says, He makes his **angels** winds, his **servants** flames of fire. **But** unto the Son he saith, **Thy throne** is God for ever and ever: a sceptre of righteousness is the sceptre of **thy kingdom**." (Hebrews 1:7-8)

This clearly shows that God established Christ as ruler over his kingdom *rather than* the angels. And the author of Hebrews *repeats* this point when he goes on to say:

> "**But** to which of the angels said he at any time, sit on my right hand, until **I** (God) **make** thine enemies thy footstool? Are they not all ministering spirits, sent forth **to serve** them who shall be heirs of salvation?" (Hebrews 1:13-14)

And he again contrasts the position of Christ as ruler with the position of the angels as servants when he afterwards says:

> "For unto the angels hath he not put in subjection the world to come, whereof we speak. **But** one in a certain place testified, saying, What is man, that thou art mindful of him ... Thou didst set him over the works of thy hands: Thou hast put all things in subjection under his feet." (Hebrews 2:5-8)

The man whom God has "put all things in subjection under" is Christ (1 Corinthians 15:27). Therefore, again, the point being made was that God established Christ as ruler rather than the angels.[254]

God *established* Christ's throne and therefore, in scriptural terminology, God *is* his throne.

> "To the Son he saith, Thy throne **is God** ... But to which of the angels said he at any time, 'Sit on my right hand until **I make** thine enemies thy footstool'?" (Hebrews 1:8, 13)

God is shown to be the one who establishes Christ's rulership by these words, "Sit on my right hand until **I make** thine enemies thy footstool." (Hebrews 1:13.) And thus the translation "Thy throne is God" is perfectly in line with the context. The author is clearly contrasting ***the position*** of Christ with the position of angels. By contrast, the argument that "Christ's divine nature" is in view here is completely disconnected from the context of Hebrews.

Westcott makes some good comments later in his entry for Hebrews 1:8, saying:

> It is commonly supposed that the force of the quotation lies in the divine title (ὁ θεός) which, as it is held, is applied to the Son. It seems however from the whole form of the argument to lie rather in the description that is given in the Son's office and endowment. The angels are subject to constant change, He has a dominion for ever and ever; they work through material powers, He—the Incarnate Son—fulfills a moral sovereignty and is crowned with unique joy. ... In whatever way then ὁ θεός be taken, the quotation establishes the conclusion which the writer wishes to draw as to the essential difference of the Son and the angels. Indeed it might appear to many that the direct application of the divine Name to the Son would obscure the thought.[255]

Hebrews 1:10-12 – Not Addressed to the Son

It is commonly thought that Hebrews 1:10 contains the Father's words spoken to the Son, but that is not the case.

Hebrews 1:8-12 says:

> "(**8**) But unto the Son he saith, Thy throne is God for ever and ever: a sceptre of righteousness is the sceptre of thy kingdom. (**9**) Thou hast loved righteousness, and hated iniquity; therefore God, even thy God, hath anointed thee with the oil of gladness above thy fellows. (**10**) And, Thou, Lord, in the beginning hast laid the foundation of the earth; and the heavens are the works of thine hands: (**11**) They shall perish; but thou remainest; and they all shall wax old as doth a garment; (**12**) And as a vesture shalt thou fold them up, and they shall be changed: but thou art the same, and thy years shall not fail." (Hebrews 1:8-12)

Hebrews 1:10-12 contains a direct quotation from Psalm 102(101):24-27. When we look at the context in Psalm 102 (101 LXX) then it becomes supremely evident that the Father is *not* speaking to the Son therein.

Psalm 102(101):24-27 (which is partially quoted in Hebrews 1:10-12) reads as follows in the Septuagint:

> "He answered him in the way of his strength: **tell me the fewness of my days. Take me not away in the midst of my days: thy years are through all generations**. In the beginning, thou, O Lord, didst lay the foundation of the earth; and the heavens are the works of thine hands. They shall perish, but thou remainest: and they all shall wax old as a garment; and as a vesture shalt thou fold them, and they shall be changed. But thou art the same, and thy years shall not fail."
> (Psalm 101:23-27 LXX)

In the *King James Version* this passage, representing the Hebrew text, reads as follows:

"He weakened my strength in the way; he shortened my days. **I said, O my God, take me not away in the midst of my days: thy years are throughout all generations**. Of old hast thou laid the foundation of the earth: and the heavens are the works of thy hands. They shall perish, but thou shalt endure: yea, all of them shall wax old as a garment; as a vesture shalt thou change them, and they shalt be changed: But thou art the same, and thy years have no end."
(Psalm 102:23-27 KJV)

This does *not* show the Father pleading to the Son to "take me not away in the midst of my days: thy years are throughout all generations." Hence, the quotation in Hebrews 1:10-12 that is taken from this text does not show the Father speaking to the Son.

Furthermore, the quote from Psalm 102 (101 LXX) is not introduced within Hebrews 1:10-12 in such a way that would make it applicable to the addressee of Hebrews 1:8-9. In the New Testament, whenever two or more Old Testament quotations are applied successively to the same subject matter, they *never* simply have the word καί (kai – *and*) joining them. Usually, whenever two Old Testament passages are successively applied to the same subject matter, you will find the word πάλιν (palin - *again*) between the two.

- "That the saying of Esaias the prophet might be fulfilled, which he spake, Lord, who hath believed our report? And to whom hath the arm of the Lord been revealed? Therefore they could not believe, because that Esaias said **again** (πάλιν), He hath blinded their eyes, and hardened their heart; that they should not see with their eyes, nor understand with their heart, and be converted, and I should heal them." (John 12:38-40)

- "For these things were done, that the scripture should be fulfilled, A bone of him shall not be broken. And **again** (πάλιν) another scripture saith, They shall look on him whom they pierced." (John 19:36-37)

- "And that the Gentiles might glorify God for his mercy; as it is written, For this cause I will confess to thee among the Gentiles, and sing unto thy name. And **again** (πάλιν) he saith, Rejoice, ye

Gentiles, with his people. And **again** (πάλιν), Praise the Lord, all ye Gentiles; and laud him, all ye people. And **again** (πάλιν), Esaias saith, There shall be a root of Jesse, and he that shall rise to reign over the Gentiles; in him shall the Gentiles trust." (Romans 15:9-12)

- "For the wisdom of this world is foolishness with God. For it is written, He taketh the wise in their own craftiness. And **again** (πάλιν), The Lord knoweth the thoughts of the wise, that they are vain."
(1 Corinthians 3:19-20)

These examples clearly demonstrate how two scriptures, when quoted in succession and applied to the same subject matter (as stated above), are regularly joined by the word "again" (πάλιν). The author of the epistle to the Hebrews demonstrates this same style as well:

- "For both he that sanctifieth and they who are sanctified are all of one: for which cause he is not ashamed to call them brethren, Saying, I will declare thy name unto my brethren, in the midst of the church will I sing praise unto thee. And **again** (πάλιν), I will put my trust in him. And **again** (πάλιν), Behold I and the children which God hath given me." (Hebrews 2:11-13)

- "For we know him that hath said, Vengeance belongeth unto me, I will recompense, saith the Lord. And **again** (πάλιν), The Lord shall judge his people." (Hebrews 10:30)

In light of this principle, let's observe its application in Hebrews chapter one.

Hebrews 1:5-6 says:

"For unto which of the angels said he at any time, Thou art my Son, this day have I begotten thee? And **again** (πάλιν), I will be to him a Father, and he shall be to me a Son? And **again** (πάλιν), when he bringeth in the firstbegotten into the world, he saith, And let all the angels of God worship him." (Hebrews 1:5-6)

These three Old Testament texts are all quoted as statements that point to the Son's position. Do you see how the word "again" (πάλιν) is used to show that the scriptures being quoted all refer to a common subject? Yet, when the subject matter is changed from the Son's position (Hebrews 1:5-6) to the angels' position (Hebrews 1:7) the author does *not* use the word "again" (πάλιν), he merely says "and" (καi):

> "For unto which of the angels said he at any time; Thou art my Son, this day have I begotten thee? **And** (καi) **again** (πάλιν), I will be to him a Father, and he shall be to me a Son? **And** (καί) **again** (πάλιν), when he bringeth in the first begotten into the world, he saith, And let all the angels of God worship him. **And** (καί) to the angels he saith, Who maketh his angels spirits, and his ministers a flame of fire." (Hebrews 1:5-7)

When the subject matter changed in those verses from what was said regarding the Son to what was said regarding the angels, the word "again" (πάλιν) was dropped. Similarly, Hebrews 1:8-12 goes on to say:

> "But unto the Son he saith, Thy throne is God for ever and ever: a sceptre of righteousness is the sceptre of thy kingdom. Thou hast loved righteousness, and hated iniquity; therefore God, even thy God, hath anointed thee with the oil of gladness above thy fellows. **And** (καί), Thou, Lord, in the beginning hast laid the foundation of the earth; and the heavens are the works of thine hands: They shall perish; but thou remainest; and they all shall wax old as doth a garment; And as a vesture shalt thou fold them up, and they shall be changed: but thou art the same, and thy years shall not fail." (Hebrews 1:8-12)

I submit that the reason why the writer does not include the word "again" (πάλιν) in Hebrews 1:10 is because he is *not* applying the scripture quoted therein to the same subject matter of Hebrews 1:8-9. If the purpose of quoting Psalm 45:6 (in Hebrews 1:8) actually *were* to show that Christ is God, and Psalm 102(101):24-27 was successively quoted in reference to the same subject (Christ being God), the author would have likely included the word "again" (πάλιν) within the introduction to the second quotation. He did not do so. I believe this is a grammatical indicator showing that the subject matter changed. The Son is the addressee of the quotation in Hebrews 1:8-9 and, as was proven by the context of Psalm 102 (101 LXX), the Father is the addressee of the quotation in Hebrews 1:10-12.

Why is Psalm 102:24-27 Quoted?

Why then did the author of the epistle to the Hebrews quote a statement made to the Father? How is such a quotation applicable in the context of this epistle? The reason why Psalm 102(101):24-27 is quoted in Hebrews 1:10-12 is not to identify the *addressee of the* quotation, but rather to point out *the facts stated within* the quotation.

Look at what it says:

> "Thou, Lord, in the beginning hast laid the foundation of **the earth**; and the heavens are the works of thine hands: **They shall perish**; but thou remainest; and **they all shall wax old** as doth a garment; And as a vesture shalt thou fold them up, and **they shall be changed**: but thou art the same, and thy years shall not fail."
> (Hebrews 1:10-12)

The content of this quotation describes how the *current* heavens and the *current* earth will be destroyed and subsequently made new (*i.e.,* "changed"). Since the earth in its current state shall *not* endure forever, but Hebrews 1:8 speaks of Christ's kingdom as something that *will* endure forever, Christ's eternal kingdom *must* pertain to the world to come (which cannot be shaken, Hebrews 12:26-27). The author of Hebrews goes on to speak of these things in Hebrews 2:5, saying:

> "For unto the angels hath he not put in subjection **the world to come**, whereof we speak." (Hebrews 2:5)

Notice that he says, "the world to come whereof we speak." He was previously referring to Christ's eternal kingdom in the world to come when he said:

> "Thy throne is God **for ever and ever**: a sceptre of righteousness is the sceptre of thy kingdom." (Hebrews 1:8)

But lest the readers should think that the Messiah was to come and reign forever in this *present* world (which *was* the expectation of many Jews), the writer goes on, after showing that the Messiah's kingdom *is* eternal, to also show that this present world is *not* eternal,[256] saying:

> "But unto the Son he saith, Thy throne is God **for ever and ever**: a sceptre of righteousness is the sceptre of **thy kingdom**. Thou hast loved righteousness, and hated iniquity; therefore God, even thy God, hath anointed thee with the oil of gladness above thy fellows. And, Thou, Lord, in the beginning hast laid the foundation of **the earth; and the heavens** are the works of thine hands: **They shall perish**; but thou remainest; and **they all shall wax old as doth a garment; And as a vesture shalt thou fold them up, and they shall be changed**: but thou art the same, and thy years shall not fail ... For unto the angels hath he not **put in subjection the world to come, whereof we speak**. But one in a certain place testified, saying, What is man, that thou art mindful of him ... Thou didst set him over the works of thy hands: Thou hast put all things in subjection under his feet. For in that he put all things in subjection under him, he left nothing that is not put under him. **But now we see not yet all things put under him**. ... But now he (God) hath promised, saying, Yet once more I shake not **the earth** only, but also the heaven. And this word, Yet once more, signifieth the removing of those things that are shaken, as of things that are made, that those things which cannot be shaken may remain. Wherefore we receiving **a kingdom which cannot be moved**, let us have grace, whereby we may serve God acceptably with reverence and godly fear: for our God is a consuming fire."
> (Hebrews 1:8-12, 2:5-8, 12:26-29)

Hence, the eternal kingdom pertains to the world to come, and that is precisely the point being conveyed by the author's use of Psalm 102(101):24-27.

Chapter Thirteen
John 1 – The Word

So many people today read John 1:1, which says *"the Word* was God," as an affirmation that *Jesus* was God. *Is that what it says?* If we assume "Word" *automatically* means "Jesus" then, yes, we would have an example in John 1:1 of Jesus being referred to as "God." Notwithstanding, this conclusion alone would not necessitate that Jesus is God in any literal sense. In chapter three, we saw that individuals were often called by the name of the archetype they represented. In the Bible, Jesus is God's representative and is even called "the image of God." (2 Corinthians 4:4, Colossians 1:15.) Now, if I show you an image of myself, like a photograph of me, and ask you, "Who is that?" you will say, "That is *you.*" So, the image *of* me *is* me, but that does not necessitate that I am somehow composed of two or more persons. Rather, there is one true me and my image is me by expression, but there yet remains only one me. So also, even if we conclude that the "Word" in John 1:1 is Jesus, this does not automatically prove that Jesus, who the Bible unambiguously identifies as the image of God, is God in any literal sense. Perhaps if religious organizations placed as much of an emphasis on Jesus being the *image* of God as they do on Jesus being *called* God, this kind of explanation would be readily preferred by the masses as more consistent with both Scripture and logic. However, due to indoctrination and an overemphasis on some parts of the Bible, to the exclusion of others, those who have been taught Trinitarianism all their lives often feel that the illogical explanation of three persons all literally being the same God *must* be what the Bible *means* before they even *study* what the Bible actually *says*. Yet, on our part, let us endeavor to examine John 1 without bringing any presuppositions or foregone conclusions to the table. Let's just look at what the text *actually* says and allow our conclusions to be drawn *only* from the Bible. *Amen?*

What Does "the Word" Mean?

The Greek word translated as "Word" in John 1:1 is λόγος (logos), which refers to *a summation of either a discourse or thinking.*

Thayer's Greek-English Lexicon of the New Testament defines λόγος as follows:

> λόγος prop. *a collecting, collection*—and that, as well of those things which are put together in thought, as of those which, having been thought *i.e.,* gathered together in the mind, are expressed in words. Accordingly, a twofold use of the term is to be distinguished: one which relates to speaking, and one which relates to thinking.[257]

The word λόγος relates to either a collection of *speaking* or *thinking*. Outside the New Testament,[258] λόγος was often used to denote the latter (*reason/thinking*).[259] However, within the New Testament, λόγος is employed to denote *something spoken*, as in *a message* of some sort.

> "For unto us was the gospel preached, as well as unto them: but **the word** (ὁ λόγος) preached did not profit them, not being mixed with faith in them that heard it." (Hebrews 4:2)

Here, ὁ λόγος (*ho logos* – the same phrase translated as "the Word" in John 1:1) refers to "the gospel." Elsewhere, ὁ λόγος is also used to denote *a prophetic saying*, as we see in the Book of John:

> "That **the saying** (ὁ λόγος) of Esaias the prophet might be fulfilled, which he spake …" (John 12:38)

And, again from the Book of John:

> "But this cometh to pass, that **the word** (ὁ λόγος) might be fulfilled that is written in their law, They hated me without a cause."
> (John 15:25)

As we just saw in the examples, ὁ λόγος isn't used in the Book of John in such a way that would automatically demand some *person* be in view. Rather, to the contrary, it is apparent that, after chapter one, ὁ λόγος is *always* used by the author to denote *that which is spoken* or a *discourse* of some kind (λόγος denotes *something said*, but with the article, ὁ, *some- things* **specific** *that was said*). Here is a list showing how ὁ λόγος (in the nominative case) is translated everywhere in the Book of John (using the KJV):

- "the Word" (John 1:1, 14)
- "that saying" (John 4:37)
- "saying" (John 6:60, 7:36, 21:23)
- "word" (John 8:37, 17:17)
- "the word" (John 10:35, 12:48, 14:24. 15:25)
- "the saying" (John 12:38, 18:9, 32)

It is easy to see that ὁ λόγος is **not** used in the Book of John outside of chapter one to denote an individual (*i.e.,* Christ). Since chapters 2-21 in the Book of John do not use ὁ λόγος in reference to a person, is it truly justifiable to read ὁ λόγος in John chapter one as if an individual is in view there? The men who translated the Greek into English *do* show that they believe ὁ λόγος is to be taken differently in John chapter one by their capitalization of the "W" in "the Word," but the Greek text has no such capitalization. Are there some *contextual* factors that would justify a departure from the impersonal use of ὁ λόγος *everywhere else* in the Book of John?

The Word – It or He?

William Tyndale was burned at the stake in 1536 for translating the Bible into English. His Bible was the first English translation that became widespread due to the advent of the printing press. This preceded the *King James Version*, which was translated in 1611. In Tyndale's translation, he does not refer to the λόγος as "him," but as "it" in John 1:3-4.

Tyndale's English translation of John 1:2-4 reads as follows (parentheses mine):

> "**The same** (οὗτος) was in the beginning with God. All things were made by **it** (αὐτοῦ), and without **it** (αὐτοῦ) was made nothing, that was made. In **it** (αὐτῷ) was life, and the life was the light of men."

Grammatically speaking, both "it" and "him" are allowable translations. This is because, in the Greek, pronouns always match the gender of the antecedent noun (*i.e.,* the noun identified by the pronouns). And, since impersonal nouns in the Greek language are often masculine, the pronouns that follow those masculine nouns will, by default, be masculine as well.

Let's look at some examples from the Book of John to illustrate this point:

> "**The world** (ὁ κόσμος) cannot hate you; but me it hateth, because I testify **of it** (αὐτοῦ), that the works thereof are evil." (John 7:7)

In the Greek language, *the world* (ὁ κόσμος) is a *masculine* noun, so the pronoun *referring back to* that masculine noun is *also* masculine, but we still translate the pronoun as "it" because we know that *the world* is not a *person*.

> "Now **the coat** (ὁ χιτὼν) was without seam ... They said therefore among themselves, Let us not rend it, but cast lots for **it** (αὐτοῦ), whose it shall be." (John 19:24)

The coat (ὁ χιτὼν) is a masculine noun, so the pronoun (αὐτοῦ) that refers back to it is also masculine. Since we understand that a coat is not a *he*, we translate the masculine pronoun into English as *it* instead.

If the KJV translators thought that *the world* and *the coat* in the examples above were conscious beings, they would have conveyed that by translating the pronouns as "he" instead of as "it." So then, whether a pronoun is rendered "it" or "he" is determined by the translator's *opinion* of whether a *he* or an *it* is in view, not by the Greek nouns and pronouns alone. Hence, if we concluded that ὁ λόγος referred to an *individual* in John 1:1, it would be best to read the corresponding pronouns as "him." Yet, since ὁ λόγος is used throughout John chapters 2-21 as an impersonal noun, denoting *that which is said*, it makes the most sense, if we are consistent, to take ὁ λόγος in John 1 in a similar fashion.

John 1:1b – The Word was "with" God?

The Greek word that is translated as "with" in John 1:1 does not inherently mean *with*. There are other words that mean *with* in the Greek, σύν (*soon*) and μετά (*meta*), but the word that is translated as "with" in John 1:1 is πρὸς (*pros*), which typically means *toward* or *unto*.

The Greek text of John 1:1b reads as follows:

καὶ	ὁ	λόγος	ἦν	πρὸς	τὸν	θεόν
and	the	Word	was	unto	the	God

Here we see the Greek phrase πρὸς τὸν θεόν, which is so often translated as "with God" in most of our English versions. However, when we look at the other places in the New Testament where πρὸς τὸν θεόν is used, we see that this phrase *always* carries the meaning of *unto/toward God*.

Adolph E. Knoch (1874–1965), producer of the *Concordant Literal New Testament,* translates John 1:1b as, "And the Word was *toward* God." He argues that "with God" is not the best translation of the Greek phrase πρὸς τὸν θεόν and makes a case for this position by examining every other instance in the New Testament where πρὸς τὸν θεόν is used. Here is every instance of that phrase in the New Testament:

- John 1:1 "the Word was **with** (πρὸς) **God** (τὸν θεόν)"

- John 1:2 "was in the beginning **with** (πρὸς) **God** (τὸν θεόν)"

- John 13:3 "he was come from God and went **to** (πρὸς) **God** (τὸν θεόν)"

- Acts 4:24 "they lifted up their voice **to** (πρὸς) **God** (τὸν θεόν)"

- Acts 12:5 "prayer was made ... **unto** (πρὸς) **God** (τὸν θεόν) for him"

- Acts 24:16 "a conscience void of offense **toward** (πρὸς) **God** (τὸν θεόν)"
- Romans 5:1 "we have peace **with** (πρὸς) **God** (τὸν θεόν)"
- Romans 10:1 "my heart's desire and prayer **to** (πρὸς) **God** (τὸν θεόν)"
- Romans 15:17 "those things which pertain **to** (πρὸς) **God** (τὸν θεόν)"
- Romans 15:30 "your prayers **to** (πρὸς) **God** (τὸν θεόν)"
- 2 Corinthians 3:4 "such trust have we ... **to** (πρὸς) **Godward** (τὸν θεόν)"
- 2 Corinthians 13:7 "now I pray **to** (πρὸς) **God** (τὸν θεόν)"
- Philippians 4:6 "your requests be made known **unto** (πρὸς) **God** (τὸν θεόν)"
- 1 Thessalonians 1:8 "your faith **to** (πρὸς) **Godward** (τὸν θεόν)"
- 1 Thessalonians 1:9 "you turned **to** (πρὸς) **God** (τὸν θεόν) from idols"
- Hebrews 2:17 "a high priest in things pertaining **to** (πρὸς) **God** (τὸν θεόν)"
- Hebrews 5:1 "high priest ... in things pertaining **to** (πρὸς) **God** (τὸν θεόν)"
- 1 John 3:21 "then have we confidence **toward** (πρὸς) **God** (τὸν θεόν)"
- Revelation 12:5 "her child was caught up **unto** (πρὸς) **God** (τὸν θεόν)"
- Revelation 13:6 "blasphemy **against** (πρὸς) **God** (τὸν θεόν)"

You see, πρὸς τὸν θεόν denotes a direction *toward God* or *unto God*. While this list is good to demonstrate how πρὸς τὸν θεόν always denotes *toward God*, John 1:1b ("And ὁ λόγος was πρὸς τὸν θεόν") presents πρὸς τὸν θεόν somewhat differently than most of the examples above. Instead of stating that something was *done* unto or toward God, John 1:1b says something *itself* was unto God. The Word *itself* was πρὸς τὸν θεόν.

To understand what it means to say the Word itself was πρὸς God, we should examine other passages where a noun is πρὸς another noun. Here are some of the examples commonly brought forth by Trinitarians.

- Mark 14:49 "I was daily **with** (πρὸς) you in the temple teaching"
- 1 Corinthians 16:6 "And it may be that I will abide, yea, and winter **with** (πρὸς) you."
- 2 Corinthians 5:8 "We are confident, I say, and willing rather to be absent from the body, and to be present **with** (πρὸς) the Lord."
- 2 Corinthians 11:9 "And when I was present **with** (πρὸς) you, and wanted, I was chargeable to no man."
- Galatians 1:18 "Then after three years I went up to Jerusalem to see Peter, and abode **with** (πρὸς) him fifteen days."
- Galatians 4:20 "I desire to be present **with** (πρὸς) you now, and to change my voice; for I stand in doubt of you."
- 1 Thessalonians 3:4 "For verily, when we were **with** (πρὸς) you, we told you before that we should suffer tribulation"

These examples involving personal nouns are often brought forth as justification for translating John 1:1b as "And the Word was **with** (πρὸς) God." And, indeed, they do show the validity of such a translation **if we take ὁ λόγος as a personal noun**. However, even those who *do* take ὁ λόγος as a personal noun in John 1:1b fail to see *why* πρὸς is actually used in all of those other passages. As the examples above show, the personal noun that was πρὸς ("with") another noun did not originally *begin* in that specified location. The whole reason why πρὸς is used is to show that one personal noun *traveled to where another stationary noun already was*. For example, Paul is talking about being with the Thessalonians *after he traveled to them*.

"For verily, when we were **with** (πρὸς) you, we told you before that we should suffer tribulation" (1 Thessalonians 3:4)

A personal noun that is πρὸς another noun has **moved** from a former location **to be where the stationary noun abides**. This is the case in all of the commonly referenced examples, listed above, where a personal noun is πρὸς another noun. So, to be consistent, if we take ὁ λόγος as a personal noun in John 1:1, the meaning would be, "the Word was *with* God" *because the Word **moved** from a former location to be at God's location.* Now, instead of trying to figure out what *that* could mean, let us rather go back to the beginning of this process and ask, "Why should we even take ὁ λόγος as a personal noun in the first place?" As we already discussed, taking ὁ λόγος as a personal noun in John 1 would be contrary to the way ὁ λόγος is used *everywhere else* in the Book of John. So, why should we *assume* a definition of ὁ λόγος in John 1 that is *foreign to the rest of the Book of John?* Isn't it better to allow the author to demonstrate *his own* definition of terms and for us to study *his* use of such terms to understand *his* intent? *Why would anyone resist such a reasonable methodology?* Regardless, on *our* part, let us approach the Bible as its student, not as its teacher. Instead of departing from the normal use of ὁ λόγος, let us accept ὁ λόγος in John 1 as it is used everywhere else throughout the Book of John.

When we take ὁ λόγος as an *impersonal* noun in John 1:1b, what should we understand by the phrase, "And ὁ λόγος ἦν πρὸς τὸν θεόν"? Was *something said* "with" God? *How could that make sense?* In our pursuit of a biblical explanation, we will first look at *another example* from the Book of John which *demonstrates* how one impersonal noun can be πρὸς another noun. Then, by discovering how one impersonal noun can be πρὸς another noun *elsewhere* in the Book of John, we can simply transfer that established principle over to our understanding of John 1:1b.

"This **sickness** (impersonal noun) **is** (ἔστιν) not **unto** (πρὸς) **death** (accusative noun)." (John 11:4)

Now, this is a good example of how one impersonal noun (sickness) can itself be πρὸς another noun. The sickness is not *doing something* to or toward death. Rather, this shows that *sickness itself* can be πρὸς death.

What this means is not entirely foreign to what we saw earlier when a *personal* noun *traveled to the location* of another noun that was stationary, because *progress toward the outcome* is still intended. Even so, when a sickness is πρὸς death, it is not because the sickness is *traveling* anywhere. Rather, it is because the sickness is *progressing* **unto the extent of** *death.* The sickness has **reached the point of** death and is now **associated with** death itself.

Here is another example from John that, while less straightforward, still demonstrates how πρὸς means *extending unto an association with*.

> "Look on the **fields** (impersonal noun); for **they are white** already **to** (πρὸς) **harvest** (accusative noun)." (John 4:35)

Here, the fields are *white unto the harvest*. This means that *the status* of the fields *progressed to a point of association with* the harvest.

And here also I will include the following example, because it conveys a similar concept.

> "Ye were willing **for a season** (πρὸς ὥραν) to rejoice." (John 5:3)

It is obvious here that πρὸς *a season* means *to the extent of* a timeframe, now retrospectively summarized as *a season*.

We see from these examples that πρὸς can denote *to the extent of association with*. Notice how these instances have more of a *conceptualized progression* in view, rather than one noun *traveling* to another. Notwithstanding, like with the personal noun examples we saw, πρὸς continues to show, *not the progression alone*, but *the outcome of that progression*. Hence, we do not think of **going toward** the destination, but rather **having arrived at** the destination, i.e., with.

Now that we have looked at how the Book of John uses πρὸς when an impersonal noun is involved, let's carry our findings over to John 1:1b.

> "The Word (that specific category of things spoken) was *traced to* and *associated with* God."

John 1:1b is saying that there was *a specific category of things spoken* which were to be *traced to God and associated with him*. Put plainly, when this λόγος was spoken, those words were *traced back to* God and identified with him.

John 1:1c – The Word was God

How can ὁ λόγος (that specific category of things spoken) which was *associated with* God also *be* God? As we discussed in chapter three, an image is called by the name of the archetype. If we were to look at a photograph (an *image*) of Abraham Lincoln, and I was to ask you, "Who is that?" You would probably say, "That is Abraham Lincoln." *Yes!* The photograph of Abraham Lincoln *is* Abraham Lincoln, *but not in an absolute sense*. It is Abraham Lincoln *by expression*, but not directly. So even though it *is* Abraham Lincoln, it is *not* the *one true* Abraham Lincoln in an absolute and unqualified sense.

Now, let's see how this principle applies to John 1:1.

> "The Word (that specific category of things spoken) was *associated with* God and the Word *expressed* God." (John 1:1)

The grammatical structure of the Greek in John 1:1 also supports this, or is at least not contrary to it. The Greek text of John 1:1b contains a direct article τὸν, which modifies the noun θεόν (God), saying:

ὁ λόγος ἦν πρὸς **τὸν** θεόν
the Word was with **the** God   (John 1:1b)

However, the author did *not* place a direct article before θεὸς (God) within John 1:1c, which says:

καὶ θεὸς ἦν ὁ λόγος
and God was the Word   (John 1:1c)

When John 1:1c says that "the Word was **God** (θεὸς)," the author *omits* the direct article before the word θεὸς, showing that he is referring to God *in a less emphatic manner*. This omission of the direct article, when ὁ λόγος is called *God,* shows that ὁ λόγος, that specific category of things spoken, truly expressed God, but it was not God itself (as if to say that God was himself a category of sayings).

John 1:1a – In the Beginning

John 1:1 begins with these words:

> "**Ἐν ἀρχῇ (in the beginning)** was the Word…" (John 1:1a)

The same author of John 1:1 also wrote these words in 1 John 2:7:

> "Brethren, I write no new commandment unto you, but an old commandment which ye had from the beginning (ἀπ' ἀρχῆς). The old commandment is **the word** (ὁ λόγος) which ye have heard from the beginning (ἀπ' ἀρχῆς)." (1 John 2:7)

The "old commandment" that they had "from the beginning" is ὁ λόγος (same terminology used in John 1:1). This commandment, referred to as ὁ λόγος, was heard by men "from the beginning." (1 John 2:7.) So, contrary to popular opinion, the phrase "the beginning" does not *automatically* denote the precise moment creation began. "The beginning" denotes just that, *when whatever is being referred to in the context began.* When people said "the beginning" in the New Testament (ἀρχῇ, as in John 1:1), they were many times only referring to *the beginning of Jesus' public ministry*, which ministry was, incontrovertibly, the focus of their writing. Notice especially the opening statements of the Book of Mark and the Book of Luke.

- "**The beginning** (ἀρχή) of the gospel of Jesus Christ, the Son of God;" (Mark 1:1)

- "Forasmuch as many have taken in hand to set forth in order a declaration of those things which are most surely believed among us, Even as they delivered them unto us, which from **the beginning** (ἀρχή) were eyewitnesses, and ministers of the word (τοῦ λόγου[260]);" (Luke 1:1-2)

Like Mark and Luke, the Book of John uses "the beginning" *after* John 1 to denote *the beginning of Jesus' ministry* when Jesus says to his disciples, "And ye also shall bear witness, because ye have been with me from **the beginning**." (John 15:27.) So, "the beginning," according to John 15:27, denotes the time when the disciples began to travel with Jesus, which was at the beginning of Jesus' public ministry.

Even though "the beginning" often refers to *the onset of Jesus' public ministry* elsewhere, the opening words of John 1:1 ("In the beginning") are usually taken as an *intentional correlation* to the opening words of Genesis 1:1. Both John 1:1 and Genesis 1:1 (LXX) begin with the exact same Greek phrase, "Ἐν ἀρχῇ" (in the beginning). This is *different* than what we find in other passages of John (and 1 & 2 John), where, instead of "**in** the beginning," we see "**from** the beginning." The phrase *from the beginning* denotes something that *extends **from the point of** the beginning **into the future***. The phrase *in the beginning* denotes a timeframe *contained **within** the stated parameter—**in** the beginning*. I believe that an intentional distinction is being made between "in the beginning" and "from the beginning" within John (and 1 & 2 John) precisely because the author is correlating "*in* the beginning" with Genesis 1:1, while using "*from* the beginning" to denote the beginning of Jesus' ministry, etc. Furthermore, the *context* of John 1 talks about creation (John 1:3, 10), so I see a connection therein to Genesis 1 as well. Thus, when discussing John 1:1 from here on, I will have the same timeframe as Genesis 1:1 in mind.

John 1:3 – "By Means of" the Word

The more ancient English translations render διά in John 1:3 as "by":

- "All things were made **by** it" (Tyndale)
- "All things were made **by** him" (KJV)

However, modern translations typically read "through" instead of "by."

- "All things were made **through** Him" (NKJV)
- "**Through** him all things were made" (NIV)
- "God created everything **through** him" (NLT)

So, which is correct? *Both* are acceptable, as long as the translations that read "by" are understood correctly. Some read "by" and think that the Word is the *originator* of the action, but that is not the case. Rather, *God* is the *originator* of the creation process, which was carried out *through* that which he spoke—all things were made *by* God, who made all things *by* [means of] the Word. So how did God create by the Word? I have already presented the evidence for why the *Word* should be understood as *something said*. Accordingly, I interpret John 1:3 as *God spoke creation into existence*. The Racovian Catechism takes the position that the Word in John 1:3 is Jesus, but asserts that the new, second creation is in view. This interpretation is difficult to maintain, because John 1:10 says that the world (ὁ κόσμος) which was made δι' αὐτοῦ *knew him not*. This could *not* be applicable to the new creation (unless ὁ κόσμος could justifiably be understood as *the Jewish system* in John 1:10). Modern-day Unitarians typically see this present creation in John 1:3, but read διά as *in view of*, e.g., *God made all things **with Christ in mind***. This interpretation finds grammatical support in the context, because of how the same phrase δι' αὐτοῦ, translated as "by him" in John 1:3 (KJV), is used in John 1:7.

> "There was a man sent from God, whose name was John. The same came for a witness, to bear witness of the Light, that all men **through him** (δι' αὐτοῦ) might believe." (John 1:6-7 KJV)

Traditionally, Trinitarians have read John 1:3 as *God performed the act of creation **through the agency of** the Word*. However, if we applied the same *action done through the agency of* reasoning to δι' αὐτοῦ in John 1:7, it would mean that *all men were to perform the act of believing **through the agency** of John the Baptist*.

> "… that all men through him (δι' αὐτοῦ) might believe."

Although most would agree that the Word *carried out the act* of creation which originated from God, we can all agree that John did not *carry out the act* of believing which originated from all men. Rather, the meaning is that all men might believe "because of" John. Since the traditional explanation of δι' αὐτοῦ in John 1:3 is not applicable just a few verses later in John 1:7, we cannot dogmatically assert that traditional view on the basis of grammar alone. See chapter twelve herein, subheading *Hebrews*

1:2 – Through Christ? where Grotius argues δι' αὐτοῦ may be translated "on whose account." Unlike Hebrews 1:2, John 1:3 is dealing with *the speaking of God*, not the "Son," per se (unless we were to take ὁ λόγος in John 1:1 as the Word *made flesh* within the archetypal *plan* of God). Although I take both passages as denoting "through," we cannot dismiss those who prefer "because of" as if they tout a grammatical impossibility.

John 1:4 – Life in the Word

Most translations render αὐτοῦ as a masculine pronoun in John 1:3.

> "All things were made by **him**; and without **him** was not any thing made that was made." (John 1:3 KJV)

However, William Tyndale, that martyr of God who translated the New Testament into English several decades before the *King James Version* even existed, renders αὐτοῦ in the neuter gender.

> "All things were made by **it**, and without **it**, was made nothing, that was made." (John 1:3 Tyndale)

As I have explained already, I believe Tyndale's rendering is correct, because ὁ λόγος denotes *a specific category of* **things spoken** *that were to be traced to God, associated with God,* and *that expressed God*. When we read that God made all things *by* or *through* the Word, we understand that God made all things *by means of* the Word.

> "By the word of the LORD were the heavens made; and all the host of them by the breath of his mouth." (Psalm 33:6)

God's ability to create life from nothing is proven by the fact that all things came to be through his Word already. By means of that which he spoke, God created all life. This establishes our hope that, just as he has made life to exist *beforehand*, so also we may live *again* by that same Word.

> "All things were made by it, and without it, was made nothing, that was made. **In it was life** …" (John 1:3-4a Tyndale)

The same author of John 1:1-4 also wrote these words regarding the eternal life manifested in the resurrected Christ:

> "For **the life was manifested**, and we have seen it, and bear witness, and **shew unto you that eternal life**, which was πρὸς τὸν πατέρα (traced back to and associated with the Father), and was manifested unto us." (1 John 1:2)

Our *hope* of a life to come is *based upon* God's historic creation of life. God *already* made the life that we see and experience now. He also evidenced that eternal life to come when he raised Jesus from death.

John 1:6-7 – John Prepares the Way for God

John the Baptist is a major figure in the first chapter of the Book of John.

> "There was a man sent from God, whose name was John. The same came for a witness, to bear witness of the Light, that all men through him might believe." (John 1:6-7)

Isaiah prophesied concerning John's ministry, saying:

> "The voice of him that crieth in the wilderness, **Prepare ye the way of the LORD**, make straight in the desert a highway **for our God**." (Isaiah 40:3)

John the Baptist applies this prophecy to himself in the Book of John:

> "Then said they unto [John the Baptist], Who art thou? that we may give an answer to them that sent us. What sayest thou of thyself? He said, I am the voice of one crying in the wilderness, Make straight the way of the Lord, as said the prophet Esaias."
> (John 1:22-23)

So, John the Baptist came to prepare the way *for God*. God was going to be revealed in the person of Christ to the nation of Israel. John came ahead of that occurrence to announce the event beforehand (and to turn people's hearts back to God through repentance).

Since **1.** John the Baptist was preparing the way for God and **2.** John 1:4 equates *the life* to *the light* by the words, "the life was the light," and **3.** John 1:4 also says *the light was in the Word*, John 1:7-10 could be appropriately interpreted as follows:

> "He [John the Baptist] was not the light [which was the life in the Word]: but [John the Baptist came] to bear witness of the light [so that men would know the way to the one who gives life]. That was the true light [the actuality of that life-giving principle], which lighteth all men that come into the world [which is the cause of life for all men]. He [the God who made life] was in the world [manifested in the person of Christ], and the world was made by him [because of the life creating principle in his Word]: and yet the world knew him not [though its very existence was due to him]."
> (John 1:7-10 Tyndale, brackets mine)

John 1:12 – His Name

John 1:12 continues to focus on God who, by his Word, is revealed in the person of Christ.

> "But as many as received him, to them gave he power to become the sons of God, even to them that believe on his name." (John 1:12)

Some may argue that this is only talking about Jesus, not God, when it says **1.** *received him* and **2.** *believe on his name*. However, we *must remember* what Jesus said about men *believing on him* and *receiving him*.

Ponder these words of Christ:

- "He that believeth on me, believeth not on me, but on him that sent me." (John 12:44)

- "Whosoever shall receive me, receiveth not me, but him that sent me." (Mark 9:37)

The speaking of God was embodied in the human Jesus, so much so that Jesus said those who believed on him did *not* believe on *him*, but on the *God* speaking *through* him. So, if someone says that John 1:12 is talking about *believing on and receiving Jesus* then, *according to Jesus*, that is *still* talking about *believing on and receiving God*.

In a similar fashion, when we read "believe on his *name*," we understand that Jesus' *name* is called *God*, etc.

> "His name shall be called … The mighty God." (Isaiah 9:6)

We will discuss the meaning of "name" a little more in the next section, but for now suffice it to say that it relates to *the attributes which someone exhibits*.

> "Proud and haughty scorner is his name, who dealeth in proud wrath." (Proverbs 21:24)

The *attributes* someone exhibits *provides their name*. So, when Jesus' name is called "The Everlasting Father," (Isaiah 9:6,) we understand that Jesus is *exhibiting the attributes of the Father*. Thus, while praying to the Father, Jesus shows that the Father's name was given to him.

> "When Jesus had spoken these words, he lifted up his eyes to heaven and said, '**Father** … this is eternal life, that they know thee the only true God, and Jesus Christ whom thou hast sent. … for I have given them the words which thou gavest me … **I have manifested thy name** to the men whom thou gavest me out of the world … Holy Father, keep them in **thy name, which thou hast given me**, that they may be one, even as we are one. While I was with them, I kept them **in thy name, which thou hast given me**.'"
> (John 17:1, 3, 6, 8, 11-12 RSV)

So, when men believed on Jesus' name, this was the name of the Father, which was given to him.

John 1:14 – The Word was Made Flesh

Christ was the embodiment of the λόγος. He was *the speaking of God in human flesh*. And, as we discussed under the heading *John 1:4 – Life in the Word*, life is in the Word, so Jesus, the embodied Word of God, also has the power to give eternal life.

> "Verily, verily, I say unto you, The hour is coming, and now is, when the dead shall hear the voice of the Son of God: and they that hear shall live. For as the Father hath life in himself; so hath he given to the Son to have life in himself." (John 5:25-26)

Interpreting "the Word was made flesh" as *the speaking of God was embodied in the human Jesus* matches the theme we find throughout the Book of John.

Consider the following sayings of Christ:

- "He that sent me is true; and I speak to the world those things which I have heard of him." (John 8:26)

- "But now ye seek to kill me, a man that hath told you the truth, which I have heard of God." (John 8:40)

- "For I have not spoken of myself; but the Father which sent me, he gave me a commandment, what I should say, and what I should speak. And I know that his commandment is life everlasting: whatsoever I speak therefore, even as the Father said unto me, so I speak." (John 12:49-50)

- "The words that I speak unto you I speak not of myself: but the Father that dwelleth in me, he doeth the works." (John 14:10)

- "All things that I have heard of my Father I have made known unto you." (John 15:15)

- While praying, Jesus says, "I have given unto them the words which thou gavest me." (John 17:8)

When ὁ λόγος, which was the expression of God, became flesh, those who heard Christ were hearing the words of God. It is no wonder, therefore, that we see Jesus identified with God and the speaking of God.

> "His name is called **the Word of God** (ὁ λόγος τοῦ θεοῦ)."
> (Revelation 19:13)

Here, as in other places, "name" is **not** used to denote *a proper title*, like *Jesus* or *Yahweh*, but to point out *attributes associated with* the one who is named. We see this *name=attributes* motif throughout the Bible.

> "For thou shalt worship no other god: for the LORD, **whose name is Jealous**, is a jealous God." (Exodus 34:14)

Here, Yahweh's *name* is Jealous because he "*is* a jealous God." His proper name is not *literally Jealous*, but since he is *identified with that attribute*, the Bible says his name is such. Similarly, since Jesus was/is identified with the revelation of God, by the speaking of God embodied in him, Revelation 19:13 says, "His name is called **the Word of God** (ὁ λόγος τοῦ θεοῦ)."

Even while we acknowledge that "he whom God hath sent speaketh the words of God," (John 3:34,) we should see *more than that alone* in the statement, "The Word was made flesh." To clarify what I mean, I will draw comparisons with what is said about Christ and believers. In that regard, when a believer is filled with the Holy Spirit, there is *a change* that is made in them. Such individuals sometimes afterward speak words given to them by the Spirit, but not always in such a manner that they are *repeating what they heard formerly* (as a student learns before repeating his teacher afterward). Rather, words are given to them *spontaneously*.

> "But when they arrest you and deliver you up, do not worry beforehand, or premeditate what you will speak. But whatever is **given you in that hour, speak that**; for **it is not you who speak, but the Holy Spirit**." (Mark 13:11 NKJV)

So, it is not that we always hear something from the Spirit beforehand and then afterward repeat what we heard. Rather, we speak the words as we are given them. Now then, *we* speak the words of *Christ* because *Christ* is in *us*, but *Jesus* spoke the words of *God* because *God* was in *him*.

> "[Jesus prayed to the Father, saying,] And the glory which thou gavest me I have given them; that they may be one, even as we are one: **I in them, and thou in me**, that they may be made perfect in one." (John 17:22-23)

Since God is speaking through Christ, Christ speaks the words of God. Since Christ is speaking through us, by the Holy Spirit, we speak the words of Christ, which are, due to Christ speaking the words of God, also the words of God. So, there is a unity in action and all things have their source in God.

> "For both he that sanctifieth [Christ] and they who are sanctified [believers in Christ] are all of one [God]: for which cause he is not ashamed to call them brethren [because we are all from the same Father]." (Hebrews 2:11, brackets mine)

Paul clearly affirms that Christ spoke in him:

> "If I come again, I will not spare: Since ye seek a proof of **Christ speaking in me**, which to you-ward is not weak, but is **mighty in you** [*i.e., among you.* Comp. ἐν ὑμῖν in 2 Cor. 12:12]. For though he was crucified through weakness, yet he liveth by the power of God." (2 Corinthians 13:3-4)

My point is that, though differing in degree, there is *a comparison* between how Christ was revealed in his followers with how God was revealed in Christ.

- Paul said, "I live; yet not I, but Christ liveth in me." (Galatians 2:20)

- Christ said, "The words I speak unto you I speak not of myself: but the Father that dwelleth in me, he doeth the works" (John 14:10)

So, when the Word became flesh, the words of God were not *simply spoken* by Christ, but this *also* means that *God was in Christ speaking*. Hence,

Christ could even pronounce someone was forgiven of their sins (Luke 5:20), because he was doing so in the person of God. And Paul, acting in the person of Christ, could also forgive sins.

> "To whom ye forgive any thing, I forgive also: for if I forgave any thing, to whom I forgave it, for your sakes forgave I it in the person of Christ." (2 Corinthians 2:10)

And this authority to forgive sins was given to the other apostles as well:

> "Then said Jesus to them again, Peace be unto you: **as my Father hath sent me, even so send I you**. And when he had said this, he breathed on them, and saith unto them, Receive ye the Holy Ghost: **Whose soever sins ye remit, they are remitted unto them**; and whose soever sins ye retain, they are retained." (John 20:21-23)

When we say we are "the body of Christ, and members in particular," (1 Corinthians 12:27,) we refer to experiencing his life in us by the Holy Spirit, not that we simply repeat what we heard Christ say. Similarly, we should not think of Christ as a man who merely *repeated words* that he heard from God. Rather, Christ was infused with the life of God (though he did not become God) and we are infused with the life of Christ (though we do not become Christ).

- "And **the Word was made flesh**, and dwelt among us, (and we beheld his glory, the glory as of the only begotten of the Father,) full of grace and truth." (John 1:14)

- "For no man ever yet hated **his own flesh**; but nourisheth and cherisheth it, even as the Lord the church: For **we are members of his body** ... For this cause shall a man leave his father and mother, and shall be joined unto his wife, and they two shall be **one flesh**. This is a great mystery: but I speak concerning **Christ and the church**."
(Ephesians 5:29-32)

As to the phrase in John 1:14, "the Word *dwelt among us,*" (KJV,) this means *the speaking of God, now embodied in the man Jesus, lived among the disciples*. They *beheld* his glory *because* he was in their midst in the person of Christ. A somewhat similar idea is presented in 1 John 1:1, where we read:

> "That which was from the beginning, which we have heard, which we have seen with our eyes, which we have looked upon, and our hands have handled, of the Word of life." (1 John 1:1)

That which was "of the Word of life" (περὶ τοῦ λόγου τῆς ζωῆς, read *concerning **that which is of** the word of life*) was not only the "message," (1 John 1:5,) but also *the embodied eternal life in the person of the resurrected Messiah,* who still had flesh that was handled by men's hands, even after his resurrection (Luke 24:39).

One final point that ought to be made regarding John 1:14 is that it was likely written in such a way so as to refute Gnostic error. False concepts of Christ (particularly, that he did not have genuine human flesh) were *already* creeping into the world when John 1:14 was written. The same author of John 1:14 also wrote these words:

> "Hereby know ye the Spirit of God: Every spirit that confesseth that Jesus Christ is come in the **flesh** is of God: And every spirit that confesseth not that Jesus Christ is come in the **flesh** is not of God: and this is that spirit of antichrist, whereof ye have heard that it should come; and **even now already** is it in the world." (1 John 4:2-3)

According the the Scriptures, Jesus had the same flesh and blood as other men.

> "Forasmuch then as the children are partakers of flesh and blood, he also himself likewise took part of the same." (Hebrews 2:14)

Chapter Fourteen

John 1:18

There has been a shift in recent years as to how John 1:18 is translated. Some versions refer to Jesus as "the only begotten *Son*" while others say, "the only begotten *God*." The different readings are due to manuscript variants. Some Greek manuscripts refer to Christ as υἱός (Son) in John 1:18, whilst others contain the word θεός (God). In this chapter we will deal primarily with this issue.

Only-Begotten or One-Of-A-Kind?

Some English Versions present John 1:18 like the *King James Version* does:

"No man hath seen God at any time; the **only begotten**…" (John 1:18)

Other English versions, however, render the text differently:

"No one has ever seen God. But the **unique One**…" (John 1:18 NLT)

The Greek word translated here as "only begotten" in the KJV and "unique one" in the NLT is μονογενής. Both translations show how μονογενής denotes a certain kind of unique position, but the translation "only begotten" carries with it the implication of a parental relationship. The word μονογενής is, as *Thayer's Greek-English Lexicon* states, "used of only sons or daughters (viewed in relation to their parents)."[261] For this reason, I prefer the translation "only begotten." Translating μονογενής as "unique one" or "one and only" or "one of a kind" does not convey the sense of the word's meaning, which applies exclusively within a parental relationship. I do not disagree, however, with the fact that Christ was and is the Son of God in a unique way.

Only Begotten Son or Only Begotten God?

The *King James Version* refers to Christ in John 1:18 as "the only begotten Son," but notice how the *New American Standard Bible* renders the passage:

> "No one has seen God at any time; the only begotten God who is in the bosom of the Father, he has explained him."
> (John 1:18 NASB)

Why does the KJV say "only begotten Son," but the NASB says "only begotten God"? Which reading is authentic?

For starters, the oldest Greek manuscript containing John 1:18 is 𝔓66, a papyrus dating to around the middle of the 2nd century. Then there is 𝔓75, which dates a little later to around the *end* of the 2nd century. Both of these papyri have the word θεός (God) rather than υἱός (Son). Added to these two witnesses are the Codex Sinaiticus and Codex Vaticanus, both from the 4th century and both also containing the word θεός (God). These are very authoritative codices. As Joseph Thayer acknowledged, the reading μονογενής θεός "is supported by no inconsiderable weight of ancient testimony."[262]

When it comes to modern-day scholarship, the μονογενής θεός reading has a great deal of backing as well. I consider *A Textual Commentary on the Greek New Testament*, which reflects the decisions of the Editorial Committee of the *United Bible Societies,* to be very authoritative. Yet, "the majority of the committee" agreed in favor of the μονογενής θεός reading. However, I am herein going to express a respectful disagreement with the majority decision. It is a disagreement that is based upon factors that I did not see brought up by Metzger (who authored *A Textual Commentary on the Greek New Testament* on behalf of the aforementioned committee). Before I propose a theory for why his entry for John 1:18 is incomplete, let me first say that Metzger was an expert in the field of textual criticism. In his comment, he is applying tried and true principles used when attempting to discover the original reading of a text. I am very appreciative to have his works in my personal library and the world owes him, and the committee he represents, a debt of gratitude for all they have done.

In a demonstration of Metzger's balanced approach to his craft, he includes the following comments from Allen Wikgren, one of the dissenting committee members:

> It is doubtful that the author would have written μονογενής θεός, which may be a primitive, transcriptional error in the Alexandrian tradition.[263]

Wikgren attributes the change from μονογενής υἱός (only-begotten Son) to μονογενής θεός (only-begotten God) to an accidental transcriptional error. This is reasonable since the early Greek manuscripts contain abbreviated forms of commonly used words, especially for υἱός (Son) and θεός (God). With the accidental switch of a single letter, the text could have been changed from the abbreviated form of θεός (θς) to the abbreviated form of υἱός (υς). Metzger addresses this hypothesis, however, as improbable. He says if the change were accidental, the text should still read, ὁ ... θς, but, in the θεός manuscripts, the article is omitted and the text only says θς. For an unintentional change from ὁ ... υς to θς the scribe(s) would not have only had to mess up a very crucial letter, but *also* omitted the article. Metzger dismisses this explanation, saying:

> There is no reason why the article should have been deleted, and when υἱός supplanted θεός it would certainly have been added.[264]

Within the breadth of his analysis, I agree with Metzger. However, the dissenting member of the committee was correct as well in some regard. As to the correctness of Metzger, the change being attributed to mistake is not favorable. As to the correctness of Wikgren, it is unlikely that the author wrote μονογενής θεός and this reading is traced back to Alexandrian tradition.

All four of the ancient Greek manuscripts we previously cited as containing μονογενής θεός are from the district of Alexandria, Egypt. While these Alexandrian manuscripts authoritatively support the μονογενής θεός reading, they do so in contrast to the *thousands* of other, admittedly less ancient, New Testament manuscripts that attest to the authenticity of μονογενής υἱός. The extant Alexandrian manuscripts boast of an earlier date, but if these Alexandrian manuscripts are correct, why is it that this reading is isolated to the region of Alexandria alone? Why is it that the μονογενής υἱός reading is found in ancient manuscripts and in numerous languages from everywhere else?

Μονογενής Υἱός – The Manuscript Evidence

The New Testament was translated into extra-biblical languages very early on in the Christian movement. We can look at these translations and, assuming the accurateness of the translations themselves, discover the readings of the Greek manuscripts from which they were translated.

The Old Latin Version – The New Testament was translated into Latin around 157 AD. Early Christians in Africa spontaneously produced Latin translations/copies which, taken together, are referred to as the *Old Latin Version*. The Old Latin text was widespread throughout the Northern African regions **west and south of Alexandria**. The Old Latin Version unanimously contains the "only begotten Son" reading of John 1:18. The oldest remaining Old Latin manuscript containing John 1:18, *Codex Vercellensis,* dates back to the 4th century.

The Syrian Version – The New Testament was also translated into Syriac around the middle of the 2nd century. The Syrian Christians who lived **far northeast of Alexandria** used the Syriac translation. The Syrian Version unanimously contains the "only begotten Son" reading. The oldest remaining Syrian New Testament manuscript containing John 1:18, the *Curetonian Version,* dates back to the 5th century.

The Latin Vulgate – The Latin Vulgate is the common name for the Latin translation of the Bible completed by Jerome in the early 5th century. Jerome is widely reputed to have been the leading Bible scholar of his time, which is why Pope Damasus asked *him* to produce the Vulgate. The Vulgate contains a Greek-to-Latin translation of the four Gospels which was actually completed by Jerome during the 4th century (384 AD). Since Jerome translated the four Gospels from Greek, this means he was using

Greek New Testament manuscripts that *were considered authoritative during the 4th century*. There are nearly 10,000 Vulgate manuscripts still in existence. The Vulgate also contains the "only begotten Son" reading.

Codex Alexandrinus – There is a 5th century *Greek* manuscript (Codex Alexandrinus) **from Alexandria** that contains the "only begotten Son" reading. Hence, no later than the 5th century, the "only begotten Son" reading was already being considered as authentic *even in Alexandria, where* μονογενής θεός was formerly prominent.

The Ante-Nicene Fathers

Within the writings of the Ante-Nicene Fathers, Christian writings that predate the Nicene Council, there is only **one** non-Alexandrian quotation of John 1:18 that contains the μονογενής θεός reading. This quotation of John 1:18 is found among the writings of Irenaeus. Yet, the extant writings of Irenaeus suspiciously contain *both* readings, and within very close proximity of one another.

Irenaeus quotes John 1:18 as reading μονογενής υἱός first, saying:

> There is one God, the Father, who contains all things and who grants existence to all, **as is written** in the Gospel: "No man hath seen God at any time, except the only-begotten **Son**, who is in the bosom of the Father; he has declared him."[265]

Irenaeus' alleged "only begotten God" quote appears only *a few paragraphs* later. The context in which the latter citation appears is as follows:

> "No man hath seen God at any time." However, as he himself desired it (and for the benefit of those who beheld the Word), his Word has shown the Father's brightness and explained his purposes (as also the Lord said: "The only-begotten **God**, who is in the bosom of the Father, he has declared him;" and he does himself also interpret the Word of the Father as being rich and great); not in one figure, nor in one character, did he appear to those seeing him, but according to the reasons and effects aimed at in his dispensations, as it is written in Daniel.[266]

Irenaeus did not vacillate between two differing readings of John 1:18 within the span of a few paragraphs, so we must discern which of these quotations is authentic and which is not. Sometimes scribes would write notes in a manuscript's margin that would afterwards be included among subsequent copies of that manuscript's text. This did not mean that the person who penned the marginal notes was *trying* to sneak the notes into the original text, but nevertheless the notes did sometimes obtain a place within latter copies of the text itself. In those instances where this has occurred, the marginal notes often do not flow well with the context, and are thereby evidenced to be interpolations. This is the case with the "only begotten God" reading that we find among Irenaeus' writings. Observe how *The Ante-Nicene Fathers* has the entire John 1:18 quote inside a larger parenthetical statement:

> But his Word, as he himself willed it, and for the benefit of those who beheld, did show the Father's brightness, and explained his purposes <u>(as also the Lord said: "The only-begotten God, which is in the bosom of the Father. He hath declared him:" and he does himself also interpret the Word of the Father as being rich and great)</u>; not in one figure, nor in one character, did he appear to those seeing him, but according to the reasons and effects aimed at in his dispensations, as it is written in Daniel.[267]

Notice how the underlined parenthetical segment doesn't quite fit in with the flow of the text. If we were to remove the underlined portion, the text would read more smoothly:

> But his Word, as he himself willed it, and for the benefit of those who beheld, did show the Father's brightness, and explained his purposes; not in one figure, nor in one character, did he appear to those seeing him, but according to the reasons and effects aimed at in his dispensations, as it is written in Daniel.

Also, notice how the parenthetical statement incorrectly attributed the words of John 1:18 to Christ, saying:

> ...his Word has shown the Father's brightness and explained his purposes (**as also the Lord said**: "The only-begotten God....")

John 1:18 was not spoken by Christ, and I seriously doubt that someone as learned as Irenaeus would have erroneously attributed the quotation to him.[268] His first quotation said:

> ... **as is written in the Gospel**: "No man hath seen God at any time, except the only-begotten Son"

This is factually correct and at odds with the "only begotten God" section that we find amongst his works. Hence, Irenaeus most likely knew the text as μονογενής υἱός. The μονογενής θεός version, therefore, was not quoted by any of the Ante-Nicene Fathers outside of Alexandria.

Μονογενής Θεός – The Phrase Never Used

If the original reading of John 1:18 did say "only begotten God" then, even apart from direct *quotations* of the passage, we should at least expect to see some early non-Alexandrian Christians *using the phrase* "only begotten God" within their writings. However, there are zero examples of this.[269] Although there is one corrupted epistle from Ignatius that contains the phrase "only begotten God," this phrase, along with multiple others, is generally agreed to be a spurious addition to his original writings (if he even had any original writing at all. See Appendix I).

The writings of Ignatius (if we assume they were his) have unfortunately been severely corrupted. The unedited versions of his works, which show a vast amount of material falsely attributed to Ignatius, are often referred to as the Long Versions (or *Longer Recensions*). Scholars have since attempted to "weed out" what they believe are fabricated additions to his epistles and have thus come up with the Short Versions (Shorter Recensions) of his works.

The "only begotten God" phrase only appears once in the *longer* version of Ignatius' epistle to the Philadelphians and is widely accepted by scholars as an unauthentic addition to his writings. If we *were* to place authority upon all of Ignatius' alleged writings, this would actually give support for the "only begotten Son" reading of John 1:18, because the spurious writings actually *quote* John 1:18 as reading "only begotten Son," saying:

> And there is also one Son, God the Word. For "the only-begotten Son," saith [the Scripture], "who is in the bosom of the Father."[270]

Nevertheless, it is obvious that the writings attributed to him have been severely tampered with and some have manifestly been forged altogether. Some scholars have even argued that all of the Ignatian epistles are forgeries.[271] We should not, therefore, make the irresponsible mistake of placing authority upon these unsubstantiated texts.

As far as I know, there are no Ante-Nicene Christian writers, outside of Alexandria, who *ever even use* the phrase "only begotten God" (in quotations or otherwise). Yet, the phrase "only begotten Son" is used consistently from the time of the apostles onward, over a very broad geographical area.

The Internal Evidence

So far we have only discussed the *external* evidence favoring the "only begotten Son" reading. The case becomes even stronger when we consider the evidence that exists within the Bible itself. The internal evidence within the Bible, and particularly within the writings attributed to John, clearly supports the μονογενής υἱός reading. The author of John 1:18 never uses "only begotten God" anywhere else in any of his writings, nor does it appear anywhere in the Bible as a whole. However, the phrase "only begotten Son" is perfectly concordant with what we find in the Scriptures, especially in the Book of John.

- "For God so loved the world, that he gave **his only begotten Son** (τὸν υἱὸν αὐτοῦ τὸν μονογενῆ), that whosoever believeth in him should not perish, but have everlasting life." (John 3:16 KJV)

- "He that believeth on him is not condemned: but he that believeth not is condemned already, because he hath not believed in the name of the **only begotten Son** (μονογενοῦς υἱοῦ[272]) **of God**." (John 3:18 KJV)

- "In this was manifested the love of God toward us, because that God sent his **only begotten Son** (τὸν υἱὸν αὐτοῦ τὸν μονογενῆ) into the world, that we might live through him." (1 John 4:9 KJV)

Based upon the internal evidence of what we find in the Scriptures, the μονογενής υἱός reading is undoubtedly the strongest.

The Testimony of Clement of Alexandria

We previously discussed how none of the Ante-Nicene Father's *outside of Alexandria* ever quoted the μονογενής θεός version of John 1:18. However, we do find the μονογενής θεός version quoted by Ante-Nicene Fathers who lived and wrote inside of Alexandria. Clement of Alexandria, as he is so called, wrote three works around the end of the 2nd century. When he actually quotes the text, he says "only begotten God."

> And John the Apostle says: "No man hath seen God at any time. **The only-begotten God**, who is in the bosom of the Father, He hath declared Him"[273]

There can be no doubt that the μονογενής θεός (God) reading was accepted within Alexandria during the 2nd and 3rd century. The writings of Clement, Origen of Alexandria,[274] and reference to Arius,[275] and the extant manuscripts prove this to be the case. However, it seems that we also see signs that the μονογενής υἱός (Son) reading was present in the thoughts of Clement as well.

Notice what Clement says elsewhere:

> For how shall he not be loved for whose sake the **only-begotten Son** is sent **from the Father's bosom**?[276]

And elsewhere:

> For the Word is "the power and the wisdom of God." Again, the expounder of the laws is the same one by whom the law was given; the first expounder of the divine commands, **who unveiled the bosom of the Father, the only-begotten Son**.[277]

Here, it looks like he is referencing a version of John 1:18 that reads "only begotten Son." Additionally, it looks like he incorporates *both* readings elsewhere, when he writes:

> And then thou shalt look into **the bosom of the Father**, whom **God the only begotten Son** alone **hath declared**.[278]

I think the duplicity in references can be attributed to a clash between a *known* version of John 1:18 and the *written* version that Clement found in his local Alexandrian manuscripts.

> In order to understand Clement rightly, it is necessary to bear in mind that he laboured in a crisis of transition. This gives his writings their peculiar interest in all times of change. The transition was threefold, affecting doctrine, thought, and life. **Doctrine was passing from the stage of oral tradition to written definition**.[279]

Valentinian Influence in 2nd Century Alexandria

Thayer's Greek-English Lexicon of the New Testament says:

> [Μονογενής θεός] is foreign to John's mode of thought and speech (3:16, 18, Un.4:9), dissonant and harsh,—appears to owe its origin to a dogmatic zeal which broke out soon after the early days of the church.[280]

The early dogmatic zeal which resulted in the alteration of John 1:18 can be traced back to the doctrine of Valentinus and his adherents (and even before Valentinus to Basilides). Valentinus was a Gnostic who began propagating his doctrines in Alexandria before the middle of the 2nd century, which is when and where we first find the μονογενής θεός reading popping up. *A Dictionary of Early Christian Biography* gives us some interesting facts about Valentinus' life that place him in precisely the right place and time to influence the earliest μονογενής θεός manuscript.

> [Valentinus'] native home was on the coast of Egypt, and he received instruction in Greek literature and science at **Alexandria**.

> Epiphanius, who makes him begin to teach in Egypt, relates further that he also went to Rome ... **We may, then, conclude that Valentinus, towards the end of Hadrian's reign (c.130), appeared as a teacher in Egypt.**[281]

The earliest manuscript containing the μονογενής θεός reading of John 1:18 is 𝔓66, which is from the region of Alexandria, Egypt and dates back to around 150 AD. Valentinus began teaching in the region of Alexandria. Egypt around 130 AD. Could it be that, during the middle of the 2nd century, manuscripts in Alexandria were being composed with a Valentinian twist? I believe so. Before the end of the 2nd century, Alexandria was very prone to Gnostic influence.

In his introduction to the book entitled *Alexandrian Christianity,* Henry Chadwick comments on the condition of the Alexandrian Church, saying:

> It is only towards the end of the second century that the Christian community at Alexandria emerges from its shroud of darkness. Earlier in the second century during the latter part of Hadrian's reign there flourished at Alexandria a distinguished Christian teacher named Basilides. Soon after him there followed the even more eminent Valentine, who moved to Rome, where, it seems, he very nearly succeeded in becoming Pope. Both these teachers, however, were prominent in the so-called "gnostic" movement of the period, and their opinions were not acceptable to the Church at large.[282]

The fact that Gnosticism "flourished in Alexandria" whilst those "opinions were not acceptable to the church at large" would coincide with how the reading of John 1:18 found in Alexandria does not match the reading we find elsewhere.

During much of the 2nd century, Christianity in Alexandria was actually saturated with Gnosticism. The primary text used by Valentinus and his followers was *the Gospel of John.*

Irenaeus wrote of how the Valentinians used John as a primary text:

> Those, moreover, who follow Valentinus make copious use of the gospel according to John to illustrate their conjunctions.[283]

Since the Valentinians favored the Book of John so much, it becomes quite shocking to discover that *the entire text of* 𝔓66, where we first see μονογενής θεός, consists *only* of John. It contains every chapter of John, but nothing more. *Is this a coincidence?* We certainly cannot conclude by this alone that 𝔓66 was a manuscript used by Gnostics, but considering the time and location of its origin, it is definitely plausible. The Valentinians used John as a primary text. 𝔓66 is from a city and a time in which Gnosticism flourished. 𝔓66 is the first manuscript we find that has the μονογενής θεός reading. 𝔓66 consists only of the Gospel of John, which was of primary use to the Valentinian sect.

While focusing much of their attention on the Book of John, Valenitinians focused especially upon the prologue itself (*i.e.,* John 1:1-18).

> Valentinian expositors shew a special preference for St. John's Gospel, and above all for its prologue.[284]

One of Valentinus' prominent adherents was a man named Ptolemy. This Ptolemy actually wrote a brief commentary on the prologue of John. In fact, it is known by the name of *Ptolemy's Commentary on the Gospel of John Prologue.*

Irenaeus speaks of this commentary when he writes:

> Furthermore they teach ... expressing themselves **in these words**: John, the disciple of the Lord, wishing to set forth the origin of all things, so as to explain how the Father produced the whole, lays down a certain principle,—that, namely, which was first begotten by God, which being he has termed both the **only begotten Son** and God, in whom the Father, after a seminal manner, brought forth all things.[285]

Now, when one examines the entire commentary of Ptolemy, it is evident that he, in accordance with the scope of the prologue, only uses appellations found within the prologue itself. Indeed, when he goes beyond that and introduces a new term for "church" he feels the need to qualify that term by saying that "men" (John 1:4) is synonymous with "church." The terms he uses are thus confined to the prologue itself, except for his introduction of a new term which he uses to expound upon the prologue terminology. When he introduced a term that was *not* found in the prologue, he forthrightly acknowledged this. Therefore, since Ptolemy used the term *Son* while writing his prologue, we can reasonably deduce that a version of the prologue containing the word υἱός (Son) was known to him during the time of his writing (around 150 AD). *The only place that "Son" is found in the prologue is John 1:18.* Thus, we have a testimony, even from one of Valentinus' adherents, that μονογενής υἱός (Son) was commonly known amongst the Valentinians and, by extension, in mid-2nd century Alexandria where 𝔓66 originated.

Valentinus Introduced Corrupted Texts

𝔓66 is the earliest manuscript containing μονογενής θεός. As we have already shown, it is plausible that the Valentinians knew of the μονογενής υἱός reading during the middle of the 2nd century. Yet, the 𝔓66 manuscript dates to mid-2nd century Alexandria and clearly contains the reading μονογενής θεός. Could it be that, despite the fact that the μονογενής υἱός reading was known beforehand, 𝔓66 was composed, not as a faithful copy of previous manuscripts, but as a modified text formed to suit Gnostic doctrine? By an examination of this 𝔓66, since it is the earliest manuscript containing μονογενής θεός, if it be seen that it was in fact not a faithful copy, but instead altered to fit doctrinal positions, we can find a root cause for the subsequent μονογενής θεός manuscripts that came after it. If 𝔓66 contains textual alterations, it stands to reason that such alterations would also have been replicated afterwards when that initial manuscript (or one like it) was copied.

We will now look for evidence in support of the notion that:

1. Valentinus changed the Scriptures to match his doctrine.

2. 𝔓66 bears signs of being modified to fit doctrinal positions.

Tertullian, writing at the close of the 2nd century, affirms that Valentinus *did* impose his own views into the text of Scripture:

> Now, inasmuch as all **interpolation** must be believed to be a later process, for the express reason that it proceeds from rivalry which is never in any case previous to, nor home-born with that which it emulates, it is as incredible to any man of sense that we should seem to have **introduced any corrupt text into the scriptures**, existing, as we have been, from the very first, and being the first, as it is that they have not **in fact introduced it**, who are both later in date and opposed (to the scriptures). One man perverts the scriptures with his hand; another their meaning by his exposition. For although Valentinus seems to use the entire volume, he has none the less laid violent hands on the truth, only with a more cunning mind and skill than Marcion. Marcion expressly and openly used the knife, rather than **the pen**, since he made such an excision of the Scriptures as suited his own subject-matter. Valentinus, however, abstained from such excision, because he did not invent Scriptures to square with his own subject-matter, but adapted his matter to the Scriptures. And **yet he took away more, and added more**, by removing the proper meaning of every particular word, and **adding fantastic arrangements** of things which have no real existence.[286]

Valentinus is shown here to have introduced corrupt texts into the Scriptures. The statement "did not invent Scriptures to square with his own subject matter" may be qualified by the words "such excision" as Marcion made. The contrast presented is Marcion inventing scriptures vs. how Valentinus seems to "use the entire volume." Although not in the manner of Marcion, who physically cut out parts of manuscripts, Valentinus is nonetheless said to "take away" the meaning and "add" his views into the Scriptures by means of "interpolation" and "the pen." By contrast, Tertullian clearly detested the alteration of Scripture, and instead affirmed that the Scriptures should be accepted as they are, therefore we should not take his following citation of John 1:18 lightly:

> It is of course the Father, with whom was the Word, "the only

begotten **Son**, who is in the bosom of the Father," and has himself declared him.[287]

How Trustworthy is Papyrus 66?

I contend that either Valentinus or his Alexandrian followers probably had a direct influence upon ℘66, which dates back precisely to that time and location in which Gnosticism flourished in Alexandria. In this section we will discuss some characteristics of ℘66. Was the ℘66 scribe careful to relay the original manuscript text he was copying? Did the scribe exercise liberty in his copying process?

The Text of the Earliest New Testament Greek Manuscripts makes some very interesting statements regarding the text of ℘66, saying:

> The large print throughout indicates that it was written to be read aloud to a Christian congregation ... The original scribe was quite free in his interaction with the text. He produced several singular readings that reveal his interpretation of the text ... Some of the singular variants also show that the scribe was interested in helping the readers understand the text.[288]

The Text of the Earliest New Testament Greek Manuscripts also indicates that the scribe *omitted* several passages from the Gospel of John as well:

> This leads us to another phenomenon in the manuscript ℘66, that of omissions. Beginning with chapter 17 and on to chapter 19, ℘66 exhibits several omissions ... many of the omissions seem so sensible that it is difficult to attribute their omission to carelessness. It is possible, then, that ℘66's exemplar had a trimmer text. However, since none of these shorter readings show up later in textual tradition, this cannot be determined with any certainty. As the Alands note, most variant readings endure; sooner or later, they show up again in the textual stream. Thus, it is more likely that the shorter text in ℘66 is not original, but redactional, the work of the scribe attempting to trim the text of whatever he perceived to be unnecessary. Some examples illustrate this. In 17:11, the scribe

omitted "that they may be one, even as we are"... In 19:15 he omitted the whole sentence: "And he says to them, 'Behold the man.'" Perhaps the scribe of 𝔓66 took exception to Jesus being presented by Pilate as a mere man ... In 19:28 he omitted the phrase "that the Scriptures might be fulfilled."[289]

Notice that he said, "Many of the omissions seem so sensible that it is difficult to attribute their omission to carelessness." The alterations were intentional, and the nature of the alterations seem to coincide with Valentinian doctrine. Valentinus had an issue with Jesus being connected to the material world like other men are, because he viewed all matter as corrupted. In the Valentinian line of reasoning, Jesus had a body, but it was not genuine flesh like that of our own. He was able to suffer, but the Valentinian Jesus was so distinct from matter that, although he ate and drank, he never really absorbed the ingested nutrients into his unique body.

Irenaeus described the Valentinian view of Christ's nature and his relation to corrupted matter as follows:

> He was invested by the Demiurge with the animal Christ, but was begirt by a [special] dispensation with a body endowed with an animal nature, yet constructed with unspeakable skill, so that it might be visible and tangible, and capable of enduring suffering. At the same time, they deny that he assumed anything material [into his nature], since indeed matter is incapable of salvation.[290]

With the doctrine of Valentinus in mind, recall how the scribe of 𝔓66 seemingly took issue with Jesus being a real man when he omitted the words, "Behold the man." Notice also that the scribe took issue with other natural men, "consisting of corrupted matter/flesh," being one with Jesus and the Father, which he shows by the omitted words, "That they may be one, even as we are." Observe also how the scribe omits the phrase "that the Scriptures might be fulfilled" in John 19:28. In this last text, Jesus is dying on the cross and says, "I thirst." Why would the scribe omit the reference to prophetic fulfillment here? Well, the Old Testament scripture that was being fulfilled (Psalm 69:21) shows a genuine thirst and a disappointment in being offered vinegar for that thirst ... Since Valentinus would not allow that Christ assimilated any matter, this statement is contrary to his opinions.

In summary, the scribe who copied 𝔓66 was very liberal with his pen when he produced the manuscript, and we see Valentinian tendencies in how he interacted with the text. Could 𝔓66 be a Valentinian manuscript? I believe it is very plausible. Whether penned by Valentinus himself, one of his adherents, or some other like-minded Gnostic, I am persuaded that 𝔓66 was a product of Gnostic influence in that Alexandrian region. Papyrus 66 *is* from Alexandria, Egypt and it *does* date *precisely* to the time that Gnosticism was flourishing in that self-same city. *Is this all just a coincidence?* Suffice it to say that the possibility of a corrupted Gnostic manuscript meeting the exact time and place specifications of 𝔓66 is very real and by no means a stretch of the imagination.

The Valentinian Motive

I will now relay why the Valentinians would have *desired* to change John 1:18. First, I will present some additional facts about Valentinian theology and then we will see how that theology could have provided the *motive* for changing John 1:18 from ὁ μονογενής υἱός to μονογενής θεός.

The Valentinians believed that the God of the Old Testament was a different kind of God than the God of the New Testament. They claimed that a higher God, named Bythos, through a feminine contemporary named Sige, emanated lower levels of God (which emanations they referred to as *Aeons*). Each level of their God emanations consisted of a male and female pair that, subsequent to being emanated themselves, also emanated a lower male-female pair, who then emanated a pair from themselves, and so on. All of the Aeons in Valentinian theology ultimately traced the origin of their emanation back to the first God. By right of their origin, the entire group of Aeons were, according to Valentinians, all God. One of these Valentinian God-emanations was *named* Μονογενής (who they also called *Nous*).

A Dictionary of Early Christian Biography shows that Μονογενής and Νοῦς (Nous) were two proper names used by the Valentinians:

> The **names** Μονογενής and Νοῦς (here Ἀείνους) meet us again among the Valentinians.[291]

Look at the following quote from Irenaeus and notice how the Valentianians **1.** identified Μονογενής as Νοῦς and **2.** say things about Nous that sound like John 1:18.

> "They proceed to tell us that the Propator of their scheme was known **only to Monogenes**, who sprang from him; in other words, **only to Nous**, while to all the others he was invisible and incomprehensible. And, according to them, Nous alone took pleasure in contemplating the Father, and exulting in considering his immeasurable greatness; while he also meditated how he might communicate to the rest of the Æons the greatness of the Father, revealing to them how vast and mighty he was, and how he was without beginning,—beyond comprehension, and altogether incapable of being seen."[292]

Do you see how Μονογενής is the same as Νοῦς and these words are used as proper titles? Do you see how the actions of Μονογενής/ Νοῦς sound strikingly familiar to John 1:18?

Valentinians taught that Μονογενής/Νοῦς was joined with his feminine counterpart emanation named Alethia (the Greek word for "truth") and together they produced another male-female couple, who in turn produced another male-female couple, and so on. This domino effect of emanations went on and on until at last the Valentinians wound up with a "divine" family of thirty God emanations.

> Valentinus was more consistent and more liberal [than Marcion]. For, having once imagined two deities, Bythos and Sige, he then poured forth a swarm of divine essences—a brood of no less than thirty Aeons.[293]

The male emanation produced from Μονογενής was named Λόγος (*Logos*, the same Greek word translated as *Word* in John 1:1). Although the many emanations in Valentinian theology were different individuals, they were all considered God.

Ptolemy, the Valentinian commentator we discussed, wrote the following:

> "And the Word was God;" reasonably so, for what is engendered from God is God. This shows the order of emanation.[294]

Since all of the Aeons emanated from Bythos, they all were alike called "God." They believed that Logos emanated out of Μονογενής/Νοῦς and that Μονογενής/Νοῦς was in fact the one called God in John 1:1.

Regarding the Valentinian belief that Μονογενής was the God in John 1:1, *A Dictionary of Early Christian Biography* states:

> By the ἀρχή of St. John 1:1, in which the Logos "was," we must understand the Μονογενής "Who is also called God" ... The Logos was ἐν ἀρχῇ means that he was in the Monogenes, in the Νοῦς and the 'Αλήθεια. The Logos is called God because he is in God, in the Νοῦς.[295]

I believe the Valentinian idea of Logos emanating from Μονογενής/ Νοῦς and 'Αλήθεια stemmed from how the Greek text of John 1:14 reads.

καὶ	ὁ	λόγος	σὰρξ	ἐγένετο	καὶ	ἐσκήνωσεν	ἐν
and	the	Word	flesh	became	and	tabernacled	among

ἡμῖν	καὶ	ἐθεασάμεθα	τὴν	δόξαν	αὐτοῦ	δόξαν	ὡς
us	and	we beheld	the	glory	his	glory	as

μονογενοῦς	παρὰ	πατρός	πλήρης	χάριτος	καὶ
only-begotten	from	Father	full	of grace	and

ἀληθείας
truth   (John 1:14)

No mention of Νοῦς here, right? However, the Valentinians interpreted the text *somewhat* similar to this:

καὶ	ὁ	**Λόγος**	σὰρξ	ἐγένετο	καὶ	ἐσκήνωσεν	ἐν
and	the	**Logos**	flesh	became	and	tabernacled	among

ἡμῖν	καὶ	ἐθεασάμεθα	τὴν	δόξαν	αὐτοῦ	δόξαν	ὡς
us	and	we beheld	the	glory	his	glory,	as

Μόνο, γε Νοῦς παρὰ πατρός πλήρης χάριτος
Monogenes, even Nous, from [his] father [Nous], full of grace,

καὶ 'Αληθείας
and Alethia [his mother] (John 1:14)

By breaking up μονογενοῦς into μονο, γε, and νοῦς we see a sudden appearance of the Valentinian νοῦς paralleled with Μόνο (taken as a shortened form of Μονγενής). This would line up with how they said the Logos comes from Monogenes/Nous in John 1:1 and also how they said the Logos came from Alethia, since here we see:

1. The Logos being as Μόνο (*i.e.* Monogenes)

2. Νοῦς paralleled with Monogenes

3. Nous as father of Logos

4. Alethia as the female counterpart with whom Nous begat Logos

This accords with what we know about Valentinian doctrine. The Valentinians thought that the logos/word coming forth from the nous/mind was just too obvious a connection to deny. As a result of parsing μονογενοῦς to show that the mind, or νοῦς, was the source of the logos/word, they were subsequently left with the scraps of μονογενοῦς, namely μονογε. By further distinction between the scraps, μονογε was read as two words, Μόνο and γε, which they apparently read as "Monogenes, even [Nous]." That's basically the only option that remained once νοῦς was removed from μονογενοῦς. In other words, "We *know* that the text is saying Nous here, because the mind is producing the word, so this Monoge in front of Nous must be equated to Nous in some way, since Nous is what is the interpretative principle here."

This accords with what Tertullian said about Valentinus:

> And yet he took away more, and added more, by removing the proper meaning of every particular word, and adding fantastic arrangements of things which have no real existence.[296]

Irenaeus says something similar of the Valentinians:

> By transferring passages, and dressing them up anew, and making one thing out of another, they succeed in deluding many through their wicked art in adapting the oracles of the Lord to their opinions.[297]

Now, if John 1:14 was taken as "Mono, ge Nous," and this Nous was supposed to be the God of John 1:1 from whom the Logos emanated, then we already have a parallel between Μόνο, γε Νοῦς (Monogenes, even Nous) in John 1:14 and Μονογενής, θεός (Monogenes, God) in John 1:18.

What I mean is this:

1. The Valentinians said that Nous is an emanation from God, who is thereby also God, and Nous subsequently emanated Logos (who is also God since he came from God).

2. The Valentinian version of John 1:1 says the "God" spoken of there is Nous, who preceded Logos (Word emanating from Mind). (Thus, they also said Arche (the "Beginning") in whom the Logos existed ('In Arche was the Logos"), was a third name[298] for Monogenes / Nous).

3. The Gnostics equated Nous to God, so for them Μονογενής, θεός ("Monogenes, God") is the same as Μόνο, γε Νοῦς ("Monogenes, even Nous").

4. Since ὁ μονογενὴς υἱός ("the only-begotten Son") in John 1:18 is obviously presenting μονογενής as modifying υἱός ("the only-begotten Son" instead of their "Monogenes [as a proper name], is God" theme), they felt that they could "clarify" the meaning by changing υς to θς, pointing the readers back to John 1:1, where Monogenes, "the God of John 1:1," is declaring Bythos by Logos.

Valentinians wanted to preserve the notion that Logos came from Nous in John 1:14, but the original reading of John 1:18 stood in opposition to their claim. Someone reading ὁ μονογενὴς υἱός in John 1:18 would logically think that μονογενής was being used adjectivally. Since μονογενής was obviously used as an adjective in John 1:18, this stood in opposition to how the Valentinians required μονογε**νοῦς** to be viewed in John 1:14. If μονογενὴς was an adjective in John 1:18 then John 1:14 didn't say Μονο, γε Νοῦς, but μονογενοῦς.[299] This would muddle the Valentinians' conclusion that *Logos/Word came from the Nous/Mind*. However, if they simply substituted θς for υς in John 1:18 *and dropped the article before* μονογενὴς, they would have a parallel to John 1:14 that protected the Logos/Nous connection therein. They were not as interested in producing an *only begotten God text* as they were in preserving their *Nous produced Logos* interpretation. By changing "the only begotten Son" to "Monogenes, God" they not only identified Nous as God, but they simultaneously strengthened their position that Nous was the "God" who preceded Logos in John 1:1. If Logos was called "God" John 1:1, then Nous, the God whom he proceeded from, had to be identified as God somewhere as well, which they procured through their own alteration of John 1:18.

What we see in the textual corruption of John 1:18 is a case of men who thought they had knowledge (gnosis) of what the text truly meant. Being persuaded that their own ideas were correct, they were unwilling to yield to the true sense of what the Scriptures actually said. In order to maintain their presupposition, they were forced to dismiss, even alter the true meaning of those Scriptures that they themselves professed to believe.

Chapter Fifteen

Fifth Chapter of John

The fifth chapter of the Gospel of John contains some profound statements regarding the relationship between the Father and the Son. The focus of this present chapter is the examination of those statements in particular (although we will branch off into a couple of other issues as well).

John 5:23 – Honor the Son Even as the Father

In John 5:23, Jesus says:

> "That all men should honour the Son, even as they honour the Father. He that honoureth not the Son honoureth not the Father which hath sent him." (John 5:23)

By honoring the image of God, a person simultaneously honors God himself. It was not because Christ was God himself that we are to honor him as we honor God, but rather because he is God's representative. Jesus knew this, and that is why, even though he said men are to honor him as they honor God, he also said:

> "I receive not honour from men." (John 5:41)

The honor given to Christ was actually given to God *through* Christ.

> "For as the image of a king would be honored for the sake of him whose lineaments and likeness it bears (and though both the image and the king received honour, one person would be honoured, and not two; for there would not be two kings, the first the true one, and the one represented by the image)."
> —*Eusebius of Caesarea*[300]

Christ did not receive the honor from men unto himself. In fact, God is to receive the glory whenever he reveals himself in *anyone.* This principle is clearly attested to within two very similar stories that are recorded in the book of Judges. In the first story an angel of the LORD appeared to a man named Gideon with a message from God. When the angel delivered the message from God he spoke *God's words* in *first person narrative:*

> "And **the LORD said** unto him (Gideon), Surely I will be with thee." (Judges 6:16)

Now, it is evident that it was an angel who was speaking to Gideon, as is seen in the context of Judges 6:11-16. However, though Gideon plainly saw that the angel was the one speaking (Judges 6:12), he also understood that God spoke *through* his angels. This is why Gideon says:

> "Show me a sign that thou talkest with me." (Judges 6:17)

Gideon obviously knew that the *angel* was speaking with him, but he was inquiring whether it was *God* speaking to him *through* the angel. This recognition of the angel as God's representative accounts for why the angel did not rebuke Gideon when he afterwards honored him with a present.

> "Depart not hence, I pray thee, until I come unto thee, and bring forth my present, and set it before thee. And he said, I will tarry until thou come again." (Judges 6:18)

Gideon recognized God was being revealed through his angel. The honor Gideon gave to the angel, when he offered him a gift, was honor given to him as God's representative, whereby he was honoring God.

In the second story, an angel of the LORD was also representing God when he appeared to a man named Manoah. Unlike Gideon, Manoah didn't acknowledge who the angel represented. Instead, Manoah was trying to give honor to *the angel himself.*

> "Manoah said **unto the angel** of the **LORD**, What is **thy name**, that when thy sayings come to pass **we may do thee honour**?"
> (Judges 13:17)

This is in contrast with Gideon, who was honoring the God whom the angel represented. The angel only received the gift from Gideon *because* he offered it in honor of God, but because Manoah was not giving God the honor when he offered to bring a gift, the angel would not accept it.

Notice what the angels says:

> "**I** will not eat of thy bread: and if thou wilt offer a burnt offering, **thou must offer it unto the LORD**." (Judges 13:16)

Why did the angel say this? The very next words in Judges 13:16 tell us exactly why:

> "For Manoah **knew not** that he was an angel of the **LORD**." (Judges 13:16)

The angel would not accept Manoah's gift because he knew that Manoah did not *know* that he was an angel of God. Consequently, Manoah was not acknowledging the fact that the angel was God's representative. Later, when "Manoah **knew** that he was an angel of the LORD" (Judges 13:21) he proclaimed, "We have seen **God**." (Judges 13:22.) The reason Manoah said that he saw God by seeing God's angel was because he realized whom it was that the angel represented. Do you see how the angel of the LORD would not receive the honor from men for what God was doing? The only time that the angels would receive the honor from men is when those men honored them as God's representatives.

In the same way, Christ says:

> "That all men should honour the Son, even as they honour the Father. He that honoureth not the Son honoureth not the Father which hath sent him." (John 5:23)

But he also says:

> "I receive not honour from men." (John 5:41)

Jesus Refused to be Called "Good Master"

Jesus clearly showed that he would not receive honor from men who did not acknowledge him as representing God. Once, a man approached him and said:

> "Good Master, what shall I do that I may inherit eternal life?" (Mark 10:17)

Jesus responded to the man by saying:

> "Why callest thou me good? There is none good but one, that is God." (Mark 10:18)

Jesus knew that it was the goodness of God being revealed through him, but the man was trying to give the credit to Jesus by calling *him* "good." Jesus corrected him by giving glory to God. The man that Jesus spoke to obviously understood the point that Jesus was conveying because the next time he spoke to Jesus (two verses later), he no longer addressed him as "**Good** Master," but simply as "Master." (Mark 10:20.)

In 160 AD, Justin Martyr said:

> The Son foretells that he will be saved by the same God. He does not boast of accomplishing anything through his own will or might. For when on earth, he acted in the very same manner. He answered to a man who addressed him as "Good Master": "Why do you call me good? One is good, my Father who is in heaven."[301]

In 248 AD, Origen wrote:

> Our Lord and Savior, hearing himself on one occasion addressed as, "Good Master," referred the person who used it to his own Father, saying, "Why do you call me good? There is no one good but one, that is, God the Father." It was in accordance with sound reason that this was said by the Son of the Father's love, for he was the image of the goodness of God.[302]

God Alone is "Good" / Christ the "Good" Shepherd

Someone might think, though I have never heard anyone assert such a thing, that Christ identifies himself as God when he says:

> "I am the **good** shepherd." (John 10:11)

And elsewhere:

> "There is none **good** but one, that is God." (Mark 10:18)

If Christ is good, and there is none good but God, then doesn't this make Christ God? Actually, the Greek words that Christ used in these two passages are entirely different from one another:

- "There is none **good** (ἀγαθὸς) but one, that is God." (Mark 10:18)

- "I am the **good** (καλός) shepherd." (John 10:11)

Since the Greek words used are different in these passages, the argument that Christ was making himself out to be the good (ἀγαθὸς) God when he presents himself as the good (καλός) shepherd falls apart. And yet the Bible *does* apply the Greek word ἀγαθὸς (which was attributed *exclusively* to God) to Joseph of Arimathea, saying:

> "And, behold, there was a man named Joseph, a counsellor, and he was a **good** (ἀγαθὸς) man." (Luke 23:50)

The exact same word that Christ used when he said, "There is none **good** (ἀγαθὸς) but one, that is God," is also applied to Joseph of Arimathea in Luke 23:50. Of course, Joseph of Arimathea was not God. We have to be careful when deducing too much from comparisons like this. Unfortunately, much of the erroneous doctrine about Christ is produced in such a way, via a "fast and loose" comparison of statements pulled out of context.

The reason why Christ said that God *alone* is good is because he was acknowledging the *source* of all goodness (God). God is the perpetual source of the goodness that makes anyone else good. Hence, a man is made good only when God's own personal attributes are revealed in him. A good man's goodness is not of himself, instead that goodness is of God.

> "He that doeth good is of God: but he that doeth evil hath not seen God." (3 John 11)

John 5:18 – Equal with God?

The fifth chapter of John records a certain miraculous healing that Christ performed on the Sabbath. Since the Jews didn't believe that anyone should do such works on the Sabbath, they persecuted him.

> "The man went away and told the Jews that it was Jesus who had healed him. And this was why the Jews persecuted Jesus, because he did this on the sabbath." (John 5:15-16 RSV)

They said that Christ shouldn't do those things on the Sabbath, but Christ responded to the Jews by showing them that God was working on the Sabbath, and thus he worked as well.

> "But Jesus answered them, My Father worketh hitherto, and I work." (John 5:17)

Since the works of the Father were revealed through the Son, when God worked Christ also worked.

Christ again expresses this same principle later on in John 9:3-4, saying:

> "[This man was born blind] that the works of God should be made manifest in him. **I must work the works of him that sent me** while it is day." (John 9:3-4)

The works were God's works, but Christ had to act in accordance with God so that God's works would be manifested through him. God worked to heal this man who was born blind, yet Christ was the channel *through* whom that healing from God was put into effect. This is also the principle upon which Jesus made his defense for healing the previous man on the Sabbath:

> "Jesus answered them, My Father worketh hitherto, and I work." (John 5:17)

The context is referring to Christ's actions being in harmony with the actions God.

In John **5:17**, Jesus says:

> "My Father worketh hitherto, and I work."

In John **5:19**, Jesus says:

> "The Son can do nothing of himself, but what he seeth the Father do: for what things soever he doeth, these also doeth the Son likewise."

In between those two passages, John **5:18** says:

> "Therefore the Jews sought the more to kill him, because he not only had broken the sabbath, but said also that God was his Father, **making himself equal with God**." (John 5:18 KJV)

The context is specifically talking about Christ's actions being in sync with the actions of God. The fact that Jesus "said also that God was his Father" does not move the contextual meaning away from actions (see chapter four herein, subheading *Begotten Explained*). The Jews understood that claiming God as one's Father implied an agreement with God in actions. In fact, they tried to make this same claim for themselves in John 8.

Jesus said to the Jews:

> "Ye **do the deeds** of your father." (John 8:41)

Notice how the Jews respond:

> "Then said they unto him, We be not born of fornication, **we have one Father, even God**." (John 8:41)

They were trying to say that God was their Father and that, instead of doing the deeds of another, they were doing the works of God. Christ did not accept this from them, but he instead reproves them, saying:

> "If God were your Father, ye would love me ... Ye are of **your father** the devil, and the lusts of your father **ye will do**."
> (John 8:42, 44)

Being a child of God denotes the works of God being revealed through a person. The Jews did not seek to kill Jesus simply because he claimed to do the works of God. The reason they sought to kill him was because **1.** Jesus "broke the Sabbath" and **2.** he attributed his "Sabbath-breaking" actions to God.

> *"Making himself equal to God,* by placing His action on the same level with the action of God."
> —B.F. Westcott[303]

The meaning of ἴσος ("equal") cannot be stressed to mean "equal in every respect." Such a meaning would be:

1. Contrary to the surrounding context both before and after John 5:18, which has Christ doing the actions of God in view.

2. Contrary to the text of John 5:18 itself, which plainly shows Christ's claim "that God was his Father" supplies the meaning for being "equal to God" (again, I refer the reader to chapter four, subheading *Begotten Explained*).

3. Contrary to how the Jews claimed the same thing for themselves to justify their own deeds. Fixing the meaning of God being their Father to their deeds, thus agreeing with the contextual usage in John 5:18.

4. Contrary to Christ's claim elsewhere when he says, "The Father is greater than I." (John 14:28.)

5. Contrary to how the word ἴσος (equal) is used elsewhere in the New Testament. It never denotes "equal in every aspect," but is always "equal in some regard." (See chapter six herein, subheading *Philippians 2:6 – Equal to God*)

John 5:19 – Actions of Christ all Actions of God?

Christ's life was truly a product of God's work in him, but he did not always reflect God's own words and actions in a direct way.

- Christ *prayed* to God, but this was not a reflection of God's own actions.

- Christ said, "My Father is greater than I," (John 14:28,) but these were not the words of God (who has no father).

The list of things which Christ did and spoke that were not reflecting God directly could go on and on. Nevertheless, there are still some who believe that all of the words and actions of the Son of God depict the very words and actions of the Father himself. They believe that Jesus is simply the Father in a body of limitations. According to this viewpoint, when Jesus prays to God it only appears as if he is corresponding with someone else, but this is in fact the Father, acting within the confines of his limited body, corresponding with his own self.[304] John 5:19 is presented as a primary proof text for this viewpoint.

> "Verily, verily, I say unto you, The Son can do **nothing** of himself, but what he seeth the Father do: for what things soever he doeth, these also doeth the Son likewise." (John 5:19)

When Christ said he could do "nothing" of himself he was not saying that he couldn't do anything in any capacity that didn't reflect the very actions and words of God himself. By way of comparison, Jesus made a similar statement regarding his disciples' relationship to himself, saying:

> "Without me ye can do **nothing**." (John 15:5)

Now, Jesus wasn't saying that his disciples couldn't do anything in any capacity without him ... If that were the case, Peter could not have denied Christ three times without Christ's involvement. Instead, the context shows that Jesus was informing his disciples that they could not *bear fruit* (*i.e.,* do the works of the kingdom of God) unless he was involved (John 15:1-8). In regard to how Christ said that his disciples could do "nothing" without him. we would clearly be in error if we interpreted this to mean that they couldn't have done anything in any capacity without him whatsoever. The "nothing" that Christ spoke of was clearly *nothing in a specified category* (bearing fruit). So also, when Christ said that he could do nothing of himself, but only what he saw the Father do, he was referring to a specific category as well, namely those miracles done in his public ministry.

> "Verily, verily, I say unto you, The Son can do **nothing** of himself, but what he seeth the Father do: for what things soever he doeth, these also doeth the Son likewise. For the Father loveth the Son, and sheweth him all things that himself doeth: and he will show him **greater works than these**, that ye may marvel." (John 5:19-20)

Contextually, Jesus was simply arguing that he couldn't have performed such a miraculous work (healing the man on the Sabbath) unless God was involved.

Chapter Sixteen

Tenth Chapter of John

The tenth chapter of John's Gospel has often been misunderstood. The section we are going to look at specifically is John 10:27-38. It is here that we find the famous statement from Christ, "I and the Father are one," (John 10:30,) as well as the statements Jesus made concerning men being "called gods." (John 10:34-35.) Since John 10:27-29 also deals with the followers of Christ being in both the hand of the Father and the Son, we will look at the implications of that passage as well. While there, we will also show the true meaning of Jesus' words regarding the security of his sheep. John 10:27-28 is probably the most commonly referred to passage in all of the Bible by proponents of "unconditional eternal security." While salvation, *per se,* is not specifically the subject matter of this present work, seeing that this prominent passage appears in a text we are already looking at, the issue merits a slight digression on our part.

John 10:30 – "I and the Father are One [Essence?]"

In John 10:30, Jesus makes the following statement:

ἐγὼ	καὶ	ὁ	πατὴρ	ἕν	ἐσμεν
I	and	the	Father	one	are

The Greek word that is used here for "one" (ἕν) is neuter in gender. The gender of Greek adjectives corresponds with the gender of the nouns they modify. If the adjective is neuter, the noun will be neuter as well. Since the gender of Greek nouns differ, the gender of the adjective "one" used to modify the nouns (*i.e.,* one ____) fluctuates accordingly. A good example of this principle can be seen in Ephesians 4:4-6, where the word "one" is used to modify several different nouns with differing genders. I will post the Greek text for Ephesians 4:4-6 below. (M) represents the masculine gender, (N) represents the neuter gender, (F) represents feminine gender.

ἓν	σῶμα	καὶ	ἓν	πνεῦμα	καθὼς	καὶ	ἐκλήθητε	ἐν
one	body	and	one	spirit	even as	also	ye are called	in
(N)	(N)		(N)	(N)				

μιᾷ	ἐλπίδι	τῆς	κλήσεως	ὑμῶν	εἷς	κύριος	μία
one	hope	of	the calling	your	one	Lord	one
(F)	(F)				(M)	(M)	(F)

πίστις	ἓν	βάπτισμα	εἷς	θεὸς	καὶ	πατὴρ	
faith	one	baptism	one	God	and	Father	(Ephesians 4:4-6)
(F)	(N)	(N)	(M)	(M)		(M)	

Do you see how the gender of the adjectives match the gender of the nouns? When a *masculine* noun (Lord, God, Father) was being described, the word "one" was masculine in gender as well (εἷς), etc. We can determine the gender of the noun by the gender of its adjective, even if the noun is not stated. So, when Jesus says, "I and the Father are ἓν (one, neuter gender)" we know that he could not have been referring to masculine or feminine gender nouns. Instead, the noun has to match the neuter gender of the adjective ἓν.

This is why A.T. Robertson, for example, can make this statement about what Christ was *not* talking about:

> *One* (ἕν). Neuter, not masculine (εἷς). Not one person.[305]

I agree with Robertson's comment concerning what Jesus was *not* talking about. The implications can be taken farther, however, than simply "not one person." Since the word for *God* (θεός) is masculine and requires the masculine adjective εἷς (as we see in the above text of Ephesians 4:6), Jesus was not saying "I and the Father are one ***God***." A.T. Robertson was correct thus far. What baffles me, however, is the conclusion Robertson made about what Jesus *was* talking about.

> *One* (ἕν). Neuter, not masculine (εἷς). Not one person, **but one essence or nature.**[306]

I do not understand his reasoning, because the word for *essence* in the Greek is οὐσία, which is feminine, not neuter. As we saw in the Greek text of Ephesians 4:4-5, feminine nouns (hope, faith) require a feminine adjective (μία).

Henry Alford says something similar to Robertson:

> Christ and the Father are one; one in essence primarily, but therefore also one in working, and power, and in will.[307]

He presents "one in essence" as his lead off statement, but eventually pulls himself back to what the text actually means as an afterthought ("**but therefore also** one in working ..."). The notion of essence is not in the text. Yet, many commentators seem to assume such and build their interpretation upon that assumed premise.

Alford goes on to say:

> It is perhaps more than is actually contained in the words : but as Meyer says, they are *founded on* the unity of essence of the Son and the Father, and so *presuppose* the homoousian doctrine.[308]

You see, he acknowledges that the homoousian (same-essence) doctrine is not stated within the text, but then says that which actually can be extracted from the text is "founded upon" the "presupposed" essence doctrine. We see, then, that the notion of **essence** is not found in the text itself, nor is it allowed inasmuch as οὐσία (essence/nature) is feminine and does not match the neuter adjective ἕν. The unity referred to in John 10:30 is something other than essence. Many commentators only "presuppose" *essence* as the foundation upon which that other, actual, allowed meaning has its basis. I hold their work in high regard, but I believe we should look at the text afresh without any such presuppositions.

Novation, writing in 235 AD, commented on John 10:30 as follows:

> He did not say "one person." For the word "one," used in the neuter gender refers to social unity, not personal unity. Note that "one" is neuter, not masculine. ... So this "one" has reference to agreement, to identity of judgment, and to the loving association itself. ... For he would not have said "are" if he meant that he, the one and only Father, had become the Son. ... [Scripture has many examples of] this unity of agreement. ... For in writing to the Corinthians, Paul said, "I have planted, Apollos watered, but God gave the increase. ... Now he that plants and he that waters are one (ἕν, neuter)." (1 Corinthians 3:6, 8.) Now, who does not realize that Apollos is one person and Paul another? ... Furthermore, the offices mentioned of each one of them are different. For he who plants is one, and he who waters is another. ... Yet, as far as respects their agreement, both are one.[309]

Understanding "I and the Father are One"

Both before and after Jesus said, "I and the Father are one," he specifically spoke of *doing the works of the* Father.

> "**The works that I do in my Father's name**, they bear witness of me. ... **I and my Father are one**. Then the Jews took up stones again to stone him. Jesus answered them, **Many good works have I shewed you from my Father**; for which of those works do ye stone me? ... **If I do not the works of my Father**, believe me not."
> (John 10:25, 30-32, 37)

Contextually, doing the works of God are in view. If I had to submit a specific neuter noun that agreed with both the neuter adjective ἕν and the context surrounding Christ's statement, I would suggest ἔργον (work). Unity in works is the pervasive theme in the context and the neuter noun ἔργον is used throughout (John 10:25, 32, 33, 37, 38).

Unity in work is the first definition also given by Henry Alford once he moved on from his presupposition of *essence,* saying:

Christ and the Father are one; one in essence primarily, but therefore also one in working.[310]

And Heinrich Meyer, whom Alford referred to in his entry, states something similar in his comments on John 10:30, writing thus:

> The unity, therefore, is one of *dynamic* fellowship, *i.e.* a unity of action for the realization of the divine decree of redemption; according to which, the Father is in the Son, and moves in him, so that the Father acts in the things which are done by the Son.[311]

There is a prayer of Jesus contained in John 17 where the Lord says some things strikingly similar to what we find in John 10. First, look at what Jesus says in the immediate context of his "I and the Father are one" statement:

> "I and the Father **are one** ... If I do not the works of my Father, believe me not. But if I do them, though ye believe not me, believe the works: **that ye may know and understand that the Father is in me, and I in the Father**." (John 10:30, 37-38 KJV)

Jesus says, "I and the Father are one," explaining his meaning afterwards as "the Father is in me and I am in the Father." Now compare his statement with the words we find in his John 17 prayer:

> "Neither for these only do I pray, but for them also that believe on me through their word; that they may all **be one; even as thou, Father, art in me, and I in thee, that they also may be**[312] **in us**: that the world may believe that thou didst send me. And the glory which thou hast given me I have given unto them; that they may **be one, even as we are one; I in them, and thou in me**, that they may be perfected into **one**." (John 17:20-23 ASV)

The parallels between these two passages is undeniable. Jesus prays for his followers, saying, "Even as thou, Father, art in me, and I in thee, that they also may be in us," and, "that they may be one, even as we are one; I in them and thou in me."

John 10:30, 38	**John 17:22-23**
"I and the Father are one ... the Father is in me, and I in the Father."	"...that they may be one, even as we are one; I in them, and thou in me"

Those men associated with Arius were recorded as saying:

> If, as we become one in the Father, so also He and the Father are one, and thus He too is in the Father, how pretend you from His saying, I and the Father are One, and I in the Father and the Father in Me, that He is proper and like the Father's Essence? For it follows either that we too are proper to the Father's Essence, or He foreign to it, as we are foreign.[313]

There is obviously a connection between being *one with* God/Jesus, being *in* God/Jesus, and God/Jesus being *in* man. Let's look at what the Bible says about man being in God and God being in man. After we see the meaning of this, the meaning of being one with God/Jesus will be self-evident.

As we said elsewhere in the book, being "in" something often denotes *acting in accordance with the attributes of* something.

> "God is love; and he that dwelleth in love dwelleth in God."
> (1 John 4:16)

To "dwell in love" clearly means to *act in accordance with attributes identifiable with* love. So, since God is love, dwelling in love is the same as *acting in accordance with the attributes of God.* Notice how the passage also includes, not only man dwelling in God, but God dwelling in man.

> "God is love; and he that dwelleth in love dwelleth in God, **and God in him**." (1 John 4:16)

God dwelling in man shows *the source* of the love that man walks in. Man dwelling in God is *the action that accords with* that source. So, we have *God in us,* providing the character, and *us in God,* walking in accordance with that character.

Now, with that being said, look at Christ's statement again:

> "I and the Father are one ... **If I do not the works of my Father**, believe me not. **But if I do them**, though ye believe not me, **believe the works**: that ye may know and understand that the Father is in me, and I in the Father." (John 10:30, 37-38)

Do you see how Christ is speaking of acting in accordance with the attributes of the Father? By believing that he was doing the works of the Father, the Jews would have known that the Father was in him (as the source of those works) and that he was in the Father (carrying out the works of the Father). This is the meaning of being one with God—*conforming to the revealed attributes of God in the carrying out of his works.*

Paul of Samosata – How God and Jesus are One

We do not have many words spoken by Paul of Samosata, bishop of Antioch from 260-272 AD, but of those we do have, we see him describing the manner in which God and Christ are one. The words of this ancient bishop of Antioch, in the city where Simon Peter and Paul of Tarsus established the local beliefs, in the city where disputes about belief were subjected to the original apostles of Christ (Acts 14:26-15:2), are as follows:

> The different natures and the different persons admit of union in one way alone, namely in the way of a complete agreement in respect of will; and thereby is revealed the One (or Monad) in activity in the case of those (wills) which have coalesced, in the manner described. ... We do not award praise to beings which submit merely in virtue of their nature; but we do award high praise to beings which submit because their attitude is one of love; and so submitting because their inspiring motive is one and the same, they

are confirmed and strengthened by one and the same indwelling power, of which the force ever grows, so that it never ceases to stir. It was in virtue of this love that the Saviour coalesced with God, so as to admit of no divorce from Him, but for all ages to retain one and the same will and activity with Him, an activity perpetually at work in the manifestation of good. ... Wonder not that the Saviour had one will with God.[314]

John 10:27-29 – The Security of the Sheep

Whilst speaking of how he was unified in action with the Father, Jesus made the following statements:

> "My sheep hear my voice, and I know them, and they follow me; and I give them eternal life, and they shall never perish, and no one shall snatch them out of my hand. My Father, who has given them to me, is greater than all, and no one is able to snatch them out of the Father's hand." (John 10:27-29 RSV)

Here we see a clear example of Christ's unity in action with the Father in securing the eternity of his followers. The Father is protecting the sheep, but the Son is as well. This accords with what we have said before of the Father and Son's unity in action. The Bible uses the phrase "in the hand" to denote *under the oversight* of or *in the possession of* (Genesis 32:13-16). When John 10:27-29 says no one can snatch the sheep out of the hand of the Father and the Son, this is to say *no one can overcome the protection provided for the sheep who are under the oversight of God and Jesus.* Jesus appeals to the indomitable power of the Father as the backing for the security that he himself provides, saying, "My Father, who has given them to me, is greater than all, and no one is able to snatch them out of the Father's hand." Jesus is not presenting himself as acting independently, but as carrying out the works of the Father and as having the full extent of the Father's power backing him up as he does so.

> "God did not let the sheep out of his hand, *i.e.* out of his protection and guidance, when he gave them to Christ. But this continued

divine protection is really nothing else than the protection of *Christ,* so far, that is, as the Father is in the Son and works in him."

—*Heinrich Meyer*[315]

Now we will examine whether John 10:27-29 contains proof for the doctrine known as *Unconditional Eternal Security,* which alleges that a person, once converted, can never "lose their salvation" thereafter. Allow me to share my entry on this passage from *The Salvation Bible Commentary.*

John 10:26-29

Kerrigan

26. Ye believe not – Jesus' claim to be the Christ. John 10:24-25
Because ye are not – What did Jesus mean by the words *because you are not of my sheep?* Are men incapable of believing Christ's claims about himself if they are not his sheep? Jesus certainly continued his attempt to persuade these same men to believe, but notice what he said:
"If I am not doing the works of my Father, then do not believe me; but if I do them, even though you do not believe me, believe the works…" (John 10:37-38 ASV)
Jesus said they should believe the *works,* even if they didn't believe *him.* Why would he say this? It is because those miraculous works that God did through Jesus were his way of *bearing witness* to Jesus. Jesus did not expect men to believe his claims about himself if they did not see God bearing witness to his words by miraculous deeds.

- "If I do not the works of my Father, believe me not." (John 10:37)
- "The Pharisees therefore said unto him, Thou bearest record of thyself; thy record is not true. Jesus answered and said unto them, … It is also written in your law, that the testimony of two men is true. I am one that bear witness of myself, and the Father that sent me beareth witness of me." (John 8 13-14, 17-18)
- "If I bear witness of myself, my witness is not true. There is another that beareth witness of me … the same works that I do, bear witness of me, that the Father hath sent me." (John 5:31-32, 36)

Jesus expected men to believe on him *based upon* their recognition of the miraculous works from the Father. Those miracles were the *foundation upon which* belief in Jesus' words were predicated.

Now, how does this tie into John 10:26? Let's look at the context leading up to that verse.

"The Jews therefore came round about him, and said unto him, How long dost thou hold us in suspense? If thou art the Christ, tell us plainly. Jesus answered them, *I told you*, and ye believe not: the *works* that I do in my Father's name, these *bear witness of me*. *But ye believe not*, because ye are not of my sheep." (John 6:24-26)

Contextually, the meaning is, "Ye believe not [my claim to be the Christ], because ye are not of my sheep." They did not believe Jesus' claims *because* they did not believe God's testimony about Jesus. Belief in God's testimony is *precisely* what causes men to become Christ's sheep. The Father testifies through the miracles that Jesus is his representative, so those who believe God's testimony regarding Jesus *respond by* becoming receptive to Jesus. Therefore, by the actions of the Father, mingled with faith, men are *thereby* placed under Christ's care. So then, by belief in *God's* actions, men *in turn* become adherent to Christ's shepherding. (Note: This can also be accomplished through belief in the Scriptures. John 5:39-47.) These men in John 10 did not believe the testimony *of* the Father, so they were not given to Jesus as sheep *by* the Father. Thus, afterwards, when Jesus spoke to them, they did not believe him either. Yet, Jesus did not abandon them as *incapable* of believing in the future, he just knew that he should not make claims about himself without first building the foundation for those claims. Hence, he went on to say, "Even though you do not believe me, believe the works, *that you may know* and understand..." (John 10:38 RSV)

Of my sheep – So many *presume* they are Christ's sheep for this reason or that, but according to the Bible the sheep are *the Israel of God*. This is a consistent testimony throughout the Old Testament. "My people hath been lost sheep ... Israel is a scattered sheep" (Jeremiah 50:6, 17) The entire chapter of Ezekiel 34 identifies Israel as the sheep of God. There we see remarkable comparisons to what is said of Christ's sheep in the New Testament:

1. They "were scattered because there was *no shepherd*" (Ezekiel 34:5), agreeing with "they were as sheep *not having a shepherd*" (Mark 6:34).

2. God says, "I will seek that which was *lost*" (Ezekiel 34:16), agreeing with "I am not sent but unto *the lost sheep* of the house of Israel" (Matthew 15:24).

3. God says he will "*save* his flock" (Ezekiel 34:22), agreeing with "the Son of man is come to seek and to *save* that which was lost" (Luke 19:10).

4. God says, And I will *bring* them out from the people, and *gather* them from the countries" (Ezekiel 34:13), agreeing with "And other sheep I have, which are not of this fold: *them also I must bring* ... and there shall be *one flock*" (John 10:16).

5. God will "judge between sheep and sheep, rams and he-goats" (Ezekiel 34:17) similar to "he shall set the sheep on his right hand, but the goats on the left" (Matthew 25:33).

6. God says "I will set up *one shepherd* over them" (Ezekiel 34:23), agreeing with "there shall be one flock and *one shepherd*" (John 10:16). The sheep who belong to God are the people of Israel. God gives these sheep to Jesus (John 10:27-28). Jesus is over them as their shepherd (John 10:11). *Thou bearest not the root, but the root thee!* Can someone cease to be included in Christ's sheep? To answer this, one only need ask if an individual could cease to be included in Israel. *The answer to that is a resounding Yes!* In the Old Testament, men who sinned presumptuously were "cut off" from Israel (Numbers 15:30). The New Testament also shows that "they are not all Israel, which are of Israel" (Romans 9:6). Natural born Jews were removed from Israel through unbelief. Furthermore, although Gentiles have now been graffed into Israel "by faith" (Ephesians 2:11-19), they should "fear" lest *they too* be "cut off" (Romans 11:20-23).

"This declaration: "they shall certainly not perish," will be accomplished in eternity. The lost sheep, *i.e.* the sheep which has been separated, and wandered away from the flock (Matthew 10:6; Luke 15:4), typifies him who is separated from the protection and gracious leading of Christ, who has fallen into unbelief. Compare the following καὶ οὐχ ἁρπάσει, etc., where this protection and gracious leading is set forth with still more concrete tenderness by the words ἐκ τῆς χειρός μου. His hand protects, bears, cherishes, leads them. Liberty and the *possibility of apostasy* are not thus excluded (in answer to Augustine and the teaching of the Reformed Church); he who has fallen away is no longer a πρόβατον [sheep]."

—*Heinrich Meyer's Critical and Exegetical Commentary on the New Testament, John 10:28*

27. My sheep hear my voice ... I know ... they follow − Each of the Greek verbs used here are present indicative verbs, which often refers to action being performed presently at that time, but present indicative verbs do not *always* denote that. In this passage we have an example of the *gnomic present*, which is used to express general, timeless truths, such as, "[God] maketh his sun to rise on the evil and on the good, and sendeth rain on the just and on the unjust." (Matthew 5:45) The truth conveyed here shows a timeless principle that is not confined to the present moment. This is what we find here in John 10 as well. Notice the timeless truth presented earlier in John 10:4 (part of "the parable" that makes up John 10:1-5), where Jesus says, "And when he putteth forth his own sheep, **he goeth (πορεύεται)** before them, and the sheep **follow (ἀκολουθεῖ)** him:

for they know his voice." Both *goeth* and *follow* are present indicative verbs, as in John 10:27-28. Jesus often uses the present indicative to express a timeless truth in his parables (e.g., the mustard seed *groweth up, becometh, shooteth out* Mark 4:32). Like sheep responding to their shepherd in John 10:4, which was a timeless truth, not a real time event, Jesus spoke a timeless truth in John 10:27 as well: "My sheep hear my voice, and I know them, and they follow me." This is not to be understood as "they are *presently* following me," but rather, "at any point in time, at the hearing of the Shepherd's voice, whether it be before now or after, they follow."

28. And I give unto them eternal life ... never perish – *Give* here is also a present indicative verb, taken as a gnomic present. When the sheep follow Christ, whether it be in the past or in the future, he gives them eternal life. The shepherd "putteth forth his own sheep" and "goeth before them" and they *in turn* "follow him." (John 10:4) See πρόδρομος (forerunner), Hebrews 6:20. So let us ponder the question, *Where did Christ go before us and where are we following him to?* In the context of John 10, Jesus spoke of how he set aside his life in this world (John 10:15, 18) in order that he might take it up again afterwards (John 10:17). In this way he has gone before us and leads us out of this present land into the green pasture of eternity (Ezekiel 34). Consider how the following examples show that *following* Christ refers to *remaining faithful unto death as he did* in order to take up the eternal life to come: "And Jesus answered them, saying, The hour is come, that the Son of man should be glorified. Verily, verily, I say unto you, Except a corn of wheat fall into the ground and die, it abideth alone: but if it die, it bringeth forth much fruit. He that loveth his life shall lose it; and he that hateth his life in this world shall keep it unto life eternal. If any man serve me, **let him follow me; and where I am, there shall also my servant be**: if any man serve me, him will my Father honour. Now is my soul troubled; and what shall I say? Father, save me from this hour: but for this cause came I unto this hour." (John 12:23-27)

"Therefore, when he was gone out, Jesus said, Now is the Son of man glorified, and God is glorified in him. ... Little children, yet a little while I am with you. Ye shall seek me: and as I said unto the Jews, **Whither I go, ye cannot come**; so now I say to you. ... Simon Peter said unto him, Lord, whither goest thou? Jesus answered him, **Whither I go, thou canst not follow me now; but thou shalt follow me afterwards**. Peter said unto him, Lord, why cannot I follow thee now? I will lay down my life for thy sake. Jesus answered him, Wilt thou lay down thy life for my sake? Verily, verily, I say unto thee, The cock shall not crow, till thou hast denied me thrice." (John 13:31, 33, 36-38)

"This spake [Jesus], signifying by what **death** [Peter] should glorify

God. And when he had spoken this, he said unto him, **Follow me**."

(John 21:19)

Compare how Jesus said Peter could not follow him with Mark 14:54, where Peter in fact *did* "follow" him *after* Christ spake thus, but "afar off" and not faithfully unto death. See also Mark. 5:37. When Jesus spoke of *following* he didn't mean *begin to follow for a* moment (John 6:2) but rather *follow so that you wind up at the same destination*. See my note on John 6:35.

Is it not clear to the reader that Christ went on before his sheep in faithfulness unto death, being the first to enter into the resurrection (Acts 26:23)? And it is in this manner, in the losing of one's life in this world by being faithful unto death, that we ultimately follow him (Hebrews 13:13). So, when the Master says, "My sheep follow me, and I give unto them eternal life," this is the same as to say, "My sheep follow me even unto the death, and to those who follow me thus, I give eternal life." As he says elsewhere, "Be thou faithful unto death, and I will give thee a crown of life." (Revelation 2:10) See my note on James 1:12 for "crown of life."

29. My Father, which gave them me – See my note on John 10:26.

And they shall never perish, etc – The sure hope of all who follow Christ unto death, after which time all their future is certain and unalterable, by the power of God, who is greater than all.

John 10:34-35 – Jesus' Defense / "Ye are Gods"

Subsequent to claiming a unity of action with God, even to the extent of giving eternal life to his followers, some of the Jews wanted to stone Jesus.

> "Then the Jews took up stones again to stone him." (John 10:31)

This is when Jesus begins to state his case for why he has done nothing worthy of being stoned, saying:

> "Many good works have I shewed thee from my Father; for which of these do ye stone me?" (John 10:32)

He shows that unity with the Father in actions is in view here as his contextual theme. Those miracles performed by Christ were beneficial and proved that God was with him backing his words and deeds. What did Jesus do that was wrong?

> "The Jews answered him, saying, 'For a good work we stone thee not; but for blasphemy; and because that thou, being a man, makest thyself God.'" (John 10:33)

Now this is a very interesting statement. They are accusing Jesus of making himself God. Let's pay very close attention to how Jesus responds. He does not say, "I really am God," but what does he say? Something quite remarkable:

> "Is it not written in your law, 'I said 'Ye are gods[316]?'" (John 10:34)

Now why would Jesus quote *this* verse? What point was he making? It is obvious that he is continuing his own defense by appealing to a scriptural precedent. He goes on to explain the passage he cited:

> "He called them gods, unto whom the word of God came." (John 10:35)

The passage Jesus cites is Psalm 82:6 (81:6 LXX). The context of Psalm 82 shows that God was being revealed in the ones called θεοί (gods). The first verse in Psalm 82 reads:

> "God standeth in the congregation of the mighty; he judgeth among the gods." (Psalm 82:1)

Now the word here that is translated as "the mighty," when it says, "God standeth in the congregation of **the mighty**," is the Hebrew word *el*, which means *God*. Hence, some English versions read like the *American Standard Version:*

> "God standeth in the congregation of God." (Psalm 82:1 ASV)

The Greek Septuagint, however, has the text as:

ὁ   θεὸς   ἔστη   ἐν   συναγωγῇ   θεῶν
the   God   stood in   the assembly of gods (Psalm 81(82):1 LXX)

The word θεῶν here is the plural, which denotes *gods*. Although the original Hebrew read אֱלֹהִים (*elohim – God/gods*), and thus could have been translated "God," the ancient Jewish scholars who translated the passage into Greek rendered it as "gods" (likely because, unlike Exodus 7:1, where Moses alone is called God, this psalm has multiple representatives of God in view). We have a vindication of this Greek translation in John 10:35, which, like the LXX, says θεοί (gods). Hence, we do have an affirmation of "gods" terminology in the Bible. However, this does not contradict the fact that there is only one true God (Isaiah 43:10, 44:6, John 17:3, 1 Corinthians 8:4-6), because we know biblically an image is called by the name of its archetype. For example: Moses was told to "make two cherubim," (Exodus 25:18,) but even though the images he made were called "cherubim," (the plural for *cherub,*) we know that Moses' formation of those cherubim did not increase the number of true and actual cherubim. The Bible could call the representations of cherubim "cherubim" while not implying that any additional cherubim were in view than actually existed. Likewise, there is only one true God, and those who are called "God" or "gods" otherwise do not exist as truly being God.

The actual statement quoted by Jesus in John 10:34 comes later in this psalm, where, again, God calls the ones being addressed *elohim* in the Hebrew, which was translated as θεοί (gods) in the Greek. Yet, the psalm not only goes on to call them θεοί (gods), but also refers to them as sons of God.

> "I said, Ye are gods, and all of you **sons of the Most High**."
> (Psalm 82:6 ASV)

The text says that they were both θεοί (gods) and sons (υἱοί) of God. We already discussed how men were sometimes called God (see chapter three herein, subheading *The Image is Called by the Name of the Archetype)*. Men were called God inasmuch as they *acted in accordance with the revealed attributes of God*. We also showed that being the son of someone means *acting in accordance with the attributes of the source-individual* (see chapter four herein, subheading *Begotten Explained)*. So, in biblical terms, Jesus was referring to a scriptural precedent where men were already identified as *acting in accordance with the attributes of God*. The men who wanted to stone him could not do so when he claimed this of himself, because the same claim already had scriptural precedent. However, Jesus also goes past proving that unity of action with God has scriptural precedent and makes it personal, drawing attention to evidence that his own claim, now vindicated as scriptural, was indeed true.

> "Jesus answered them, Many good works have I shewed you from my Father; for which of those works do ye stone me? The Jews answered him, saying, For a good work we stone thee not; but for blasphemy; and because that thou, being a man, makest thyself God. Jesus answered them, Is it not written in your law, I said, Ye are gods? If he called them gods, unto whom the word of God came, and the scripture cannot be broken; Say ye of him, whom the Father hath sanctified, and sent into the world, Thou blasphemest; because I said, I am the[317] Son of God? **If I do not the works of my Father, believe me not. But if I do, though ye believe not me, believe the works: that ye may know, and believe**." (John 10:32-38 KJV)

As we have seen all along, the context deals entirely with Jesus doing the miraculous works of the Father. The works themselves testified to Jesus' claim.

Before we move on, let's briefly touch on Psalm 82 a little more. The ones being addressed by God are contextually being reproved by God, so how could they simultaneously be carrying out his works? At one time they *were* acting in accordance with the attributes of God, but, apparently, they *ceased to* do so, which brought about the contextual rebuke from God. Aorist indicative verbs show a past event. We see such verbs used in Psalm 82(81):1, 6, relating these events to a historic declaration. The pertinent verbs highlighted below are aorist indictive verbs.

> "God **hath stood** (ἔστη) in the company of God ... I **have said** (εἶπα), 'Gods ye are ...'" (Psalm 82:1, 6 YLT)

The declaration that these men were θεοί (gods) and sons (υἱοὶ) was a past event. At some time in the past, God referred to these men as acting in accordance with his attributes, but now, as the rebuke shows, they were no longer doing so. Hence, though he "said" they were θεοί (gods) and sons (υἱοὶ) before, this past affirmation seems to afterwards be nullified.

> "**I have said**, Ye are gods; and all of you are children of the most High. **But** ye shall die like men, and fall like one of the princes."
> (Psalm 82:6-7 KJV)

Chapter Seventeen

John 12:37-41

Not One, but Two Texts Being Quoted

John 12:37-41 incorporates a quotation from Isaiah 53:1 as well as a subsequent quotation from Isaiah 6:9-10, saying

> "But though he (Jesus) had done so many signs before them, yet they believed not on him: that the word of Isaiah the prophet might be fulfilled, which he spake, **Lord, who hath believed our report? And to whom hath the arm of the Lord been revealed?** For this cause they could not believe, for that Isaiah said again, **He hath blinded their eyes, and he hardened their heart; Lest they should see with their eyes, and perceive with their heart, and should turn, and I should heal them**. These things said Isaiah, because he saw his glory; and he spake of him."
>
> (John 12:37-41 ASV)

The second set of bold letters indicate a quotation from Isaiah chapter six, in which chapter Isaiah also says that he **saw** the "the Lord sitting upon a throne," whom he afterwards also identifies as "the LORD of hosts." (Isaiah 6:5.) The quotation from Isaiah 6 is then qualified with these words, "These things said Isaiah, because he **saw** his glory; and spake of [Christ]." (John 12:41 ASV.) Some say that John 12:37-41 parallels seeing God with seeing Christ. They thereby assert that Christ must have been the LORD (Jehovah) whom Isaiah saw. Is that an accurate conclusion? Is Christ identified as the LORD whom Isaiah saw here in John 12:39-41?

We must remember that there are *two* quotations from the book of Isaiah in John 12:37-41 (Isaiah 6:9-10 *and* Isaiah 53:1). The author refers back to *both* of these quotations when he says:

> "**These things** (*plural = both of these sayings*) said Isaiah, because he saw his glory; and spake of him." (John 12:41 ASV)

Many interpretations of John 12:41 have been presented to explain the *second* quotation from Isaiah 6:9-10, but few have *also* acknowledged the *first* quotation from Isaiah 53:1. Indeed, Isaiah 53, and a large amount of text preceding and following Isaiah 53, truly speaks in great detail about events in Christ's life that Isaiah saw[318] beforehand. Nevertheless, while acknowledging the quote from Isaiah 53:1 in John 12:38, we must not forget to *also* acknowledge the quote from Isaiah 6:9-10 in John 12:40. No matter how much emphasis we place on *one* of the author's quotes, the proper explanation of this passage must necessarily comply with *both* of the texts that he refers to.

How Were They Blinded?

Isaiah 6:9-10, the second passage quoted in John 12:37-41, shows God speaking to Isaiah, saying:

> "Go, and say to this people, ye shall hear indeed, but ye shall not understand; and ye shall see indeed, but ye shall not perceive. For the heart of this people has become gross, and their ears are dull of hearing, and their eyes have they closed; lest they should see with their eyes, and hear with their ears, and understand with their heart, and be converted, and I should heal them." (Isaiah 6:9-10 LXX)

God told Isaiah to tell the people that the time was coming when they would see and not perceive, hear and not understand. Jesus shows that this prophecy was fulfilled during the time of his own ministry, saying:

> "Therefore speak I to them in parables: because they seeing see not; and hearing they hear not, neither do they understand. And **in**

them is fulfilled the prophecy of Esaias, which saith, By hearing ye shall hear, and shall not understand; and seeing ye shall see, and shall not perceive: For this people's heart is waxed gross, and their ears are dull of hearing, and their eyes they have closed; lest at any time they should see with their eyes, and hear with their ears, and should understand with their heart, and should be converted, and I[319] should heal them." (Matthew 13:13-15)

The prophecy of Isaiah 6:9-10 was "fulfilled" during Christ's ministry. This is the same prophecy that the author quotes in John 12:39-40. Yet, *how* was such a prophecy (regarding the people seeing and not perceiving, hearing but not understanding) fulfilled in the ministry of Christ?

Albert Barnes comments on how the people's eyes were blinded and their hearts were hardened, saying:

> **He hath blinded their** eyes – The expression in Isaiah is, "Go, make the heart of this people fat, and shut their eyes." That is, go and proclaim truth to them—truth that will *result* in blinding their eyes. Go and proclaim the law and the will of God, and the *effect will be,* owing to the hardness of their heart, that their eyes will be blinded and their hearts hardened.[320]

This kind of truth, which upon being proclaimed resulted in men's eyes being blinded, was heralded by Christ, as the author says:

> "Therefore they could not believe, because that Esaias said again, He (Christ) hath blinded their eyes, and hardened their heart; that they should not see with their eyes, nor understand with their heart..." (John 12:39-40)

When the author says, "*He* hath blinded their eyes," he is not quoting Isaiah 6:9 verbatim, because *there is no manuscript that reads,* "*He* hath blinded their eyes." The author instead says, "He hath blinded their eyes," to show that this prophecy was fulfilled in Christ. This point is of great importance, because God is the one speaking in Isaiah 6:9-10. Yet, the author shows a *distinction* between the speaker (God) and the one who blinds the peoples' eyes (Christ), saying:

> "Therefore they could not believe, because that Esaias said again, **He** (Christ) hath blinded their eyes, and hardened their heart; that they should not see with their eyes, nor understand with their heart, and be converted, and **I** (God) should heal them." (John 12:39-40)

God was speaking in the *first*-person narrative, and he, according to the author of John, was speaking of Christ in the *third*-person narrative; therefore Christ is not identified as the God who was speaking, but rather as the one of whom God spoke.

God sent Christ to proclaim truth to the people in such a way that they would hear it, but not understand it.[321] This was the fulfillment of Isaiah's prophecy to Israel, "Ye shall hear indeed, but ye shall not understand; and ye shall see indeed, but ye shall not perceive." (Isaiah 6:9 LXX) But what was it about Jesus' teachings that caused the people to hear but not understand, and see but not perceive? This blinding principle is attributed to Jesus' usage of parables … Jesus *always* spoke in parables to the crowds:

> "But without a parable spake he not unto them: and when they were alone, he expounded all things to his disciples." (Mark 4:34)

Jesus only *explained* the parables to those who remained with him after the crowds dispersed:

> "And when he was alone, they that were about him with the twelve asked of him the parable. And he said unto them, Unto you it is given to know the mystery of the kingdom of God: but unto them that are without, all these things are done in parables: **That** seeing they may see, and not perceive; and hearing they may hear, and not understand; lest at any time they should be converted, and their sins should be forgiven them." (Mark 4:10-12)

Jesus spoke to the crowds in parables. The crowds did not understand the *meaning* of the parables, but neither did they *seek to* understand the meaning. Nevertheless, Christ *did* give the explanation of those parables to those who remained with him.

How could the masses of people not seek to truly understand Christ's words even though they saw all of the miracles that Christ performed? Those miracles clearly *proved* that he was from God. This is why Nicodemus came to Jesus, saying:

> "Rabbi, we know that thou art a teacher come from God: for no man can do those miracles that thou doest, except God be with him." (John 3:2)

Jesus was obviously of God, so why did the crowds not take his words to heart? Multitudes of people flocked to Jesus because of the miracles that he performed, but when it came to his teachings few people even believed what he said. Why didn't they seek to *learn* from Jesus? It was this lack of belief regarding the teachings of Christ that caused many of the Jews to be blinded.

The Glory Pertained to the Miracles

The Jews'[322] failure to believe in Christ despite the many miracles that they saw him perform is precisely what the author is referring to in John 12:37-43, saying:

> "But **though he had done so many miracles** before them, **yet they believed not on him: That** the saying of Esaias the prophet might be **fulfilled**, which he spake, Lord, who hath believed our report? And to whom hath the arm of the Lord been revealed? Therefore they could not believe, because that Esaias said **again**, He hath blinded their eyes, and hardened their heart; that they should not see with their eyes, nor understand with their heart, and be converted, and I should heal them. **These things said Esaias, because he saw his glory, and spake of him**. Nevertheless among the chief rulers also many believed on him; but because of the Pharisees they did not confess him, lest they should be put out of

the synagogue: For they loved the praise of men more than the praise of God." (John 12:37-43)

Isaiah prophetically saw the coming and ministry of Christ (including seeing his miracles).[323] Isaiah also saw that the people would not receive Christ despite the many miracles that he would perform. These are the things the author was referring to in John 12:37-41. Someone might object to this by saying that such an understanding does not account for the author saying, "These things said Isaiah, **because he saw his glory**; and he spake of him." (John 12:41 ASV.) I disagree. The **context** of John 12 *does* refer to Christ's miracles as being the glory that is seen and rejected by the Jews during Christ's ministry. What is more, the Bible specifically identifies Christ's miracles as the way in which Christ's glory was revealed:

> "This beginning of **miracles** did Jesus in Cana of Galilee, and **manifested forth his glory**; and his disciples believed on him."
> (John 2:11) (c.f. John 11:4, 40)

Christ manifested his glory by the performance of miracles. The context of John 12:37-41 refers to the miracles of Christ, therefore it makes perfect sense to interpret the glory of Christ that Isaiah saw as being the miraculous nature of Christ's ministry.

The Common Explanation Fails

In summary, the correct understanding of John 12:37-41 is as follows:

> "But though [Jesus] had done **so many miracles** before [the Jews], yet they believed not on him: That the saying of Esaias the prophet might be fulfilled, which he spake, Lord, who hath believed our report? And to whom hath the arm of the Lord [that is, the miraculous works of God] been revealed? Therefore they could not believe, because that Esaias said again, [Christ] hath blinded their eyes [using parables], and hardened their heart [using parables]; that they should not see with their eyes, nor understand with their

heart, and be converted, and [God] should heal them. These things said Esaias, because he saw [the miraculous ministry of Christ], and he spake of him." (John 12:37-41)

On the other hand, those who say that the author of John was identifying Christ as the LORD whom Isaiah saw sitting upon the throne adhere to an interpretation of the text, which:

1. Fails to acknowledge the true and entire *context* of John 12:37-43.

2. Does not provide a logical explanation as to why Isaiah said those things "*because*" he saw Christ's glory.[324]

3. Doesn't account for how the author refers to Isaiah 53:1 as well (which referenced Christ's coming ministry rather than Christ appearing in a glorious form).

4. Is contrary to Daniel 7:9-14 as well as Revelation 4:2-5:7, which both portray *God* sitting on a throne while being *distinct* from Christ.

5. Does not give an adequate reason as to why the author quotes Isaiah 6:9-10 saying, "He (Christ) hath blinded their minds ... lest I (the LORD whom Isaiah saw) should heal them."

Chapter Eighteen

Christ and Worship

In our modern culture we use the word *worship* in reference to an act of reverence given only to someone who is divine. However, in times before ours the word *worship* was simply used to signify a giving of high honor and/or adoration. In fact, examples of how the word *worship* was formerly used like this, even in our English language, can still be found in the historic *King James Version,* which, for instance, translates Luke 14:10 as follows:

> "But when thou art bidden, go and sit down in the lowest room; that when he that bade thee cometh, he may say unto thee, Friend, go up higher: **then shalt thou have worship** in the presence of them that sit at meat with thee." (Luke 14:10 KJV)

This antiquated translation (AD 1611) shows how men formerly did not consider the English word *worship* as something applicable *only* to God. Just as the word *worship* was not used exclusively of God in the English vocabulary, so also the Hebrew and Greek words for *worship* were not used in biblical times exclusively of God either.[325]

The Worship that is Given to Jesus

When the Bible speaks of worship directed towards Christ, the Greek word usually translated as "worship" is προσκυνέω (proskuneō).

- "Then they that were in the ship came and worshipped (προσκυνέω) him, saying, Of a truth thou art the Son of God."
(Matthew 15:25 KJV)

- "And it came to pass, while he blessed them, he was parted from them, and carried up into heaven. And they **worshipped** (προσκυνέω) him, and returned to Jerusalem with great joy."

    (Luke 24:51-52 KJV)

The Strong's Concordance defines προσκυνέω as follows:

> Προσκυνέω – (mean. to *kiss* like a dog *licking* his master's hand); to *fawn* or *crouch to,* i.e. (lit. or fig.) *prostrate* oneself in homage (do *reverence* to, *adore*): – worship.[326]

Albert Barnes comments accurately on the meaning of προσκυνέω, saying:

> So far as the word is concerned, it may refer either to spiritual homage, that is, the worship of God; or it may mean respect as shown to superiors.[327]

And John Calvin states:

> We read, indeed, frequently, of men having been worshipped, but that was civil honour.[328]

In the Septuagint, the Greek translation of the Old Testament, προσκυνέω is applied, not only to God (Exodus 34:14), but also to David (1 Samuel 25:23), to David's servants (1 Samuel 25:41), to angels (Genesis 19:1), etc.[329]

1 Chronicles 29:20 records an event where the Israelites worshipped both the LORD and King David, saying:

> "And David said to the whole congregation, Bless the Lord our God. And all the congregation blessed the Lord God of their fathers, and they bowed the knee and **worshipped** (προσκυνέω) **the LORD and the king**." (1 Chronicles 29:20 LXX)

Nowhere in this chapter (1 Chronicles 29) does it speak of God as "the king," but it speaks of "David the king" *several* times (1 Chronicles 29:1,

9, 24, 29, etc.). Thus, when it says they "worshipped the king" it is obvious that the king being worshipped is "David the king." (1 Chronicles 29:1.)

In the New Testament, Jesus states that the Christians at Philadelphia would receive worship (προσκυνέω), saying:

> "Behold, I will make them of the synagogue of Satan, which say they are Jews, and are not, but do lie; behold, **I will make them to come and worship** (προσκυνέω) **before thy feet**, and to know that I have loved thee." (Revelation 3:9)

Some say that Christ's words here should be *interpreted* as:

> "...behold, I will make them to come and **worship [God]** before thy feet."

However, that is not what Christ was saying at all. Compare Christ's statement in Revelation 3:9, "worship before thy (the Christian's) feet," to Revelation 22:8-9, where John tried to "worship before the feet of the angel" and was rebuked for *trying to worship the angel **himself***, not for trying to worship *God* at the angel's feet.

> "And I John saw these things, and heard them. And when I had heard and seen, I fell down to **worship before the feet of** the angel which shewed me these things. Then saith he unto me, See thou do it not: for I am thy fellowservant, and of thy brethren the prophets, and of them which keep the sayings of this book: worship God."[330] (Revelation 22:8-9 KJV)

It is clear in the Book of Revelation that "worshipping before" someone signified worshipping them.

> "Who shall not fear thee, O Lord, and glorify thy name? for thou only art holy: for all nations shall come and **worship before thee**; for thy judgments are made manifest." (Revelation 15:4)

Thus, when Jesus told the church at Philadelphia, "I will make them to come and worship (προσκυνέω) before thy feet," he was definitely letting these Christians know that he would cause their persecutors to come and worship them. Therefore, προσκυνέω cannot exclusively mean *worship as God.* Some other examples of where προσκυνέω is used in the Bible are as follows:

- Abraham "bowed himself (προσκυνέω)" to the people of Canaan. (Genesis 23:7, 12 LXX)

- Isaac blessed Jacob, saying, "Let nations **bow down** (προσκυνέω) to you ... and let your mother's sons **bow down** (προσκυνέω) to you." (Genesis 27:29 LXX)

- "David stooped and **bowed himself** (προσκυνέω) to the earth" to king Saul. (1 Samuel 24:8 LXX)

- Abigail "**bowed herself** (προσκυνέω) to the ground" to David (1 Samuel 25:23), and again to David's representatives. (1 Samuel 25:41)

- "When Mephibosheth ... was come unto David, he fell on his face and **did reverence** (προσκυνέω)." (2 Samuel 9:6 LXX)

- Jesus shows that he himself is a worshipper of God, saying, "Ye worship ye know not what: **we** [Jews] know what **we** worship." (John 4:22)

- The servant in Jesus' parable worshipped his human king. (Matthew 18:26)

Why the Angel Would Not Let John Worship Him

The Greek word for *worship,* προσκυνέω, denotes the homage given to one's *superior.* This is why the angel in Revelation 19:10 *refused* to receive worship from John.

> "And I (John) fell at his feet to worship him. And he said unto me, See thou do it not: I am thy fellowservant, and of thy brethren that have the testimony of Jesus." (Revelation 19:10)

The angel wasn't in a position of *authority* over John, but he was instead in a position of *equality* with John. The angel explains his reason for not receiving worship from John right there in the text—He was John's fellow servant.

> "See thou do it not: **I am thy fellow servant**." (Revelation 19:10)

John was told not to worship the angel *because* they were both "fellow servants." Contrast this with Joshua 5:14, where the angel who was "**captain** of the host of the LORD" was, due to his position, worshipped by Joshua. The angel speaking to John here in Revelation 19:10 was one of those seven angels who had the seven vials (Revelation 17:1,3,15 19:9), so John knew that this was just an angel. Therefore, John obviously did not think that he was falling down to worship either God or Jesus. **If worship was applicable only to God himself then what would that say about the character and integrity of John who tried to worship an angel??? Especially since he tried to worship an angel *again* three chapters later in Revelation 22:8???**

> "And I John saw these things, and heard them. And when I had heard and seen, I fell down to worship before the feet of the angel which shewed me these things. Then saith he unto me, See thou do it not: for I am thy fellowservant." (Revelation 22:8-9)

John wasn't trying to commit a blasphemous act by worshipping someone who wasn't God, because *worship,* as it is used in the Scriptures, doesn't always mean *worship as God.*

Why Peter Would Not Let Cornelius Worship Him

There is also a scenario in Acts 10:25-26 where a Roman centurion named Cornelius tried to "worship" Peter. Unlike the angel whom John was trying to worship, Peter did not say, "I am thy fellow servant," but he instead says:

> "Stand up; **I myself am also a man**." (Acts 10:26)

Peter knew that the Romans mostly believed in Greek mythology, which claimed that gods took on the forms of men. This is why he said, "I myself am **also** a man," so that those who were present would not think that he was some kind of god.

A similar incident happened in Acts 14:11-15, which says:

> "And when the people saw what Paul had done, they lifted up their voices, saying in the speech of Lycaonia, The gods are come down to us in the likeness of men. And they called Barnabas, Jupiter; and Paul, Mercurius, because he was the chief speaker. Then the priest of Jupiter, which was before their city, brought oxen and garlands unto the gates, and would have done sacrifice with the people. Which when the Apostles, Barnabas and Paul, heard of, they rent their clothes, and ran in among the people, crying out, And saying, Sirs, why do ye these things? **We also are men**."
> (Acts 14:11-15)

Notice how Paul and Barnabas were clearing up any misconceptions by saying, "We also are men." (Acts 14:15) Peter was doing this same thing at Cornelius' house when he said, "I myself also am a man." (Acts 10:26) Against the backdrop of Roman paganism, Peter was simply protecting against being worshipped as something that he was not.

Matthew 4:10 / Luke 4:8 – Worship [Only?] God

Although Matthew 4:10 and Luke 4:8 are often misquoted as if they say, "Worship God alone," all they *actually* say is:

> "Thou shalt worship (προσκυνέω) the Lord thy God, and him only shalt thou serve." (Matthew 4:10 / Luke 4:8 KJV)

This Old Testament commandment being quoted by Christ here simply says, "Worship the Lord thy God," not, "Worship *only* the Lord thy God." So why do so many people cite Matthew 4:10 as evidence that we are to worship *only* God? It is because of the context in which this statement was made.

Jesus spoke those words in Matthew 4:10 as a *reply* to Satan, who said:

> "All these things will I give unto thee, **if thou wilt fall down and worship** (προσκυνέω) **me**." (Matthew 4:9)

The logic applied to this scenario is as follows:

> Since Satan's request was that Christ worship him, then by Christ saying, "It is written, Thou shalt worship the Lord thy God," he was affirming that the reason he could not worship *Satan* was because that Old Testament commandment actually means worship *God alone.*

Although I *do* believe that Jesus quoted this passage to show that he was obligated by the commandment to worship God, the fact of the matter is that the text still does not say "worship *only* God."

Even though it isn't explicitly stated, it does not make sense to say that a person who worships God also worships Satan. How can someone worship God "in spirit and in truth" (John 4:23) while simultaneously worshipping the one who would oppose God on every hand? To worship Satan cancels out the worship of God. The Bible says God is a jealous God:

> "For thou shalt worship no other god: for the LORD, whose name is Jealous, is a jealous God." (Exodus 34:14)

Notice that he demands worship of himself as opposed to worship of false gods. In regard to false gods, the Bible says:

> "The gods of the nations are idols." (Psalm 96:5 KJV)

A person cannot, therefore, worship both God and an idol/god because God will not allow such. Now, the truth is that idols are presentations of demons, and those who do homage to idols are actually doing homage to demons, as the Scripture says.

> "What say I then? that the idol is any thing, or that which is offered in **sacrifice to idols** is any thing? But I say, that the things which the Gentiles sacrifice, they **sacrifice to devils**, and not to God: and I would not that ye should have fellowship with devils. Ye **cannot** drink the cup of the Lord, and the cup of devils: ye **cannot** be partakers of the Lord's table, and of the table of devils. **Do we provoke the Lord to jealousy**?" (1 Corinthians 10:19-22)

It is impossible to worship God and demons. How much more is it impossible to worship both God and Satan? The impossibility is based upon the character of God. A woman can say that she loves her husband and another man, and she very well may in some regard. However, due to the character of the husband, if he is jealous, he would never tolerate the wife giving the other man messages of adoration in hopes of receiving some great benefit from him. Should Satan have his way in your life, you would blaspheme God. Compare the temptation of Christ, to whom Satan promised power over the kingdoms of the world if he would worship (Luke 4:6-7), to what we see in Revelation 13, where the Antichrist's government worships Satan (the dragon), is given its authority by Satan, and also blasphemes God (Revelation 13:3-4, 6).

Some things are simply incompatible:

> "You adulterous people, don't you know that friendship with the world means enmity against God? Therefore, **anyone who chooses to be a friend of the world becomes an enemy of God**. Or do you think Scripture says without reason that he jealously longs for the spirit he has caused to dwell in us? But he gives us more grace. That is why Scripture says: 'God opposes the proud but shows favor to the humble.' Submit yourselves, then, to God. Resist the devil, and he will flee from you." (James 4:4-7 NIV)

APPENDIXES

Appendix A

Common Inquiries: The Old Testament

The meaning of Echad This Hebrew word simply means *one* and is used as our English word *one* is used. It can mean one thing composed of many, like one cluster of grapes (Numbers 13:23); or one thing consisting of one, like one ram (Leviticus 16:5).

The meaning of Elohim Why is the plural used of God? Many people assume too much by the usage of the Hebrew plural for God (Elohim) that is used in the Old Testament. The plural form of *el* (god) is *elohim* (gods), but when used of one being (as of Yahweh), the plural is used to express grandeur. This usage of the plural in reference to a single individual is known as *the plural of majesty*.
Consider how the plural form of *adon* (lord) is used when Joseph is described as the "lord" (*adonim* – plural) of the land.
"The man, who is the lord (*adonim*) of the land, spake roughly to us, and took us for spies of the country." (Genesis 42:30)
Joseph was not many people in one being. We cannot extract that doctrine from the plural of majesty used in regard to Joseph, nor can we do so when God is called *Elohim*. Elohim, with multiple referents, literally means *gods*. Those who assert that Elohim means *many persons* in one God are simply fabricating a definition based upon their presuppositions. Again, elohim, when having multiple referents, does not mean *more than one person*, but *more than one god*.

Genesis 1:26 "Let us make man" Compare the proximity of these two statements: In Genesis 11:4 the men in Shinar say to one another, "**Go to, let us** build us a city and a tower." Three verses later, God says, "**Go to,**

let us go down, and there confound their language." (Genesis 11:7.) When God makes these "us" statements, he is evidently referencing himself and those heavenly beings (e.g., angels) present with him (1 Kings 22:19-20, Isaiah 6:6-8, Job 38:4-7, Psalm 89:5-8). Ancient Jews interpreted God's "us" statement in Genesis 1:26 as God speaking with his angels. Targum Jonathan (probably 2nd century AD) renders Genesis 1:26 as:

"And the Lord said to the angels who ministered before Him, who had been created in the second day of the creation of the world, Let us make man in Our image, in Our likeness."[331]

Philo of Alexandria, a Jewish contemporary of Jesus, writes:

"And the practicer of virtue, Jacob, bears his testimony in support of this doctrine of mine, where he says, 'The God who has nourished me from my youth up, the angel who delivered me from all my evils.' For the most ancient benefits, those by which the soul is nourished, he attributes to God, but the more recent ones, which are caused by the errors of the soul, he attributes to the servant of God. On this account, I imagine it is, that when Moses was speaking philosophically of the creation of the world, while he described everything else as having been created by God alone, he mentions man alone as having been made by him in conjunction with other assistants; for, says Moses, 'God said, Let us make man in our image.' The expression, 'let *us* make,' indicating a plurality of makers. Here, therefore, the Father is conversing with his own powers, to whom he has assigned the task of making the mortal part of our soul, acting in imitation of his own skill while he was fashioning the rational part within us, thinking it right that the dominant part within the soul should be the work of the Ruler of all things, but that the part which is to be kept in subjection should be made by those who are subject to him."[332]

I have historically taken Genesis 1:26 as God speaking to the *resurrected* Christ during a *future* creation (also during his *conceptualized plan* for that New Heaven and Earth. See chapter two, subheading *The Doctrine of Arius*). Jeremiah 4:23-26 seems to show that the conditions of Genesis 1:2 are due to God's wrath. As such, God could plausibly be speaking to Christ in Genesis 1:26 during a future creation event (Revelation 21:1). Since Jesus is the image of God (2 Corinthians 4:4), God could say to him, "Our image." For example, one identical twin might say to the other, "Let's draw a man that looks like us." Comp. Romans 8:29, where God's children are "conformed to the image of his Son." Theophilus "of

Antioch" (late 2nd century) corresponds the creation account in Genesis with man's future resurrection (see Appendix K herein). The Epistle of Barnabas (late 1st–early 2nd century) says, "He has created us anew by His Spirit. For the Scripture says concerning us, while He speaks to the Son, 'Let Us make man after Our image, and after Our likeness'"[333] See *The Salvation Bible Commentary*, entry for Hebrews 4:3, where I contrast the two creation narratives found in Genesis 1-2. I am currently leaning toward Genesis 1:2-7 as descriptive of Noah's flood, while the waters yet covered the Earth. Comp. 2 Peter 3:5-7. At this point, it is a *very* undeveloped proposition. "As it is possible even now for man to form men, according to the original formation of Adam, He no longer now creates, on account of His having granted once for all to man the power of generating men, saying to our nature, 'Increase, and multiply, and replenish the earth.'" (ANF, Vol. 2, p. 584.) Comp. "I have created a man just as the LORD did!" (Genesis 4:1 NET.)

Genesis 11:7 "Let us go down" Compare the story of Sodom and Gomorrah, where God sent angels (Genesis 18:1-2, 16, 19:15). There the LORD says, "I will go down now," (Genesis 18:21,) but he sends his angels. Biblically, representatives were sometimes spoken of as if they *were* the one they were acting on behalf of. Jesus was said to be baptizing in John 3:22-26, but John 4:1-2 says these baptisms were actually done by Jesus' disciples. Compare Matthew 8:5-13 with Luke 7:6-10.

Genesis 19:24 The LORD rained from the LORD Two LORDs are not in view here. Compare 1 Kings 8:1, "Solomon assembled the elders unto King Solomon." Only one Solomon and only one LORD are intended.

Genesis 22:8 God will provide himself a lamb Not God will *be* the lamb provided. Better, "God will provide for himself a lamb." (NKJV.) And, not *to be crucified,* but, as the rest of the verse says, "for a burnt offering." The ram in Genesis 22:13 was a male sheep offered as a burnt offering.

Leviticus 26:12 I will walk among you (ἐμπεριπατήσω ἐν ὑμῖν)**, and will be your God** This text, according to 2 Corinthians 6:16, meant that *God would inhabit believers by his Spirit*. Compare 1 Corinthians 3:16.

Psalm 49:7 God can't be paid off by man The context is clearly dealing with men who trust in riches and how riches can't save anyone from death, therefore their trust is vain (read the verse in context, starting at Psalm 49:6). Albert Barnes writes, "There is here no particular reference to the *means* to be employed, but only an emphatic statement of the fact that *it cannot by any possibility be done*. ... Wealth can do *nothing*—literally, *nothing*—in saving the soul of its possessor, or in enabling its possessor to save his best friend. Nothing but the blood of the cross can avail then." Compare Mark 8:36-37 and 1 Peter 1:18-19.

Isaiah 9:6 "Mighty God, Everlasting Father"? The Septuagint reads, "Messenger of Mighty Counsel (μεγάλης βουλῆς ἄγγελος)." However, the Hebrew reading is ancient as well. Notwithstanding, it does not say, "He shall be," but, "His name shall be called." He is not the Father himself, although he expresses his attributes. See chapter three herein, subheading *The Image is Called by the Name of the Archetype*.

Isaiah 40:3 Prepare the way of the LORD The point of John's proclamation was to prepare the people's hearts to receive the truth that Christ was going to show them. Jesus was the messenger of this truth, but the teaching was of God (John 7:16-17). Compare Mark 9:37.

Isaiah 43:11 "Beside me there is no savior" Meaning *without God* or *apart from his involvement* there is no ability to save. Other men from God were called "saviors" (2 Kings 13:15, Nehemiah 9:27, Obadiah 21).

Isaiah 44:6 "The First and the Last" Likely idiomatic and may be understood as *having the first say and the last say in a matter* (*i.e.,* God is unable to be thwarted when he determines a matter). Compare comments on Revelation 1:11. Revelation 1:17 and 2:8 are not quoting Isaiah 44:6, because the Greek text of Isaiah 44:6 (LXX) reads differently, "I am the first, and **I am after these things** (ἐγὼ μετὰ ταῦτα)."

Isaiah 48:16 And now the Lord GOD, and his Spirit, hath sent me The one who is sent is either the Messiah or Isaiah. The Messiah is meant in 49:6 (Compare Luke 2:32, Acts 26:23 w/ 13:47). The words of the sent one should be punctuationally separated from the prior statement of God.

"From the first announcement I have not spoken in secret; at the time it happens, I am there." And now the Sovereign LORD has sent me, endowed with his Spirit. (NIV with unaltered punctuation)
Compare how Revelation 22:8-16 abruptly alternates between speakers.

Jeremiah 23:5-6 The LORD our Righteousness In Exodus 17:15 Moses called the altar "Jehovahnissi" or "The LORD is my Banner." It was a remembrance of the help of Yahweh in battle. How much more should the work of Yahweh in Christ for our redemption merit our Lord being referred to as "The LORD our Righteousness"? See also Jeremiah 33:16.

Daniel 3:25 Like the Son of God The NIV, RSV, NASB, etc. translate this portion as "a son of the gods." The LXX translates it as "a son of a god (ὁμοία υἱῷ θεοῦ)." The KJV translation of the Aramaic ("the Son of [the] God") is grammatically possible. Even so, Nebuchadnezzar never says the fourth *was* the Son of God. Rather, he says he is *like* (ὅμοιος) "the Son of God." Compare ὅμοιος in John 9:9. In the Apocrypha, the Prayer of Azariah says of this event, "The angel of the Lord (Ὁ ἄγγελος Κυρίου) came down into the furnace." (Prayer of Azariah 25.) It is likely that water was involved in the angel's activity, because he "**smote** the flame of the fire out of the oven; and made the midst of the furnace as it had been a **moist** whistling wind." (Prayer of Azariah 26.) Since, in Babylonian myths, Enki was **1.** depicted as a man surrounded by water and **2.** the son of "the supreme god," Anu, Nebuchadnezzar possibly meant "like Enki."

Zechariah 11:13 I was priced Applied to Jesus in Matthew 27:9. As with Matthew 1:22-23, the Matthean interpolator shows ignorance by attributing this prophecy to Jeremiah. See my entry on Zechariah 12:10.

Zechariah 12:10 Yahweh pierced? There is some debate over the correct translation of this text. Most will read like the KJV, "Look upon me whom they have pierced," but others like the RSV, "Look on him whom they have pierced." Thankfully, we have a direct quote of this text in John 19:37, which says, "And again another scripture saith, They shall look on him whom they pierced." (KJV.) A more literal translation of the Greek text of John 19:37 would be, "They shall look to him whom they did pierce." (YLT.) This is how the earliest, extra-biblical Christian writings extant quote Zechariah 12:10 as well (Justin Martyr, Irenaeus, Tertullian). Even if we take the text as it reads in the KJV, "They shall look upon **me** whom they have pierced and mourn for **him**," they wouldn't have *literally* pierced the "me" (Yahweh) in the text, but rather the "him" (Jesus). Compare Matthew 25:40, "Inasmuch as ye have done it unto one of the least of these my brethren, ye have done it unto me," etc. See also, "I am Jesus whom thou persecutest." (Acts 9:5.) Biblically, an agent may be spoken of as if they are the person they are representing. See Appendix F herein.

Zechariah 14:3-5 His [the LORD's?] feet "His feet" are likely the feet of the shepherd (Jesus) in Zechariah 13:7. Compare Exodus 7:17, "Thus saith the LORD, In this thou shalt know that I am the LORD: behold, I will smite with the rod that is in **mine hand**." See entry for Genesis 11:7. For a discussion on how a representative is spoken of as if they were the one whom they represent, see Appendix F herein.

Malachi 3:1 The way before me ... The Lord Applied to John the Baptist's ministry in the Synoptics. The Septuagint reads, "I send my messenger and he shall survey the way before me." The difficulty is that Malachi 3:1 is repeatedly *quoted* as reading "thee" instead of "me" within the New Testament (Matthew 11:10, Mark 1:2, Luke 7:27). See also Luke 1:76. Still, a harmony can be found between the two in explanation. See entry for Isaiah 40:3 here.

When we read "the Lord," the Hebrew has the article before *Adon*, which is important, because this only occurs eight times in the Hebrew Tanakh (*i.e.,* the Old Testament), and every other instance refers to God (Exodus 23:17, 34:23, Isaiah 1:24, 3:1, 10:6, 10:33, 19:4). Hence, being consistent, this should be taken as a reference to God as well, which is supported by the fact that he comes to "his" temple. This is a prophecy of how God, *in the person of Christ Jesus*, would come to his temple (either to the temple in Jerusalem or, some may think, to "the temple" that was Jesus' body. John 2:21.). Since "God was in Christ" (2 Corinthians 5:19), we understand that the readings "before me" and "before thee" are not at odds with one another, because Jesus, in whom God was revealed, is intended in "thee." I think all would agree with this interpretation of the text, but some go beyond the text and say that Jesus must also *be* the God who was manifested in him in an absolute sense. See the comment on Genesis 11:7.

Appendix B

Common Inquiries: The New Testament

Matthew 28:18 Jesus given all power Although the disciples received power as well (Acts 1:8), this did not diminish from Christ's power. The power is shared, but has its source in the Father.

Matthew 28:19 Name of the Father, Son, Spirit All of the extant Greek MSS that contain this Trinitarian baptismal formula are dated no earlier than the 5th century AD (post-Nicaea). Eusebius of Caesarea wrote, "Matthew, who had at first preached to the Hebrews, when he was about to go to other peoples, committed his Gospel to writing in his native tongue."[334] Eusebius also quotes Papias, bishop of Hierapolis, who wrote around 100 AD, as saying, "So then Matthew wrote the oracles in the Hebrew language, and every one interpreted them as he was able."[335] The Hebrew text of Matthew was known during the time of Jerome (347-420 AD), who said it was still found in the Hebrew language in the library of Caesarea. "Matthew, who is also Levi, and who from a publican came to be an apostle, first of all composed a Gospel of Christ in Judaea **in the Hebrew language** and characters for the benefit of those of the circumcision who had believed. Who translated it after that in Greek is not sufficiently ascertained. Moreover, **the Hebrew itself is preserved to this day in the library at Caesarea**, which the martyr Pamphilus so diligently collected. I also was allowed by the Nazarenes who use this volume in the Syrian city of Beroea to copy it."
   —*Jerome: De viris inlustribus (On Illustrious Men), chapter III*
There is a Hebrew manuscript containing Matthew 28:19 known as *Shem-Tov's (or Tob's) Hebrew Gospel of Matthew*, which contains the reading, "Go and teach them to carry out all the things which I have commanded

you forever." This manuscript dates to 1385 AD, but is believed by some to contain the original reading of Matthew 28:19.

Greg Howard, Professor of Religion at the University of Georgia, published a book entitled *The Hebrew Gospel of Matthew*, wherein he writes: "Shem-Tob's Hebrew Matthew is the most unusual text of the First Gospel extant. It contains a plethora of readings which are not to be found in any of the Christian codices of the Greek Gospel. Its unusual nature may be explained by the fact that it underwent a different process of transmission than the Greek, since it was preserved by Jews, independent from the Christian community. A textual profile of Shem-Tob's Matthew reveals that it sporadically agrees with early witnesses, both Christian and non-Christian. Sometimes it agrees with readings and documents that vanished in antiquity only to reappear in recent times. The profile thus suggests that a Shem-Tob type text of Matthew was known in the early Christian centuries."[336]

So far, we have seen evidence that: **1.** Matthew's Gospel was originally written in Hebrew. **2.** A Hebrew version of Matthew's Gospel (Shem Tov's) is still in existence that, according to Professor George Howard, is likely similar to a Hebrew version of Matthew known in the early Christian centuries. **3.** During the time of Jerome, the Hebrew text of Matthew still existed in the city of Caesarea.

Since there is so much evidence pointing to Caesarea as the city where the original reading of Matthew was most likely to be found, it is quite amazing when we see Eusebius, the bishop of Caesarea, quoting the text of Matthew 28:19 several times as, "Go ye, and make disciples of all the nations, teaching them to observe all things, whatsoever I have commanded you." I found four[337] quotations that read thus in Eusebius' work *The Proof of the Gospel (Demonstratio Evangelica)*, written 314-318 AD. Frederick C. Conybeare (1856-1924), former Professor of Theology at the University of Oxford, is still a primary scholar of note on this subject. After his research, Conybeare made the following conclusion on page 75 of his book *History of New Testament Criticism*:

"It is clear, therefore, that of the MSS which Eusebius inherited from his predecessor, Pamphilus, at Caesarea in Palestine, some at least preserved the original reading, in which there was no mention either of Baptism or of Father, Son, and Holy Ghost."

There is a single 11th century Greek manuscript of the *Didache* (or *Teaching of the Apostles*) that includes the Trinitarian baptismal formula of Matt. 28:19 within its 7th chapter (contradicted in Didache 9:5 where baptism is done "in the name of the Lord"). This is the only Didache manuscript containing the Trinitarian text. A couple of 4th century papyrus scraps of the Didache exist, but these only contain portions of the first two chapters. The 10th century Latin manuscript has the Didache *closing* shortly after chapter 5 and "by its variations suggests the presence of many textual corruptions."[338] The only other manuscript of the Didache is a 4th century Coptic translation containing portions of chapters 10-12, which it presents as the *end* of the Didache. Thus, the Latin and Coptic versions are at variance with the extant Greek version, which alone contains the Trinitarian formula and has enough text for 16 chapters.

"The simple Christology of Acts confronts us again in the so-called *Teaching of the Apostles*, a composite work, of which the first six chapters seem to be a Christian redaction of a Jewish document entitled *The Two Ways*, while the rest is the work of several Christian writers, the earliest belonging to the first century and the latest perhaps to the fourth. … The formula of baptism in the name of the Trinity, which is given in Chap. VII, must come from a later hand, though possibly earlier than Justin Martyr, who is familiar with it."
—*A. D. Howell-Smith Jesus Not a Myth, 1942, p. 120*

Mark 2:7 Jesus forgave sins See comment here on Luke 5:21-24.

Mark 2:27-28 "Lord of the Sabbath" This has been confused with "Lord of Sabaoth" in Romans 9:29 and James 5:4, but they do not mean the same thing. *Sabaoth* does not refer to a day. It is a Greek translation of the word *saba* which means *armies, host* (Strong's #G4519).

Luke 5:21-24 Jesus forgave sins He did not act independently. Paul forgave sin "in the person of Christ." (2 Corinthians 2:10.) Jesus said the Apostles could forgive sins, but this was predicated upon the Holy Spirit (John 20:22). Jesus said, "As I hear, I judge." (John 5:30.) See John 12:49.

Luke 8:39 God/Jesus cast out demons God did this through the agency of Christ Jesus. See Acts 2:22. Jesus cast out demons by the "finger of God" (Luke 11:20) or "Spirit of God." (Matthew 12:28.)

Luke 17:15-16 Fell down at the feet of "God"? This is not saying "fell down at his (God's) feet." The pronoun "his" contextually has Jesus as its antecedent. The NLT captures the sense, "One of them, when he saw that he was healed, came back to Jesus, shouting, 'Praise God!' He fell to the ground at Jesus' feet, thanking him for what he had done."

John 1:15 & 30 Jesus was before John the Baptist A footnote in the Racovian Catechism says:

"In proof of the existence of Christ before his nativity are adduced John 1:15 and 30. "John bare witness of him, and cried, saying, This was he of whom I spake, He that cometh after me is preferred before me: for he was before me." "This is he of whom I said, After me cometh a man which is preferred before me: for he was before me." But that the word πρῶτός (BEFORE) in this passage denotes a priority in DIGNITY and not in TIME, has been sufficiently proved by Erasmus, Grotius, and Beza (who reads here *antepositus est mihi,* "he is placed before me.") Cingallus, in the work above referred to, gives a catalogue, p. 127, of other writers, both ancient and modern, who held the same opinion. The same thing is illustrated by parallel places in Matt. iii. 11 ; "He that cometh after me is mightier than I, whose shoes I am not worthy to bear." Mark i. 7 ; "There cometh one mightier than I after me, the latchet of whose shoes I am not worthy to stoop down and unloose." Luke iii. 16 ; "One mightier than I cometh, the latchet of whose shoes I am not worthy to unloose." Genesis xlviii. 20 may also be considered, "And he blessed them that day, saying, In thee shall Israel bless, saying, God make thee as Ephraim and as Manasseh: and he set Ephraim BEFORE Manasseh." B. Wissowatius." (*The Racovian Catechism, pp. 150-151.*)

John 2:24 Jesus knew all men Jesus did not know everything in every category. See Mark 13:32. The word *all* is used in a relative sense. Compare 1 John 2:20. The meaning of "knew all men" is shown in the next verse, "For he knew what was in man."

John 8:24 If ye believe not that I am Christ was *possibly* saying, "ἐγώ (I) εἰμι (am) from above ... if ye believe not that ἐγώ (I) εἰμι (am) [from above]." (John 8:23-24.) However, as in John 8:58 (see chapter eight herein), I take ἐγώ εἰμι as a reference to his *perpetual existence* (by resurrection) *despite his execution*. Jesus was killed by crucifixion. This death is indicated contextually in John 8:28. The Law said crucifixion made a man cursed by God (Deuteronomy 21:22-23, Acts 5:30). Unless the Jews believed in eternal life apart from the works of the Law, proven by Christ's death and resurrection, they would continue to seek justification by the Law and thus die in their sins. Comp. 1 Corinthians 15:17.

John 16:30 Jesus knew all things See entry for John 2:24. Jesus "knew their thoughts," (Luke 6:8,) etc. Sometimes this means *"perceived what they were thinking,"* but even this can be by the unction of the Spirit. All things are made open by the Holy Spirit at work in Christ. Compare "sheweth him all things." (John 5:20.) See Isaiah 11:1-2 for wisdom, understanding, knowledge produced by the Spirit. See John 3:34, Acts 1:2.

John 17:24 Before the foundation of the world In *The Salvation Bible Commentary* (entry for Ephesians 1:4), I discuss how "the foundation of the world" denotes *the commencement of Israel as a nation*. Here, *before the saints are gathered to form the nation of Israel in the future*.

John 20:28 My Lord and my God Compare Matthew 16:23, where Jesus "said unto Peter, Get thee behind me, Satan." Peter was not literally Satan, nor was Jesus literally God. See chapter three herein.

Acts 7:59 Calling upon God Rather, "As he called out." The word "God" appears in italics in the KJV because it is not in the Greek text. In the KJV, *italics* represent words added for clarity by the translator. Regardless, it is biblical to speak to the heavenly Messiah, whom God has made Lord.

Romans 8:9 Spirit of God/Christ I take "spirit" here as an *unseen force* from God, *through* (so now *of*) Christ. Acts 2:33. See Appendix E.

Romans 9:5 God is the Blessed The word εὐλογητός, translated as *blessed* in Romans 9:5, is used like a descriptive title and is applied exclusively to the Father in the New Testament. Here is every instance of the word in the NT: Mark 14:61, Luke 1:68, Romans 1:25, Romans 9:5, 2 Corinthians 1:3, 2 Corinthians 11:31, Ephesians 1:3, 1 Peter 1:3. The RSV has the sense of the verse correct when it presents "God who is over all be blessed for ever. Amen," as an independent sentence. It is the manner of Paul to interject praise within his writings, followed by an "Amen." Compare Romans 1:25, Romans 11:33-36, Galatians 1:5, Ephesians 3:21, Philippians 4:20, 1 Timothy 1:17, 6:16.

Romans 10:13 Whosoever shall call upon the name of Yahweh This passage quotes Joel 2:32, which refers to calling on the name of Yahweh. Paul is saying salvation is available to "Jew and Greek" and "all" (Romans 10:12). The contextual force of the quotation is in the "whosoever," showing that salvation is available to all. That is why he cites the text.

1 Corinthians 2:8 "Lord of Glory"? Not connected grammatically to "King of Glory" in Psalm 24:7-10. The phrase τὸν κύριον τῆς δόξης should be taken as "glorious Lord" (NLT).

1 Corinthians 10:4 The Rock was Christ Paul is not referring to Deuteronomy 32:31, but to Exodus 17:6, where Moses struck the rock and water came out for Israel to drink. Jesus was not *literally* the rock struck by Moses. Nor was he *literally* the manna from heaven, though he himself says, "I am the bread which came down from heaven." (John 6:41.) Jesus was the fulfilment of those representative events that transpired in the wilderness. Within Scripture, the fulfilment of a representative type is sometimes transposed into the place of that type. For example, Paul said earlier in 1 Corinthians, "Christ our passover is sacrificed for us." (1 Corinthians 5:7.) Jesus was not *literally* the Passover lamb that was slain while Israel was yet in Egypt. He was not *literally* the rock struck by Moses, either. These things are allegorical. Compare 2 Corinthians 3:13-15, "the same vail" over the heart of the Jews was not *literally* the vail Moses wore over his face.

There was a rabbinic tradition that said a rock literally rolled behind Israel as they walked. Many commentators think Paul adopted this view. That is, however, not likely. I concur with Albert Barnes: "This evidently cannot mean that the rock itself literally followed them ... it means they drank of the water that flowed from the rock ; so when it is said that the 'rock followed' or accompanied them, it must mean that the water that flowed from the rock accompanied them. This figure of speech is common everywhere. Thus the savior said, (1 Corinthians 11:25) 'This cup is the new testament,' that is, the wine in this cup represents my blood etc." (*Barnes' Notes on the Bible,* 1 Corinthians 10:4.) There were over a million Israelites who had to drink of the water. The water came from the area of Mt. Horeb (Exodus 17:6). It wasn't a fountain where men *came* to drink, rather "He opened the rock, and the waters gushed out; they *ran in the dry places like a river."* (Psalm 105:41.) This river like current of water flowed from behind them as they went, and they proceeded onward drinking of it as the water followed.

1 Corinthians 10:9 Neither let us tempt Christ, as some of them also tempted – Some very authoritative mss. read "Lord" instead of "Christ," but the latter is most likely the original according to *A Textual Commentary on the New Testament,* UBS, 2nd edition, p. 494. There are several respected scholars who would disagree with that conclusion. I believe the correct reading is, "Neither let us tempt *the Lord."* This is what we find in Codex Sinaiticus and Codex Vaticanus. The reading in Codex Alexandrinus says "God," agreeing with "the Lord," but *not* with "Christ" (which is found in 𝔓46). Normally, the more difficult reading would be preferred when there is doubt, but "Christ" is not necessarily the most difficult reading in this instance, because *1 Corinthians 10:4 just finished placing "Christ" in that same wilderness*. If the copyists were inclined to "remove the difficulty of Christ in the wilderness," we would expect to see some corroborating variants within verse 4. There are no such variants in *any* of the mss. *All* read "Christ." Hence, there was no attempt to remove Christ from the wilderness in 1 Corinthians 10. Instead, a copyist, being driven along by that universally accepted theme of verse 4, brought verse 9 into conformity, changing "Lord" to "Christ." Although Codex Alexandrinus' "God" variant was probably not the original reading, it was likely chosen as a substitute for "Lord" to resolve the evident confusion introduced by verse 4. It was Yahweh who was "tempted" [to the point of destroying those men] in the wilderness (Numbers 14:20-23).

Allowing that the reading *could have been* "Christ," the theme of interpretation applied in 1 Corinthians 10:4 could easily be applied to this verse as well. See my comments on verse 4 herein as well as my comments on Jude 5.

2 Corinthians 8:9 "Though he was rich, yet for your sakes he became poor" Some think this must mean Christ existed before becoming a man. They interpret "becoming poor" as "becoming a man after previously being wealthy in heaven." Such a notion is foreign to the context, however. Paul is exhorting the Corinthians to imitate what Christ did and share their abundance with the poor (2 Corinthians 8:14-15). The notion that Paul had any preexistence in mind is only *inferred* by others, because it is never *stated* by Paul. Paul became poor that others might be rich (2 Corinthians 6:10) and he urges others to be imitators of him as he also was of Christ (1 Corinthians 11:1), but we do not infer from such a statement that Paul preexisted his humanity.

Jesus spoke to a "rich" man and told him to sell all he had and give to the poor, which would result in him having "treasure in heaven." (Luke 18:22-23.) This was an invitation to the rich man to "follow" Jesus. If the rich man *had* done as Jesus instructed and "become poor" to live as a disciple of Christ (Luke 14:33), he could have helped many obtain the true riches in heaven. Thus, without any notion of preexistence, we could say that man became poor so that by his poverty others could be made rich. This would especially be true if helping others into the kingdom of heaven was a primary motivation for him to leave his own riches behind. Now, is there anyone who argues that Christ was not motivated to bring others into the eternal inheritance of the saints when he abandoned his self-interests in this life and went out to seek and save the lost? Was Jesus instructing the rich man to "follow" him down a path that he himself did not trod? Jesus was ever exhorting men to abandon personal wealth and follow his example. He himself said, "Foxes have holes, and birds of the air have nests; but the Son of man hath not where to lay his head." (Luke 9:58.) Does anyone think this was because he could not *afford* a home? Imagine if someone was doing what Jesus did in our day. What type of offerings do you think would be at their disposal? The people even wanted to make him a king! (John 6:15.) Jesus even had a man carrying his offerings around for him (John 12:6.) Grammatically speaking, the argument can be made that he was poor *while* being rich, because the text literally says, "*Being* (ὤν) rich he was poor (ἐπτώχευσεν)." The picture is that Christ had material wealth at his disposal (John 13:29) and yet suffered the life of a homeless wanderer to fulfill his mission of redemption for others. In order to follow the self-denying example of Christ, the "rich" Corinthians

(1 Corinthians 4:8) should also turn aside from selfish living in order to meet the needs of others.

Colossians 2:9 "Fulness of the Godhead" Compare "God was in Christ." (2 Corinthians 5:19.) Compare "Ye might be filled with all the fulness of God." (Ephesians 3:19.) Christians are not empowered by God in an abstract way, but we "partake of the divine nature." (2 Peter 1:4.) The actual power, righteousness, etc. that is inherent to God is in us by the indwelling of his Spirit. This is not of ourselves but provided for us in its fullness within the person of Christ. Compare Ephesians 4:13. That is the contextual meaning of Colossians 2:2-12. See Colossians 2:3.

1 Timothy 1:17 Not spoken of Christ Henry Alford writes:
The doxology is to the Father, not to the Trinity (Thdrt.), nor to the Son (Calov., al.): cf. ἀοράτῳ, incorruptible (in ref. Rom. only, used of God), invisible (reff: see also 1 Timothy 6:16; John 1:18. Beware of taking ἀφθάρτῳ, ἀοράτῳ with θεῷ, as recommended by Bishop Middleton, on the ground of the articles being wanting before these adjectives. It is obvious that no such consideration is of any weight in a passage like the present. The abstract adjectives of attribute are used almost as substantives, and stand by themselves, referring not to βασιλεῖ immediately, but to Him of whom βασιλεύς is a title, as well as they: q. d. 'to Him who is the King of the ages, the Incorruptible, the Invisible, ...'), the only God (σοφῷ has apparently come from the doxology at the end of Romans, where it is most appropriate), be honour and glory to the ages of the ages (the periods which are made up of αἰῶνες, as these last are of years,—as years are of days: see note, Ephesians 3:21; and Ellic. on Galatians 1:5), Amen.[339]

1 Timothy 3:16 "God manifested in the flesh"? The original text did not read, "God was manifest in the flesh," but, "Who was manifest in the flesh." See *A Textual Commentary on the New Testament,* UBS, 2nd edition, pp. 573-574. Compare Colossians 1:27

Titus 2:13 "Great God and Savior, Jesus"? The text should be read as *the glory of the great God and our Savior, Jesus Christ*. Some have argued, based upon the Greek syntax of this verse, that the text *must* be read

as *the glory of our great God and Savior, Jesus Christ*. Those who argue in favor of this view refer to *Sharp's Rule*. This proposed rule was introduced by Granville Sharp in 1798 and is defined as follows:
"When the copulative καὶ connects two nouns of the same case, if the article ὁ, or any of its cases, precedes the first of the said nouns or participles, and is not repeated before the second noun or participle, the latter always relates to the same person that is expressed or described by the first noun or participle."
To maintain this as a rule without contradiction in the New Testament, certain exceptions had to be applied by Sharp (excluding examples containing plural nouns, impersonal nouns, or proper names). Once the exceptions to Sharp's Rule were sectioned off, Sharp argued that the singular, personal, common nouns θεοῦ (God) and σωτῆρος (Savior) in Titus 2:13 and 2 Peter 1:1, having only one article (the) before *God* but not before *Savior*, while being joined by καὶ (and), required a common referent, namely Jesus Christ. Thus, Sharp argued that Jesus was identified as "God and Savior" in both Titus 2:13 and 2 Peter 1:1. However, a contradiction to Sharp's conclusion is found within the Septuagint (LXX) text of Proverbs 24:21. Although meeting all of Sharp's stipulations, the verse still winds up with *two referents* (God and the king). A supplemental modifier was introduced by Daniel B. Wallace, who formed what he calls *the Sharper Rule*. Wallace's rule dismisses exceptions that are not from a native Greek source. So, the LXX, containing a Greek *translation* of Hebrew, would be excluded from consideration, along with its Proverbs 24:21 exception to Sharp's Rule. There is really no syntactical reason why translation Greek should be excluded. In fact, there isn't really a strictly syntactical basis for Sharp's Rule (or Wallace's Sharper Rule) at all. As Greg Stafford points out, Sharp's Rule is inconsistent, because it *begins* by focusing on the semantic weight of the nouns in the text, but abandons that methodology once the agenda-based requirements have been conveniently satisfied. Stafford has come up with a rule that remains consistent throughout the interpretive process. *Stafford's Sharpest Rule* states: "When reading or translating ancient Greek, if a text uses two or more substantives (nouns, pronouns, or other terms as nouns) in grammatical agreement, and if each substantive is separated by kai ("and"), but only the first substantive has the article, determine the semantic weight of each term in its context to identify the correct number of subjects."[340] In short,

Stafford does not automatically take the word "God" as a common noun. Nor should he. When monotheists are writing or speaking to other monotheists, the term "God" is usually used as a proper noun. This is why Proverbs 24:21 (LXX), Titus 2:13, and 2 Peter 1:1, all texts where monotheists refer to "God," cannot be interpreted using Sharp's Rule.

Hebrews 2:16 Took on our nature? The Greek text of Hebrews 2:16 reads, "Οὐ (not) γὰρ (for) δήπου (verily) ἀγγέλων (of angels) ἐπιλαμβάνεται (he/it lays hold of) ἀλλὰ (but) σπέρματος (seed) Ἀβραὰμ (of Abraham) ἐπιλαμβάνεται (he/it lays hold of)." The words "the nature of" are in *italics* in the KJV because they were *added* by the translators. They do not reflect anything found in the Greek manuscripts. Furthermore, the present middle indicative verb which the KJV renders *"took"* should instead read *"takes."* The middle voice would indicate a *taking to himself*. Compare the crowd **taking** (ἐπιλαβόμενοι aorist middle participle) Paul to themselves in Acts 21:30. Darby presents Hebrews 2:16 as, "For he does not indeed take hold of angels *by the hand*, but he takes hold of the seed of Abraham." The concept of *laying hold of to help* is reflected in most English translations (NKJV, ASV, NLT, NIV, etc.). Some have said that Jesus *not* helping angels would contradict Colossians 1:20, but I do not see such a conclusion as warranted. An alternative view of Hebrews 2:16 is that the text refers to how *death*, or *the one who has the power of death* (Hebrews 2:14-15), does not lay hold of angels, but of the seed of Abraham. I consider this view of Hebrews 2:16 as most likely correct.

Hebrews 3:1-6 Christ/God built the house Compare 1 Corinthians 11:12, Woman is ἐκ (from) τοῦ (of the) man, but all things ἐκ (from) τοῦ (of the) God. "For *every house* is builded by *some man;* but he that built all things is God." (Hebrews 3:4.) Without God there would be none to build and nothing to be built. See also Psalm 127:1.

James 2:1 "Lord of Glory"? See entry for 1 Corinthians 2:8. Should be taken as "our glorious Lord." (NASB.)

2 Peter 1:1 "Our God and Savior, Jesus Christ"? The text should likely either be read as *the righteousness of our God and **a** Savior* (c.f., Acts 5:31, 13:23) or ***the** Savior*. "Sharp's Rule" has been cited by some to identify Jesus as God here, but see my comments on Titus 2:13 herein. Though not likely the original reading, Codex Sinaiticus along with some Vulgate and Syriac texts read κυρίου (Lord) instead of θεοῦ (God).

1 John 3:16 "God" laid down his life? The word "God" appears in italics in the KJV because it is not in the original Greek. The text actually says, "By this we know love, that he laid down his life for us; and we ought to lay down our lives for the brethren." (RSV.)

1 John 4:2-3 Christ is come in the flesh This passage was written to refute Docetism, which alleged that Jesus did not have a flesh body like we do. This does not mean *Jesus preexisted and went into a body of flesh*. Rather, it is an attestation that Christ, the man, had flesh that is common to us all (Hebrews 2:14). Jesus is come in the flesh. *Not* some *other version* of flesh, but the flesh that is common to all men. For texts that help give a correct view of what is meant by "coming," see Matthew 2:6, 11:3, 17:12, etc., John 1:9, 1:31, 7:41-42, 9:39 (comp. John 17:18), 10:10, 11:48, 12:15, etc., 2 John 1:10, 12, 3 John 1:10. Cf. ANF, Vol. 3, p. 259.

1 John 5:7 "Three are one" None of the ancient Greek manuscripts have this passage in them. It does appear in some Latin manuscripts, but not any as ancient as the Latin Vulgate, which does not have the text either. In the 16th century, Erasmus refused to include the text in his Greek New Testament, because he did not find it in any of the Greek manuscripts he had access to. In response, a Greek text was reverse-engineered from the Latin and subsequently given to Erasmus as a means to push him to include the text. He then placed this passage into the 3rd edition of his work, which then found its way into English versions. See *A Textual Commentary on the Greek New Testament*, pp. 647-649. The interpolation clashes with the context wherein it was written, which has in view affirmations that Christ was a genuine man—*By water* (through woman. John 3:4-5), but not simply through the woman, but also *by blood* (of her body. John 1:13). The Spirit affirms this testimony. This was to combat Docetism.

2 John 1:7 Christ is come in the flesh See comment on 1 John 4:3-4.

Jude 5 "Jesus"? *A Textual Commentary on the Greek New Testament* favors "the Lord" as the authentic reading in Jude 5.[341] Even so, there is some weighty evidence behind reading "Jesus." If the latter be preferred, the explanation of 1 Peter 3:19 (pp. 123 ff. herein) may be considered, where I discuss the fulfilment of a type being set forth in the place of the type itself. Jude says the slanderers in his day "perished in the gainsaying of Core." (Jude 11.) This is a reference to Numbers 16:1-35, where Korah gets destroyed for his opposition to Moses. Jude clearly exhibits a stylistic tendency to place his contemporaries within the historical narratives of Scripture, as if they were present and active during those ancient events when they were not. The slanderers in Jude 11 were not destroyed along with Korah, nor did Jesus do any destroying during that same timeframe.

Revelation 1:7 "the Almighty"? Some have tried to say that since Christ is spoken of in Revelation 1:7, he must be the "Almighty" spoken of in Revelation 1:8 as well. Revelation 1:7-8 says this: "Behold, he cometh with clouds; and every eye shall see him, and they also which pierced him: and all kindreds of the earth shall wail because of him. Even so, Amen. I am Alpha and Omega, the beginning and the ending, saith the Lord, which is, and which was, and which is to come, the Almighty." Notice that an "amen" is spoken at the end of Revelation 1:7, showing the conclusion of the matter being discussed in that verse. This same principle is shown in Revelation 22:20, where it says: "Surely I come quickly. Amen. Even so, come Lord Jesus." Now, when we look at this verse are we to assume that the one who said, "Surely I come quickly," is also the one who said, "Come Lord Jesus"? No, of course not. Just because a quote appears in one verse does not mean it is quoting the person speaking in the previous verse: Revelation 1:7-9 says: (1:7) "Behold, he cometh with clouds; and every eye shall see him, and they also which pierced him: and all kindreds of the earth shall wail because of him. Even so, Amen." (1:8) "I am Alpha and Omega, the beginning and the ending, saith the Lord, which is, and which was, and which is to come, the Almighty." (1:9) "I John, who also am your brother, and companion in tribulation, and in the kingdom and patience of Jesus Christ, was in the isle that is called Patmos, for the word of God, and for the testimony of Jesus Christ." If we must conclude that Revelation 1:7 is speaking of the same person in Revelation 1:8, then why are we not to conclude that Revelation 1:8 is speaking of the same person in Revelation 1:9? The truth is, Revelation 1:8 contains the words of God. An example of how speakers in Revelation change without any introduction can be seen in Revelation 22:6-18. Some have also said that since the Almighty is said "to come" that must denote the coming Christ. However, it also says he is the one who "is." It doesn't have in view "is on earth" or "coming to earth" but *was, is, and shall exist.* Here, God uses the same Greek phrase, ἐγώ (I) εἰμι (am) ὁ (the) ὤν (one who is), as is used in Exodus 3:14 LXX.

Revelation 1:11 "Alpha and Omega" The KJV has, "I am Alpha and Omega, the first and the last," among the words of Christ. This is not in the original Greek text however. Every authentic claim to be Alpha and Omega in the Book of Revelation is spoken by God. The phrase "First and Last" is spoken by God and Christ. Like Alpha and Omega, this is likely an idiomatic phrase similar to *having the first and the last say in a matter.* The point being, none can thwart them.

Revelation 2:23 In the Book of Revelation, the speakers sometimes pivot without any notice (Revelation 1:7-9, 19:9-10, 22:6-16). The angel speaking in Revelation 2:23 (see Appendix F) conveys "the word of God, and of the testimony of Jesus Christ." (Revelation 1:2.) Sometimes he is speaking the words of God, sometimes of Jesus. In Revelation 2:23, the angel says he is the one who searches the hearts and gives to everyone according to their works. God spoke this of himself in Jeremiah 17:10. Hence, it is plausible that the angel is speaking the words of God. Yet, since God has made Jesus Lord (Acts 2:36), given him all power (Matthew 28:18), and committed all judgment to him (John 5:22), Jesus also judges in harmony with God's method and ability described in Jeremiah 17:10.

Revelation 22:1 w/ v. 3 Same throne *Throne* here denotes *a seat of authority.* God reigns through the person of Christ. Comp. Revelation 3:21.

Revelation 22:6 w/ v. 16 Same angel Both God and Christ are involved. Compare who sent the men in Acts 10:5, 10:20, and 10:23. See also John 17:10 "All mine are thine, and thine are mine."

Appendix C

Revelation 3:14 Ἀρχή contd.

Although "beginning of the creation of God" in Revelation 3:14 means *God's first creation*, two alternate translations of Jesus' words are frequently proposed by those who disallow any such possibility. Objective research only points to the "beginning of the creation of God" reading.

The alternative meanings proposed are:

1. The Greek word ἀρχή in Revelation 3:14 should not be translated as "beginning," but as "source" (NRSV).

2. The Greek word ἀρχή in Revelation 3:14 should not be translated as "beginning," but as "ruler" (NIV).

Albert Barnes rejected the source interpretation of Revelation 3:14, saying:

> **The beginning of the creation of God** - [to say] that he is the author of the creation, and in that sense the beginning – though expressing a scriptural doctrine, is not in accordance with the proper meaning of the word used here - ἀρχή. The word properly refers to the "commencement" of a thing, not its "authorship."[342]

The word ἀρχή is translated in the KJV New Testament as follows:

- **beginning (x38)** – Matthew 19:4, 8, 24:8, Mark 1:1, 10:6, 13:19, Luke 1:2, John 1:1, 1:2, 2:11, 6:64, 8:25, 8:44, 15:27, 16:4, Act 11:15, Philippians 4:15, Colossians 1:18, 2 Thessalonians 2:13, Hebrews 1:10, 3:14, 7:3, 2 Peter 3:4, 1 John 1:1, 2:7(x2), 13, 14, 24(x2), 3:8, 11, 2 John 5, 6, Revelation 1:8, 3:14, 21:6, 22:13

- **beginnings (x1)** – Mark 13:8

- **principality (x2)** – Ephesians 1:21, Colossians 2:10

- **principalities (x6)** – Romans 8:38, Ephesians 3:10, 6:12, Colossians 1:16, 2:15, Titus 3:1

- **principles (x2)** – Hebrews 5:12, 6:1

- **corners (x2)** – Acts 10:11, 11:5

- **power (x1)** – Luke 20:20

- **magistrates (x1)** – Luke 12:11

- **rule (x1)** – 1 Corinthians 15:24

- **at the first (x1)** – Hebrews 2:3

- **the first (x1)** – Acts 26:4

- **first estate (x1)** – Jude 6

As you can see ἀρχή is *never* translated as *source/beginner/author* in the Greek New Testament. The vast majority of the passages in which the word ἀρχή is used bear reference to the *beginning* of a thing. But what about those other places in New Testament Greek where the word ἀρχή is translated as "principality"? And what about the instance in Luke 20:20 where ἀρχή is translated as "power"? How do we know that one of those meanings is not represented by ἀρχή in Revelation 3:14 as well? Doesn't this justify the NIV translation, "the *ruler* of the creation of God"? Let's consider the factors.

First, *all* of those passages in the New Testament where ἀρχή does refer to *authority* (*i.e., principality* or *power*) clearly imply this meaning within the immediate context *every time*. Yet, there is nothing to suggest any other meaning than that which is principally inherent to the word ἀρχή within the context of Revelation 3:14. Well then, apart from the contextual considerations, is the NIV translation, "the ruler of the creation of God," *grammatically* possible? No, I do not believe that it is grammatically possible in Revelation 3:14, because the evidence simply will not allow it.

- It is based upon an unwarranted neglect of the primary meaning of ἀρχή.

- **Every time** ἀρχή is used in the New Testament within a partitive genitive construction, it is **always** included as part of the stated category.

Also, the writings commonly attributed to John (who wrote Revelation) *always* use the word ἀρχή to signify *beginning* (John 1:1, 1:2, 2:11, 6:64, 8:25, 8:44, 15:27, 16:4, 1 John 1:1, 2:7(x2), 13, 14, 24(x2), 3:8, 11, 2 John 5, 6, Revelation 1:8, 3:14, 21:6, 22:13). Indeed, in these writings the word ἀρχή is uniformly translated as "beginning" (KJV) *all twenty-three times* that it is used. Hence, to translate "John's" usage of ἀρχή as anything *other than* "beginning" in Revelation 3:14 is contrary to what we see in the works attributed to him (I do not believe that John wrote the Gospel of John. I did, but after reading *The Disciple Whom Jesus Loved*, I changed my opinion. Regardless, the same is true of how ἀρχή is unanimously used in Revelation).

Consider also that when John *does* refer to Christ elsewhere as *ruler*, specifically within the same book, he does *not* use the word ἀρχή to do so.

The NIV translates Revelation 3:14 as:

> "These are the words of the Amen, the faithful and true witness, the **ruler** of God's creation." (Revelation 3:14 NIV)

Notice how the NIV renders Revelation 1:5 similarly:

> "Christ ... who is the faithful witness, the firstborn from the dead, and the **ruler** of the kings of the earth." (Revelation 1:5 NIV)

The NIV translates both Revelation 3:14 and Revelation 1:5 as "ruler." However, the Greek word that the NIV translates as "ruler" in Revelation 1:5 is *not* the same Greek word that the NIV translates as "ruler" in

Revelation 3:14. *The Strong's Concordance*, for example, has them listed as two separate entries. In Revelation 1:5, the NIV translates the word "ruler" from the *masculine* Greek word ἄρχων (archōn) (Strong's #G758). This is the *correct* Greek word for *ruler*. However, the Greek word that the NIV translates as "ruler" in Revelation 3:14 is not ἄρχων, but it is rather ἀρχή (Strong's #G746), which is *feminine* in gender and is referring to a beginning rather than a ruler. If the meaning that was intended by John in Revelation 3:14 was *ruler* then why wouldn't John have simply repeated the word that he used for *ruler* (ἄρχων) in Revelation 1:5? Why would he use two *different* words in Revelation 1:5 and Revelation 3:14 to refer to the *exact same thing*?

Someone might suggest that the difference is due to the fact that John was writing in his own personal style in Revelation 1:5, but was *quoting Christ* in Revelation 3:14. By this reasoning such a one might assert that John's style of writing is not an applicable standard by which the meaning of Revelation 3:14 can be discerned. However, we already said that the Gospel of John does not have any place where ἀρχή means anything other than *beginning*, including the times when Christ was speaking. Furthermore, in the Synoptic Gospels, Jesus' statements only use the word ἀρχή as "beginning" in Matthew and Mark. Luke, however, does have Jesus using the plural form of ἀρχή as "power" in Luke 12:11. This is the single instance where Jesus is shown to use ἀρχή thus. Notwithstanding, this still does not present ἀρχή in a partitive genitive phrase, like Revelation 3:14. Luke 20:20 doesn't have ἀρχή in a partitive genitive phrase either,[343] although there too we see ἀρχή translated as "power."

Why would Christ want John to quote him using terminology that was not harmonious with John's own writing style? Why would Jesus use ἀρχή in a partitive genitive construction to mean something different than the other places where he always means "beginning" while using the exact same word in the same construction? Especially in light of the fact that the alleged "alternative" expression for *ruler* uses language that undeniably favors a *created* Christ and is contrary to the term used by John for *ruler* in the same book? Wouldn't this promote *confusion* rather than "revelation"? The reality of the matter is that translating ἀρχή as anything other than "beginning" in Revelation 3:14 is simply unjustifiable. It is for theological considerations, not a weighing of the evidence, that the primary and principle definition of the word ἀρχή is abandoned by some in Revelation 3:14.

Some may think that John does not always use the word ἀρχή to signify beginning in his writings, because God says:

> "I am Alpha and Omega, **the beginning** and the end."
> (Revelation 21:6)

And again God says:

> "I am Alpha and Omega, **the beginning** and the end, the first and the last." (Revelation 22:13)

Surely God was not saying that he is the beginning of creation. Indeed, he was not, and the context in which these statements are made do not in any way imply such a thing.

The fact of the matter is that God refers to himself in both of these passages using two *idiomatic expressions* that are similar in meaning—"Alpha and Omega" and "the beginning and the end." We should not look at "Alpha" and "Omega" as two individual titles, but rather as two parts of one unified phrase. "Alpha" is literally the first letter of the Greek **alpha**bet, but it takes on an idiomatic meaning when presented in unison with "Omega" (otherwise God is literally referring to himself as two letters of the Greek alphabet). Just as we cannot separate "Alpha" from "Omega" when seeking to understand the contextual implications of "Alpha," neither can we remove "the beginning" from "the end" in an attempt to discover an alternate meaning for the word ἀρχή. This presents a wholly different context that is distinct from that of Revelation 3:14. The phrases "Alpha and Omega" and "the beginning and the end" are *idioms*.

> Among the Jewish Rabbins, it was common to use the first and the last letters of the Hebrew alphabet to denote the whole of anything, from beginning to end.[344]

In our modern vernacular we have a similar idiom, *Everything from A to Z*. Just as we use this idiomatic expression in order to express a *principle* that has absolutely no literal correlation with either the letters *A* or *Z*, the same holds true for the idiomatic expressions "Alpha and Omega" and "the beginning and the end." God was not defining himself as literally being either Alpha or Omega, nor was he defining himself as either a beginning or an end. These are idiomatic expressions that are not to be broken down and taken separately while being defined. Hence, we would be imprudent to base our understanding of ἀρχή in Revelation 3:14 on Revelation 21:6 and Revelation 22:13. God was using an idiomatic expression. Christ was not. Even so, ἀρχή does not lose its meaning in those "beginning and the end" passages. Instead, ἀρχή is clearly presented as the *opposite* of "the end," which is, incontrovertibly, "the beginning."

The Septuagint reading of Job 40:14 (Job 40:19 in the Hebrew text) is considered as a proof text showing that ἀρχή can also refer to a *ruler* of creation. Job 40:14 (LXX) refers to the *Behemoth* as the ἀρχή of the creation of God, saying:

τοῦτ'	ἔστιν	ἀρχὴ	πλάσματος	κυρίου	
This	is	a beginning	**of formation**	of the Lord	(Job 40:14 LXX)

Christ is the first "creation" in regard to the new creation, but Behemoth is **a** first "formation" in regard to this present creation. Behemoth is a creature "formed" from the dust of the earth. The word πλάσματος that is used here is from the Greek root word πλάσσω, which refers to *molding* (as from clay) (c.f. Romans 9:20-21). The word used in regard to Christ in Revelation 3:14 is κτίσις, which properly refers to creation in general. Another notable fact regarding the Behemoth passage is that the Septuagint text does not include a direct article before the word ἀρχή when it says:

τοῦτ'	ἔστιν	ἀρχὴ	πλάσματος	κυρίου	
This	is	**a beginning**	of formation	of the Lord	(Job 40:14 LXX)

The absence of a direct article before the word ἀρχή allows this to denote *a* beginning in a broader sense rather than *the* beginning. Contrarywise,

Christ does employ the direct article when he refers to himself as "the beginning of the creation of God," saying:

ἡ **ἀρχὴ**	τῆς κτίσεως	τοῦ θεοῦ	
the beginning	of the creation	of the God	(Revelation 3:14)

Christ is the *precise* beginning of God's new creation.

In the context of Job 40:10-19, God is relaying several facts regarding Behemoth (which I believe is a brontosaurus type of an animal): He eats grass like an ox (Job 40:10 LXX); his tail is like a cypress tree (Job 40:12 LXX), etc. Among these facts regarding the Behemoth, God also states that this type of animal is among his first formations. The immediate context in the Septuagint refers to the *origin* of Behemoth: "This is **a beginning** of the **formation** of the Lord; **made** to be played with by his angels." (Job 40:14 LXX.) It is also noteworthy that (according to the extant Hebrew Old Testament) the word translated as ἀρχή in the Septuagint is the Hebrew word re'shiyth, which does *not* mean *chief* (although the KJV translates it as such). Hence, we see *Young's Literal Translation* render re'shiyth as "a beginning," saying:

> "He is **a beginning** of the ways of God, his maker bringeth nigh his sword." (Job 40:19 YLT)

Re'shiyth is the exact same Hebrew word used in Genesis 1:1, when it says, "In the **beginning** (re'shiyth) God created the heaven and the earth."

Some people may also think that ἀρχή is not included as a member of the group that is specified within the partitive genitive construction of Proverbs 9:10 (LXX), which says:

> "The fear of the LORD is the beginning (ἀρχή) of wisdom."
> (Proverbs 9:10 LXX)

However, since the fear of the LORD is wisdom (in the sense that it is the first part of the wisdom being described), then this may not be an exception to the normal use of ἀρχή in the partitive genitive construction. In fact, some manuscripts of Job even state forthrightly that the fear of the LORD is wisdom, saying:

> "Behold, **the fear of the LORD, that is wisdom**; and to depart from evil is understanding." (Job 28:28 KJV)

Notice that this text *also* says, "to depart from evil is understanding." This clearly refers to how applied understanding = departing from evil. Likewise, applied wisdom (even the initial part) = fearing God. The same may hold true for the passage that refers to the fear of the LORD as "the beginning of *knowledge*." (Proverbs 1:7) The phrase "fear of the LORD is the beginning of knowledge/wisdom" (Psalm 111:10 (110:10 LXX), Proverbs 1:7, 9:10) obviously does not have any random category of knowledge in mind. I take it as the first part of a *certain kind* of knowledge that is only contemplated and known with such fear as its beginning. Once a person has the fear of God, they have the first part of the knowledge/wisdom that proceeds afterwards.

Appendix D

Firstborn in the Old Testament

There are five Old Testament texts commonly referred to by those who assert a *non-literal* definition for the word firstborn. However, *all* of these passages actually *do* retain the literal meaning of the word, therefore the primary argument used to dismiss the literal meaning of Colossians 1:15 is not a scriptural reality.

Note: We should remember that there are *one hundred and sixteen* instances in the Bible (KJV) wherein the word *firstborn* is used, and the following *five* instances represent the texts out of this number that are the most difficult to understand. Seeing that they are somewhat difficult, we should be patient in our examination, taking the necessary time to consider the relative factors carefully.

Exodus 4:22 – Those who deny the creation of Christ sometimes cite this verse as presenting a non-literal definition for the word *firstborn*.

> "And thou (Moses) shalt say unto Pharaoh, Thus saith the LORD, Israel is my son, even my firstborn." (Exodus 4:22)

God is speaking to Moses in this particular passage about telling Pharaoh to let the Israelites go free ... Notice what God says:

> "Thus saith the LORD, Israel is **my son, even my firstborn**."
> (Exodus 4:22)

If God says that Israel is his "son" and his "firstborn" then what does this say about Christ? Surely Christ is not God's *second-born* Son? And if *firstborn* means *first in rank* within this passage, which is the foremost alternative definition proposed for *firstborn*, does this mean that Israel is the son with the ranking authority over all of God's *other* sons? Well then, is Israel God's "firstborn son" over Christ as well? Not at all. How then does the proposed definition of *first-in-rank* apply here? It doesn't. So then, should we just make up another non-literal definition for the word *firstborn* that we feel *would* fit in this passage? No, that is not necessary, because, as we shall see, the word retains its literal meaning in this passage as well.

The category that is referred to in Exodus 4:22 is literally God's "firstborn son." This is evident because God immediately follows his statement regarding Israel being his firstborn son by saying:

> "And I (God) say unto thee, Let **my son** go, that he may serve me: and if thou refuse to let him go, behold, I will slay **thy son**, even **thy firstborn**." (Exodus 4:23 KJV)

This may be addressed to Moses, who afterwards (the next verse) was found in an inn (delaying?). The angel was about to slay "him," which possibly denotes the uncircumcised firstborn son of Moses. Moses' Ethiopian wife (Numbers 12:1-15) cut off the foreskin of Moses' son, probably as a sign of commitment to becoming one with Israel and fulfilling the call of God toward Moses. Such is the view of Adam Clarke as well. In this way, since Moses' literal son was in view, *firstborn* is literal. However, I am not sure this is correct. The common view is, because Pharaoh did not free *God's firstborn son* then God would slay Pharaoh's firstborn son. In this way also, it was *literally* Pharaoh's *son* that God slew (Exodus 11:4-7).

> "And it came to pass, that at midnight the LORD smote all the firstborn in the land of Egypt, from the firstborn of Pharaoh that sat on his throne unto the **firstborn of the captive** that was in the dungeon; and all the **firstborn of cattle**." (Exodus 12:29 KJV)

Highest ranking captive? Highest ranking cow? *No!* God didn't slay Pharaoh's highest-ranking official, but he rather slew that son of Pharaoh that was born first. The term *firstborn* did not take on some foreign and non-literal meaning when God said that he would slay *Pharaoh's* firstborn

(Exodus 4:23), so why should we say that it took on a non-literal definition when God used the term of his own firstborn in the previous verse (Exodus 4:22)? Yet, how can Israel truly be God's firstborn if Christ is God's firstborn? This is an important question.

Some might think that Israel was called God's firstborn son because Israel prophetically *symbolized* Christ. The Old Testament is full of symbolism that represents a shadow of the New Testament fulfillment (Hebrews 10:1, Colossians 2:16-17, Galatians 4:24-29, Romans 2:28-29). Therefore, it *could be* that Israel was referred to as God's firstborn son in a symbolic sense—as a type of God's *true* firstborn (even as the Mosaic Passover lamb served as a type of the true and coming Passover lamb. 1 Corinthians 5:7). This does not present a new definition for the word *firstborn*, but simply applies the literal definition in an allegorical sense, because Israel prophetically represented God's true firstborn.

Although the type/fulfillment principle is itself valid, I do not believe that is necessarily the reason why Israel is referred to as God's firstborn son in Exodus 4:22. Rather, I believe that Israel is God's firstborn in the sense that Israel was the first nation of people established by God.

Moses speaks of Israel as having been begotten by God:

> "Of the Rock that **begat** thee thou art unmindful, and hast forgotten God that formed thee." (Deuteronomy 32:18)

This is not to mean that Israel came out of God's substance (see chapter four herein on the meaning of *begotten*), but that God established them as the first nation through whom he was represented (Deuteronomy 4:32-34).

Job 18:13 – This text is also sometimes used by those who assert that the word *firstborn* doesn't always literally mean *first-born*.

> "It shall devour the strength of his skin: even **the firstborn of death** shall devour his strength." (Job 18:13)

Those who deny the creation of Christ say that the "firstborn of death" refers to the *worst* thing that death could throw at you. By this they attempt to redefine *firstborn* as *supreme one*. However, the "supreme one of death" is not what is being described within this passage.

In Job 18:13, Bildad the Shuhite was speaking his mind to Job regarding how a wicked man's life would come to an end. Notice what he says:

> "His strength shall be hungerbitten, and **destruction shall be ready at his side**. It shall devour the strength of his skin: **even the firstborn of death** shall devour his strength." (Job 18:12-13)

When Bildad says that destruction is "ready" (*i.e.,* waiting) at the wicked man's side he was speaking of how the wicked man's time to die was *approaching*. Then, in continuation of this thought, he says:

> "It shall devour the strength of his skin: **even the firstborn of death** shall devour his strength." (Job 18:13)

Bildad was not speaking of the *worst* disease imaginable, but he was instead referring to the *first signs* or *first symptoms* of death. The destruction that was waiting at his side comes upon the wicked, and the first product of that destruction is what Bildad refers to as "the firstborn of death."

Anyone or anything that is firstborn is produced (*i.e.,* born) out of a certain category and is always included in and among that category. This means that the firstborn of death is included in the category of death (as in the dying process). This is clearly seen in the context of Job 18, where we see (1) the destruction waiting at his side, (2) the first product of death come upon him, and (3) the final fulfillment of that dying process.

> "His strength shall be hungerbitten, and destruction shall be ready at his side. It shall devour the strength of his skin: even the firstborn of death shall devour his strength. His confidence shall be rooted out of his tabernacle, and it shall bring him to the king of terrors. It shall dwell in his tabernacle, because it is none of his: brimstone shall be scattered upon his habitation. His roots shall be

dried up beneath, and above shall his branch be cut off. His remembrance shall perish from the earth, and he shall have no name in the street. He shall be driven from light into darkness, and chased out of the world." (Job 18:12-18)

When Job 18:13 refers to "the firstborn of death" this is describing the *first offspring* or *first product* of death in the wicked man's life. Hence, the word *firstborn* retains its literal meaning in Job 18:13 as well.

Psalm 89:27 – Psalm 89 speaks of "David," and then God says, "I will make *him* my firstborn." Those who say that *firstborn* means something other than *first-born* probably cite this passage of Scripture more than any other as a "proof text" for their argument.

Psalm 89 records these words from God:

> "I have found **David** my servant; with my holy oil have I anointed him: With whom my hand shall be established: mine arm also shall strengthen him. The enemy shall not exact upon him; nor the son of wickedness afflict him. And I will beat down his foes before his face, and plague them that hate him. But my faithfulness and my mercy shall be with him: and in my name shall his horn be exalted. I will set his hand also in the sea, and his right hand in the rivers. He shall cry unto me, Thou art my father, my God, and the rock of my salvation. Also **I will make him my firstborn**, higher than the kings of the earth." (Psalm 89:20-27)

Those who have sought to invent a new meaning for the word *firstborn* look at this passage of Scripture and say:

> "It is obvious that David was not the firstborn of God, nor the firstborn of Jesse (David's father), so God was referring to David's *rank* rather than the *order in which he was born*."

However, the literal meaning of the word *firstborn* remains intact in this passage as well, because God used the name *David* in reference to *Christ* (who was the seed of David). God is speaking of Christ in this passage rather than of David himself. Am I making this up, or do the Scriptures prove this? God also calls Christ by the name "David" in Ezekiel 34:23 as well, saying:

> "And I will set up one shepherd over them, and he shall feed them, even my servant **David**; he shall feed them, and he shall be their shepherd." (Ezekiel 34:23)

John Wesley comments accurately on this passage in Ezekiel, saying:

> **Ezekiel 34:23 One shepherd** – Christ, the great, good, chief, only shepherd, that laid down his life for his sheep. **My servant David** – The seed of David, the beloved one, who was typified by David, and is in other places called by his name, as [in] Jeremiah 30:9, Ezekiel 37:24.[345]

If God calls Christ by the name of "David" in other passages of the Bible (Ezekiel 34:23, 37:24, Jeremiah 30:9) then why can't Christ be referred to as "David" in Psalm 89:27 as well? Indeed he can be, and indeed he is.

Matthew Henry agrees with this conclusion, saying:

> **Psalm 89:19-37** – The covenant God made with David and his seed was mentioned before (v. 3, 4); but in these verses it is enlarged upon, and pleaded with God, for favour to the royal family, now al- most sunk and ruined; yet certainly it looks at Christ, and has its accomplishment in him much more than in David; nay, some passages here are scarcely applicable at all to David, but must be understood of Christ only (who is therefore called *David our king*, Hosea 3:5) ... *I will make him my firstborn.* I see not how this can be applied to David.[346]

God speaks of Christ as "David" several times within Old Testament prophecies, so it should not seem strange that God would do the same in Psalm 89:27 as well. Sometimes people in the Bible are called by the name of the one from whom they have descended (hence the descendants of Israel are called "Israel").

Someone might also inquire how God could speak of the future and say, "I *will* make him my firstborn"? This statement is to be understood in the same way as some of God's other statements, "Thou art my Son, *this day* have I begotten thee," etc. These things are discussed in chapter nine, under the subheading *Christ Begotten Completely at the Resurrection*.

Isaiah 14:30 – This scripture has also been referred to as if it redefines the word *firstborn*:

> "And **the firstborn of the poor** shall feed, and the needy shall lie down in safety: and I will kill thy root with famine, and he shall slay thy remnant." (Isaiah 14:30)

Those who deny that Christ was created say that this gives a non-literal meaning for the word *firstborn* because, according to them, the firstborn of the poor is referring to *the poorest of the poor*. However, that is not what is being said here at all.

The context clearly presents God telling Philistia not to rejoice because of the fact that their oppressor has died, because God was going to kill *all* of the Philistines as well:

> "In the year that King Ahaz died came this oracle: Rejoice not, O Philistia, all of you, that the rod which smote you is broken, for from the serpent's root will come forth an adder, and its fruit will be a flying serpent. And **the first-born of the poor will feed**, and the needy lie down in safety; but **I will kill your root** with famine, and **your remnant I will slay**." (Isaiah 14:28-30 RSV)

The Philistines were going to be slain by God, even their remnant, until there were no more Philistines left. Thus, the continuation of the Philistine generations was about to come to an end. This, however, was *contrasted* with the fact that (during the time that the Philistine generations were being cut off) even the firstborn of the poor would be cared for (the firstborn son was the initial guarantee that the family name would be continued). God was not describing *the poorest of the poor* when he referred to "the firstborn of the poor," but he was instead *literally* referring to the *firstborn of the poor*. The meaning of the passage is simply this: Even the poor man's bloodline would continue, but there would be no continuation of the Philistine generations.

It is noteworthy that the word *firstborn* does not even appear in the Septuagint translation of this passage, which says:

> "And the poor shall feed by him, and poor men shall rest in peace: but he shall destroy thy seed with hunger, and shall destroy thy remnant." (Isaiah 14:30 LXX)

Notice how the Septuagint says God will destroy the Philistines' "seed." This gives further proof that God was contrasting how the *children* of the poor would live on, but he would cut off the *children* (the seed) of the Philistines (thus discontinue their generations). And God did this very thing, which is why the Philistines are no longer around.

Jeremiah 31:9 – As in Exodus 4:22, God speaks of Israel in this passage as well, saying:

> "They shall come with weeping; and with petitions will I lead them: I will cause them to walk by rivers of waters, in a straight way in which they shall not stumble; for **I am a father to Israel, and Ephraim is my firstborn**." (Jeremiah 31:9)

At this time, Israel was divided into a northern kingdom, referred to as Israel or Ephraim, and a southern kingdom, referred to as Judah. God's prophet to the northern kingdom was Jeremiah. When God spoke through Jeremiah and said, "Israel is my son, and Ephraim is my firstborn," he was referring to the northern kingdom (known both as Israel and Ephraim). Thus, since Israel was in view, the same understanding which applied to the previous study on Exodus 4:22 is applicable here as well.

Appendix E

Holy Spirit

What or *who* is the Holy Spirit? Generally speaking, I take the word *spirit* as *unseen force* (invisible power or influence, that which motivates or causes actions) and the *Holy Spirit* as *God's* unseen force, whereby the things of God are made known to his creation. I also recently concluded, after reading *The Two Treatises of Servetus on the Trinity*, that the Holy Spirit is often tied to the agency of *angelic beings* as well. I will quote the relative passage from Servetus' own work at the end of this present appendix. It seems to me that "Holy Spirit" may be applicable to the entire economy of God's spiritual activity, with certain elements of that economy being singled out and distinguished. Compare the Holy Spirit to "the wind" (John 3:8). We can refer to an *entire kind* of wind as "warm wind," but also specify "*a* warm wind" or "*the* warm wind." Perhaps a thorough treatment of the subject will come at a later date. In the meantime, I will relay some of my current thoughts here in this appendix.

The Holy Spirit is the Manifestation of God in the Earth

In reference to casting out demons, Jesus spoke in the following manner:

> "But if I cast out devils by the Spirit of God, then the kingdom of God is come unto you." (Matthew 12:28)

So, Jesus cast out devils *by the Spirit of God*. Yet, in another instance he says he did so *by the finger of God.*

> "But if I with the finger of God cast out devils, no doubt the kingdom of God is come upon you." (Luke 11:20)

Similarly, the Ten Commandments were "two tables of testimony, tables of stone, written **with the finger of God**." (Exodus 31:18.) Paul compares this to how the New Covenant is written, "not with ink, but **with the Spirit of the living God** (πνεύματι θεοῦ ζῶντος); not in tables of stone, but in fleshy tables of the heart." (2 Corinthians 3:3.) So, God's Spirit is compared to his finger. Now, do we think of someone's finger as a distinct person? Of course not. Our finger is included in us, being a part of us. So also, when Paul talks about the Spirit of God writing on our hearts, he says, "Now the Lord is that Spirit (ὁ δὲ κύριος τὸ πνεῦμά ἐστιν)." (2 Corinthians 3:17.) Notwithstanding, there is more to God's Spirit that is not conveyed by the above comparison to his finger.

> "But God hath revealed them unto us by his Spirit: for the Spirit searcheth all things, yea, the deep things of God. For what man knoweth the things of a man, save the spirit of man which is in him? even so the things of God knoweth no man, but the Spirit of God." (1 Corinthians 2:10-11)

Here, we see that the Spirit of God searches the deep things of God and this is compared to how our own spirits know what is going on within us. Paul compares the function of the Spirit of God with that of the spirit of a man. Now, does a man think that his own spirit is functioning as *a distinct person?* Of course not. When a man says his spirit is affected in some manner, we understand that the man *himself* is affected thus (Psalm 77:3). The spirit of a man is simply an aspect of his own being. The same is true of God's own Spirit.

Paul says that God's Spirit searches what pertains to God in a similar way that man's spirit searches what is going on within man. In the past, I have compared the way that our own spirit knows what is going on in us to how a librarian could function inside of a library. When we learn something new, the figurative librarian (our spirit) takes the information and places it on the bookshelves of our memories. Now, no matter how much we have learned, we *never* have *all* of our memories present simultaneously, though they are, if you will, all simultaneously in our library. However, when we *do* want to recall some old information, our spirit goes to those library shelves and finds the specific book with the information desired, then presents that to our consciousness (or rather *as* our consciousness). Now then, God *has* all knowledge, but when we are taught by the Holy Spirit, we do not receive the *entirety* of God's knowledge (the thought of that is inconceivable). Rather, if I may use the analogy thus, we get just what we need from the library of our Father. And, furthermore, unlike man, God is all-powerful. His Spirit not only produces what he desires to share in matters of knowledge, but it also pulls from his being that power inherent to him and carries out whatsoever he wills.

What about the Holy Spirit sent in Jesus' Name?

In Ephesians 4:4, Paul refers to the one Spirit that is common to all of God's people, saying:

> "Endeavouring to keep the **unity of the Spirit** in the bond of peace. There is **one body**, and **one Spirit**, even as ye are called in one hope of your calling; One Lord, one faith, one baptism, One God and Father of all." (Ephesians 4:3-6)

This one Spirit that all Christians partake of is the Spirit of Christ.

> "God hath sent forth **the Spirit of his Son** into your hearts, crying, Abba, Father." (Galatians 4:6)

Notice that it is the Spirit of Christ (God's Son) that cries "Abba, Father." Since the attributes of Christ are revealed through Christ's Spirit, and Christ's Spirit is in us, then the attributes of Christ are revealed through us as well. That is why the Scriptures also say:

> "For ye have not received the spirit of bondage again to fear; but ye have received **the Spirit of adoption, whereby we cry, Abba, Father**." (Romans 8:15)

It is the Spirit of God's Son that cries "Abba, Father," yet as that Spirit is revealed in us, we *also* cry "Abba, Father" as well (Romans 8:15). In this way, it is Christ who has the communication with the Father, but we are made partakers of that communication as the Spirit of Christ is revealed in us.

> "For through him we both have **access by one Spirit unto the Father**." (Ephesians 2:18) (c.f. Ephesians 3:12)

Since it is the Spirit of Christ that cries to God *through* us, it is in response to that same Spirit that God answers. This does not mean that Christ is in need of the things that we are in need of when we pray, but it rather means that the Spirit of Christ is interceding unto God on our behalf (Romans 8:26-27).

> "And in like manner **the Spirit joins also its help to our weakness**; for we do not know what we should pray for as is fitting, but the Spirit itself makes intercession with groanings which cannot be uttered." (Romans 8:26 Darby)

There is a certain sharing and union that occurs between our spirits and Christ's when Christ's Spirit is revealed in us. Christ helps us, but it is as if the help that he gives to us does not simply come in the form of advice on how *we* should do a thing, but it instead comes in the form of Christ's own characteristics and attributes being revealed *through* us. It is like we are needy vessels and Christ inhabits us by his Spirit so that we can share in what is his.

Christ's Spirit is so intricately joined to the spirit of a Christian that Paul says:

> "But he that is joined unto the Lord is **one spirit**." (1 Corinthians 6:17)

That is not to say that our spirit *is* Christ's Spirit,[347] but rather that there is such a union and a sharing between the two spirits that the things of Christ's Spirit have become interwoven into the Christian's spirit. This results in the attributes of Christ being revealed through the one who is joined unto him as their own spirits are brought into subjection to the leading of the Spirit of Christ. Thus, it is Christ who is revealed in us (because the Spirit of Christ reveals Christ), and we are vessels through whom he is revealed (*i.e.,* members of his body). This is what Paul referred to when he said:

> "I am crucified with Christ: nevertheless I live; yet not I, but Christ liveth in me." (Galatians 2:20)

He did not say, "I *became* Christ," because Paul continued to remain an individual soul, as did Christ. What Paul said was, "Christ lives *in* me."

- Paul said, "I live; yet <u>not I</u>, <u>but Christ</u> liveth <u>in me</u>." (Galatians 2:20)
- Christ said, "The words I speak unto you I speak <u>not of myself</u>: but <u>the Father</u> that dwelleth <u>in me</u>, he doeth the works." (John 14:10)

Just as we partake of the attributes of Christ, so also Christ partakes of the attributes of God. In a similar way that we are "one Spirit" with Christ, so also God and Christ may be said to be "one Spirit" as well.

Imagine that we have three glasses, and the first glass is the only one with water in it. Now, if we pour the water from glass one into glass two, and then pour the water from glass two into glass three, we can say that the water that glass three receives proceeded from glass one. And yet it is also the water of glass two as well in an intermediate sense. Again, suppose that glass two had a few drops of blue food coloring in it. When the water from glass one is poured into glass two, then the water from glass one would take on the blue color of the liquid that was already in glass two. When the water in glass two is then poured into glass three, glass three will contain both what proceeded from glass one and *also* what pertained to glass two. Likewise, the Spirit of God proceeds from God, but since it is sent *through* Christ, the Spirit of Christ and the Spirit of God are *joined*. Hence the Spirit that we receive is the Spirit that is of God and *also* of Christ. And just as the drops of blue food coloring from glass two could not have filled up glass three if it had not been combined with the water of glass one, so also the Spirit of Christ could not fill us all without being joined to the Spirit of God. This explains how *Christ* sent forth the Spirit that proceeds from the Father (John 15:26), but it is also true that "*God* hath sent forth the Spirit of his Son." (Galatians 4:6.) Perhaps it is by an omnipresent ability of the Spirit of God in Christ that the Spirit of Christ (now united to the Spirit of God) may now indwell us all.[348]

> "He that descended is the same also that ascended up far above all heavens, that he might fill all things." (Ephesians 4:10)

God sent his own Spirit (revealing his own attributes) into Christ. The intertwining of the Spirit of God and of Christ produces "one Spirit" in the same way that "he that is joined unto the Lord is one Spirit." (1 Corinthians 6:17.) This "one Spirit" consists of both the attributes of God *and* of Christ. The Holy Spirit that we receive is of God *originally*, but it is also of Christ *intermediately*. The attributes of God are revealed in Christ, and the attributes of Christ are revealed in us.

Christ receives the things of God, and we receive the things of Christ (John 17:22). In this way, the things *of God* that we receive are also *of Christ*, being sent to us *through* Christ. This is why Jesus prayed to God for all Christians, saying:

> "**The glory which thou gavest me I have given them**; that they may be one, even as we are one: **I in them**, and **thou in me**, that they may be made perfect in one." (John 17:22-23)

This understanding also makes perfect sense of Christ's statements in John 14-16 as well:

- "And **I will pray the Father**, and **he shall give** you another Comforter, that he may abide with you for ever." (John 14:16)

- "The Comforter, which is the Holy Ghost, whom **the Father will send in my name**, he shall teach you all things." (John 14:26)

- "But when the Comforter is come, whom **I will send** unto you **from the Father**, even the Spirit of truth, which **proceedeth from the Father**, he shall testify **of me**." (John 15:26)

- "[The Comforter] shall glorify me: for he shall **receive of mine**, and shall shew it unto you. **All things that the Father hath are mine**:

therefore said I, that he shall take **of mine**, and shall shew it unto you." (John 16:14-15)

The point of this last statement was to show that the things of God have been given to Christ, and thus the Spirit can reveal the things of God by revealing what is Christ's. Compare also how God took

Why is the Spirit Referred to in the English Versions as a He?

As we have seen, the Holy Spirit is the expression of God and of Christ. Apparently, this expression is embodied or actualized through the agency of angels and thus identified with them. In other words, when the Bible speaks of the Holy Spirit, this sometimes correlates to an angel. We cannot come to this conclusion simply because we find the Holy Spirit referred to with masculine pronouns (e.g., *he*). While it is true that the Holy Spirit is accurately identified by masculine pronouns when described as the παράκλητος (*i.e.,* Comforter) within John 14-16, this is because, in the Greek, παράκλητος is itself a masculine noun. Those corresponding pronouns, therefore, that refer *back* to παράκλητος are, by default, also masculine. This is a rule of Greek grammar and does not necessitate that a literal *he* is in view, because **Greek nouns that have masculine or feminine gender are not always a *he* or *she***. For example, the Greek word for *charity* in 1 Corinthians 13 is *feminine* and, in the Greek, has *feminine pronouns*. If someone wanted to argue that *charity* was a *female*, they might open up the *King James Version* and read:

> "**Charity** suffereth long, and is kind; charity envieth not; charity vaunteth not itself, is not puffed up, Doth not behave itself unseemly, seeketh not **her** own." (1 Corinthians 13:4-5)

Aha! Charity must be a distinct female person with emotions! I mean, just look at all the "personal attributes" displayed by "her"! Surely these things could only be said of someone with feelings and a mind and a will! And look! We see proof that Charity is a female because the Bible clearly says "her" right there in the text! Although I am being sarcastic, this does demonstrate the nature of reasoning many have used while arguing that the Holy Spirit must be a "he" because personal traits are sometimes associated with it, or because of the appearance of masculine pronouns. In reality, the Greek word for *spirit* (πνεῦμα) is actually neuter in gender, so we normally find that the pronouns referring back to the Spirit are neuter as well (e.g., *itself*, Romans 8:16, 26; *it*, 1 Peter 1:11, etc.).

Notwithstanding the former point, some early Christians evidently viewed *the Comforter* in John chapters 14-16 as *an angel*. As proof of this I will cite Clement of Alexandria, writing around 200 AD. Clement speaks of how Christ is our παράκλητος (which is the exact same Greek word translated as *comforter* in John 14-16 KJV, translated *advocate* in the NIV, NLT, NET). Clement is clearly referring to how Jesus is called our παράκλητος in 1 John 2:1 and how, before his ascension, Jesus promised to send *another* παράκλητος. This undoubtedly refers to "the Spirit of truth" in John 14-16, yet Clement identifies this Spirit with the *angels*.

> "For so the Lord is an advocate with the Father for us. So also is there, **an advocate, whom, after His assumption, He vouchsafed to send**. For **these** primitive and first-created virtues are unchangeable as to substance, and **along with subordinate angels and archangels, whose names they share, effect divine operations**. Thus also Moses names the virtue of the angel Michael, by an angel near to himself and of lowest [proximity]. The like also we find in the holy prophets; but to Moses an angel appeared near and at hand. Moses heard him and spoke to him manifestly, face to face. On the other prophets, through the agency of angels, an impression was made, as of beings hearing and seeing."
>
> —*Clement of Alexandria*[349]

According to Clement of Alexandria, the advocate/comforter promised by Christ was counted among the angels. Thus, in 200 AD, the Comforter of John 14-16 was being identified as an angelic being.

Biblically, angels are presented as *different* than spirits.

> "For the Sadducees say that there is no resurrection, **neither angel, nor spirit** (μήτε ἄγγελον μήτε πνεῦμα): but the Pharisees confess both. And there arose a great cry: and the scribes that were of the

Pharisees' part arose, and strove, saying, We find no evil in this man: but if **a spirit or an angel** (πνεῦμα ἐλάλησεν αὐτῷ ἢ ἄγγελος) hath spoken to him, let us not fight against God." (Acts 23:8-9)

However, although angels and spirits are different, we also find God making his angels *to be* spirits. "And of the angels he saith, **Who maketh his angels spirits** (Ὁ ποιῶν τοὺς ἀγγέλους αὐτοῦ πνεύματα)." (Hebrews 1:7.) So, how does God make his angels spirits? Perhaps the word "spirits" denotes *invisible influences* and God makes his angels, which are inherently visible, to be invisible influences in the earth. Or, perhaps, they are made "spirits" in the same manner of Psalm 82:6, where God says to men, "Ye are gods (אֱלֹהִים)." Those men were not *literally* "gods," but it was only because the one true God was being revealed through *each* of them that they were *collectively* called "gods." Compare אֱלֹהִים in Psalm 8:5. Likewise, it may be that "that one and the selfsame Spirit" (1 Corinthians 12:11) is revealed through the many angels of God, who are in turn called *spirits*, acknowledging the plural number of that one Spirit's agents. Yet, they are also called the Spirit (singular) of God. For, the Bible says "the Spirit of God" is "every spirit" (*each one of a group*) that confesses that Christ has come in the flesh.

> "Beloved, believe not every spirit, but try the **spirits** whether they are of God: because many false prophets are gone out into the world. Hereby know ye **the Spirit of God: Every spirit** that confesseth that Jesus Christ is come in the flesh is **of God**: And every spirit that confesseth not that Jesus Christ is come in the flesh is not of God: and this is that spirit of antichrist, whereof ye have heard that it should come; and even now already is it in the world."
> (1 John 4:1-3)

Hence, when 1 John 4 speaks of "the Spirit of God" as "every spirit" with right doctrine, we understand that those are *each* called the Spirit of God. Thus, there are spirits (plural) which are referred to as "the Spirit of God." 1 John 4 afterward says, "Hereby know we the spirit of truth, and the spirit of error." (1 John 4:6.) Now, if "every spirit" with correct doctrine is "the spirit of truth," (τὸ πνεῦμα τῆς ἀληθείας,) when we find **that exact same phrase**, "the Spirit of truth" (τὸ πνεῦμα τῆς ἀληθείας), in John chapters

14-16, we can easily take this as referencing "every spirit" that is of the truth as well. The plurality of angelic agents may account for why, in the Greek text, *Holy Spirit* is often anarthrous (lacking a definite article). In other words, this is possibly why the Greek text actually reads *a Holy Spirit* in some instances (Luke 11:13, 1 Corinthians 12:3).

In the following quote, notice how Clement of Alexandria refers to the Spirit (singular) of Christ and then says this correlates to an angelic being, who is one of the *several* spirits of Christ.

> "'Of which salvation,' he says, 'the prophets have inquired and searched diligently,' and what follows. It is declared by this that the prophets spake with wisdom, and that **the Spirit of Christ** was in them, according to the possession of Christ, and in subjection to Christ. For God works through **archangels and kindred angels**, who are **called spirits of Christ**."
> —*Clement of Alexandria*[350]

Is it possible that the Holy Spirit that is *in* a man also, in some way, relates to an angel? Consider this next quote from *The Shepherd of Hermas*, written around 150 AD. He initially says angels are *with* men but then also says *the angels* can *enter* a man.

> "There are two angels **with** a man—one of righteousness, and the other of iniquity." And I said to him, "How, sir, am I to know the powers of these, for both angels dwell with me?" "Hear," said he, "and understand them. The angel of righteousness is gentle and modest, meek and peaceful. When, therefore, **he ascends into your heart**, forthwith he talks to you of righteousness, purity, chastity, contentment, and of every righteous deed and glorious virtue. **When all these ascend into your heart**, know that the angel of righteousness is with you. These are the deeds of the angel of righteousness. Trust him, then, and his works. Look now at the works of the angel of iniquity. First, he is wrathful, and bitter, and foolish, and his works are evil, and ruin the servants of God. When, then, **he ascends into your heart**, know him by his works." And I said to him, "How, sir, I shall perceive him, I do not know." "Hear and understand" said he. "When anger comes upon you, or

> harshness, know that **he is in you**; and you will know this to be the case also, when you are attacked by a longing after many transactions, and the richest delicacies, and drunken revels, and divers luxuries, and things improper, and by a hankering after women, and by overreaching, and pride, and blustering, and by whatever is like to these. **When these ascend into your heart, know that the angel of iniquity is in you**. Now that you know his works, depart from him, and in no respect trust him, because his deeds are evil, and unprofitable to the servants of God. These, then, are the actions of both angels. Understand them, and trust the angel of righteousness; but depart from the angel of iniquity, because **his instruction** is bad in every deed. For though a man be most faithful, and **the thought of this angel ascend into his heart**, that man or woman must sin. On the other hand, be a man or woman ever so bad, yet, if **the works of the angel of righteousness ascend into his or her heart**, he or she must do something good. You see, therefore, that it is good to follow the angel of righteousness, but to bid farewell to the angel of iniquity."[351]

Hermas correlates the thoughts of angels being in a man's heart to the angel being in a man. Tertullian, writing 197 AD, said "demons and angels breathe into the soul" of men.[352] Interestingly, the Greek word πνεῦμα (*pneuma*) that is usually translated as *spirit* can also mean *breath*. This reminds me of how Jesus "breathed on them, and said to them, 'Receive the Holy Spirit.'" (John 20:22.)

Origen wrote that each person has an angel assigned to them and that those angels take our prayers to God (or at least to Christ, who in turn presents them to God as our High Priest).

> "And the Christian will suffer nothing [from demons], for 'the angel of the Lord will encamp about them that fear Him, and will deliver them,' and his 'angel,' who 'always beholds the face of his Father in heaven,' offers up his prayers through the one High Priest to the God of all, and also joins his own prayers with those of the man who is committed to his keeping." —*Origen, 248 AD*[353]

Origen said the angel joins his own prayers with the prayers of the man to whom he is assigned. This reminds me of how "the Spirit itself maketh intercession for us." (Romans 8:26.) Consider also how men in the Bible "spoke in tongues as *the Spirit gave them utterance*"? (Acts 2:4.) Does this mean that they spoke words that were impressed upon them by angels? What else could Paul mean when he, *while referencing the gift of tongues*, says, "Though I speak with *the tongues ... of angels*"? (1 Corinthians 13:1.) According to Paul, speaking in tongues was associated with the language of angels.

- "Then there appeared to them divided tongues, **as of fire**, and **one sat upon each of them**. And they were all filled with the Holy Spirit and **began to speak with other tongues, as the Spirit gave them utterance**." (Acts 2:3-4 NKJV)

- "And **of the angels** he saith, Who maketh his angels **spirits**, and his ministers **a flame of fire**." (Hebrews 1:14)

Since angels are "ministering **spirits, sent forth**" (Hebrews 1:14) this may also explain "the seven **Spirits of God sent forth** into all the earth" in Revelation 5:6. Angels ascend and descend between heaven and earth (Genesis 28:12). Jesus even said that the angels of God would be seen "ascending and descending upon the Son of man." (John 1:51.) This reminds me of how John the Baptist previously "saw the Spirit of God descending like a dove, and lighting upon him." (John 1:32.)

Isaiah 63:9-10 seems to correlate "the angel of his presence" to the Holy Spirit.

> "In all their affliction he was afflicted, and **the angel of his presence** saved them: in his love and in his pity he redeemed them; and he bare them, and carried them all the days of old. But they rebelled, and vexed **his holy Spirit**: therefore he was turned to be their enemy, and he fought against them." (Isaiah 63:9-10)

Concluding Thoughts

The Bible refers to our bodies as the temple of the Holy Spirit (1 Corinthians 6:19), which makes us the temple of God (2 Corinthians 6:16). So, the Holy Spirit of God, being God himself, abides in us. Whatever we conclude about the process of *receiving* that Spirit, let's remain careful to acknowledge that the angels of God and of Christ are not representing themselves.

By the time of Tertullian's writings, shortly after Clement of Alexandria's writings, angels were being considered "a secondary deity" by some.

> "Respecting, then, this [body] ... if it had been the work of angels ... it would be quite enough for securing respect for the body, that it had the support and protection of even a secondary deity. The angels, we know, rank next to God."   —*Tertullian, 210 AD*[354]

The angels were being elevated to a position of divinity already, whilst the *agency* of those angelic beings associated with the Holy Spirit was simultaneously becoming obscured. This is apparently how the Trinity doctrine came about. As mainstream beliefs shifted in favor of one multi-personal God consisting of both Jesus and the Father, it would have been quite natural for the Holy Spirit, now mingled with that "secondary deity" of angels, to be included within that same entity as well. Compare the literal reading of Luke 9:26, "His glory (singular), and of the Father, and of the holy angels" (τῇ δόξῃ αὐτοῦ καὶ τοῦ πατρὸς καὶ τῶν ἁγίων ἀγγέλων), with Matthew 28:19, "The name (singular) of the Father, and of the Son, and of the Holy Spirit" (τὸ ὄνομα τοῦ πατρὸς καὶ τοῦ υἱοῦ καὶ τοῦ ἁγίου πνεύματος).

Michael Servetus was burned alive at the stake in 1553 AD after being betrayed by John Calvin, who reportedly smiled as Servetus' executioners led him away. The executioners did not first choke Michael Servetus into unconsciousness, as happened to others who were burned. They were instead intent on making Servetus' death as painful as could be (sprinkling sulfur onto his head to increase his pain and even using green wood to make the fire around him burn slow). The reports say that he cried out in pain for half an hour. Notwithstanding, even when facing such torments, Servetus refused to deny his assertion that Jesus had a beginning. When told to recant and say Jesus was "the eternal Son of God," he instead cried out, "*Jesus, Son of the Eternal God, have mercy on me!*" And thus, Servetus gave his life, refusing to denounce his faith. Before being betrayed, this martyr of God made some very compelling points while discussing the Holy Spirit. I am grateful to have learned from his teachings. Here is an excerpt from his work entitled *The Two Treatises of Servetus on the Trinity*.

Excerpt from The Two Treatises of Servetus on the Trinity

Servetus: "I have said above what else can be understood by the paraclete, and this is also drawn from their words; for they say that appearances of fire are something proper to the Holy Spirit, though these occur by means of angels, as when the Lord appeared to Moses in the bush; and through an angel the voice of the Lord there came to Moses. Hence, according to this, the voice of God uttered through the mouth of the angel is called the voice of the Holy Spirit. And after the Holy Spirit descended upon Jesus, he said, *Verily I say unto you, ye shall see the angels of God ascending and descending upon the Son of man*. And Isidore, from the fact that it says, *He shall declare unto you the things that are to come*, infers that it was an angel, because angel bears the meaning of messenger. Add to this the fact that all angels are called *ministering spirits, sent forth to do service*, and, *He maketh his angels spirits, and his ministers a flame of fire*. And this is the flame of fire which appeared in Acts ii, 3. Again, just as an angel is called a lying spirit, so in a contrary passage an angel is to be called the spirit of truth and the Holy Spirit, even as it also says, *Spirits of God*. ...

That we may define the Holy Spirit more clearly, let us see how the Spirit also *proceeds* from the Son; for he gives us the Spirit, saying, *The words which thou gavest me, I have given unto them*. For the Spirit is derived from the Word, and if his words abide in us, the Spirit flows from us as rivers of living water. See also the reasoning of the Master: *He shall take of mine*, saith he, *and shall declare it unto you. All things whatsoever the Father hath are mine: therefore said I, that he shall take of mine.* And when it says, *proceeds*, the Greek is ἐκπορεύεται, which some would have mean, *sets out*, rather than *proceeds*; likewise it also means to *go out*; and as many as are sent by God, as messengers, are all said to go out from his face, and also to proceed and to set out, as I could prove from many other passages of Scripture where the same Greek word is used. Indeed, when a man sets out anywhere, it is expressed by this word. But investigate for yourself, for Scripture interprets itself clearly if you rightly compare passage with passage.

Nor will other passages of Scripture suggest to you those metaphysical and inner emissions of beings; but setting out in visible character from the Father, sent by Christ, it came to the Apostles. And Christ sent it, just as if I, drawing something forth from the bowels of my father, imparted it to my brethren. And this is what Christ says: *Whom I will send unto you from the Father*; and it is sent by God through Jesus Christ. For all things are given us by the Father, yet through Jesus Christ. And Peter, proclaiming this very thing, says, *Having received of the Father the promise of the Holy Spirit, he hath poured forth this gift, which ye see.* And in this the Psalmist agrees with Paul: *When he ascended on high, he received and gave gifts* — received them from the Father, and gave them *unto men*. For in the saying of Peter there is a clear agreement, and Christ said that he was from the Father, as much as to intimate that the Spirit would not be a deceiver, but would be from God; as John says, *Prove the spirits, whether they are of God.* … And Christ teaches that the Spirit is from the Father, saying that he gives the good Spirit to them that ask him; for he pours it out plentifully and liberally. Again, if you read with clear sight, all the words of Christ are concerning the Spirit which he was going to send upon the Apostles. It is something altogether silly to infer from these words eternal processions of aeons, and to be mad with this Cabalistic metaphysics. But this matter is settled on other grounds. First, that the *disposition* is a power and gift from God. Second, that the being that comes is itself a messenger, or a ministering spirit sent by Christ. Third, that in this messenger is the hypostasis itself, or the very image of the Godhead, as I shall show below. Fourth, that all these things aim at the sanctification of our spirits. Yet the one who thus visibly sets out, who shall not speak from himself, who shall take of Christ, is truly a ministering spirit, or else there is no ministering spirit in heaven.

And he is also called the Spirit of truth, and the Holy Spirit; and consequently, as we have spoken of an external breath, much more may we speak of a ministering Spirit. It is not to be wondered at if, being separated by God for a certain work, he is called Holy Spirit, or Spirit of God; for they set out from the profounder treasures of God, and in a far more remarkable way God makes them his own by his own acts. Christ also often calls the holy ones angels. If, then, what God employs is a spirit, and a sort of holiness is appropriate to it, why shall it not be called the Holy Spirit? And, to make few words of it, every breath, every breathing and impulse of the mind through which God breathes, is called holy, and accordingly the Holy Spirit, or a holy spirit, or the Spirit of God. Nor is there any other briefer explanation of this word; and it is not a single expression, but two: holy, and spirit. And in Greek it is written now the Holy Spirit, now a holy spirit; indeed, in Hebrew it is expressed, Spirit of holiness. This at least is a good point against those who hold to their usage so strictly that they are scandalized if one little word be changed. And I would that they might give up their metaphysical habit of speaking, because they would then consider the heavenly spirits not in accordance with the Nature of a being (for of this Scripture never makes mention), but as to scripture how far the very image of the Godhead shines forth in them, that all things may at length tend to the glory of God. For for this reason they are called the souls of God, and the spirits of God; and the very names of the angels indicate this, since nothing else about them is perceived by us save the power of God, the healing of God, which are God, as it were, and manifest nothing else than the brightness of the *hypostasis* of God, although they are appointed for our service.

After this, it is for me very easy to say, another Comforter; and I speak truly of an otherness of the being, for he said of a distinct being without qualification, *He shall take of mine*. And he is said by Christ to be another, and something other, unless perchance you take *other* as marking a lack of harmony; for in that case I shall not admit that the comforting Spirit is something other than Christ. On the contrary, they are one.

In this sense the Holy Spirit testifies as to what I refrained from mentioning above: that when the Spirit descended upon Christ in the Jordan, he bore distinct witness to John, distinctly witnessed that this Jesus is the Son of God, whom you deny to be the Son of God. And to prove this, John appealed to his witness; and these three are one because they agree, and they are one because they are distinguished by marks of one and the same divinity. Behold the singular, *one*, which you were seeking; and in a most singular way are they said to be one, because in the three there is one and the same Godhead. And so I admit one Person of the Father, another Person of the Son, another Person of the Holy Spirit; and I admit Father, Son, and Holy Spirit, three Persons in one Godhead; and this is the true Trinity. But I should prefer not to use a word foreign to the Scriptures, lest perchance in future the philosophers have occasion to go astray. And I have no controversy with the earlier writers, because they employed this word sensibly. But may this blasphemous and philosophical distinction of three *beings* in one God be rooted out from the minds of men.

By this means another account is settled, of which many stand in dread, namely, why the term Holy Spirit is more frequently employed in the New Testament than in the Old. For from this it seems to them that the new being is revealed anew, just because, by the addition of a single note, Christ said, *the Comforter, even the Spirit*. To the first it is replied that this is not for the reason that in the New Testament God has just arrived; for there is no other God than the God of our fathers, יהוה, and he is the Father of Jesus Christ. And the reason of the difference, which you are seeking, is this: that the Jews were not concerned, as we are, with making the Spirit holy. ... And mark these differences; for they always treated of things in an outward fashion. They called upon the Spirit of God, whereas we always call upon the Holy Spirit for the different reason which I have mentioned, that a kind of sanctity was not yet ascribed to the Spirit. Neither the word spirit, nor the word holy, is new. But formerly spirit was regarded otherwise, and there was another kind of holiness, than now. Then the flesh was made holy; but now the spirit is holy. And this is indicated when the words are joined together, and a kind of holiness is ascribed to the Spirit. From this it is evident that it is not a separate being; but every holiness of spirit is referred to man; and, excepting the messenger who when he descends is called the Holy Spirit, I say that nothing else outside of man is called the Holy Spirit. And John well said, *The Spirit was not yet*, though they are unwilling to have the words stand as God uttered them, as though God were in need of their lying. For in the very act of giving it says, Holy Spirit; nor is it said to be before it is given. And now I say that there is no longer a Holy Spirit, it is nowhere, because no one believes that Jesus Christ is the Son of God; for in the same passage this proof is conclusive.

Nor let it vex you that Christ, adding the article, said *the* Comforter; for, if I have decided to send one of my messengers to you at a certain time, I shall say to you, The messenger whom I send from my father's house will be a truthful man, or he will do thus and so. Again, if you refer to what was said above, the sense of the words of Christ is very clear. For he says, The messenger (he, that is, who I said is to be sent to you), *he shall teach you*. And this sense is so appropriate that it can be understood by a mere grammarian. For after Christ had said that they should have another true Comforter in place of him, he added to it, *The Comforter*, that is, the one of whom I spoke, is not any man, but is *the Spirit*, separated by the Father, to be sent to *teach you all things*. Add to this that the Greek article has not so much force as a relative pronoun, so that you may suppose that a being is there indicated. Again, the office of the messenger was there a single one, and the appearance, or person, of the divinity was single. Thus it could be represented by the singular article, and by a special mark, because the like was never seen either in the Prophets or in other men."

—*Michael Servetus*[355]

Appendix F

Angel of the LORD

Some think that a preincarnate version of Jesus appeared within the Old Testament as one particular angel of the LORD. They think this angel was God himself and assert that Jesus, as that angel, is shown to be God. This appendix will explain why such assertions are not true.

To begin with, the Bible *contrasts* Jesus with angels in Hebrews 1-2 in such a way that would *exclude* him from being an angel.

> "For unto which of the angels said he at any time, Thou art my Son, this day have I begotten thee? And again, I will be to him a Father, and he shall be to me a Son?" (Hebrews 1:5)

Some might say that this contrast only applies to Jesus *as a man*, arguing that it did not apply to his *preincarnate* state while he was still the angel of the LORD. However, "the angel of the Lord" continues to appear even after Jesus is born, so how can anyone say that this angel became Jesus?

- "The angel of the Lord descended from heaven, and came and rolled back the stone from the door, and sat upon it." (Matthew 28:2)

- "And the angel of the Lord spake unto Philip, saying, Arise, and go toward the south." (Acts 8:26)

- "The angel of the Lord came upon him, and a light shined in the prison" (Acts 12:7)

"The angel of the Lord" is still present after Jesus' birth. There are also passages within the New Testament that speak of "an" angel of the Lord (Matthew 2:19, Luke 1:11). Yet, in truth, all of these New Testament texts use the same anarthrous Greek phrase ἄγγελος κυρίου, which means "an angel of the Lord." So, does that exclude all of those angels from being "**the** angel of the LORD" we read about in the Old Testament? Actually, when Stephen talks about "the" angel of the LORD that appeared unto Moses, he still uses that same anarthrous Greek phrase, ἄγγελος κυρίου, which means "an" angel of the Lord.

> "There appeared to him in the wilderness of mount Sina **an angel of the Lord** (ἄγγελος Κυρίου) in a flame of fire in a bush." (Acts 7:30)

Since there is no article in the Greek text of Acts 7:30, it is correctly translated "an" angel of the Lord. Yet, the story in Exodus that Stephen referred to identifies that same "angel of the LORD" (Exodus 3:2) with God. That angel who appeared unto Moses spoke as God (Exodus 3:3-14). The Bible even says, regarding that angel, that Moses "hid his face; for he was afraid to look upon God." (Exodus 3:6.) According to prominent Trinitarians, this particular angel was actually the preincarnate Jesus. Such assertions are not new. Around 160 AD, Justin Martyr, though alleging the angel was "another God," also said that angel who appeared to Moses in the burning bush was the preincarnate Jesus.[356] Regardless, the Bible itself certainly does not say this. The biblical truth is, when the Bible speaks of *an* angel of the LORD, or even *the* angel of the LORD, it is simply referring to *one of many angels* through whom God worked or delivered his words.

- "And when Gideon perceived that he was **an** angel of the LORD (LXX has ἄγγελος κυρίου, lit. "**an** angel of the Lord"), Gideon said, Alas, O Lord GOD! for because I have seen **an** angel of the LORD (LXX has τὸν ἄγγελον κυρίου, lit. "**the** angel of the Lord") face to face." (Judges 6:22)

- 1 Chronicles 21:12 speaks of "**the** angel of the LORD," but this same angel is then referred to in 1 Chronicles 21:15 as "**an** angel."

- Zechariah 1:12 shows "**the** angel of the LORD" making a plea to Yahweh. This same angel is *given a command by a **different** angel* in Zechariah 2:3-4, which reads, "And, behold, the angel that talked with me went forth, and **another** angel went out to meet him, And said unto him, Run, speak to this young man…"

The LORD has many angels (Psalm 103:20). The singular phrase "the angel of the LORD" simply refers to the particular angel acting as God's agent in any given situation. By comparison, some of the schools in America have truancy officers assigned to the campus. We might describe them as officers (plural), but then, when speaking of a certain event at a particular school, "The truancy officer (singular) did so and so." Although we say "the truancy officer," we in no way affirm that there is only one truancy officer in existence. We are only describing the action of one particular officer at one particular campus. Likewise, the Bible refers to one of many angels when it says, "The angel of the LORD encampeth round about them that fear him, and delivereth them." (Psalm 34:7.)

There are several passages in the Bible that speak of the angel of the LORD in such a way that identifies him with God and his actions (Genesis 16:10-13, 22:15-17, 31:11-13, etc.). Trinitarians assert that the angel in such instances is therefore shown to be God himself (a standard they also apply to the Targumic use of *Memra*). Yet, they do not apply this same standard to Moses when it identifies *him* with God and his actions.

In Exodus 7:14-17, Moses is commanded by God to say the following unto Pharaoh.

> "Thus saith the LORD, In this thou shalt know that I am the LORD: behold, I will smite with the rod that is in mine hand upon the waters which are in the river, and they shall be turned to blood." (Exodus 7:17)

Moses is told to say, "In this thou shalt know that I am the LORD: behold, I will smite with the rod that is in mine hand." Interestingly, although God told Moses to say, "I will smite with the rod," the one who actually smote with the rod was Aaron (Exodus 7:19). There are numerous examples where God tells Moses to do something that is actually carried out by Aaron (e.g., Exodus 7:1-2). Yet, the Bible still says Moses did those things (Exodus 8:9). Moses was acting as God's agent and Aaron was acting as the agent of Moses (Exodus 4:16). The point is that an agent, acting as the representative of another, is often *identified as* and also *as doing the actions of* the one whom they represent. This biblical identification of someone's agent with themselves is referred to as *the Jewish law of agency*. The Jewish Mishnah says, "We have found everywhere in the Torah that the legal status of a person's agent is like that of himself." (Nedarim 72b.) Not surprisingly, we find the same concept within the Jewish New Testament as well.

- When Jesus enters Capernaum, Matthew 8:5-13 clearly has a certain centurion coming to Jesus, speaking to Jesus, and even being spoken to by Jesus. Yet, when we compare the parallel passage in Luke 7:1-10, we find that only the centurion's messengers came to Jesus while the centurion stayed behind.

- Mark 10:35-41 says James and John came to Jesus, but Matthew 20:20-24 says it was actually their mother who came to Jesus on their behalf.

- John 4:1 says, "Jesus made and baptized more disciples than John," but John 4:2 says, "Jesus himself baptized not, but his disciples."

- In the Book of Revelation, the figure speaking to John says things that could only apply to Jesus (Revelation 2:8, 18), but Jesus was actually speaking through "his angel" (Revelation 1:1). Jesus clearly says, "I Jesus have sent mine angel to testify unto you these things in the churches." (Revelation 22:16.) Compare how the angel sent by Jesus (Revelation 1:13-15) matches the description of the angel who spoke to Daniel (Daniel 10:5-6). See also Revelation 15:6, where seven angels are clothed in linen with golden sashes. Compare also the similarities of Daniel 12:7 and Revelation 10:1-7.

In summary, the Bible sometimes speaks in such a way that identifies a person's agent with that person. This is why God's agents, such as his angels, are sometimes spoken of as if they are God, though they are not.

Appendix G

Infancy Narratives Spurious?

Did the Bible *originally* teach that Jesus was born of a virgin? If that is so, why is it that outside of the first two chapters of Matthew and Luke this astounding detail concerning Jesus' origin is not even mentioned? Scholars recognize that the Book of Mark was written first, before Matthew and Luke, so why is it that Mark *never even mentions this?* Why didn't *Paul*, who also wrote before the books of Matthew and Luke, *ever* mention a virgin birth? Although the earliest *extant* manuscripts of Matthew and Luke *do* contain the virgin birth theme, *none* of those manuscripts date any earlier than the latter half of the 2nd century. Were the virgin birth narratives *added* to the original texts of Matthew and Luke *after* they were already written? This will be the subject of our investigation here.

Contradictory Infancy Narratives

Contrary to popular opinion, there are irreconcilable differences between the infancy narratives we find in Matthew and in Luke. When the details of both books are laid side by side, it is easy to see that the infancy narratives of Matthew and of Luke are two different stories.

Matthew Infancy	**Luke Infancy**
Matthew has 41 names in the genealogy between Jesus and Abraham (1:2-16). After David, 23 out of the 26 names do not match Luke's genealogy.	Luke has 56 names in the genealogy between Jesus and Abraham. (3:23-34). After David, only 3 out of 41 names match what we find in Matthew (Salathiel, Zorobabel, and Joseph).

Matthew Continued	**Luke Continued**
Jechonias is listed in the Matthew genealogy (1:12) as having "**begat** Salathiel," but it was prophesied that, "No man of his seed shall prosper, sitting upon the throne of David." (Jeremiah 22:30.)	Jechonias is *not* included in the Lucan genealogy (3:27), but the *grandson* of Jechonias (Salathiel) *is* included. Assir, Salathiel's father, is called *Jechonias' son* (1 Chronicles 3:17), but since Jechonias died *childless* (Jeremiah 22:30), this is not a son of *natural* descent, but a son according to the Law (Deuteronomy 25:5-6). Jechonias' name was possibly avoided due to the prophecy of Jeremiah.
Joseph and Mary begin in Bethlehem (2:1-9).	Joseph and Mary begin in Nazareth (2:4)
No mention of the census Luke describes.	A Roman census is the reason Joseph and Mary travel from Nazareth to Bethlehem (2:1-5). History tells us this census happened in 6 AD, the first year that "Quirinius was governor of Syria." (Luke 2:2 ASV.) Herod the Great died in 4 BC. Therefore, the census in Luke occurred *ten years after Herod was already dead*. In Luke's account, Jesus is born "after" the days of Herod—Compare "in the days of Herod" (Luke 1:5) with "after those days" (Luke 1:24).

__Matthew Continued__	__Luke Continued__
Joseph and Mary are in a "house" in Bethlehem (2:11). No mention of any manger, etc.	They could not find a place to lodge, so Mary had the child "in a manger; because there was no room for them in the inn." (2:7)
Magi come from the East following a star (2:2, 7, 9). (*Magi* is translated from the word μάγος, which means *sorcerer*, and is actually translated *sorcerer* in Acts 13:6, 8).	There is no mention of any star or of any magi (sorcerers) in Luke.
Magi visit Herod the Great (2:7).	Herod the Great is already dead. Note: Herod the Great is *the father of* "Herod the Tetrarch," who had John the Baptist executed, etc.
Herod has all the infants 2 years old and under killed "in Bethlehem, and in all the coasts thereof." (2:16.)	Luke has Herod already dead. There is no mention of any slaughter of children in Bethlehem and in all the coasts thereof.
Joseph flees to Egypt with Mary and the child to escape Herod's slaughter of the children (2:14). They are fleeing from Herod, who is in Jerusalem (Matthew 2:1-3).	No mention of Egypt in Luke or the family fleeing from Herod. In fact, Matthew says Herod is in Jerusalem (Matthew 2:1-3), which is exactly where Joseph and Mary go forty days after she has her child (2:22).

Matthew Continued	**Luke Continued**
There is never any mention of a visit to Jerusalem by Joseph and Mary.	Joseph and Mary go to Jerusalem (2:22), where, according to Matthew, Herod is located.
There is no mention of Joseph and Mary fulfilling the Levitical law for a firstborn (Luke 2:22-24), which required that an offering should be made in Jerusalem after her forty days of purification were fulfilled (Leviticus 12:1-6).	Joseph and Mary perform the legal requirement for their firstborn son at the Temple in Jerusalem (2:22-24).
Jesus is being hidden away by Joseph in Egypt, who is running from Herod, who was himself in Jerusalem.	While the child is present in Jerusalem, there are public announcements made that he is Christ. Simeon announces it first (2:25-35). Anna, a prophetess, also announces it and "spake of him to all them that looked for redemption in Jerusalem." (2:36-38.)
Joseph and his family head back toward "Judaea"—Bethlehem is in Judea—but "being warned of God in a dream, he **turned aside**" from his initial destination in Judea and goes instead into Galilee (2:22), where Nazareth is (2:23).	After leaving Jerusalem, they "**returned** into Galilee, to **their own city Nazareth**." (2:39.)

The Genealogies Pertain to Joseph

To the Jews, it was absolutely necessary that the Messiah be a physical descendant of King David.

> "God had sworn with an oath to him [David], that of the fruit of his loins, according to the flesh, he would raise up Christ to sit on his throne." (Acts 2:30)

This is why the New Testament authors would *constantly* affirm that Jesus was a descendant of David according to the flesh.

- "Concerning his Son Jesus Christ our Lord, which was made of the seed of David according to the flesh." (Romans 1:3)

- "Remember that Jesus Christ of the seed of David was raised from the dead according to my gospel." (2 Timothy 2:8)

Accordingly, we find that the "genealogy of Christ" is traced back to David in both of the genealogical records found in Matthew and Luke.

> **Matthew:** "The book of the generation of Jesus Christ, the son of David, the son of Abraham. Abraham begat Isaac; and Isaac begat Jacob; and Jacob begat Judas and his brethren; ... And Jesse begat David the king; and **David** the king begat Solomon ... And Jacob begat Joseph the husband of Mary, of whom was born **Jesus**, who is called Christ." (Matthew 1:1-2, 6, 16)

> **Luke:** "And **Jesus** himself began to be about thirty years of age, being (as was supposed) the son of Joseph, which was the son of Heli ... which was the son of Nathan, which was the son of **David**, Which was the son of Jesse ... which was the son of Juda, Which was the son of Jacob, which was the son of Isaac, which was the son of Abraham." (Luke 3:23, 31-34)

If these were, in fact, the genealogical records of *Mary*, they would demonstrate how *she* was a descendant of David, and thus, from *her* bloodline, Jesus would be a descendant of David as well. However, what we find in the infancy narratives are genealogies that *specifically trace to Joseph*, not to Mary. Read them both carefully.

> **Matthew:** "… Eliud begat Eleazar; and Eleazar begat Matthan; and Matthan begat Jacob; And **Jacob begat Joseph** the husband of Mary, of whom was born Jesus, who is called Christ."
> (Matthew 1:14-15)

> **Luke:** "And Jesus himself began to be about thirty years of age, being (as was supposed) the son of **Joseph, which was the son of Heli**, Which was the son of Matthat, which was the son of Levi…"
> (Luke 3:23-24)

These genealogies are traced to Joseph, not to Mary. How could tracing a genealogy back to David *through Joseph* mean that Jesus was an ancestor of David *if Jesus was born of a virgin?* How could *Joseph's* genealogy, who was not even related to Jesus by blood, prove that Jesus was related to David? And if it does *not* prove that (or *anything* about Jesus' bloodline) then why even relay such tedious information when introducing Jesus? Joseph's genealogy is so fundamental to Luke that he traces it *all the way back to Adam! Why would the genealogy of Joseph even matter if Joseph was not physically related to Jesus?*

Eusebius (4th century) affirms that the genealogy is properly traced to Joseph, but then, in a roundabout way, says that this itself proves Mary was of a similar descent, writing thus:

> And the lineage of Joseph being thus traced, Mary also is virtually shown to be of the same tribe with him, since, according to the law of Moses, intermarriages between different tribes were not permitted. For the command is to marry one of the same family and lineage, so that the inheritance may not pass from tribe to tribe.[357]

This assertion from Eusebius is *misrepresenting* that Mosaic prohibition to which he refers (Numbers 36:6-7), which was *only* applicable when a woman, having no brothers, became the heir of her father's inheritance.

Usually, a father's inheritance went to his *sons*, but *if he had no son* the inheritance would instead go to his daughter and in turn be passed on to the daughter's husband whenever she was married. And thus, in the specific instance where a woman was the heiress (which the Bible never says about Mary), she would be obligated to marry someone of her same tribe. Otherwise, by marrying into another tribe, the land originally allotted to her father's tribe would eventually be lost to men of other tribes. The argument that Eusebius makes *assumes* that Mary was *both* originally from the tribe of Judah *and* that she had no brothers. Notwithstanding, even if we did assume these things of Mary, this would still only mean that she was from the same *tribe* as Joseph. Since Joseph was from the tribe of Judah (Luke 3:33), this would only necessitate that she also was from that same *tribe*. This would *not* mean that she was therefore a descendant of David, who came ten generations after the tribe of Judah began. For example, Judah, who started the tribe, began with five sons (Genesis 46:12), so even if Mary was from Judah, there was *from the very first generation* only a 20% probability that she came from Judah's particular son who eventually had King David somewhere in *his* family tree. When we also factor in the numerous generations between Judah and Jesse (David's father), the odds of a descendent of Judah also being a descendent of David become much less than 0.01%. Hence, it is easy to see that the entire argument of Eusebius does not prove anything at all, except that it *might* have been true that Mary was from the tribe of Judah, provided that she actually *was* an heiress. Even so, this still would not come close to proving that Jesus was, therefore, from the line of David. Only a genealogical record traced back to David could prove such a thing. And those genealogies in Matthew and Luke that *do* trace to David pertain to *Joseph*, not Mary.

Julius Africanus

Julius Africanus (160-240 AD) was a famous historian and chronicler. An extant fragment[358] of his from around 221 AD begins with a rebuke of others for trying to *invent* themes by which to harmonize the genealogies in Matthew and Luke. Initially, Julius addresses those who say Matthew is bouncing around names to prove that Jesus was related to kings and priests, showing his disdain for such inventions as follows:

> Some indeed incorrectly allege that this discrepant enumeration and mixing of the names both of priestly men, as they think, and royal, was made properly, in order that Christ might be shown rightfully to be both Priest and King; as if any one disbelieved this, or had any other hope than this ... Let us not therefore descend to such religious trifling as to establish the kingship and priesthood of Christ by the interchanges of the names.

After this, Julius also shows a fear of God, asserting the possibility of judgment for anyone inventing unsupported claims about the genealogies. He then promises to relay the truth on this subject.

> For if the generations are different, and trace down no genuine seed to Joseph, and if all has been stated only with the view of establishing the position of Him who was to be born—to confirm the truth, namely, that He who was to be would be king and priest, there being at the same time no proof given, but the dignity of the words being brought down to a feeble hymn,—it is evident that no praise accrues to God from that, since it is a falsehood, but rather judgment returns on him who asserts it, because he vaunts an unreality as though it were reality. Therefore, that we may expose the ignorance also of him who speaks thus, and prevent any one from stumbling at this folly, I shall set forth the true history of these matters.

Julius then tries to harmonize the two accounts himself. Even though Matthew says Joseph was the son of *Jacob* while Luke says Joseph was the son of *Heli*, Julius presents a solution by focusing on how Matthew says "Jacob **begat** Joseph the husband of Mary." (Matthew 1:16.) This obviously meant that Joseph's father in the *natural, physiological sense* was a man named Jacob. Since Luke words things *differently*—"Joseph, which was **the son of** Heli"—no biological process was indicated. Therefore, according to Luke, Joseph could be the son of Heli according to Jewish law *without* actually being the *physical* offspring of Heli.

Julius continues:

> For whereas in Israel the names of their generations were enumerated either according to nature or according to law,—according to nature, indeed, by the succession of legitimate offspring, and according to law whenever another raised up children to the name of a brother dying childless; for because no clear hope of resurrection was yet given them, they had a representation of the future promise in a kind of mortal resurrection, with the view of perpetuating the name of one deceased;—whereas, then, of those entered in this genealogy, some succeeded by legitimate descent as son to father, while others begotten in one family were introduced to another in name, mention is therefore made of both—of those who were progenitors in fact, and of those who were so only in name. Thus neither of the evangelists is in error, as the one reckons by nature and the other by law.

So, in contrast to others who were inventing themes, Julius Africanus says Matthew is speaking of natural descent and Luke is describing how Joseph was the son of Heli because of the Jewish law which says a man should marry his brother's widow and raise up children for him whenever that brother died childless. The Bible records this law in Deuteronomy 25.

> "If brethren dwell together, and one of them die, and have no child, the wife of the dead shall not marry without unto a stranger: **her husband's brother** shall go in unto her, and take her to him to wife, and perform the duty of an husband's brother unto her. And it shall be, that **the firstborn which she beareth shall succeed in the name of his brother which is dead**, that his name be not put out of Israel." (Deuteronomy 25:5-6)

Thus, according to Julius Africanus, Luke's genealogy is not always demonstrating biological descent. Rather, it is sometimes *listing the name of a man who died childless* as if he were the father when in fact it was *that man's brother* who, taking the widow as his wife, inseminated the mother. Her firstborn son would then be known in Israel as the son of the deceased individual. The child's "father," therefore, would have already died before his mother even became pregnant. This would have definitely been a practiced reality in 1st century BC Jewish society. When this practice took place, the firstborn child would not be known as the child of his living, *biological* father, but *only* as the child of that man's deceased brother. Accordingly, the Jewish genealogical records *would* reflect this whenever that child's genealogical lineage was recorded.

Julius Africanus assures us that his assertion about Luke's genealogy is based upon an account given *by Jesus' own relatives*.

> This interpretation is neither incapable of proof nor is it an idle conjecture. For **the relatives of our Lord according to the flesh**, whether with the desire of boasting or simply wishing to state the fact, in either case truly, **have handed down the following account**: Some Idumean robbers, having attacked Ascalon, a city of Palestine, carried away from a temple of Apollo which stood near the walls, in addition to other booty, Antipater, son of a certain temple slave named Herod. And since the priest was not able to pay the ransom for his son, Antipater was brought up in the customs of the Idumeans, and afterward was befriended by Hyrcanus, the high priest of the Jews.
>
> And having been sent by Hyrcanus on an embassy to Pompey, and having restored to him the kingdom which had been invaded by his brother Aristobulus, he had the good fortune to be named procurator of Palestine. But Antipater having been slain by those who were envious of his great good fortune was succeeded by his son Herod, who was afterward, by a decree of the senate, made King of the Jews under Antony and Augustus. His sons were Herod and the other tetrarchs. These accounts agree also with those of the Greeks.
>
> But as **there had been kept in the archives up to that time the genealogies of the Hebrews** as well as of those who traced their lineage back to proselytes, such as Achior the Ammonite and Ruth the Moabitess, and to those who were mingled with the Israelites and came out of Egypt with them, Herod, inasmuch as the lineage

of the Israelites contributed nothing to his advantage, and since he was goaded with the consciousness of his own ignoble extraction, burned all the genealogical records, thinking that he might appear of noble origin if no one else were able, from the public registers, to trace back his lineage to the patriarchs or proselytes and to those mingled with them, who were called Georae.

A few of the careful, however, **having obtained private records of their own**, either by remembering the names or by getting them in some other way from the registers, pride themselves on preserving the memory of their noble extraction. Among these are those already mentioned, called *Desposyni*, on account of their connection with the family of the Saviour. Coming from Nazara and Cochaba, villages of Judea, into other parts of the world, **they drew the aforesaid genealogy from memory and from the book of daily records as faithfully as possible**.

Whether then the case stand thus or not no one could find a clearer explanation, according to my own opinion and that of every candid person. And let this suffice us, for, although we can urge no testimony in its support, we have nothing better or truer to offer. In any case the Gospel states the truth.

According to Julius Africanus, the genealogical record we find in Luke was provided by Jesus' own relatives. The account he relays does make sense, because **1.** Jews *did* regard the genealogical history as fundamentally important and *would have* valued its preservation **2.** The Jews *would have* sometimes counted a nephew as a son in accordance with their laws.

Julius clearly identified *Joseph* as the son of Heli *according to Jewish law*, but *not* according to the flesh.

> And of these, the one Jacob having taken the wife of his brother **Heli, who died childless**, begat by her the third, Joseph—his son by nature and by account. Whence also it is written, "And Jacob begat Joseph." But **according to law he was the son of Heli, for Jacob his brother raised up seed to him**.

Julius is talking about the contents of Luke 3:23, which says, "Jesus himself began to be about thirty years of age, **being (as was supposed) the son** of Joseph, which was the son of Heli." Yet, Julius says this phrase, "as was supposed," is not only used in regard to Jesus supposedly being the son of Joseph, but that it is also applied to how *Joseph* was supposedly the son of Heli.

> But Luke, on the other hand, says, "Who was the son, as was supposed (for this, too, he adds), of Joseph, the son of Heli, the son of Melchi."

Now, that is the English translation found in *The Ante-Nicene Fathers* and it hides what is going on in the corresponding Greek text.[359] Even so, a footnote in that same location makes the concession, reading as follows:

> Africanus refers the phrase "as was supposed" not only to the words "son of Joseph," but **also** to those that follow, "the son of Heli;" so that **Christ would be the son of Joseph by legal adoption, just in the same way as Joseph was the son of Heli**, which would lead to the absurd and impious conclusion that **Christ was the son of Mary and a brother of Joseph** married by her after the death of the latter. [360]

According to Julius Africanus' explanation, "Christ would be the son of Joseph by legal adoption, just in the same way as Joseph was the son of Heli." Since Julius said Joseph was Heli's son *because Heli's brother raised up seed to him*, then, *following that logic*, Jesus was the son of Joseph *because Joseph's brother inseminated Mary and raised up a seed to Joseph after Joseph died*. This explanation apparently did not begin with Julius Africanus either, because he claims this is actually the historical account passed on by Jesus' own relatives.

Julius describes the origin of Jesus' genealogy [in Luke] as follows:

> Coming from Nazara and Cochaba, villages of Judea, into other parts of the world, **they** drew the aforesaid genealogy from

memory and from the book of daily records as faithfully as possible.

This was *a peer-reviewed* genealogy *presented by Jesus' own family!* Now, in the Greek text of Julius' writings, his *explanation*, corresponding to Jesus being born to Joseph by his brother, *is shown to have passed down from Jesus' family as well!* After Julius says that the phrase "as was supposed" in Luke 3:23 also defined how Joseph was the son of Heli, he *then* says, "This interpretation is neither incapable of proof nor is it an idle conjecture. For the relatives of our Lord according to the flesh, whether with the desire of boasting or simply wishing to state the fact, in either case truly, παρέδοσαν καὶ τοῦτο [have handed down **also**] the following account [etc.]"

> "The καὶ occurs in all the mss. and versions of Eusebius ... The καὶ is certainly troublesome if we suppose that all that precedes is Africanus' own interpretation of the Biblical lists, and not a traditional account handed down by the 'relatives of our Lord.'"
>
> —*Arthur Cushman McGiffert, Ph. D.*[361]

Both the genealogy *and* the explanation thereof conveyed in Julius' writings were passed down by Jesus' own relatives. This means that, according to their account, *Joseph was dead before Jesus was even conceived in the womb*. So, the scenario is *not* that, *due to a virgin birth*, Jesus was *incorrectly thought to be Joseph's son* while Joseph was still alive. The scenario was instead *Joseph died without children and his widow was remarried to Joseph's brother. Then, once she had a child by Joseph's brother, the family now "supposed" (Luke 3:23) her firstborn, Jesus, to be Joseph's son (according to the Deuteronomic injunction)*.

According to Julius Africanus, Jesus' relatives came from villages in Judea named Nazara and Cochaba. We can assume that by *Nazara* he means *Nazareth*, but what about the village of *Cochaba*?

> "Cochaba, according to Epiphanius (Hær. XXX. 2 and 16), was a village in Basanitide near Decapolis. It is noticeable that this region was **the seat of Ebionism**. There may therefore be

> significance in the care with which these Desposyni preserved the genealogy of Joseph, for the Ebionites believed that Christ was the real son of Joseph, and therefore Joseph's lineage was his."
>
> —*Arthur Cushman McGiffert, Ph. D.*[362]

Cochaba is where the Ebionites (also known as *Nazarenes*) were from. The Ebionites did not believe that Jesus was born of a virgin. In fact, the version of Matthew used by the Ebionites did not even *contain* Matthew 1-2. Some scholars (like Bart D. Ehrman) see the Book of Luke as a text that originally began at chapter three as well. If that is the case, *none* of the original Gospels contained *any* record of Joseph being alive during Jesus' lifetime. Outside of those opening chapters of Matthew and Luke, the only[363] passage that seems to *hint* at Joseph being yet alive would be John 6:42, where Jesus' Jewish audience says, "Is not this Jesus, the son of Joseph, whose father and mother we know?" Yet, even scholars who believed in the virgin birth recognized that "the verb will bear the sense of knowing as matter of fact who they were, and need not be confined to personal knowledge."[364]

> "Nothing can be inferred from this [John 6:42] as to Joseph's being alive at this time: the probability is that he was not, as he nowhere appears in the Gospel narrative; but this cannot be proved."
>
> —*A. Plummer, M.A., D.D.*[365]

It has been said that the Ebionites believed Jesus "was *begotten* by Joseph."[366] But, what if that was only *inferred* by their opponents? Was their position misrepresented? The Jewish Ebionites *would have* said Joseph was Jesus' father, which he *would have been* according to their laws. So, when they also affirmed that Jesus was "the fruit of the intercourse between a man with Mary,"[367] it was only natural for their Gentile opponents to think they meant Joseph. Maybe the Ebionite's opponents were *misinterpreting* what the Ebionites *actually* asserted. Was Epiphanius doing so when he said they believed "Christ is the offspring of *a man, that is, of Joseph?*"[368] Perhaps some of the Ebionites *did* believe Jesus was the physical offspring of Joseph. Yet, if Julius Africanus' report is correct, Jesus's relatives (in contrast to the broader Ebionite sect) were in possession of the actual records themselves, which would add credibility to their assertion. As such, Jesus would not have been the biological son of Joseph, but he *still* would have been the biological son of *Joseph's brother*, thus of the same *descent* as Joseph. Hence, a genealogy traced back through Joseph to David *would* represent Jesus' physical descent as well. How could there have been such confusion as to who fathered Jesus? To the Jews, the most important issue was that Jesus was from David. If that happened because of Joseph or because of Joseph's brother, it ultimately did not matter. After initially accepting that Jesus *was* from David, they may have simply followed their customs and spoken of him as the son of Joseph. With the passing of only a few decades, it is easy to see how confusion over such minute details could have arisen. If we were going to get an accurate genealogy, a testimony from Jesus' relatives would be the ideal place to look. And the assertion of Julius, that they took pride in their familial connection to Jesus, does make sense and explains why they would pay closer attention to such things.

Julius Africanus' writings present to us a picture of Jesus that is quite different from what we are accustomed to. Jesus would have been called the son of a man, Joseph, who was already dead. Legally, Jesus' biological father, Joseph's brother, would not even be *counted* as his father. And now that Mary was remarried, Jesus would have been the only son of Joseph amidst a family of others. He could have felt very isolated and disconnected from his family as a youth. He could have longed for a father that he never had. And God, seeing this fatherless child, could have felt compelled to take him as his own.

> "When my father and my mother forsake me, then the LORD will take me up." (Psalm 27:10)

Jesus, Son of Man

Jesus never says he was born of a virgin, but he does continuously refer to himself as "the Son of man (ὁ υἱὸς τοῦ ἀνθρώπου)" and even once as "*a* son of [a] man" (υἱὸς ἀνθρώπου) (John 5:27). Outside of the first two chapters of Matthew and of Luke, we never see anything that would lead us to believe that Jesus was born of a virgin. *Why?* Surely that would be a monumental occurrence if it *did* happen. Yet, it is never even *mentioned* outside of those opening chapters of Matthew and Luke (which contradict one another). There is not even one single mention of any virgin birth in Mark, John, Acts, any of Paul's lengthy writings, James, Jude, Peter, etc. So, what is more likely? That it was *not important enough to even mention?* Or that those infancy narratives were something that the biblical authors simply didn't know about, much less affirm?

Some will say that Paul had a virgin birth in mind in Galatians 4:4.

> "But when the fulness of the time was come, God sent forth his Son, **made of a woman**, made under the law." (Galatians 4:4)

In our English versions this may look like God sent forth his Son *to be* made of a woman, but that is not the case in the original Greek. The phrase "made of a woman" uses an aorist participle verb for "made," which shows that this action *preceded the main verb*. This means that God sent forth his Son *after* he was from a woman (compare John 17:18). Similarly, Hebrews 10:5 says Christ's body was *previously* "prepared" (aorist indicative) for him (compare Job 10:8-11 w/ Lamentations 3:4) *before* he was "coming" (present participle) into the world (John 7:41-42 w/ John 18:20). Paul's statement in Galatians 4:4 does *not* imply a virgin conception. Compare "born of women" in Job 14:11, Matthew 11:11, and Luke 7:28. Paul's word usage in Galatians 4:4 places *even less* emphasis on *how* Jesus came to be from a woman than those texts. And notice how Paul used the exact same verb to describe Jesus c*oming to be* under the Law.

> "God sent forth his Son, **made** (γενόμενον) of a woman, **made** (γενόμενον) under the law." (Galatians 4:4)

The Greek could even be read as, "God sent forth his Son, who *came on the scene* from a woman, who *came on the scene* under the law." So, why does Paul say that Jesus is *from* a woman? Possibly to counter that heathen notion that Jesus was a god from heaven (Acts 14:11). Possibly to connect Jesus to that messianic seed of a woman in Genesis 3:15.[369] Regardless of *why*, he does *not* say anything about a virgin birth here.

> "When Paul tells us that Jesus was "born of a woman" in Galatians 4:4, could he have refrained from mentioning (it would take only one word) that that woman was in fact a virgin, had he known such a thing? It seems unlikely to me. My hunch is that Paul simply had never heard of it. Paul, of course, was writing before the Gospels of Matthew and Luke."
>
> —*Bart D. Ehrman*[370]

The absence of any mentions of a virgin birth outside of Matthew 1-2 and Luke 1-2, coupled with the fact that those two accounts contradict one another, caused some, like Faustus the Manichean, to *abandon* Matthew and Luke altogether and only use Mark and John.

> "Do I believe in the incarnation? For my part, this is the very thing I long tried to persuade myself of, that God was born; but the discrepancy in the genealogies of Luke and Matthew stumbled me, as I knew not which to follow. For I thought it might happen that, from not being omniscient, I might take the true for false, and the false for true. So, in despair of settling this dispute, I betook myself to Mark and John, two authorities still, and evangelists as much as the others."
>
> —*Faustus, 383 AD*[371]

Augustine rejected Faustus' assertion that Matthew contradicts Luke. However, you can tell by the following reply from Augustine that the first two chapters of Matthew were, at least sometimes, thought to be corrupted by "someone else under his name."

> Matthew himself mentions that she was called Joseph's wife by the angel; as it is also from Matthew that we learn that Mary conceived not by Joseph, but by the Holy Spirit. But if this, **instead of being a true narrative written by Matthew the apostle, was a false narrative written by some one else under his name**, is it likely that he would have contradicted himself in such an apparent manner, and in passages so immediately connected, as to speak of the Son of David as born of Mary without conjugal intercourse, and then, in giving His genealogy, to bring it down to the very man with whom the Virgin is expressly said not to have had intercourse,

unless he had some reason for doing so? Even supposing there were **two writers**, one calling Christ the Son of David, and giving an account of Christ's progenitors from David down to Joseph; while the other does not call Christ the Son of David, and says that He was born of the Virgin Mary without intercourse with any man; those statements are not irreconcilable, so as to prove that one or **both writers** must be false.[372]

As I said, the Ebionites rejected the virgin birth, so they would have had a problem with the infancy narrative now found in Matthew 1-2. In his book *Lost Christianities*, Bart D. Ehrman writes, "The Matthew used by the Ebionite Christians would have lacked the first two chapters."[373] I agree with Ehrman. Still, it seems from Augustine's reply that some also suspected that the words, "Christ was the Son of David," (Matthew 1:1,) were written by one man, but the subsequent virgin birth narrative was written by another. Do the first two chapters of Matthew contain an amalgamation of two contradictory texts?

Notice what Epiphanius says of the Ebionites' version of Matthew.

> For by supposedly using their same so-called Gospel according to Matthew, Cerinthus and Carpocrates want to prove from the beginning of Matthew, by the genealogy, that Christ is the product of Joseph's seed and Mary. But these people have something else in mind. They falsify the genealogical tables in Matthew's Gospel and make its opening, as I said, "It came to pass in the days of Herod, king of Judaea, in the high-priesthood of Caiaphas, that a certain man, John by name, came baptizing with the baptism of repentance in the river Jordan" and so on.[374]

From this, we see that Cerinthus and Carpocrates (two men living from the latter half of the 1st century) were using the genealogy of Matthew to prove that Jesus was begotten by Joseph. *How could they have done that if the virgin birth narrative appeared immediately after that genealogy?* It seems to me that *their* text began with the assertion that Jesus was, in fact, a physical descendant of David and of Abraham (1:1) and it continued on with the genealogy (1:2-16) in an attempt to validate that claim. The subsequent introduction of a virgin birth would have thus been (and is now) contrary to the entire trajectory of the first 16 verses of Matthew 1.

It is my theory that the original Hebrew Matthew text was used to produce a corresponding Greek text, but those who possessed that Greek text also took liberties with it and added the genealogy. After this, according to my theory, another scribe (Basilides?) copied that text and added the infancy narrative along with the misapplied prophecies we find throughout Matthew and probably some of the narrative between Jesus' sayings. As we proceed you will see that **1.** The authentic Matthew was in Hebrew letters and **2.** The Greek Matthew is not a faithful copy of that Hebrew Matthew.

Symmachus, the Expert Witness

The Jewish Ebionites rejected the virgin birth while tracing their origins back to Jesus' original disciples in Jerusalem (see chapter one, *The Ebionites*). A very interesting passage in *Eusebius' Ecclesiastical History* (4th century) shows how one such Ebionite named Symmachus not only translated the Hebrew Old Testament into Greek, but also wrote commentaries denouncing the virgin birth narrative found within the New Testament Greek copies of Matthew.

Eusebius' record reads as follows:

> So earnest and assiduous was Origen's research into the divine words that he learned the Hebrew language, and procured as his own the original Hebrew Scriptures which were in the hands of the Jews. He investigated also the works of other translators of the Sacred Scriptures besides the Seventy. And in addition to **the well-known translations** of Aquila, **Symmachus**, and Theodotion, he discovered certain others which had been concealed from remote times … Having collected all of these, he divided them into sections, and placed them opposite each other, with the Hebrew text itself. He thus left us the copies of the so-called *Hexapla*. He arranged also separately an edition of Aquila and Symmachus and Theodotion with the Septuagint, in the *Tetrapla*.

> As to these translators it should be stated that **Symmachus was an Ebionite**. But the heresy of the Ebionites, as it is called, asserts that **Christ was the son of Joseph and Mary, considering him a mere man**, and insists strongly on keeping the law in a Jewish manner, as we have seen already in this history. **Commentaries of Symmachus are still extant in which he appears to support this heresy by attacking the Gospel of Matthew**. Origen states that he obtained these and other commentaries of Symmachus on the Scriptures from a certain Juliana, who, he says, received the books by inheritance from Symmachus himself.[375]

This is quite remarkable, because Origen lived 184-253 AD, and yet there was a "well known" translation from an Ebionite scholar in circulation during his time. Just how old *was* Symmachus' translation? We don't know exactly, but some have suggested that Origen's placement of Symmachus *between* Aquila and Theodotion demonstrate a *chronological* order—Thus, Symmachus wrote *after* Aquila (130 AD) and *before* Theodotion (150 at the latest). Most scholars will suggest late 2nd century. Whichever the case, we still find a well-known Christian scholar writing commentaries denouncing the virgin birth narrative in Matthew within the mid to late 2nd century (140-200 AD). I believe we should take this objection from Symmachus seriously.

Symmachus was a respected scholar, known for making good translations. His work was held in high esteem by Origen in the early 3rd century. Jerome also praised Symmachus' Hebrew-to-Greek translation of the Old Testament and made use of it while producing his Latin Vulgate.[376] The impeccable nature of Symmachus' work in translating biblical texts is enough to deem him an *authority* in his particular field of expertise, namely, *translating Hebrew manuscripts into Greek*. Now, couple that with the fact that *Matthew* was *originally* written in the Hebrew language and was *afterward* translated into Greek. Such translations are precisely where Symmachus expert assessment should be highly respected.

Jerome, also an expert in the field of manuscripts and translation, wrote the following in 393 AD:

> "Matthew, also called Levi, apostle and aforetimes publican, composed a gospel of Christ at first published in Judea **in Hebrew** for the sake of those of the circumcision who believed, but this was **afterwards translated into Greek though by what author is uncertain**. The Hebrew itself has been **preserved until the present day in the library at Cæsarea** which Pamphilus so diligently gathered. I have also had the opportunity of having the volume described to me **by the Nazarenes** of Beroea, a city of Syria, **who use it**."[377]

Now see how this all comes together. Matthew was *originally* written in Hebrew. The one who *translated* the Hebrew text of Matthew into Greek was *unknown*. After that anonymous translation begins circulating, we find a well-known and reliable authority on such matters decrying its contents. *Furthermore*, and this is important, Jerome says the *original* Hebrew text was *still in the hands of the Nazarenes!* Symmachus was himself a Nazarene (which, as I explained in chapter one, is synonymous with *Ebionite*). The Nazarenes were even being called *Symmachians*[378] during the times of Jerome, who said they possessed the *Hebrew* Matthew text that was, quote, "preserved until the present day." It gets even better. Jerome said that the preserved Hebrew text was kept "in the library at *Caesarea*." Now, *where* did Symmachus do his translation work? We don't have much to go on, but it was *most likely Caesarea*.

> "The book I found in the house of Juliana the virgin **in Caesarea**, when I was hiding[379] there; who said that **she received it from Symmachus himself**, the interpreter of the Jews." —*Origen*[380]

Symmachus was a reputable *authority* on Hebrew-to-Greek translations who had strong ties to *Caesarea, where the original Hebrew text was preserved*. If Symmachus said there was a corrupt version of Matthew going around, his assertion should be accepted. He was a Christian who believed in Jesus Christ. He affirmed, with other Ebionites, that Matthew was authentic. He was not attacking the *preserved* Hebrew Gospel of Matthew, he was only attacking the version of Matthew that contained the virgin birth infancy narrative.

> "Symmachus was an Ebionite. ... Ebionites, as it is called, asserted that Christ was born of Joseph and Mary and supposed him to be a mere man ...There are commentaries of Symmachus still extant in which he appeared to direct his remarks against the Gospel of Matthew in order to establish this heresy."
> —*Eusebius*[381]

Jerome and "The Authentic Gospel of Matthew"

In 398 AD, Jerome wrote a commentary on the Gospel of Matthew, stating the following:

> In the Gospel which the Nazarenes and Ebionites use, which we have recently translated from Hebrew to Greek, and which most people call **the authentic Gospel of Matthew**, the man who had the withered hand is described as a mason who begged for help in the following words: "I was a mason, earning a living with my hands; I beg you, Jesus, restore my health to me so that I need not beg for my food in shame."[382]

This is quite informative. Jerome says that, during his day, most people considered the Hebrew[383] Gospel *used by the Ebionites* "the *authentic* Matthew." Jerome says he "recently translated [it] from Hebrew to Greek." Now, if the Hebrew Matthew was *identical* to the Greek Matthew text that was *already* in circulation (as we discussed under the former heading), then *why translate the Hebrew Matthew into Greek all over again?* We need not speculate *if* it was different, because Jerome confirmed that it was when talking about the man with the withered hand.

Advocates of the virgin birth narratives accused their opponents of altering Matthew to suit their own beliefs. For example, Epiphanius said the Ebionites falsified the genealogy in Matthew and had an altered text.

> They falsify the genealogical tables in Matthew's Gospel and make its opening, as I said, "It came to pass in the days of Herod, king of Judaea, in the high-priesthood of Caiaphas, that a certain

man, John by name, came baptizing with the baptism of repentance in the river Jordan" and so on.[384]

Was the Ebionite Matthew corrupted? As we will see from other examples, false accusations of textual corruption were often made against the Ebionites. For instance, Irenaeus accused the Ebionites of altering Isaiah 7:14 to read "the young woman" instead of "the virgin," writing thus:

> Let those, therefore, who **alter the passage of Isaiah** thus, "Behold, a young woman shall conceive," and who will have Him to be Joseph's son, also alter the form of the promise which was given to David, when God promised him to raise up, from the fruit of his belly, the horn of Christ the King. But they did not understand, otherwise **they would have presumed to alter even this passage also**.[385]

Irenaeus thought he was *amending* a recent textual corruption, but he was actually only imposing an anachronistic definition for παρθένος upon the Septuagint text. His accusations of textual corruption were false. Scholars know that the text of Isaiah 7:14 *always* meant *young woman*. Tertullian also falsely accused others of altering the text of John 1:13.[386] According to him, the text originally read, "**Who was** [singular] born, not of blood, nor of the will of the flesh, nor of the will of man, but of God." Tertullian used this version of John 1:13 as a proof text for the virgin birth theme. Yet, scholars recognize that Tertullian's accusations of a textual corruption in John 1:13 are also false.[387] Hence, we have two examples of very prominent theologians falsely accusing others of altering Scripture when, in fact, they had not. Nor were these accusations unrelated to our present investigation. These men specifically accused others of changing the Bible so they could correspondingly deny that Jesus was born of a virgin. If they were wrong about those other "virgin birth proof texts," were they also wrong when asserting that the Ebionites removed Matthew 1-2 as well?

Trypho's Gospel, Justin's Memoirs

Justin Martyr's book titled *Dialogue with Trypho* was written around 155 AD and recounts his interactions with a certain group of contemporaneous Jews. The main character from that group was a Jewish man named *Trypho*, hence the title *Dialogue with Trypho*. Near the outset of their discussion, Trypho says he is familiar with the Gospel and has read it carefully.

> **Trypho:** "Moreover, I am aware that your precepts in the so-called **Gospel** are so wonderful and so great, that I suspect no one can keep them; for **I have carefully read them**."[388]

Here we see a 2nd century Jew who is familiar with Christianity and had carefully read that which was commonly referred to as "the Gospel." Justin did not have to ask Trypho *which* Gospel it was that he read. When the Jewish man said he read the Gospel, Justin knew exactly which text that was. Accordingly, Justin goes on to quote sayings of Jesus, knowing that they would be *familiar* to Trypho *since* they were contained within that Gospel text.

> **Justin:** "For He appeared distasteful to you when He cried among you, 'It is written, My house is the house of prayer; but ye have made it a den of thieves!' He overthrew also the tables of the money-changers in the temple, and exclaimed, 'Woe unto you, Scribes and Pharisees, hypocrites! because ye pay tithe of mint and rue, but do not observe the love of God and justice. Ye whited sepulchres! appearing beautiful outward, but are within full of dead men's bones.' And to the Scribes, 'Woe unto you, Scribes! for ye have the keys, and ye do not enter in yourselves, and them that are entering in ye hinder; ye blind guides!' "For **since you have read**, O Trypho, as you yourself admitted, the doctrines taught by our Saviour, I do not think that I have done foolishly in adding some short utterances of His to the prophetic statements."[389]

Some of those sayings of Christ that Justin cites from "the Gospel" known to Trypho are verses *common*[390] to both Luke and Matthew. However,

Justin *goes on* to quote texts *only* found in Matthew, as if those were the texts that would be familiar to Trypho (*i.e.,* as if they were in that Gospel Trypho read).[391] Here is a prime example where Justin identifies the source text as "the Gospel," then quotes a verse that is *only found in Matthew*.

> **Justin:** "Also in **the Gospel** it is **written** that He said: 'All things are delivered unto me by My Father;' and, 'No man knoweth the Father but the Son; nor the Son but the Father, and they to whom the Son will reveal Him.'"[392]

The text Justin quotes is not found in Mark, Luke, or John, but *only in Matthew* (Matthew 11:27). Hence, "the Gospel" known to the Jews at that time was composed of texts specifically found in Matthew. Therefore, if that Matthew text circulating among the Jews contained the infancy narrative, Trypho should have been familiar with that as well, right? Let's see if he was. Let us also see whether Justin quotes the infancy narrative as something found in "the Gospel," or whether he introduces a new source for that information.

The very first time that Justin says Jesus was born of a virgin, he does *not* quote anything from "the Gospel," but specifically identifies the virgin birth with a message *told* to him by an old man.

> **Justin:** "I used to go into a certain field not far from the sea. And when I was near that spot one day, which having reached I purposed to be by myself, a certain old man, by no means contemptible in appearance, exhibiting meek and venerable manners, followed me at a little distance. And when I turned round to him, having halted, I fixed my eyes rather keenly on him. And he said …'There existed, long before this time, certain men more ancient than all those who are esteemed philosophers, both righteous and beloved by God, who spoke by the Divine Spirit, and foretold events which would take place, and which are now taking place. They are called **prophets**. … They were entitled to credit on account of the miracles which they performed, since they both glorified the Creator, the God and Father of all things, and **proclaimed**

> **His Son, the Christ** [sent] by Him.' ... [Justin then says to Trypho] "When he had spoken these and many other things, which there is no time for mentioning at present, he went away, bidding me attend to them; and I have not seen him since. ... Wherefore, Trypho, **I will proclaim to you**, and to those who wish to become proselytes, the divine message **which I heard from that man**. Do you see that the elements are not idle, and keep no Sabbaths? Remain as you were born. For if there was no need of circumcision before Abraham, or of the observance of Sabbaths, of feasts and sacrifices, before Moses; no more need is there of them now, <u>after that, according to the will of God, Jesus Christ the Son of God has been born without sin,</u> **of a virgin** <u>sprung from the stock of Abraham.</u>[393]

Here is the very first time that Justin mentions a virgin birth. He does not relate it to that "Gospel" already being discussed (Matthew), but rather to a message that an old man told him one day. That old man said Jesus was *God's Son*, but we are not initially told what the old man meant by that phrase (or at least what Justin *understood* that phrase to mean). Yet, when Justin decides to expound upon that message from the old man in greater detail, he instantly starts saying Jesus was born of a virgin. In fact, the Greek text[394] translated as the underlined portion in the previous quote above would more literally be rendered as:

> "After that, according to the will of God, separated, without sin, of a virgin (from the stock of Abraham) was begotten the Son of God, Jesus Christ."

Justin is saying that God begat his Son from a virgin. Thus, the *Son* and *begetting* aspect, according to Justin's lead off statement here, relates to Jesus being *born of a virgin*.

Trypho *already* said he read "the Gospel" in chapter 10 of the *Dialogue with Trypho*, before this virgin birth concept was mentioned in chapter 21. In chapter 18, Justin *already* felt at liberty to repeat things he knew were in the Jew's Gospel *before* he brought up the virgin birth in chapter 21. Why didn't Justin relate the virgin birth to something that was already in the Gospel? I mean, the Gospel is brought out in chapter 10, and they are talking about its contents as something familiar to them both in chapter 18. Yet, there is *another source* of information brought out in chapter 21 when introducing the virgin birth. *Why?*

So far, Justin Martyr is not citing any *written* records of Jesus' birth, even though "the Gospel" Trypho "read" was familiar to both men and contained texts exclusive to Matthew. As we will see, when Justin *finally* cites a text that is found *only in Luke* (much later on in chapter 86), he introduces it as *part of* ***a single text*** *that contains quotations from* ***both*** *Luke and Matthew*.

This is the first instance where Justin cites a text exclusive to Luke (Luke 10:19). Notice how it *also* contains a text exclusive to Matthew as well (Matthew 25:41).

> **Justin:** "Again, **in other words** (ἐν ἄλλοις λόγοις), by which He shall condemn those who are unworthy of salvation, He said, 'Depart into outer darkness, which the Father has prepared for Satan and his, angels.' And again, **in other words** (ἐν ἑτέροις λόγοις), He said, 'I give unto you power to tread on serpents, and on scorpions, and on scolopendras, and on all the might of the enemy.'"[395]

This might not look like much to the English reader, but there is an important dynamic going on here in the Greek text. First, Justin began by referring to "other (ἄλλοις) sayings (λόγοις)" of Jesus. Then he quotes a text that can *only* be traced to Matthew 25:41. What happened next is crucial, though. Justin *then* said, "Again in (ἐν) other (**ἑτέροις**) sayings (λόγοις)." What this means is, *Justin's second quote is coming **from the same text as the first one!*** This may sound confusing, but it is not. The word Justin uses to introduce his *second* quote is *heterois* (ἑτέροις), which is a plural form of *heteros* (ἕτερος). *Heteros* is where, for example, we get our word *hetero*-sexual. Now, when a person is heterosexual, this means they desire *the other* sex. We do not have to guess *which* other sex is meant, because there are *only two*. This is an easy way to understand how *heteros* (ἕτερος) is used. It refers to *one of the two*.

Greek Grammar, by Herbert Weir Smyth, affirms what I am saying here in the following entry.

> **1271.** ἄλλος strictly means *other* (of several), ἕτερος other (of two).[396]

Justin initially introduced the new category of sayings as "other (ἄλλοις) sayings"—other out of several—but once *that* other group of sayings was delineated, Justin's subsequent words specify *that* other—other out of two—set of sayings. Thus, Justin has now introduced a second set of sayings which contain texts from *both* Matthew and Luke.

Look closely and see how he initially quotes texts only found in Matthew, without qualifying the source, but when he introduces the new text, he qualifies it. Yet, after that introduction is made, he subsequently begins quoting from that second text without additional qualification as well.

> **Justin** (the underlined text is my own commentary)**:** "For He alone taught openly those mighty counsels which the Father designed both for all those who have been and shall be well-pleasing to Him, and also for those who have rebelled against His will, whether men or angels, when **He said** [Justin does not qualify his source material, because he has been using Matthew all along]: 'They shall come from the east [and from the west], and shall sit down with Abraham, and Isaac, and Jacob, in the kingdom of heaven: but the children of the kingdom shall be cast out into outer darkness.'[Matthew 8:11] And, 'Many shall say to Me in that day, Lord, Lord, have we not eaten, and drunk, and prophesied, and cast out demons in Thy name? And I will say to them, Depart from Me.'[Matthew 7:22] Again, **in other words** (ἐν ἄλλοις λόγοις), by which He shall condemn those who are unworthy of salvation, **He said** [sayings of Jesus now being quoted from another source], 'Depart into outer darkness, which the Father has prepared for Satan and his angels.' [this can *only* be traced to Matthew 25:41, though it has several differences] And again, **in other words** (ἐν ἑτέροις λόγοις), **He said** [quoting from *that same source*], 'I give unto you power to tread on serpents, and on scorpions, and on

scolopendras [*i.e.*, centipedes³⁹⁷], and on all the might of the enemy.' [This is Justin's *first* use of a quote, now in chapter 76 of his *Dialogue with Trypho*, that is found *exclusively* in a Gospel *other* than Matthew. This can *only* be traced to Luke 9:22.] And now we, who believe on our Lord Jesus, who was crucified under Pontius Pilate, when we exorcise all demons and evil spirits, have them subjected to us. For if the prophets declared obscurely that Christ would suffer, and thereafter be Lord of all, yet that [declaration] could not be understood by any man until He Himself persuaded the apostles that such statements were expressly related in the Scriptures. **For He exclaimed before His crucifixion** [Justin now *continues* to quote sayings not found in "the Gospel," but he has *discontinued* prefacing these as from that second source]: 'The Son of man must suffer many things, and be rejected by the Scribes and Pharisees, and be crucified, and on the third day rise again.'" [This last quote can only be traced to either Luke 9:22 or Mark 8:31. The Luke text is a closer match.] ³⁹⁸

It is apparent that Justin's new source for quotations contains a combination of Jesus' sayings from both Matthew and Luke. Interestingly, Justin's disciple, Tatian, famously produced *Tatian's Diatessaron*, which is a harmonization of Matthew, Mark, Luke, and John. As the saying goes, "The apple doesn't fall far from the tree." Like Tatian, Justin is utilizing a harmonization of texts as well. And, although he was formerly only quoting the Gospel of Matthew, now that Justin has introduced this *other* source, we instantly see him quoting texts exclusive to Luke as well. Yet, after his *initial introduction* of the "other" source material, he leaves off referencing it (for now) and then continues to quote texts outside of Matthew without specifying that source. The clarification of Justin's second source did not occur until chapter 76 of his *Dialogue with Trypho*. Isn't it interesting that we first find him referring to the Matthew infancy narrative in the very next chapter (77)? Although Justin formerly relayed the old man's message, which he took to mean that Jesus was born of a virgin, and although Justin has been trying to back up that claim with prophecies from the Tanakh (the Old Testament), he has not yet quoted *any* infancy narrative[s] or even told any of their stories. Suddenly, in chapters 77-78, immediately after bringing his "other" source of quotes into play in chapter

76, Justin begins relaying *both* of those infancy narratives from that single, harmonized text.

> **Justin** (the underlined text is my own commentary): "For at the time of His birth, Magi who came from Arabia worshipped Him, coming first to Herod, who then was sovereign in your land, and whom the Scripture calls king of Assyria on account of his ungodly and sinful character. ... [This whole narrative about sorcerers coming to worship Jesus is only found in the Matthew infancy narrative] Now this king Herod, at the time when the Magi came to him from Arabia, and said they knew from a star which appeared in the heavens that a King had been born in your country, and that they had come to worship Him, learned from the elders of your people that it was thus written regarding Bethlehem in the prophet: 'And thou, Bethlehem, in the land of Judah, art by no means least among the princes of Judah; for out of thee shall go forth the leader who shall feed my people.' Accordingly the Magi from Arabia came to Bethlehem and worshipped the Child, and presented Him with gifts, gold and frankincense, and myrrh; but returned not to Herod, being warned in a revelation after worshipping the Child in Bethlehem. And Joseph, the spouse of Mary, who wished at first to put away his betrothed Mary, supposing her to be pregnant by intercourse with a man, *i.e.*, from fornication, was commanded in a vision not to put away his wife; and the angel who appeared to him told him that what is in her womb is of the Holy Ghost. Then he was afraid, and did not put her away; [This next part about a census is from the Luke infancy narrative] but on the occasion of the first census which was taken in Judæa, under Cyrenius, he went up from Nazareth, where he lived, to Bethlehem, to which he belonged, to be enrolled; for his family was of the tribe of Judah, which then inhabited that region. [Now the story mixes the two infancy narratives together. Notice that it also says Jesus was born in a cave, which is traced to the apocryphal *Protoevangelium of James*] Then along with Mary he is ordered to proceed into Egypt, and remain there with the Child until another revelation warn them to return into Judæa. But when the Child was born in Bethlehem, since Joseph could not find a lodging in that village, he took up his

quarters in **a certain cave** near the village; and while they were there Mary brought forth the Christ and placed Him in a manger, and here the Magi who came from Arabia found Him.[399]

After Justin relays this infancy narrative to Trypho, asserting that Isaiah 7:14 was fulfilled thereby, *Trypho's very next words* are, "The utterances of God are holy, but your expositions are mere contrivances, as is plain from what has been explained by you."[400] Does this sound like Trypho was familiar with Justin's position? No. Yet, Justin *was* familiar with "the Gospel" that Trypho carefully read. However, despite Justin's *continued* reference to a virgin birth, he *never* quotes the infancy narrative in Matthew [or Luke] until *after* he introduced a second source, which consists of texts and narratives from *both* [our] Matthew and Luke.

Trypho's assertion that Justin was fabricating explanations happened in chapter 79 of Justin's *Dialogue with Trypho*. In chapter 81, Justin again quotes a text exclusive to Luke (Luke 20:35-36). This, as I have stated, is now coming from a single source that has a *combination* of texts from Matthew and Luke. The source of this second collection of sayings has not yet been *named*, but Justin does say the following in chapter 88.

> **Justin:** "And then, when Jesus had gone to the river Jordan, where John was baptizing, and when He had stepped into the water, a fire was kindled in the Jordan; and when He came out of the water, the Holy Ghost lighted on Him like a dove, [as] the apostles of this very Christ of ours wrote."[401]

It is plausible that Justin could mean the apostles *each* wrote about the Holy Ghost coming down, but it is likely that when he refers to the *apostles'* (plural) writings (since his new source text is a *combination* of at least Matthew and Luke), he is describing his second source. Justin is quoting a text which was distinct from "the Gospel" and contains texts from both Matthew and Luke and he has now [possibly] said it [singular] contains the writings of the apostles [plural]. This assessment of Justin's statement is supported by what I will show next.

Justin continues to quote texts that are from his second collection of sayings. In chapter 100, Justin eventually gives a precise quote—not the paraphrasing he has been doing—of a text *only* found in Matthew, which he specifies as coming from "the Gospel."

> **Justin:** "Also in **the Gospel** it is written that He said: 'All things are delivered unto me by My Father;' and, 'No man knoweth the Father but the Son; nor the Son but the Father, and they to whom the Son will reveal Him.'[Matthew 11:27]"[402]

This is it for Justin. He is about to refer to those other sayings once again, correlate a Gospel text one last time, and afterward move on to emphasizing that second source with no further mentions of the former.

> **Justin** (the underlined text is my own commentary)**:** "Also in **the Gospel** it is written that He said: 'All things are delivered unto me by My Father;' and, 'No man knoweth the Father but the Son; nor the Son but the Father, and they to whom the Son will reveal Him.'[Matthew 11:27]" Accordingly He revealed to us all that we have perceived by His grace out of the Scriptures [Justin asserts here that Christ has revealed these things to them from the prophecies, but why isn't he citing the Gospel Trypho knew of?], so that we know Him to be the first-begotten of God, and to be before all creatures; likewise to be the Son of the patriarchs, since He assumed flesh by the Virgin of their family, and submitted to become a man without comeliness, dishonoured, and subject to suffering. Hence, also, among His words [ἐν τοῖς λόγοις αὐτοῦ - in *those sayings of his*] He said, when He was discoursing about His future sufferings: 'The Son of man must suffer many things, and be rejected by the Pharisees and Scribes, and be crucified, and on the third day rise again.' [This text is *common* to Matthew and Luke] He said then that He was the Son of man, either because [Notice the uncertainty of Justin on this matter, which demonstrates there was no official, preestablished explanation for this] of His birth by the Virgin, who was, as I said, of the family of David, and Jacob, and Isaac, and Abraham; **or** because Adam was the father both of Himself and of those who have been first enumerated from whom

Mary derives her descent. For we know that the fathers of women are the fathers likewise of those children whom their daughters bear. For [Christ] called one of His disciples— previously known by the name of Simon—Peter; since he recognized Him to be Christ the Son of God [this record of *Simon being named Peter because of this* is **only** found in Matthew 16:18], by the revelation of His Father: **and** since we [there is no "since" in the Greek[403] here. It simply reads "and we"] find it recorded in the memoirs of His apostles that He is the Son of God, and **since** [again, there is no "since" in the Greek] we call Him the Son, we have understood [νενοήκαμεν – *we have conquered*] that [there is no "that" here in the Greek. The text *transitions* with καί (and), so should be read, "…we call him Son. We have conquered. And…" Justin has assembled his witnesses and now claims victory for their assertions. Now he proceeds to *elaborate* on who this one vindicated as *Son of God* is] He proceeded before all creatures from the Father by His power and will (for He is addressed in the writings of the prophets in one way or another as Wisdom, and the Day, and the East, and a Sword, and a Stone, and a Rod, and Jacob, and Israel); and that [no "that" here in the Greek, only καί (and)] He became man by the Virgin."[404]

Justin has compiled his witnesses. He says **1.** Christ showed them that the prophecies in the Old Testament announced he would be the Son of God. **2.** In "the Gospel" Jesus is called the Son of God—Justin quotes two texts *only* found *in Matthew* (Matthew 11:27 and 16:18), both of which say Christ is the Son of God. **3.** Justin then adds his *third witness*, which he calls *The Memoirs of the Apostles*,[405] wherein Christ is called Son of God as well. He thus distinguishes this text from "the Gospel." **4.** Finally, drawing on the testimony of Christians in his day as the fourth witness, he says, "And we call him Son." Then, in view of his collection of witnesses, Justin declares, "We have conquered." What follows *thereafter* is a *recap* of Justin's assertions that Jesus existed before his humanity and was afterward born of a virgin.

Feeling as if his position has been vindicated here in chapter 100, Justin now frees himself to parade that second source which he has passively referenced since chapter 76. Consider how Justin did not even introduce this text until chapter 76, then passively referenced it until chapter 88, where he says it was written by the apostles, then names it for the very first time upon his declaration of victory in chapter 100. After chapter 100, where Justin first names *The Memoirs of the Apostles* and declares victory, he suddenly goes into a frenzy and names *The Memoirs* as his source multiple times—in chapters 101, 102, 103 (twice), 104, 105 (thrice), 106 (thrice), and finally again in chapter 107. *Clearly there has been a shift in his primary text!*

As I intimated formerly, the fact that Justin's text *combines* apostolic content into one manuscript accounts for the plural "apostles." It would be incorrect to call the *composite* text *Memoirs of the Apostle* (singular) because Justin's text contained passages from *both* Matthew *and* Luke. He never quotes a text from the Gospel of John and, when singling out an account *only found in Mark,* he differentiates the source as the "memoirs of *him*" (Peter)[406]—It was well known that Mark recorded Peter's recollections. Distinguishing Mark as the *Memoirs of Peter* indicates to me that it was a separate text from Justin's *Memoirs of the Apostles*. Thus, I propose that *The Memoirs of the Apostles* is a single text containing material from Mathew and Luke, but not from Mark and John. Although Justin does refer to the memoirs *individually* as "Gospels" elsewhere,[407] two of these "Gospels" could have easily been combined to form a single text and still be referred to as "Gospels." Compare how Justin's disciple, Tatian, composed *The Diatessaron* shortly after Justin wrote these things. The Diatessaron takes *all four of the Gospels* (with the infancy narratives, but without the genealogies) and merges them into one chronological narrative. *Diatessaron* means *harmony-of-four*, so referring to *Gospels* (plural) does not prohibit a single text composed of *two Gospels* (plural) from being called *The Memoirs of the Apostles*. This composite text containing material from Mathew and Luke *also has both infancy narratives* found in [our] Matthew and [our] Luke as well.

When Justin brings *The Memoirs of the Apostles* forward by name in chapter 100, this is specifically in relation to Jesus being the Son of God (which Justin relates to a virgin birth). Right after stating that Jesus is called the

Son of God in *The Memoirs of the Apostles*, Justin quotes the virgin birth narrative we find only in [our] Luke *for the first time* in that *same chapter*.

> **Justin:** "And since **we find it recorded in the memoirs of His apostles that He is the Son of God**, and since we call Him the Son, we have understood that He proceeded before all creatures from the Father by His power and will (for He is addressed in the writings of the prophets in one way or another as Wisdom, and the Day, and the East, and a Sword, and a Stone, and a Rod, and Jacob, and Israel); and that **He became man by the Virgin**, in order that the disobedience which proceeded from the serpent might receive its destruction in the same manner in which it derived its origin. For Eve, who was a virgin and undefiled, having conceived the word of the serpent, brought forth disobedience and death. But the Virgin Mary received faith and joy, when the angel Gabriel announced the good tidings to her that the Spirit of the Lord would come upon her, and the power of the Highest would overshadow her: **wherefore also the Holy Thing begotten of her is the Son of God**. [Luke 1:35]" [408]

This is Justin's first reference to the Luke infancy narrative. We have already established that, while Justin was quoting "the Gospel" that Trypho knew of (and read), those texts were from the Book of Matthew. We also saw that, after Justin introduced a second set of source material, he instantly and for the first time began quoting texts that are found only in Luke. Now we see that this other text, *The Memoirs of the Apostles*, also contains the infancy narrative of Luke as well. Yet, what about the infancy narrative of Matthew? Justin *never* says that the infancy narrative of Matthew is found in that Matthew text known to Trypho, but in chapter 106 of his *Dialogue* he *does* say it is found in The Memoirs of the Apostles.

> **Justin:** "Accordingly, when a star rose in heaven at the time of His birth, **as is recorded in the memoirs of His apostles**, the Magi from Arabia, recognizing the sign by this, came and worshipped Him."[409]

Thus, Justin lets us know that the infancy narrative of Matthew was found in that secondary text of his.

Trypho was familiar with that version of Matthew circulating among the Jews. He read it carefully. He knew it was authentic to Christianity. It was at the forefront of his conversation with Justin. Why would Justin *bypass* that "Gospel" when specifying where the Matthew infancy narrative was recorded? Why refer to undocumented hearsay when *introducing* the virgin birth? Why didn't Justin even *mention* a documented source for the infancy narratives until after he introduced a second source text? Why was Trypho *shocked* by Justin's correlation of Isaiah 7:14 to the Matthew infancy narrative events? It is apparent in Justin's *Dialogue with Trypho, the Jew*, that Trypho has been exposed to Ebionite Christians prior to his encounter with Justin. Trypho continuously contrasts an Ebionite Christology with what is being proposed by Justin.[410] He acts like what Justin is saying is new to him.[411] This Jewish man was indeed familiar with Christianity and the Gospel of Matthew, but it was the Christianity of the Ebionites and the Gospel of Matthew in circulation amongst *them*. The Ebionites asserted that the infancy narrative was not originally part of the Matthew text. Their assertion is vindicated here yet once again. The infancy narrative obviously did not exist in Trypho's Matthew.

Origin of the Matthew Infancy

The notion that Jesus did not have genuine flesh and blood was being spread in the earliest days of the Christian movement.

> "Little children, it is the last time: and as ye have heard that antichrist shall come, even now are there many antichrists; whereby we know that it is the last time. ... Hereby know ye the Spirit of God: Every spirit that confesseth that Jesus Christ is **come in the flesh** is of God: And every spirit that confesseth not that Jesus Christ is come **in the flesh** is not of God: and this is that spirit of antichrist, whereof ye have heard that it should come; and even now already is it in the world." (1 John 2:18, 4:2-3)

There was a fight going on. Some were professing to be Christians while asserting that Jesus did not have genuine flesh. The earliest man said to have taught this doctrine, that Jesus did not have human flesh, was mentioned by name in the Bible.

> "But there was a certain man, called Simon, which beforetime in the same city used sorcery, and bewitched the people of Samaria, giving out that himself was some great one: To whom they all gave heed, from the least to the greatest, saying, This man is the great power of God. ... And when Simon saw that through laying on of the apostles' hands the Holy Ghost was given, he offered them money, Saying, Give me also this power, that on whomsoever I lay hands, he may receive the Holy Ghost. But Peter said unto him, Thy money perish with thee, because thou hast thought that the gift of God may be purchased with money. For I perceive that thou art in the gall of bitterness, and in the bond of iniquity."
>
> (Acts 8:9-10, 18-23)

After Simon was rebuked by Peter, history tells us that he began to form his own version of Christianity.

> "There is the (infamous) Simon of Samaria in the Acts of the Apostles, who chaffered for the Holy Ghost: after his condemnation by Him, and a vain remorse that he and his money must perish together, he applied his energies to the destruction of the truth, as if to console himself with revenge."
>
> —*Tertullian, 210 AD*[412]

Simon began to claim that he himself was the Son of God who had recently "come down" to the people in Samaria. He also said he was Jesus who appeared formerly to the Jews, but that he did not really suffer even though he appeared to have died on the cross.

> "Simon was a sorcerer, and came from Gitthon, the city in Samaria—though it is a village now. He deluded the Samaritan people by deceiving and catching them with his feats of magic, and said that he was the supreme power of God and had **come down**

> **from on high**. To the Samaritans he called himself the Father; but **to Jews he said he was the Son**, though he had **suffered without suffering**, but **suffered only in appearance**."
>
> —*Epiphanius, 375 AD*[413]

Thus, Simon asserted that Jesus did not have a genuine human body, which *would* have been subject to suffering. His successors taught the same thing. One was named Saturninus.

> "Saturninus … has also laid it down as a truth, that **the Saviour was without birth, without body**, and without figure, but was, **by supposition, a visible man**."
>
> —*Irenaeus, 180 AD*[414]

So far, these men deemed Jesus as a phantasmal being who only appeared to be a man. Saturninus said Jesus was "without birth." This is what Marcion believed as well, namely that Jesus first appeared among men in an adult form. Yet, there was another of Simon the Sorcerer's successors named Basilides who, according to Irenaeus, began to develop his own form of doctrine as well.

> "Arising among these men [Simon and Menander], Saturninus (who was of that Antioch which is near Daphne) and **Basilides** laid hold of some favourable opportunities, and promulgated different systems of doctrine—the one in Syria, the other at Alexandria. … Basilides again, **that he may appear to have discovered something more sublime and plausible, gives an immense development to his doctrines**."
>
> —*Irenaeus, 180 AD*[415]

Basilides taught his doctrines from around 117 to 138 AD in Egypt. What changes would he make to his predecessors' doctrine? Would he *retain* the notion that Jesus did not have genuine flesh but *add* an origin story as well? What would be his motivation? Remarkably, Basilides *was* the *first* man who ever referred to the virgin birth infancy narrative of Luke *or* of Matthew. Realize what is going on here. In accordance with what Simon taught, Basilides' version of Jesus does not have human flesh. So, a virgin birth narrative (coming into the world *absent* the normal process of procreation) *would* match his persuasion.

Here are the oldest references of those infancy narratives in Matthew and Luke, contained within quotes from Basilides.

> Now [according to Basilides] this (mystery) was not made known to previous generations, as he says, it has been written, "By revelation was made known unto me the mystery;" and, "I have heard inexpressible words which it is not possible for man to declare." The light, (therefore,) which came down from the Ogdoad above to the Son of the Hebdomad, descended from the Hebdomad upon Jesus the son of Mary, and he had radiance imparted to him by being illuminated with the light that shone upon him. This, he says, is that which has been declared: "**The Holy Spirit will come upon thee**," (meaning) that which proceeded from the Sonship through the conterminous spirit upon the Ogdoad and Hebdomad, **as far as Mary; "and the power of the Highest will overshadow thee**," (meaning) the power of the anointing, (which streamed) from the (celestial) height above (through) the Demiurge, as far as the creation, which is (as far as) the Son. ... And that each thing, says (Basilides), has its own particular times, the Saviour is a sufficient (witness) when He observes, "Mine hour is not yet come." **And the Magi (afford similar testimony) when they gaze wistfully upon the (Saviour's) star**. For (Jesus) Himself was, he says, mentally preconceived at the time of the generation of the stars, and of the complete return to their starting-point of the seasons in the vast conglomeration (of all germs). ... According to them, this constitutes the gospel. Jesus, however, was born, according to these (heretics), as we have already declared. And when the generation which has been previously explained took place, all the events in our Lord's life occurred, according to them, in the same manner as they have been described in the Gospels.[416]

Basilides affirms *both* infancy narrative accounts. How did we get to this point? Where did he get his references from? Let's look at the life of Basilides and see what occurred.

According to Archelaus (3rd century), Basilides was associated with *the Persians* (perhaps he came from Persia).

> **Among the Persians** there was also a certain promulgator of similar tenets, one Basilides, of more ancient date, who lived no long time after the period of our apostles.[417]

According to Clement of Alexandria (195 AD), the magi in Matthew 2 were believed to have come from Persia as well.

> The **Magi of the Persians**, who foretold the Saviour's birth, and came into the land of Judaea guided by a star. [418]

Basilides was associated with Simon Magus, who was *a sorcerer* (Acts 8:9). The reason why he was even known as Simon *Magus* is because *magos* (μάγος) in the Greek—*magos* comes from *magus* in Old Persian—means *sorcerer*. The plural of *magos* is *magoi* (μάγοι), which our English Bibles render as either *magi* or, obscuring the matter more, *wise men*. So, thus far we find *sorcerers* coming from *Persia* in the Matthew infancy narrative. Was Basilides, who was associated with Persia, also a sorcerer?

> "These men [Basilides and Saturninus], moreover, **practice magic**; and use images, incantations, invocations, and every other kind of curious art."
> —*Irenaeus, 180 AD*[419]

In Matthew 2 we find *sorcerers* coming from *Persia*. Basilides is a *sorcerer* associated with *Persia*. See the connection? There is more.

In Matthew 1:1-17 we have a genealogy listed for Jesus. Yet, whoever decided to count these was apparently more desirous of mathematical symmetry than he was of an accurate count. He says the genealogy is composed of *three sets of 14*. However, *there are only 41 names* (including Jesus) and 14 x 3 = 42.

> "So all the generations from Abraham to David are **fourteen** generations; and from David until the carrying away into Babylon are

fourteen generations; and from the carrying away into Babylon unto Christ are **fourteen** generations." (Matthew 1:17)

Why is someone trying to *force* mathematical symmetry here?

> "They [Basilides and his adherents] make out the local position of the three hundred and sixty-five heavens in the same way as do **mathematicians**. For, accepting the theorems of these latter, **they have transferred them to their own type of doctrine**."
>
> —*Irenaeus, 180 AD*[420]

Is it just a *coincidence* that the very first man ever recorded as citing the virgin birth narratives looks like a perfect match for someone who might invent that infancy narrative we find in Matthew? So, was this sorcerer from the east *known* to invent writings and say they were of God? *Yes, he was*.

Jerome, writing in 398 AD, says Basilides wrote things that showed he was more interested in telling a story than he was in the truth.

> That there were many who **wrote gospels**, both Luke the evangelist testifies, when he says: "Since indeed many have tried to tell a story of the things that have been completed among us, just as they themselves who from the beginning saw the word and ministered to him have handed down to us," and the literary monuments that endure unto the present time show, monuments which, published by various authors, have been **the beginning of various heresies**—for example, the gospels according to the Egyptians: and Thomas and Matthias and Bartholomew. There is also a Gospel of the Twelve Apostles, and **of Basilides** and of Apelles, and of others whom it would be too long to list. For the present it is only necessary to say that certain men have arisen who without the Spirit and without the grace of God **"tried to tell a story" rather than to compose historical truth**.[421]

So, this teller of stories was not only the first man to ever reference the infancy narrative in Matthew, he was also the perfect candidate to invent it as well. As I said formerly, Basilides taught from around 117 to 138 AD in Egypt. This is *well* before the oldest *extant* manuscript containing the Matthew infancy narrative text.[422] Furthermore, this was early enough to account for the use of *every* extant *reference* to the Matthew infancy narrative in *anyone's* writings.

So, if we conclude that Basilides wrote much of the Matthew infancy narrative, what is he doing quoting the Luke infancy narrative as well? I am now going to present *a hypothetical scenario*, based upon known evidence, for how all this could have played out.

Basilides may have traveled from Persia to Alexandria, Egypt with two of his acquaintances, becoming acquainted with Christianity during their journey through "Glaucias, the interpreter of Peter."[423] After arriving in Alexandria, they are exposed to the same version of Matthew used by Carpocrates of Alexandria (see p. 422 herein), a Greek translation of Matthew's Gospel containing the genealogical record found in Matthew 1:1-16. Carpocraties' followers have gnostic tendencies and practice magic, but they also use their Matthew genealogy, traced to Joseph, to prove that Jesus was a physical descendent of David.

> "Carpocrates, again, and his followers maintain that the world and the things which are therein were created by angels greatly inferior to the unbegotten Father. They also hold that Jesus was the son of Joseph, and was just like other men. ... They practice also magical arts and incantations."
>
> —*Irenaeus, 180 AD*[424]

There are other magic-using "Christians" that interact with the followers of Carpocrates in Alexandria, but these are the adherents of Simon Magus, who previously travelled to and established a following in Alexandria (ANF, Vol. 8, pp. 232-233). Basilides and the other two magi join themselves to this latter sect and he takes up a role as successor to Simon Magus. Eventually, the two sorcery sects are joined into one group, with Basilides as their leader. Basilides never openly denounces anything from Carpocrates' version of Matthew, knowing his fellow sorcerers from the Carpocrates' sect hold it in high esteem. Whatever doctrinal issues arise, he and his two Persian acquaintances seek a way to explain the text as if it matches their own beliefs. Jesus *had* come from the lineage of David, like Carpocrates' text said, even if he did not have flesh. But why wouldn't he have the flesh like other men if he was a descendent of David? One day Basilides and his two friends find a solution in the Greek version of Isaiah 7:14. There it was. A *virgin* birth. Jesus must have been born of a virgin. Concluding that he and his two friends were the first to recognize Jesus' true origin, Basilides correspondingly adds a narrative in Matthew about three magi (*i.e., sorcerers*) knowing about Jesus' birth while everyone else around remained ignorant.

A Dictionary of Christian Biography, quoting Clement of Alexandria, inadvertently provides us with the names of these three magi.

> **Basilides** "named as prophets to himself **Barcabbas** and **Barcoph**, providing himself likewise with certain other [? prophets] who had no existence, and that he bestowed upon them barbarous appellations to strike amazement into those who have an awe of such things."[425]

Basilides, Barcabbas, and Barcoph were represented in the three Persian magi who knew the truth about Jesus. Those three Persian sorcerers were the good guys in his text. *They* were the knowledgeable ones. *They* had the gnosis (knowledge). Everyone needed to listen to *them* now. Like those three magi, *they* were even able to ***interpret the stars*** and predict the future, a practice identified with ***the Persian Zoroastrian*** religion.

A Dictionary of Christian Biography went on to describe the nature of the prophecies that these magi associated with Basilides gave.

> The alleged prophecies apparently belonged to the apocryphal **Zoroastrian** literature popular with various Gnostics.[426]

Basilides' sect is fascinated by him, but his Carpocrates copy of Matthew (with its freshly added infancy narrative) is now at odds with a copy used by others in Alexandria who are not part of his sorcery group. These Alexandrian Christians are already making use of the Gospel of Luke and have never even *heard* of Basilides' infancy narrative in Matthew. These two sects, Basilides' group and the Christians at Alexandria, are about to enter into a dispute over which text is to be accepted.

Basilides' Claim to Matthias/Matthew

We have already seen several correlations that point to Basilides as the author of the infancy narrative in Matthew. Yet, how could Basilides *justify* adding anything to Matthew? What would he tell others who knew Matthew did not originally contain such additional content? Interestingly, Basilides actually claimed to relay the views of *Matthew himself*.

> "Of the heresies, some receive their appellation from a [person's] name, as that which is called after Valentinus, and that after Marcion, and that after **Basilides**, although **they boast of adducing the opinion of Matthew** (Ματθου)."
>
> —*Clement of Alexandria*[427]

The Ante-Nicene Fathers translation above says "Matthew" but there is also a footnote beneath the text that says, "Miller erroneously reads Matthew." The assertion being made in the footnote is that the text refers to *Matthias* instead of Matthew. *Which is correct?* Did Basilides claim to relay the views of *Matthias* or the views of *Matthew?* The Greek word being translated here as "Matthew" is Ματθου, which is now commonly interpreted as representing *Matthias* (Ματθίας) rather than *Matthew* (Ματθαῖος). Yet, there was not always such a distinction. In fact, according to the *Strong's Concordance*, Matthew and Matthias are *both* a shortened *Greek* form of *the same Hebrew name*, מתתיה (*Mattithia*).[428] So, *to the Jews, Matthias would have been the same as Matthew.*

By the time Clement wrote the *Stromata* (around the end of the 2nd century) a distinction between the names Matthias and Matthew was regularly being employed by Greek-speaking Christians. However, we also find an indicator within Clement's writings that Matthew was, by some, still being identified as Matthias as well. Clement refers to "Ματθίαν (read *Matthias*), the chief of the publicans."[429] If Matthias was a publican (*i.e.*, a tax collector), this, according to the Gospels, would identify him with *Matthew the tax collector* (known to have authored the Gospel of Matthew). We also find evidence that Matthias was believed to be the selfsame Matthew in later Christian writings, because Didymus the Blind (313-398 AD) says Levi, the tax collector in Luke 5:27-29, is Matthias.

> "[Scripture] seems to call Matthew (τὸν Μαθθαῖον) "Levi" in the Gospel of Luke. Yet, it is not a question of one and the same person. Rather, Matthias (ὁ Μαθθίας), who was installed (an apostle) in place of Judas, and Levi are the same person with a double name. This is clear from the Gospel of the Hebrews."
>
> —*Didymus the Blind* [430]

Didymus says Levi the tax collector from Luke 5:27-29 is Matthias from Acts 1:23-26. Yet, we know from comparing Luke 5:27-31 to Matthew 9:9-12 that this tax collector was also known as "Matthew." Therefore, according to Didymus, Matthias was Levi, who was also known as Matthew, author of the Gospel of Matthew. Now, my point in all this is not to argue that the Matthias of Acts 1 is Matthew the tax collector. Rather, I am demonstrating that the names Matthias and Matthew were used interchangeably within early Christian circles.

> "Both the name Matthew and Matthias are translations of the Hebrew מתתיה. However, this name is also rendered in Greek by words like ματθαθίας, ματθίας, ματταθίας, ματταθία, μαθθίας, μαθθαθίας, μαθθανίας and ματθιας. From this it appears that the name Matthias was known among Greek-speaking Jews. If Hebrew- or Aramaic-speaking Jewish-Christian circles knew an apostle by the name מתתיה, it is easy to explain how that this name was translated as Matthias by some Greek-speaking Christians and as Matthew by others."
>
> —*A. F. J. Klijn* [431]

Historically, the names Matthew and Matthias were used synonymously. Therefore, when we see Basilides claiming secret knowledge from *Matthias*, we can easily take this as denoting *Matthew*, author of that very

Gospel corrupted by Basilides. A claim from Basilides to possess knowledge from Matthew makes sense, because Basilides' text is, to some extent, traced back to the authentic Gospel of Matthew. On the other hand, why would he claim a connection to the Matthias of Acts 1:23-26? Such a connection would have been less authoritative by comparison and entirely unrelated to that personalized Gospel of Matthew in his possession.

As Christianity became increasingly distanced from its Jewish roots, the fact that Matthew and Matthias were synonymous was often overlooked. Eventually, this oversight led to a miscategorization of Basilides' claims to Matthew, associating him instead with an illusive "Gospel of Matthias."

> "We know very little about [the Gospel of Matthias], but Lipsius conjectures that it was 'identical with the παραδόσεις Ματθίου which were in high esteem in Gnostic circles, and especially among the Basilidaeans.'"
>
> —*Arthur Cushman McGiffert, Ph. D.*[432]

The phrase παραδόσεις Ματθίου means *traditions of Matthias*. Clement wrote about these "traditions" from Matthias (and gives us a couple of sayings alleged to be from him), but it is unlikely that these Traditions of Matthias are identical to the Gospel of Matthias.

> "In the work known to Clement the speaker is not our Lord, but Matthias. Neither this fact nor the title 'Traditions' is favourable to the hypothesis that it was in reality a Gospel."
>
> —*James Hastings*[433]

We really don't know what book was called the "Gospel of Matthias," but I suspect that it was the *Hebrew* Gospel of Matthew (since the Jews would have called it by that name). After Basilides' version of Matthew was declared orthodox, the Hebrew version of Matthew would have been viewed as an imposter and disassociated from Basilides' text. An overemphasis on the different Greek spellings of "Matthew" may have provided the semantical opportunity to distance the Greek Matthew text from its Hebrew counterpart and, once declared a heretic, even from Basilides himself.

Luke, Without an Infancy Narrative

There were men within the 2nd century who said Luke did not originally have an infancy narrative. Marcion of Sinope lived from around 85-160 AD and was accused of using such a text.

> "Besides this, [Marcion] mutilates the Gospel which is according to Luke, removing all that is written respecting the generation of the Lord."
> —*Irenaeus*[434]

Did Marcion actually *remove* the infancy narrative from his version of Luke? Or was it *never there to begin with?* Remember, Irenaeus accused others of changing Isaiah 7:14 when they had not. Irenaeus wanted to defend the virgin birth narrative and was making accusations against those who would challenge the validity of his "proof texts." Yet, we must ask, *where did Irenaeus get **his** texts from?* Irenaeus quotes Justin Martyr at times, so we know he had access to Justin's writings. On one occasion he quotes from Justin's book entitled *Against Marcion*.[435] This was the same Marcion that Irenaeus accused of removing the infancy narrative of Luke. So, let's put the pieces together:

1. Justin used a version of Matthew and Luke that contained at least one spurious infancy narrative (as we saw under the heading *Trypho's Gospel, Justin's Memoirs*).

2. Marcion used a version of Luke that did not contain an infancy narrative at all.

3. Irenaeus is influenced by Justin Martyr and quotes Justin's work *Against Marcion*.

4. Irenaeus *concludes* that Marcion used a redacted version of Luke.

Marcion was accused of removing other texts as well, which, in my estimation, he probably did. Yet, why would he feel at liberty to do so? Was it because he knew for sure that Luke did not have the infancy narrative that was suddenly being propagated as genuine? Could Marcion have abandoned the view that Scripture was preserved because he knew it was being corrupted right in front of him?

> "As early as Irenaeus's *Adversus Haereses* (1. 27. 2) Marcion was accused of excising the first two chapters of his Gospel because they did not coincide with his view that Jesus appeared from heaven in the form of an adult man in the fifteenth year of Tiberius Caesar—that is that he was not actually born into the world. But who is to say that Irenaeus, Tertullian, and their successors were right, that these are chapters that Marcion <u>excised</u> from his account? It is at least possible, has occasionally been recognized, that the version of Luke in circulation in Marcion's home church in Sinope, on the coast of the Black Sea, didn't have these chapters, and that his view that Jesus simply appeared on the scene as an adult was surmised from the text as it was available to him."
>
> —*Bart D. Ehrman*[436]

Scholars, like Bart D. Ehrman, have pointed out that the third chapter of Luke looks like it was *originally the beginning of the Luke text*. In Ehrman's post entitled *Did Luke Originally Have Chapters 1-2?*[437] he gives the following reasons (among others) for why Luke probably originally began at chapter three.

1. The language of Luke 1-2 shows that the writing style seems to differ from the rest of the Gospel. The first two chapters appear much more Septuagintal in character.

2. The beginning of chapter 3 reads like the *beginning* of a narrative, not the continuation of a narrative.

3. Some of the central themes of chapters 1-2 are never referred to elsewhere in either the rest of the Gospel or the book of Acts (e.g., Jesus having come from Bethlehem; his mother being a virgin), even though lots of other themes from early chapters (e.g., the baptism by John) *are* referred to later.

4. The genealogy that is given in chapter 3 doesn't make sense if the Gospel already had chapters 1-2. The genealogy is given *after* the baptism. But the natural place for a genealogy is at the point in which a person is *born* (since the genealogy traces the bloodline up to the time of birth), not at the point of baptism.

These are solid reasons to conclude that Luke 1-2 were later additions to the Gospel of Luke. Yet, if Luke did not *originally* have the infancy narrative, why was it added and when?

The infancy narrative in Luke was being quoted by Justin Martyr around 160 AD, so it must have come before then. Marcion was excommunicated by the church in Rome around 144 AD, so it is plausible that he began to encounter the new content in Luke shortly before that date (removing passages of Scripture from the texts was one of the matters he was, at some point, reprimanded for). If we use the year of Marcion's excommunication as our starting point—the year he possibly became exposed to an infancy narrative in Luke—we only need to go back a little further than 144 AD to locate the initial propagation of that infancy text. This takes us to the time of Basilides, who taught in Egypt from around 117 to 138 AD.

The First Infancy Narrative Added to Luke

As we already discussed, the original Luke text started at chapter three and didn't contain any account of Jesus' birth whatsoever. It may have been an exposure to Basilides' Matthew text that caused the Christians in Alexandria to respond with their own infancy narrative (which we now find in Luke 2). This reaction to Basilides' Matthew may have even eventually occasioned the opening statement we find in Luke 1:1.

Origen commented on that opening statement in Luke as follows:

> You should know that not only four Gospels, but very many, were composed. ... We can know this from Luke's own prologue, which begins this way: "Because many have tried to compose an account." The words "have tried" imply an accusation against those

who rushed into writing gospels without the grace of the Holy Spirit.[438]

The opening line in Luke 1:1 shows us that competing versions of the Gospel were floating around. It is plausible that someone added an infancy narrative to the front of Luke's Gospel, which infancy narrative did not originally contain a virgin birth, as a response to Basilides' text. Yet, after this new version of Luke was formed, and when the virgin birth faction eventually became "orthodoxy," a *later* revisionist subsequently interwove a virgin birth narrative *into* that *first* infancy narrative, bringing it into doctrinal conformity. This double-infancy narrative theory may sound far-fetched, but we can find evidence for this within the extant version of Luke itself.

The bulk of the virgin birth based narrative is found in the *first* chapter of Luke. If Luke 1 did not exist, no one would read the account of Jesus' actual birth in Luke 2 (when accurately rendered from the Greek) and think Jesus was born of a virgin. In Luke 2, we don't find any mention at all of Mary being a virgin. To the contrary, we see the author identifying Joseph as Jesus' *father*. Furthermore, Joseph and Mary together are called Jesus' *parents*.

- "And **his father and his mother** marveled at what was said about him." (Luke 2:33 RSV)

- "And when they saw him, they were amazed: and his mother said unto him, Son, why hast thou thus dealt with us? behold, **thy father** and I have sought thee sorrowing." (Luke 2:48)

- "Now **his parents** went to Jerusalem every year at the feast of the passover. ... and when the feast was ended, as they were returning, the boy Jesus stayed behind in Jerusalem. **His parents** did not know it." (Luke 2:41-43 RSV)

These things are at odds with the whole virgin birth theme we find in the first chapter of Luke. Unsurprisingly, the wording of these passages was altered as time went on, so sometimes you will find variants that obscure the meaning of the text (like "*Joseph* and his mother" instead of "*his father* and his mother"). The quotes I have provided above reflect the true forms of the text. This information is easy to come by, so I do not want to spend time discussing these particular variants.

The fact that Joseph is called Jesus' *father* and he and Mary together are called Jesus' *parents* lets us know that this was not written by someone conveying a virgin birth theme. Notwithstanding, although *the bulk* of Luke 1 is an addition to *the bulk* of Luke 2, separating the original infancy narrative from the latter additions is not so simple. As I said, the virgin birth content was *interwoven* into the account. Thus, even in chapter 2 we find a parenthetical reference to the angel who announced the virgin conception in Luke 1. Furthermore, Mary is now described as Joseph's "**espoused** wife" (Luke 2:5) to match Luke 1:27, where Mary is described as "a virgin espoused to a man whose name was Joseph." If we take out the word "espoused," which basically means they were *engaged to be married*, the text simply says Joseph traveled with "Mary *his wife*, being great with child." Even if we *retained* "espoused" in the text, no one would read chapter 2 and think Mary was still a virgin, unless they were already told that in chapter 1. Thankfully, the changes in chapter two were very minor, which is why we can still find the original infancy narrative therein. Even so, this really is not a crucial issue, because, as we saw earlier, Luke *originally* didn't contain an infancy narrative at all. All I am pointing out now is that *there was an infancy narrative attached to the front of Luke which, at some point, did not have the virgin birth theme*. If we deem it as a *true* infancy narrative (with the virgin birth theme extracted), it will contradict the account of Jesus' relatives (at least as relayed by Julius Africanus). According to Jesus' relatives, Joseph was already deceased at the time of Mary's conception. I do not know which account is true. If the words "as was supposed" in Luke 3:23 were not added by the 2nd Lucan revisionist, that clause would seem to validate the testimony of Jesus' relatives. Fortunately, I don't see the events surrounding Jesus' birth as fundamental to the Gospel. Mark and John never even mention such things.

As long as we understand that Jesus was the descendant of David (as the genealogy of Luke 3 already established) and that he had flesh, like us, I believe we have what we need. It seems to me that, apart from Jesus' relatives, the early Christians felt the same way I do. At least they *did*, until Basilides brought in a false infancy narrative, showcasing himself and his fellow magi. Basilides' infancy narrative needed to be countered. For the Alexandrians to do so effectively, they needed to provide an infancy narrative of their own. After doing so, and adding it to the front of Luke, that first infancy narrative would itself eventually be altered as well (once the virgin birth concept overshadowed its competition).

"Isn't Luke that Ebionite Adoptionist?"

To demonstrate the doctrinal split in Alexandria, we will now look at a well-known, early Christian writing titled *The Dialogue of Jason and Papiscus* (usually dated to around 140 AD). Interestingly, this writing was believed by some to have been written by Luke.

The writings of John of Scythopolis (536-550 AD)—his writings were mistakenly attributed to Maximus the Confessor—relayed how Clement of Alexandria mistook Luke as the author of *Jason and Papiscus*.

> I have found this expression *Seven heavens* (says Maximus, in *Scholia on the work concerning the Mystical Theology*, ascribed to Dionysius the Areopagite, cap. i.) also in the *Dispute between Papiscus and Jason*, written by Aristo of Pella, which **Clement of Alexandria, in the sixth book of the *Outlines*, says was composed by Saint Luke.**[439]

Clement of Alexandria, writing at the end of the 2nd century, believed that Luke was the author of *Jason and Papiscus*. We even see the work attributed to Luke a second time by Sophronius of Jerusalem (560-638 AD), where he writes:

> The most illuminating Luke, then, reveals this splendid and welcome knowledge to us, not by putting down the information in his divine Gospel nor by writing it into the Acts of the Apostles, but by recording it in a different work of his, one that he composed in

dialogue form and to which he gave the title *Dialogue of Jason and Papiscus*.[440]

Why were these men convinced that Luke wrote *Jason and Papiscus*? Clement lived in Alexandria, Egypt. This is possibly where *Jason and Papiscus* was composed, because Celsus, writing around 175 AD, "tells us that Jason was a Hebrew Christian, while his opponent was **a Jew of Alexandria**."[441] The bulk of *Jason and Papiscus* is no longer extant. Therefore, we must learn about it from those who read and described its contents within their own extant writings. According to Celsus, the two men dialoguing in *Jason and Papiscus* were Jews, one of which was an Alexandrian Jew. Clement, living in Alexandria, had been exposed to this writing and was under the impression that it was composed by Luke. *Why? What would lead him to that conclusion?* We will get to that, but first we need to learn more about *Jason and Papiscus*.

1. Origen wrote the following about *Jason and Papiscus*, "In it a Christian is described as disputing with a Jew from the Jewish scriptures and as showing that the prophecies about the Messiah fit Jesus." (ANF, Vol. 8, p. 750.) This is precisely the format adopted in Justin's *Dialogue with Trypho*. Justin is doing the same thing as Jason was doing, namely, "disputing with a Jew from the Jewish scriptures to show that prophecies about the Messiah fit Jesus." When all of the factors are considered, it makes sense to think Justin's work was inspired by its predecessor. In fact, that seems to be the *consensus* of scholars on the matter. Justin's *Dialogue with Trypho* was inspired by *Jason and Papiscus*.[442] Since Justin's *Dialogue with Trypho* is dated 155-160 AD, *Jason and Papiscus* must have been written beforehand.

2. Origen said Jason showed Papiscus "that the prophecies about the Messiah fit Jesus." Since Justin tried to correlate Jewish prophecies to Jesus in his *Dialogue with Trypho* **by referencing events** associated with *Jesus' birth*, we can reasonably expect that Jason did the same in *Jason and Papiscus*. Therefore, like the *Dialogue with Trypho*, *Jason and Papiscus* probably contained an infancy narrative somewhere in its contents as well (or at least *referenced* an infancy narrative *known* to the Jews in Alexandria).

3. The author of *Jason and Papiscus* likely informed the reader about the *source* of the infancy narrative content, like Justin did in his *Dialogue with Trypho*. If that sourced infancy narrative was found in Luke, and if the author of *Jason and Papiscus*, while referencing that source, also claimed to be the author of that source, he could have been confused for Luke.

4. The extant fragments of *Jason and Papiscus* do show Jason claiming knowledge of when Jesus was born. He says, "We are completely justified in honoring the first of the week as the beginning of all creation, because *on this day* Christ was manifested on the earth."[443] Sophronius of Jerusalem, the man who copied this fragment, probably had access to the entire text of *Jason and Papiscus*. After Sophronius quoted this portion he made the following comment, "And this was the teaching of the inspired Luke when he composed the *Dialogue of Jason and Papiscus*, namely that the Day of the Lord is splendid, illustrious and the first in time of the rest of the days; **it is acknowledged as the day of our Savior's nativity in the flesh**."[444] It is reasonable to conclude that there was much more written in *Jason and Papiscus* on this subject. Evidently, Jason was claiming to have already relayed enough information about Jesus' birth to reference the day of its occurrence.

So, *Jason and Papiscus* contained infancy narrative material, but how can we know whether or not that infancy narrative contained a virgin birth? We have to dig a little deeper.

1. Justin Martyr did not know much about the Hebrew language. He asks the Jews listening to him for *help* understanding what the Hebrew word *Israel* means (ANF, Vol. 1, p. 262). He also makes no interaction with the Hebrew language in the Tanakh, though, in his *Dialogue with Trypho*, he combs the prophecies therein for minute details. He only ever uses the Greek translation (the Septuagint).

2. The only instance where we find Justin *confidently* expounding upon the Hebrew language is when he breaks down the etymology of *Satanas*. Justin was obviously exposed to a Hebrew/Jewish source

explaining this information beforehand. If that source was in writing from a Jew, it must have been composed in the Greek language for Justin to have even read it. This matches what we find in *Jason and Papiscus*. It was written by a Jew, but, per Jerome, was "composed in Greek." (ANF, Vol. 8, p. 749.)

3. When Justin recounts the Hebrew based etymology of *Satanas* he immediately associates this *Satanas* with a narrative of Jesus' post-baptismal temptation (ANF, Vol. 1, p. 262). Hence, it is plausible that the Jewish writing, composed in Greek, told the narrative of Jesus' baptism and temptation as well.

4. Jason was trying to cite Old Testament texts as fulfilled in Jesus, which would also account for the awkward application of Psalm 2:7 to Jesus' baptism as relayed by Justin. Justin writes: "For 'Sata' in the Jewish and Syrian tongue means apostate; and 'Nas' is the word from which he is called by interpretation the *serpent, i.e.,* according to the interpretation of the Hebrew term, from both of which there arises the single word *Satanas*. For this devil, when [Jesus] went up from the river Jordan, at the time when the voice spake to Him, 'Thou art my Son: this day have I begotten Thee.'" (ANF, Vol. 1, p. 262). This application of Psalm 2:7 *is consistent* with the theme in *Jason and Papiscus*, but it is *contrary* to how Justin viewed Jesus as God's Son *because of a virgin birth*. Justin shows discomfort with the affirmation that Jesus was begotten of God at his baptism and tries to explain the announcement away as symbolic (ANF, Vol. 1, p. 244). The fact that Justin quotes Psalm 2:7 as fulfilled in Jesus' baptism, even though he tries to explain away the point (and never emphasizes it), shows that this did not originate with Justin. He is quoting a source that *formerly* said this. A source that was trying to correlate prophecies to events in Jesus' life. This matches what we would expect to find in *Jason and Papiscus*.

5. The application of Psalm 2:7, "This day have I begotten thee," to Jesus' baptism is at odds with Jesus being begotten of God by virgin birth. Therefore, because *Jason and Papiscus* **did** apply Psalm 2:7 to Jesus' baptism, we can surmise that the author of *Jason and Papiscus* **did not** believe Jesus was born of a virgin. Hence, *Jason and Papiscus*,

like the first infancy narrative of Luke, represents a viewpoint contrary to Basilides, in Alexandria, within the first half of the 2nd century.

So, *Jason and Papiscus* predates Justin Martyr's *Dialogue with Trypho*, declared knowledge of Jesus' birth, but was written by a Jew who did not believe in the virgin birth account. Our assessment that *Jason and Papiscus* did not contain a virgin birth narrative is also reflected in the identity of its author. As we saw earlier, John of Scythopolis corrected Clement of Alexandria's misconception, informing us that "the *Dispute between Papiscus and Jason* [was] written by Aristo of Pella." Usually, *Aristo* is called *Ariston*, but that is beside the point. Ariston *of Pella* is clearly associated with *Pella*, which is where the Ebionites (or Nazarenes) were located (we discussed this in chapter one). Since the Ebionites did not believe in a virgin birth, our assertion regarding *Jason and Papiscus* finds *confirmation* via its Pellaian authorship. The connection of Ariston with the Ebionites is also evidenced in Justin's *Dialogue with Trypho*, where Justin says, "When [Jesus] had stepped into the water, a fire was kindled in the Jordan."[445] This concept of a fire kindled in the Jordan came from *The Gospel of the Ebionites*. Hence, the *Gospel of the Ebionites* was used by Ariston of Pella, who wrote *Jason and Papiscus*.

In *The Ante-Nicene Fathers*, the footnote for Justin's reference to fire in the Jordan says:

> "Justin learned this either from tradition or from apocryphal books. Mention is made of a fire both in the Ebionite Gospel and in another publication called *Pauli praedicatio*."[446]

This latter work mentioned, *Praedicatio Pauli*, is dated to the 3rd century, so it is not even old enough to be the source for Justin's fire reference. Thus, it comes from *The Gospel of the Ebionites*, repeated by Ariston of Pella when he wrote *Jason and Papiscus*, which was the precursor to Justin's *Dialogue with Trypho*. Note: *The Gospel of the Ebionites* is a Greek text, not to be confused with the Hebrew Matthew text known as *the Gospel of the Nazarenes* or *the Gospel of the Hebrews*.

Why was this Ebionite adoptionist text, *Jason and Papiscus,* attributed to Luke? I believe a theological battle occurred in Alexandria over which Gospel tradition was true. On the one side, you had Basilides and his personalized *Matthew* text, on the other side, Ebionite adoptionist Christians at Alexandria who held to *Luke's* Gospel. If the controversial split was defined in terms of *Matthew vs. Luke*, one could understand how any text that opposed the Matthew infancy narrative might have been identified with Luke as well. On the other hand, maybe it was Ariston of Pella himself who authored the first infancy narrative added to Luke (and changed Luke 3:22 to match his Psalm 2:7 application). Maybe several years had passed and Ariston had simply become known as "that guy who wrote the Luke narrative" by the time he penned *Jason and Papiscus*.

The Adoptionists Lose

Philo of Alexandria, who lived in Egypt and wrote during the time of Jesus, spoke of the Word (λόγος) as the Father's "archangelic and most ancient Word."[447] Philo had a habit of allegorizing everything in the Old Testament. When Philo said that God gave men the faculty of *reason* (λόγος), he sometimes allegorized that as a distinct, conscious, angelic being. Correspondingly, if the Judean Christians were identifying an angel with the Holy Spirit, those Alexandrian Jews would have naturally assumed the angelic Word became flesh when the Holy Spirit descended at Jesus' baptism. Thus, you would have Christ identified as the Word, who is a preexistent angel, becoming Jesus at his baptism. This was an extremely common theme amongst Alexandrian Gnostics.

Lucian, the disciple of Paul of Samosata and mentor to Arius, opposed the allegorical methods of Philo.

> "Lucian proposed to limit the symbolic interpretation characteristic of the Alexandrian allegorical tradition by emphasizing the primacy of the literal sense, whether expressed directly or metaphorically."
>
> —*The New Encyclopedia Britannica*[448]

Although this form of adoptionism traced to Philo's λόγος eventually died out, it was initially very prominent in the early years of the Christian movement. While it did not begin with the apostles of Christ, we do find this view being propagated as early as the 1st century by a man named Cerinthus, "a man who was educated in the wisdom of the Egyptians."[449] Like the Ebionites, Cerinthus "represented Jesus as having not been born of a virgin, but as being the son of Joseph and of Mary according to the ordinary course of human generation, while he nevertheless was more righteous, prudent, and wise than other men."[450] Probably while equating "Christ" to Philo's angelic λόγος, Cerinthus also taught that "after [Jesus'] baptism, Christ descended upon him in the form of a dove." This view may have eventually been adopted by *some* of the Ebionites.[451] Still, this concept of a normal human being merging with a heavenly angel as an adult was not familiar to Roman society at large. Within Greco-Roman society, calling Jesus "the Son of God" meant that he was born from a god in a similar manner to "Perseus, the son of Zeus."

While presenting a defense of Christianity to men who believed in Greek mythology, Justin Martyr acknowledged the similarities between what they believed and his assertion that Christ was born of a virgin.

> And when we say also that the Word, who is the first-birth of God, was **produced without sexual union**, and that He, Jesus Christ, our Teacher, was crucified and died, and rose again, and ascended into heaven, **we propound nothing different from what you believe regarding those whom you esteem sons of Jupiter**. For you know how many sons your esteemed writers ascribed to Jupiter: … And what kind of deeds are recorded of each of these reputed sons of Jupiter, it is needless to tell to those who already know. This only shall be said, that they are written for the advantage and encouragement of youthful scholars; for **all reckon it an honourable thing to imitate the gods**.[452]

It was deemed "an honorable thing" to imitate the gods, and Zeus was said to have a son born of a woman without sexual union. Hence, that Greco-Roman society surrounding 1st century Christianity would also lean in *that* direction when they heard that Jesus was God's Son. It was *that* kind of sonship which was being taught by Basilides. Basilides had a Jesus who was conceived in the womb without sexual union, like Perseus. Whichever doctrines matched Greco-Roman ideas about gods and goddesses the *closest* were bound to grow the *fastest* in that society dominated (quite literally) by Greco-Roman influences. Basilides claimed a pedigree that traced back to the apostles and he even had his own Gospel text. Who was going to argue with him that Jesus was born by natural means? Even if they did, that society surrounding them was steeped in Greek mythology, so the scales were tipped in Basilides' favor.

The Ebionites were also under tremendous social pressure during the time of Basilides' activity in Alexandria due to the Bar Kokhba revolt (132–136 AD). During this Jewish war, Jews were often seen as enemies of Rome. Consequently, Ebionite influence waned while Basilides' grew. Soon, someone added a virgin birth account to the existing Gospel of Luke (Proto-Luke + first infancy narrative). The new additions to Luke 1 likely targeted an Ebionite-associated audience, because the *Gospel of the Ebionites* names John the Baptist's parents, but lacks their story.

> "But the beginning of their Gospel is, 'It came to pass in the days of Herod, king of Judaea, in the high-priesthood of Caiaphas, that a certain man, John by name, came baptizing with the baptism of repentance in the river Jordan, and he was said to be of the lineage of Aaron the priest, **the son of Zacharias and Elizabeth**, and all went out unto him.'"
>
> —*Epiphanius, 375 AD*[453]

The new text in Luke 1 would have appealed to a group of people *already* familiar with those names. That same group was *also* now provided with the first, ear-tickling encounter of John the Baptist and Jesus while they were yet in their mothers' wombs. Since John the Baptist's responsibility was to announce the coming of Jesus, as soon as the pregnant mother of Jesus enters the room where he is, "John the Fetus" suddenly "*leaps* in the womb"! (Luke 1:41.) *Never too early for practice!* Yet, later on, John did not even know who Jesus was (John 1:33-34). Maybe after those awesome events in Luke 1 everyone involved just forgot what happened. Of course,

I am being sarcastic, but only toward the invented content of someone who actually *was* irreverent with the text.

Now that the Alexandrian group had a Gospel matching that of Basilides, at least in the affirmation of a virgin birth, the two groups began to coalesce under that virgin birth concept. As the original proponent of that doctrine, it is no surprise that we find Basilides referencing the Luke 1 account alongside his own magi text. That was his victory lap. Yet, there were still hurdles. The two Gospels now contained infancy narratives that just didn't match up. Even so, both groups viewed their own texts as authoritative. Someone needed to explain how *both* texts, though they contradicted one another, were yet true. Eventually, someone attempted the task. It was probably the same author of the Luke 1 virgin birth additions that also produced the *Protoevangelium of James* (150 AD). The *Protoevangelium of James* took blocks of the two infancy narratives and combined them together as one story. And, by saying that the work was written by Jesus' brother, James (though at some point he also claims to be speaking the words of Joseph[454]), it now had a pedigree on par with all of the other Gospels.

It was final! The two Gospels were *both* authoritative. Someone even produced a harmonization of their entire contents, minus the genealogies, while incorporating material from *Jason and Papiscus*. A few years later, with Basilides out of the picture, Justin Martyr would obtain a copy of that text and use it in his *Dialogue with Trypho*, referring to it as *The Memoirs of the Apostles*. Around that same time, while *individual* copies of the two Gospels are being spread far and wide, Symmachus also begins writing his commentaries on Matthew, telling everyone who will listen that something has gone awry. This account has been a simplified *theory* of what *might* have occurred.

Aristides of Athens

If truly dated to Hadrian's reign, there may be a record from around 135 AD where Aristides of Athens says Jesus was born of a virgin. Outside of Basilides, this would be the earliest affirmation of such a concept. The earliest *extant* manuscript containing Aristides' speech is dated to the 11th century. Since the extant texts do not agree with one another—they contain different titles and wording—and because the textual witness is so limited,[455] we have to be careful assuming too much here (texts were sometimes changed as time passed to match orthodoxy). In one of the versions of his speech he says, "God came down from heaven, and from a Hebrew virgin assumed and clothed himself with flesh." In the other version, "The son of the most high God, who came down from heaven for the salvation of men. And being born of a pure virgin, unbegotten and immaculate, He assumed flesh." Let's assume that at least the virgin birth part and the taking on the flesh part are both authentic (since the two themes are present in both versions).

Aristides was not just any man, he was a *Greek philosopher from Athens*. Jerome describes him as, "Aristides a most eloquent Athenian philosopher," adding that he presented his speech "while yet retaining his philosopher's garb."[456] What record do we have regarding the city of Athens? Athens was known to have been *saturated with Greek mythology*.

> "Now while Paul waited for them at Athens, his spirit was stirred in him, when he saw **the city wholly given to idolatry**. ... Then certain philosophers of the Epicureans, and of the Stoicks, encountered him. And some said, What will this babbler say? other some, He seemeth to be a setter forth of **strange gods**: because he preached unto them **Jesus**, and the resurrection. ... Then Paul stood in the midst of Mars' hill, and said, **Ye men of Athens**, I perceive that in all things ye are **too superstitious**. For as I passed by, and beheld your devotions, I found an altar with this inscription, TO THE UNKNOWN GOD. Whom therefore ye ignorantly worship, him declare I unto you." (Acts 17:16, 18, 22-23)

I don't doubt the Athenians thought Jesus was a god, because they thought this already when Paul was there. If we accept the *Syriac* version of Aristides speech, Aristides attributes his information to the Gospel, saying, "This is taught in the gospel, as it is called, which a short time ago was preached among them." The fact that he says it was preached "a short time ago" might even be taken as the recent position of the Alexandrian Jews who held that Jesus was a normal man born of a virgin. If Basilides was teaching in Egypt from 117-138 AD and the 2nd Luke infancy coincided with that timeframe, then we could fathom a new announcement of doctrine in Alexandria, tied into the Gospels, happening in 120 AD, the word of which was spread to Athens by 130 AD.

> "For all the Athenians and strangers which were there spent their time in **nothing else**, but either to **tell**, or to **hear** some **new** thing."
> (Acts 17:21)

Even though Aristides of Athens is said to have declared a virgin birth as early as Hadrian's reign, there was another individual who presented a defense of Christianity to Hadrian as well, namely, *Ariston of Pella*, that same *Ebionite* whom we discussed formerly.

> "In this year (134 CE), the Pellaian Ariston, who is mentioned by Eusebius Pamphilus in his *Ecclesiastical History*, (he) presented a composition (in the form of an) apology concerning our religion to the Emperor Hadrian."
> —*The Chronicon Paschale, 640 AD*[457]

The virgin birth assertions about Christ were *never* more ancient than the belief that Jesus was conceived by natural generation.

Concluding Remarks

We have now seen enough evidence to justifiably conclude that the virgin birth infancy narratives of Matthew and Luke are spurious. Let's briefly review some of the points made.

1. Isaiah 7:14 was not even about a virgin giving birth. The application of the prophecy to Jesus' birth in Matthew 1:23 is erroneous (discussed on pp. 78-84 herein).

2. Outside of Matthew 1-2 and Luke 1-2, the virgin birth theme is *never even mentioned* in the entire Bible.

3. The infancy narratives contain *contradictory* accounts. Both cannot be true. In Matthew's account, Herod the Great is trying to kill Jesus, but in Luke Herod the Great was already dead when Jesus was born.

4. The genealogies pertain *only* to Joseph, not Mary, and thus would be *irrelevant* if Jesus were born of a virgin. This shows that the virgin birth theme was added after the Gospels' genealogical records were already present.

5. Jesus' relatives reportedly passed on the genealogy in Luke, which Julius Africanus affirmed while simultaneously rebuking others for fabricating their own explanations. According to this account, Jesus was the son of Joseph's brother, but was accounted as Joseph's son due to a Levirate marriage.

6. Jesus often referred to himself as the Son of Man, and even once as "a Son of [a] man."

7. Jerome said most considered the Hebrew Gospel used by the Ebionites to be "the authentic Matthew." However, the Ebionites did not accept the virgin birth theme. Since those who used the authentic Matthew did not believe in a virgin birth, it was evidently *non-existent* in the authentic version of Matthew.

8. Symmachus was a reliable expert in Hebrew to Greek translations. He most likely did his work in Caesarea, where the authentic version of Matthew was known to exist. Yet, we find him writing commentaries on Matthew in the 2nd century denouncing the virgin birth theme as false.

9. Trypho the Jew was already familiar with the Gospel of Matthew in the mid. 2nd century, yet Justin Martyr had to bring up *other* sources of information to introduce the virgin birth theme during their discussion.

10. Basilides and his two magi counterparts were most likely responsible for the Matthew infancy narrative fabrication. Those three magi were

suspiciously identifiable with the Zoroastrian magi from the East found within that Matthew infancy narrative account.

11. Basilides was the first man in known history to affirm the account of the three magi in Matthew.

12. The third chapter of Luke (in our versions) was considered the *beginning* of Luke's Gospel by Marcion in the middle of the 2nd century. We saw several points from Bart D. Ehrman demonstrating that this was indeed the case.

13. Marcion was accused of removing the infancy narrative account from Luke by Irenaeus and Tertullian, but those men mistakenly accused others of changing texts regarding Jesus' birth as well, when no such alterations occurred.

14. Basilides went to Alexandria, Egypt, where he taught in the first half of the 2nd century. There was also an Ebionite adoptionist influence present in Alexandria as well, which is evident because Ariston of Pella wrote *Jason and Papiscus* (about an Alexandrian Jew) in the same timeframe.

15. Variations between Gospel texts accounts for the opening statement of Luke 1:1, where other written accounts are said to have occasioned that Lucan edition.

16. The *first* infancy narrative added to Luke did not even contain a virgin birth theme, instead referring to Joseph as Jesus' "father."

17. That first infancy narrative in Luke was possibly tied to the work of the Ebionite adoptionist Ariston of Pella, which would explain why Clement of Alexandria afterward thought *Jason and Papiscus*—the work of Ariston—was also written by Luke.

18. Eventually the Luke text, after its "Ariston additions," was also modified to incorporate the virgin birth theme as well.

Appendix H
Paul of Samosata on Jesus' Birth

Here, I will relay the source material commonly brought forth by those who say Paul taught a virgin birth, demonstrating that no such conclusion is justified.

Athanasius wrote "the Samosatene held that the Son was not before Mary, but received from her the origin of his being."[458] This was not stated in the context of whether Christ was born of *a virgin* (it actually only says *Mary*). The context only relates to whether Christ preexisted before he was conceived in the womb of his mother. Any of us might be said to have received the origin of our existence in our mother's womb, yet this in no way entails a virgin conception.

There are a couple of other texts related to Paul of Samosata called the *Acta* and *The Letter of the Six Bishops* where similar statements ("from the body of Mary" and "born of Mary"[459]) are made. These things related specifically to *when* Jesus began to exist—He was *from* Mary. These do not indicate virgin birth.

I have seen allegations that "the Virgin bore [Jesus] by the Holy Spirit" is found in the excerpts from *Paul to Sabinus*. These excerpts are preserved in a book entitled *Doctrina Patrum de Incarnatione Verbi*. I was not able to find an English translation of the text, but the Greek text is printed at length in the German edition by Franz Diekamp. I personally examined the quotes from Paul of Samosata therein (pp. 303-305) and there is *no mention at all* of virgin birth there. The passage *associated* with Paul that *does* talk about Christ ἐκ παρθένου (from a virgin) is located in an entirely separate area of the text (p. 14, modified and repeated on p.176). This is completely unrelated to Paul's quotes in *Paul to Sabinus*. Furthermore, the ἐκ παρθένου (from a virgin) text is *not* quoting Paul of Samosata. It is contained in a statement of faith meant to *contradict* Paul and defend the Nicene usage of ὁμοούσιος (homoousios). Hence, when that synodic statement of faith goes on to say Jesus was "begotten from a virgin according to the flesh," this is stated within a text that *contradicts* Paul. Now, this does not *necessitate* that the *specific mention* of virgin birth was contradicting Paul, but it could have been. A modified version of the ἐκ παρθένου (from a virgin) statement—now claiming that Mary is the *Mother of God*—is repeated on page 176, which is explicitly countering the doctrine of Nestorius (who rejected calling Mary the "Mother of God"). Since that *modified* statement *was* used as a *counter* to Nestorius, it makes sense to think the *original* statement regarding virgin birth was possibly meant to counter Paul of Samosata as well. And if so, it means that Paul did *not* teach a virgin birth.

The only other place that I know of where Paul of Samosata is alleged to affirm a virgin birth is in a work attributed to Athanasius called *On the Incarnation of Our Lord Jesus Christ, Against Apollinaris*. In the common English translation of this text, we find the words, "Paul of Samosata acknowledges God from the virgin."[460] Yet, those who say this is Paul affirming a virgin birth have failed to account for the statement made immediately afterward in that same text, "And Marcion and Manichaeus say that God has come among us through the virgin."[461] It is *well* known that *neither* Marcion *nor* Manichaeus claimed Jesus was born of a virgin. According to Marcion, who rejected the first two chapters of Luke,[462] Jesus simply descended from heaven in his adult form.[463] Additionally, the same can be found in the writings "of Manichaeus, where it is **denied** that Jesus was born of a virgin."[464] *Clearly, something is amiss here! Those who assert that Paul of Samosata affirms a virgin birth in this text have completely misunderstood it!* What the text is *actually* saying is that Paul, Marcion, and Manichaeus all held that *the notion* of God being born of a virgin **would mean** that *God himself* had an *origin from a virgin*, which is a conclusion **they all rejected**. The common English translation of this text is incorrect when it says, "Paul of Samosata **acknowledges** God from the virgin." There is no Greek word in the text that means "acknowledges." The text only says, "Tell us then, how you suppose God to have come into being at Nazareth: for all heretics are wont to say this, as **Paul of**

Samosata, 'God from the virgin,' 'God seen as from Nazareth' (ὡς Παῦλος ὁ Σαμοσατεὺς Θεὸν ἐκ τῆς Παρθένου ὁμολογεῖ, Θεὸν ἐκ Ναζαρὲτ ὀφθέντα)." The *meaning* is, "Paul of Samosata *pretenses* that our doctrines *imply God began to exist in a virgin* and *God is seen as originating from Nazareth*." This is clearly the dynamic of the text, which is *proven* by Athanasius'[?] *rebuttal* to that allegation, which reads thus:

> Tell us then, how is it that you say that "God" **came into being from Nazareth, affirming** [ἀπαγγέλλοντες, read ***presenting***] with Paul of Samosata a sort of beginning of existence for the Godhead, or with Marcion and the other heretics denying the nativity of the flesh: not walking in a line with the definite teaching of the Gospel, but choosing to speak from your own resources. **For this is your motive for saying, "God was born of the virgin," instead of** "God" and "man," according to the gospel definition, **that** you may not, while acknowledging a nativity of flesh, call it "natural," and in so speaking keep to the truth, but **may speak of a "God" as having been born**, and having "shown" flesh of his own, as if in mere appearance. **For God does not "exhibit" a beginning of existence from Nazareth**.[465]

Thus, there is no real evidence that Paul of Samosata taught the virgin birth. The fact that Paul's doctrine was correlated to that of Artemon, whose doctrine was correlated to that of Theodotus (as we discussed in chapter one), leads us toward the conclusion that, like Theodotus, Paul taught "Christ was a mere man begotten of a man's seed."

Appendix I

Epistles of Ignatius Spurious?

This appendix is composed solely of passages from *The Ignatian Epistles Entirely Spurious* by W. D. Killen, D.D. Professor of Ecclesiastical History, and Principal of the Presbyterian Theological Faculty, Ireland, 1886.

THE IGNATIAN EPISTLES ENTIRELY SPURIOUS

The question of the genuineness of the Epistles attributed to Ignatius of Antioch has continued to awaken interest ever since the period of the Reformation. That great religious revolution gave an immense impetus to the critical spirit; and when brought under the light of its examination, not a few documents, the claims of which had long passed unchallenged, were summarily pronounced spurious. Eusebius, writing in the fourth century, names only seven letters as attributed to Ignatius; but long before the days of Luther, more than double that number were in circulation. Many of these were speedily condemned by the critics of the sixteenth century. Even the seven recognized by Eusebius were regarded with grave suspicion; and Calvin—who then stood at the head of Protestant theologians—did not hesitate to denounce the whole of them as forgeries. The work, long employed as a text-book in Cambridge and Oxford, was the *Institutes* of the Reformer of Geneva;[466] and as his views on this subject are there proclaimed very emphatically,[467] we may presume that the entire body of the Ignatian literature was at that time viewed with distrust by the leaders of thought in the English universities.

From time to time, however, these Epistles were kept before the eyes of the public by Archbishop Wake and other editors; and more recently the appearance of a Syriac copy of three of them—printed under the supervision of the late Rev. Dr. Cureton—reopened the discussion. Dr. Cureton maintained that his three Epistles are the only genuine remains of the pastor of Antioch. In a still later publication,[468] Bishop Lightfoot controverts the views of Dr. Cureton, and makes a vigorous effort to uphold the credit of the seven letters quoted by Eusebius and supported by Pearson. Dr. Lightfoot has already acquired a high and deserved reputation as a scholar and a commentator, and the present work furnishes abundant evidence of his linguistic attainments and his perseverance; but it is somewhat doubtful whether it will add to his fame as a critic and a theologian. In these three portly octavo volumes—extending to upwards of 1800 pages of closely printed matter—he tries to convince his readers that a number of the silliest productions to be found among the records of antiquity, are the remains of an apostolic Father.

It would be hopeless to attempt to settle a disputed question of criticism by enumerating authorities on different sides, as, after all, the value of these authorities would be variously discounted. We must seek to arrive at truth, not by quoting names, but by weighing arguments. Not a few, however, whose opinion may be entitled to some respect, will not be prepared to agree with Bishop Lightfoot when he affirms that those who reject these Ignatian letters are, with few exceptions, only to be found in the "list of second and third rate names" in literature.[469] We have seen that Bentley and Porson disagree with him—and he can point to no more eminent critics in the whole range of modern scholarship. ... But whilst the internal evidence testifies against them, they are not noticed by any writer for considerably more than a century after they are said to have appeared.

The date commonly assigned for the martyrdom of Ignatius, and consequently for the writing of the letters ascribed to him, is the ninth year of Trajan, corresponding to A.D. 107. This date, Dr. Lightfoot tells us, is "the one fixed element in the common tradition."[470] It is to be found in the *Chronicon Paschale*, and in the Antiochene and the Roman "Acts," as well as elsewhere.[471] This same date is assigned by the advocates of the Ignatian Epistles for the writing of Polycarp's letter. "Only a few months at the outside," says Dr. Lightfoot, "probably only a few weeks, after these Ignatian Epistles purport to have been written, the Bishop of Smyrna himself addresses a letter to the Philippians."[472] In due course it will be shown that Polycarp was at this time only about four-and-twenty years of age; and any intelligent reader who pursues his Epistle can judge for himself whether it can be reasonably accepted as the production of so very youthful an author. It appears that it was dictated in answer to a communication from the Church at Philippi, in which he was requested to interpose his influence with a view to the settlement of some grave scandals which disturbed that ancient Christian community. Is it likely that a minister of so little experience would have been invited to undertake such a service?

There are other indications in this letter that it cannot have been written at the date ascribed to it by the advocates of the Ignatian Epistles. It contains an admonition to "pray for *kings* (or *the* kings), *authorities*, and *princes*."[473] We are not at liberty to assume that these three names are precisely synonymous. By kings, or *the* kings, we may apparently understand the imperial rulers; by authorities, consuls, proconsuls, praetors, and other magistrates; and by princes, those petty sovereigns and others of royal rank to be found here and there throughout the Roman dominions.[474] Dr. Lightfoot, indeed, argues that the translation adopted by some—"*the* kings"—is inadmissible, as, according to his ideas, "we have very good ground for believing that the definite article had no place in the original."[475] He has, however, assigned no adequate reason why the article may not be prefixed. His contention, that the expression "pray for kings" has not "anything more than a general reference,"[476] cannot be well maintained. In a case such as this, we must be, to a great extent, guided in our interpretation by the context; and if so, we may fairly admit the article, for immediately afterwards Polycarp exhorts the Philippians to pray for their persecutors and their enemies,—an admonition which obviously has something more than "a general reference." Such an advice would be inappropriate when persecution was asleep, and when no enemy was giving disturbance. But, at the date when Ignatius is alleged to have been martyred, Polycarp could not have exhorted the Philippians to pray for "the kings," as there was then only *one* sovereign ruling over the empire.

That this letter of Polycarp to the Philippians was written at a time when persecution was rife, is apparent from its tenor throughout. If we except the case of Ignatius of Antioch—many of the tales relating to which Dr. Lightfoot himself rejects as fabulous[477]—we have no evidence that in

A.D. 107 the Christians were treated with severity. The Roman world was then under the mild government of Trajan, and the troubles which afflicted the disciples in Bithynia, under Pliny, had not yet commenced. The emperor, so far as we have trustworthy information, had hitherto in no way interfered with the infant Church. But in A.D. 161 two sovereigns were in power, and a reign of terror was inaugurated. We can therefore well understand why Polycarp, after exhorting his correspondents to pray for "the kings," immediately follows up this advice by urging them to pray for their persecutors and their enemies. If by "kings" we here understand emperors, as distinguished from "princes" or inferior potentates, it must be obvious that Polycarp here refers to the two reigning sovereigns. It so happened that, when two kings began to reign, persecution at once commenced; and the language of the Epistle exactly befits such a crisis.

The simple solution of all these difficulties is to be found in the fact that the Ignatius mentioned by Polycarp was a totally different person from the pastor of Antioch. He lived in another age and in another country. Ignatius or Egnatius—for the name is thus variously written—was not a very rare designation;[478] and in the neighborhood of Philippi it seems to have been common. The famous *Egnatian* road,[479] which passed through the place, probably derived its title originally from some distinguished member of the family. We learn from the letter of Polycarp that his Ignatius was a man of Philippi. Addressing his brethren there, he says, "I exhort you all, therefore, to be obedient unto the word of righteousness, and to practice all endurance, which also ye saw with your own eyes in the blessed Ignatius, and Zosimus, and Rufus, and IN OTHERS ALSO AMONG YOURSELVES" (Sec. 9). These words surely mean that the individuals here named were men of Philippi. It is admitted that two of them, viz. Zosimus and Rufus, answered to this description; and in the Latin Martyrologies, as Dr. Lightfoot himself acknowledges,[480] they are said to have been natives of the town. It will require the introduction of some novel canon of criticism to enable us to avoid the conclusion that Ignatius, their companion, is not to be classed in the same category.

Let us now call attention to another passage in this letter of Polycarp to the Philippians. Towards its close the following sentence appears somewhat in the form of a postscript. "Ye wrote to me, both ye yourselves and

Ignatius, asking that if anyone should go to Syria, he *might* carry thither the letters *from you*." We have here the reading, and translation adopted by Dr. Lightfoot; but it so happens that there is another reading perhaps, on the whole, quite as well supported by the authority of versions and manuscripts. It may be thus rendered: "Ye wrote to me, both ye yourselves and Ignatius, suggesting that if anyone is going to Syria, he might carry thither *my letters to you*."[481] The sentence, as interpreted by the advocates of the Ignatian Epistles, wears a strange and suspicious aspect.

If we are to be guided by the statements in the Ignatian Epistles, we must infer that the letters to be sent to Antioch were to be forwarded with the utmost expedition. A council was to be called forthwith, and by it a messenger "fit to bear the name of God's courier"[482] was to be chosen to carry them to the Syrian metropolis. There are no such signs of haste or urgency indicated in the postscript to Polycarp's Epistle. The letters of which he speaks could afford to wait until someone happened to be travelling to Syria; and then, it is suggested, he *might* take them along with him. If we adopt the reading to be found in the Latin version, and which, from internal evidence, we may judge to be a true rendering of the original, we are, according to the interpretation which must be given to it by the advocates of the Ignatian Epistles, involved in hopeless bewilderment. If by Syria we understand the eastern province, what possibly can be the meaning of the words addressed by Polycarp to the Philippians, "If anyone is going to Syria, he might *carry thither my letters to you*"?[483] Anyone passing from Smyrna to Philippi turns his face to the north-west, but a traveller from Smyrna to Syria proceeds south-east, or in the exactly opposite direction. How could Polycarp hope to keep up a correspondence with his brethren of Philippi, if he sent his letters to the distant East by anyone who might be going there?

This explanation throws light on another part of this postscript which has long been embarrassing to many readers. After adverting to the request of Ignatius and the Philippians relative to the conveyance of the letters, Polycarp adds, "which request I will attend to if I get a fit opportunity, either personally, or by one whom I shall depute to act likewise on your behalf."[484] According to the current interpretation, Polycarp here suggests the probability of a personal visit to the eastern capital, if he could find no one else to undertake the service. ... The letter of Polycarp was written, not as Dr. Lightfoot contends, in A.D. 107 but, as we have seen, about A.D. 161, when, as the whole strain of the Epistle indicates, he was far advanced in life.

The only two vouchers of the second century produced in support of the claims of the Epistles attributed to Ignatius, are the letter of Polycarp to the Philippians and a sentence from the treatise of Irenaeus *Against Heresies*. The evidence from Polycarp's Epistle has been discussed in a preceding chapter. When examined, it has completely broken down, as it is based on an entire misconception of the meaning of the writer. The words of Irenaeus can be adduced with still less plausibility to uphold the credit of these letters. The following is the passage in which they are supposed to be authenticated: "*One of our people said*, when condemned to the beasts on account of his testimony towards God—'As I am the wheat of God, I am also ground by the teeth of beasts, that I may be found the pure bread of God.'"[485] It is worse than a mere begging of the question to assert that Irenaeus here gives us a quotation from one of the letters of Ignatius. In the extensive treatise from which the words are an extract, he never once mentions the name of the pastor of Antioch. Had he been aware of the existence of these Epistles, he would undoubtedly have availed himself of their assistance when contending against the heretics—as they would have furnished him with many passages exactly suited for their refutation. The words of a man taught by the apostles, occupying one of the highest positions in the Christian Church, and finishing his career by a glorious martyrdom in the very beginning of the second century, would have been by far the weightiest evidence he could have produced, next to the teaching of inspiration. But though he brings forward Clemens Romanus, Papias, Justin Martyr, Polycarp,[486] and others to confront the errorists, he ignores a witness whose antiquity and weight of character would have imparted peculiar significance to his testimony. To say that though he never names him elsewhere, he points to him in this place as "one of our people," is to make a very bold and improbable statement. Even the Apostle Paul himself would not have ventured to describe the evangelist John in this way. He would have alluded to him more respectfully. Neither would the pastor of a comparatively uninfluential church in the south of Gaul have expressed himself after this fashion when speaking of a minister who had been one of the most famous of the spiritual heroes of the Church. Not many years before, a terrific persecution had raged in his own city of Lyons; many had been put in prison, and some had been thrown to wild beasts;[487] and it is obviously to one of these anonymous sufferers that Irenaeus here directs attention. The "one of our people" is not certainly an apostolic Father; but some citizen of Lyons, moving in a different sphere, whose name the author does not deem it necessary to enroll in the record of history. Neither is it to a *written* correspondence, but to the *dying words* of the unknown martyr, to which he adverts when we read,—"One of our people *said*, As I am the wheat of God, I am also ground by the teeth of beasts, that I may be found the pure bread of God."

The two witnesses of the second century who are supposed to uphold the claims of the Ignatian Epistles have now been examined, and it must be apparent that their testimony amounts to nothing. Thus far, then, there is no external evidence whatever in favor of these letters. The result of this investigation warrants the suspicion that they are forgeries.[488] The internal evidence abundantly confirms this impression. Anyone who carefully peruses them, and then reads over the Epistle of Clemens Romanus, the Teaching of the Apostles, the writings of Justin Martyr, and the Epistle of Polycarp, may see that the works just named are the productions of quite another period. The Ignatian letters describe a state of things which they totally ignore.

The internal evidence furnished by the Ignatian Epistles seals their condemnation. I do not intend, however, at present to pursue this subject. In a work published by me six and twenty years ago,[489] I have called attention to various circumstances which betray the imposture; and neither Dr. Lightfoot, Zahn, nor anyone else, so far as I am aware, has ever yet ventured to deal with my arguments. I might now add new evidences of their fabrication, but I deem this unnecessary.

If, as there is every reason to believe, the Ignatian Epistles are forgeries from beginning to end, various questions arise as to the time of their appearance, and the circumstances which prompted their fabrication. Their origin, like that of many other writings of the same description, cannot be satisfactorily explored; and we must in vain attempt a solution of all the objections which may be urged against almost any hypothesis framed to elucidate their history. It is, however, pretty clear that, in their original form, they first saw the light in the early part of the third century. About that time there was evidently something like a mania for the composition of such works,—as various spurious writings, attributed to Clemens Romanus and others, abundantly testify. Their authors do not seem to have been aware of the impropriety of committing these pious frauds, and may even have imagined that they were thus doing God service.[490] Several circumstances suggest that Callistus—who became Bishop of Rome about A.D. 219—may, before his advancement to the episcopal chair, have had a hand in the preparation of these Ignatian Epistles. His history is remarkable. He was originally a slave, and in early life he is reported to have been the child of misfortune. He had at one time the care of a bank, in the management of which he did not prosper. He was at length banished to Sardinia, to labor there as a convict in the mines; and when released from servitude in that unhealthy island, he was brought under the notice of Victor, the Roman bishop. To his bounty he was, about this time, indebted for his support.[491] On the death of Victor, Callistus became a prime favorite with Zephyrinus, the succeeding bishop. By him he was put in charge of the cemetery of the Christians connected with the Catacombs; and he soon attained the most influential position among the Roman clergy. So great was his popularity, that, on the demise of his patron, he was himself unanimously chosen to the episcopal office in the chief city of the empire. Callistus was no ordinary man. He was a kind of original in his way. He possessed a considerable amount of literary culture. He took a prominent part in the current theological controversies,—and yet, if we are to believe Hippolytus, he could accommodate himself to the views of different schools of doctrine. He had great versatility of talent, restless activity, deep cunning, and much force of character. Hippolytus tells us that he was sadly given to intrigue, and so slippery in his movements that it was no easy matter to entangle him in a dilemma. It may have occurred to him that, in the peculiar position of the Church, the concoction of a series of letters, written in the name of an apostolic Father, and vigorously asserting the claims of the bishops, would help much to strengthen the hands of the hierarchy. He might thus manage at the same time quietly to commend certain favorite views of doctrine, and aid the pretensions of the Roman chief pastor. But the business must be kept a profound secret; and the letters must, if possible, be so framed as not at once to awaken suspicion. If we carefully examine them, we shall find that they were well fitted to escape detection at the time when they were written.

The internal evidence warrants the conclusion that the Epistle to the Romans was the first produced. It came forth alone; and, if it crept into circulation originally in the Imperial city, it was not likely to provoke there any hostile criticism. ... The words reported by Irenaeus as uttered by one of the martyrs of Lyons are adroitly appropriated by the pseudo-Ignatius as if spoken by himself; and, in an uncritical age, when the subject-matter of the communication was otherwise so much to the taste of the reader, the quotation helped to establish the credit of the Ignatian correspondence. Another portion of the letter was sure to be extremely acceptable to the Church of Rome—for here the writer is most lavish in his complimentary acknowledgements. That Church is described as "having the presidency in the country of the region of the Romans, being worthy of God, worthy of honor, worthy of felicitation, worthy of praise, worthy of success, worthy in purity, and having the presidency of love, filled with the grace of God, without wavering, and filtered clear from every foreign stain."

"The Epistle to the Romans," says Dr. Lightfoot, "had a wider popularity than the other letters of Ignatius, both early and late. It appears to have been circulated apart from them, sometimes alone."[492] It was put forth as a feeler, to discover how the public would be disposed to entertain such a correspondence; and, in case of its favorable reception, it was intended to open the way for additional Epistles. It was cleverly contrived. It employed the Epistle of Polycarp to the Philippians as a kind of voucher for its authenticity, inasmuch as it is there stated that Ignatius had written a number of letters; and it contained little or nothing which any one in that age would have been disposed to controvert. The Christians of Rome had long enjoyed the reputation of a community ennobled by the blood of martyrs, and they would be quite willing to believe that Ignatius had contributed to their celebrity by dying for the faith within their borders. It is very doubtful whether he really finished his career there: some ancient authorities attest that he suffered at Antioch;[493] and the fact that, in the fourth century, his grave was pointed out in that locality, apparently supports their testimony.[494] The account of his hurried removal as a prisoner from

Antioch to Rome, in the custody of ten fierce soldiers—whilst he was permitted, as he passed along, to hold something like a levee of his co-religionists at every stage of his journey—wears very much the appearance of an ill-constructed fiction. But the disciples at Rome about this period were willing to be credulous in such matters; and thus it was that this tale of martyrdom was permitted to pass unchallenged. In due time the author of the letters, as they appeared one after another, accomplished the design of their composition. The question of the constitution of the Church had recently awakened much attention; and the threat of Victor to excommunicate the Christians of Asia Minor, because they ventured to differ from him as to the mode of celebrating the Paschal festival, had, no doubt, led to discussions relative to the claims of episcopal authority which, at Rome especially, were felt to be very inconvenient and uncomfortable. No one could well maintain that it had a scriptural warrant. The few who were acquainted with its history were aware that it was only a human arrangement of comparatively recent introduction; and yet a bishop who threatened with excommunication such as refused to submit to his mandates, could scarcely be expected to make such a confession. Irenaeus had sanctioned its establishment; but, when Victor became so overbearing, he took the alarm, and told him plainly that those who presided over the Church of Rome before him were nothing but presbyters.[495] This was rather an awkward disclosure; and it was felt by the friends of the new order that some voucher was required to help it in its hour of need, and to fortify its pretensions. The letters of an apostolic Father strongly asserting its claims could not fail to give it encouragement. We can thus understand how at this crisis these Epistles were forthcoming. They were admirably calculated to quiet the public mind. They were comparatively short, so that they could be easily read; and they were quite to the point, for they taught that we are to "regard the bishop as the Lord Himself," and that "he presides after the likeness of God."[496] Who after all this could doubt the claims of Episcopacy? Should not the words of an apostolic Father put an end to all farther questionings?

As we read these Ignatian letters, it may occur to us that the real author sometimes betrays his identity. Callistus had been originally a slave, and he here represents Ignatius as saying of himself, "I am a slave."[497] Callistus had been a convict, and more than once this Ignatius declares, "I am a convict."[498] May he not thus intend to remind his co-religionists at Rome that an illustrious bishop and martyr had once been a slave and a convict like himself? Callistus, when laboring in the mines of Sardinia, must have been well acquainted with ropes and hoists; and here Ignatius describes the Ephesians as "hoisted up to the heights through the engine of Jesus Christ," having faith as their "windlass," and as "using for a rope the Holy Spirit."[499] Callistus had at one time been in charge of a bank; and Ignatius, in one of these Epistles, is made to say, "Let your works be your deposits, that you may receive your assets due to you."[500] Callistus also had charge of the Christian cemetery in the Roman Catacombs; and Ignatius here expresses himself as one familiar with graves and funerals. He speaks of a heretic as "being himself a bearer of a corpse," and of those inclined to Judaism "as tombstones and graves of the dead."[501] It is rather singular that, in these few short letters, we find so many expressions which point to Callistus as the writer. There are, however, other matters which warrant equally strong suspicions. Hippolytus tells us that Callistus was a Patripassian. "The Father," said he, "having taken human nature, deified it by uniting it to Himself, ... and so he said that the Father had suffered with the Son."[502] Hence Ignatius, in these Epistles, startles us by such expressions as "the blood of God,"[503] and "the passion of my God."[504] Callistus is accused by Hippolytus as a trimmer prepared, as occasion served, to conciliate different parties in the Church by appearing to adopt their views. Sometimes he sided with Hippolytus, and sometimes with those opposed to him; hence it is that the theology taught in these letters is of a very equivocal character. Dr. Lightfoot has seized upon this fact as a reason that they are never quoted by Irenaeus. "The language approaching dangerously near to heresy might," says he, "have led him to avoid directly quoting the doctrinal teaching."[505] A much better reason was that he had never heard of these letters; and yet their theology is exactly such a piebald production as might have been expected from Callistus.

The forger, whoever he may have been, has displayed no little art and address in their fabrication. From all that we know of Callistus, he was quite equal to the task. Like the false Decretals, these letters exerted much influence on the subsequent history of the Church. Cyprian, though he never mentions them,[506] speedily caught their spirit. His assertion of episcopal authority is quite in the same style. Origen visited Rome shortly after they appeared; he is the first writer who recognizes them; and it is worthy of note that, of the three quotations from them found in his works, two are from the Epistle to the Romans. It is quite within the range of possibility that evidence may yet be forthcoming to prove that they emanated from one of the early popes. They are worthy of such an origin. They recommend that blind and slavish submission to ecclesiastical dictation which the so-called successors of Peter have ever since inculcated.

This letter is a strange mixture of silly babblement, mysticism, and fanaticism; but throughout it wants the true ring of an honest correspondence. … It was accommodated to the taste of an age of deteriorated Christianity. Polycarp would have sternly condemned its extravagance. But, in the early part of the third century, the tone of public sentiment in the Christian Church was greatly changed, and the writings of Tertullian contributed much to give encouragement to such productions as the Ignatian Epistles. Tertullian, however, in his numerous writings, never once names Ignatius. It would appear that he had never heard of these letters.

Appendix J
Trinity in 1 Clement?

It seems to some that Clement of Rome presented the Trinity doctrine in 1st century epistle known as 1 Clement. Although the epistle does not present any such *theme*, Trinitarians have pointed out a single *statement* found in 1 Clement 58:2 as a proof that Clement was a Trinitarian.

> "For as God lives, and as the Lord Jesus Christ lives, and the Holy Spirit (who are the faith and hope of the elect)" (Lightfoot)

Although this is how it has been translated (and thus quoted) by Trinitarians, it is not the best translation of the Greek text, which reads as follows:

> ζῇ γὰρ ὁ Θεός καὶ ζῇ ὁ Κύριος Ἰησούς Χριστός καὶ τὸ πνεῦμα τὸ ἅγιον, **ἥ τε** πίστις **καὶ ἥ** ελπίς των εκλεκτών

We can take τε here to either mean *in addition to* or to mean *both*. The *Loeb Classical Library* translation accords with the meaning *in addition to* and has the primary translation of the text as:

> "For as God, the Lord Jesus Christ, and the Holy Spirit all live— as do the faith and the hope of those who are chosen"

Yet, even if we took τε to mean *both*, the Greek can be translated thus:

> "For God lives and the Lord Jesus Christ lives and the Holy Spirit, both the faith and hope of the elect"

There is nothing in the text that can be translated as "who are" (as the Trinitarian translators render it). Notwithstanding, when anyone takes the final clause of the text as *summarizing* what came beforehand, they are *forced* to *define* the previous contents being summarized. Instead of choosing to take the summary as a reference to *three persons*, which the text does not say, I propose that we define the content being summarized by the factors presented *within the summary itself*. In other words, since the summary is "the faith and hope of the elect," we are given a guide on how to interpret the preceding content. In this framework, I suggest the following English translation be adopted.

> "For God lives and the Lord Jesus Christ lives and the Holy Spirit, **which amounts to** both the faith and hope of the elect"

Now that we have assessed the text itself, let's turn our attention toward biblical examples to see how we might *interpret the meaning* of the text in accordance with early Christian beliefs.

What is the faith and hope of the elect according to the Bible?

> "Who by him do believe in God, that raised him up from the dead, and gave him glory; that **your faith and hope** might be in God."
> (1 Peter 1:21)

Our faith and hope is specifically related to Christ's resurrection that was brought about by God. The resurrection of Christ is the basis of our own hope for life after we die, and that hope is associated with the Holy Spirit.

> "But if the Spirit of him that raised up Jesus from the dead dwell in you, he that raised up Christ from the dead shall also quicken your mortal bodies by his Spirit that dwelleth in you." (Romans 8:11)

Accordingly, the Spirit is deemed the affirmation of our hope to come.

> "After that ye believed, ye were sealed with that holy Spirit of promise, which is the earnest of our inheritance." (Ephesians 1:13-14)

So, if we interpret the statement in 1 Clement 58:2 by the substantiated beliefs of the early Christians, we come up with the following.

"For God lives [who raised Jesus from the dead, in whom we thereby have faith] and the Lord Jesus Christ lives [having been raised from the dead and now embodying our hope of life] and the Holy Spirit [the evidence of our future life and the means by which that resurrection will occur], which [in summary] amounts to both the faith and hope of the elect."

It is noteworthy that this entire text we are discussing *does not even exist* within the *oldest* manuscript containing 1 Clement, *Codex Alexandrinus*. However, the argument for its original inclusion in Codex Alexandrinus rests on the fact that a single leaf (a page) is *missing* from the 5th century codex where this passage *would have* appeared.

> Junius (Pat. Young), who examined the MS. before it was bound into its present form, stated that a whole leaf was here lost. The next letters that occur are ιπον, which have been supposed to indicate εἶπον or ἔλιπον. Doubtless some passages quoted by the ancients from the Epistle of Clement, and not now found in it, occurred in the portion which has thus been lost.[507]

It is important to note that there are *textual variants* in the newer manuscripts that demonstrate *some* different wordings than what we find in the more ancient Codex Alexandrinus (which existed over five hundred years before any of the other extant manuscripts containing 1 Clement). If we had the missing leaf, we might find that the phrase "and the Holy Spirit" did not exist in the earlier text. In my opinion, the text would read more like the New Testament if it simply said, "For God lives and the Lord Jesus Christ lives, both the faith and hope of the elect." Compare "God our Savior and the Lord Jesus Christ, our hope." (1 Timothy 1:1.) As to why the leaf is missing, we can only speculate. Since the extant text that *would have* appeared on the missing leaf consists almost entirely of a lengthy prayer, the leaf may have simply been removed by someone who wanted to use it as a prayer script. Maybe they pulled it out to copy the prayer and it somehow never made its way back into the codex.

Appendix K
Theophilus "of Antioch"

There was a Theophilus of Antioch who served as a bishop in Antioch sometime before Paul of Samosata. The only *extant* work attributed to him is known as *To Autolycus*. This work consists of three books, all allegedly written by Theophilus of Antioch, to a certain man named Autolycus. The purpose of this appendix is to present evidence demonstrating that Theophilus of Antioch did not actually author that work. I do believe *To Autolycus* was written by someone with the name Theophilus, likely from Alexandria, so I will refer to the author of *To Autolycus* as Theophilus, but with the qualifier that I am not speaking of Theophilus "of Antioch."

To begin with, there is nothing within the text of *To Autolycus* that would justify the assertion that it was written by Theophilus of Antioch. *A Dictionary of Early Christian Biography* says the following in its entry for Theophilus of Antioch while discussing *To Autolycus*:

> He makes no reference to his office in his existing writings.[508]

The author of *To Autolycus* never even claims to be a bishop. Nor does he say anything at all about Antioch. *Not even a single mention! A Dictionary of Early Christian Biography* **infers** that the birthplace of Theophilus was near the Tigris and Euphrates rivers (the Euphrates border Syria, where Antioch is located).

> We gather from his writings that he was born a heathen, not far from the Tigris and Euphrates.[509]

This assertion regarding Theophilus' place of birth is unsubstantiated. When Theophilus mentions the Tigris and Euphrates, it is not in the context of divulging personal details, but strictly about approximating the geographical location of the Garden of Eden by identifying the rivers in Genesis 2:10-14. Theophilus describes the Tigris and Euphrates as, "[Rivers that] border on our own regions (γειτνιῶσιν ἕως τῶν ἡμετέρων κλιμάτων),"[510] but this is simply a reference to the borders of the Roman Empire during the 2nd century (many Bibles will have a map in the back where you can see how these two rivers met or ran along the Imperial border). Hence, this assertion that "our own regions (plural)" indicates a place of birth is unsupported. Theophilus is simply speaking to Autolycus within the Roman Empire about two rivers that border that same empire's territory. If his references to the rivers tells us anything about his location, it is that he is *not* in Syria (not in Antioch, Syria) because in one place he says the Tigris "goeth toward Syria"[511] (not "cometh toward Syria").

There is nothing *internal* to *To Autolycus* that would lead us to believe Theophilus of Antioch wrote it, so where do we get that tradition? I suspect *To Autolycus* was initially associated with Antioch by someone who saw that the author was called "a Christian"[512] and tied this to the disciples being called "Christians" at Antioch (Acts 11:26). If this is how the rumor started, it was started without good reason. The account in Acts 11 happened over a hundred years before *To Autolycus* was written and the fact that Acts 11:26 says "the disciples were called Christians **first** in Antioch" lets us know that the appellation was *already* being used abroad. Regardless, the origin of the rumor is left to speculation. The earliest *recorded* assertion that Theophilus of Antioch wrote *To Autolycus* is found within the 4th century work of Eusebius entitled *Ecclesiastical History*. Within *Nicene and Post-Nicene Fathers* there is a footnote regarding Eusebius' assertion that reads as follows:

> We have only Eusebius' words (Jerome simply repeats Eusebius' statement) for the fact that Theophilus was bishop of Antioch (his extant works do not mention the fact, nor do those who quote from his writings).[513]

As you can see, the traditional belief that Theophilus of Antioch wrote *To Autolycus* is founded "only" on Eusebius' *Ecclesiastical History*. Jerome would afterward repeat the claim of Eusebius, but, as we shall see, Jerome eventually dissented from that assertion. Before we discuss Jerome, let's show why, *according to Eusebius' own claims*, Theophilus of Antioch could not have written *To Autolycus*.

The same comment within *Nicene and Post-Nicene Fathers* we referenced earlier states:

> Eusebius here calls Theophilus bishop of Antioch, and in chap. 20 makes him the sixth bishop ... The accession of his successor Maximus is put into the seventeenth year (177); but this date is at least four years too early, for his work, *ad Autolycum*, quotes from a work in which the death of Marcus Aurelius (who died in 180) was mentioned, and hence cannot have been written before 181 or 182.[514]

Eusebius has Theophilus of Antioch as the sixth bishop of Antioch and says his successor, Maximus, became bishop of Antioch in 177 AD. The problem is, *To Autolycus* actually **records the death** of Marcus Aurelius, which occurred in 180 AD. Hence, according to Eusebius' own history, Theophilus of Antioch was **already deceased** when *To Autolycus* was written. *Amazing! Eusebius contradicts his own historical records when he says Theophilus of Antioch wrote To Autolycus!* From the outset of our investigation we find that the "only" record tying Theophilus of Antioch to *To Autolycus* is unreliable.

Jerome would *initially* repeat the claim of Eusebius within his earlier writings, but as time progressed we see evidence that Jerome began attributing the authorship of *To Autolycus* to a *different* Theophilus, one whose style of writing did not match that of Theophilus of Antioch. What I mean is this, Jerome had *other* writings that were *also* attributed to Theophilus of Antioch, a commentary on Matthew and a commentary on Proverbs. Jerome stated that the style of writing found in those commentaries did not match that of *To Autolycus*, though they were all attributed to Theophilus of Antioch. Hence, in his work *On Illustrious Men*, Jerome, holding to the tradition of Eusebius, expresses doubts that those commentaries were actually written by Theophilus of Antioch. Now, *On Illustrious Men* was completed by Jerome sometime in 392-393 AD, but a few years after this, in his own commentary on Matthew, Jerome affirms that the commentary on Matthew attributed to Theophilus of Antioch actually *was* written by him. Hence, Jerome eventually says that those works *at odds* with *To Autolycus* were the genuine works of Theophilus of Antioch.

Jerome, 392-393 AD	**Jerome, 398 AD**
"**Theophilus, sixth bishop of the church of Antioch**, in the reign of the emperor Marcus Antoninus Verus composed a book *Against Marcion*, which is still extant, also three volumes *To Autolycus* and one *Against the heresy of Hermogenes* and other short and elegant treatises, well fitted for the edification of the church. **I have read, under his name, commentaries On the Gospel** and *On the proverbs of Solomon* which do not appear to me to correspond in style and language with the elegance and expressiveness of the above works."[515]	"You want me to explain **Matthew** briefly, to touch upon it lightly with a few words, yet to open up its wider meaning. ... I confess that years ago I read Origen's twenty-five books on Matthew and just as many of his homilies and a kind of verse-by-verse interpretation. **I have also read the commentary of Theophilus, bishop of the city of Antioch.**"[516]

Jerome eventually began to view *To Autolycus* as a work at odds with the genuine style of Theophilus of Antioch, and thus not written by him. Since Jerome no longer viewed Theophilus of Antioch as the author of *To Autolycus*, unto whom did he attribute its authorship? We may find the answer to this question within *Lives of Illustrious Men* (*de Viyis Iliustribus*) written by Jerome's successor, Gennadius.

> The *de Viyis Iliustribus* in its most commonly accepted form was probably published c. 495. and contains, in some ten folio pages, short biographies of ecclesiastics between 392 and 495. Although

lacking the lively touches of his great predecessor, Jerome, the catalogue of Gennadius exhibits a real sense of proportion. The greater men stand out in its pages, and it conveys much real and valuable information. With due allowance for the bias referred to, it may be regarded as a trustworthy compilation.

Gennadius' work, *Lives of Illustrious Men*, was the sequel to Jerome's work *On Illustrious Men*. Gennadius definitely had access to Jerome's work. It is very interesting, therefore, that the copy of *To Autolycus* Gennadius encountered was actually attributed to a Theophilus of Alexandria (not Antioch). Gennadius mentions this in his entry on a certain Theophilus of Alexandria who was bishop in Alexandria 385–412 AD.

A Dictionary of Early Christian Biography comments on Gennadius' statement when recounting the history of *To Autolycus* (which is sometimes referred to as the *Apology*, etc.).

> The silence regarding the *Apology* of Theophilus in the East is remarkable. We find the work nowhere mentioned or quoted by Greek writers before the time of Eusebius. Several passages in the works of Irenaeus shew an undoubted relationship to passages in one small section of the *Apology* (Iren. v. 23, 1; *Autol.* ii. 25 *init.*: Iren. iv. 38, 1, iii. 23, 6; *Autol.* ii. 25: Iren. iii. 23, 6; *Autol.* ii. 25, 26), but Harnack (p. 294) thinks it probable that the quotations, limited to two chapters, are not taken from the *Apology*, but from Theophilus's work against Marcion (cf. Möhler, *Patr.* p. 286; Otto, *Corp. Apol.* II. viii. p. 357; Donaldson, *Christ. Lit.* iii. 66). In the West there are certain references to the *Autolycus*, though not copious. It is quoted by Lactantius (*Div. Inst.* i. 23) under the title *Liber de Temporibus ad Autolycum*. There is a passage first cited by Maranus in Novatian (*de Trin.* c. 2) which shews great similarity to the language of Theophilus (*ad Autol.* i. 3). In the next cent. the book is mentioned by Gennadius (c. 34) as "tres libelli de fide." He found them attributed to Theophilus of Alexandria, but the disparity of style caused him to question the authorship.[517]

Gennadius shows that he is unfamiliar with *To Autolycus* when he simply refers to the work (which consists of three books) as "three books on faith" ("tres libelli de fide"). He only knows that the 4th–5th century bishop of Alexandria named Theophilus is not the same Theophilus of Alexandria who authored the work in question.

> "Theophilus, bishop of the church of Alexandria, wrote one great volume *Against Origen* in which he condemns pretty nearly all his sayings and himself likewise ... He also wrote *Against the Anthropomorphites*, heretics who say that God has the human form and members, confuting in a long discussion and arguing by testimonies of Divine Scripture and convincing. ... I have read also three books *On faith*, which bear his name but, as their language is not like his, I do not very much think they are by him."
>
> —*Gennadius of Massilia, 495 AD*[518]

Gennadius says the writing style in *To Autolycus* does not match the works of the 4th century Theophilus of Alexandria. Yet, *To Autolycus* was apparently attributed by someone (Jerome?) to another Theophilus from that same city. Was that a justified attribution? If so, who was this *other* Theophilus of Alexandria that authored *To Autolycus*?

There are factors within *To Autolycus* that point toward Alexandrian authorship. One of the prominent themes within *To Autolycus* is the difference amongst Egyptian, Greek, and Christian writings. We see this in Theophilus' eventual recap.

> Hence one can see how our sacred writings are shown to be more ancient and true than those of the Greeks and Egyptians, or any other historians.[519]

This comparison to the writings of Greeks and Egyptians seems to play out in such a fashion that infers the addressee, Autolycus, is actually an Egyptian. Theophilus contrasts the writings of the Egyptians with that of the Greeks and says the Egyptian poets pertain to Autolycus.

> And these, indeed, are the milder kinds of legends; since the god who is called Osiris is found to have been torn limb from limb, whose mysteries are celebrated annually, as if he had perished, and were being found, and sought for limb by limb. For neither is it known whether he perished, nor is it shown whether he is found. And why should I speak of Atys mutilated, or of Adonis wandering in the wood, and wounded by a boar while hunting; or of Æsculapius struck by a thunderbolt; or of the fugitive Serapis chased from Sinope to Alexandria; or of the Scythian Diana, herself, too, a fugitive, and a homicide, and a huntress, and a passionate lover of Endymion? Now, it is not we who publish these things, but **your own** writers and poets. Why should I **further** recount the multitude of animals worshipped by the **Egyptians**, both reptiles, and cattle, and wild beasts, and birds, and river-fishes; and even wash-pots and disgraceful noises? **But if you cite the Greeks** and the other nations, they worship stones and wood, and other kinds of material substances,—the images, as we have just been saying, of dead men.[520]

After Theophilus talks about Osiris and how Serapis came to Alexandria, Egypt, he says to Autolycus, "Now, it is not we who publish these things, but your own writers and poets." Theophilus then abstains from "further" discussion of Egyptian practices and, as if introducing a new source of contrast, says, "But if you cite the Greeks." Hence, since Theophilus says to Autolycus, the Egyptian sources are "your own," we can infer that Autolycus was also Egyptian in his beliefs.

Some may reply that Theophilus could have been in Antioch and sending his letters to Autolycus from afar, but this is contradicted by what we find in *To Autolycus*. The two men were friends and would meet frequently in person and then return to their own houses (not to their own countries). Theophilus also himself states that *the reason* he is writing is because he is less skilled at speaking in person. This lets us know that person-to-person speaking was an available option when he wrote his three books to Autolycus.

> When we had formerly some conversation, my very good friend Autolycus, and when you inquired who was my God, and for a little paid attention to my discourse, I made some explanations to you concerning my religion; and then having bid one another adieu, we went with much mutual friendliness each to his own house, although at first you had borne somewhat hard upon me. For you know and remember that you supposed our doctrine was foolishness. As you then afterwards urged me to do, I am desirous, though not educated to the art of speaking, of more accurately demonstrating, by means of this tractate, the vain labour and empty worship in which you are held; and I wish also, from a few of your own histories which you read, and perhaps do not yet quite understand, to make the truth plain to you.[521]

Thus, Theophilus and Autolycus lived near enough to one another that regular conversation was a viable option and the writing of books was only chosen because Theophilus, at least according to his own humble admission, lacked oratorical prowess. Even so, Theophilus encourages follow-up meetings with Autolycus where they can discuss these matters in person, writing thus, "Endeavour therefore to meet [with me] more frequently, that, by hearing the living voice, you may accurately ascertain the truth."[522] Hence, both men were living proximate one another.

Theophilus himself shows his knowledge of Egyptian history when he gives an extensive chronology of the Egyptian kings, recounting the number of years each king was in power.[523] Furthermore, although the readership of the Egyptian writer Apollonides Horapius was largely confined to Egypt,[524] Theophilus shows personal familiarity with *several* of Apollonides' works, which means he was likely in Egypt himself.

> ... of the Egyptian gods,—or, rather, vain men, as Apollonides, surnamed Horapius, mentions in the book entitled *Semenouthi*, and in **his other histories** concerning the worship of the Egyptians and their kings, and the vain labours in which they engaged.[525]

It was in Egypt that the annual Osiris festival took place. Theophilus refers to the procession of that Egyptian festival with familiarity.

> And these, indeed, are the milder kinds of legends; since the god who is called Osiris is found to have been torn limb from limb, whose mysteries are celebrated annually, as if he had perished, and were being found, and sought for limb by limb. For neither is it known whether he perished, nor is it shown whether he is found.[526]

Theophilus also speaks of Satyrus, who wrote about the "history of the Alexandrine families," asserting "the relationship of the Alexandrine kings to Bacchus."[527] Such references to Alexandria in Theophilus' books would support the hypothesis that Autolycus was a resident of Alexandria, Egypt. Alexandria's libraries, most famously the Mouseion and the Serapeum, would also readily account for Theophilus' reference to "libraries" (plural) as something locally accessible to Autolycus. "For," he says to Autolycus, "if it were possible for you, you would not grudge to spend the night in the libraries."[528] Alexandria was a coastal city, which would provide the context for Theophilus' multiple references to the harbor and ships. Alexandria had a "gymnasium," which is something Theophilus refers to as well when he asks, "And what man, when he enters into this life or into the gymnasium, is not anointed with oil?"[529]

The greatest evidence I see in opposition to the Alexandrian connection is when Theophilus refers to Egypt as "there" (instead of "here"). This occurs only once when he is recounting the history of Israel and says they were "obliged to migrate to Egypt for the sake of buying food **there** (ἐκεῖ)." Typically, ἐκεῖ denotes a *different* geographical location. However, ἐκεῖ is also used when referring to a historic scenario that does not correspond to the present system of things. Events occurring in the *present* system would be described as happening "here" and events occurring in the *former* system would be described as happening "there." For example, Hebrews 7:8 says:

> "And **here** (ὧδε) men that die receive tithes; but **there** (ἐκεῖ) he receiveth them, of whom it is witnessed that he liveth." (Hebrews 7:8)

In Hebrews 7:8, ἐκεῖ is not describing a different geographical location. The events occurring with Abraham and Melchisedec transpired within the *same geographical region* in which the Levitical priests *afterward* received tithes. So, ἐκεῖ can be used of the same geographical location when referring to a system of things that does not correspond to the speaker's present environment. Theophilus is living in the Roman Empire, a system that was completely different than that old Egyptian kingdom ruled by Pharaoh and Joseph. Hence, Theophilus' use of ἐκεῖ when describing that old Egyptian system agrees with what we find in Hebrews 7:8. If such was not Theophilus' intention, and he actually did intend a different location, he may have been simply recounting the migration of Israel *from their own perspective*—Israel had to leave their present location and go somewhere else (*i.e.,* "there"). Theophilus often exhibits the narration style of one who *distances* himself from the subject matter within his discourse. For example, although he clearly identifies himself as a Christian, he speaks of Christians as "them" (rather than "us").

> But far be it from Christians to conceive any such deeds; for with **them** temperance dwells.[530]

We cannot say that Theophilus wasn't a Christian because he speaks of Christians as "them." Nor can we say Theophilus was outside of Egypt when he speaks of Egypt as "there" within his narration of history.

Enough has been said to establish that **1.** *To Autolycus* was not written by Theophilus of Antioch and **2.** The Theophilus who did write *To Autolycus* was probably a resident of Alexandria, Egypt. Remember that, according to Gennadius, someone actually *had* attributed *To Autolycus* to a Theophilus of Alexandria. So, who was this Theophilus of Alexandria? What can we know about him?

Theophilus of Alexandria was evidently a Jew. He refers to the writings of the Jews as "our writings" and "our books,"[531] to Moses as "our prophet,"[532] to the ancient Hebrews as "our ancestors,"[533] and to other Jews as "those of our own stock."[534] It may seem to some readers that Theophilus couldn't possibly be a Jew since he speaks of the Jewish Scriptures as something newly introduced to him.

> I myself also used to disbelieve that this would take place, but now, having taken these things into consideration, I believe. At the same

time, I met with the sacred Scriptures of the holy prophets, who also by the Spirit of God foretold the things that have already happened, just as they came to pass, and the things now occurring as they are now happening, and things future in the order in which they shall be accomplished.[535]

Theophilus' lack of familiarity with the Jewish Scriptures is likely due to the lasting repercussions of the Bar Kokhba revolt (132–136 AD) within the Roman Empire. As a result of Rome's war with the Jews, Hadrian, Rome's emperor from 117 to 138 AD, wiped out Jewish society in the Judean province. Jews could no longer even live within sight of their homeland. The Jews' religious scrolls in Judea were burned. A temple to Jupiter was built in Jerusalem and Hadrian had the name of the city changed to Aelia Capitolina. Throughout the Roman Empire, Jews were no longer allowed to practice circumcision nor were they allowed to observe Jewish holidays. There was clearly an anti-Jewish sentiment within the Empire during Hadrian's reign that would have crushed, and did crush, much of the Jewish culture. Hadrian's death (138 AD) brought an end to Rome's anti-Jewish campaign. His successor, Antoninus Pius (emperor from 138 to 161 AD) reversed much of Hadrian's anti-Jewish legislation. Jews began to find acceptance within Roman society again, but the effects of Hadrian's conquest against Judaism had been brutal. It makes sense that some of the Jews, like Theophilus, would have, either willingly or unwillingly, become unfamiliar with the religion of their Jewish ancestors due to Hadrian's actions.

The evidence so far leads us toward the conclusion that Theophilus was a late 2nd century Jew living in Alexandria, Egypt. Apparently, probably prior to his conversion to Christianity, Theophilus was assigned a governmental position within Alexandria during the reign of Antoninus Pius. This accounts for how Theophilus refers to the Roman provinces as "our own regions."[536] In my opinion, there is a good possibility that this was the same Theophilus to whom the final editions of Luke and Acts were addressed. In Luke 1:3, Theophilus' governmental position is indicated by the Greek adjective κράτιστος (translated in Luke 1:3 as "most excellent").

> "It seemed good to me also, having had perfect understanding of all things from the very first, to write unto thee in order, **most excellent** (κράτιστε) Theophilus." (Luke 1:3)

Within the New Testament, this adjective is only used when government officials are being addressed (Acts 23:26, 24:3, 26:25). Hence, Theophilus was evidently some kind of official when the final edition of Luke was addressed to him. When we see the adjective *dropped* in Acts 1:1, this may indicate to us that Theophilus (perhaps because of his conversion) was eventually removed from his position in government.

> "The former treatise have I made, O Theophilus, of all that Jesus began both to do and teach." (Acts 1:1)

John Wesley's research led him to the conclusion that the Theophilus to whom Luke and Acts are addressed was "a person of eminent quality at Alexandria" who was afterward, when Acts was addressed to him, probably a private man.

> "*Most excellent Theophilus*—This was an appellation usually given to Roman governors. Theophilus (as the ancients inform us) was a person of eminent quality at Alexandria. In Acts i. 1, St. Luke does not give him this title. He was then, probably, a private man."
>
> —*John Wesley*[537]

Wesley's conclusion matches my own. Though I cannot prove the Theophilus who wrote *To Autolycus* is the self-same individual to whom the final editions of Luke and Acts are addressed, I do not know of anything that would negate this conclusion.

- There aren't any extant manuscripts of Luke and Acts that predate *To Autolycus* (sometime shortly after 180 AD) where any Theophilus is mentioned.

- There aren't any correlations of any Theophilus to Luke or Acts in any extra-biblical writings that predate *To Autolycus*.

- The first-person pronouns found in Acts 27-28 can be relegated to the original words of Luke left unchanged by the subsequent copyist. The current scribe is apparently compiling an account and conveying it "**even as** (καθὼς) they delivered them." (Luke 1:2.)

- Not long after *To Autolycus* was written, Hippolytus (170-235 AD) composed *Treatise on Christ and Antichrist* which begins with these words, "As it was your desire, my beloved brother Theophilus, to be thoroughly informed on those topics which I put summarily before you, I have thought it right to set these matters of inquiry clearly forth to your view…" (ANF, Vol. 5, p. 204.) The closing remarks begin with, "These things, then, I have set shortly before thee, O Theophilus…" (ANF, Vol. 5, p. 219.) I believe Luke and Acts, as we have them, may very well have been addressed to this same Theophilus.

We may find a hint that ties the final edition of Luke to the author of *To Autolycus* inasmuch as Luke 1:1-3 answers to that criteria set forth by Theophilus himself.

To Autolycus, Book III, Ch. 2	Luke 1:1-3
"For it was fit that they who wrote should themselves have been eye-witnesses of those things concerning which they made assertions, or should accurately have ascertained them from those who had seen them; for they who write of things unascertained beat the air."	"Forasmuch as many have taken in hand to set forth in order a declaration of those things which are most surely believed among us, Even as they delivered them unto us, which from the beginning were eyewitnesses, and ministers of the word; It seemed good to me also, having had perfect understanding of all things from the very first, to write unto thee in order, most excellent Theophilus."

I personally find the phrase in Luke 1:2, "Eyewitnesses and ministers of **the word** (τοῦ λόγου)," to be unusual when compared to the rest of Luke and Acts. It may have been inserted due to Theophilus' own emphasis on the Logos in *To Autolycus*. Theophilus does not go so far as to say that Jesus is the Word, but he does present the Word as an entity who is distinct from the Father in some respects (and he does quote John 1:1 as answering to that entity).

Although *To Autolycus* contains the earliest mention of God as a Trinity, it does not say that God is "Father, Son, and Holy Spirit." The sole instance where Theophilus says "Trinity" reads as follows.

> In like manner also the three days which were before the luminaries, are types of **the Trinity** (τῆς Τριάδος), of God, and His Word, and His wisdom.[538]

Here, Theophilus is interpreting the days of creation in Genesis 1. When summarizing the first *three* days, he says these days are a type of the Trinity of God, his Word, and his Wisdom. Notice that he does not say "Spirit" but "Wisdom." Furthermore, Theophilus describes the *Word* as being πνεῦμα θεοῦ (God's Spirit),"[539] tying this in with "the Spirit of God (πνεῦμα θεοῦ)" in Genesis 1:2 LXX. The "Wisdom" Theophilus refers to is something internal to God. Hence, *To Autolycus* does not contain an affirmation of the modern-day Trinity formula.

After correlating a Trinity with the first three days of creation, Theophilus moves to the *fourth* day and adds man alongside God, his Word, and his Wisdom.

> In like manner also the three days which were before the luminaries, are types of the Trinity, of God, and His Word, and His wisdom. And the fourth is the type of man, who needs light, that so there may **be God, the Word, wisdom, man**.

It seems Theophilus was asserting that man could become part of God (making God consist of more than three parts). Indeed, he says elsewhere that man, if he is obedient, will *become God* at the resurrection.

> Was man made by nature mortal? Certainly not. Was he, then, immortal? Neither do we affirm this. But one will say, Was he, then, nothing? Not even this hits the mark. He was by nature neither mortal nor immortal. For if He had made him immortal from the beginning, **He would have made him God** (θεόν αὐτόν ἐπεποιήκει). Again, if He had made him mortal, God would seem to be the cause of his death. Neither, then, immortal nor yet mortal did He make him, but, as we have said above, capable of both; so that if he should incline to the things of immortality, keeping the commandment of God, he should receive as reward from Him immortality, and **should become God** (γένηται θεὸς).[540]

So, according to Theophilus, man will (in some aspect) become God at the resurrection. Theophilus ties this future resurrection of man into one of the two creation accounts found in Genesis 1-2.

> Wherefore also, when man had been formed in this world, it is mystically written in Genesis, as if he had been twice placed in Paradise; so that the one was fulfilled when he was placed there, and the second will be fulfilled after the resurrection and judgment.[541]

The resurrection of man is also what Theophilus is referencing when he mentions God as a Trinity and then places man alongside that Trinity.

> On the fourth day the luminaries were made ... And these contain the pattern and type of a great mystery. For the sun is a type of God, and the moon of man. And as the sun far surpasses the moon in power and glory, so far does God surpass man. And as the sun remains ever full, never becoming less, so does God always abide perfect, being full of all power, and understanding, and wisdom, and immortality, and all good. But the moon wanes monthly, and in a manner dies, being a type of man; then it is born again, and is crescent, for a pattern of **the future resurrection**. In like manner also the three days which were before the luminaries, are types of the Trinity, of God, and His Word, and His wisdom. And the fourth

> is the type of man, who needs light, that so there may be God, the Word, wisdom, man.

According the Theophilus, man is, as a result of the resurrection, "made God." If we do not take this to be true, we should not hastily affirm that God is a Trinity either, simply because we find a semblance to that modern tradition within his works. If we do take Theophilus' assertion to be true, that man becomes God at his resurrection, we should understand this in a qualified sense. This would, in turn, mean we should probably take the Word and Wisdom in *To Autolycus* as God in a qualified sense as well. Regardless, my intent here in this appendix was not to discuss the theology of Theophilus, but to refute the common assertion that *To Autolycus* was written by Theophilus of Antioch.

REFERENCE NOTES 505

[1] *Ante-Nicene Fathers, Hendrickson, Vol. 3, pp. 21-22.* We have no record of Tertullian's account, nor of Eusebius' account, ever being disputed. Tertullian was the son of a Roman centurion and wrote to the Romans in Latin, their own language, encouraging them to consult their own histories. Eusebius was writing a great deal about Roman history and its Emperors, while the Roman Empire was yet in existence. He was a well-known bishop. His work had prominence. Yet, we never see his record being disputed, either. I think it is harder to believe that news of Jesus would not have been reported to Tiberius than it is to believe Tiberius would have been ignorant of such happenings and indifferent to such claims. Regardless, we have a historical account from 200 AD that says these things occurred.

[2] *Nicene and Post-Nicene Fathers, Hendrickson, Series 2, Vol. 1, p.105*

[3] *Ante-Nicene Fathers, Hendrickson, Vol. 1, p. 223*

[4] *Ante-Nicene Fathers, Hendrickson, Vol. 1, p. 219*

[5] *Ante-Nicene Fathers, Hendrickson, Vol. 1, p. 219. Compare "Jesus was born man of men" w/out brackets in ANF, 1, p. 231.*

[6] *Ante-Nicene Fathers, Hendrickson, Vol. 1, p. 170*

[7] *Ante-Nicene Fathers, Hendrickson, Vol. 4, p. 429*

[8] *Nicene and Post-Nicene Fathers, Hendrickson, Series 2, Vol. 1, p. 159*

[9] *The Jewish Annotated New Testament, Oxford University Press, p. 336*

[10] *Ante-Nicene Fathers, Hendrickson, Vol. 4, p. 570*

[11] Epiphanius mistakenly refers to an "Ebion" as the founder of a separate sect of the Nazarenes. He does, however, trace this Ebion and the Nazarenes back to the same town (30.2.8). Epiphanius says Ebion "was of the Nazoraeans' school, but preached and taught other things than they" (30.1.1). Yet, he afterward says, "For a while now, however, various of [Ebion's] followers have been giving conflicting accounts of Christ" (30.3.1). It seems Epiphanius is confusing views "which are current among them" (30.15.5) with what the original Ebionite/Nazarene group believed. See also note 12.

[12] "It has been the custom of historians to carry this distinction back into apostolic times, and to trace down to the time of Epiphanius the continuous existence of a milder party—the Nazarenes—and of a stricter party—the Ebionites; but this distinction Nitzsch (*Dogmengesch. p. 37 sqq.*) has shown to be entirely groundless. The division which Epiphanius makes is different from that of Justin, as well as from that of Origen and Eusebius;

in fact, it is doubtful if he himself had any clear knowledge of a distinction, his reports are so contradictory. The Ebionites known to him were most pronounced heretics; but he had heard of others who were said to be less heretical, and the conclusion that they formed another sect was most natural. Jerome's use of the two words is fluctuating; but it is clear enough that they were not looked upon by him as two distinct sects. The word 'Nazarenes' was, in fact, in the beginning a general name given to the Christians of Palestine by the Jews (cf. Acts xxiv. 5), and as such synonymous with 'Ebionites.'" —*Arthur Cushman McGiffert, Ph. D.* (*NPNF, Series 2, Vol. 1, p.159*)

[13] *Epiphanius, Panarion, 29. 7 (7-8)*

[14] As to the accusations against the Ebionites found in early Christian writings, written by men who were not Jews themselves, these largely centered around the Ebionites' observance of Jewish laws and practices. However, Paul himself participated in Jewish customs while amongst the Jews (1 Corinthians 9:20), even circumcising Timothy (Acts 16:3). Perhaps we should not precipitously fault *other* early Jewish Christians for having conducted themselves likewise while living amongst their fellow Jews. See also note 16.

[15] *Eusebius' Ecclesiastical History, Hendrickson, p. 93 (Book. 3, ch. 27)*

[16] "The Ebionites were not originally heretics. ... In the time of Justin there were two opposite tendencies among such Christians as still observed the Jewish law: some wished to impose it upon all Christians; others confined it to themselves. Upon the latter Justin looks with charity; but the former he condemns as schismatics (see *Dial. c. Trypho. 47*). For Justin the distinguishing mark of such schismatics is not a doctrinal heresy, but an anti-Christian principle of life. ... as the Church, in its strife with Gnosticism, laid an ever-increasing stress upon Christology, the difference in this respect between itself and these Jewish Christians became ever more apparent until finally left far behind by the Church in its rapid development, they were looked upon as heretics." —*Arthur Cushman McGiffert, Ph. D.* (*NPNF, Series 2, Vol. 1, p.159*)

[17] Generally, Ebionites were recognized as rejecting the virgin birth. For example, even though Eusebius mentions two views among the Ebionites, later on he does not, writing, "The heresy of the Ebionites, as it is called, asserts that Christ was the son of Joseph and Mary, considering him a mere man." (*Nicene and Post-Nicene Fathers, Hendrickson, Series 2, Vol. 1, p. 264*). Cf. ANF Vol. 4, p. 570. See also, Ebionites say Jesus begotten by Joseph, ANF Vol. 1. p. 451, 527; Tertullian says they deny the Son of God, ANF Vol. 3, p. 259; Jerome, Ebionites/Nazarenes in his day believed Jesus was born of virgin, NPNF, Series 1, Vol. 1, p. 338; Cf. ANF Vol. 5, p. 114; ANF Vol. 7, p. 452.

[18] *Eusebius' Ecclesiastical History, Hendrickson, p. 186 (Book. 5, ch. 28)*

[19] *Eusebius' Ecclesiastical History, Hendrickson, p. 186 (Book. 5, ch. 28)*

[20] *Nicene and Post-Nicene Fathers, Hendrickson, Series 2, Vol. 1, p. 246, footnote 3*

[21] *Epiphanius, Panarion, 54. 1 (2)*

[22] *Epiphanius, Panarion, 54. 1 (3-7), 2 (3)*

[23] *Ante-Nicene Fathers, Hendrickson, Vol. 5, p. 147*

[24] How could Theodotus say that Christ was born a man and afterward Christ descended upon Jesus at his baptism? Could he have meant *what caused Jesus to be the Christ* descended upon him when "God anointed Jesus of Nazareth with the Holy Spirit" (Acts 10:38) at his baptism? Thus, Jesus, who was "made Christ," (Acts 2:36,) was *previously* born a normal man before that event. Although it is evident that *Gnostics* spoke of Christ as *a different being* than Jesus, it seems plausible that this concept may have been assumed of others who said Jesus *became* Christ at his baptism. See Appendix E.

[25] *Ante-Nicene Fathers, Hendrickson, Vol. 5, p. 115, bracket mine*

[26] *Ante-Nicene Fathers, Hendrickson, Vol. 5, p. 114*

[27] *Lost Christianities, Bart D. Ehrman, Oxford University Press, pp. 152-153*

[28] *A Dictionary of Early Christian Biography, Hendrickson, p. 1023*

[29] *A Dictionary of Early Christian Biography, Hendrickson, p. 1024*

[30] *Epiphanius, Panarion, 65. 1 (4)*

[31] *Eusebius' Ecclesiastical History, Hendrickson, p. 186 (Book. 5, ch. 28)*

[32] *Eusebius' Ecclesiastical History, Hendrickson, p. 250 (Book. 7, ch. 13)*

[33] *A Dictionary of Early Christian Biography, Hendrickson, p. 816*

[34] *Eusebius' Ecclesiastical History, Hendrickson, p. 265 (Book. 7, ch. 28)*

[35] *Eusebius' Ecclesiastical History, Hendrickson, p. 266 (Book. 7, ch. 29)*

[36] *A Dictionary of Early Christian Biography, Hendrickson, p. 681*

[37] *A Dictionary of Early Christian Biography, Hendrickson, p. 816*

[38] *Eusebius Ecclesiastical History, Hendrickson, p. 269 (Book. 7, ch. 30)*

[39] *Eusebius Ecclesiastical History, Hendrickson, p. 268 (Book. 7, ch. 30)*

[40] *Eusebius' Ecclesiastical History, Hendrickson, p. 186 (Book. 5, ch. 28)*

[41] *Eusebius' Ecclesiastical History, Hendrickson, p. 265 (Book. 7, ch. 27)*

[42] *Eusebius' Ecclesiastical History*, Hendrickson, p. 268 (Book. 7, ch. 30)

[43] *A Dictionary of Early Christian Biography*, Hendrickson, p. 816

[44] *Eusebius' Ecclesiastical History*, Hendrickson, p. 268 (Book. 7, ch. 30)

[45] *On the Incarnation of Our Lord Jesus Christ, Against Apollinaris*, Book 2, Section 3

[46] *Epiphanius, Panarion*, 65. 3 (4), 7 (3)

[47] *Epiphanius, Panarion*, 29. 7 (1)

[48] *Epiphanius, Panarion*, 65. 2 (5)

[49] *Ante-Nicene Fathers*, Hendrickson, Vol. 1, p. 569. First two brackets and bold mine.

[50] *Eusebius' Ecclesiastical History*, Hendrickson, p. 425 (Life of Const., Book 3, ch. 18)

[51] *A Dictionary of Early Christian Biography*, Hendrickson, p. 12

[52] *The Catholic Encyclopedia, First Edition, Volume 2*, p. 36

[53] *Letter from Arius to Alexander, Athanasius, De Synodis, 16.*

[54] *A Dictionary of Early Christian Biography*, Hendrickson, p. 915

[55] *A Dictionary of Early Christian Biography*, Hendrickson, p. 12

[56] *Sozomen, History of the Church*, Translated by Edward Walford, 1855, London, p. 36

[57] *Eusebius' Ecclesiastical History*, Hendrickson, p. 414 (Epiphanius, Pan. 69. 6)

[58] *Nicene and Post-Nicene Fathers*, Hendrickson, Series 2, Vol. 3, p. 42

[59] The underlined portion is evidently an interpolation from a later date. The statement of faith being read was produced by Eusebius of Caesarea who *repeatedly* quoted Matthew 28:19 as reading, "Go ye, and make disciples of all the nations, teaching them to observe all things, whatsoever I have commanded you." (see Appendix B, *Matthew 28:19 Name of the Father, Son, Spirit*.) Yet, the underlined portion contains a different version of Matthew 28:19 than Eusebius made use of. This letter was written to Eusebius' own adherents in Caesarea, who would have been the most familiar with his historic citations of Matthew 28:19. How could he possibly have included the alternate reading of Matthew 28:19 in his letter, affirmed therein that he had *always* believed and preached accordingly, then sent it to his people who *knew* he historically did not? The underlined portion does not show up in the finalized version of the creed, which I relay on page 26 herein. If the council did remove the underlined portion, this would have been *contrary* to the pleasure of Constantine, who, upon hearing it, praised it. Additionally, the

underlined portion comes across like a *revisiting* of material that was *already* covered (*i.e.*, as a later addition to the original text). It appears right at the end of the creedal language, precisely where a later addition might be expected.

[60] *Eusebius' Ecclesiastical History, Hendrickson, p. 417 (Theodoret, H.E. 1.11)*

[61] *Eusebius' Ecclesiastical History, Hendrickson, p. 417 (Theodoret, H.E. 1.11)*

[62] *Eusebius' Ecclesiastical History, Hendrickson, p. 418 (Theodoret, H.E. 1.11)*

[63] *Eusebius' Ecclesiastical History, Hendrickson, p. 414 (Theodoret, H.E. 1.5)*

[64] *Nicene and Post-Nicene Fathers, Hendrickson, Ser. 2, Vol. 4, p. 458*

[65] *Eusebius' Ecclesiastical History, Hendrickson, p. 391 (Socrates, Bk. 1, ch. 8)*

[66] *Eusebius' Ecclesiastical History, Hendrickson, p. 397 (Theodoret, H.E. 1.8)*

[67] *Eusebius' Ecclesiastical History, Hendrickson, p. 397-398 (Socrates, Bk. 1, ch. 8)*

[68] *Eusebius of Ceasarea's letter to his home diocese:* This letter is preserved in *Socrates Scholasticus' History of the Church, Bk. 1, ch. 8.* See this citation in *Jesus the Evidence (first edition only), Ian Wilson, Harper and Row, 1984, p. 168.*

[69] *Nicene and Post-Nicene Fathers, Hendrickson, Ser. 2, Vol. 4, p. 458*

[70] "According to the faith of God's elect, God's prudent ones, Holy children, rightly dividing, God's Holy Spirit receiving, Have I learned this ... Along their track, have I been walking, with like opinions." —*Arius* (*NPNF, Ser. 2, Vol. 4, p. 308*)

[71] *Epiphanius, Panarion, 69. 6 (6). Cf. The Search for the Christian Doctrine of God, RPC Hanson, pp. 5 & 15.*

[72] A certain creed was said to have been found in Lucian's home after he died. I doubt the assertion. That creed does not accord well with beliefs held by Paul, his mentor, and by Arius, his student. That creed allegedly found in Lucian's home along with two other creeds were presented at the Synod of Antioch in 341 AD. There was somewhat of a scramble going on to find a *replacement* for the Nicene Creed. Lucian pedigree *would have* given authority to any creed and an authoritative creed *was* being pursued at that time. If it really was found in Lucian's home after his death, it may have even been something submitted to him for evaluation. The fact that the creed was never made public before Lucian's death should give pause to anyone claiming he wrote it or approved it.

[73] *The New Encyclopedia Britannica, 15th ed., Vol. 7, p. 541*

[74] *Nicene and Post-Nicene Fathers, Hendrickson, Series 2, Vol. 4, p. 407*

[75] *Nicene and Post-Nicene Fathers, Hendrickson, Series 2, Vol. 4, p. 355*

[76] *Eusebius' Ecclesiastical History, Hendrickson, p. 414 (Theodoret, H.E. 1.5)*

[77] Arius was tied to the school of Lucian. "Lucian proposed to limit the symbolic interpretation characteristic of the Alexandrian allegorical tradition by emphasizing the primacy of the literal sense, whether expressed directly or metaphorically." (*The New Encyclopedia Britannica, 15th ed., Vol. 7, p. 541*)

[78] *Ante-Nicene Fathers, Hendrickson, Vol. 9, pp. 254-255*

[79] *The Apostolic Fathers, 2nd ed., Baker Book House, 1989, p. 197. Brackets mine.*

[80] *Philo, Creation 15-20*

[81] *Philo, Cherubim 1.28.*

[82] *Nicene and Post-Nicene Fathers, Hendrickson, Series 2, Vol. 4, p. 458*

[83] *Philo, Heir 206*

[84] *Athanasius, De Synodis, 16*

[85] *Nicene and Post-Nicene Fathers, Hendrickson, Series 2, Vol. 4, p. 458*

[86] "You, having been taught of God, are not ignorant that the teaching at variance with the religion of the Church which has just arisen, is the same as that propagated by Ebion and Artemas, and rivals that of Paul of Samosata, bishop of Antioch." —*Alexander of Alexandria* (*Nicene and Post-Nicene Fathers, Hendrickson, Series 2, Vol. 3, p. 38*)

[87] *Nicene and Post-Nicene Fathers, Hendrickson, Series 2, Vol. 3, p. 35*

[88] *The Catholic Encyclopedia, 1912, Vol. 13, p. 57*

[89] "[Theodosius] fell ill while in this city, and after receiving instruction from Ascholius, the bishop, he was initiated, and was soon restored to health. The parents of Theodosius were Christians, and were attached to the Nicene doctrines; he was pleased with Ascholius, who maintained the same doctrines." —*Sozomen* (*NPNF, Ser. 2, Vol. 2, p. 378*)

[90] *A Dictionary of Early Christian Biography, Hendrickson, p. 974*

[91] *Theodosian Code XVI.1.2; see also NPNF, Ser. 2, Vol. 2, p. 378*

[92] Some groups did reject Catholic Trinitarianism during the Reformation. "Ludwig Hetzer, a young preacher who had broken away from Zwingli at Zürich, rejected all sacraments and denied the deity of Christ. The Anabaptists ... commonly rejected the dogmas of the Trinity." (*The Reformation, A.T. Robertson, p. 113.*) In 1550, Anabaptists held a

forty-day convention in Venice, where, "Among the theological points agreed upon by the convention was one specifying that Jesus Christ was not God and that he was the normally-conceived child of Joseph and Mary." (*Declaratio, Matteo Gribaldi, p. xxvii.*)

[93] *John Calvin, Institutes of the Christian Religion, Paul T. Jones Publishing, 1843, p. 155.* I do *not* agree with the doctrines of Calvin. See my book *The Salvation Bible Commentary.*

[94] *Barnes' Notes on the Bible, entry for Matthew 11:14*

[95] Compare 2 Kings 2:9. "Elijah said unto Elisha, Ask what I shall do for thee, before I be taken away from thee. And Elisha said, I pray thee, let a double portion of thy spirit be upon me."

[96] *Nicene and Post-Nicene Fathers, Hendrickson, Series 2, Vol. 4, p. 309*

[97] *Brooke Foss Westcott, The Epistles of St John, Eerdmans, p. 196*

[98] *A Textual Commentary on the Greek New Testament, United Bible Society, 2nd edition, p. 650*

[99] The author of 1 John uses the neuter τοῦτο as an encapsulation of the preceding context in 1 John 3:10. I believe he does so here as well, only using the masculine οὗτος in regard to the primacy of ὁ θεός, with ζωὴ αἰώνιος taking a subsidiary role under ὁ θεός, as something pertaining to him, rather than paralleled with him.

[100] *Meyer's Commentary on the New Testament, Hendrickson, Vol. 10, p. 623*

[101] *Philo, Dreams 1.232.* The portion "so that they fancy that it is his image, not an imitation of him, but the very archetypal appearance itself" is translated from ὡς τὴν εἰκόνα οὐ μίμημα, ἀλλ' αὐτὸ τὸ ἀρχέτυπον ἐκεῖνο εἶδος ὑπολαμβάνειν εἶναι. Like λόγος, Philo also uses εἰκών in a manner different than the apostles. Paul refers to man, contextually distinct from Christ and woman, as εἰκὼν καὶ δόξα θεοῦ ("the image and glory of God." 1 Corinthians 11:7).

[102] *Ante-Nicene Fathers, Hendrickson, Vol. 1, p. 420*

[103] *Mere Christianity, C.S. Lewis, Macmillan Publishing Company, 1960, p. 157*

[104] *Ante-Nicene Fathers, Vol. 3, p. 604*

[105] *Philo, Giants 60-61*

[106] *Philo, Giants 62-63*

[107] *Philo, Confusion of Tongues 145-147*

[108] *Philo, Allegory 1. 32, 40-43*

[109] *Philo, Worse 83*

[110] Those who taught a Christ who did not come in the flesh were rejected by the same author (2 John 7). Paul also spoke of "false apostles" who teach "another Jesus, whom we have not preached." (2 Corinthians 11:4.) The authentic Jesus and his authentic teachings are in view whenever the Bible refers to believing in Jesus. One of the dangers behind the belief that Christ did not come in the flesh was that it put him in such a different category than we are. If sin is produced by the flesh, and he didn't have it, then he could abstain from sin, but we can't.

[111] *Clarke's Bible Commentary, Abingdon Press, Vol. 6, p. 911*

[112] The parenthetical words are mine. The text reads, "For both he that sanctifieth and they who are sanctified are all of one: for which cause he is not ashamed to call them brethren."

[113] The Greek text of Eusebius of Caesarea's work *Gospel Problems and Solutions* has recently been translated into English by David J. D. Miller. You can find the first segment of this quote on page 33 and the second segment on page 35 therein (I emboldened segments in this quote for emphasis). See the full text in EUSEBIUS OF CAESAREA, GOSPEL PROBLEMS AND SOLUTIONS QUAESTIONES AD STEPHANUM ET MARINUM (CPG 3470), Edited by Roger Pearse, Translated by David J. D. Miller (Greek, Latin), Adam C. McCollum (Syriac, Arabic), Carol Downer (Coptic), and others, *Chieft ain Publishing*, 2010.

[114] This does not mean do good in a *moral* sense. The Greek text means *he bestowed benefits*. I believe that Jesus was *already* doing good in the moral sense and was thus, in the Matthew 5:44-45 definition, *already* a son of God.

[115] See *The Orthodox Corruption of Scripture* by Bart D. Ehrman, Oxford University Press, pp. 73-85.

[116] *A Textual Commentary on the Greek New Testament, United Bible Society, 2nd edition, pp. 112-13*

[117] This is from a Jewish Midrash, cited by John B. Lightfoot in his *Commentary on the New Testament from the Talmud and Hebraica*, Hendrickson, Vol. 3, p. 53. The source of the quote is "Schemoth Rabba, fol. 160. 4." This must correlate to something in *Semot Rabbah*, 1000-1200 AD, but the folio address is for Lightfoot's own catalogue system.

[118] Compare Galatians 1:15, *Who separated me from my mother's womb* – Paul speaks of *birth* in this way, "My little children, of whom I travail in birth again until Christ be formed in you." (Galatians 4:19.) Now, *this birth* is not natural birth, but *a birth of*

conversion. When Paul speaks of *his birth* in Galatians 1:15, he likely has the time of *his own conversion* in mind. The context surrounding Paul's statement is **1.** Paul's conversion experience. **2.** God separating Paul from others immediately after that conversion experience. If "separated me from my mother's womb" can be used by Paul in such a manner, it is plausible that the mother/child terminology could imply something similar in Psalm 22. This would mean that Jesus was cast upon God from the time of his baptism when he was *begotten of God*. The phrase "I am a worm" in Psalm 22:6 is obviously figurative. Jerome writes: "In the Gospel according to the Hebrews, which is written in the Chaldee and Syrian language, but in Hebrew characters, and is used by the Nazarenes to this day (I mean the Gospel according to the Apostles, or, as is generally maintained, the Gospel according to Matthew, a copy of which is in the library at Caesarea), we find, "Behold, the mother of our Lord and His brethren said to Him, John Baptist baptizes for the remission of sins; let us go and be baptized by him. But He said to them, what sin have I committed that I should go and be baptized by him? Unless, haply, the very words which I have said are only ignorance (Nisi forte hoc ipsum quod dixi, ignorantia est)." (*Nicene and Post-Nicene Fathers, Hendrickson, Series 2, Vol. 6, p. 472.*) According to this testimony, Jesus did not know of any sin he committed, but allowed the possibility of having sinned in ignorance.

[119] There are early witnesses that have the text as "water and blood *and spirit.*" Notwithstanding, "water and blood" is likely the original reading. See *The Orthodox Corruption of Scripture* by Bart D. Ehrman, Oxford University Press, pp. 70-71.

[120] $\mathfrak{P}41$, $\mathfrak{P}74$, *Codex Sinaiticus, Codex Alexandriunus, Codex Vaticanus, Codex Ephraemi Rescriptus, Codex Bezae, Codex Clarotnontanus, etc.*

[121] *John Darby, The Holy Scriptures: A New Translation from the Original Languages, 1961 edition, note on Acts 20:28*

[122] *The NIV Study Bible, Zondervan, note on Acts 20:28*

[123] *A Textual Commentary on the Greek New Testament, UBS, 2nd edition, p. 427*

[124] *Alford's Greek Testament, Baker, Vol. 2, p. 230*

[125] Such as Alford, Robertson, Meyer, etc.

[126] The other places in the Greek NT where the word ἰδίου appears are as follows: Luke 6:44, Romans 8:32, 1 Corinthians 7:4 (x2), 1 Corinthians 7:37, 1 Timothy 3:4, 1 Timothy 3:5, 2 Peter 3:17. The word ἰδίου always appears before the noun that it modifies.

[127] *A Textual Commentary on the Greek New Testament, UBS, 2nd edition, p. 427*

[128] *The Bart Ehrman Blog, February 26, 2016*

[129] *Justin Martyr in ANF Vol. 1, pp. 234-235; Irenaeus ad loc., p. 453*

[130] *Commentary on Matthew, St. Jerome, translated by Thomas P. Scheck, the Fathers of the Church, vol. 117, p. 63*

[131] Compare 1 Chronicles 7:23 LXX, "Καὶ εἰσῆλθεν πρὸς τὴν γυναῖκα αὐτοῦ **καὶ ἔλαβεν ἐν γαστρὶ** καὶ ἔτεκεν υἱόν," with Isaiah 7:14, "Ἰδοὺ ἡ νεᾶνις **ἐν γαστρὶ συλλαμβάνει** καὶ τίκτει υἱόν καὶ καλέσεις ὄνομα αὐτοῦ Εμμανουηλ." (Aquila.) Jerome probably preferred λήψεται (Codex Vaticanus) over συλλαμβάνει.

[132] *Heinrich Meyer, Meyer's Commentary on the New Testament, entry for Matthew 1:22-23*

[133] *John Bengel, New Testament Word Studies, entry for Matthew 1:23*

[134] *Ante-Nicene Fathers, Hendrickson, Vol. 3, p. 161*

[135] See also Jeremiah 32:6-16, where Jeremiah bought a field in Israel despite the impending exile to Babylon as a sign from God that, "Houses and fields and vineyards shall be possessed again in this land."

[136] *Philo, Worse 88-89*

[137] *Deuteronomy 13:6*

[138] *Leviticus 16:17*

[139] *Philo, Heir 83-84*

[140] See *The Disciple Whom Jesus Loved* by James Phillips. I believe the initial cause for associating this Gospel with John was due to how *John the Baptist* says much more regarding Jesus and his mission therein than anywhere else.

[141] *Vincent's New Testament Word Studies, MacDonald Publishing, Vol. 2, p. 99*

[142] *Tatian's Diatessaron (160-175 AD)*

[143] *See A Textual Commentary on the Greek New Testament, United Bible Society, 2nd edition, pp. 174-175*

[144] *The NIV Study Bible, Zondervan Publishing House, 1995, Introduction to John's Gospel, under the subheading, Date, (p. 1588)*

[145] Mark 8:31 & Mark 9:9

[146] *Daniel B. Wallace, Greek Grammar Beyond the Basics, pp. 535-536*. Bold emphasis added by me.

[147] *Daniel B. Wallace, Greek Grammar Beyond the Basics, p. 581*

REFERENCE NOTES

[148] J.B. Lighfoot, *St. Paul's Epistle to the Philippians*, Hendrickson, p. 110

[149] J.B. Lighfoot, *St. Paul's Epistle to the Philippians*, Hendrickson, p. 127

[150] J.B. Lighfoot, *St. Paul's Epistle to the Philippians*, Hendrickson, p. 110

[151] J.B. Lighfoot, *St. Paul's Epistle to the Philippians*, Hendrickson, p. 127

[152] *Thayer's Greek-English Lexicon of the New Testament*, Zondervan, 1978, p. 418

[153] See Lightfoot's comments on the *Clementine Homilies of St. Peter* in Lightfoot's *Commentary on Philippians*, Hendrickson, p. 132

[154] *Thayer's Greek-English Lexicon of the New Testament*, Zondervan, 1978, p. 418

[155] *Thayer's Greek-English Lexicon of the New Testament*, Zondervan, 1978, p. 172

[156] ὑπάρχω is translated in Philippians 2:6 as "subsisting" in *The Interlinear Literal Translation of the Greek New Testament* by George R. Berry, Chicago, 1946, p. 515

[157] The usage of ὁμοίωμα in Romans 8:3 as "*likeness* of sinful flesh" does not mean "not actual flesh," instead it means "not actual *sinful* flesh." The potential for sin was there as in our flesh, but he overcame it, hence "condemned sin in the flesh." See also 2 Corinthians 7:1.

[158] See Meyer's note 1, bottom of p. 76, in *Meyer's Commentary on the New Testament*, Hendrickson, Vol. 9

[159] 1 John 4:2-3, etc. is written to counter the notion of Docetism.

[160] This definition for σχῆμα is found in *A Greek-English Lexicon of the New Testament and Other Early Christian Literature*, 2nd edition, p. 797.

[161] See *A Textual Commentary on the Greek New Testament*, UBS, 2nd edition, p. 213

[162] *The Racovian Catechism*, translated by Thomas Rees, London, 1818, pp. 144-145

[163] E.W. Bullinger, *The Companion Bible*, ad loc

[164] A.T. Robertson, *Robertson's Word Pictures in the New Testament*, 1 Peter 3:19

[165] Philo, *Questions and Answers on Genesis* 186

[166] I would like to acknowledge Ronald Day here. I learned of these examples in the Bible years ago while reading his postings. Although we differ in our view of salvation, I honor him for his labor.

[167] The New Testament was translated into the Syriac language around the middle of the 2nd century. The ancient copies that have come down to us in Syriac are now referred to as *the Syriac*.

[168] *Barnes' Notes on the Bible, ad locum*

[169] *Daniel B. Wallace, Greek Grammar Beyond the Basics, Zondervan, pp. 530-531*

[170] *The New Testament, J. A. Kleist and J. L. Lilly, Milwaukee, 1956*

[171] *The New Testament in the Language of Today, William F. Beck, St. Louis, 1963*

[172] See *Truth in Translation: Accuracy and Bias in English Translations of the New Testament, Jason BeDuhn, University Press, pp. 107-108.*

[173] *Greek Grammar, Herbert Weir Smyth, Benediction Classics, Oxford, 2014, pp. 422-423.*

[174] The most authoritative reading for 2 Thessalonians 2:2 is, "the day of the Lord," not, "the day of Christ."

[175] *Barnes' Notes on the Bible, entry for John 8:56*

[176] The seven verses where γενέσθαι is used within John are 1:12, 3:9, 5:6, 8:58, 9:27, 13:19, 14:29. I hadn't noticed the unanimity in John after my initial research on γενέσθαι within the New Testament. While discussing how γενέσθαι is often futuristic, the unanimity as such within the Book of John was mentioned to me by Mark Rich (who recalls hearing the point on a Bill Schlegel podcast). I also checked and found that, lacking γενέσθαι throughout, 1, 2, and 3 John contain no exceptions.

[177] I translate γενέσθαι as "comes to be" in these examples, but a more literal translation may read "shall have come to be," because πρὶν (*before*) + an aorist infinitive verb (like γενέσθαι) carries "the force of the Latin future perfect of things future: πρὶν ἀλέκτορα φωνῆσαι, before the cock shall have crowed, Matthew 26:34." —*Thayer*

[178] *John Lightfoot, Commentary on the New Testament from the Talmud and Hebraica, Hendrickson, Vol. 3, p. 336.*

[179] *A.T. Robertson, Word Pictures in the New Testament, entry for John 8:24*

[180] *Ante-Nicene Fathers, Hendrickson, Vol. 1, p. 576*

[181] I am quoting this representation of Grotius' view from *Alford's Greek Testament*, entry for John 8:58. Alford says Grotius' view, along with the view of proposal 5 here, "are little better than *dishonest quibbles*."

[182] Note that in the Septuagint (LXX) 1st and 2nd Samuel are 1st and 2nd Kings, so what we think of as 1st and 2nd Kings are actually 3rd and 4th Kings in the LXX. I use our standard references in the verses listed after this, so 2 Samuel and 2 Kings match our English Bibles.

[183] *The Racovian Catechism, translated by Thomas Rees, London, 1818, pp. 68-69.*

[184] *Nicene and Post-Nicene Fathers, Hendrickson, Vol. 14., p. 199.* NOTE that I reverse translated "I Am" (the English translation in NPNF) to "ἐγώ εἰμι" here. As it reads in NPNF it is, "But wherefore said He not, "Before Abraham was, I was," instead of "I Am"? As the Father uses this expression, "I AM," so also does Christ; for it signifies continuous Being, irrespective of all time."

[185] *Calvin's Commentary on the Bible, entry for Zephaniah 2:15*

[186] *Greek Grammar, Herbert Weir Smyth, Benediction Classics, Oxford, 2014, p. 422*

[187] *Ray Rogers, Thermochimica Acta 425 (2005), p. 189*

[188] *Giulio Fanti and Pierandrea Malfi, The Shroud of Turin, Pan Stanford Publishing, p. 286*

[189] *Nicene and Post-Nicene Fathers, Hendrickson, Series 2, Vol. 3, p. 362*

[190] *Philo, Allegory 1.31*

[191] *New Strong's Exhaustive Concordance, Hendrickson, 2007, p. 1622*

[192] The Greek text does not say "the spirit." It *could* be translated with "the," but πνεῦμα is anarthrous—it is not preceded by an article—so "a spirit" is absolutely a grammatical possibility here.

[193] *Meyer's Commentary on the New Testament, Hendrickson, Vol. 5. p. 34. Entry for Romans 1:4.*

[194] *Ante-Nicene Fathers, Hendrickson, Vol. 1, p. 454*

[195] *Nicene and Post-Nicene Fathers, Hendrickson, Series 2, Vol. 3, p. 36*

[196] The KJV has the word *"God"* in italics in v.16 because it is not in the original Greek, but was added by the translators.

[197] *Barnes' Notes on the New Testament, note on John 10:11*

[198] This reading is in agreement with the translation found in the *NASB*, but I have translated ἐξουσία as "freedom" rather than the *NASB's* "authority."

[199] *New Strong's Exhaustive Concordance*, Hendrickson, 2007, p. 1626. Bold mine.

[200] Yet, just because Jesus was commanded to lay down his life for the sheep does not mean that he did so only out of obedience to God. Just as God commands us to give to the poor and yet we are willing to do so out of love for them, so also God commanded Jesus to lay down his life for us and he was willing to do so out of his love for us as well. Nevertheless, God did command Christ to lay down his life in this world, and Christ obeyed God in doing so.

[201] Just as our bodies are "the temple of God" because the Spirit of God resides in us (1 Corinthians 6:19, 2 Corinthians 6:16, Ephesians 2:21-22), so also the fact that "God was in Christ" (2 Corinthians 5:19) made Christ's body the "temple" of God as well. This is also why Christ's 'flesh' is called "the veil" in Hebrews 10:20 (which is a reference to the veil of the temple).

[202] The Old Testament prophets would often say, "Thus saith the LORD," prior to reciting God's words in the first-person narrative. They did this in order to acknowledge God as the source of those words. Although Christ is not on record as having said, "Thus saith the LORD," he did acknowledge God as the source of his words in other ways (see John 8:26, 28, 38, 40, 14:10, 24, etc.). Christ openly declared that he "came in his Father's name" rather than his own name (John 5:43, 17:6, 26). These declarations serve the same purpose as an Old Testament prophet's, "Thus saith the LORD." Nevertheless, I do believe that the revelation of God was more spontaneous and innate in Christ than it was in the prophets of old (John 3:34, Revelation 19:10).

[203] *Barnes' Notes on the New Testament*, note on Acts 2:22.

[204] *Alford's Greek New Testament*, ad locum.

[205] *Barnes' Notes on the Bible*, ad locum.

[206] In reality, the Greek word for *firstborn*, (prototokos) is actually a composite word formed from two smaller Greek words: πρῶτος (protos) – *first* and τίκτω (tikto) – *be born*. Prototokos literally means *first-born*, and it retains this definition every single time that it is used within the Bible.

[207] Colossians 1:15 says, "firstborn **of** all creation," but Colossians 1:18 says, "firstborn **from** the dead." This is because Christ *came out from* the category of "the dead" (*i.e.,* he was raised from the dead). He ceased to be included among the dead, but he did not cease to be included among creation. The difference in structure does not give a new meaning to πρωτότοκος.

[208] Daniel B. Wallace, *Greek Grammar Beyond the Basics*, pp. 563-564

[209] I take "no more sea" as reference to the sea dividing lands. New Pangaea.

REFERENCE NOTES

[210] *Greek Grammar*, Herbert Weir Smyth, Benediction Classics, Oxford, 2014, p. 432

[211] This is the best rendering of the text. It has been translated thus in the *Hebrew Names Version*. The bold and Greek parenthetical texts are added here by me.

[212] *Meyer's Commentary on the New Testament*, Hendrickson, Vol. 10. p. 432. Entry for 2 Thessalonians 1:10.

[213] *A Bible Commentary for English Readers*, Charles Ellicott, Cassel and Company, Limited, Vol. 8, p. 153. Entry for 2 Thessalonians 1:10.

[214] *Alford's Greek Testament*, Baker, Vol. 3, p. 286. Entry for 2 Thessalonians 1:10.

[215] Meaning his body was made anew, just as the earth, though remaining, will be made anew and "created."

[216] *Pre-eminent* here in the RSV is translated from πρωτεύω, which means "to be first."

[217] *Alexander, Encyclical Epistle*. I here implement a translation found in *Early Arianism: A View of Salvation*, Gregg and Groh, pg. 105

[218] *Nicene and Post-Nicene Fathers*, Hendrickson, Series 2, Vol. 4, p. 159

[219] *Epiphanius, Panarion, 69. 24 (2-4)*

[220] *Early Arianism—A View of Salvation*, Robert C. Gregg and Dennis E. Groh, Fortress Press, 1981, p. 23

[221] *Ante-Nicene Fathers*, Hendrickson, Vol. 1, p. 35, brackets mine

[222] The fact that our English translations do not capitalize the "L" in "lord" when Sarah calls Abraham κύριος (Lord) is only a matter of preference on the part of the English translator. The only time that the Greek text capitalizes a letter is when it is at the beginning of a proper name, the beginning of a quotation, or the beginning of a new paragraph. The original Greek has the same capitalization when both Christ and Abraham are called "Lord."

[223] **Kyrios** is the same Greek word as **kurios**. The two different spellings are just based on varying English pronunciations of the same Greek word κύριος.

[224] *The NIV Study Bible*, Zondervan Publishing House, 1995

[225] "By" is the rendering found in the KJV, but, if referring to *redemption* (compare 2 Corinthians 5:18), "through" is preferable to "by." If taken of *creation*, the Greek word διά (+ a genitive) should probably be rendered here as "for" instead of "by." See my entry on Hebrews 1:2 (p. 227 herein).

[226] God made Jesus both Lord and Christ—Jesus was already anointed with the Spirit of God when he was baptized by John (Acts 10:37-38, Luke 4:18). There is also another kind of anointing that has to do with becoming king (1 Samuel 15:17, 16:1), etc. Someone who is anointed as a sign of future appointment (1 Samuel 16:13) can be anointed again when that appointment is actualized (2 Samuel 2:4).

[227] This is ὁ κύριος, but in the dative case. The dative just shows that an action was done toward/for/beside the noun, etc.

[228] *Alford's Greek Testament, Baker, Vol. 4, p. 602*

[229] *Robertson's Word Pictures of the New Testament, ad loc.*

[230] *Alford's Greek Testament, ad loc.*

[231] *Meyer's Commentary on the New Testament, Hendrickson, Vol. 10. p. 432*

[232] *Alford's Greek Testament, ad loc.*

[233] *A similar phrase is applied to Christ in Revelation 17:14 as well, the order is just reversed from, "King of kings and Lord of lords," to, "Lord of lords and King of kings."*

[234] *Albert Barnes, Barnes' Notes on the Bible, entry for Daniel 2:37*

[235] Nebuchadnezzar is not called *lord of lords*, but the title *lord of lords* simply means *ruler of rulers* and is therefore similar to *king of kings*. A ruler is someone in a general position of authority while a king is someone in a specific position of authority.

[236] *Ante-Nicene Fathers, Hendrickson, Vol. 7, pp. 124-126*

[237] *The Racovian Catechism, Translated by Thomas Rees, London, 1818, pp. 94-95.*

[238] *A Greek-English Lexicon of the New Testament and Other Early Christian Literature, 2nd edition, pp. 180-181.*

[239] *Alford's Greek Testament, ad loc.*

[240] I believe the author of Hebrews uses φέρω consistently in every instance with the definition "bear unto the end" (Hebrews 1:3, 6:1, 9:16, 12:20, 13:13). Like Hebrews 13:13, which has the present active participle of φέρω to denote a bearing forth from now on unto its end, the same is true of the present active participle of φέρω in Hebrews 1:3.

[241] The words are the same. They just appear slightly different due to how they are used in the sentence. We will touch on the appearance of Greek nouns in the next section for Hebrews 1:8.

[242] Same word used in Hebrews 1:3, in both instances regarding the resurrected Messiah.

²⁴³ Some try to disprove the translation, "Thy throne is God," by pointing to the fact that there is no word in the Greek text of Hebrews 1:8 that can be translated as "is" ("Thy throne *is* God"). It is odd, however, that by such an objection they think to advance the alternate translation ("Thy throne, O God, *is* forever") which **also** requires an understood verb that isn't stated in the corresponding Greek text. Without the inclusion of an understood linking verb, none of the English translations would have any verb at all.

²⁴⁴ *Vincent's Word Studies of the New Testament, Baker, Vol. 4, p. 390*

²⁴⁵ He often quotes passages that coincide with the Septuagint text which do not match the reading of the Hebrew text. Example: Deuteronomy 32:43 is quoted in Hebrews 1:6 as it reads in the LXX as opposed to the reading found in the extant Hebrew OT, etc.

²⁴⁶ The reason why Psalm 45 is Psalm 44 in the LXX is because the Septuagint does not contain Psalm 10.

²⁴⁷ I am not affiliated with the Jehovah's Witness organization. I purchased this book shortly after becoming a Christian (while still a Trinitarian) in order to refute that organization's doctrine and to defend the Trinitarian doctrine.

²⁴⁸ *Ron Rhodes, Reasoning from the Scriptures with the Jehovah's Witnesses, p. 96*

²⁴⁹ *The Septuagint with Apocrypha, ed. Sir Lancelot C.L. Brenton, Hendrickson, p. 724*

²⁵⁰ *B.F. Westcott, The Epistle to the Hebrews, Eerdmans, 1967, pp. 25, 26*

²⁵¹ *B.F. Westcott, The Epistle to the Hebrews, Eerdmans, 1967, p. 26*

²⁵² *A Textual Commentary on the Greek New Testament, UBS, 2ⁿᵈ edition, p. 593*

²⁵³ *See A Textual Commentary on the Greek New Testament, UBS, 2ⁿᵈ edition, p. 593*

²⁵⁴ We do not yet see all things under man (Hebrews 2:8). This pertains to the world to come. During this age angels do have some rule (as do some men opposed to Christ). See "rulers" (Ephesians 6:12), "prince" and "one of the chief princes" (Daniel 10:13).

²⁵⁵ *B.F. Westcott, The Epistle to the Hebrews, Eerdmans, 1967, p. 26*

²⁵⁶ Hence the omission of πάλιν. Hebrews 1:8-9 shows the eternity of Christ's kingdom, while Hebrews 1:10-12 is antithetical, showing that this present world will pass away.

²⁵⁷ *Thayer's Greek-English Lexicon of the New Testament, Zondervan, 1978, p. 380*

²⁵⁸ "The term λόγος never has the sense of *reason* in the New Testament." —*Westcott, The Gospel According to St. John, John 1:1.*

²⁵⁹ Ian Wilson's *Jesus the Evidence* makes an interesting case that the Dead Sea Scroll's *Manual of Discipline* has a style of speaking similar to the Book of John. Wilson compares John 1:1 with Manual of Discipline 11:11, which reads, "All things come to pass by his knowledge, He establishes all things by his design And without him nothing is done." (p. 41, 1ˢᵗ edition.) If, indeed, similar concepts *were* in view, one might think *reason* could be meant by ὁ λόγος in John 1:1. Was the author of John 1:1 an Essene? See *The Disciple Whom Jesus Loved* by James Phillips for a compelling argument that "the disciple whom Jesus loved" was actually Lazarus (John 11:3). Even if he *was* an Essene, this does not give us leave to take ὁ λόγος as *reason* in John 1, since ὁ λόγος is not used that way anywhere else in the New Testament.

²⁶⁰ This is ὁ λόγος in the Genitive (possessive) case.

²⁶¹ *Thayer's Greek-English Lexicon of the New Testament, Zondervan, 1978, p. 417*

²⁶² *Thayer's Greek-English Lexicon of the New Testament, Zondervan, 1978, p. 418*

²⁶³ *A Textual Commentary on the Greek New Testament, UBS, 2ⁿᵈ edition, p. 170*

²⁶⁴ *A Textual Commentary on the Greek New Testament, UBS, 2ⁿᵈ edition, p. 169*

²⁶⁵ *Ante-Nicene Fathers, Hendrickson, Vol. 1, p. 489*

²⁶⁶ *Ante-Nicene Fathers, Hendrickson, Vol. 1, p. 491*

²⁶⁷ *Ante-Nicene Fathers, Hendrickson, Vol. 1, p. 491. Underline is by me.*

²⁶⁸ But comp. "He says" before quoting John 1:18 as reading "Son of God" in ANF, Vol. 1, p. 427.

²⁶⁹ There are two references to "only begotten God" in what is called, *"The Constitutions of the Holy Apostles," (ANF, Vol. 7, pp. 431, 484,)* but it is dated to after the Council of Nicaea.

²⁷⁰ *Ante-Nicene Fathers, Hendrickson, Vol. 1, p. 116*

²⁷¹ See *The Ignatian Epistles Entirely Spurious* by W. D. Killen (See Appendix I herein)

²⁷² This is the possessive / genitive case of μονογενής υἱός

²⁷³ *Ante-Nicene Fathers, Hendrickson, Vol. 2, p. 463*

²⁷⁴ *Ante-Nicene Fathers, Hendrickson, Vol. 9, p. 343*

²⁷⁵ Arius, who also lived in Alexandria, seems to use the notion as "God-only begotten" as in "only begotten in God." *(Athanasius, De Synodis, 15.)* Athanasius says *The Epistle of Dedication in Antioch, (341 AD,)* where Arius was tried, was revised to read τὸν υἱὸν

αὐτοῦ τὸν μονογενῆ θεόν, which some render as, "His Son, the Only-Begotten God," but the Greek does not match the Alexandrian reading of John 1:18. It should be translated, "His Son, the only-begotten, God," or perhaps as it is translated by Hanson in *The Search for the Christian Doctrine of God*, "His only-begotten Son, God."

[276] *Ante-Nicene Fathers*, Hendrickson, Vol. 2, p. 211

[277] *Ante-Nicene Fathers*, Hendrickson, Vol. 2, p. 214

[278] *Ante-Nicene Fathers*, Hendrickson, Vol. 2, p. 601

[279] *A Dictionary of Early Christian Biography*, Hendrickson, p.181

[280] *Thayer's Greek-English Lexicon of the New Testament*, Zondervan, 1978, p. 418

[281] *A Dictionary of Early Christian Biography*, Hendrickson, pp. 998-999

[282] Henry Chadwick, B.D., *Alexandrian Christianity*, Westminster Press, 1997, pp. 15-16

[283] *Ante-Nicene Fathers*, Hendrickson, Vol. 1, p. 428

[284] *A Dictionary of Early Christian Biography*, Hendrickson, p. 1004

[285] *Ante-Nicene Fathers*, Hendrickson, Vol. 1, p. 328

[286] *Ante-Nicene Fathers*, Hendrickson, Vol. 3, p. 262

[287] *Ante-Nicene Fathers*, Hendrickson, Vol. 3, p. 611

[288] *The Text of the Earliest New Testament Greek Manuscripts*, Tyndale, pp. 381-383

[289] *The Text of the Earliest New Testament Greek Manuscripts*, Tyndale., pp. 383-384

[290] *Ante-Nicene Fathers*, Hendrickson, Vol. 1, p. 324

[291] *A Dictionary of Early Christian Biography*, Hendrickson, p. 1003

[292] *Ante-Nicene Fathers*, Hendrickson, Vol. 1, p. 317

[293] *Ante-Nicene Fathers*, Hendrickson, Vol. 3, p. 274

[294] *Ante-Nicene Fathers*, Hendrickson, Vol. 1, p. 328

[295] *A Dictionary of Early Christian Biography*, Hendrickson, p. 1003

[296] *Ante-Nicene Fathers*, Hendrickson, Vol. 3, p. 262

[297] *Ante-Nicene Fathers*, Hendrickson, Vol 1, p. 326

[298] The Valentinians also referred to Monogenes as Arche, corresponding with "the beginning" in John 1:1. Irenaeus points this out in ANF, Vol. 1, p. 329, where he says, "These men, by a plausible kind of exposition, perverting these statements, maintain that there was another Monogenes, according to production, whom they also style Arche." So, according to them, "In Arche [Monogenes] was Logos."

[299] Μονογενὴς and μονογενοῦς are the same word, it just appears different due to its use since μονογενὴς is nominative but μονογενοῦς is genitive (showing possession). Both are used elsewhere as well, μονογενὴς in Luke 7:12, 9:38; μονογενοῦς in John 3:18.

[300] *The Proof of the Gospel, Eusebius of Caesarea, Veritatis Splendor Publications, LLC, 2019, p. 295*

[301] *Ante-Nicene Fathers, Hendrickson, Vol. 1, p. 249*

[302] *Ante-Nicene Fathers, Hendrickson, Vol. 4, p. 548*

[303] *B.F. Westcott, The Epistle to the Hebrews, Eerdmans, 1967, p. 84*

[304] Consider Hebrews 10:5, where Jesus speaks to the Father as both distinct from the body and the Father. How could he do that if he were simply the Father in a body? Comp. 2 Peter 1:13-14.

[305] *Word Pictures in the New Testament, ad loc.*

[306] *Word Pictures in the New Testament, ad loc.*

[307] *Alford's Greek Testament, ad loc.*

[308] *Alford's Greek Testament, ad loc.*

[309] *Ante-Nicene Fathers, Hendrickson, Vol. 5, p. 637*

[310] *Alford's Greek Testament, on John 10:30.*

[311] *Meyer's Commentary on the New Testament, ad loc.*

[312] There are many weighty manuscripts that read "one in us" rather than just "in us." *A Textual Commentary on the New Testament* states that the latter is the original reading (2nd edition, p. 214).

[313] *Nicene and Post-Nicene Fathers, Hendrickson, Series 2, Vol. 4, p. 403.*

[314] *1911 Encyclopedia Britannica (11th edition), Entry for Paul of Samosata.* The Greek text of his sayings can be found in *Doctrina Patrum de Incarnatione Verbi, Franz Diekamp, pp. 303-305.*

REFERENCE NOTES

[315] *Meyer's Commentary on the New Testament, Hendrickson, Vol. 3, p. 330*

[316] The Greek does not capitalize the word "God." The fact that this is written without capitalization is inconsequential.

[317] There is no article in the Greek text. The text literally means "a son."

[318] Although future events may not be seen visibly, they can be "seen" by faith, prophetic revelation, or by vision (Hebrews 11:13, 27, Revelation 20:11-15, etc.).

[319] Jesus is quoting the prophecy text, not identifying himself as the one who was speaking therein.

[320] *Albert Barnes, Barnes' Notes on the Bible, entry for John 12:40*

[321] Although there are other passages of Scripture that speak of God blinding the minds of the unbelievers, Isaiah 6:9-10 is referring to Christ rather than to God. Nevertheless, it can be said that God blinded the people through Christ's teachings. Christ went on to say in John 12:49: "For I did not speak of my own accord, but the Father who sent me commanded me what to say and how to say it." (John 12:49 NIV.) Since God commanded Christ to say what he said, then both Christ and God took part in blinding the eyes of the people.

[322] A time is coming when all of the Jews, although they will be a remnant, will understand the truth concerning Jesus and accept him as the Messiah. This is their inheritance. Romans 9:4-5. See Isaiah 53.

[323] The quotation from Isaiah 53:1, "To whom is the arm of the LORD revealed," also speaks of how God worked miracles through Christ. See Isaiah 52:10, Luke 11:20, Acts 2:22

[324] The original reading says: "These things said Isaiah because (ὅτι) he saw his glory, and spake of him." (John 12:41) See *A Textual Commentary on the New Testament, UBS, 2nd edition, p. 203*. Hence, many of the newer English translations also read, "because he saw his glory," (NIV, NLT, NASB, RSV, Darby, ASV) rather than, "when he saw his glory." (KJV.)

[325] The Hebrew word usually translated as "worship" is (shachah) which means the same as the Greek word προσκυνέω (proskuneō) and is translated in the Septuagint as προσκυνέω.

[326] *Strong's Exhaustive Concordance of the Bible, Hendrickson, #4352, p. 1664*

[327] *Barnes' Notes on the New Testament, loc. Rev. 3:9*

[328] *Institutes of the Christian Religion, Paul T. Jones Publishing, 1843, Vol. 1, p. 114.* I do not agree with the doctrines of Calvin. See *The Salvation Bible Commentary.*

[329] Even though some of the English translations don't translate the word as "worship" in some of these verses, it is the same Greek word (in the Septuagint) as is used when referring to the "worship" of Christ in the New Testament (προσκυνέω).

[330] When John fell down to worship before the angel who showed him future events, the angel said, "Worship God: for the testimony of Jesus is the spirit of prophecy." (Revelation 19:10.) What did he mean? Jesus says, "I Jesus have sent mine angel to testify unto you these things," (Revelation 22:16,) but we know that the revelation was given to Jesus by God (Revelation 1:1). Therefore, Jesus' testimony (Revelation 1:2) is equated to the Spirit of prophecy which originated from God, who is to be acknowledged as the source of these things.

[331] *Targum Pseudo-Jonathan, edited by Tov Rose, 2016, p. 8*

[332] *Philo, On Flight, 67-69*

[333] *Ante-Nicene Fathers, Hendrickson, Vol. 1, p. 140*

[334] *Nicene and Post-Nicene Fathers, Hendrickson, Series 2, Vol. 1, p. 152*

[335] *Nicene and Post-Nicene Fathers, Hendrickson, Series 2, Vol. 1, p. 173*

[336] *George Howard, The Hebrew Gospel of Matthew, pp. 190-191*

[337] *The Proof of the Gospel, Eusebius of Caesarea, Veritatis Splendor Publications, LLC, 2019, pp. 61, 65, 82, 194 (book 1, ch. 3, 4, 6; book 3, ch. 6)*

[338] *M. B. Riddle, D.D., Ante-Nicene Fathers, Hendrickson, Vol. 7, p. 374*

[339] *Alford's Greek Testament, ad locum.*

[340] Greg Stafford, from a video titled *Bible & the Trinity in Conflict #27---Sharp's Rule Wallace's Sharper Rule & Stafford's Sharpest Rule.* He has been working on finishing a book titled *The Sharpest Rule: Greek's Most Tragic Rule.*

[341] *A Textual Commentary on the Greek New Testament, UBS, 2nd edition, p. 657*

[342] *Albert Barnes, Barnes' Notes on the Bible, ad locum.*

[343] Τῇ ἀρχῇ is *Roman power in general* (Alford). "The second article renders the separation of the two [Roman power and the authority of the governor] necessary." —*Alford*

[344] *Albert Barnes, Barnes' Notes on the Bible, entry for Revelation 1:8*

³⁴⁵ *John Wesley's Explanatory Notes on the Whole Bible, entry for Ezekiel 34*

³⁴⁶ *Matthew Henry, Matthew Henry Commentary on the Whole Bible, entry for Psalm 89*

³⁴⁷ The Bible speaks of how a man and a woman will become one flesh (not one spirit or soul), as Jesus said: "He which made them at the beginning made them male and female, And said, For this cause shall a man leave father and mother, and shall cleave unto his wife: and they two shall be one flesh? Wherefore they are no more two, but one flesh. What therefore God hath joined together, let not man put asunder." (Matthew 19:4-6.) So, Christ says that a man and a woman are no longer two, but one flesh after they are joined. This is not to say that a husband and a wife are no longer distinct from one another, but instead it emphasizes the bond and union that exists between the two. In a somewhat similar way, the Bible also says: "What? know ye not that he which is joined to a harlot is one body? for two, saith he, shall be one flesh. But he that is joined unto the Lord is one spirit." (1 Corinthians 6:16-17)

³⁴⁸ This is according to the will of God. "The same God ... distributing to each one individually just as He wills." (1 Corinthians 12:6, 11.) Compare also how God took of the Spirit that was on Moses and gave it to other men (Numbers 11:25).

³⁴⁹ *Ante-Nicene Fathers, Hendrickson, Vol. 2, p. 575.* I substitute "grade" with the *proximity* here, because the former sounds like a defamation, which is not the author's intent.

³⁵⁰ *Ante-Nicene Fathers, Hendrickson, Vol. 2, p. 571*

³⁵¹ *Ante-Nicene Fathers, Hendrickson, Vol. 2, p. 24*

³⁵² *Ante-Nicene Fathers, Hendrickson, Vol. 3, p. 36*

³⁵³ *Ante-Nicene Fathers, Hendrickson, Vol. 4, p. 654*

³⁵⁴ *Ante-Nicene Fathers, Hendrickson, Vol. 3, p. 548*

³⁵⁵ *The Two Treatises of Servetus on the Trinity, Harvard University Press, 1932, pp. 94-102*

³⁵⁶ *Ante-Nicene Fathers, Hendrickson, Vol. 1, p. 184*

³⁵⁷ *Nicene and Post-Nicene Fathers, Hendrickson, Series 2, Vol. 1, p. 94*

³⁵⁸ These quotes are from *The Epistle to Aristides* as found in *The Ante-Nicene Fathers, Hendrickson, Vol. 6, pp. 125-127*, but for the longer quote that relays the account from Jesus' relatives, I switch to the translation found in *Nicene and Post-Nicene Fathers, Hendrickson, Series 2, Vol. 1, pp. 91-94.*

[359] ὁ δὲ Λουκᾶς ἀνάπαλιν 'ὃς ἦν, ὡς ἐνομίζετο 'καὶ γὰρ καὶ τοῦτο προστίθησιν' τοῦ Ἰωσὴφ τοῦ Ἠλὶ τοῦ Μελχί.'

[360] *Ante-Nicene Fathers, Hendrickson, Vol. 6, p. 126, footnote 7.* This is recapped and expounded upon afterward by McGiffert in *Nicene and Post-Nicene Fathers, Hendrickson, Series 2, Vol. 1, p. 92, footnote 120.*

[361] *Nicene and Post-Nicene Fathers, Hendrickson, Series 2, Vol. 1, p. 92, footnote 122*

[362] *Nicene and Post-Nicene Fathers, Hendrickson, Series 2, Vol. 1, p. 93, footnote 136*

[363] I am aware that some point to the antagonists' statement, "We be not born of fornication" and say this indicates Jesus' human father was unknown to them. This interpretation, however, is contradicted by the context and that very same statement of those Jews, who said, "We be not born of fornication; *we have one Father, even God.*" (John 8:41.) They were *not* speaking of natural birth. If so, then they were all claiming to have been born *without a human father*. Their statement is about *the origin of their conduct*. They wanted to portray their actions as pure and unquestionably sourced in God.

[364] *Alford's Greek Testament, Baker, Vol. 1, p. 764*

[365] *Cambridge Greek Testament for Schools and Colleges, The Gospel According to S. John, Cambridge University Press, 1891, p. 152*

[366] *Irenaeus, Ante-Nicene Fathers, Hendrickson, Vol. 1, p. 451*

[367] *Eusebius, Nicene and Post-Nicene Fathers, Hendrickson, Series 2, Vol. 1, p. 159*

[368] *Epiphanius, Panarion, 30. 3 (1)*

[369] Being born of a woman does not indicate virgin birth. The same is true regarding Genesis 3:15, where some say a virgin birth is intended by *the seed of the woman*. Such a claim is contradicted by Genesis 16:10, where God says to Hagar, "I will multiply thy seed exceedingly." Hagar's seed was not born of a virgin. Some contrast Galatians 4:4 with Galatians 4:23, where Paul talks of being "born (γεγέννηται) after the flesh." There, the manner of birth is the focus. If Paul wanted to emphasize Jesus' manner of birth in Galatians 4:4 as being of a virgin, he could have. He did not. He could have simply written "virgin" instead of "woman."

[370] *Bart D. Ehrman, Reader's Mailbag February 26, 2016*

[371] *Nicene and Post-Nicene Fathers, Hendrickson, Series 1, Vol. 4, p. 159*

[372] *Nicene and Post-Nicene Fathers, Hendrickson, Series 1, Vol. 4, p. 159*

[373] *Lost Christianities, Bart D. Ehrman, Oxford University Press, p. 102*

[374] *Epiphanius, Panarion, 30. 14 (2-3)*

[375] *Nicene and Post-Nicene Fathers, Hendrickson, Series 2, Vol. 1, pp. 262-264*

[376] *Jewish, Christian, and Classical Exegetical Traditions in Jerome's Translation of the Book of Exodus, Matthew A. Kraus, pp. 111-115*

[377] *Nicene and Post-Nicene Fathers, Hendrickson, Series 2, Vol. 3, p. 362*. Immediately after this quoted portion, Jerome says that the prophecies in Matthew 2:15 and 2:23 are from the Hebrew Old Testament (as opposed to the LXX). However, even while arguing for their Hebrew origins in his subsequent commentary on Matthew (398 AD), Jerome never says those prophecies are found within the Matthew text used by the Nazarenes.

[378] Faustus said: "If one of the Nazareans, or Symmachians, as they are sometimes called, were arguing with me from these words of Jesus that he came not to destroy the law, I should find some difficulty in answering him." Augustine replies: "These are the people of whom Faustus speaks under the name of Symmachians or Nazareans. Their number is now very small, but the sect still continues." (400 AD, *Nicene and Post-Nicene Fathers, Hendrickson, Series 1, Vol. 4, pp. 240, 246*)

[379] Symmachus' translation was in use long before the persecution of Christians under Maximinus Thrax. *A Dictionary of Early Christian Biography* (p. 918) says, "Eusebius speaks of the version of Symmachus (vi. 16) as being, like those of Aquila and Theodotion, in common use in Origen's day. ... Origen's extant remains shew that he knew and used Symmachus's version long before the time of Maxim (236-239)."

[380] *A Dictionary of Early Christian Biography, Hendrickson, p. 918*

[381] *Eusebius' Ecclesiastical History, Hendrickson, p. 207 (Book 10, ch. 9)*

[382] *Jerome, Commentary on Matthew 12:13*, quoted here from *Gospel Parallels: A Comparison of the Synoptic Gospels, 5th edition, Nelson, p. 59*

[383] This is a Hebrew text. There is a difference between this text and the Greek text that came to be known as *The Gospel of the Ebionites*. This *Hebrew* text would be identified commonly as either *The Gospel of the Hebrews* or *The Gospel of the Nazarenes*. "This particular Gospel of the Ebionites appears to have been a 'harmonization' of the New Testament Gospels of Matthew, Mark, and Luke. ... The Gospel of the Ebionites was evidently written in Greek." —Bart D. Ehrman (*Lost Christianities, pp. 102-103*)

[384] *Epiphanius, Panarion, 30. 14 (3)* The opening to this Gospel used by the Ebionites sounds a lot like Luke 3:1-2. Although Epiphanius says it is the Gospel of *Matthew*, sometimes Luke was referred to as Matthew. Even the oldest manuscript fragments containing the Luke infancy narrative (𝔓4/ 𝔓64/ 𝔓67) were found with the title *Gospel according to Matthew* (εὐαγγέλιον κατὰ μαθθαῖον). See *The Text of the Earliest Greek New*

Testament Manuscripts, Comfort and Barrett, 1st edition (single volume), p. 53. There were *only* texts from Luke in these fragments, so I deduce that the title fragment, found with those Luke texts, most likely answers to that text. Also, Epiphanius apparently cites an Arian's mocking comment as, "But according to Matthew God's incarnation came after seventy-two generations." *(Panarion 69. 21, 6)*. This is much closer to the number of generations in Luke than Matthew. See also ANF, Vol. 3, pp. 423-424, where passages only found in Matthew are attributed to Luke. *The Gospel of the Ebionites* (so called at that time) was apparently a composite of other texts (*Panarion 30. 13. 6-8*), so flavors of Luke (like mentioning that John the Baptist was from Zecharias and Elizabeth) may not be as meaningful as one might think. Generally, scholars say the Ebionites Gospel began at our Matthew chapter three.

[385] *Ante-Nicene Fathers, Hendrickson, Vol. 1, p. 453*

[386] *Ante-Nicene Fathers, Hendrickson, Vol. 3, pp. 538-539*

[387] See *The Orthodox Corruption of Scripture* by Bart D. Ehrman, Oxford University Press, p. 123, note 72.

[388] *Ante-Nicene Fathers, Hendrickson, Vol. 1, p. 199*

[389] *Ante-Nicene Fathers, Hendrickson, Vol. 1, p. 203*

[390] Justin is familiar with various readings, as he will demonstrate later, but these are tied to Matthew with flavors of other readings. For example, when he quotes Matthew 23:23, which, unlike Luke, begins with, "Woe unto you, *scribes and Pharisees*," (Luke only says "Pharisees,") the *ending* of his quotation accords better with Luke, where we find "judgment and the love of God" (Luke 11:42) instead of Matthew's "judgment, mercy, and faith." Contrast this with Tatian's Diatessaron reading, "the law, judgement, and mercy, and faith, and the love of God."

[391] Justin does not preface his quotes of Christ from Matthew, but simply says things like, "He said," showing no need to qualify the source of those sayings. He does this repeatedly (ANF, Vol. 1, pp. 218, 221, 236, 240, 242, 247, 248, 249). Justin probably could not read Hebrew, so he must have learned these from a Greek translation (oral or written).

[392] *Ante-Nicene Fathers, Hendrickson, Vol. 1, p. 249 (ch. 100)*

[393] *Ante-Nicene Fathers, Hendrickson, Vol. 1, pp. 195,198 (ch. 3, 7-8, 23)*

[394] The Greek text corresponding to the underlined portion is: "μετά τὸν κατὰ τὴν βουλὴν τοῦ θεοῦ δίχα ἁμαρτίας τῆς ἀπὸ γένους τοῦ Ἀβραὰμ παρθένου γεννηθέντα Υἰὸν Θεοῦ Ἰησοῦν Χριστόν."

[395] *Ante-Nicene Fathers, Hendrickson, Vol. 1, p. 236 (ch. 76)*

[396] *Greek Grammar, Herbert Weir Smyth, Benediction Classics, Oxford, 2014, p. 311*

[397] Per the footnote on p. 236 of *The Ante-Nicene Fathers, Hendrickson, Vol. 1.*

[398] *Ante-Nicene Fathers, Hendrickson, Vol. 1, pp. 236-237 (ch. 76)*

[399] *Ante-Nicene Fathers, Hendrickson, Vol. 1, p. 237 (ch. 77, 78)*

[400] *Ante-Nicene Fathers, Hendrickson, Vol. 1, p. 238 (ch. 79)*

[401] *Ante-Nicene Fathers, Hendrickson, Vol. 1, p. 243 (ch. 88)*

[402] *Ante-Nicene Fathers, Hendrickson, Vol. 1, p. 249 (ch. 100)*

[403] The Greek text starting at "and" is: καί (and) Υἱὸν (Son) Θεοῦ (of God) γεγραμμένον (has been written) αὐτὸν (he is) ἐν (in) τοῖς (those) ἀπομνημονεύμασι (memoirs) τῶν (of the) ἀποστόλων (apostles) αὐτοῦ (his) ἔχοντες (they are having).

[404] *Ante-Nicene Fathers, Hendrickson, Vol. 1, p. 249 (ch. 100)*

[405] I capitalize *The Memoirs of the Apostles* because I believe the text Justin is using is a single manuscript.

[406] "And when it is said that He changed the name of one of the apostles to **Peter**; and when it is written in **the memoirs of Him** that this so happened, **as well as** that He changed the names of other two brothers, the sons of Zebedee, to Boanerges, which means **sons of thunder** [this is only found in Mark 3:17]; this was an announcement of the fact…" (*Ante-Nicene Fathers, Hendrickson, Vol. 1, p. 252 (ch. 106)*)

[407] *Ante-Nicene Fathers, Hendrickson, Vol. 1, p. 185 (1ˢᵗ Apology, ch. 66)*

[408] *Ante-Nicene Fathers, Hendrickson, Vol. 1, p. 249 (ch. 100)*

[409] *Ante-Nicene Fathers, Hendrickson, Vol. 1, p. 252 (ch. 106)*

[410] It seems like Trypho has been wrestling with whether to become a Christian. Yet, his questions do not stay on the track Justin pushes, but bring up his view of what a *Jewish* Christian might be. After Justin brings up the virgin birth theme and goes to great lengths to convince Trypho that Jesus is "another God," Trypho has not incorporated *any* of that into his view of Christianity. Trypho: "But if some, even now, wish to live in the observance of the institutions given by Moses, and yet believe in this Jesus who was crucified, recognizing Him to be the Christ of God, and that it is given to Him to be absolute Judge of all, and that His is the everlasting kingdom, can they also be saved?" (ANF, Vol. 1, p. 217.) And, "Those who affirm him to have been a man, and to have been anointed by election, and then to have become Christ, appear to me to speak more plausibly than you who hold those opinions which you express. For we all expect that Christ will be a

man [born] of men, and that Elijah when he comes will anoint him. But if this man appear to be Christ, he must certainly be known as man [born] of men." (ANF, Vol. 1, p. 219.)

[411] Trypho to Justin: "We are not prepared for such perilous replies; since never yet have we heard any man investigating, or searching into, or proving these matters." (ANF, Vol. 1, p. 224.)

[412] *Ante-Nicene Fathers, Hendrickson, Vol. 3, p. 215*

[413] *Epiphanius, Panarion, 21. 1 (2)*

[414] *Ante-Nicene Fathers, Hendrickson, Vol. 1, p. 349*

[415] *Ante-Nicene Fathers, Hendrickson, Vol. 1, p. 349*

[416] *Ante-Nicene Fathers, Hendrickson, Vol. 5, p. 108*

[417] *Ante-Nicene Fathers, Hendrickson, Vol. 6, p. 233*

[418] *Ante-Nicene Fathers, Hendrickson, Vol. 2, p. 316*

[419] *Ante-Nicene Fathers, Hendrickson, Vol. 1, p. 350*

[420] *Ante-Nicene Fathers, Hendrickson, Vol. 1, p. 350*

[421] *Commentary on Matthew, St. Jerome, translated by Thomas P. Scheck, the Fathers of the Church, vol. 117, pp. 51-52, bold emphasis mine*

[422] $\mathfrak{P}$1 is dated to the middle of the 3rd century and is the oldest extant manuscript with the Matthew infancy narrative. It contains Matthew 1:1-9, 12, 14-20. The verses reflect the fragmented papyrus, not textual omissions. See *The Text of the Earliest Greek New Testament Manuscripts*, 1st edition, p. 39 for more information.

[423] "It was later, in the times of Adrian the king, that those who invented the heresies arose; and they extended to the age of Antoninus the elder, as, for instance, Basilides, though he claims (as they boast) for his master, Glaucias, the interpreter of Peter."
—Clement of Alexandria (*Ante-Nicene Fathers, Vol. 2, p. 554*)

[424] *Ante-Nicene Fathers, Hendrickson, Vol. 1, p. 350*

[425] *A Dictionary of Early Christian Biography, Hendrickson, p. 110*

[426] *A Dictionary of Early Christian Biography, Hendrickson, p. 110*

[427] *Ante-Nicene Fathers, Hendrickson, Vol. 2, p. 555*

[428] *New Strong's Exhaustive Concordance, Hendrickson, 2007, p. 1646*

⁴²⁹ *Ante-Nicene Fathers*, Hendrickson, Vol. 2, p. 415

⁴³⁰ Didymus the Blind, Psalm Commentary (Tura papyrus) III, ed. and trans. M. Gronewald, *Papyrologische Texte und Abhandlungen* 8, 1968, p. 198:, p. 184. 9-10

⁴³¹ A. F. J. Klijn, *Jewish-Christian Gospel Tradition*, Brill, 1991, p. 78

⁴³² *Nicene and Post-Nicene Fathers*, Hendrickson, Series 2, Vol. 1, p.157, footnote 808

⁴³³ James Hastings (summarizing the arguments of Adolf von Harnack), *A Dictionary of the Bible*, p. 437

⁴³⁴ *Ante-Nicene Fathers*, Hendrickson, Vol. 1, p. 352

⁴³⁵ *Ante-Nicene Fathers*, Hendrickson, Vol. 1, p. 468

⁴³⁶ *The Bart Ehrman Blog, Luke's First Edition*, December 23, 2012

⁴³⁷ *Bart D. Ehrman, Did Luke Originally Have Chapters 1-2?, Reader's Mailbag*, August 15, 2013

⁴³⁸ Hom. in Luc. 1.1, trans. Joseph T. Lienhard, *Origen: Homilies on Luke, Fragments on Luke* (FC 94; Washington, D.C.: The Catholic University of America Press, 1996), 5

⁴³⁹ *Ante-Nicene Fathers*, Hendrickson, Vol. 8, p. 750

⁴⁴⁰ Bovon, François, and John M. Duffy. "A New Greek Fragment from Ariston of Pella's 'Dialogue of Jason and Papiscus.'" *The Harvard Theological Review*, vol. 105, no. 4, 2012, p. 462

⁴⁴¹ *Ante-Nicene Fathers*, Hendrickson, Vol. 8, p. 749

⁴⁴² This is also demonstrable in other ways. For example, in the extant fragment of *Jason and Papiscus*, Jason focuses on distinguishing *the eighth day* as *more honorable* than *the seventh*. Justin follows suit and (using a *plural* personal pronoun), says, "Now, sirs, it is possible for us to show how the eighth day possessed a certain mysterious import, which the seventh day did not possess, and which was promulgated by God through these rites." (ANF, Vol. 1, p. 206). When Clement of Alexandria (who attributes *Jason and Papiscus* to Luke) talks about the eighth day in such a way, he also says Christ is called "the Day." (ANF, Vol. 2, p. 514.) This is also how Justin refers to Christ (ANF, Vol. 1, p. 249). According to Clement, when David says, "This is the day which the Lord hath made," (Psalm 118:24,) this means *God made Jesus, who is called the Day*. Clement probably got this from *Jason and Papiscus*, the source of the eighth day material mentioned immediately prior. Thus, when Justin says Christ is called *the Day* in the Tanakh (the "Old Testament"), he is revealing his source as *Jason and Papiscus* as well.

[443] *Bovon, François, and John M. Duffy. "A New Greek Fragment from Ariston of Pella's 'Dialogue of Jason and Papiscus.'" The Harvard Theological Review, vol. 105, no. 4, 2012, p. 462. Italics mine.*

[444] *ad loc.* Bold emphasis added by me. This is the translation found in the article. The actual Greek text for the bold section (found in the same article) reads: καί τής ένσάρκου τού Σωτήρος γεννήσεως ἡμέρα γνωρίζεται.

[445] *Ante-Nicene Fathers, Hendrickson, Vol. 1, p. 243 (ch. 88)*

[446] *Ante-Nicene Fathers, Hendrickson, Vol. 1, p. 243 (ch. 88)*

[447] *Philo, Heir 205*

[448] *The New Encyclopedia Britannica, 15th ed., Vol. 7, p. 541*

[449] *Ante-Nicene Fathers, Hendrickson, Vol. 1, p. 351*

[450] *Ante-Nicene Fathers, Hendrickson, Vol. 1, p. 352*

[451] Epiphanius writes, "And at first, as I said, Ebion declared that Christ is the offspring of a man, that is, of Joseph. For a while now, however, various of his followers have been giving conflicting accounts of Christ, as though they have decided on something untenable and impossible themselves. ... But others among them say that he is from above; created before all things, a spirit, both higher than the angels and Lord of all; and that he is called Christ, the heir of the world there. But he comes here when he chooses, as he came in Adam and appeared to the patriarchs clothed with Adam's body. And in the last days the same Christ who had come to Abraham, Isaac and Jacob, came and donned Adam's body, and appeared to men, was crucified, rose and ascended. But again, when they choose to, they say, 'No! The Spirit—that is, the Christ—came to him and put on the man called Jesus.' And they get all giddy from making different suppositions about him at different times. They too accept the Gospel according to Matthew. Like the Cerinthians and Merinthians, they too use it alone." (Epiphanius, Panarion, 30. 3. 1-6). Though the Ebionites' exclusive use of the Gospel of Matthew appears to conflict with their use of the Gospel of Luke, it seems possible that, historically, in some ways, Matthew was once confounded with Luke. In fact, the oldest fragments of Luke ($\mathfrak{P}$4) were found with the title "Gospel According to Matthew" even though there were *only* texts from Luke found among those fragments. See *The Text of the Earliest Greek New Testament Manuscripts*, Comfort and Barrett, 1st edition, pp. 45-48 and 53-54. Tertullian (200 AD) also attributed texts found in Luke to Matthew (ANF, Vol. 3, pp. 423-424).

[452] *Ante-Nicene Fathers, Hendrickson, Vol. 1, p. 170*

[453] *Epiphanius, Panarion, 30. 13 (6)*

[454] In chapter 18, he says, "And I, Joseph," before he describes the events allegedly experienced by Joseph at Jesus' birth. It seems to me that they *claimed* to be *prophesying* by those deceased individuals' spirits. "At this very time, even the heretical dupes of Simon [Magus] are so much elated by the extravagant pretension of their art, that they try to bring up from Hades the souls of the prophets themselves." —*Tertullian, 210 AD* (*Ante-Nicene Fathers, Vol. 3, p. 234.*) Such spiritism supports the association of the *Protoevangelium of James* with Basilides, who was himself associated with Simon Magus.

[455] A version of his speech was also included in a fictitious writing *The Life of Barlaam and Josaphat* that was written around the 6th century. Additionally, there are a couple of fragments dated to the 3rd or 4th century, which are "very fragmentary."

[456] *Nicene and Post-Nicene Fathers, Hendrickson, Series 2, Vol. 3, p. 368*

[457] *The Chronicon Paschal*, from *Ariston of Pella's Lost Apology for Christianity*, (*Ariston of Pella: An Investigation of His Works, Name, and Toponym*, p. 93), Harry Tolley

[458] *Nicene and Post-Nicene Fathers, Hendrickson, Series 2, Vol. 4, p. 474*

[459] I read these quotes in books on the subject, but I have not been able to examine those source texts myself. From what I have seen, Paul only says Jesus was *from* Mary in both. Ehrman says of the *Acta* that the "most recent investigators have discounted their authenticity." In the same location, Ehrman says of The Letter of the Six Bishops (called the *Epistula*) "is now widely considered authentic" but "proves problematic for knowing what Paul himself believed because it expresses only the theological affirmations of his orthodox opponents, not the heretical views it was drafted to oppose." (See *The Orthodox Corruption of Scripture* by Bart D. Ehrman, Oxford University Press, p. 62.)

[460] *On the Incarnation of Our Lord Jesus Christ, Against Apollinaris, Book 2, Section 3*

[461] *On the Incarnation of Our Lord Jesus Christ, Against Apollinaris, Book 2, Section 3*

[462] *Ante-Nicene Fathers, Hendrickson, Vol. 1, p. 352*

[463] *Ante-Nicene Fathers, Hendrickson, Vol. 3, p. 351*

[464] *Nicene and Post-Nicene Fathers, Hendrickson, Series 1, Vol. 4, p. 325*

[465] *On the Incarnation of Our Lord Jesus Christ, Against Apollinaris, Book 2, Section 5*

[466] *Carwithen, Hist. Ch. of England, i. 554, 2nd ed.*

[467] *Instit. I. c. xiii. § 29.* "There is," says Calvin, "nothing more abominable than that trash which is in circulation under the name of Ignatius."

[468] *The Apostolic Fathers, Part II., S. Ignatius, S. Polycarp. Revised texts, with Introductions, Notes, Dissertations, and Translations. By J. B. Lightfoot, D.D., D.C.L., LL.D., Bishop of Durham. London 1885.*

[469] *Vol. i. p. 316*

[470] *Vol. ii. sec. i. p. 446*

[471] *Ibid.*

[472] *Vol. i. p. 380.* He says elsewhere "almost simultaneously," *vol. i. p. 382*

[473] The words "for kings" of this part of the letter are extant only in a Latin version. The passage in the Latin stands thus: "Orate etiam, pro regibus et potestatibus et principibus."

[474] As the great monarch of Assyria surveyed the potentates under his dominion, he was tempted to exclaim vaingloriously, "Are not my princes all of them kings?" Isa. x. 8, Revised Version. The emperor of Rome might have uttered the same proud boast.

[475] *Vol. i. p. 576*

[476] Ibid. In support of this view Dr. Lightfoot appeals to 1 Tim ii. 2, where the apostle says that "supplications, prayers, intercessions, and giving of thanks," as circumstances required, should be made "for kings and all that are in authority." Paul is here giving general directions suited to all time; but Polycarp is addressing himself to the Philippians, and furnishing them with instructions adapted to their existing condition.

[477] *Vol. i. p. 407*

[478] See Dr. Lightfoot, vol. i. p. 23, and Zahn, *Ignatius von Antiochien,* pp. 28 and 401.

[479] This road was several hundred miles in length.

[480] *Vol. ii. sec. ii. p. 921, note.*

[481] "Si quis vadit ad Syriam, deferat literas meas, quas fecero ad vos." This is the reading of the old Latin version, which, as Dr. Lightfoot tells us, "is sometimes useful for correcting the text of the extant Greek MSS." *Vol. ii. sec. ii. p. 901.* Even some of the Greek MSS. read, not [Greek: par humon] but [Greek: par haemon]. This reading is found in some copies of Eusebius and in Nicephorus, and is followed by Rufinus. *See Jacobson, Pat. Apost. ii. 488, note.*

[482] *Epistle to Polycarp, § 7.*

[483] The words may be literally translated, "If any one is going to Syria, he might convey to you my letters which I shall have finished," that is, which I have ready. Friendly letters

were then generally much longer than in our day, as the opportunities of transmitting them were few; and much longer time was occupied in their preparation.

[484] *Bingham's Origines Ecclesiasticae, iii. 196. London 1840.*

[485] *Contra Haer. lib. v. c. 28. §4.*

[486] Dr. Lightfoot seems to have been in a condition of strange forgetfulness when he asks, "Why does not Irenaeus quote Polycarp's Epistle?"—vol. i. p. 328. The simple answer is that he mentions the Epistle, and quotes Polycarp by name as a witness against the heretics. *Contra Haer. book iii. c. 3. § 4.*

[487] Eusebius, v. c. i. The writer here mentions a number of individuals by name, who were at this time "led into the amphitheatre to the wild beasts."

[488] Professor Harnack says: "If we do not retain the Epistle of Polycarp, then we must allow that *the external evidence on behalf of the Ignatian Epistles is exceedingly weak, and hence is highly favourable to the suspicion that they are spurious."—Expositor* for Jan. 1886, p. 11. We have seen, however, that the Epistle of Polycarp furnishes no evidence in their favour. See Chap. II.

[489] The Ancient Church, Period II. sec. ii. chap. ii., iii.

[490] Even Eusebius has given some countenance to this practice. See his *Evangelical Preparation*, xii. c. 31.

[491] Döllinger's *Hippolytus and Callistus*, p. 113.

[492] Vol. ii. sec. i. p. 186.

[493] Lightfoot, vol. ii. sec. i. pp. 435, 445.

[494] Vol. i. p. 46.

[495] Euseb. v. c. 24.

[496] Eph. § 6; Magn. § 6.

[497] Rom. § 4.

[498] Eph. § 12; Rom. § 4; Trallians, § 3.

[499] Eph. § 9.

[500] Polycarp, § 6.

[501] Smyrnaeans, § 5; Philad. § 6.

[502] Philosophumena, Book IX.

[503] Eph. § 1.

[504] Rom. § 6.

[505] Vol. i. p. 329.

[506] Cyprian could not sympathize with this Ignatius in his passion for martyrdom. The Bishop of Carthage incurred some odium by retiring to a place of safety in a time of persecution.

[507] *Ante-Nicene Fathers Vol. 1 (p. 20) footnote 15*

[508] *A Dictionary of Early Christian Biography, Hendrickson, p. 981*

[509] *A Dictionary of Early Christian Biography, Hendrickson, p. 981*

[510] *Ante-Nicene Fathers, Hendrickson, Vol. 2, p. 104*

[511] *Ante-Nicene Fathers, Hendrickson, Vol. 2, p. 102*

[512] *Ante-Nicene Fathers, Hendrickson, Vol. 2, p. 89*

[513] *Nicene and Post-Nicene Fathers, Hendrickson, Series 2, Vol. 1, p. 203*

[514] *Nicene and Post-Nicene Fathers, Hendrickson, Series 2, Vol. 1, p. 203*

[515] *Nicene and Post-Nicene Fathers, Hendrickson, Series 2, Vol. 3, p. 369*

[516] *Commentary on Matthew, St. Jerome, translated by Thomas P. Scheck, the Fathers of the Church, vol. 117, pp. 56-57*

[517] *A Dictionary of Early Christian Biography, Hendrickson, p. 982*

[518] *Nicene and Post-Nicene Fathers, Hendrickson, Series 2, Vol. 3, p. 392*

[519] *Ante-Nicene Fathers, Hendrickson, Vol. 2, p. 119*

[520] *Ante-Nicene Fathers, Hendrickson, Vol. 2, p. 92*

[521] *Ante-Nicene Fathers, Hendrickson, Vol. 2, p. 94*

[522] *Ante-Nicene Fathers, Hendrickson, Vol. 2, p. 110, brackets from the source material*

[523] *Ante-Nicene Fathers, Hendrickson, Vol. 2, p. 117*

[524] "We even hear of one Greek work with an Egyptian title—the 'Semenouthi,' attributed to Apollonides Horapios, the 'arch-prophet' (second century CE); the title probably means 'Sacred Scroll' in Egyptian ... In most cases, the readership of 'Greco-Egyptian' literature seems to have been confined to Egypt." —Ian Rutherford, *Greco-Egyptian Interactions: Literature, Translation, and Culture, 500 BC-AD 300,* Oxford University Press, p. 7

[525] *Ante-Nicene Fathers,* Hendrickson, Vol. 2, p. 96

[526] *Ante-Nicene Fathers,* Hendrickson, Vol. 2, p. 92

[527] *Ante-Nicene Fathers,* Hendrickson, Vol. 2, p. 96.

[528] *Ante-Nicene Fathers,* Hendrickson, Vol. 2, p. 112

[529] *Ante-Nicene Fathers,* Hendrickson, Vol. 2, p. 92

[530] *Ante-Nicene Fathers,* Hendrickson, Vol. 2, p. 115

[531] *Ante-Nicene Fathers,* Hendrickson, Vol. 2, p. 111

[532] *Ante-Nicene Fathers,* Hendrickson, Vol. 2, p. 116

[533] *Ante-Nicene Fathers,* Hendrickson, Vol. 2, p. 117

[534] *Ante-Nicene Fathers,* Hendrickson, Vol. 2, p. 115

[535] *Ante-Nicene Fathers,* Hendrickson, Vol. 2, p. 93

[536] *Ante-Nicene Fathers,* Hendrickson, Vol. 2, p. 104

[537] *Wesley's Notes on the New Testament,* Bacon Hill Press, entry for Luke 1:3

[538] *Ante-Nicene Fathers,* Hendrickson, Vol. 2, pp. 100-101

[539] Book 2, ch. 10. Translated "Spirit of God" in the *Ante-Nicene Fathers*, Vol. 2, p. 98

[540] *Ante-Nicene Fathers,* Hendrickson, Vol. 2, p. 105

[541] *Ante-Nicene Fathers,* Hendrickson, Vol. 2, p. 104

SCRIPTURE INDEX

Genesis

1:1 ... 268, 373
1:1-2:3 ... 348
1:26 ... 347
1:27 ... 348
3:15 ... 528
3:20 ... 189
4:1 ... 349
4:21 ... 66
6:5-18 ... 224
11:6-7 ... 348
11:7 ... 349
16:10-13 ... 403
17:4-5 ... 152
18:1-19:16 ... 349
19:1 ... 338
19:24 ... 349
22:8 ... 349
22:15-17 ... 403
23:7 ... 340
27:9 ... 340
28:12 ... 394
31:11-13 ... 403
32:13-16 ... 318
37:9 ... 72
42:30 ... 43, 347
48:15-16 ... 348

Exodus

3:2-14 ... 402
3:14 ... 135, 137, 152, 368
4:10 ... 136
4:16 ... 41, 403
4:22 ... 186, 375
4:23 ... 376
5:1-3 ... 40
7:1 ... 40, 54, 203, 325
7:17 ... 352, 403
8:25-29 ... 40
11:4-7 ... 376
12:29 ... 376
13:17-18 ... 351
17:4 ... 123
17:6 ... 358
17:15 ... 351
24:10 ... 51
25:18 ... 325
31:18 ... 384
32:34 ... 351
34:14 ... 112, 275, 338

Leviticus

16:5 ... 347
16:17 ... 86
26:12 ... 349

Numbers

12:1-5 ... 376
14:20-23 ... 359
15:30 ... 321
36:6-7 ... 410

Deuteronomy

4:32-34 ... 377
13:16 ... 86
18:17-19 ... 41, 174
25:5-6 ... 406, 413
30:13 ... 98
32:3-4 ... 59
32:6-12 ... 69
32:7-8 ... 129
32:18 ... 59, 377
32:31 ... 358
32:43 ... 412

Joshua

5:14 ... 341

Judges

6:11-18 ... 302
6:18 ... 150
6:22 ... 402
11:34 ... 65
13:16-17 ... 302
13:21-22 ... 38, 50, 303

1 Samuel

15:17 ... 519
16:1 ... 519
16:13 ... 520
25:23 ... 338, 340
25:41 ... 338, 340
28:4 ... 340

2 Samuel

2:4 ... 520
2:20 ... 136
9:6 ... 340
7:12-14 ... 68, 161
13:28 ... 150
24:17 ... 150

1 Kings

8:1 ... 349
22:9-10 ... 348

2 Kings

10:9 ... 150
13:15 ... 350
22:20 ... 150

1 Chronicles

16:25-26 ... 54
21:12 ... 402
28:6 ... 68
29:20 ... 338

Ezra

7:12 ... 219

Nehemiah

9:27 ... 350

Job

7:9 ... 98
18:13 ... 186
40:15 ... 43
40:19 ... 372

Psalms

2 ... 162
2:7 ... 66, 178, 459
8:5 ... 391
16:5 ... 245
16:10 ... 178
22:1 ... 69, 122
22:9-10 ... 69
24:7-10 ... 358
27:10 ... 419
33:6 ... 270
34:7 ... 403
40:7-8 ... 238
45:2-4 ... 240
45:5-6 ... 241
45:6 ... 242
49:7 ... 350
63:9 ... 99
68:5 ... 70

68:18 ... 92
69:21 ... 295
71:3 ... 245
82:1 ... 324
82:6 ... 324, 391
82:6-7 ... 327
89:20-27 ... 379
89:27 ... 186, 379
96:5 ... 343
102:23-27 ... 250, 254
104:4 ... 248
105:41 ... 359
111:10 ... 375
115:16 ... 223
118:14 ... 246
127:1 ... 365
132:11 ... 72

Proverbs

1:7 ... 374
7:4 ... 197
8:1-4 ... 196
8:12-31 ... 197
8:22 ... 195
9:3-16 ... 197
9:10 ... 373
24:21 ... 362
30:2 ... 241

Isaiah

1:2 ... 59
6 ... 329
6:6-8 ... 348
6:9-10 ... 177, 329
7:1 ... 81
7:10-16 ... 81
7:14 ... 74, 78, 427
8:3-4 ... 82
8:8-10 ... 83
9:6 ... 273, 350

9:7 ... 161, 224
11:1 ... 72
11:1-2 ... 357
12:2 ... 245
14:28-30 ... 381
14:30 ... 186, 381
40:3 ... 271, 350
41:4 ... 153
43:10 ... 153, 325
43:11 ... 350
44:6 ... 325, 350
45:23 ... 114
46:4 ... 153, 155
47:10 ... 151, 155
48:16 ... 350
49:20-21 ... 64
50:4-6 ... 70
53:1 ... 329, 525
53:2-3 ... 241
53:3 ... 122
53:4-10 ... 197
53:10 ... 64
55:4 ... 218
63:9-10 ... 394
65:17 ... 183

Jeremiah

3:4 ... 69
3:19 ... 70
4:23-26 ... 348
16:2-4 ... 83
17:10 ... 366
22:30 ... 406
23:5-6 ... 351
23:24 ... 51
27:6-8 ... 219
30:9 ... 380
31:9 ... 69, 186, 382
33:16 ... 351
50:6 ... 320
50:17 ... 320

SCRIPTURE INDEX

Lamentations

1 ... 198

Ezekiel

1:26-28 ... 50
33:29 ... 153
33:33 ... 153
34 ... 320
34:23 ... 39, 380
37:24 ... 380

Daniel

2:21 ... 220
2:37-38 ... 219
3:14 ... 220
3:25 ... 351
4:17 ... 219
4:24-25 ... 220
4:31 ... 220
4:36 ... 220
7:9 ... 50
7:9-14 ... 335
7:13-14 ... 209, 218, 221
7:14 ... 220
7:16-27 ... 221
7:18 ... 224
10:5-6 ... 404
10:6 ... 50
10:13 ... 521
12:7 ... 404

Hosea

3:5 ... 380
11:1 ... 69

Joel

2:32 ... 358

Obadiah

21 ... 350

Micah

5:2 ... 129
7:14 ... 130

Zephaniah

2:15 ... 154

Zechariah

1:12 ... 403
11:13 ... 351
12:10 ... 351
14:3-5 ... 352

Malachi

3:1 ... 352
4:5-6 ... 38

Matthew

1:1 ... 39, 65, 422
1:2-16 ... 405 ff.
1:17 ... 444
1:19 ... 467
1:21-23 ... 78, 466
2:1 ... 407, 444
3:11 ... 356
3:16 ... 89
4:10 ... 342
5:34 ... 244
5:44-45 ... 64

5:45 ... 321
10:5 ... 39
10:6 ... 321
10:8 ... 172
10:19-20 ... 118
10:25 ... 39
10:39 ... 172
11:3 ... 148
11:13-14 ... 38
11:27 ... 204, 429
12:24 ... 39
12:26-28 ... 37
12:28 ... 356, 383
13:13-15 ... 331
13:54 ... 175
13:57 ... 175
15:24 ... 320
15:25 ... 337
16:23 ... 37, 357
16:27 ... 361
18:10 ... 389
18:26 ... 340
19:4-6 ... 527
20:21 ... 218
20:23 ... 218
20:26 ... 143, 145
21:11 ... 175
23:9 ... 64
23:9-10 ... 213
23:34 ... 117
23:37 ... 117
24:5 ... 148
25:31 ... 361
25:33 ... 321
25:34 ... 192
25:40 ... 352
25:41 ... 431
25:45 ... 345
26:21-22 ... 137
27:46 ... 237, 239
27:59-60 ... 160
28:2 ... 401

28:18 ... 213, 353, 366
28:19 ... 353, 395, 508

Mark

1:1 ... 184, 267
1:7 ... 356
1:10 ... 89
1:17 ... 143
2:7 ... 355
2:27-28 ... 355
3:28 ... 222
4:10-12 ... 332
4:32 ... 322
4:34 ... 332
5:37 ... 323
5:39 ... 158
6:34 ... 320
8:11 ... 86
9:37 ... 36, 88, 272, 350
10:17-20 ... 304
10:18 ... 305
10:44 ... 143
11:30 ... 87
12:35-36 ... 68
12:36 ... 206
13:11 ... 118, 275
13:32 ... 216, 356
14:54 ... 323
14:61 ... 357
14:61-64 ... 150
14:62 ... 137
15:34 ... 122, 239
16:9-14 ... 103
16:12 ... 102
16:20 ... 277

Luke

1:1 ... 453
1:1-2 ... 267
1:1-3 ... 501
1:17 ... 38
1:31-32 ... 72
1:35 ... 65, 439
1:41 ... 463
2:5 ... 455
2:32 ... 350
2:33 ... 454
2:41-43 ... 454
2:42-52 ... 70
2:48 ... 454
3:8 ... 74
3:16 ... 356
3:22 ... 66, 89, 461
3:23 ... 416, 455
3:23-38 ... 132, 405 ff.
3:38 ... 74
4:6-7 ... 344
4:8 ... 342
4:18 ... 410, 150
5:21-24 ... 355
6:8 ... 357
6:13 ... 213
6:20 ... 5
7:16 ... 175
8:39 ... 356
9:26 ... 395
9:42 ... 64
9:58 ... 360
10:19 ... 431
10:22 ... 59
11:13 ... 392
11:20 ... 356, 383
11:49 ... 118
12:11 ... 370
12:32 ... 157
13:2 ... 190
13:5-9 ... 212
13:31-33 ... 175
13:32 ... 156
14:10 ... 42, 337
15:4 ... 321
16:13 ... 214

17:15-16 ... 356
17:22-23 ... 276
17:24 ... 140, 141
19:10 ... 320
19:11-18 ... 225
20:20 ... 368, 370
20:27 ... 119
20:35-36 ... 141, 435
20:36 ... 187
21:8 ... 148
21:14-15 ... 118
22:25-27 ... 109
22:69 ... 114
24:15-31 ... 103
24:19 ... 174
23:50 ... 305
24:39 ... 278
24:51-52 ... 338

John

1 ... 257 ff.
1:1 ... 258, 261, 266, 267
1:1-18 ... 290
1:2-4 ... 260
1:3 ... 268
1:4 ... 270, 272, 291
1:6-7 ... 271
1:7 ... 269
1:7-10 ... 272
1:10 ... 268
1:11 ... 76
1:12 ... 144, 272
1:13 ... 72, 366, 427
1:14 ... 274, 297
1:15 ... 356
1:18 ... 279
1:21 ... 38
1:22-23 ... 271
1:30 ... 356
1:32 ... 89, 394
1:33-34 ... 463

SCRIPTURE INDEX

1:51 ... 394
2:11 ... 184, 334
2:19 ... 173, 176
2:21 ... 352
2:22 ... 177, 178
2:24 ... 177, 180, 356
3:2 ... 333
3:3-12 ... 94
3:4-5 ... 366
3:4-6 ... 71
3:8 ... 383
3:9 ... 144
3:11-13 ... 95
3:13 ... 86, 94
3:13-21 ... 91
3:16 ... 94
3:17 ... 99
3:27 ... 86
3:31 ... 86, 88
3:31-34 ... 90, 95
3:34 ... 89, 175, 275
3:35 ... 213
4:19 ... 174
4:22 ... 340
4:23 ... 343
4:25 ... 142
4:35 ... 265
4:52 ... 134
5:3 ... 265
5:15-17 ... 306
5:18 ... 107, 306
5:19 ... 35, 309
5:19-20 ... 66, 310
5:22 ... 204, 213, 366
5:21-26 ... 173
5:22-27 ... 222
5:23 ... 301
5:27 ... 419
5:28-29 ... 96
5:30 ... 36, 205, 355
5:37-39 ... 105
5:41 ... 301, 303

6:2 ... 323
6:32 ... 86, 96
6:33 ... 95
6:38 ... 86, 95
6:39-40 ... 96
6:42 ... 418
6:44 ... 99
6:51 ... 95
6:61-63 ... 98
6:62 ... 86, 97
6:70 ... 37
7:16-17 ... 35, 350
7:28 ... 90
7:34-36 ... 157
7:42 ... 131
8:14 ... 90
8:15 ... 205
8:23 ... 100, 357
8:24 ... 146, 148, 357
8:28 ... 155, 357
8:29 ... 171
8:37 ... 68, 70
8:38 ... 90, 356
8:39-44 ... 63
8:41 ... 69, 307, 528
8:42-44 ... 301, 308
8:43-47 ... 105
8:44 ... 68
8:51-53 ... 141, 156
8:53 ... 69, 147, 148, 150
8:56 ... 63, 70, 140, 142
8:57 ... 146
8:58 ... 135
8:59 ... 146, 148, 149, 150, 151, 156
9:3-4 ... 306
9:9 ... 136, 153
10:1-5 ... 322
10:11 ... 305
10:11-12 ... 168
10:14-18 ... 169
10:15-18 ... 167, 322

10:16 ... 321
10:25-37 ... 314
10:26-29 ... 319
10:27-29 ... 318
10:30 ... 108, 311
10:30-38 ... 317
10:31-32 ... 323
10:33 ... 324
10:34-35 ... 323
10:36 ... 99
10:37 ... 276
10:37-38 ... 315
11:4 ... 264
11:23-25 ... 148
11:24 ... 142
11:25 ... 46, 173
11:25-27 ... 149
11:26 ... 148, 155
12:17 ... 172
12:23-27 ... 322
12:25 ... 172
12:26 ... 157
12:31-38 ... 323
12:32-33 ... 155
12:33-34 ... 162
12:34 ... 148, 156, 157
12:37-41 ... 329
12:39-40 ... 177
12:41 ... 142, 416, 525
12:44 ... 36, 88, 272
12:45 ... 88
12:49 ... 42, 175, 525
12:49-50 ... 66, 88, 171
13:12-15 ... 109
13:19 ... 144, 153
13:31-32 ... 119
14-16 ... 388 ff.
14:3 ... 157
14:6 ... 46
14:7-9 ... 48
14:7-11 ... 105
14:9 ... 47, 104, 140

14:10 ... 88, 276, 387
14:12 ... 276
14:16 ... 388
14:26 ... 388
14:28 ... 108, 302, 308
14:29 ... 144
15:5 ... 309
15:10 ... 171
15:19 ... 75
15:26 ... 387, 388
15:27 ... 139
16:14-15 ... 39
16:28 ... 90
16:30 ... 357
17:1-12 ... 273
17:3 ... 43, 44, 46, 202
17:5 ... 118
17:6 ... 120
17:8 ... 89, 90
17:10 ... 368
17:11 ... 113
17:14 ... 100
17:18 ... 66, 100
17:20-23 ... 276, 315
17:22 ... 119, 388
17:22-23 ... 276, 388
17:24 ... 157, 357
18:36 ... 120
19:37 ... 351
20:1-9 ... 93
20:17 ... 92
20:21-23 ... 277
20:22 ... 355, 393
20:28 ... 357

Acts

1:1 ... 500
1:2 ... 205, 357
1:7 ... 216
1:8 ... 353
1:12 ... 205
1:23-26 ... 449
2:3-4 ... 394
2:22 ... 173, 356
2:22-32 ... 157
2:25-28 ... 178
2:25-31 ... 123
2:26-31 ... 179
2:30 ... 67, 409
2:36 ... 203, 213, 217, 366, 507
3:20-26 ... 41, 174
4:33 ... 468
7:30 ... 402
7:59 ... 357
8:9-23 ... 441
8:32-33 ... 170
8:26 ... 401
9:5 ... 352
10:5 ... 368
10:20 ... 368
10:23 ... 368
10:25-26 ... 341
10:37-38 ... 410, 520
10:38 ... 66, 507
10:40 ... 145
10:42 ... 220
11:26 ... 490
12:7 ... 401
13:10 ... 64
13:22-33 ... 161
13:30-35 ... 161
13:32-33 ... 163
13:33 ... 66, 94, 161, 234
13:47 ... 350
14:11-13 ... 1
14:11-15 ... 342
14:26-15:2 ... 317
17:18 ... 2
17:30-31 ... 221
17:31 ... 115
20:28 ... 74
23:8-9 ... 391
24:5 ... 6
26:22-23 ... 188
26:23 ... 151, 323, 350
26:28 ... 143
28:25-27 ... 176

Romans

1:3 ... 67, 409
1:3-4 ... 166
1:4 ... 164
1:28 ... 53
2:4 ... 211
2:28-29 ... 377
4:12-18 ... 63
4:18 ... 143, 151
6:4 ... 228, 232
8:3 ... 165, 515
8:5-14 ... 166
8:9 ... 357
8:11 ... 486
8:15 ... 377, 385
8:17-25 ... 194
8:23 ... 94, 164
8:26 ... 386, 394
8:29-30 ... 193, 349
9:3-5 ... 67
9:4-5 ... 525
9:5 ... 357
9:6 ... 321
9:29 ... 355
10:7 ... 98
10:9 ... 200
10:13 ... 358
11:8 ... 52
11:15 ... 151
11:20-23 ... 321
12:1 ... 229
13:1 ... 220
14:10-12 ... 115
15:30 ... 229
16:26 ... 357

SCRIPTURE INDEX

1 Corinthians

1:8 ... 140
1:24 ... 195
1:30 ... 196
2:8 ... 358
2:10-11 ... 384
3:6-8 ... 314
4:15-16 ... 62
4:19-20 ... 276
4:21 ... 394
5:7 ... 68, 377
6:16-17 ... 527
6:17 ... 386, 388
6:19 ... 395
7:22 ... 214
8:4-6 ... 54, 325
8:6 ... 202
9:18-22 ... 110
10:4 ... 128, 358
10:9 ... 359
10:19-22 ... 344
11:1 ... 61, 360
11:2 ... 359
11:3 ... 199, 349
11:12 ... 365
11:25 ... 358
12:11 ... 391, 527
13:1 ... 394
13:4-5 ... 389
15:8 ... 216
15:17 ... 357
15:20 ... 145
15:20-23 ... 181, 188
15:20-49 ... 163
15:24-26 ... 207
15:24-28 ... 205, 224
15:27 ... 112, 190, 203, 249
15:42-43 ... 232
15:42-44 ... 164
15:42-53 ... 187
15:45 ... 150
15:51-54 ... 207

2 Corinthians

2:10 ... 277, 355
3:3 ... 384
3:17 ... 384
4:4 ... 35, 48, 51, 257
5:19 ... 352, 361, 518
6:10 ... 360
6:16 ... 395, 518
8:9 ... 360
8:14-15 ... 360
11:4 ... 512
12:2 ... 87
13:4 ... 165, 276
17:24 ... 140

Galatians

1:15 ... 512
2:15 ... 110
2:20 ... 276, 387
3:7 ... 63
3:16 ... 67, 72
3:19 ... 349
4:4 ... 65, 420
4:6 ... 385, 387
4:19 ... 72, 512
4:24 ... 68
4:24-25 ... 358

Ephesians

1:13-14 ... 487
2:11-19 ... 321
2:18 ... 386
3:19 ... 361
4:3-6 ... 385
4:4-6 ... 213, 311
4:9 ... 99

4:10 ... 388
5:27 ... 213
5:29-32 ... 277
6:5-7 ... 214

Philippians

1:6 ... 140
2:3-7 ... 107
2:6 ... 101, 107
2:6-8 ... 108, 110
2:7 ... 109
2:8-9 ... 112
2:9-11 ... 111, 114
3:20 ... 114
3:20-21 ... 164
4:9 ... 62

Colossians

1:15 ... 104, 186, 189, 258, 375, 518
1:16 ... 190, 191
1:18 ... 151, 161, 188
2:2-12 ... 361
2:9 ... 361
2:16-17 ... 377

1 Thessalonians

1:9-10 ... 43
3:13 ... 360
4:16 ... 96, 140

2 Thessalonians

1:10 ... 192
2:2 ... 140, 516
2:10-12 ... 52

1 Timothy

1:1 ... 363, 487
1:15-16 ... 211
1:17 ... 49, 361
2:3-5 ... 357
2:12-13 ... 151
3:16 ... 361
6:14-16 ... 215
6:15 ... 217
6:16 ... 51

2 Timothy

2:8 ... 67, 68, 409

Titus

1:3 ... 364
2:10-11 ... 364
2:13 ... 361, 366

Philemon

10 ... 61

Hebrews

1:1-2 ... 71, 175, 227
1:3 ... 230
1:3-5 ... 234
1:5 ... 68, 401
1:6 ... 521
1:7 ... 125, 253, 391
1:7-8 ... 248
1:8 ... 234 ff., 521
1:9 ... 166
1:10-12 ... 250
1:13 ... 113, 249
1:13-14 ... 248
1:14 ... 394
2:5 ... 120, 254
2:5-8 ... 248
2:5-9 ... 223
2:8 ... 111, 190, 521
2:11 ... 64, 276
2:14 ... 73, 165, 278, 364
2:16 ... 363
2:17 ... 223
3:1-6 ... 363
4:2 ... 258
4:3 ... 342
5:5-6 ... 162
5:7 ... 180
6:1 ... 520
6:5 ... 119
6:20 ... 322
7:3 ... 131
7:8 ... 497
7:16 ... 232, 234
7:17-25 ... 162
8:1-5 ... 44
9:3-7 ... 233
9:11-12 ... 233
10:1 ... 349, 377
10:5 ... 420, 524
10:7 ... 238
11:1 ... 231
11:13 ... 142, 415
11:16 ... 192
12:20 ... 520
12:26-27 ... 254
13:8 ... 134
13:13 ... 323, 520
13:14 ... 192

James

1:1 ... 205
2:1 ... 363
2:17 ... 86
4:4-7 ... 344
5:4 ... 355

1 Peter

1:10-11 ... 120
1:19 ... 121
1:21 ... 486
3:6 ... 199
3:14-16 ... 127
3:18-20 ... 123
3:21-22 ... 128
3:22 ... 92
4:4-5 ... 127

2 Peter

1:1 ... 361, 364
1:4 ... 361
2:4-9 ... 126
2:14 ... 278
3:4 ... 185
3:5-7 ... 127, 349
3:3-13 ... 224
3:13 ... 183
3:14 ... 212
3:15 ... 210
3:15-16 ... 211

1 John

1:1 ... 278
1:2 ... 271
1:5 ... 50, 278
1:7 ... 76
2:1 ... 390
2:7 ... 267
2:18 ... 440
2:29 ... 60
2:29-3:10 ... 62
3:7-8 ... 385
3:9 ... 66
3:16 ... 167, 364
3:16-17 ... 168
4:1-3 ... 391

4:2-3 ... 71, 278, 364, 440, 515
4:6 ... 391
4:9 ... 99, 287
4:12 ... 49, 216
4:16 ... 316
5:1 ... 60
5:6 ... 71
5:7 ... 364
5:20 ... 43

2 John

7 ... 365, 512

3 John

11 ... 306

Jude

4 ... 205
5 ... 365
6-8 ... 125
13-15 ... 125

Revelation

1:1 ... 50
1:1-2 ... 526
1:5 ... 161, 369
1:7-9 ... 365
1:8 ... 136
1:11 ... 366
1:13-15 ... 404
1:14 ... 50
1:17 ... 350
2:8 ... 350
2:10 ... 323
2:23 ... 368
3:9 ... 42, 339
3:12 ... 113
3:14 ... 183, 189, 190, 367
4:1-2 ... 87
4:2-5:7 ... 335
4:3 ... 51
4:6 ... 51
4:11 ... 208
4:11-5:12 ... 209
5:6 ... 394
10:1-7 ... 404
11:15 ... 206
12:1-5 ... 72
13:3-6 ... 344
15:4 ... 339
17:14 ... 218, 520
19:10 ... 340, 518, 526
19:13 ... 275
19:16 ... 217
20:5 ... 224
21:1 ... 192, 348
21:5 ... 192
21:6 ... 371
22:1 ... 366
22:3 ... 366
22:6-18 ... 366
22:8-9 ... 339, 341
22:8-16 ... 351
22:13 ... 371
22:16 ... 366, 526
22:20 ... 365

www.ingramcontent.com/pod-product-compliance
Lightning Source LLC
LaVergne TN
LVHW012248070526
838201LV00091B/156